The Sociology of Cities

Titles of Related Interest

Specialized Texts

Martin Marger, *Elites and Masses*, 2d

Martin Marger, *Race and Ethnic Relations: American and Global Perspectives*

Arnold Sherman/Aliza Kolker, *The Social Bases of Politics*

Robert Atchley, *Social Forces in Aging*, 4th

Robert Atchley, *Aging: Continuity and Change*, 2d

Donald Cowgill, *Aging Around the World*

Judith Perrolle, *Computers and Social Change: Information, Property, and Power*

John Weeks, *Population*, 3d

David Miller, *Introduction to Collective Behavior*

James Wood/Maurice Jackson, *Social Movements: Development, Participation, and Dynamics*

Research Methods and Statistics

Earl Babbie, *The Practice of Social Research*, 4th

Earl Babbie, *Observing Ourselves: Essays in Social Research*

Earl Babbie, *Survey Research Methods*

Margaret Jendrek, *Through the Maze: Statistics with Computer Applications*

John Lofland/Lyn Lofland, *Analzying Social Settings: A Guide to Qualitative Observation and Analysis*, 2d

Joseph Healey, *Statistics: A Tool for the Social Sciences*

June True, *Finding Out: Conducting and Evaluating Social Research*

John Hedderson, *SPSS-X Made Simple*

Computer Software for the Social Sciences

William Bainbridge, *Sociology Laboratory: Computer Simulations for Learning Sociology*

Cognitive Development Company, *Showcase: Demonstrating Sociology Live in the Classroom* with demonstration scripts by Rodney Stark

The Sociology of Cities

Second Edition

James L. Spates
*Hobart and
William Smith Colleges*

John J. Macionis
Kenyon College

*Wadsworth Publishing Company
Belmont, California
A Division of Wadsworth, Inc.*

Sociology Editor: Sheryl Fullerton
Assistant Editor: Liz Clayton
Editorial Assistant: Cynthia Haus
Production Editor: Gary Mcdonald
Cover and Interior Designer: Andrew H. Ogus
Print Buyer: Karen Hunt
Copy Editor: Noel Deeley
Compositor: Thompson Type, San Diego
Cover Photo: Peter Menzel/Stock, Boston

Acknowledgments and credits for quotations are found
on pages 501–503.

Printed in the United States of America   49

1 2 3 4 5 6 7 8 9 10—91 90 89 88 87

ISBN 0-534-07254-2

Library of Congress Cataloging-in-Publication Data

Spates, James L.
    The sociology of cities.

    Bibliography: p.
    Includes index.
    1. Sociology, Urban.   I. Macionis, John J.
II. Title.
HT119.S66 1987   307.7′64   86-22460
ISBN 0-534-07254-2

To Our Teachers

Kingsley H. Birge (1916–1980)

Master sociologist and friend: who first taught me about the challenge of sociology and the importance of cities; and who also taught me that sociology without a conception of the good isn't good sociology at all.

E. Digby Baltzell

Sociologist, historian, and teacher—loved and respected by his students with whom he has shared his wisdom and warmth.

And to Our Parents

James Lyle Spates and Gladys Ramsey Spates

Who, in love and support, taught me just about everything else that has been important in my life.

John Joseph Macionis and May Johnston Macionis

Who have, from the beginning, been the most important people in my life.

Contents

Preface

This book explores one of the most exciting and vital of human creations: the city. Our fundamental approach to the study of the city is sociological, reflecting the classic contributions of eminent European thinkers such as Max Weber, Georg Simmel, Emile Durkheim, and Karl Marx, as well as the theories of American scholars like Robert Park and Louis Wirth. In addition, we discuss the central ideas of contemporary urbanists such as Herbert Gans, Claude Fischer, Brian Berry, Alejandro Portes, and Anthony Downs, whose research continues to illuminate the many dimensions of urban life. In preparing this second edition of *The Sociology of Cities*, we have included the most current debates from journals such as the *American Sociological Review* and *Urban Affairs Quarterly* as well as up-to-date statistical information from such diverse sources as the Bureau of the Census and the World Bank.

By itself, however, the sociological approach provides only a limited foundation for understanding the complexity of cities. Because they are at the center of contemporary social life, cities have become an important topic of study in all the social sciences. The richest urban sociology, then, must integrate outstanding material from *many* diverse fields. As in the first edition, this revision incorporates work of urbanists working in history (Chapters 2 and 3), social psychology (Chapter 5), geography, ecology, and economics (Chapter 6), and anthropology (Chapters 2, 7–10).

This revision has been improved in a number of respects, thanks largely to suggestions made by faculty and students who have used the text. First, carefully reviewing the entire manuscript has allowed us to provide a revision with all the richness of the original in a trimmer format. Second, the chapters concerned with the historical development of cities have been moved to the front of the text, improving the logical flow. Third, a considerable amount of new material has been incorporated throughout the text. As a result—in terms of theory, research, and statistical data—this revision truly reflects the state of urban studies in the mid-1980s.

The book is organized in the following manner. After a brief introduction to the main themes of the book in Chapter 1, we begin to pursue a major objective: understanding how cities vary in time and in different cultural contexts. This is an important lesson for most beginning students whose firsthand experience with cities probably is limited to urban places in North America within the last two decades. Chapters 2 and 3 present the historical development of cities. We begin with urban origins in prehistory and follow the city's changes up to the Industrial Revolution in Europe (Chapter 2). The next chapter deals with urban development in the United States from the 1600s until the present.

This foundation laid, the next four chapters outline the concerns of urbanists from various disciplines. Chapter 4 presents the classic sociological theorists, including Ferdinand Toennies, Georg Simmel, Robert Park, and Louis Wirth. The validity of their work today is also assessed. Chapter 5 considers the social psychology of cities: the "urban experience" of urban dwellers and visitors. Chapter 6 covers the crucial work of urban geographers, urban ecologists, and urban economists. Finally, Chapter 7 is unique to texts of this kind, providing a systematic introduction to the interplay of cities and culture.

The next three chapters focus on the city in non-industrial settings. Chapter 8 describes the rapidly growing cities of Latin America. Chapters 9 and 10 extend the discussion to Africa, the Middle East and Asia. In addition, Chapter 10 concludes with an analytical overview of world urbanization. These chapters reveal how different American cities can be from their counterparts in other societies. Just as important, such comparisons suggest that the conventional thinking about cities, which emerged within the industrialized West, is, in itself, insufficient to understanding the variety of world urban patterns.

The next three chapters provide a detailed analysis of American cities. Chapter 11 examines the variety of American urban life-styles, and provides a close-up look at the suburbs. Chapter 12 turns to the crucial issues of stratification, race, and power as these have appeared on the urban stage. Chapter 13 continues the analysis by examining a select group of urban problems—poverty, housing, crime, urban violence, and city finances. These particular issues have been chosen because they, more than others, are emblematic of the major ills of contemporary American cities.

Finally, the last two chapters explore the issues of the quality and planning of urban life. How do cities become positive, humane environments? What detracts from that elusive goal? Chapter 14 considers the history of urban planning, the fate of the New Towns movement in the United States and elsewhere, planning in socialist cities, and the realities of urban politics. Chapter 15 asks first if it is possible to develop a model of the ideal or "good" city that could be used by urban planners (we suggest that it is). Second, the chapter assesses the likely future of cities in America and abroad.

Two other special features of the book deserve mention. First, the *Boxes* and longer *Cityscapes* that were such a popular feature of the first edition have been retained (and in some cases revised). These are excerpts from a wide range of observers who have a keen eye for the urban scene: novelists, poets, journalists, as well as more conventional urbanists. These materials are linked directly to the chapter discussion and should be read as one proceeds. All have been chosen because of their intrinsic interest, and because of their ability to make cities "come alive."

Second, this revision contains nine case studies that provide a detailed look at actual cities. Like the Boxes and Cityscapes, they provide clear and compelling illustrations of key text points. Three major cities in the United States are represented: New York (Chapter 3), Chicago (Chapter 12), and San Francisco (Chapter 15). Case studies of cities in other historic and cultural settings include London (Chapter 2); Periclean Athens, Ming Peking, and contemporary Beijing (Peking), all in Chapter 7; La Paz, Bolivia (Chapter 8); and Kano, Nigeria (Chapter 9). Taken together, the case studies provide a comparative overview of the striking diversity and vitality of cities.

Acknowledgments

Anyone who has undertaken even the smallest piece of writing knows the substantial debt owed to others. Our debts are legion; our thanks, we hope, adequate to the generosity bestowed.

This book originated from a most happy collaboration between the authors and the college department of St. Martin's Press. This revision continues to reflect the efforts of many talented people who helped us prepare the first edition. To them, particularly to Bob Woodbury, who signed the project, and to Emily Berleth, who was an indefatigable project editor, we once again offer our sincere thanks.

Our present publishers at Wadsworth have been no less helpful. Sheryl Fullerton, our editor, is a delight to work with and provided enthusiastic assistance from the first moment we "signed up." She is truly one of the best in the business. No less talented is Gary Mcdonald, who took major responsibility for the production process. He always had the goals of the book at heart as he worked us through the complicated process of revising 15 chapters. Andrew H. Ogus was responsible for the design of the cover and the interior. In addition, skillful copyediting was provided throughout by Noel Deeley. To all of them goes our appreciation.

Careful reviews of the complete manuscript by Ralph Thomlinson and Gordon F. Lewis were a major contribution to the first edition. In the preparation of this revision, these colleagues have once more generously given of their knowledge. Thoughtful and helpful reviews are too often the exception in text publishing and we are privileged to have had two people of high caliber commenting on our work.

Still others contributed specialized knowledge. Bill Egelman and his students at Iona College read the whole first edition carefully and made many useful suggestions. Ilene Nicholas commented on sections of Chapter 2; David Eaton and Gundars Rudzitis did the same for por-

tions of Chapter 6; and Alan Frishman commented on Chapter 9. Additional thanks are due to Amy L. Marsh, who prepared the index for this edition. Lynne B. Harris, who did everything from soup to nuts, helped us with references, photocopying, and permissions.

Finally, we must once again offer our thanks to our mutual friend, the nearly legendary parochial antiurbanist. Such friends are rare; such unfettered biases rarer. In the preparation of the first edition he kept us thinking and laughing by hurling antiurban invective in all directions. Ironically, since the first edition of this book, he has become an independent businessman and his life a textbook case of the power of cities to transform human life! Beginning operations at home, he moved his office to a small town to take advantage of a larger population. He next proceeded to a small city where business has never been better. He himself has moved closer to the city to be nearer work, a classic example of central place theory (Chapter 6). Harried in his success, he dashes about, trying to jack up trade ever further. His type, the true urban character, is discussed at length in Chapter 11.

James L. Spates
Hobart and William Smith Colleges
Geneva, New York

John J. Macionis
Kenyon College
Gambier, Ohio

The Sociology of Cities

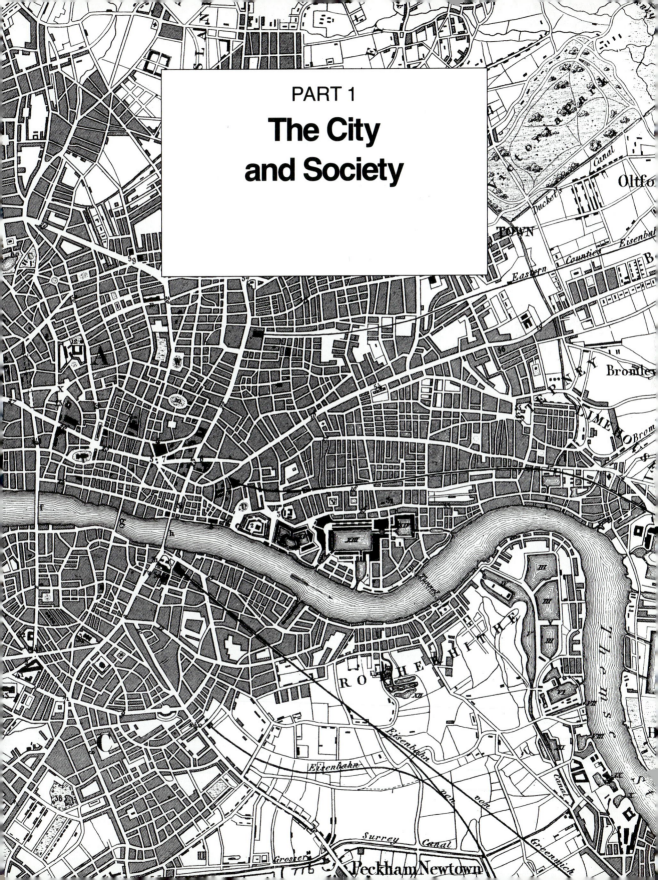

PART 1

The City
and Society

CHAPTER 1

The Living City

'This music crept by me upon the waters'
And along the Strand, up Queen Victoria
    Street.
O City city, I can sometimes hear
Beside a public bar in Lower Thames Street,
The pleasant whining of a mandolin
And a clatter and a chatter from within
Where fishmen lounge at noon: where the
    walls
Of Magnus Martyr hold
Inexplicable splendour of Ionian white and
    gold.

T. S. ELIOT, "THE WASTE LAND"

Let us go then, you and I,
When the evening is spread out against the
    sky
Like a patient etherised upon a table;
Let us go, through certain half-deserted
    streets,
The muttering retreats
Of restless nights in one-night cheap hotels
And sawdust restaurants with oyster-shells:
Streets that follow like a tedious argument
Of insidious intent
To lead you to an overwhelming question . . .

Oh, do not ask, 'What is it?'
Let us go and make our visit.

T. S. ELIOT,
"THE LOVE SONG OF J. ALFRED PRUFROCK"

Why Study the City?

Cities! Like the poet T. S. Eliot, who was speaking of London, most of us are fascinated by these cauldrons of excitement, where human joy and terror often intermingle. With the poet, most of us would agree that cities are places we would all like to visit (but, of course, we wouldn't want to live there!). Let's imagine a recent visit to Washington, D.C., our nation's capital. Checking into a major hotel we would experience the latest wrinkle on urban security. We would be given a room key imprinted with an incorrect room number! For example, if we were staying in Room 412, our key, which actually fits Room 412, might have the number 749 on it. That way, if we lost the key and someone with larcenous intent picked it up, the would-be burglar would try to open Room 749 to no avail. Ordering breakfast the next morning

London in the 1870s. (Bettmann Archive)

in the hotel coffeeshop we would get a sense of the cost of living in major cities. We would find that two eggs, toast, and coffee cost a mere $7.50 (without tip). Reading the morning paper we would encounter the following story by Ronald White, a staff writer for *The Washington Post*:

> I am walking home alone, heading west on M Street to my apartment at 14th and Corcoran streets at 2 A.M. A crowd of people, including several transvestites, is massing ahead of me. Two men are prepared to fight and the crowd wants blood. A fat man dressed as a woman yells: "This is the Thunderdome. Two enter. One must die."
>
> My apartment is three blocks away. I realize that these bizarre people are actually my neighbors. I spend the rest of my walk home looking to see if I am being followed. (Aug. 30, 1985)

This is one unnerving and recurrent image of the city: that it is a volatile, even dangerous place. But this image is too simplistic and certainly not the whole urban story. Reading further in the same article, we would find other, more positive, evidence about Washington. We would learn that the same neighborhood described by White is in a general process of transformation—for the better:

> Cabdrivers once refused to go to Corcoran Street. Now, the houses have been exquisitely restored. Young and successful black and white people live there. A smattering of expensive autos are parked on a street where stolen cars were once stripped and drugs sold openly. Now, like a tide that moves in years but never ebbs, the . . . gentrification [process] moves inexorably east. (Aug. 30, 1985)

Such contrasting images are the heart of the urban experience, an experience we all know, regardless of whether, like the author of the above passages, we actually live in the city or are only visitors. We all know and are stimulated by the city's people, sounds, shapes, rhythms.

Consider that many of us build our lives around cities. Many of our favorite entertainments—concerts or sports—are city based. We identify our homes with cities ("I come from Norwalk. It's a suburb of Los Angeles"). Consider as well that the adage already cited, about the city being a nice place to visit but a place where

few would want to live, is, for most of us, a saying with little connection to reality. For nearly 75 percent of all Americans are classified as living in urban areas. "Sooner or later," said *Saturday Review* critic Karl Meyer, Americans are going to have "to come to terms with a reality we have sought to deny or ignore—that we are a nation of city slickers, that the urban way of life is the norm" (1979, p. 16). To study the city, therefore, is to study ourselves.

But the city is more than our personal experiences reveal. It is a dynamic entity unto itself, the most powerful "drawing card" in human history. In 1900, cities were the home of a mere 9 percent of the world's population. Now, almost 90 years later, over 40 percent of the world's people live in them. If present trends continue, this figure will mushroom to well over 50 percent by the year 2000.

Such growth has made the city an increasingly important stage on which all aspects of the human drama are performed: the highest learning and the grossest ignorance, unimaginable levels of wealth and the most abject poverty exist side by side. Historically, most people drawn to the city have been able to increase their material standard of living, but how are cities to meet the needs of populations increasing by millions? Many major world cities—among them Mexico City, Rio de Janeiro, Cairo, New Delhi, and Tokyo (see the world map after the table of contents to locate these and other prominent cities)—are growing with such enormous speed that presently they cannot provide basic services (water, housing, electricity) to many of their people. If such growth is not checked in the near future, poverty and suffering for billions will be inescapable and ecological disasters unparalleled in recent history may be inevitable. To study the city, therefore, is to study a uniquely powerful form of human settlement: a physical and social environment with the potential for satisfying *and* frustrating the entire spectrum of human needs.

But, powerful as it is, the city is not an entity entirely to itself. All cities are inextricably part and parcel of the larger societies in which they exist. Thus, for centuries the city has been the heart, the lifeblood, of various civilizations, the epicenter of economic, political, and artistic activities. There we find both the zenith and the nadir of the human story. We associate Hellenic Athens, Renaissance Florence, and Elizabethan London with unparalleled triumphs of the human spirit, while we link classical Rome and Nazi Berlin with degradations of that same spirit. But the success or failure of these cities was not a simple product of the cities themselves. The cultural setting of which they were a part helped shape their character. There was something special about Greek civilization in the fourth century B.C. that made Athens a pinnacle of history. Likewise, another—radically different—cultural milieu permitted the rise of Nazism in Germany in the post–World War I era and led to Berlin's infamous decadence.

The connection between the city and a society's qualities is no less evident today. In American cities exists much of what is great about American society: intellectual excellence, political freedom, and artistic vitality. The same cities exhibit America's greatest failings: continuing poverty for millions, racial prejudice, inhuman exploitation. To study the city, then, is also to examine the society in which it exists.

Understanding the city is therefore crucial in coming to comprehend modern existence. But *how* we choose to study the city also is important. The city is a complex, multifaceted reality that will not admit to easy answers and yield up its intricacies to cursory glances.

We believe that we must study the city much as we would a poem. In encountering a poem for the first time, most people wonder, "What does it mean?" They may ask, "What is the poem's topic?" "What meter does it use?" "What is its place in the poet's works?" For example, someone might ask what T. S. Eliot means by "the walls of Magnus Martyr" in the lines that opened this chapter (a reference to a particularly beautiful London church—Saint Magnus Martyr—built by Sir Christopher Wren in the seventeenth century). What does he mean by the walls holding "inexplicable splendour of Ionian white and gold" (a reference to the startling white and gold interior of Magnus Martyr, which reminded Eliot of the glories of the Ionian period of classical Greece).

Central as these "what" questions are, American poet John Ciardi (1959, Chap. 1) believed that if they were the *only* questions one asked, a poem would never be understood. Such questions ignore the mood the poem creates in us, its readers, as well as the deeper subtleties that are conveyed in how the poem's words work together. Our concern, wrote Ciardi, should not be "to arrive at a definition and close the book, but to arrive at an experience" (1959, p. 666). Only by asking *how* a poem transmits its meaning—by experiencing and understanding through repeated encounters how all its complex elements fit together—does Ciardi believe we can grasp the poem completely. The same is true of cities.

If we look only at the facts of urban life, we shall surely miss its vital, dynamic essence. The city will appear dull and lifeless, somehow outside of us. We shall see only concrete buildings, bureaucracies, unemployment rates. But if we also ask the "how" questions, if we see *how* these factual elements of the city are linked together as part of human lives, the city will spring to life as a set of vital, dynamic forces. Real people—not abstract numbers—work in those buildings, are affected by decisions made in those bureaucracies, and suffer the difficulties of being unemployed.

In studying the city, we must not merely ask "what is it?" We must, as Eliot suggests in his poem, "go and make our visit." We must probe beyond the descriptions and the statistics to the deeper dimensions of ongoing urban life. It is the purpose of this book to help us develop this understanding; the remainder of this chapter gives an overview of the steps we will follow.

The Complexity of the City: Various Perspectives

The city is one of the most complex of all human creations. As a result, it cannot be understood using any single point-of-view. While this book is fundamentally sociological in its orientation, we believe that the best sociology is continuously informed by insights from a wide variety of related disciplines, among them history, archaeology, psychology, geography, economics, and political science. As will become obvious in the next few pages, all these perspectives are vital for grasping the living entity that is the contemporary city.

The City in History

Cities are so much a part of our life in modern society that they seem both natural and inevitable. Yet you may be surprised to learn that in the larger picture of human history, cities are a very recent development. Although the human species has existed on the earth for at least a quarter of a million years, cities began to appear a scant 10,000 years ago. Moreover, it wasn't until the last 3,000 years that cities became relatively numerous and populated by significant numbers of people.

Even more important, the style of life experienced by urban dwellers has changed dramatically as time has progressed. As an example, consider the massive changes undergone by San Francisco. Today San Francisco is a thoroughly modern American city, famed for its hills, cable cars, fog, and natural beauty. It also has a particularly easy-going lifestyle, about which Geoffrey Moorhouse wrote recently:

> No one who visits San Francisco for the first time can fail to be aware of the pleasantly relaxed atmosphere. You are not perpetually admonished by well-wishers about the dangers of getting mugged, as visitors usually are in New York. It seems true that shop assistants here are more amiable than elsewhere, less bent on treating their customers as components of the cash register; when they say "Have a nice day," they sound as though they mean it and not as if it were a ritual phrase learned to help trade. Watch people move about the streets if you want to appreciate what San Francisco has done to them. Except at rush hour, they tend to stroll. There is nothing comparable here to downtown New York or the heart of London, where the word "perambulation" may now be considered redundant except at weekends, having long since been banished by the general push and shove. (1979, p. 24)

But it was not always thus. The changes San Francisco has been through in its brief century and a half of existence are profound, as only historic documents can show. One such document is Richard Henry Dana's *Two Years Before the Mast* (1947, originally published in 1862), one of the greatest of nineteenth-century seagoing journals, which is excerpted in Cityscape 1-1. (Cityscapes and the shorter Boxes, which we include in each chapter, illustrate points made in the main text. They are an integral part of the book, a central part of our presentation. So, when reference is made to a particular Cityscape or Box, it is important to read that material before going on with the chapter.)

What had happened to San Francisco was *gold*, discovered in 1849. Almost overnight the sleepy little village of Yerba Buena, the nearest port for outfitting the Sierra Nevada mines, was transformed into a feverish city. Only after another seventy years would Moorhouse's sophisticated, "laid back" San Francisco begin to appear.

Such an example shows how crucial it is to study the city historically. Without such a perspective we may have the mistaken notion that cities, although perhaps smaller, were always something like those we know today.

Luckily, our understanding of past cities is not reliant only on historical documents such as Dana's account of early San Francisco. In recent years urban archaeologists have made major strides in the study of urban settings from which little or no written material is available.

When cities are abandoned or rebuilt on earlier foundations, traces of earlier development remain. Archaeologists are trained in the careful excavation and analysis of artifact material. Each piece of evidence provides a clue as to how the city's people lived: how their houses were organized, what they thought important enough to paint, what level of technology they had, what they drank or ate. If enough clues can be found, the city, even though long dead, can spring to life once more.

One of the most important finds in recent years has been the discovery of Gran Pajaten, a legendary lost city of Peru. Imagine trekking through the high jungles of South America and finding the ruins of a vast system of

> . . . walls and terraces, buildings and tombs and statuary, all perched on the steep, cloud-shrouded eastern slope of the Andes [Mountains] overlooking

---

CITYSCAPE 1-1:
San Francisco's Massive Changes

Shipping from New York, Dana first visited San Francisco, then called Yerba Buena (good herbs), in 1835. Here is what he saw:

Our place of destination had been Monterey, but as we were to the Northward of it when the wind hauled ahead, we made a fair wind for San Francisco. This large bay, which lies in latitude 37′ 58″, was discovered by Sir Francis Drake and by him represented to be (as indeed it is) a magnificent bay, containing several good harbors, great depth of water, and surrounded by a fertile and fine wooded country. . . . [Near the] mouth of the bay . . . is a high point on which the Presidio [Mexican military outpost] is built. Behind this point is the little harbor, or bight, called Yerba Buena, in which trading vessels anchor, and, near it, the Mission of Delores. There was no other habitation on this side of the Bay, except a shanty of rough boards put up by a man named Richardson, who was doing a little trading between the vessels and the Indians. . . . We came to anchor near the mouth of the bay, under a high and beautifully sloping hill, upon which herds of hundreds and hundreds of red deer, and the stag, with his high branching of antlers, were bounding about, looking at us for a moment, and then starting off, affrighted at the noises we made at seeing the va-riety of their beautiful attitudes and motion. . . .

That was hardly the San Francisco of Geoffrey Moorhouse; nor was this description of Dana's, written in 1859 after a second visit:

We bore round the point toward the old anchoring ground of hide ships, and there, covering the sand hills and the valleys, stretching from the water's edge to the base of the great hills, and from the old Presidio to the Mission, flickering all over with lamps of its streets and houses, lay a city of one hundred thousand inhabitants. . . . The dock into which we drew, and the streets about it, were densely crowded with express wagons and hand-carts to take luggage, coaches and cabs for passengers, and with men,—some looking out for friends among our hundreds of passengers,—agents of the press, and a greater multitude eager for newspapers and verbal intelligence from the great Atlantic and European world. Through this crowd I made my way, along the well-built and well-lighted streets, as alive as by day, where boys in high-keyed voices were already crying the latest New York papers; and between one and two o'clock in the morning found myself comfortably abed in a commodious room, in the Oriental Hotel, which stood, as well as I could learn, on the filled-up cove, and not far from the spot where we used to beach our boats from the Alert.

When I awoke in the morning, and looked from my windows over the city of San Francisco, with its townhouses, towers, and steeples; its courthouses, theaters, and hospitals; its daily journals; its well-filled learned professions; its fortresses and light houses; its wharves and harbor, with their thousand-ton clipper ships, more in number than London or Liverpool sheltered that day; itself one of the capitals of the American Republic, and the sole emporium of a new world, the awakened Pacific; when I looked across the bay to the eastward, and beheld a beautiful town on the fertile wooded shores of the Contra Costa [the area of today's Oakland and Berkeley] and steamers, large and small, the ferryboats of the Contra Costa, and capacious freighters and passenger-carriers to all parts of the great bay and its horizon—when I saw all these things, and reflected on what I once was and saw here, and what now surrounded me, I could scarcely keep my hold on reality at all, or the genuineness of anything, and seemed to myself like one who had moved in "worlds not realized."

Source: Richard Henry Dana, *Two Years Before the Mast* (New York: Heritage, 1947), pp. 196, 203, 320–322.

---

a nameless river, [ruins] of an early, resourceful and mysterious people whose civilization flourished long before the glory days of the Incas. (Wilford 1985, p. A1)

Lost for centuries, Gran Pajaten appears to be only one of a series of lost urban sites in the area. According to the team of American and Peruvian archaeologists that found it in the summer of 1984, the ruins may be as extensive and impressive as the already famous remnants of Machu Picchu, also in Peru, hundreds of miles to the south. What astonishes the scholars is how the city, clearly one with a highly developed civilization and agriculture, thrived in a most inhospitable environment—a place of almost perpetual clouds and rain some 8,600 feet above sea level surrounded by dense jungle. They estimate that it will take at least 15 years for them to finish exhuming the city and understand how its people lived.

Equally important is archaeology in contemporary cities. Most cities exist on the rubble of their own past. London is an example. Over 2,000 years old, it is a city that has grown literally 30 feet higher on its own refuse. At present a major excavation is under way to unearth Roman London—established in the first century A.D. In great 30-foot holes surrounded by modern skyscrapers hundreds of feet high, archaeologists are digging up the remains of the Emperor Claudius's bath and billet. Two other archaeologists, Nan Rothchild and Diana Rothman, have recently reported completion of excavation on Wall Street in New York. They have uncovered artifacts from the original Dutch settlement of 1625 (National Public Radio, Jan. 26, 1981).

An understanding of the city in history is so important that we devote two full chapters to the subject. In Chapter 2 we review what is known about cities from their beginnings some ten millenia ago (the ruins of Jericho in present-day Israel are the site of the oldest known city) to the seventeenth century. We shall see that the urban story is one of enormous and continuing change. In Chapter 3 we bring this analysis home, studying how cities have developed in the United States. Here, too, there are astonishing changes— changes hinted at in Dana's account of San Francisco. We shall see the alterations of American urban life as cities have grown from small, isolated colonial centers of the seventeenth century to environments in which populations often reach 3 to 7 million.

The Emergence of Urban Sociology

It is just as vital to understand how sociologists have looked at the city. Although historians have been looking at cities for centuries, sociologists are more recent arrivals on the scene. As we shall see in Chapter 4, urban sociologists only began

their study of the city in the late nineteenth century, a period of dramatic urban upheaval. Largely as the result of the Industrial Revolution, cities in both Europe and America were changing from small, manageable centers to huge, chaotic places. A remarkable description of a seemingly insatiable seventeenth-century London is provided by novelist Charles Dickens in Box 1-1. The full-page drawing near the beginning of this chapter illustrates his concerns.

Dickens's pessimistic vision was shared by many early sociologists of the city. In many of their works, the city is portrayed as a dangerous place where the traditional values of social life— a sense of community, a caring for other people— were being inevitably and irretrievably lost. However, recent research by sociologists has shown that many of these concerns about the uncontrollable destructiveness of the city were based on inadequate evidence. In the light of contemporary research, the city emerges more as a neutral phenomenon. Not good or bad in itself, cities have been pushed in one direction or the other by the historical epoch and society in which they exist. Thus, the horrors of nineteenth-century London appear to have been primarily a product of the massive industrialization taking place within a capitalist society, and not a result of something in the nature of the city itself.

The Urban Experience

The city is not something merely to be studied, however. It is something that is *experienced*. And because the city is the home of nearly three-quarters of the American population, it is essential for us, as students of the city, to understand that experience. How does the city stimulate the individual? How does it change people's psychology? How does it change social arrangements? These are all questions that demand our attention.

We know that the city affects our reactions: We behave differently in the city than in other environments. An example is provided in Cityscape 1-2, a recollection by Jim Spates (coauthor of this book) of his first visit to "the big city"—New York. Spates's reactions may be very personal, but they

BOX 1-1
London, The Devouring City

[Harriet Carker] often looked with compassion . . . upon the stragglers who came wandering into London by the great highway hard by, and who, footsore and weary, and gazing fearfully at the huge town before them, as if foreboding that their misery there would be but as a drop of water in the sea, or as a grain of sea-sand on the shore, went shrinking on, cowering before the angry weather, and looking as if the very elements rejected them. Day after day, such travellers crept past, but always, as she thought, in one direction—always towards the town. Swallowed up in one phase or other of its immensity, towards which they seemed impelled by a desperate fascination, they never returned. Food for the hospitals, the churchyards, the prisons, the river, fever, madness, vice, and death—they passed on to the monster, roaring in the distance, and were lost.

Source: Charles Dickens, *Dombey and Son* (London: Chapman and Hall, 1848), Chap. 33.

are *social* in two senses. First, they are generated by the social environment of the city itself. Second, they are also social in the sense that other people have similar urban experiences. We know, for example, that the experiences described in Cityscape 1-2 are rather typical of newcomers to a big city. Likewise, we expect long-time city residents to experience the city with greater sophistication and to display more street-wise behavior.

Such social aspects of the urban experience make possible the systematic study of people's responses to the city and city living. Thus, Chapter 5 provides an overview of the social psychology of the city, the study of the individual within the urban environment.

Urban Geography, Economics, and Ecology

Why did people form cities in the first place? In the fourth century B.C., the Greek philosopher Aristotle provided this insightful answer: Men come together in cities for security; they remain there in order to live the good life. For the ancient Greeks, cities satisfied a need for security. Inter-

national law did not exist, and groups frequently preyed upon one another. For protection, people came together in a single location, often one that possessed natural fortification (such as the Acropolis in the Athens of Aristotle). Where natural defenses were not available, people built walls for protection. But these sites could become cities only if they had other geographical assets: water, access to transportation routes, and the ability to produce (by local effort or import) enough to meet their population's needs.

Once cities began, a remarkable thing happened. People discovered that mixing together in large numbers not only afforded protection but generated more complex and more profitable trade and stimulated their thinking. They began to see that the city had the possibility of facilitating what Aristotle called "the good life." They stayed.

The importance of a city's physical location, and how people come to arrange themselves within it, have continually intrigued urbanists. Three subfields have emerged: (1) *urban geography*, which focuses on the significance of the city's location and resources; (2) *urban economics*, which is concerned with how goods and resources are produced and distributed within the city; and (3) *urban ecology*, which analyzes how people are located within the urban area. Let us illustrate each of these areas of study.

A city's geographical location has a great deal to do with how life in that city is lived. Take America's two largest cities, New York and Los Angeles. New York is centered on Manhattan Island, is surrounded by rivers, and has a land base physically able to support tall buildings. By contrast, Los Angeles is laid out across a semiarid basin surrounded at some distance by hills and has a geographical underpinning that makes the building of skyscrapers shaky business indeed. These different settings translate into very different daily routines, as Joseph Giovannini, a part-time resident of both cities, notes:

New York and Los Angeles have fundamentally different spatial premises. Space in New York collects people; in Los Angeles it separates them. New Yorkers occupy a community; Angelenos occupy their own privacy. New York is an environment of

CITYSCAPE 1-2
New York, New York!

As a child, I lived in a suburb of Springfield, Massachusetts. I must've been about eleven years old the first time I ever went to New York City. I remember I was so excited that I could hardly sleep for a week before.

New York? It seemed absolutely *incomprehensible*. To my mind, Springfield and Boston weren't even *cities* compared to *New York*. They were outposts, back country. New York was in a class by itself—gargantuan, mysterious, the city of cities, the place where everything important (other than the Red Sox) happened. I had read about it; I had seen it in the movies; I knew about people who lived there. I was going.

We took the train from Springfield. Four hours! Imagine being eleven years old and waiting four hours on a train to get to New York! I counted the cities (hardly looked at them, couldn't care less) as we went by—Hartford, New Haven, Stamford, whatever. Finally: the outskirts!

Our approach was through the Bronx and Harlem, tenement areas. I had never seen so many buildings. They went on for miles and all seemed huge and alike. I saw the back alleys, the clothes strung from windows, and pigeon cages on the roofs. I *knew* tremendously exciting things were happening here. This was where the boxer Rocky Graziano grew up (I had read his autobiography, *Somebody Up There Likes Me*, a dozen times), where *West Side Story* gang wars took place, where the people who worked *On the Waterfront* lived. (In retrospect, it seems crass, even cruel, this attitude about the poor. I had no comprehension of the suffering, the degradation that more often than not accompanied such existences. I was a suburban kid, hyped up by all the media I had been exposed to.)

After what seemed an eternity, during which the train repeatedly slowed, stopped, and went slowly forward again, we finally stopped for good. All the people on the train except my mother and myself (bumpkins both!) got up, put their coats on, grabbed their briefcases, and started out. We piled onto the platform; I pulled myself, our three suitcases, and my mother after the crowd. Inside the main lobby of Grand Central, I was awestruck. I knew it was going to be big, but this was *cavernous! I mean, you could hardly see the roof!* And there were the haze, the incredible echoes, the indecipherable voices of the train announcers, and no fewer than five hundred thousand people going every which way. We were in New York!

Somehow, we got to the street—I have no recollection how—and once again I was stupefied, this time by the traffic, the hurrying people, the huge buildings. My mother suggested we take a cab to the hotel. Although excited by this prospect, I argued against it: "Let's not," I said, "It's only 14 blocks to our hotel. It's just around the corner. Nobody can get lost in New York. Everything's numbered, the streets go one way, the avenues another (I wasn't sure which). Let's walk." A bit skeptical, my mother agreed. Carrying our not inconsiderable baggage, we headed over to Fifth Avenue.

---

people; Los Angeles is an environment of vehicular movement. New York is a vertical city, and Los Angeles, despite its hills and mountains, is horizontally organized. . . .

The urban patterns that shape attitudes in the two cities are as simple as the daily commute. In Los Angeles, I coasted downhill in my '59 Studebaker Lark, accompanied by FM music. If I timed the freeways correctly to avoid bottlenecks, the drive to work from my office in Venice was a rumination. . . .

In New York, the half-hour commute is a very different half hour. It starts in the elevator, where I might encounter another tenant: We chat. Then, a brief conversation with the doorman; perhaps a passing greeting to a neighbor on the street, and then another chat at the corner newsstand. [After my subway ride, when] I arrive at Times Square, I sometimes head for my morning coffee and pastry at the Lucky Star Delicatessen, where I talk to Mervat, an Egyptian waitress; then, on the elevator in The Times building, I meet more people before sitting down at my desk (1983, p. 147).

Just as important as a city's geographical setting is its ability to generate trade, to be economically viable. Aristotle said that initially people were drawn to cities for security. True enough, particularly at the time he was writing. But throughout history people also have gone to the city for other

What do I remember? The lions on the steps of the New York Public Library. They were larger than any statues I had ever seen. The library itself was huge: the library in Springfield was about a third the size, and the library in my suburb wasn't even as large as one of the lions. People: in suits, in dresses, in uniforms and clothing that I hardly imagined existed. Orthodox Jews in their traditional raiment; blacks and Asians; young kids in motorcycle jackets with their hair slicked back (delinquents!); bums lying in the street or panhandling.

And, I remember the street—the newsstands, with more papers and magazines than I could believe. I took mental notes on one block: a department store, a book store, a record store, a fashion shop, a Florsheim shoe store. Then another: a department store, a Kelly Girls office, a restaurant (Tad's Steak House, I think, "Complete Steak Dinner: $1.49"), and *another* Florsheim shoe store! How was this *possible*? Springfield had three shoe stores within its entire city limits, all different companies. Two Florsheim shoe stores in two blocks? I could hardly believe it. How could they stay in business?

The next thing I remember is my mother grabbing my shoulder and yelling at me to be careful. I was three steps into the street on a "Don't Walk" signal. Yellow cabs and Cadillacs were coming at me, honking like crazy. They weren't about to stop. In my daze I had just kept walking, looking at everything and astonished by a *third* Florsheim shoe store across the street. As I leaped back onto the curb, the horns were honking and the cabbies were glaring and shaking their fists.

At this point, my mother said we were taking a cab the rest of the way to the hotel, no matter how close it was. I didn't argue. I was exhausted. I hailed a cab like a native (I'd seen them do it in hundreds of movies). We got in. The cabbie looked around and said, "Where to, Mack?" A bit ruffled by his demeanor, I said in a confident, firm voice: "The Hotel _____" (I've forgotten the name). The cabbie looked at me, frowned, looked impatient, and then asked gruffly, "Where's that, Mack?"

What? In every story I'd ever read, in every film I'd ever seen about New York, you just got into the cab, said the name of the hotel, and the cab took off. Cabbies *knew* all the hotels in New York. I suddenly realized New York was *so* big they *didn't* know all the hotels. And this cabbie couldn't care less. I fumbled about for the address, my suave façade completely blown. My mother finally found it. The cabbie grabbed it, snorted, and turned around. We roared off.

I smashed back into the seat, sliding through a piece of fresh gum thoughtfully left by a prior passenger. All I remember about the ride is that we almost got in twelve accidents, that the cabbie yelled at other drivers a lot, that the meter went up awfully fast, and that we passed eight more Florsheim shoe stores on the way.

Source: James L. Spates

---

reasons, chief among them the notion that, in the city, they would be able to significantly improve their material standard of living. An excellent case in point is Hsiang Tzu, a Chinese peasant who went to Peking, China's capital city, in the 1930s:

> When he saw the bustle of people and horses, heard the ear-piercing racket, smelled the dry stink of the road, and trod the powdery, churned-up gray dirt, Hsiang Tzu wanted to kiss it, kiss that gray stinking dirt, adorable dirt, dirt that grew silver dollars! He had no father or mother, brother or sister, and no relatives. The only friend he had was this ancient city. This city gave him everything. Even starving here was better than starving in the country. There were things to look at, sounds to listen to, color and voices everywhere. All you needed was to be willing to sell your strength. There was so much money it couldn't be counted. There were ten thousand kinds of grand things here that would never be eaten up or worn out. Here, if you begged for food, you could even get things like meat and vegetable soup. All they had in the village was cornmeal cakes. (Lao 1979, p. 31)

Although Hsiang Tzu's experience occurred half a world away, it is not atypical. His hope that life in the city would fulfill his dreams is not so different from the hopes and dreams of the millions upon millions of immigrants who came to

The West German city of Heidenheim retains many medieval qualities: There is no central business district and the city is visually dominated by the cathedral. (Nat Norman/Photo Researchers)

the United States from rural and poor backgrounds around the turn of this century. These people, the grandparents and great-grandparents of many of us, settled in cities across the nation in an attempt to make their fortunes.

Comparisons of medieval and contemporary cities also reveal the growing importance of the economic function of cities over the centuries. In the Middle Ages, although cities were already important centers of trade, other areas of life also were thriving. All someone has to do is look at the physical layout of cities built in the Middle Ages to see the importance of religion in the lives of the people (see, for example, the photo of Heidenheim, West Germany). With the coming of the Industrial Revolution, however, all that began to change. Cities became evermore important as centers of wealth. Skyscrapers, large factories, and office buildings sprang up to meet the economic demands of millions. The churches, which previously dominated the skyline were dwarfed or totally obscured (see the photo of Columbus, Ohio).

As we are beginning to see, cities are by no means static entities. They are continually changing—and not only during times of radical upheaval such as the Industrial Revolution. Urban ecology seeks to understand how people choose to locate and rearrange themselves in urban space. One ecological process, now fairly well understood, is called *invasion and succession*. It is a process by which whole sections of the city change. An old industrial district may be rather suddenly upstaged by a new "high-tech" area in an adjacent suburb. Overnight the older district becomes tawdry. Once respectable businesses are invaded by fly-by-night operations and pornographic bookstores and movie houses. Before long, income levels in the area drop as the few remaining original businesses close their doors. Where once executives and working people trod the city sidewalks, there are only prostitutes, drug dealers, and petty criminals. Thus is succession completed.

The same process of invasion and succession may occur in residential areas as new categories

Rather than having a central cathedral, like that in the medieval city of Heidenheim, West Germany, expressways and a skyline dominated by commercial buildings are familiar American urban patterns, as shown in this view of Columbus, Ohio. (Georg Gerster/Photo Researchers)

of people enter an established neighborhood. An example is contained in Cityscape 1-3, where novelist Paul Theroux describes the reaction of Mr. Gawber, a traditional British civil servant and long-term London resident, to ethnic changes in his neighborhood. Mr. Gawber is greatly offended by the presence of these new people. He refuses to see any positive qualities in his neighbors—a reaction not likely to foster good relations.

Are Mr. Gawber's reactions completely unreasonable? To find out, the urban ecologist might look to some historical data to gain a deeper understanding of the reasons for his rancor.

Gawber is a member of a traditional, now dying, London middle class. His father, impoverished, had come to London in the early part of this century to work for the huge civil service that had evolved to control London's growth. Over the years, the Gawbers, proud of their accomplishments, enjoyed solid, well-ordered lives in their neighborhood.

After World War II, however, London changed radically. The soldiers came home, to be followed closely by thousands upon thousands of the British Empire's far-flung subjects: Africans, Asians, islanders from such places as Trinidad and Tobago, immigrants from India. The immigration was occasioned by postwar conditions. The war had devastated many colonies' economies. To make matters more complicated, many colonies were demanding independence and were politically unstable. In such a climate, many of the Empire's colonial subjects decided to try their hand at life in England. Many who arrived in London, however, had little money and few skills to support themselves.

They had to live somewhere. Gawber's neighborhood was one place they settled because the massive wartime bombing of London had decreased property values in that area significantly. Speculating real-estate agents had bought up the available housing cheaply and rented it to the newcomers at affordable prices. The poverty and colonial lifestyles of the newcomers offended and threatened traditionalists, many of whom packed up and left. Gawber was among the few who re-

CITYSCAPE 1-3
Mr. Gawber's London—A Neighborhood
in Transition

Volta Road . . . was in [Mr. Gawber's] eyes a corridor of cracked Edwardian aunts in old lace, shoulder to shoulder, shawled with tiles and beaked with sloping roofs; the upper gables like odd bonnets with peaks jutting over the oblongs of window lenses and the dim eyes blinded by criss-crossings of mullioned veils. With the long breasts of their bay-fronts forward and their knees against bruised, clawed steps, they knelt in the road, as if—gathering dust—they were dying in their prayers. . . .

Once, this road had the preserved well-tended look of . . . painted trim, owned by families for their cozy size and kept in repair. But the houses on Volta—with servants' bells in every room and names like The Sycamores—had fallen into the hands of speculators and building firms and enterprising landlords, who partitioned them with thin walls, sealing off serving hatches and doors, building kitchens in back bedrooms, installing toilets in broom cupboards, bolting a sink or a cooker on a landing so the stacked dishes were in full view of the street. . . .

Mr. Gawber had been born in number twelve and he had grown up in it. . . . He had attended the boys' school, Saint Dunstan's, at the top of the road and the Anglican church at the bottom. Now the church was Baptist and mostly black . . . he stayed away. He had seen the street's residents grow old and die or retire to the country, and after the war the houses had moved into a phase of decline that was, even now, unchecked. The new occupants were numerous, they were every human color, and the street was made nearly impassable by their parked cars. . . . The window boxes were empty, the hedges torn out, the gardens paved for cars and motorbikes. . . . It was not a bad road—there were many worse—but it would never improve. Eventually it would be bought wholesale by the council and boarded up and rained on, then pulled down and tall apartment blocks built on it. That was the pattern. . . .

Mr. Gawber thought: I am a relic from that other age. Lately, he had studied the new families. They were . . . Negroes and Irishmen who wore bicycle clips; dog-faced boys in mangy fur coats and surly mothers with red babies and children with broken teeth and very old men who inched down the sidewalk tapping canes. . . . There was a tall Chinese man and his wife in number eight and an Indian with a blue Land Rover next door—he washed the huge thing on Sunday mornings with his radio going. Mr. Gawber . . . did not know them well; they did not seem to know each other, and oddest of all, none of the darker people wore socks. Tropical folk with tropical names: Wangoosa, Aroma, Palmerston, Churchill, Pang. . . .

Mr. Gawber walked down the sidewalk feeling spied upon. In the warm weather . . . the life in those houses spilled into Volta Road—babies were wheeled out for approval, youths met and tinkered with motorbikes and taunted girls; arguments turned into fights, shameless courtships into loud weddings. . . . This evening they were out: Wangoosa mending his bicycle, Churchill dandling his baby, the Indian tuning his Land Rover, each one claiming his portion of the road. He wished these families away.

Mr. Gawber destroyed it with his eyes. He policed the ruins and found the idlers guilty of causing a nuisance and a breach of the peace, of unlawful assembly, uttering menaces, outraging the public modesty, and tax evasion. He blew a shrill whistle and had them carted off, then leveled the road, reducing the houses to a field of broken bricks and lumber, and he let the grass reassert itself and cover the rubble with its green hair. It would serve them right.

Source: Paul Theroux, *The Family Arsenal* (Boston: Houghton Mifflin, 1976), pp. 34–37.

mained to fume intransigently at the newcomers who symbolized the demise of his "orderly and decent life."

Taken together, then, these three aspects of the urban setting—its geography, economy, and ecological arrangements—are interrelated. These topics are discussed in Chapter 6.

The City and Culture

As we have already suggested, the city does not exist in a vacuum. It is "powered" by its people who represent a particular way of life, or culture. By the term *culture*, we mean the basic beliefs, values, and technology that characterize a society in a particular historical era. Any society's culture is reproduced and intensified in the city.

Technology provides a good example. If we were to visit the London of a century and a half ago, we likely would be shocked to see how different it was from the cities of today. Yes, we would find a bustling business district and lots of people—but there the similarity would end. Rather than a sprawling metropolitan area with extensive suburbs and shopping centers, crisscrossed by superhighways and adorned with skyscrapers, we would find a relatively compact city, with all its hustle going on in narrow, winding streets of astonishing filth. Once again, Charles Dickens, who lived there, provides us with an illustration:

> LONDON. . . . Implaccable November weather. As much mud in the streets as if the waters had but newly retreated from the face of the earth. . . . Smoke lowering down from chimney pots, making a soft black drizzle, with flakes of soot in it as big as full-grown snow-flakes—gone into mourning, one might imagine, for the death of the sun. Dogs, undistinguishable in mire. Horses, scarcely better; splashed to their very blinkers. Foot passengers, jostling one another's umbrellas, in a general infection of ill-temper, and losing their foothold at street-corners, where tens of thousands of other foot passengers have been slipping and sliding since the day broke (if this day ever broke), adding new deposits to the crust upon crust of mud . . . and accumulating at compound interest. (1853, p. 1)

Inevitable as they seem to us, clean, paved streets, clean air, the skyscraper, the superhighway, and the large, sprawling suburb are very recent urban phenomena, all products of a certain level of technological development. The skyscraper only became feasible in the latter part of the nineteenth century, when steel-frame buildings and electrically powered elevators were developed. Similarly, sprawling suburbs are unthinkable without superhighways or mass public transportation; these, in turn, are dependent on technological innovations such as steel, railroads, electricity, and the private automobile. Finally, paved streets became common in cities only in this century, and it wasn't until the 1950s and 1960s that clean air acts were passed in the United States to curtail exhaust excesses like those Dick-

ens described. A given level of technology, then, has much to do with the urban experience.

In the same way, cultural beliefs play a major role in shaping city life. Americans, for instance, live out distinctly American beliefs and values in an urban setting. Consider that well-known urban institution, the cabdriver, who earns a living in a society based on capitalistic free enterprise. Americans take as axiomatic that each individual is responsible for his or her own life and is in competition with others for the scarce resources that presumably make life better: wealth, power, and prestige. The operation of the taxi industry in New York is only one illustration of the influence of such distinctive cultural values on urban life.

Before the introduction of the automobile taxicab in 1907, most cabdrivers in New York owned their own carriage and horse and worked for themselves. The newly available automobile offered a strong competitive advantage, and, before long, taxi companies appeared. These companies distributed cars—too expensive for most individuals to own—to hired drivers, who received a cut of the fare paid by passengers. Soon, control of the New York market by cab companies was complete. Despite the appearance in recent years of "gypsy cabs"—taxis privately owned by drivers, who work out of their homes—most of New York's cabs still are controlled by large companies (Vidich 1976).

Understanding the situation of New York City cabdrivers depends on seeing how the central American value of maximizing private profit has shaped this facet of urban life. To maximize their profit, fleet owners try to pay drivers the smallest amount of the fare possible. Since they control the market, the percentage paid to the driver historically has been quite low, as low as one-third in some periods. Hence, to maximize *their* profit—indeed, to make a decent wage at all—cabdrivers frequently have employed two strategies: (1) cheating the fleet owner and sometimes the public and (2) learning to skillfully maximize tips.

One traditional, though illegal, technique is to take on fares without running the meter or to charge more than the meter reads (4 A.M., Greenwich Village: "You want to go to Queens? That'll be forty bucks!"). Faced with the loss of such revenue, angry fleet owners have employed private investigators—known as the "gestapo"—who drive about the city looking for cheating cabbies. Since 1968, however, owners have used a more efficient, electronic means of controlling cheating: the "hot seat." This is a device that immediately triggers the meter when a fare sits in the cab. Not surprisingly, this enterprising, sophisticated check on cheating produced an equally enterprising and sophisticated counterattack:

> It took several short months before the drivers realized that the hot seat, like all machines, was capable of being sabotaged and business could go on as usual. . . . Some of the more prominent counter devices to the hot seat have been the giant magnet, banana plugs and false back seats, requiring short circuiting and deadening of the electrical system of the entire cab. . . . As long as the driver can return his cab to the garage in the same electrical condition as he took it, the fleet owner has little to suspect. (Vidich 1976, pp. 35–36)

The desire to maximize tips has produced another intriguing technique, not necessarily geared to the most efficient or egalitarian service. Unlike waiters and bellhops, who also rely on tips, the cabdriver can never be assured of the same clientele. The service offered is essentially a one-shot interaction with a stranger. Also problematical is the fact that the driver's clientele is a mixed, even unpredictable, lot: city people, tourists, drunks, women in labor, people of all ethnic and racial backgrounds. Experience has taught the cabbie that all these people tip differently, that some may not tip at all, and that some may even try to jump fare or rob the cab (Davis 1959; Vidich 1976).

As a result, drivers use a screening system to evaluate potential fares before people get into the cab. If the cabbies like what they see, people ride; if they don't, people walk. Vidich (1976, pp. 15–16) reported that cabbies evaluate potential fares by considering (1) the quality of the neighborhood where the hail is made (poor neighborhoods are not likely to produce big tippers, and entertainment areas are likely to produce more tourists, notoriously bad tippers); (2) the people with or near the potential fare (a street gang will be passed by; a nicely dressed couple will ride); (3) where the person wants to go (someone going into town is likely to tip more than someone leaving town); and (4) the racial or ethnic characteristics of the person hailing (on the whole, blacks and other ethnic minorities tip more poorly than whites).

Once a potential fare has passed the tests and entered the cab, the driver has to decide what tactic to use to increase the tip. With city people, the trick is to be efficient. As a Chicago cabbie put it:

> Now, take a businessman. He's in a hurry to get someplace and he doesn't want a lot of bullshit and crapping around. With him you've got to keep moving. Do some fancy cutting in and out, give the cab a bit of a jerk when you take off from a light. Not reckless, mind you, but plenty of zip. He likes that. (Davis 1959, p. 161)

Old people may receive special treatment:

> They're more afraid than anyone of getting hurt or killed in a cab. Take it easy with them. Creep along, open doors for them, help them in and out, be real folksy. Call them "Sir" and "Ma'am" and they'll be calling you "young man." They're suckers for this stuff and they'll loosen up their pocketbooks a little bit. (Davis 1959, p. 164)

Or, when a driver anticipates a small tip, he or she may launch into a hard-luck story about the problems of being a "hack," of long hours, of insulting and unappreciative passengers. Another tactic is the "making change" ploy. "Depending on the tariff and the amount handed him, the driver can fumble about in his pocket for change, or make change in such denominations as often to embarrass a fare into giving a larger tip than he had intended" (Davis 1959, p. 162).

The behavior of the cabdriver reveals that the urban environment that we experience is not a product of the city alone. True, the urban setting has given rise to a need for quick, convenient, flexible transportation, and cabs have emerged to meet this need. But beyond this, the nature of the relationship among cabdriver, fleet owner, and passenger is influenced deeply by the specifically American cultural emphases on individual com-

BOX 1-2
Life in the Fast Lane: A New York Cab Ride

The Checker cab zoomed along Madison Avenue at a pace that guaranteed an interrupted string of green lights. Soon, Leslie H. ben-Zvi, the passenger, was aware that the cab's increasing speed and the lights were losing their synchronism and the greeting at the crosswalks was yellow rather than green. As the cab sped uptown ever more swiftly to overcome the sequence of yellow, Mr. ben-Zvi's view became one of panic-stricken pedestrians flying out of the way of the oncoming vehicle. When a red light finally forced the driver to screech to a heart-stopping halt, passenger remarked to driver that some of the pedestrians had barely got clear of the vehicle.

The driver turned around. "Yeah," he said. "It's sorta like a video game."

Source: *New York Times*, November 13, 1985, p. C2.

petition and maximization of private profits at almost any cost. Box 1-2 illustrates the adventure of taking a cab in New York City.

An examination of London cabbies would turn up rather striking differences. First, there is little conflict between drivers and fleet owners. A prime reason is that a full 40 percent of London's drivers (compared with a mere handful in New York) own their own cabs and are beholden to no one but themselves. This difference also has profound effects upon the remaining 60 percent, who work for fleets. Because of the threat that any driver may "go independent," fleet owners cannot impose rigid terms that drivers must meet. The same threat makes fleet owners more solicitous to drivers and more competitive with other fleets in terms of benefits offered (Buckland 1968).

Second, the British maintain far more government control of the cab industry than is the case in the United States. Although cities in both countries view cab driving as a public service, in England there are stringent requirements concerning the character and ability of drivers, and regulations on the upkeep of cabs are strictly enforced (Buckland 1968; Georgano 1973). This

control has reinforced a traditional value that competes with profit making in the minds of London's drivers and owners: pride. With cabs in good repair and personnel "up to a certain mark," London's taxi people have the *esprit de corps* of an elite group. Although restricted from cutting corners to maximize profit, most British drivers and fleet owners would not do so even if they could. Similarly, although many of London's cabbies struggle to make ends meet, they find it undignified to manipulate passengers for tips, as often happens in American cities (Buckland 1968, Chap. 7).

In comparison, government control is anathema to many Americans. New York fleet owners have lobbied long, hard, and successfully to keep government regulation to a minimum. With fewer restrictions and a powerful profit motive, they have been able to hire less experienced drivers and let cabs deteriorate tremendously (Vidich 1976, Chaps. 6–7). The result is more profit but also a lower quality of service and noticeably less pride.

It would be impossible to understand the differences between English and American cabdrivers without a careful study of the role that cultural beliefs play in the urban setting. So central is this issue to the study of cities that we devote all of Chapter 7 to it.

Chapters 2 through 7 will provide the basic framework for a detailed analysis of the cities of the contemporary world. With these six chapters as a starting point, we will examine next two regions of the globe in depth: first, the nonindustrial urban world—specifically the cities of Latin America, Africa, the Middle East, and Asia—and, then, American cities. Let us briefly note what some of our concerns will be in these excursions.

The City in World Perspective

If there is one thing that should absolutely rivet our attention when we consider the cities of the world, it is how astonishingly popular they become. Cities are only 10,000 years old as a human

TABLE 1-1
Percentage of Urban Population in Major Areas of the World, 1920–1985

Area	1920	1940	1960	1985
Europe (except Soviet Union)	32	37	41	73
Soviet Union	10	24	36	64
North America	38	45	57	74
Latin America (Central and South America)	14	19	32	66
Africa	5	7	13	31
Asia	7	11	17	27
Oceania	34	38	50	71
The World	14	19	25	41

Sources: "Growth of the World's Urban and Rural Population: 1920–2000," *International Social Development Review* 1 (1969), p. 52; Frisbie (1976); Population Reference Bureau (1985).

invention, and as the centuries have passed, people have continued to migrate to them in droves. To put it slightly differently, once people began to be aware of the advantages of cities—protection, increased material standard of living, a more stimulating mental and social life—the popularity of cities spread. The process of *urbanization*—the growth of cities and of their influence on human life—was under way. People are *still* moving to the cities, and they are *still* staying—in record numbers.

For example, in 1950 there were 906 urban places in the world with populations over 100,000. By 1984, there were 2,202 such places (Kurian 1984, p. 27). Table 1-1 makes the point even more powerfully. Reporting the percentage of urban people living in the world's seven major geographical areas between the years 1920 and 1985, the table shows that the continuing trend is toward the increasing urbanization of the population. Nor is this trend expected to decrease by the end of the century; by the year 2000, the world's urban population is likely to go over 50 percent.

On another level, however, the figures of Table 1-1 don't tell us enough. If we examine the table for the percentages of growth between 1960 and 1985, we can see that all regions increased in urban population. But this information hides the fact that in the more industrialized areas of the world—North America, Europe, and the Soviet Union—urban growth has either stopped or slowed considerably in recent years. For instance, the urban population of the U.S. in 1970 was 73.5 percent; in 1980 it was 73.7 percent.

The area of greatest urban growth is now in the non-industrial world, in Latin America, Africa, the Middle East, and Asia. In fact, when we consult the figures on urban growth rates by country, we find that the ten countries with the *highest* urban growth rates are all in these four regions; those with the *lowest* rates, with one exception (Uruguay, in South America), are all in Western Europe. Moreover, when we scan the list of all the world's countries and their urban growth rates, we reach the ninety-eighth highest country (Spain) before encountering an industrial society (Kurian 1984, p. 30).

What does all this mean? Why should it concern us? Aren't growing cities generally a good thing? After all, they produce jobs and generate better health care and stimulate improvements in technology and the arts, don't they? The answer to this question is two-edged: *sometimes* they do these things, but not always; and often, when they do them, they do them for very few of the city's people.

For the truth of the matter, all over the non-industrial world, is that the urban situation is desperate and in most places is getting more so daily.

BOX 1-3
A Shantytown Disaster in Ponce, Puerto Rico

Oct. 10, 1985. Tens of thousands of poor Puerto Ricans are living in unhealthy and dangerously situated shantytowns like the one that was struck by a landslide here four days ago, government officials and housing experts said today.

The communities of squatters, so poor that they cannot pay any amount of rent, have sprouted on the outskirts of the island's main cities.

Many of them cling perilously to steep hillsides, as did the community of Mameyes on the northern edge of [Ponce]. The landslide Monday morning literally wiped it off the earth, burying, the authorities say, as many as 500 people. Others, built of castoff scraps of lumber and tin by people who often have not even heard of building codes, sprawl across river flood plains and low-lying coastal strips where tidal flooding is common.

Aides to Governor Rafael Hernandez Colon and other government officials estimated in interviews today that more than 200,000 lived in the shantytowns built here, as in many countries of Latin America, Africa and Asia, by people who abandoned the countryside in search of better jobs and were unable to find affordable housing. . . .

Municipal officials here and state officials in San Juan said, however, that many of the shantytowns lacked proper sanitation facilities and nearly all of them piled together too many people in too little space.

In Mameyes, for example, many houses were without indoor plumbing. Some of the houses were stacked so close to one another that the edges overlapped.

There was no plan for the drainage of the latrines. . . .

Mayor Dapena said Ponce's housing shortage was closely related to the economic decline of the city that followed the closing of the oil refinery here and numerous small byproducts factories in 1980 and 1981. Some government officials estimate that the unemployment rate is up to nearly 50 percent and they said that nearly 90 percent of the people were receiving food stamps and other kinds of federal aid. . . .

"If we can't solve our economic problem," he [Dapena] said, "no matter what we do in housing, people will still be scratching. People won't be able to pay even a minimum amount for housing."

Source: Joseph B. Treaster, "Shantytowns Termed Widespread in Puerto Rico," *New York Times*, Oct. 11, 1985.

Enticed by the promise of a better life, hundreds of millions of people have moved into the cities of Latin America, Africa, the Middle East and Asia in the last decade and a half. Most of these cities *cannot* keep up with the incoming tide. The results are extreme poverty, malnutrition, disease, and, frequently, disaster for the bulk of many of these people. Box 1-3 provides an example, all the more poignant because it concerns the island of Puerto Rico in the Caribbean Sea. Despite the fact that Puerto Rico is usually considered part of Latin America, it is also a commonwealth of the United States. Hence, the description is of *American citizens.*

The situation in Puerto Rico is common throughout the non-industrial world. Although there are exceptions to the pattern—Japan, Hong Kong, and Singapore in Asia and some countries in the Middle East—the situation is grave and in need of attention. For this reason we devote three chapters to the study of the cities of these regions. Chapter 8 examines the cities of Latin America, Chapter 9 looks at those in Africa, and Chapter 10 concludes our analysis with a look at the urban problems and successes of Asia and the Middle East.

The Anatomy of Modern American Cities

Having viewed cities and urban life in world perspective, our attention returns to North America for detailed analysis of the cities most of us know best. The fact that urban population growth has slowed or stopped in the United States by no means suggests that the situation of our cities is stagnant and unchanging. Far from it. The last decade and a half has been a period of enormous change for American cities.

The much publicized movement to Sunbelt (southern and western) cities is one such change.

In *San Juan, Puerto Rico*, city trucks enter a slum area street to move fifty families from this squalor to a new life in a new housing development.
(UPI/Bettmann Newsphotos)

As Table 1-2 indicates, southern and western cities have gained markedly in population in the last decade, while midwestern and northeastern cities have generally declined. Growing significantly were the cities of Houston, Phoenix, and San Jose, all in the Sunbelt. Declining substantially were Chicago, Philadelphia, and Detroit, all in the Midwest or Northeast. Even New York City lost 9.3 percent of its population. The overall trend toward the South and West is expected to continue into the 1990s. The urban hegemony of the Northeast and Midwest seems to be drawing to a rapid close.

A second important development revealed by the 1980 census is a nationwide trend toward living in smaller cities or areas further away from large central cities. For instance, the census shows that the exurbs—the areas surrounding the suburbs—are growing rapidly. Thus, just as people moved from central cities to suburbs a generation ago, now they are moving still further out from the urban core.

Why have such marked changes occurred? These trends are still under study by demographers, but the following seems likely. First, as more affluent Americans reach retirement age, they are less willing to endure the severe winters and increased heating costs of living in the North. The little retirement house in Dade County, Florida (Miami's home county), in Brownsville, Texas, or in Sun City, Arizona (near Phoenix), has become an attraction that millions have no desire to resist. Second, the last decade has seen an increasing exodus of business and industry from center cities, occasioned by a desire to escape high taxation, congestion, outmoded plants, high union wages, and excessive heating costs (the latter two factors primarily in the North). In many cases, these firms have moved south or west. In others, they have moved to areas on the periphery of the center city. In either case, they have pulled their employees with them. The choice by these employees to live in smaller cities, exurbs, and rural areas is explained in part by their desire to be near relocated business or industry and in part by a long-standing American desire to be free of congestion and to have "living space." Earlier suburbs, built primarily in the 1950s and 1960s, were the first manifestation of this cultural value. The decentralization indicated by recent census data shows that this trend is continuing.

Whatever the final explanations for these demographic changes, their effects will be profound. Those cities with declining population will lose both federal funds and political representation, which are based on population. (Standing to lose millions of dollars and four seats in the House of Representatives as a result of population loss, in 1980 New York City sued the federal government for a census recount.) As a result, such cities will have to cut budgets, services, and aid to the poor and elderly, decreasing further their attractiveness as places to live. Because of lost revenues, inner suburbs also will begin to deteriorate

TABLE 1-2
Ranking of the Thirty Largest American Cities, 1984

1984 Ranking	City	1984 Population	1970 Population	1970 Ranking	Percent Change
1	New York	7,165,000	7,896,000	1	− 9.3
2	Los Angeles	3,097,000	2,812,000	3	+ 10.1
3	Chicago	2,992,000	3,369,000	2	− 11.2
4	Houston	1,706,000	1,234,000	6	+ 38.3
5	Philadelphia	1,647,000	1,949,000	4	− 15.6
6	Detroit	1,089,000	1,514,000	5	− 28.1
7	Dallas	974,000	844,000	8	+ 15.4
8	San Diego	960,000	697,000	14	+ 37.7
9	Phoenix	853,000	584,000	20	+ 46.0
10	San Antonio	843,000	654,000	15	+ 28.8
11	Baltimore	764,000	905,000	7	− 15.7
12	San Francisco	713,000	716,000	13	− 0.4
13	Indianapolis	710,000	737,000	11	− 3.7
14	San Jose, Calif.	686,000	460,000	29	+ 49.2
15	Memphis	648,000	624,000	17	+ 3.9
16	Washington, D.C.	623,000	757,000	9	− 17.7
17	Milwaukee	621,000	717,000	12	− 13.5
18	Jacksonville, Fla.	578,000	504,000	26	+ 14.6
19	Boston	571,000	641,000	16	− 11.0
20	Columbus, Ohio	566,000	540,000	21	+ 4.8
21	New Orleans	559,000	593,000	19	− 5.8
22	Cleveland	547,000	751,000	10	− 27.2
23	Denver	505,000	515,000	24	− 1.9
24	Seattle	488,000	531,000	22	− 8.0
25	El Paso	464,000	322,000	45	+ 44.0
26	Nashville-Davidson, Tenn.	462,000	426,000	32	+ 8.5
27	Oklahoma City	443,000	368,000	37	+ 20.4
28	Kansas City, Mo.	443,000	507,000	25	− 12.7
29	St. Louis	429,000	622,000	18	− 31.0
30	Atlanta	426,000	495,000	27	− 13.9

Source: Bureau of the Census, 1985.

as people move away. On the other hand, the small cities and exurbs gaining population are likely to "get rich quick." However, this growth will be a mixed blessing. Many residents of outlying areas, long accustomed to traditional rural lifestyles, will find themselves assailed by an "invasion of the city slickers" (as we will see later, in Cityscape 7-1).

What is life like in these cities of ours? Who lives in them? Why do they live there? What are the problems that these cities face? These and related questions will be dealt with in three chapters that look at American urban social structure. By *social structure*, we mean the recurrent patterns of city life that are shaped significantly by the unequal distribution of important urban resources, including wealth, power, and prestige.

One aspect of social structure concerns the wide variety of life-styles within our cities. Often, these life-styles are associated with different geographical districts of the city. In downtown areas, for example, we are likely to see well-dressed businesspeople—many of whom live in apartments; older residential neighborhoods may provide

CITYSCAPE 1-4

Wealth and Power—and the Lack of it—in the City

J. Pierpont Morgan

The offices of the J. P. Morgan Company were at 23 Wall Street. The great financier came to work one morning dressed in a dark blue suit, a black overcoat with a collar of lamb's wool and a top hat. He affected fashions slightly out of date. When he stepped out of his limousine the car robe fell around his feet. One of the several bank officers who had rushed out to meet him disentangled the robe and hung it over the robe rail on the inside of the door. The chauffeur thanked him profusely. Somehow the speaking tube had come off its hook and another officer of the bank replaced it. In the meantime Morgan had marched into the building, assistants, aides and even some of the firm's customers circling him like birds. Morgan carried a gold-headed cane. . . . Accepting the obeisances of his employees, he strode to his office, a modest glass-paneled room where he was visible to everyone and everyone was visible to him. He was helped with his hat and coat. He was wearing a wing collar and an ascot. . . . Pierpont Morgan was that classic American hero, a man born to extreme wealth who by dint of hard work and ruthlessness multiplies the family fortune until it is out of sight. He controlled 741 directorships in 112 corporations. He had once arranged a loan to the United States Government that had saved it from bankruptcy. . . . Moving about in private railroad cars or yachts he crossed all borders and was at home everywhere in the world. He was a monarch of the invisible, transnational kingdom of capital whose sovereignty was everywhere granted.

Source: E. L. Doctorow, *Ragtime* (New York: Bantam, 1975), pp. 157–159.

Jurgis and Ona Rudkis

The Arrival: Where They Lived. [That] afternoon [Jurgis] and Ona went out to take a walk and look about them, to see more of this district which was to be their home. In back of the yards the dreary two-story frame houses were scattered farther apart, and there were great spaces bare— that seemingly had been overlooked by the great sore of a city as it spread itself over the surface of the prairie. These bare places were grown up with dingy, yellow weeds hiding innumerable tomato cans; innumerable children played upon them, chasing one another here and there, screaming and fighting. . . .

[The streets] through which Jurgis and Ona were walking resembled streets less than they did a miniature topographical map. The roadway was commonly several feet lower than the level of the houses, which were sometimes joined by high boardwalks; there were no pavements—there were mountains and valleys and rivers, gullies and ditches, and great hollows full of stinking green water. In these pools the children played, and rolled about in the mud of the streets; here and there one noticed them digging in it, after trophies which they had stumbled on. One wondered about this, and also about the swarms of flies which hung about the scene, literally blackening the air, and the strange, fetid odor which assailed one's nostrils, a ghastly odor, of all the dead things of the universe. It impelled the visitor to questions—and then the residents would explain, quietly, that all this was "made" land, and

---

the sights, sounds, and even smells of exotic cultural diversity; in many suburban areas, single-family homes dominate—replete with children and the ever-present automobile. The understanding of these diverse urban life-styles is the topic of Chapter 11.

Life-styles are, of course, much more than matters of individual choice. They reflect dimensions of social difference, which often takes the form of social inequality—the focus of Chapter 12. Like virtually all other societies, the United States is characterized by marked patterns of *social stratification*, the hierarchical ranking of people whereby some have more resources than others. Wealth is certainly one important dimension of social stratification; American cities typically provide striking contrasts between well-heeled urbanites who live lives of material comfort and others who struggle on a daily basis to survive.

Very often, this difference is closely related to another dimension of social difference: *race and ethnicity.* Historically, immigrants of different races and ethnic origin have been attracted to American cities; on arrival many have found

that it had been "made" by using it as a dumping ground for the city garbage. After a few years the unpleasant effect of this would pass away, it was said; but meantime, in hot weather—and especially when it rained—the flies were apt to be annoying. Was it not unhealthful? the stranger would ask, and the residents would answer, "Perhaps; but there is no telling."

Three years later, Jurgis got a job in the stockyards, and, after much scrimping, he, Ona, and the family bought a house. Or so they thought. In actuality, the house they had "bought" had been rented to them by land speculators taking unscrupulous advantage of the Rudkises' ignorance of the fine print in the contract. When another family came along who could pay more, the Rudkises were unceremoniously turned out into the cold. What follows is Jurgis's realization of what has happened and his powerlessness to do anything about it.

The whole long agony came back to him. Their sacrifices in the beginning, their three hundred dollars that they had scraped together, all they owned in the world, all that stood between them and starvation! . . . Why, they had put their very souls into their payments on that house, they had paid for it with their sweat and tears—yes, more, with their very life blood. Dede Antanas had died of the struggle to earn that money—he would have been alive and strong today if he had not had to work in Durham's dark cellars to earn his share. And Ona, too, had given her health and strength to pay for it—she was wrecked and ruined because of it; and so was he, who had been a big, strong man three years ago, and now sat there shivering, broken, cowed, weeping like a hysterical child. . . .

Jurgis could see all the truth now. . . . Ah, God, the horror of it, the monstrous, hideous, demoniacal wickedness of it! He and his family, helpless women and children, struggling to live, ignorant and defenseless and forlorn as they were—and the enemies that had been lurking for them, crouching upon their trail and thirsting for their blood! That first lying circular, that smooth-tongued slippery [real estate] agent! That trap of the extra payments, the interest, and all the other charges that they had not the means to pay, and would never have attempted to pay! And then all the tricks of the packers, their masters, the tyrants who ruled them—the shutdowns and the scarcity of work, the irregular hours and the cruel speeding up, the lowering of wages, the raising of prices! The mercilessness of nature about them, of heat and cold, rain and snow; the mercilessness of the city, of the country in which they lived, of its laws and customs that they did not understand! All of these things had worked together for the company that had marked them for its prey and was waiting for its chance. And now, with this last hideous injustice, its time had come, and it had turned them out bag and baggage, and taken their house and sold it again! And they could do nothing, they were tied hand and foot—the law was against them, the whole machinery of society was at their oppressors' command!

Source: Upton Sinclair, *The Jungle* (New York: Viking, 1947), pp. 28–29, 176–177.

themselves at or near the bottom of the social stratification system. With time, many have managed to improve their situation, but others continue to suffer from a wide range of problems associated with poverty. Consider, for example, black novelist James Baldwin's assertion that racial difference is a fundamental element of American city life (Box 1-4).

Social power—the ability to achieve one's ends and to shape events—is yet another important dimension of inequality. For those with considerable wealth, urban living is often the experience of shaping their own lives (and, indeed, the lives of others); for poorer urbanites, however, many of whom are members of racial and ethnic minorities, life in the city is a grim matter of trying to cope with forces that often seem overwhelming and out of control.

It should be clear immediately that none of these structural patterns is found exclusively in cities. Social stratification is as important in small towns in New Hampshire as it is in Concord, the capital; racial distinctions are perceived as keenly in rural Tennessee as they are in Knoxville; and

---

BOX 1-4
Race and the City

The life of the city is hard for everybody. But, baby, try it if you're black. We began to move across the river [from Harlem] to the Bronx and . . . all those [white people] fled in terror. One of the results is the present disaster called the South Bronx where nobody can live. The movement of white people in this country has been—and it is terrifying to say this, but time to face it—a furious attempt to get away from the niggers.

Source: James Baldwin in "Symposium: Literature and the Urban Experience," *Humanities*, 1:4 (July/Aug. 1980), p. 3.

"power politics" is the name of the game in rural Wyoming, just as it is in Cheyenne. Nevertheless, because these structural patterns have shaped our cities so strongly, they can hardly be ignored.

On another level, however, because cities concentrate everything human in a small space, there is a tendency for the effects of class, race, and power to be intensified. If we care to look, we can be buffeted by visions of wealth and poverty, of power and powerlessness of such extremity as to be nearly incomprehensible. Cityscape 1-4 gives such contrasting visions. It depicts the phenomenal wealth and power of J. Pierpont Morgan, the late-nineteenth-century industrialist, and contrasts his life with the shattering poverty and powerlessness of Lithuanians Jurgis and Ona Rudkis, new arrivals in the immigrant camps of Chicago in the same period. Both Morgan and the Rudkises worked extremely hard. Yet, because of his early advantages, Morgan gained fabulous wealth and power, while the Rudkises, despite all their efforts, were doomed to failure. The structural organization of wealth and power in the city was against them from the start.

The horrific poverty experienced by the Rudkises has by no means disappeared, as a walk through the poor neighborhoods of almost any major American city will reveal. Indeed, poverty for millions continues as only one of the significant problems that beset the American urban environment. Others are housing, crime, violence,

and inadequate financial resources. An analysis of all these problems and their implications is found in Chapter 13.

Urban Sociology and the Quality of City Life

The city is a dynamic, enduring, living entity. After society itself, the city is perhaps the most important phenomenon on the current world stage. This is because, of all human "inventions" (and make no mistake about it, the city *is* an invention), it contains the most potential for improving the quality of human life.

From its beginnings millenia ago, people have come to the city with hopes and dreams of a better existence. Aristotle said it best nearly 2,500 years ago: people went to cities, initially, for security, but they stayed there in order to live the good life. But what is this "good life"? When all is said and done, has the city truly enhanced human existence? True, material living standards are higher than they ever have been in history in many cities—but not for all of the city inhabitants. Further, in many cities of the non-industrial world material living standards are appallingly low—destitution in these cities is the rule, not the exception. Moreover, to focus on material standards alone may be a mistake. What about security, Aristotle's first concern? Many areas in American cities are so dangerous that people cannot go out alone or at night without fear of being mugged. What about strong, community-oriented neighborhoods? Once a primary element of American cities, these too have weakened—and in some areas disappeared altogether—in the past few decades.

All of these questions need to be addressed. We need to understand the whole spectrum of conditions that contribute to a more stimulating, fulfilling urban life. Similarly, can we identify conditions that diminish the quality of urban life?

In bits and pieces throughout this book, evidence regarding the positive and negative elements of the city will emerge. We shall comment on some of this evidence as we proceed and, in the final two chapters, pull together these ideas as we examine urban planning (Chapter 14) along with models of "the good city" and speculations about the future of cities (Chapter 15).

Because of the ever-increasing importance of the city as the fulcrum of contemporary existence, such an evaluative assessment of its humane potential is absolutely essential. Are we inevitably heirs to the city of rage, racial prejudice, and exploitation that Mr. Gawber, James Baldwin, and Jurgis and Ona Rudkis encountered? Or can the city become the ideal suggested by historian Lewis Mumford in the following passage?

The mission of the city is to further [the human being's] conscious participation in the cosmic and historic process. Through its own complex and enduring structure, the city vastly augments [human beings'] ability to interpret these processes and take an active, formative part in them, so that every phase of the drama it stages shall have, to the highest degree possible, the illumination of consciousness, the stamp of purpose, the color of love. That magnification of all the dimensions of life, through emotional communion, rational communication, technological mastery, and above all, dramatic representation, has been the supreme office of the city in history. And it remains the chief reason for the city's continued existence. (1961, p. 576)

To answer, we need go and make our visit.

(Menschenfreund)

PART 2

Cities in Historical Perspective

CHAPTER 2

The Origin and Development of The City

From our contemporary perspective the city seems almost synonymous with civilization itself. Could we imagine the United States without such great cities as New York, Chicago, or San Francisco? The same holds true if we look to Europe, where societies are far older than the United States. Can we imagine England without London? France without Paris? Greece without Athens? Italy without Rome? Difficult—perhaps impossible. Indeed, as we shall see in this chapter, much of the story of human civilization *is* centered on the city.

But this was not always the case. We readily recognize the importance of cities because we live in an era in which the city is the dominant form of human association and is becoming more so every day. In the larger picture of human history, however, the city is a mere "babe in the woods"— a very *recent* arrival on the human scene.

Origins

When and where did the first cities develop? What were they like? How did they change over time? Here we shall attempt to answer these crucial questions. But, before we can do so, we must

look far back into time to see just how recently we human beings began making history on this earth.

Astronomer Carl Sagan (1977) suggests that we do this by imagining the entire history of our planet compressed into a single calendar year. What does such a vision suggest? To begin, for almost the entire history of the earth (roughly from January 1—the date of the "Big Bang"), the human species as we know it did not even *exist*. In fact, anatomically modern humans (*Homo sapiens sapiens*) appeared on earth a mere 50,000 years ago (December 31 in Sagan's year). Another 40,000 years passed before permanent settlements—even in the form of small villages—existed. The emergence of the first cities, then, and with them the way of life we commonly call "civilization," occurred only about *10,000* years ago (8000 B.C.)—in the last minute of Sagan's year! It would be several thousand more years, around 3000 B.C., before cities became common. Even then they contained only a small proportion of the world's population.

Indeed, it is only in the last several centuries (the last *second* in Sagan's year) that the world has acquired a sizable urban population. As recently as 1950 the proportion of the world's population living in cities was only 16 percent. Today, this

28

figure has grown to about 32 percent. The existence of the city and the urban way of life that we so readily take for granted, in other words, are very recent and enormous changes in the history of the world.

Archaeology and the Early City

Learning about the first cities has been a gradual process fraught with difficulties. Traditionally, urban sociologists and anthropologists have relied heavily on the work of archaeologists to gain an understanding of early settlements. Through excavation and techniques for determining the age of artifacts, we have learned much about the social life of people who left little formal record of their existence. Often, however, simply *finding* the sites of early cities—frequently buried beneath the surface, hidden by dense plant growth, or even covered by a current metropolis—is a matter of hard work and a bit of luck. Once an ancient city is found, excavation must proceed carefully to avoid damaging the remains. Finally, even when a city has been excavated successfully, archaeologists do not always agree in their interpretations of findings at a given site.

Moreover, our understanding of early urban settlements is continually subject to revision. Ongoing investigation at old sites and the discovery of new locations (such as the recent excavation at Gran Pajaten in Peru) may provide new data. In addition, techniques of analysis continually improve, often leading to a reformulation of many beliefs urbanists held with certainty only a few years ago.

We still have much to learn; nevertheless, this chapter presents what we now know about early cities. We examine cities as they first took form in the ancient world and consider how, as the centuries passed, they reflected the changing character of human civilization.

The First Permanent Settlements: Why They Began

Human beings as we know them today first appeared on the earth about 50,000 years ago. All the evidence now at hand suggests that, for the next 40,000 years, our ancestors lived as hunters and gatherers—hunting game and gathering vegetation for food over large areas. Most lived in small groups, ranging in size from 25 to 50 individuals. Nomads, these people had no truly permanent settlements. Frequently they would camp in a place for a few weeks because the hunting was good or the vegetation was plentiful. When the game left the area or the vegetation went out of season, the people moved on.

Then, around 10,000 years ago, near the end of the last Ice Age, a change occurred. It happened slowly and without any evident drama. Nonetheless it was to be one of the most momentous changes in human history: People began to settle in places *permanently* and to evolve more complex social structures. Civilization as we know it was beginning. Why?

Many archaeologists now think it had something to do with *population density* (Cohen 1977). As time went on, the number of hunter-gatherer tribes grew. Gradually but inexorably, they began to deplete the natural resources that had formed the mainstay of their existence for millenia. Game became less abundant; vegetation didn't grow back as quickly.

How could these nomads solve the food shortage problem? They could wander over larger areas, but that would be difficult and threatened to place them in direct competition with other groups. They could eat less nutritious food, but that would be undesirable unless absolutely necessary. They could carry extra food from areas of abundance, but this would be burdensome without the use of animals—which had not yet been domesticated. One more possibility was to settle in the most fertile areas and attempt to raise their own food. This option, over time, was the one that won out.

The choice had crucial consequences for human history. Just as hunting and gathering required almost continuous movement, so raising crops and domesticating animals demanded permanent settlements. Thus villages began and, over a period of some 5,000 years, they began to multiply.

As permanent settlements flourished, patterns of social structure were transformed. To take one important example, these settlements were all characterized by a more complex *division of labor*. For the first time people began doing many different, *specialized* tasks to "earn a living." This was a radical shift from the social structure that prevailed in hunter-gatherer tribes. While nomadic groups clearly divided up life's responsibilities—by age or sex, for example—they were not specialists. Everyone knew a bit about everything; no one was a full-time doctor, lawyer, priest, or farmer. Permanent settlements, however, could afford people specializing in religion or military affairs. Others could specialize in producing food. Indeed, by such an arrangement, all benefited: the farmer gained the protection of the military and the value of the priest's greater insight into matters religious, while the priest and the soldier received the fruits of the farmer's labors. In short, these early settlements provided, from their beginnings, the possibility of living a life based more on *choice* than tradition. As Dora Jane Hamblin has suggested, "No longer was every man forced to be a hunter or a farmer, every woman a mother and a housekeeper." Such a tantalizing variety, "offering the possibility of following a personal bent rather than a parent's footsteps, must have been as powerful a lure in 8000 B.C. as in the twentieth century" (Hamblin 1973, pp. 9–10).

Linked to the more complex division of labor was a second major element in the social structure of these early settlements: a *hierarchical power structure*. Hunting and gathering societies tend to be egalitarian. That is, while people perform different tasks in daily life, all tasks are deemed equally important to the welfare of the group. For example, hunting (typically done by men) is held to be no more important than gathering food or caring for children (usually women's tasks). Furthermore, with the limited productive technology possessed by hunter-gatherers, there are few resources beyond those needed for daily life; no one is able to amass much more wealth than anyone else.

All that began to change as permanent settlements developed. Fried (1967) suggests that the use of *power*—the ability to demand compliance of others—increased as settlements became more complex. There is a good reason for this. A more complex division of labor requires the *unequal*

distribution of power for activity to be efficient. For instance, if agricultural workers were to support a large number of nonagricultural people engaged in other specialized activities, someone would have to oversee the collection and distribution of the food surplus. Some form of administrative leadership—a king, a council of elders—would therefore appear necessary. This leadership could oversee other important tasks as well, such as the construction of buildings, of walls for defense, of irrigation systems, the collection of taxes, and long-range planning (Sjoberg 1973, p. 19).

Of course, there was another advantage of a hierarchical power structure, at least for those nearer the top. Higher-ups were rewarded for their efforts (or by their very control over others) with greater amounts of wealth and prestige. Both provided these people with the ability to enjoy more of "the finer things in life." There is ample historical (as well as modern) evidence that suggests that positions of power are not always used for the good of all people.

Given a more complex division of labor and the development of a hierarchical power structure, a third element was probably necessary for cities to emerge: the development of a *productive surplus*. Earlier in this section we mentioned that many archaeologists now believe that the development of agriculture as a response to population pressure was the main reason people gave up hunting and gathering for permanent settlements. Many also believe that a similar process was at work in the gradual transition from village to town to city. Specifically, a growing population could not be supported without a surplus of food. This notion of "agricultural primacy"—food surplus first, then permanent settlements—has been fostered by the discovery, in many early sites around the world, of the remains of domesticated plants and animals.

In summary, then, we can conclude the following about the emergence of the first permanent human settlements. Around 8000 B.C., hunting and gathering societies began to increase in number. As a response to this population increase, people began to settle down and take up agriculture as a way of life. These permanent settlements were characterized by increasingly complex social structures organized around a division of labor and a hierarchical power structure. Also associated with the largest of these settlements was a productive surplus of some kind. As these elements coalesced, they fed on each other: The division of labor led to more efficient use of human and natural resources, which in turn led to a greater division of labor and a more intricate power structure, and so on. As this happened, villages turned into towns and then towns into the first cities.

The City Emerges

What do we know of these earliest cities? We begin with what currently is understood to have been the first city: Jericho. The modern city and its ancient ruins lie just to the north of the Dead Sea, in present-day Israel (see Figure 2-1).

Jericho

When it is approached by air, Jericho stands out as a tiny green oasis set in a glittering expanse of desert. The modern city is a cluster of lush parks, palm trees and attractive homes. . . . Just north of the modern city is a bulging mound, which is of far greater significance to archaeologists than the present Jericho. They have carved up the mound into a network of trenches to study the layers of civilization below the surface; for beneath this now welted and pock-marked ground lies the evidence of a much earlier Jericho, and in fact the oldest city yet to be discovered anywhere in the world. (Hamblin 1973, p. 29)

With the excavation of Jericho, the history of cities has been largely rewritten. Previously, it was believed that the first cities arose in the Fertile Crescent region of Mesopotamia (present-day Iraq) about 3500 B.C. The work of archaeologists at Jericho, notably Kathleen Kenyon, has established the fact that Jericho was a "developing city" ten millennia ago; it was a city that had become "ancient when the pyramids were new" (Hamblin 1973, p. 29).

Research at Jericho, however, has sparked a debate: At which point could one speak of a permanent settlement as being a "city"? Kenyon (1957, 1970) argues that the size (about 600 people) and the architectural construction of Jericho were sufficient to allow it to be considered a city about 8000 B.C. Others disagree, observing that Jericho was, at that time, very small: only 500 or 600 people settled in an area of about ten acres. Size, however, is not the only important factor. Density and the complexity of social life—involving a broad range of activities and a hierarchy of power relations—added to Jericho's claim to city status.

What made Jericho different from other settlements of its time was the presence of a surrounding wall, a tower, and a large trench, all suggesting an advanced division of labor and a hierarchical social order that could oversee large-scale public works. The wall further points to a recognition of the need for defense and protection from the elements. Even after 10,000 years of erosion, its ruins are some 12 feet high and 6 feet thick at the base. The trench, cut into solid rock, is about 27 feet across and 9 feet deep. Although archaeologists are not sure what it was used for (to hold water?), certainly a complex, cooperative effort was necessary to create it. Jericho may have developed a system of irrigation to take oasis spring water to the surrounding fields. The houses its settlers built appear to have been round and constructed of handmade, sun-dried brick.

A short account of the later history of the city holds an interesting lesson in the history of urban settlements. It seems that the original settlers of Jericho did not remain past about 7000 B.C., when a second group took up residence. This second group was more technologically advanced than the original settlers, constructing rectangular houses of bricks and mortar with plaster walls and floors. Around this time, trade with outsiders appears to have developed, adding to Jericho's cosmopolitan character. Then, about 1,000 years later—near 6000 B.C.—the site was inexplicably abandoned and remained so for a millennium.

Resettlement began about 5000 B.C., providing yet another twist to Jericho's story. The later settlers were markedly *less* advanced in their technology, digging only primitive shelters, and no public works are traceable to this period. Then,

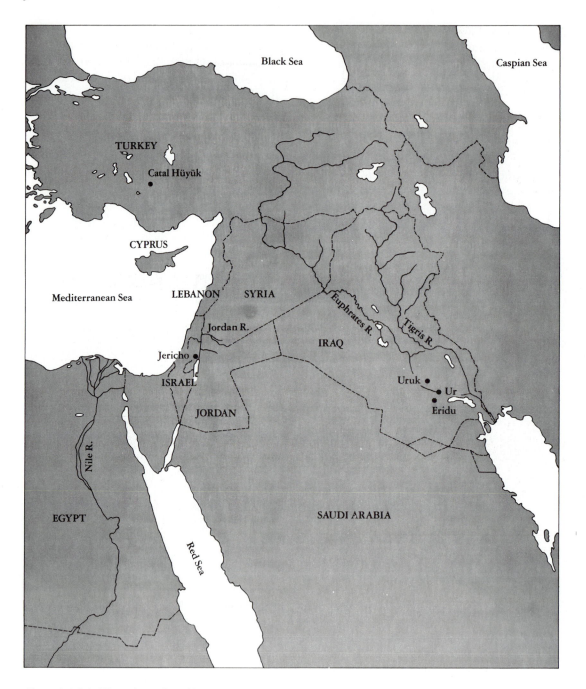

Figure 2-1 *Asia Minor: the earliest cities.*

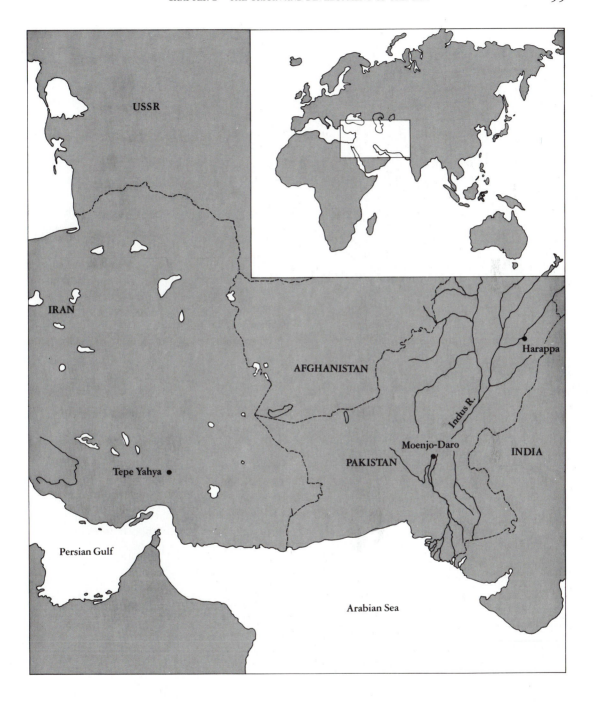

with the coming of the Bronze Age about 3000 B.C., a far more advanced culture prevailed. Artwork is evident, possibly linked to the civilization in Mesopotamia to the east or Egypt to the southwest. By the time settlement of ancient Jericho came to an end about 1500 B.C., many other groups had lived within the city.

The story of Jericho teaches us that the history of cities must not be oversimplified. Cities do *not* always grow incrementally in population and gradually gain in size and technical capacity, as our modern preconceptions might suggest. Discontinuity and unexpected events change developmental patterns again and again, as we shall see in the remainder of this chapter.

Catal Hüyük

Evidence produced by excavation at Jericho has placed the beginning of city life between 7000 B.C. and 8000 B.C. By 6000 B.C., other sites, such as Catal Hüyük (pronounced Sha-tal Hoo-yook) in present-day Turkey, had become well developed. Originally settled on a 32-acre site, Catal Hüyük eventually supported a population of some 6,000. Archaeological work there has been extensive. So much has been learned that it is possible to reconstruct a portrait of daily life, as is done in Cityscape 2-1.

The First Urban Revolution: City-States and Urban Empires

Although scattered cities such as Jericho and Catal Hüyük thrived in the period between 7000 B.C. and 4000 B.C., it was not until about 3500 B.C. that urban development accelerated to a point where large numbers of cities were in existence.

What seems to have happened is this: The earliest cities, like Jericho, clearly demonstrated the ability of this form of human organization to generate security and wealth for fairly large numbers of people. Thus, more and more people came to the city to share in these benefits. The *idea* of the city was taking hold. No longer were many people content to live the "backward" life of the tribe, the village, or the town. They wanted

the benefits of the city: more choice, material wealth (at a level undreamed of in hunting and gathering societies), excitement, and, not least, personal power.

So cities grew in number and in population. But growth brought with it problems: Production had to be increased to take care of these people, and the rising standard of living, especially among the elite, gave rise to dreams of even greater wealth. As important, there had to be a way to manage the city's inhabitants as their number grew. Some cities responded to this challenge by making their social structure even more complex: they created *the state* (Fried 1967).

The central feature of the state is its ability to wield power over many people, to more or less dictate the rights and responsibilities of everyone: who has to live where, who has to serve in the military, and so on. With such power the city's leaders can do pretty much what they like to solve (or create) the city's problems—they can reorganize production in this way or that, they can determine who is educated and who is not, and, perhaps most important, they can make alliances and wage war to capture land, population, and resources.

With the emergence of the state form of social organization came the first *city-states*, cities that controlled surrounding regions including a number of other towns, villages, and rural lands. As time passed, some of these city-states conquered or made alliances with others to form the world's first *urban empires*, much larger regions, usually dominated by a single central city. As we shall see, these first urban empires emerged in particular areas of the world—in Mesopotamia, Egypt, the Indus River Valley, China, Central America, and South America—and they "pushed" the city as a form of human settlement to ever greater complexity and population size.

In the regions where this change occurred, cities became an indispensable fact of political life. To maintain their independence as well as to continually increase their material standard of living, people *had* to be organized as a city. Anything less would make them nearly defenseless against the predatory advances of other groups who *were* organized in such a fashion. As anthro-

---

CITYSCAPE 2-1
Daily Life in Catal Hüyük, 6000 B.C.

When the first light of dawn struck . . . on a spring morning in the year 6000 B.C., it brushed lightly across the flat roofs of tightly built mud-brick houses. . . . The houses turned blank, doorless walls to the world. The household entrance was by way of the roof through either a wooden doorway or a thatch opening onto a ladder. Doors at ground level could have let in anything from floodwaters to wild animals: the roof holes and ladders provided security. . . .

Inside one of the houses the father stirred. . . . From his leather pouch he grasped a lump of yellowish, crystalline sulfur collected on his last trip to the hills, and a flint tool that he had fashioned to his needs. . . . With this prehistoric Boy Scout knife the man could make wood shavings, strike a spark, feed the spark with sulfur and produce a fire within min-

utes. . . . The man made a fire on the hearth while his wife went through a small doorless opening in the mud-brick wall to the family food-storage niche. In it was a bin about a yard high, made of clay and very clean. She drew some grain from a small hole at the bin's bottom: it was always filled from the top and emptied from the bottom so that the oldest grain, or that most exposed to damp, would be used first. The wife moved slowly. She was heavy with another child, and she was getting old: almost 28.

On that mythical morning the family ate a gruel of grain and milk, supplemented by bits of meat left over from a previous meal. The mother nursed the baby while she fed the next-oldest with a spoon made from a cow's rib bone. . . .

Then there was work to do. . . .

The man and the woman might have tended fields or flocks, but not many townsfolk could have been farmers—no compact community of 6,000 people could have grown enough food to support itself while doing all the other things that Catal Hüyük residents did. The city must have traded goods and services for supplies from the surrounding region. The woman of the house might conceivably have made baskets for such trade. Or the man might have spent his days as a craftsman, for although no specialized tools were found in his home, there is ample evidence in the city of skillfully woven textiles, good pottery and beautiful art work.

Source: Dora Jane Hamblin, *The First Cities* (New York: Time-Life, 1973), pp. 43–46, excerpts.

---

pologist Richard Sipes (1973) has argued, when one group attacks another, the group attacked has little choice but to respond aggressively (whether its members wish to or not) if it is going to survive.

This, then, was the period of the *first urban revolution* (Childe 1950). From approximately 4000 B.C. to A.D. 500, the city began to take on a life of its own. Urban sites multiplied and their populations grew to sizes unknown before in human history (Rome at its apex was over a million; in comparison, hunter-gatherer societies typically have fewer than 50 people).

In retrospect, the first urban revolution appears to be a bit of a mixed blessing. The city's greatest positive attributes are its ability to increase a people's standard of living, provide choice in the conduct of life, and stimulate the human mind in new and different ways. There is little doubt that the earliest cities did this. On the other hand, the evidence is clear that these first cities also had rigid social class divisions that allowed access to

the city's benefits to only a small minority of the urban population. With the emergence of city-states and urban empires, human warfare and bloodshed rose to unparalleled levels.

Recent evidence suggests that the city, as a form of human organization, was not intrinsically at fault regarding these more negative attributes. Rather, it appears that the division of society into discriminatory social classes and the incidence of warfare had been increasing for more than four thousand years before cities became common. Recall that one major characteristic of the first permanent settlements, which began about 8000 B.C., was the development of a productive surplus—more wealth, food, and material resources than were absolutely necessary to sustain life at a minimum standard. It was a desire to partake in this surplus that drew others from the countryside to these settlements, which allowed an increase in living standards for those already there. However, this same surplus also caught the eyes of a

---

BOX 2-1
The Perilous Life of Ancient Cities

The archaeological record makes it very clear that warfare was common among the earliest cities. Along with their many benefits such as an increased standard of living and more choice of life-style, many of the residents of these urban centers must have lived in some trepidation that, sooner or later, they would have to pay the price for having such amenities. This is illustrated in the following excerpts. In the first, historian Lewis Mumford relates how the first cities allowed human aggression to be transformed into a much more virulent form. In the second, Ilene Nicholas gives an example of an ancient city that ran afoul of some other group's belligerence.

Once the city came into existence, with its collective increase in power in every department, [the whole situation regarding aggression] underwent a change. Instead of raids and sallies for individual victims [the hallmark of hunter-gatherer societies], mass extermination and mass destruc-

tion came to prevail. . . . Much of this aggression was unprovoked, and morally unjustified by the aggressor. . . . To accumulate power, to hold power, to express power by deliberate acts of murderous destruction—this became the constant obsession of [the earliest cities' kings]. In displaying such power the king could do no wrong. By the very act of war the victorious king demonstrated the maximum possibilities of royal control. . . . [Such cities] invited a centralized military control, systematic robbery, and economic parasitism—all institutions that worked against the life-promoting aspects of urban civilization, and finally brought one city after another to its ruin. . . . As soon as war had become one of the reasons for the city's existence, the city's own wealth and power made it a natural target. The presence of thriving cities gave collective aggression a visible object that had never before beckoned: the city itself, with its growing accumulation of tools and mechanical equipment, its hoards of gold, sil-

ver, and jewels, heaped in palace and temple, its well-filled granaries and storehouses. . . .

Consider the small Iron Age city of Hasanlu, near the south shore of present-day Lake Urmia in northwestern Iran. Around 800 B.C. this flourishing settlement was abruptly conquered and destroyed. The archaeological record at Hasanlu . . . is strikingly clear: Invaders . . . attacked and set the settlement afire. The elaborate citadel buildings burned and collapsed, trapping many in their ruins. Other individuals were massacred in the streets by the raiders. No one ever returned to bury these victims, although later a few squatters briefly lived at the site. . . . [This battle] essentially ended Hasanlu's life as an important cultural center as abruptly and as finally as the eruption of [Mount] Vesuvius ended the life of Pompeii [in Italy in A.D. 79].

Source: Lewis Mumford, *The City in History* (New York: Harcourt, Brace and World, 1961), pp. 42–43 (excerpts); Ilene Nicholas, "Extinct Cities." In *Cities*, Lisa Taylor, ed. (New York: Cooper-Hewitt Museum, 1982), p. 6.

---

covetous few. It did not take such people long to figure out that, if they could grasp power for themselves and keep it from others, they could possess more of the surplus. Nor did it take some settlements long to understand that if one settlement made war on another and conquered it, the victors could have the conquered settlement's surplus for their own coffers (Harris 1977). This desire to accumulate more and more wealth, prestige, and power is what anthropologists Richard Leakey and Roger Lewis (1977) call *psychomaterialism*, and it was on the increase from the time the first permanent settlements arose. As cities appeared in significant numbers around 3500 B.C., the competition and aggression already rampant among them magnified and intensified (see Box 2-1).

With all this in mind, then, we now turn to brief descriptions of some of the first urban empires.

The Near East: Mesopotamia and Egypt

Mesopotamia. The first such empire, most recent evidence suggests, was in the Fertile Crescent region of the Tigris and Euphrates Rivers in the southern portion of present-day Iraq. This region, commonly known in ancient times as Mesopotamia or Sumer, began evolving significant cities as early as 4000 B.C. Cities such as Uruk, Eridu, and Ur (see Figure 2-1) represent a significant extension of world urbanization not only because they were larger than their earlier counterparts but also because of their more complex social structures. Wheat and barley were important domesticated crops, and city dwellers enjoyed the advantages of oxen-pulled plows and the wheel, major technological advances (Sjoberg 1965; Stavrianos 1983).

The cities of the region reached their greatest development about 2800 B.C. Uruk, it is estimated, covered an area of about 1,100 acres (Adams 1966, p. 69) and supported a population as high as 50,000 (Hamblin 1973, p. 89). All the Mesopotamian cities were theocracies, ruled by a king who was also the main priest. The priest-king led a ruling elite, who controlled and protected the area about the city, including its agricultural land, exacted a portion of the agricultural surplus as tribute, and stored it in the major temple (Sjoberg 1965), clearly evidence of a strong commitment to psychomaterialism.

Uruk and other Mesopotamian cities had highly complex social structures including a power hierarchy and a pronounced division of labor. Excavations have established the existence of monumental public buildings, including ziggurats (religious shrines); extensive trade arrangements; a system of writing (cuneiform); mathematics; and a code of law. Sumerian texts noting the concerns of everyday life still survive. In these accounts, sheep, goats, and cattle are tabulated, taxed, and exchanged; children are shepherded to school—as always, much against their will—by concerned parents; a council of elders meets to consider grievances against the inhabitants of an adjoining city-state; and a politician attempts to win the favor of the populace with tax reductions (Wenke 1980). Clearly these cities had advanced to a point at which parallels may be easily drawn with cities of our own experience.

Early Mesopotamian urban life was centered, however, on the temple and on religious beliefs. Thousands of gods were recognized by the populace, and temples, like the palaces, were correspondingly large and opulently decorated. People of less favorable social position lived in irregularly organized houses about the narrow, unpaved, winding streets (Sjoberg, 1965). The complex social structure also resulted in a strong military elite and made possible an increasing capacity to wage war. Frequently under attack, Mesopotamian cities were walled defensively (Hamblin 1973).

After about 3500 B.C., the cities began to be organized as politically distinct city-states, each exerting its influence over a broad region. Although these city-states were independent of one another and often at war, they did represent a common civilization. They had a common cultural heritage and, as far as the outside world was concerned, saw themselves as possessors of a unique, even superior, culture (Wenke 1980).

About 2350 B.C., the city-states were forcibly united into one of the first urban empires. Sargon, a general from the city of Akkad, fought battle after battle with rival city-states, vanquishing all. According to an Akkadian document, as each southern city fell to his marching armies, Sargon captured "many kings, smashed many city walls," and finally "cleansed his weapons in the sea"—the Persian Gulf (Wenke 1980, p. 419). The Gulf region under control, Sargon then turned his eyes on cities in what are now Syria, Lebanon, and Iran, attempting to spread his empire westward.

Control of the conquered cities was apparently tenuous, as Sargon's successors had to refight his battles again and again to maintain Akkadian dominance. Even with this effort, their control was short-lived. Around 2200 B.C., the empire crumbled under attack from seminomadic peoples. It reasserted itself once more around 2100 B.C., when the invaders were cast out and an empire based at Ur—the Ur III Dynasty—was established. One ruler, Ur-Nammu, like Sargon before him, set his sights on faraway borders and reconquered much of the territory previously occupied by the Akkadian leader. He rebuilt the cities, constructed irrigation systems and roads, and reestablished the rule of law in many of these urban areas. But time was to take the measure of his dynasty as well; in 2004 B.C., the Elamites invaded from the north and led the then king of Ur away in captivity, shattering the empire.

The history of the region until the birth of Christ was much the same: group after group conquered the cities and established short-lived empires. The Assyrian Empire dominated the region around 700 B.C., and the Persian Empire followed around 500 B.C. The importance of this continual trading of urban dominance was that it spurred the development of cities and their influence throughout the Near East. In an effort to maintain control of their empire, each set of rulers tried to develop their cities as much as their culture and technology would permit. The cities of the region were continually renewed with inventions, innovations, and new ideas supplied by trade and people of different backgrounds.

Although it would be too much to say that these cities contained *all* of civilization in their era, they were important *centers*. They were "containers" in a double sense: they literally encircled their population and their valued goods with walls and, more figuratively, served as the place where all the themes of Mesopotamian culture could be found.

Egypt. The Great Pyramids of Giza are modern reminders of an empire that flourished shortly after the rise of cities in Mesopotamia. The archaeological record of Egyptian cities is less detailed than that of their Mesopotamian counterparts, but it appears that by 3100 B.C. the cities of Memphis and Hierakonopolis were established under the control of Menes, the first pharaoh of a united Egypt.

There are a number of reasons why the record of the earliest Egyptian cities is less clear. First, their buildings were built of unbaked brick and other materials that have not stood the test of time. Second, the early Egyptians apparently built and abandoned their cities frequently. As a result, although the cities were crucial centers of Egyptian civilization, none maintained its dominance long enough to reach a very large size (Sjoberg 1951; Kemp 1977–78). The sites of many of these cities are mapped in Figure 2-2.

Although the cities that emerged in Egypt went through what we now think is the normal process of early development—from village to town and, finally, to city—they were rather distinct from those in Mesopotamia. Egyptian civilization was focused on the ruling pharaoh, and each had his city—a religious and political center built to reflect his power, which, by 2500 B.C.,

was virtually absolute. More than a secular leader or a priest, the pharaoh was believed to be a god, and his singular dominance of the Nile region created a relatively peaceful history—we find little evidence in early Egypt of city walls. Each capital city became the pharaoh's administrative center, and much of the activity of urban artisans was directed toward construction of a palace for his pleasure in this life and an opulent tomb to provide for his needs in the life to come. Although not as large as those of Mesopotamia, these Egyptian cities were characterized by important urban traits, including a clear power structure and division of labor, social inequality, and an administrative organization (utilizing hieroglyphic writing, papyrus paper, and ink) to oversee public needs and maintain the pharaoh's control.

But if the early Egyptian cities were peaceful, those that followed were not. Egypt's later history, like that of Mesopotamia, is riddled with conflict within the empire and with other empires.[1] During the period known as the Old Kingdom (2700–2180 B.C.), the pharaohs made forays into neighboring territories to procure goods. Successful in many of these adventures, the pharaohs used the surplus wealth (both material and *human*—the latter in the form of slaves) to build cities and palaces. It was the pharaohs of this period—Cheops and his son, Cephren—who built the Great Pyramids of Giza between 2600 and 2500 B.C., still the most colossal monuments ever constructed. Cephren was also responsible for the Sphinx at Giza.

For reasons still not clear, the Old Kingdom lost power around 2180 B.C. and left Egypt to a fate of power struggles among warring factions. Apparently the whole social structure collapsed, famine spread, and rioting in the cities was rampant. One document of the time, written by the sage Ipuwer, suggests that the general populace, rising in anger against their condition, deposed the politically weak pharaoh, entered the hall of justice, ransacked its offices, carried off its archives, destroyed the official census, and

---

[1]The following history is based on Jacquetta Hawkes, *The First Great Civilizations* (New York: Knopf, 1973), part VI.

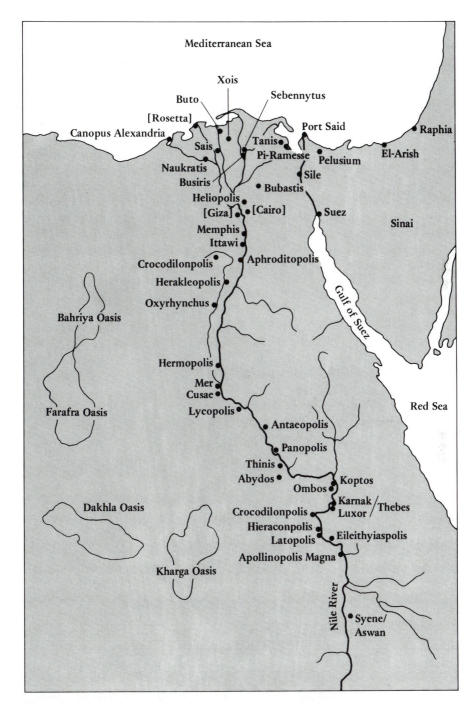

Figure 2-2 *Egypt and the Nile: the pharaonic cities (modern cities are bracketed). Source: Adapted from Jacquetta Hawkes,* The First Great Civilizations *(New York: Knopf, 1973), p. 287.*

murdered the hall's officials. This ushered in a period of terror and redistribution of wealth. Wrote Ipuwer:

> The wrong doer is everywhere. . . . A man takes his shield when he goes to plough. A man smites his brother, his mother's son. Men sit in the bushes until the benighted traveller comes, in order to plunder his load. The robber has riches. . . . He who possessed no property is now a man of wealth. The poor man is full of joy. Every town says: Let us subdue the powerful among us. . . . The owners of robes are now in rags. . . . Gold and lapis lazuli, silver and turquoise are fastened on the necks of female slaves (Quoted in Hawkes 1973, p. 298)

The First Intermediate Period, characterized by the rule of kings whose tenure was very short-lived, lasted less than 200 years, until Menthu-hotep I reunited Egypt and proclaimed his capital at Thebes. The general pattern then repeated itself. For 200 years—the Middle Kingdom—Egypt regained its power and rebuilt its cities. One pharaoh, Amenemhet III, undertook a massive soil reclamation project, constructing canals to divert the Nile into previously uncultivatable areas and increasing productive capacity immensely. After his death, things once again fell into disarray. A Second Intermediate Period lasted about 200 years (1800–1570 B.C.), during which no fewer than 217 kings ruled in Egypt, a figure probably explained by multiple dynasties rising and falling and frequent coups.

Urban greatness once again reappeared in the New Kingdom era (1500–1100 B.C.). This was the period of the minor pharaoh Tutankhamun—the only pharaoh whose grave site in the Valley of the Kings was undisturbed by pillaging robbers—and of Ramses II, the pharaoh who conquered much of the Near East for Egypt and may have confronted Moses' attempts to free the Jews from Egyptian servitude. Ramses rebuilt many of Egypt's cities, created a new capital, Pi-Ramesse, on the Mediterranean, and constructed the self-glorifying yet magnificent temples at Karnak, Luxor, and Abu Simbel. The Asian territories were lost around 1100 B.C. and the next 300 years saw the last decline of pharaonic Egypt. From 800 to 671 B.C., the rulers of Kush—a former Egyptian outpost (described in Box 9-1)—controlled Egypt.

The final indignities were visited by Near Eastern empires. The Assyrians conquered Egypt in 671 B.C. and, though expelled less than 20 years later, were followed by the Persians in 525 B.C. The Persians more or less dominated the region until 332 B.C., the year Alexander the Great arrived, was accepted as pharaoh, and built his city, Alexandria, at the head of the Nile. From then on, Egypt was at the mercy of foreign overlords.

The development of cities in the Nile region raises an interesting question as to the possible diffusion of urban influence from Mesopotamia. History records frequent contact between the two regions. Were the Egyptian cities created independently, or was the city idea imported? Debate continues, but the currently dominant belief is that some urban influences were carried by traders or nomads from early cities in Mesopotamia toward both Egypt in the west and the Indus Valley in the east (Stavrianos 1983). In all three regions, however, city life emerged, as Sjoberg notes, in its own "special fashion" and included clearly distinct and unique aspects that revealed the "stamp" of the local civilization (1965, p. 49).

The Indus Region

To the east of Mesopotamia, along the Indus River of present-day India and Pakistan, was a third ecologically favorable area where early cities emerged. Excavations have yielded the remains of two highly developed cities that were centers of a regional civilization beginning about 2500 B.C. Both were prominent in urban history until about 1500 B.C. Moenjo-Daro (see photograph) was situated on the Indus River about 175 miles from the Arabian Sea; Harappa was about 350 miles further north on one of the river's tributaries. Each had a population as high as 40,000 and represented an urban civilization distinct in many ways from those we have considered thus far.

Research by C. C. Lamberg-Karlovsky and Martha Lamberg-Karlovsky (1973) suggests that the Indus cities probably were linked by trade routes from Mesopotamian cities through other outposts such as Tepe Yahya, midway between

The excavated site of ancient Moenjo-Daro in the Indus River Valley reveals a surprisingly modern grid pattern of housing (left) and a sanitation system (trench, bottom and right). (© Larry Burrows Collection)

the two areas (Figure 2-1). It is also likely that trade of such products as jade linked this area eastward with central Asia.

Moenjo-Daro would have been familiar to a modern visitor. A thriving seaport, the city was constructed with the same gridiron pattern common to most Western cities today. Hamblin writes:

> As long ago as 2500 B.C., [Moenjo-Daro] and the half dozen cities of the Indus Valley had already put to use the crisscross gridiron system of street layout—an urban convention long thought to have been invented by the Greeks of a later era. Moenjo-Daro was planned with a broad boulevard 30 feet wide, running north and south, and crossed at right angles every 200 yards or so by somewhat smaller east-west streets. Along these impressive avenues were shops and food stands. The blocks between were served by narrow curving lanes five to ten feet wide. (1973, p. 123)

Perhaps the most remarkable discovery about this city was the uncovering of a well-established city sanitation system. Along the streets there are brick-lined open sewers that carried away house

drainage. Bathrooms—including several sit-down toilets—have been discovered by archaeologists, indicating the presence in 2500 B.C. of an urban luxury not commonly found in European cities until the nineteenth century! (This strikingly illustrates that history seldom exhibits any regular pattern of progress.) The city also had what appears to be a large public bath (Hamblin 1973).

Within the city numerous craft specialists were in operation, including potters, weavers, brick makers, and copper and bronze metalworkers (Sjoberg 1965). A citadel, the city's administrative center, may have included a granary for storage of food surplus.

Unlike either Mesopotamia or Egypt, however, Moenjo-Daro does not show evidence of a single, all-powerful leader or a preoccupation with temples and god-monuments. Rather, Moenjo-Daro shows evidence of extensive "good living." Hamblin suggests that the city

> . . . must have been among the first places to provide its citizens with a broadly based, comparatively high standard of living. Most of its people seem to

have lived in considerable comfort, in near identical mud-brick houses, along near identical streets that were served by near identical drainage systems. The ruins of residential areas struck one archaeologist as "miles of monotony." But that monotony suggests, in its uniformity, an even distribution of the population, and thus the well-being that goes with a large, prosperous middle class. (1973, p. 144)

Until 20 or 30 years ago it was commonly thought that Mesopotamia, Egypt, and the Indus River Valley contained the cities from which all later cities took their pattern. Recent archaeological research now makes this claim doubtful. Apparently, cities emerged in many places around the world independently of one another. Two other regions where this occurred were China and the Americas.

A Glance Eastward: China

Cities in China go back to at least 2000 B.C. Present knowledge suggests that the earliest was Po, the first capital of the Shang Dynasty. Very little is known about this city because excavations are incomplete.

Fortunately, the second and third Shang capitals have been studied in more detail. The second capital, Cheng-chou, was at its height about 1600 B.C. A rectangular wall 4.5 miles in length and over 30 feet high enclosed an area of about 1.5 square miles, which contained the city's administrative and ceremonial centers. In this fortified area the political and religious elite lived apart from the common people. Outside the enclosure resided artisans—bronze workers and craftspeople.

An-yang was the third Shang capital. Archaeological excavation has uncovered remnants of its larger pattern, by which the central city was linked to the surrounding area. As in Cheng-chou, the residences of artisans and craft workers were just outside a walled area. In the region immediately beyond, numerous villages formed a network of trade, supplying agricultural and other specialized products to the city (Chang 1977).

What existed in China, then, was a type of urban settlement somewhat more diffused than the areas already considered. Rather than concentrating all their political, religious, and craft activities in a single, center-city area, the Chinese set priests and rulers apart from the remainder of the urban population. At some distance from their protected, walled enclosure, residents of satellite villages participated in the life of the urban area as a whole.

A Glance Westward: The Americas

The last major region in which early cities developed was nearer home—in Mesoamerica, specifically the area of present-day central Mexico, the Yucatan Peninsula, and Guatemala; and in South America, particularly the western part of that continent. The history of these areas reveals, once again, several familiar patterns: a more productive agricultural technology and the formation of a complex social structure accompanied the rise of cities. But the case of Mesoamerica is also of interest because it represents several significant areas of contrast to urban development elsewhere.

The area was inhabited at least as early as 20,000 B.C. Cultivation of plants had been achieved by 7000 B.C., but, in contrast to other areas of the world where cities arose, the area was not well suited to the production of large surpluses partly because of its high mineral content and mountainous terrain and partly because the people lacked domestic animals and a solid source of agricultural protein. The traditional digging stick rather than the plow remained the primary tool of cultivation for millennia, and Mesoamerica never embraced farming in the sense that other regions did. Rather, its groups developed a mixed economy in which hunting and other undomesticated resources continued to play a very important part. Nevertheless, one cultivated crop, maize (corn), contributed to a sturdy and nutritious diet.

By 1500 B.C. early villages of mud-walled houses had been established. Because hunting continued to play a major part in the economy, these village sites moved with some frequency. In some villages Olmec and Maya tribes built elaborate ceremonial centers that served large populations and employed many craftspeople in their design and construction. Serving as a place of permanent residence for only a small number of priests at the outset, these ceremonial centers slowly grew in size and complexity. Before the birth of Christ they had become full-fledged cities.

The same process occurred later on the western coast of South America in present-day Peru and Bolivia. Perhaps the most famous urban empire of this region was the Inca, with its capital in the city of Cuzco. Less well known, but as important, was the urban empire of Chimor on the north coast of Peru (Moseley 1975). Its capital, Chan Chan, began as a city around the same time that the Inca urban centers evolved—about A.D. 800. At its height (approximately A.D. 1450), Chan Chan ruled over a large hinterland as a major challenger to the Inca empire.

Perhaps most interesting is the fact that this was a *regal/ritual* city—that is, a large city that contained a fairly small population, probably no more than 25,000–30,000. As the term suggests, a regal/ritual city is used primarily by the ruling class: Chan Chan's rulers lived there year round and used most of the city's buildings for their own pleasure and for the rituals of Chimor culture. Only a small group of artisans, servants, and peasants were allowed to share in that part of the urban environment. All the rest of the empire's people were forced to live in the surrounding towns or rural areas and do the ruling class's bidding, including working on city projects and paying taxes.

In 1470 Chan Chan's challenge provoked the Incas to conquer the Chimor empire and subjugate its inhabitants. However, even this dominance was not to last. By the end of the century, Columbus was to land in the New World. Not long after, the Spanish, and later the Portuguese, would arrive in Mesoamerica and South America in droves. Under the European onslaught these proud urban empires were to fall like dominoes and a new type of city would arise—a process we describe in Chapter 8.

Nevertheless, we can conclude that cities arose indigenously in the Americas as they had in other regions of the world. These cities, from a historical standpoint, were highly sophisticated and equal in complexity to those found elsewhere. For example, Teotihuacán in Central Mexico, an urban center that was at its height around A.D. 500, supported a population of perhaps 200,000 in a city physically larger than Imperial Rome itself (Millon 1970; Kornberg 1975).

Summary: Traits of Early Cities

Cities began appearing about 10,000 years ago. As shown graphically in Figure 2-3, they had become quite common in the Near East by 4000 B.C., in the Indus River Valley by 2500 B.C., and in China by 2000 B.C. Their appearance in the Americas was somewhat later, around 500 B.C.

All these cities were characterized by some combination of favorable ecological conditions, some sort of trade or food surplus, and a complex social structure (a fairly sophisticated division of labor and a power hierarchy). Beyond these important characteristics, a few other similarities and differences may be mentioned.

First, the early cities do not show any smooth progression of growth. On the one hand, the transition from first permanent settlements to full-fledged cities took a long time—from around 8000 B.C. to 3000 B.C. On the other hand, city histories the world over are marked by discontinuity and change, rise and fall. Sometimes, as in Teotihuacán, one group occupied a city for its entire duration; sometimes, as in Jericho, many groups came and went.

Second, as population centers, early cities were small. Most were mere towns by today's standards. A population of about 10,000 was common, and even the largest settlements never went much beyond the quarter-million mark.

Third, regarding the power structure, many early cities had a theocratic character—a fused religious and political elite where kings were also priests and, not infrequently, "gods." This fusion allowed a type of double control over the city's population and its problems. Royalty could, in the name of heaven, impose taxes and even servitude. Of course, the character of this elite structure varied. It was sharply evident in Egypt, China, and Teotihuacán, while it was more subdued in the Indus city of Moenjo-Daro. But we must make no mistake about it—the first cities

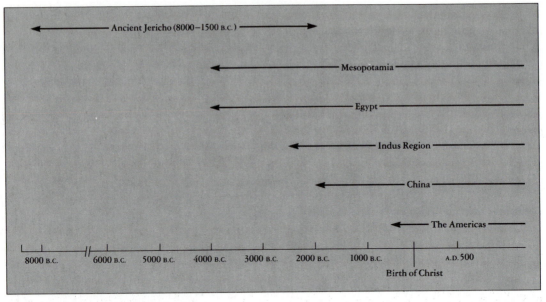

Figure 2-3 *The chronology of the first cities.*

were characterized by inequalities in power and benefits: usually few prospered and the many got by as best they could.

Finally, what of the quality of life in early cities? In comparison to modern Western cities, life was probably hard, relatively short, and subject to considerable uncertainty. Yet there is substantial variation here as well. Moenjo-Daro appears to have afforded a higher standard of living to more residents than was the case in more sharply class-divided cities elsewhere. Other factors, such as war and slavery, also must have had a powerful effect upon the quality of life experienced by many early city dwellers.

For the city, particularly after it reached the state and empire stage, was more often than not an instrument of death and destruction as one urban center tried to conquer another. To some extent this increase in bloodshed cannot be blamed on the city as such. Rather, the use of systematic warfare seems more coincident with primitive agriculture and the coming of the first permanent settlements around 8000 B.C. Apparently agricultural techniques produced a productive surplus for the first time. This surplus, in turn, attracted people to settlements and induced some of them to conquer other groups in an effort to procure even more surplus, a desire that has been called psychomaterialism. When urban areas became common around 4000 B.C., these disturbing human qualities (a psychomaterialist attitude and a willingness to make war) were magnified to a level unknown before in history because of the tendency of cities to magnify *any* trait that people bring to them.

In short, the development of the city was a most decisive event in human history. The early city magnified human activity in all its dimensions. People knew more, did more, and found more possibilities open to them. Such has always been the city's promise: to provide a better life. As we turn to the development of Western cities in the next section, we shall find that cities in our own tradition also have held out the promise of "the good life." Certainly some progress has been made along that road. We shall find, however, that these cities, like their earlier counterparts, have had a tragic capacity for harboring the human indignities of coercive inequality, militaristic expansion, and war.

Western Cities in History

Western cities—those of Western Europe and North America—are relative latecomers in the urban story. Cities had been in existence for many thousands of years before urbanization took hold in the northern Mediterranean region on the island of Crete.

Early European Civilizations

Crete and Greece. About 1800 B.C. urban settlement occurred in Crete, probably by traders or migrants from the urban settlements of Mesopotamia. Little is known of these early cities, yet by all accounts they were thriving centers. On a series of ornamental tiles found in the Palace of Minos, what appears to be a typical city is depicted. Writes Sir Arthur Evans: "The central features consisted of the towers and houses and a fortified town. . . . Also depicted were: trees and water, goats and oxen, marching warriors, spearmen and archers, arms and equipment, the prow apparently of a ship. . . ." (quoted in Mumford 1961, p. 121). Then for some reason the record breaks off inconclusively about 1400 B.C. (Carlton 1977). Like Teotihuacán two centuries later, the cities of Crete were abandoned. No one knows why this happened—a thriving civilization seemed to vanish in a twinkling. One current hypothesis is intriguing. Around 1400 B.C. the island of Santorini, in the Mediterranean Sea north of Crete, exploded in a volcanic eruption. The city of Akroteri on Santorini was totally buried in ash. The explosion sent forth ash and tidal waves in all directions. If recent volcanic eruptions, such as that of Mount Saint Helens in Oregon, are any indication, the Santorini explosion, which was larger, could have devastated life over an enormous region—Crete included. It may also be that Santorini was the fabled "continent" of Atlantis, which supposedly disappeared at about the same time (Doumas 1974). In any event, it was not until seven centuries later that urban development appeared again in Europe, this time in Greece.

The early Greek polis, or city-state, did not follow the pattern of the cities of Mesopotamia and Egypt, which magnified the power of the elite at the expense of its other citizens. The fiercely independent Greek city-states—among them Athens, Corinth, and Sparta—experienced war, as well as peaceful rivalry symbolized by the Olympic games. Compared to earlier cities of the Near East, Greek cities were more egalitarian; in Lewis Mumford's phrase, they were cities "cut closer to the human measure . . . and delivered from the claims of quasi-divine monarchs. . . ." (1961, p. 124).

These cities were led by classes whose commercial influence reached outward from Sicily to Northern Africa. The Greeks founded such cities as Messina in Sicily and Marseilles in France (Sjoberg 1965). Unfortunately, however, in the end the Greek city-states turned on themselves in the destructive Peloponnesian Wars (431–404 B.C.), leaving behind a remarkable legacy that highlighted the positive possibilities of urban civilization, including outstanding painting, sculpture, and architecture, as well as a political system and body of philosophy that influence the world to this day.

Rome. As Greek culture went into decline, another great civilization was gathering strength to the west. It was centered, perhaps more than any cultural system before or since, on a single city; indeed, the city's name is synonymous with the culture itself. As Aelius Aristedes claimed in the second century B.C.: "Rome! Everything is found here. All the skills which exist or have existed, anything that can be made or grown. If something can't be found here, then it simply doesn't exist!"

Aristedes was right. By the final centuries of the pre-Christian era, Rome was the dominant power of the Western world. By the time of Christ, the city on which the Roman Empire was based was gargantuan by all previous urban standards, approaching a population of approximately 1 million.

Rome displayed the same characteristics we have encountered in the earliest cities: a favorable ecological setting, the ability to produce an economic surplus, and a complex social structure. Also, like Greece, Rome was characterized by developed arts and sciences and public monuments and buildings.

Yet Rome was an urban civilization based almost exclusively upon the expression of militaristic power. For the several centures during which the city thrived, Rome explored and revealed for all history the consequences of concentrating the city's resources almost exclusively upon the accumulation of power and wealth.

If the Greek conception of the good life was a city founded upon the principles of moderation, balance, and human participation, the Roman conception was based on the celebration of sheer excess and unremitting domination. At its height the empire extended from Rome across the Mediterranean to northern Africa, from present-day Germany to the British Isles, from Egypt to the Near East; it included almost half the world's population (Gibbon 1879; Stavrianos 1983).

What can we say of the city that served as the center of this vast empire? In physical design Rome was similar to cities discussed earlier. At its center were a market, a forum, and a complex of monumental buildings. Radiating outward in orderly fashion across the breadth of the city— some 7 square miles overall—were major broad thoroughfares constructed according to careful plan. Indeed, roads were one of Rome's greatest achievements. In all, over 50,000 miles of roads were constructed by the Roman work force. Extremely well built, they served as links between Rome and the empire's vast hinterland, from which the city drew tribute (Roebucks 1974). Many of the major cities of Europe today—including London, York, Vienna, Bordeaux, Paris, and Cologne—were once provincial outposts of Rome.

Waterworks were another engineering achievement. The city had large public baths, fountains, hydrants along main streets, and a system of water drainage begun as early as the sixth century B.C. (Mumford 1961). Perhaps most striking was the city's aqueduct system, completed during the second century B.C. and copied in many provincial cities founded by the Romans

throughout Europe. These spillways provided fresh water often from some distance to the city, just as today's underground water system from upstate New York serves New York City.

The motive for all of this impressive engineering was ultimately to serve the interests of the ruling military and political elite. While the elite enjoyed incredible riches, Rome's poorer residents shared little in the wealth that was brought continuously to the city, living in largely unplanned and squalid tenements. Where

> the need was greatest, the mechanical facilities were least. Though the mass of the population might by day patronize at a small fee the public toilets in the neighborhood, they deposited their domestic ordure in covered cisterns at the bottom of the stairwells of their crowded tenements, from which it would be periodically removed by dungfarmers and scavengers. Even punctual nightly removal would hardly lessen the foul odor that must have pervaded the buildings. (Mumford 1961, p. 216)

This underside of Roman life had a further dimension—one which could hardly find sharper contrast with the Greek ideal of human dignity:

> The main population of the city that boasted its world conquests lived in cramped, noisy, airless, foul smelling, infected quarters, paying extortionate rents to merciless landlords, undergoing daily indignities and terrors that coarsened and brutalized them, and in turn demanded compensatory outlets. These outlets carried the brutalization even further, in a continuous carnival of sadism and death. (Mumford 1961, p. 221)

The enduring, if horrible, example of Rome's "carnival of sadism and death" was the Circus. In Cityscape 2-2 Mumford describes this ritual around which the later city revolved.

Taken as a whole, Rome was a parade of contrasts: engineering excellence and technical achievement juxtaposed with human debasement and militaristic cruelty. Eventually, extended so far afield that it no longer could control itself, and rotting from within, Rome sank into decline. It "fell" in A.D. 476 under the onslaught of northern invasion, and by the sixth century it had become a mere "town" of 20,000.

CITYSCAPE 2-2
The Dance of Death: Classical Rome

The existence of a parasitic economy and a predatory political system produced a typically Roman urban institution that embraced both aspects of its life and gave them a dramatic setting: the old practice of the religious blood sacrifice was given a new secular form in the arena.

Roman life, for all its claims of peace, centered more and more on the imposing rituals of extermination. In the pursuit of sensations sufficiently sharp to cover momentarily the emptiness and meaninglessness of their parasitic existence, the Romans took to staging chariot races, spectacular naval battles set in an artificial lake, theatrical pantomimes in which the strip tease and lewder sexual acts were performed in public. But sensations need constant whipping as people become inured to them: so the whole effort reached a pinnacle in the gladiatorial spectacles, where the agents of this regime applied a diabolic inventiveness to human torture and human extermination. . . . So, to recover the bare sensation of being alive, the Roman populace, high and low, governors and governed, flocked to the great arenas to participate in person in similar entertainments, more vividly staged, more intimately presented. Every day, in

the arena, the Romans witnessed in person acts of vicious torture and wholesale extermination, such as those that Hitler and his agents later devised and vicariously participated in—but apparently lacked the stomach to enjoy regularly in person. . . . To make attendance at these spectacles even easier, as early as the reign of Claudius, 159 days were marked as public holidays, and as many as 93, a quarter of the whole year, were devoted to games at the public expense. Vast fortunes were spent on staging even a single one of these events. . . .

No body of citizens, not even the Athenians at the height of their empire, ever had such an abundance of idle time to fill with idiotic occupations. Even the mechanized United States, with the five-day week, cannot compare with Rome; for after the hour of noon, in addition, the Roman workers, who had doubtless risen at daybreak, suffered no further demand on their time. The transformation of the active, useful life of the early Republican city into the passive and parasitic life that finally dominated it took centuries. But in the end, attendance at public spectacles, terrestrial and nautical, human and animal, became the principal occupation of their

existence; and all other activities fed directly or indirectly into it. . . .

The gladiatorial games were first introduced into Rome in 264 B.C. by the consul Decimus Junius Brutus on the occasion of his father's funeral; but the Romans gave them a more utilitarian turn by employing the deadly contests as a popular means for the public punishment of criminals, at first presumably as much for an admonitory deterrent as an enjoyment. Too soon, unfortunately, the ordeal of the prisoner became the welcome amusement of the spectator; and even the emptying of the jails did not provide a sufficient number of victims to meet the popular demand. As with the religious sacrifices of the Aztecs, military expeditions were directed toward supplying a sufficient number of victims, human and animal. Here in the arena both degraded professionals, thoroughly trained for their occupation, and wholly innocent men and women were tortured with every imaginable body-maiming and fear-producing device for public delight. And here wild animals were butchered, without being eaten, as if they were only men.

Source: Lewis Mumford, *The City in History* (New York: Harcourt, Brace and World, 1961), pp. 229–232.

Decline: The Middle Ages

As Rome collapsed, so did the empire that had sustained urban life throughout much of Europe. With this eclipse came a period of about 600 years during which European cities either fell into a pattern of minimal survival or ceased to exist entirely. The commercial trade that had been the source of life to the empire and its cities was drastically curtailed. The danger of pillaging by barbarians increased. Once-great cities, which had boasted populations in excess of 100,000, became virtually isolated hamlets. There evolved an almost singular concern for security. Surviving cities became fortified by great walls—a revival of an older urban trait rendered unnecessary by the establishment of Roman control of nearly the entire continent.

At its height Imperial Rome was the center of a vast militaristic empire. In the foreground can be seen the Roman Forum, the heart of the city's ceremonial life; in the background lies the circular Colosseum, the site of the infamous Roman Circus (see Cityscape 2-2). (The Bettmann Archive, Inc.)

The pattern of settlement typical of the fifth through the eleventh centuries was a mosaic of local manors, villages, and small towns in many ways reminiscent of the earliest urban settlements we considered at the beginning of this chapter. The dominance over a large hinterland so characteristic of Greek and Roman cities all but vanished. This is, of course, the essence of the image carried by the phrase, "Dark Ages."

It was during this period that a feudal system, in which security was given by a local lord in exchange for service on his lands, came into widespread existence. In most cases, however, manors were situated in the countryside, weakening even further any possible urban influence. A few highly fortified small cities and manor towns survived, but a delicate balance was struck in these settlements. Given the state of medieval technology, protection could be provided only for a limited population. A small population made a low level of production inevitable, and this, in turn, made the city stagnant.

Revival: The European Urban Renaissance

The low point of urban life in Europe was reached in the ninth century (Roebucks 1974). Then, around the eleventh century, a general "awakening" began to take place. The reasons for this change, which occurred gradually over several centuries, are numerous and complex, but a general development of urban trade and crafts was a key factor.

The Crusades (armed marches by Christian European groups against the holders of "The Holy Land," where, more often than not, the Europeans found ultimate defeat) took place between 1096 and 1291; they contributed to a rebirth of trade routes linking Europe and the Near East. Pirenne (1952) contends that the reopening of trade began bringing new ideas and products to cities in Europe by the twelfth century. Mumford (1961) turns the argument around and suggests that trade rebounded as cities once again became effective "stepping stones" across Europe and

TABLE 2-1
The Population of Selected Medieval Cities (in thousands)

City	Year						
	1000	1100	1200	1300	1400	1500	1600
Cologne	—	—	50	54	—	—	—
Florence	—	—	—	60	61	70	65
Genoa	—	—	—	100	100	62	—
Lisbon	—	—	—	—	55	70	110
London	—	—	—	—	—	75	187
Madrid	—	—	—	—	—	—	79
Milan	—	45	60	100	125	—	119
Naples	—	—	—	(22)	—	125	275
Palermo	75	90	—	—	—	—	105
Paris	—	—	110	228	275	225	250
Prague	—	—	—	—	95	70	100
Rome	—	—	(35)	—	—	—	109
Rouen	—	—	—	50	70	75	68
Venice	45	55	70	110	110	115	151

Source: Adapted with permission from T. Chandler and G. Fox, *3000 Years of Urban History* (New York: Academic Press, 1974), pp. 308–319. Estimates in parentheses taken from J. C. Russell, *Late Ancient and Medieval Population* (Philadelphia: The American Philosophical Society, 1958), pp. 60–62.

Asia. In any event, the growth of local trade began stimulating the long-dormant urban division of labor.

The emergence of a complex and competitive commercial class at the center of this trade, dominated from the eleventh century on by craft guilds, contributed to a newly vibrant city life. However, the merchants alone did not dominate these cities. Many groups—including the church, the landed gentry, and the feudal royalty—vied for position. Small and self-contained, medieval cities allowed no single focus to dominate urban life in the way the military and political elements had dominated Rome.

As for their populations, medieval cities were small—both in relation to Roman cities (many of which supported over 100,000 people) and in comparison to the industrial cities that would follow them. Table 2-1 presents the populations of several important European cities during this period.

Although a few cities such as Paris and Venice approached 1,000 acres, the physical dimensions of medieval cities also were modest, typically limited to a few hundred acres (the size of a small town of about 5,000 people today). Walls surrounding the cities often were supplemented by a moat, as shown in Figure 2-4. Major roads connected the city gates to the center of the city—generally the cathedral, the marketplace, or major buildings such as the guilds or town halls. Mumford (1961) suggests that if any one center was of greatest importance, it was the cathedral, often towering over the rest of the city. Indeed, the importance of the church to the social life of medieval Europe is not easily exaggerated:

. . . to be fully functioning human beings both urban and rural medieval people had to be members of the Roman Catholic Church. Religious minorities, notably Jews, were recognized as being mostly outside the mainstream of society. . . . [The] Catholic Church was the one, largely unchallenged church. To be cast out from it was the ultimate rejection of society, for without its acceptance, an individual was a spiritual leper whose situation was in some ways worse than that of a physical leper, who was at least allowed to receive charity. . . . (Roebucks 1974, p. 57)

The city of Carcassonne in France remains an outstanding example of a medieval walled city. Compare this picture to Figure 2-4. Such cities were characteristic of Europe for nearly 1,000 years after the Fall of Rome (A.D. 479). (The Bettmann Archive, Inc.)

The medieval city would not have produced the sense of awe and massive scale that a modern Western city does. Other than the cathedral and perhaps a palace, there were no tall buildings, and streets were likely to be narrow and winding rather than wide and straight as they are today. Paving of streets, done on a large scale in Rome during the empire, did not become common in medieval European cities until the twelfth and thirteenth centuries. Houses typically were built together—in rowhouse fashion—often with open space for cultivation in the rear. Despite the lack of such conveniences as indoor plumbing, the small population and relatively low density of these cities allowed life to proceed under conditions far more healthful than those of many postindustrial tenements today (Mumford 1961).

Social life also thrived. The late medieval city was a true community, as Lauro Martines observes in Box 2-2.

These European cities grew gradually—not only in population and area, but with a renewed idea of the human possibilities of the city. The period from the twelfth century until about the sixteenth century was an age of general urban rebirth, or renaissance. First evident in Italian city-states such as Venice, Florence, Palermo, and Milan, this rebirth is easily linked to the humanistic conception of city life that flourished some 1500 years earlier in Athens. During the Renaissance, the city gradually recaptured an interest in art, literature, and architecture.

The Renaissance humanists saw learning as the path to human virtue, dignity, freedom, and happiness—to becoming a perfect human being. The vehicles for attaining these goals were interpersonal dialogue and the possibilities offered by the city. Yet, there was an irony in this vision. In actuality it was a vision of the perfected *upper-class* person. Indeed, humanists and nobility alike spoke disdainfully of the uneducated "masses" that surrounded them.

> However general the heroic view of man's dignity, however much it purported to depend upon a notion of human potentiality, none came closer to the realization of the ideal than the men with the resources for learning, culture, patronage, and the *trained* capacity for enjoyment of the world's goods. This is so obvious it seems trivial, yet in surveying the age, historians constantly suppose, like the humanists themselves, that the heroic vision spoke for all men. Not at all. It spoke for an elite. . . . (Martines 1979, p. 217)

Thus, the real contradiction of the era was that, although once again the city generated the ideal of full human development, it was an ideal that the great bulk of the city's citizens had little possibility to realize. Wealth, for example, was

BOX 2-2
The Little World of the Renaissance City

Life in the Italian walled-in city about 1300 went on in a tight world of personal relations and public settings. Gossip and rumor rippled back and forth across the warp and woof of close family ties, inherited family friendships and animosities, numerous street acquaintances and peripheral contacts that were endlessly being renewed. These relations were especially dense for the rich citizens in politics, because such bonds were multiplied and vitalized by property and influence. . . . The personal-public texture of life in the Italian commune [city] lies beyond anything in our experience, but we catch glimpses of that vanished reality in the age's lyric poetry, which teems with personal allusions . . . references to streets, direct discourse, and dedications to friends. . . .

The same people walked the same streets daily. There was mutual instant recognition. . . . Every neighbor had his or her particular identity associated with a trade, a name, a reputation, a clan or family. Strangers were immediately picked out in the streets and doubtless stared at. Births, marriages, and deaths were neighborhood events—for the common knowledge and feeling of all.

Source: Lauro Martines, *Power and Imagination: City-States in Renaissance Italy* (New York: Knopf, 1979), pp. 76, 78.

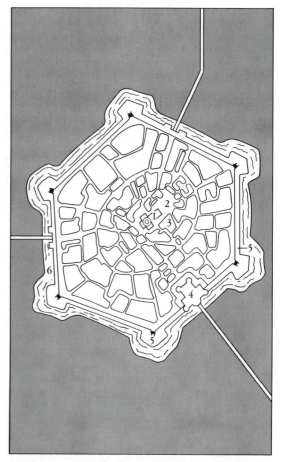

Figure 2-4 *The medieval city, circa 1350, developed on a new site in response to the needs and patterns of the new trading system and for defense. The site was chosen at the intersection of rivers and roads, a natural route center that offered plentiful water, natural defenses, and an ample food supply from the surrounding agrarian area of the valley. The city was a trading and commercial center; craft industries produced goods for trade and for exchange with farmers of the surrounding area who supplied food, as well as many of the items involved in long-distance trade. Movement within the city was mainly pedestrian so narrow streets with many angles were not constricting. Some wider, more open streets allowed passage of horse traffic involved in long-distance trade.*
1 Cathedral
2 Market plaza
3 Guildhalls, craft and trade centers
4 Fortress of local lord
5 Defensive walls with turrets at intervals
6 Moat outside defensive walls
Source: Janet Roebuck, The Shaping of Urban Society, *pp. 48–49. Copyright © 1974 by Jane Roebuck. Reprinted with permission of Charles Scribner's Sons.*

highly concentrated. In Lyon, a French city, in 1545, over half the wealth belonged to a mere 10 percent of the population (Hohenberg and Lees 1985, p. 147).

The Second Urban Revolution: The Rise of Modern Cities

Within the walls of the Renaissance city as the centuries passed, the seeds of another type of city altogether were being sown. The old feudal power structure was breaking down, giving people more freedom to live their lives where they chose; trade was becoming more important, increasing the available wealth; and cities were gaining rapidly in prominence. People took to the road in significant numbers, providing an important link between urban centers. "It sometimes seems as if

TABLE 2-2
Population of Selected European Cities, 1700–1982 (in thousands)

City	Year			
	1700	1800	1900	1982
Amsterdam	172	201	510	687
Berlin	—	172	2,424	3,041*
Hamburg	70	130	895	1,637
Lisbon	188	237	363	812
London	550	861	6,480	6,765
Madrid	110	169	539	3,368
Naples	207	430	563	1,212
Paris	530	547	3,330	2,189
Rome	149	153	487	2,840
Vienna	105	231	1,662	1,531

*West Berlin and East Berlin
Source: Adapted with permission from T. Chandler and G. Fox, *3000 Years of Urban History* (New York: Academic Press, 1974), pp. 321–341 and John Tepper Marlin, Immanuel Ness, and Stephen T. Collins, *Book of World City Rankings* (New York: Free Press, 1986), pp. 527–528.

[everyone] was on the move: touring journeymen, pilgrims, soldiers, piepowder [literally "dusty feet"], merchants, rogues, clerics, peddlers and players." (Hohenberg and Lees 1985, pp. 92–93)

Throughout Europe commerce slowly began to replace agriculture as the dominant mode of making a living. A new middle class began to rise to power. This class—the bourgeoisie (the French word means, literally, "of the town")—was composed of shopkeepers, traders, bureaucrats, government officials, and people engaged in commercial ventures of all sorts. As their wealth increased, cities began to attract, in ever larger numbers, people who hoped to share in the obvious material benefits of this process.

By the mid–seventeenth century, feudalism was all but dead, and with it went the last remnants of the rural-centered life of the Middle Ages. In its place stood capitalism, a mode of life fundamentally grounded in the trade possibilities offered by the city. By the eighteenth century, the Industrial Revolution had begun, a process that fueled even more the dominance of the city-based market economy.

The change was striking: city population everywhere exploded (see Table 2-2). If the first urban revolution took place when cities first appeared some 10,000 years before, the *second urban revolution* occurred from about 1650 on: Europe became a continent of cities.

The preindustrial era had been characterized by low-efficiency technology and health care. Both birth and death rates were high. People typically had many children, but many did not live to maturity. Even for those who did, life expectancy was much shorter than today (usually under 40 years). As a result, natural population growth (the difference between the birth and death rates) was slow and frequently checked by massive numbers of deaths occasioned by outbreaks of plague (see Box 2-3).

But plague, did not wreak its vengeance forever. Whatever the problems and excesses of the shift to capitalism and industrialization in Europe, in time a larger portion of the urban population enjoyed more wealth, more efficient means of production, and better health and sanitation conditions. In the long run, death rates went

---

BOX 2-3
The Black Plague

Black Plague was actually an organism, *Bacillus pestis*, transmitted most often by fleas carried by rodents such as rats. It is perhaps difficult for most of us to imagine the effect of so great a pestilence, which in the course of only *two years* after its outbreak in Italy in 1347 killed at least *one-fourth* of the European population. The loss of life was even greater in cities and towns. Langer (1973, pp. 106–107) notes that during the 1347 outbreak the population of Florence was cut in half—from 90,000 to 45,000—while in Hamburg the loss of life was greater still. The effects of this event, and subsequent plagues that menaced until the seventeenth century, can hardly be exaggerated. Even so, we find a rebounding of population after each attack, and cities continued to grow.

---

down dramatically, while birth rates remained high: what population experts call a *demographic transition* (Nam and Philliber 1984). A major population explosion began throughout Europe, primarily centered in the cities. Although much urban growth resulted from migration—that is, from people coming to the city from the countryside—natural population growth was also extremely high. Together, both forces began to produce cities with population sizes undreamed of in antiquity. Recall that Rome, at its peak, contained around a million people. London in 1982 (Table 2-2) contained *seven times* that number.

In European and North American countries, the urban demographic transition continued well into this century. Recently, however, an increasing standard of living—making more children for "productive purposes" unnecessary—and effective means of contraception have begun to halt the trend. In most industrial nations population growth has slowed as both birth and death rates have continued to decline. The situation is not so hopeful in many other areas of the world, however. As will be made clear in Chapters 8 through 10, overpopulation produced by an even more powerful demographic transition continues to create incredible suffering and threatens to overwhelm many nations.

To conclude this chapter we turn to Case Study 2-1, focusing on London, a city which many consider, perhaps with Paris and Rome, the greatest of European urban centers. As we examine this city of kings, queens, Shakespeare, Dickens, and Churchill, we shall see reflected all the stages of urban development we have just discussed.

CASE STUDY 2-1
London, The History of a World City

> *When a man is tired of London, he is tired of life;*
> *For there is in London all that life can afford.*
>
> DR. SAMUEL JOHNSON (1709–1784)

There are certain great cities, suggests British urban geographer Peter Hall (1979, p. 1), in which a disproportionate part of the world's most important business is conducted. These are "world cities." London is such a city.

For nearly 1,000 years, London has been a focus of European urban life. It is one of the three or four most important economic centers of the world. Its metropolitan area has a population of over 12 million people, and it is besieged by over 8 million foreign tourists a year.

Despite this vitality, the city has problems. Even though tourism brings in over $3 billion each year, the time-honored, relatively sedate character of the city is changing rapidly. As an article in *The Sunday Times* remarked,

> Some Londoners feel the quality of life is being destroyed. People urinate in Pimlico streets while waiting for Freddie Laker's skytrains. They bring in cats, without going through quarantine; jam the pavements in Oxford Street; ask awkward questions about how to get to Abbey Road, where they wish to be photographed on the pedestrian crossing featured on the Beatles' album; block up hospital casualty wards, police stations and magistrate's courts. . . . Shoplifting is a difficulty. (Aug. 20, 1978)

BOX 2-4
"A Bit of a Punch-Up": London, 1978

For the first time in London's history there are sizeable segments of the city where foreign-born citizens are in a majority—and not just foreign-born, but actually black or brown, a different category of alien to the intensely race-conscious English. Racial bigotry thrives and indeed seems to fulfill some sort of psychological need; it is different in kind, I think, from the American variety and often seems not exactly a social attitude, even less a political conviction, but rather a category of sport.

I was walking with a friend on Saturday down Lewisham Way, when we felt in the air some hint or tremor of trouble. . . . [T]his sensation of impending evil was embodied in a clutch of short-cropped youths in jeans, high boots, and spangled leather jackets. . . . Over and over again, as they drew nearer, they sang the same couplet of the old song, as though they knew no more:

"Rule Britannia, Britannia rules the waves,
Britons never, never, never shall be slaves. . . ."

"What's happening?" we asked as they passed, and they stopped at once, without resentment, and clustered around us as though they had discovered some side-walk curiosity, and were about to learn something themselves. They spoke a particular kind of debased Cockney and tended to talk all at once.

"Big rally dahn the High Street, innit? Us [the National Front] against the Socialist Revolutionaries, know what I mean? Coupla football [soccer] games in tahn, too."

"What's it all about, then?"

"Well, it's a bit of a punch-up, innit? Look, the coons and reds give us a bit of aggro, know what I mean? The Paks and them, the nig-nogs and the football mobs, then we're in there, aren't we? Bit of violence, know what I mean? That's what it's all abaht, innit? Nig-nogs Saturday night!"

Source: Jan Morris, "London Intermezzo," *Rolling Stone*, April 20, 1978, pp. 55–60.

More seriously, the city lost 750,000 jobs between 1966 and 1975 (Hall 1979, p. 47). Most of its middle class has moved to the suburbs, leaving the city bereft of its traditional tax base and increasingly polarized into a home of the very rich and the poor. As we saw in Mr. Gawber's reaction to his new neighbors (Cityscape 1-3), there is increasing tension between whites and minorities. Jan Morris comments further on this in Box 2-4.

So London remains, as Dr. Johnson put it, a pastiche of "all that life can afford." Why? What forces are at work in making a city a world city? To answer, we need look at London's history.

Beginnings: 55 B.C.–A.D. 1066

London's story begins with Rome and Julius Caesar.[2] After his conquest of Gaul in the first century B.C., Caesar was told of a large island to the north that had important natural resources.

His expedition to the island in 55 B.C. met with little success: he encountered fierce resistance from the local Celtic tribes and so retreated to Rome to enjoy his other victories. But he brought back with him knowledge of the island.

A hundred years later, in A.D. 43, the fifth Caesar, the Emperor Claudius, conquered the island. Claudius set up his main encampment at the first point upstream on the River Thames (pronounced "tems"; see Box 2-5) where a bridge could be built, thereby allowing access across the river by troops to the south. The place was called "Londinium" (meaning "wild" or "bold" place), following the Celtic name for the area.

A deep-water port, London's site facilitated the shipment of goods into the heart of England. The Romans built major roads in all directions and enclosed the city with a wall for protection. By A.D. 60 London was thriving: the Roman historian Tacitus wrote that the city was "famed for commerce and crowded with traders."

The Romans remained nearly 400 years. By the beginning of the fifth century, Roman rule was being challenged continually by the rem-

---

[2]Much of the following is based on Robert Gray's *A History of London* (London: Hutchinson, 1978).

BOX 2-5
"te Temmes"

Why are the spelling and pronunciation of London's river so different? Helene Hanff recently was offered this doubtful explanation.

Driving back to London we passed a village called Thame—pronounced as spelled, like "same" with a lisp—and the Colonel told me why the Thames is pronounced Temmes. Seems the first Hanover king [George I] had a thick German accent and couldn't pronounce th. He called the river "te Temmes" and since the-king-is-always-right everybody else had to call it the Temmes and it's been the Temmes ever since.

Source: Helene Hanff, *The Duchess of Bloomsbury Street* (New York: Avon, 1973), p. 75.

---

nants of the Celtic tribes (long before forced into the nether regions of the country: Cornwall, Wales, and Scotland) and by invading tribes from northern Europe. Eventually, the cost of maintaining the British Isles, combined with the necessities of protecting the empire closer to Rome itself, became too great and the islands were abandoned in A.D. 410. Virtually all remnants of the Roman occupation, including the Roman remains in London, were destroyed with great relish by the reemergent tribes. Nevertheless, the Romans left two legacies crucial to London's later history: the established city and a superior road system that linked it with the hinterland.

From the Roman retreat until the Norman Conquest in 1066, Britain came under a variety of political overlords. Different tribes—the original Celts, Danes, Angles, Saxons, and Vikings—vied for control of the island, gaining and losing it numerous times. To take but one example, in 1013 the Danes conquered the city, driving out the Saxon king, Ethelred. Ethelred formed an alliance with King Olaf of Norway and together they quickly reattacked the city. Knowing that London Bridge was the key to London's southern supply route, they attached ropes to its huge pilings and sailed downstream, pulling the bridge in their wake (hence the origin of the eleventh-century song, "London

Bridge Is Falling Down"). Following the Saxon-Norwegian takeover, the Danes attacked again in 1016 and again they took the city. This see-saw pattern was typical.

Despite changing political fortunes, London thrived. Eager to maintain their success, its merchants often threw in with whoever was in power, thus maintaining and strengthening London's importance as the economic center of England.

The Medieval City: 1066–1550

The year 1066 brought political stability. The Norman invader, William the Conqueror, defeated the Saxon king, Harold, in the Battle of Hastings and marched on London. Finding the city well fortified and recognizing the vital importance of the trade connections it maintained elsewhere, William fired on the community of Southwark (pronounced "sutherk") at the opposite end of London Bridge. Leaving a standing army, he took the remainder of his forces to the smaller, less protected cities to the west and north. These he systematically destroyed (ravaged might be a better word), always sending back news of his conquests. The message to Londoners was all too clear: Surrender or face utter devastation. Londoners opened the gates and welcomed William as their king. Without a shot fired, William had gained his prize. By not sacking the city, William not only gained access to virtually all its present wealth but ensured that the city would be able to produce more wealth in the future. Slaughtered merchants trade with no one.

Twenty-five years before William's conquest, the Saxon king, Edward the Confessor, a devout Christian, had decided to build a great abbey west of the original City of London, around a sharp bend in the Thames. (Technically, then as today, the "City of London" is the original one-square-mile area encompassed by the Roman walls.) It was in this abbey, called Westminster (literally, "the church in the west"), that William chose to have himself crowned king of all England. He then took up residence in the nearby palace that had been constructed by Edward.

The site of William's coronation and residence was critical to the history of London for three reasons. First, an important political residence was established in the immediate vicinity of the financial capital, giving London the power of a "double magnet" as a financial center and a political center as well. Second, the establishment of the City of Westminster to the west of the City of London meant that the land between would be filled with incoming people, thus "dragging" greater London in a westward sprawl out of the original Roman walled city. Third, the establishment of the royal residence in London inextricably tied London's *local* history to the *nation's* history. Henceforth, the history of London would be, to a large degree, part of the history of England.

For five and a half centuries, medieval London grew steadily. Nevertheless, it was an out-of-the-way place, an important, but not major, European city. This changed radically with the onset of world exploration. By 1550 London had become *the* world city.

The World City Emerges: 1550–1800

There are three reasons for this transformation. First, with the discovery of the Americas, London suddenly became "on the way" for most northern European expeditions heading west to the Americas. It thus became a place where goods could be unloaded conveniently and transferred to the ships of other nations or processed in some manner for reshipment.

Second, because of its geographic isolation from the rest of Europe and the paucity of its natural resources, England became a seafaring nation with the world's most efficient sailing fleet.

Third, there was wool. Isolated from war-ravaged Europe for centuries, England was able to produce more of this precious material than any other country. With wool in ever increasing demand, London quickly became the port where by far the largest proportion of the world's wool was traded and London merchants established a virtual monopoly.

As a result of all these factors, London exploded in population, wealth, power, and influence. By the mid-1500s, the English Renaissance—comparable to those of Florence and Venice—had begun. Not only did commerce thrive, so did art, literature, music, and drama. It was the era of Henry VIII, Sir Thomas More, Elizabeth I, Roger Bacon, Sir Walter Raleigh, and, of course, Shakespeare.

Shakespeare, in fact, is a marvelous example of a city's nourishing effect on human creativity. Shakespeare arrived in London—the only place where serious dramatists could have their work produced—in the late 1500s. There he found patrons and competitors who pushed him to his peak. All his greatest work was written in London. As Oscar Wilde, the great nineteenth-century poet and playwright, put it, "Town life nourishes and perfects all the more civilized elements in man. . . . Shakespeare wrote nothing but doggerel lampoon before he came to London and never penned a line after he left."

It is important to see the link between a thriving city and the advance of cultural ideas. There are two key factors. First, a dynamic city draws to it people from different backgrounds. As the population grows, the possibilities of permutations and combinations of ideas and life-styles become legion. Second, a thriving city is usually a wealthy city, and there has been a very intimate historical link between wealth and the development of cultural ideas. Simply, wealth supports leisure. Creative artists with wealthy patrons or buyers for their work can literally afford to develop their art in ways that would be impossible if leisure time were not available. In addition, the rich demand drama, architecture, and music, thereby enhancing the creative arts in another way.

People came to Renaissance London in droves. In 1500 the city was home to 75,000 people. By 1600 that number had nearly tripled to 220,000; by 1650 it had doubled again to over 450,000.

But London had no plan for accommodating these huge numbers of people. Housing became scarce and overcrowded, streets virtually impassable. The water became polluted, as—not surprisingly—did the streets themselves.

A whole network of officials, from the mayor down to the four [officials] attached to each ward, were continuously battling with the problems of street cleaning. People like . . . Ward, who caused great nuisance and discomfort to his neighbors by throwing out horrible filth onto the highway, the stench of which was so odious that none of his neighbors could remain in their shops, were prosecuted as public menaces. Many people defied regulations and simply emptied their slops into the street, or, like one ingenious fellow, piped them into the cellar of a neighbor. (Gray 1978, pp. 133–134)

Then, in a single year, the city was hit twice by catastrophe. The first was directly connected with the unsanitary conditions we have just described. Black plague had visited London before, but never with the virulence of the epidemic of 1665–1666 (see Box 2-6). The population of the city was nearly halved; over 100,000 people died in the space of eight months. Just as the city began to recover, on the evening of September 2, 1666, someone upset a wood stove in Pudding Lane and the entire square-mile area of the original city of London burned to the ground in four days. The horrible devastation is recorded in Box 2-7.

But, like the mythical phoenix, London arose from its own flames. Less than 40 years later, by 1700, the London area had a population of over half a million people and the city was entirely, even spectacularly, rebuilt. It was more powerful than ever. By 1750 the population had grown to over 675,000; by 1800 it was nearly 900,000, almost twice the size of Paris.

Industrialization and Colonization: 1800–1900

The onset of the Industrial Revolution in the late 1700s spurred the growth of London incredibly. London was already the center of British trade; what the city did not produce, it shipped; what it did not ship was simply not available for human consumption. To fuel its voracious industrial machine, England needed cheap raw materials in huge portions. Unable to supply all these materials itself, England, like many European nations of the period, colonized much of the globe

as quickly as possible. Thus grew the British Empire, on which the sun never set and which, from its center in London, "controlled the destinies of a quarter of the earth's population" (Morris 1985, p. 21).

To accommodate the burgeoning empire and its industry, the city grew immensely. The docks

---

BOX 2-6
The Great Plague of London, 1665–1666

There was no one way of dying. Some simply became sleepy and never woke up. The less fortunate endured an agonizing series of symptoms—shivering, violent vomiting, searing headache, fever and delirium—from which death came as a merciful deliverance. The buboes, or swellings, appeared in the groin and under the arms. Only if these tumours burst and let forth their evil might the stricken recover, but victims were driven crazy by the pain involved in lancing their sores. There was one sign, a rash which could spread over the whole body, which was regarded as a certain indication of approaching death, even though the patient was sometimes feeling perfectly well when he or she first noticed it. "The tokens," as these spots were called, are commemorated in what has now become an innocent children's rhyme:

> Ring a ring a Roses,
> A pocketful of posies,
> 'Tishoo, 'tishoo
> We all fall down.

"A pocketful of posies" refers to the herbs which people used to carry in order to ward off the plague. Sometimes the healthy were smuggled away from under the eyes of . . . watchmen, but doors marked with red crosses could only legally be opened to remove corpses on to the carts which trundled out at the dead of night to the pits at Finsbury, Shoreditch, Tothill Fields (south-west of Westminster) and elsewhere. There were gruesome stories about these carts; the drivers might fall dead on the way, leaving the horses to plunge where they would with their dreadful cargo, or to stand stock still in the streets awaiting discovery at dawn. It was all the town could manage to bury its dead.

Source: Robert Gray, *A History of London* (London: Hutchinson, 1978), pp. 170–171.

BOX 2-7
The Citty in Dreadfull Flames, 1666

This fatal night about ten, began that deplorable fire . . . in London.

After dinner I took coach with my wife and son and went to the Bank side in Southwark, where we beheld the dismal spectacle, the whole Citty in dreadfull flames neare the waterside. The fire having continu'd all . . . night (if I may call that night which was light as day for ten miles round about, after a dreadfull manner). . . . The conflagration was so universal, and the people so astonish'd, that from the beginning, I know not by what despondency of fate, they hardly stirr'd to quench it, so that there was nothing heard or seen but crying out and lamentation, running about like distracted creatures, without at all attempting to save even their goods. . . . Oh the miserable and calamitous spectacle! . . . God grant mine eyes may never behold the like, who now saw above 10,000 houses all in one flame; the noise and crackling and thunder of the impetuous flames, the shrieking of women and children, the hurry of people, the fall of Towers, Houses and Churches, was like an hideous storme, and the aire all about so hot and inflam'd that at the last one was not able to approach it, so that they were forc'd to stand still and let the flames burn on, which they did for neere two miles in length and one in bredth. . . . This I left it this afternoone burning, a resemblance of Sodom, or the last day. London was, but is no more!

Source: John Evelyn, *Diary*, 1666.

BOX 2-8
The Battle of Britain

From 7 September until 3 November 1940 London was attacked every night but one. . . . If the intention had been to stun the population into submission the bombardment proved entirely counterproductive. . . . Far from turning into gibbering neurotic wrecks in line with psychiatric predictions, Londoners actually began to shed their neuroses. Not only did total strangers risk their lives for one another; they even managed to talk to each other. As long as the bombs fell, all those nice distinctions of class and status which the English are wont to measure so carefully before committing themselves to anything as daring as a "Good morning" were swept aside. . . .

There is a photograph of St. Paul's rising unscathed above the smoke and fire which movingly symbolizes the town's indestructible spirit. Anyone in search of a miracle could do worse than ponder the survival of St. Paul's. Nearly all buildings around the cathedral [were] annihilated. . . . But the great church did not fall. Just what it meant to Londoners was movingly expressed by a woman from Bethnal Green who recorded her memories of 29 December 1940 thus: "I went up on the roof with some of the firemen, to look at the City. And I've always remembered how I was choked, I think I was crying a little. I could see St. Paul's standing there, and the fire all around, and I just said: Please God, don't let it go. I couldn't help it, I felt that if St. Paul's had gone, something would have gone from us. But it stood in defiance, it did. And when the boys were coming back, the firemen said: It's bad, but, oh, the old church stood it. Lovely, that was."

Source: Robert Gray, *A History of London* (London: Hutchinson, 1978), pp. 309–312.

expanded and provided huge numbers of jobs in the East End; the government civil service expanded to oversee the empire; growing industry provided still more jobs. London became like a huge, expanding mouth, swallowing up people by the millions. Nineteenth-century reformer William Cobbett called the city "The Great Wen" (literally, a tumorous cyst). By 1861 the population of London had risen to nearly 3 million. By 1901, the figure was almost 6.5 million. London's population had increased by more than 3 million in less than 50 years.

The city developed a level of poverty, visited on millions, never experienced before. The suffering of nineteenth-century London's poor has been articulated by many—Dickens, Mayhew, sociologists Charles Booth, Karl Marx, and Friedrich Engels—but few capture it as well as the French illustrator Gustav Doré, whose drawing accompanies this discussion.

The Modern Era: 1900 to the Present

After 1900, life improved. World War I united the country against a common enemy, and, iron-

The Industrial Revolution brought a tide of urban migration to cities such as London. Misery and despair were the lot of many, as poignantly shown in this picture of London's Harrow Alley, drawn by French artist Gustav Doré in the 1870s. (The Bettmann Archive, Inc.)

ically, the Great Depression of the 1930s helped equalize the suffering, as it cut the economic bottom out from under the country's middle and upper-middle classes. Then, in 1940, much of the city was destroyed once again. This time the culprit was Adolf Hitler's Luftwaffe.

Having overrun Europe in the late 1930s, Hitler believed that England was the key to toppling Western morale. He sought to destroy London's productive capacity, demoralize the population, and weaken England's will to resist. The first objective was largely accomplished; the second and third were never approached (see Box 2-8).

Once more the city regenerated itself. Rebuilt offices in the devastated city boomed, tourists came by the millions; and yet, much *was* lost in the war. The docklands and many of the factories were never repaired and thousands of jobs were lost; the empire disappeared and with it the im-

mense wealth that made the city grow; more and more industry moved out of town.

In recent years the country has become more socialistic and has adopted policies that assure basic housing, food, and medical services for all. On another level, socialism's costs and an annual inflation rate of over 20 percent continually threaten the city's economic stability. Racial tensions and economic frustrations are growing, as the 1981 and 1985 riots between blacks and (essentially white) police in London's Brixton district demonstrated.

Jan Morris (1978) thinks that present-day London is "a city between performances," not yet sure which direction to take in the modern world. She sees self-interest and lack of concern for the welfare of others rampant. After encountering the National Front youths in Lewisham Way that Saturday afternoon (Box 2-4), Morris returned home to watch what had happened on TV. There had been a riot, "a bit of a punch-up," as one of the boys had put it; cars had been burned, people beaten. The police had come. One thing Morris saw symbolized to her the city's current malaise: the television showed three "hatless policemen, ties askew, helmets half off . . . struggling with a youth, whose ferocious writhings, kickings, and mouthings made him the very embodiment of a snarl" (1978, p. 60).

More hopeful, even optimistic, is Bernard Nossiter, long-time London correspondent for the *Washington Post*. He notes that people in London are still truly nice to one another and that the city is one of the most humane urban environments in the world:

> The tourist horde marvels at the patience, and the sense of fairness of Britons who stand in queues for buses, theatres, goods in a shop. . . . Outsiders notice too the remarkable courtesy, particularly among workers, that governs most transactions. The lady from the council house asks, "Have you a News of the World, luv?" The news agent replies with a smile, "Here, dear." And she responds, "Thank you, luv."
>
> The "dear" and "luv" are ritual, unthought, the common vocabulary. But they also suggest a kinship, a oneness, a decency that is not part of the

Hitler's Luftwaffe virtually demolished the city of London in the blitz of 1940. Although the bombs fell all about Wren's masterpiece, St. Paul's Cathedral, the church continued to stand, symbolizing the unflagging British resistance. (Syndication International Ltd.)

ritual vocabulary in New York, Munich, Cleveland, Stockholm or Marseilles. London [is] the last inhabitable great city. To be sure, the skyline is pockmarked by the excrescences of the property speculator, huge and rude towers of glass, steel and cement. But it is not dominated by them. You can walk through miles of city streets where buildings are five-storeys high or less. These terraces do not crush the human spirit; they are built on a human scale. In strictly economic terms, measuring profit and loss, they are no doubt an inefficient use of land that would be better exploited by some forty-storey monster. The survival of a human skyline, however, is another aspect of the British choice, an insistence that things must not always take pride of place before people. (1978)

Perhaps Dr. Johnson was right after all. Between two such conflicting views as those of Morris and Nossiter, there is little room for compromise. London in the modern era is still as it was in Johnson's day: a world city that inevitably contains "all that life can afford."

Conclusion

Cities have been with us for 10,000 years. They began after the last ice age in favorable ecological settings in many areas of the world. Slowly and tentatively they established themselves, fueled by a surplus of goods and materials, whether developed by agriculture, trade, or military dominance. As they grew, they evolved a complex social structure—most particularly, a specialized division of labor and a hierarchical power structure. All these elements allowed cities, in time, to increase their dominance in human affairs. Thus began the first urban revolution.

The earliest cities, such as Jericho and Catal Hüyük, were scattered, independent units, often linked by trade but not much more. Sometime after 4000 B.C., however, the first urban empires began to appear. In Mesopotamia and later in Egypt, China, the Indus River Valley, and the Americas, systems of cities emerged. These became not only centers of culture but centers of regional domination as well. This link between city and empire was a central factor in the development of civilization for nearly 5,000 years. Urban empires pulled into their sphere diverse peoples, ideas, and great wealth and power. This was as true of Teotihuacán in North America as it was of Egypt in the Middle East.

Early Western civilization also centered around its cities—first those of Greece and then those of the Roman Empire. When the latter finally dissembled in the late fifth century A.D., most of the other cities of Europe—outposts in the Roman chain—lost their reason for being. The next 500 years—roughly from A.D. 500–1000—were a decidedly antiurban period. Many cities disappeared entirely. The few that managed to survive limped along, shadows of what they had been.

In the first few centuries of the second millennium after Christ, a halting urban revival began. Slowly trade began to revive and the old feudal system began to break down as a new merchant class gained power. This revival reached its peak between 1400 and 1600 with the evolution of the Renaissance cities—most effectively symbolized by the Italian city-states of Florence, Venice, and Milan.

Then, around 1600, a turning point was reached. The old feudal social order was weakened beyond repair, and the merchant class, generating greater wealth by increasingly successful business ventures, began to control urban life throughout Europe. Seeing new possibilities for a better life in material terms, people streamed into cities all over the continent. This influx, coupled with technological improvement and advances in health and sanitation services, created what is known as a demographic transition. Europe generally, but cities especially, exploded in population as death rates plummeted, birth rates stayed high, and migrants arived in millions. From 1650 on, cities—many huge in number and dominance—began sprouting all over Europe and North America. This was the second urban revolution, spurred on primarily by the twin engines of capitalism and industrialization.

Today, cities exist in the farthest reaches of the globe. In many cases the growth of cities created immense problems and widespread suffering amid successes. Now, in areas of the world where the urban demographic transition first occurred (notably Europe and North America), urban growth has slowed dramatically. Unhappily, in others areas—as we shall show poignantly in Chapters 8 through 10—it most assuredly has not.

Our case study of London illustrates, in the life of a single city, nearly all of these processes. London began as an outpost of the Roman Empire, achieved initial success, and then, with the Roman retreat in 410, fell into its own dark age—unheard of for centuries and the object of multiple invasions. It began to recover after the victory of William the Conqueror in 1066. For five centuries it built its prominence as the center of British life and, around 1600, blossomed into one of the greatest Renaissance cities in history. Its success was linked primarily to international trade. Throughout the next two centuries London grew and gained even greater control of world markets. Then, with the Industrial Revolution and intensive British colonization in the nineteenth and early twentieth centuries, the city exploded in population, undergoing a major demographic transition. Despite its incredible wealth-generating capacity, London has had massive problems that it has carried into this century. It now faces, as do many Western industrial cities, a future of declining population and industrial capacity.

The emergence of cities as a dominant force in human affairs is one of the crucial events of history. In many instances, cities have been the driving wheel behind the development of civilization. They have combined ideas in new ways, produced great wealth, wielded incredible power (often injudiciously and inhumanely), and become the home of an increasing proportion of the world's population.

Yet, throughout history, cities have not always had the same character. As we suggested at the opening of this chapter, the city is largely synonymous with civilization itself. Each chapter in the story of human civilization has thus brought distinctive cities: cities of the early empires, the medieval city, the Renaissance city and, most recently, the industrial-capitalist city.

Thus, there is both a constancy and a flux to city history. Together, both processes create the urban phenomenon. We shall see both clearly evident again as we consider the development of American cities in the next chapter.

CHAPTER 3
The Development
of American Cities

Come hither, and I will show you an admirable Spectacle! 'Tis a Heavenly CITY. . . . A CITY to be inhabited by an Innumerable Company of Angels, and by the Spirits of Just Men. . . .

Put on thy beautiful garments, O America, the Holy City!

COTTON MATHER, SEVENTEENTH CENTURY PREACHER

American urban history began with the small town—five villages hacked out of the wilderness . . . each an "upstart" town with no past, an uncertain future, and a host of confounding and novel problems. . . .

ALEXANDER B. CALLOW, JR. (1969)

To the visitor from London, the cities of America may seem to lack the rich texture that accumulates over centuries of history. In no city of North America, for example, does a single building rival in age the Tower of London—whose foundations were erected in the eleventh century during the reign of William the Conqueror. Indeed, even the current Houses of Parliament and Buckingham Palace—relative newcomers on the London

scene from the mid–nineteenth century—are older than all but a few urban structures in the United States.

Yet, although they may be very recent developments in the course of world urban history, the cities of North America have a fascinating history of their own, spanning some 350 years. In this chapter we examine American urban history from its earliest settlements on the Atlantic coast, literally "hacked out of the wilderness," to the massive metropolitan regions of the 1980s, which contain over 175 million urban Americans.

The first European settlements in North America were founded in the early seventeenth century when the medieval city was being transformed by industrialization in Europe. Perhaps not surprisingly, the first American cities were founded specifically as trade- and wealth-generating centers to fuel the growth of cities in Europe. Urban settlement in the United States was primarily shaped by the forces of postmedieval culture—commercial trade and, shortly thereafter, industrial production. These cities, like the nation itself, began with the greatest of hope. Cotton Mather was so enticed by the idea of the city that he saw its growth as the fulfillment of the Biblical promise for a heavenly city. Has that promise been realized? To find out we shall examine the development of urban America in terms of four phases:

1. *The Colonial Era.* Extending from the first settlements in the early 1600s to just after the Revolutionary War, this was the pre-industrial period

2. *The Era of Initial Urban Growth and Westward Expansion.* Lasting from about 1800 to 1870, this was a transitional period that saw the shift from an agricultural and trade-based economy to an industrial economy.

3. *The Era of the Great Metropolis.* Running from 1870 to 1940, this was the period of full industrialization.

4. *The Modern Era.* Extending from 1940 to the present, this has been a period of emerging urban regionalism and a post-industrial economy.

The Colonial Era: 1600–1800

If one could return to the North America of the late sixteenth century, the only human populations one would find would be those of Native American groups that later European colonists would dub "Indians." These groups lived in many small societies spread across the continent. Some, such as the Cheyenne and the Sioux of the western plains, were nomadic; others, like the Hopi and the Navajo tribes of Arizona and New Mexico and the eastern Iroquois, maintained seasonal or permanent settlements of up to 500 people.

It is also likely that some cultures from Central America and Mexico (discussed in the last chapter) spread into North America from the Southwest, moving as far east as the state of Mississippi. One such group was the Natchez, who lived in permanent settlements of perhaps 1,000 people and had considerable diversity and specialization of occupations, including priests and artisans. Until the Europeans arrived, the Natchez probably were the most "urban" people on the continent.

Beginnings

Although the Spanish founded St. Augustine in Florida in 1565, this settlement never became much more than an outpost. The seventeenth century, however, began a far-reaching transformation. The English settled in Jamestown, Virginia, in 1607. Although, like St. Augustine, Jamestown long remained little more than a village, it established a pattern—there was a continent to be exploited. As word of successful British settlement in North America spread, more northern Europeans made the trek across the Atlantic. In 1620 the Puritans arrived in Massachusetts and established Plymouth Colony. By 1630 some of their number had moved a few miles to the north and established the city of Boston at a particularly fortuitous port site. In 1639 a group, breaking away from the strict Puritanism of Boston, founded the town of Newport in present-day Rhode Island. In 1624 the Dutch arrived at the tip of Manhattan Island and decided to call their town "New Amsterdam," as the eighteenth-century humorist, Washington Irving, writing under the pseudonym Dietrich Knickerbocker, recalls in Box 3-1.

By 1664 New Amsterdam had been ceded to the British and was named New York after King Charles II's brother James, the Duke of York. In the 1680s two more urban settlements were added to the New World list. Charles Town (Charleston) was established in 1680 by the English on the eastern shore of what later would be the state of South Carolina. So impressed were they with this site, early Charlestonians boasted that the Ashley and Cooper Rivers met at Charleston to form the Atlantic Ocean! Also impressive was the town founded by William Penn, leader of the Quaker religious group, at the point of confluence of the Schuylkill and Delaware Rivers. In 1682 Penn christened his City of Brotherly Love, Philadelphia.

The Character of Early American Cities

These were the beginnings. With the exception of Newport (which was usurped in prominence by Providence in the nineteenth century), all of these settlements became important American cities.

During their earliest stages, however, they were so different from the cities we know today that they would appear virtually unrecognizable were we to visit them.

To begin with, they were exceptionally small, both in physical size and population. New Amsterdam, for example, occupied only the southernmost tip of Manhattan Island, a far cry from the huge, five-borough City of New York that was incorporated in 1898. Similarly, neither New Amsterdam nor any of the other urban settlements of North America had populations approaching 10,000 until the eighteenth century. Indeed, as Table 3-1 makes clear, it was not until the Revolutionary War that some of these cities began to develop populations even remotely resembling cities by today's standards.

Second, the small size of these settlements and the common ethnic and religious background of most of their population resulted in a very personalized urban existence: "the social life of the town dwellers represented what anthropologists would call a dense collective experience through the daily contact of neighbors and townsfolk, the expectation of regular church attendance, and the continuous association of young people among themselves as they were growing up" (Still 1974, p. 11).

Third, the building patterns of these towns were unlike those of today. Boston was ". . . one story structures, covered with thatch, and flung at random over the peninsula" (Bridenbaugh 1938, p. 9). The lack of regular street patterns in early Boston and New York gave both settlements the look of a medieval town. Even today that original pattern can be observed: both central Boston and Manhattan below 14th Street still retain their initial pattern of irregular streets. Furthermore, hard-surfaced streets were not commonly found in the United States until well into the eighteenth and nineteenth centuries. Only Philadelphia, settled half a century later, was built from the beginning upon the more familiar grid system now found in many American cities (see Figure 6-3).

Despite the fact that many of these cities were founded as religious havens and had a medieval tinge to them, such qualities were deceptive. Beneath the surface they were part and parcel of the

---

BOX 3-1
How New Amsterdam Got Its Name (Maybe)

The land being thus fairly purchased of the Indians, a circumstance very unusual in the history of colonization, and strongly illustrative of the honesty of our Dutch progenitors, a stockade fort and trading house were forthwith erected. . . .

Around this fort a progeny of little Dutch-built houses, with tiled roofs and weathercocks, soon sprang up, nestling themselves under its walls for protection, as a brood of half-fledged chickens nestle under the wings of the mother hen. The whole was surrounded by an enclosure of strong palisadoes, to guard against any sudden interruption of the savages. Outside of these extended the corn-fields and cabbage-gardens of the community; with here and there an attempt at a tobacco plantation; all covering those tracts of country at present called Broadway, Wallstreet, William-street and Pearl-street.

And now the infant settlement having advanced in age and stature, it was thought high time it should receive an honest Christian name. Hitherto it had gone by the original Indian name Manna-hata, or as some will have it, "The Manhattoes"; but this was now decried as savage and heathenish, and as tending to keep up the memory of the pagan brood that originally possessed it. Many were the consultations held upon the subject, without coming to a conclusion, for though every body condemned the old name, nobody could invent a new one. At length, when the council was almost in despair, a burgher, remarkable for the size and squareness of his head, proposed that they should call it New-Amsterdam. The proposition took every body by surprise; it was so striking, so apposite, so ingenious. The name was adopted by acclamation, and New-Amsterdam the metropolis was thenceforth called.

Source: Washington Irving, *Diedrich Knickerbocker's History of New York* (Norwalk, Conn.: Heritage, 1968), pp. 80–81.

---

change that was sweeping European urban civilization: they were unabashed trading centers bent on profit and growth. New Amsterdam was probably the most clearly commercial, but Puritan Boston and Quaker Philadelphia were no slackers when it came to money-making either. Box 3-2 notes how vigorously founder William

TABLE 3-1
Population of the Earliest Cities of the United States, 1630–1776

Major Cities

Year	New Amsterdam (New York)	Boston	Newport	Philadelphia	Charles Town (Charleston)
1640	400	1,200	96	—	—
1660	2,400	3,000	700	—	—
1680	3,200	4,500	2,500	—	700
1700	5,000	6,700	2,600	5,000	2,000
1720	7,000	12,000	3,800	10,000	3,500
1742	11,000	16,382	6,200	13,000	6,800
1760	18,000	15,631	7,500	23,750	8,000
1775	25,000	16,000	11,000	40,000	12,000

Secondary Cities

New Haven, Conn.	(1771)	8,295	Middletown, Conn.	(1775)	4,680
Norwich, Conn.	(1774)	7,032	Portsmouth, N.H.	(1775)	4,590
Norfolk, Va.	(1775)	6,250	Marblehead, Mass.	(1776)	4,386
Baltimore, Md.	(1775)	5,934	Providence, R.I.	(1774)	4,361
New London, Conn.	(1774)	5,366	Albany, N.Y.	(1776)	4,000
Salem, Mass.	(1776)	5,337	Annapolis, Md.	(1775)	3,700
Lancaster, Pa.	(1776)	5/6,000	Savannah, Ga.	(1775)	3,200
Hartford, Conn.	(1774)	4,881			

Source: Adapted with permission from figures compiled by Bayrd Still in *Urban America* (Boston: Little, Brown, 1974), p. 12. Original source: Carl Bidenbaugh, *Cities in the Wilderness* (New York: Ronald Press, 1938), pp. 6n, 143, 303n; and Carl Bridenbaugh, *Cities in Revolt* (New York: Ronald Press, 1955), pp. 5, 216–217.

Penn promoted his town of Philadelphia in a 1684 prospectus.

The underlying theme of all these cities was that they would serve as export centers for American raw materials going to the European home country. Boston, for example, supplied lumber for the ships of the British Royal Navy; for its part, Charleston shipped rice and indigo back to the British Isles; New York served as a base for the lucrative fur trade.

As time wore on, however, American cities, distant from England geographically, became more and more independent. Colonial merchants began to compete with the British and established separate trade agreements with the West Indies and even Europe. Enterprising craftspeo-

ple produced goods for local consumption equal to those imported from England. On the civic front, more and more city governments, technically responsible to their "home offices" in Europe, found reason to cave in to local demands for more freedom in trade (McKelvey 1969).

Through all this the cities prospered, attracting more and more diverse people. Although Boston was able to maintain its Puritan stamp for a time, New York attracted Jews and Swedes; Philadelphia absorbed significant numbers of Germans, Irish, Welsh, and Dutch; and Charleston became home for groups of French Huguenots and Scots (McKelvey 1969, p. 18). Many of these people moved inland as the eighteenth century progressed, and numerous new, secondary cities, such as New Haven and Baltimore (Table 3-1), were established. Although only a small fraction of the population lived in towns, an urban society was emerging along the eastern shore of what soon would become a new nation.

By the late 1760s, the 13 colonies had at least 12 major cities and a total population (city and hinterland) of 2 million English, half a million of other European backgrounds, and nearly 400,000 slaves, almost all of whom were in the South (McKelvey 1969). The major cities were losing their "backwater" status rapidly.

The Revolutionary War Era

Just as the events of the French Revolution centered on Paris, many significant events of the American Revolutionary era unfolded in cities. Most prominent were the Boston Massacre (1770), the Boston Tea Party (1773), the Philadelphia meetings of the Continental Congress (1774 and 1775), and the Constitutional Convention (1787). Although the struggle for independence did not take place entirely in cities, it was in many ways a city-instigated war. The bulk of the economic trade of the colonies was carried out in its cities. American merchants and colonists wanted freedom to pursue their life's interests as they saw fit. In most cases economic interests were what were uppermost in their minds ("No taxation without representation!"). After the war, leadership of the new nation continued to be urban centered. New York became the first capital in 1789, and Philadelphia took over the title in 1790.

Despite this urban dominance, however, most of the population was not urban at this point. When the first census was completed in 1790, only about 5 percent resided in urban places (2,500 or more persons) and only 24 such places existed. Philadelphia was the largest settlement, with a population of but 42,000.

If the first phase of the urban history of the United States was marked by the establishment of a chain of important urban settlements on the East Coast, the next phase revealed a dramatic shifting of attention westward as the new nation began an expansion which, before mid-century, would reach the Pacific Ocean.

BOX 3-2

Town Lots in Philadelphia: A Good Investment in 1684

Philadelphia . . . our intended Metropolis . . . is two Miles long, and a Mile broad, and at each end . . . upon a Navigable River. . . . From [August, 1683 to August, 1684] . . . the Town advanced [from 80] to Three hundred and fifty-seven Houses; divers of them large, well built, with good Cellars, three stories, and some with Balconies. . . . There is also a fair [dock] of about three hundred foot square . . . to which a ship of five hundred Tuns may lay her broadside. . . . There inhabits most sorts of useful Tradesmen, As Carpenters, Joyners, Bricklayers, Masons, Plasterers, Plumers, Smiths, Glasiers, Taylers, Shoemakers, Butchers, Bakers, Brewers, Glovers, Tanners, Felmongers, Wheelrights, Millrights, Shiprights, Boatrights, Ropemakers, Saylmakers, Blockmakers, Turners, etc. . . . .

There are Two Markets every Week, and Two Fairs every year. . . . Some Vessels have been here Built, and many Boats; and by that means a ready Conveniency for Passage of People and Goods. . . . The Town is well furnish'd with convenient Mills. . . . The Improvement of the place is best measur'd by the advance of Value upon every man's Lot . . . the worst Lot in the Town, without any Improvement upon it, is worth four times than it was when it was lay'd out. . . .

Source: William Penn, cited in Bayrd Still, *Urban America* (Boston: Little, Brown, 1974), pp. 16–17.

Growth and Expansion: 1800–1870

Transportation Links Westward

At the outbreak of the Revolutionary War, the western frontier of the northern colonies extended barely past the Hudson River, and the southern colonies reached outward only to the Appalachian Mountains. By the time the war was over, the territory of the United States extended roughly to the Mississippi River. The tremendous economic potential of this new region captured the interest of business leaders in established cities, and by the early decades of the nineteenth century plans were under way to link the new territories

The colonial city in the United States had many village-like qualities. Personal relationships and religious beliefs were central elements of early New York and other cities of the colonial era. (The Bettmann Archive, Inc.)

with cities in the East. All this was decidedly competitive, as Constance Green notes: "The older Atlantic port cities were . . . increasingly aware that whoever captured the bulk of the Ohio valley trade would prosper at the expense of all other competitors" (1957, p. 36).

The first of these links westward was established in 1818: the National Road (now Interstate 40) was built, which pushed through the Appalachians from the city of Baltimore. This trade route, along with Baltimore's large shipbuilding industry, caused that city to grow in size and wealth. Philadelphia attempted to keep pace, opening both canal and turnpike routes west, although with more modest success. Not to be outdone, New York opened the Erie Canal in 1825. Although it was not fully recognized at the time, the canal was to be the key to New York's increasing hegemony over East Coast urban trade in the mid–nineteenth century. By cutting across upstate New York from the Hudson, the canal opened a water route to the entire Great Lakes region and much of Canada. Undaunted, Balti-

more began another round in this interurban rivalry by opening a railroad line to Ohio in 1828. Other cities followed suit. Soon many railroad lines stretched westward, linking coastal cities to the hinterland.

By 1830 New York, Philadelphia, and fast-growing Baltimore had emerged as the main coastal American cities, largely due to their control of the lion's share of commerce with the Ohio Valley. The remarkable rate of growth of these cities in comparison to Charleston, an original East Coast city still focused on tobacco and cotton production, is suggested in Table 3-2. As westward expansion proceeded, many new cities were incorporated. A glance at Table 3-3 shows that fully 39 major urban areas appeared between 1816 and 1876, the height of the westward expansion movement.

Cities as Big Business

There can be little question that economic gain was the major objective of the urban growth of the early nineteenth century. As Europe had

TABLE 3-2
Population Growth of Selected East Coast Cities, 1800–1870

	1790	1810	1830	1850	1870
New York	33,131	—	202,589	515,547	942,292
Philadelphia	42,000	—	80,462	121,376	674,022
Baltimore	13,500	—	80,620	169,054	267,354
Charleston	16,500	—	30,289	42,985	48,956
Entire U.S.A., Percent Urban	(5.1)	(7.3)	(8.8)	(15.3)	(25.7)

Source: Adapted with permission from Bayard Still, *Urban America* (Boston: Little, Brown, 1974), pp. 58, 79.

TABLE 3-3
Incorporation Dates of the Fifty Largest U.S. Cities by Historical Period

Pre-1776 (2)	1776–1815 (5)	1816–1848 (22)	1849–1876 (17)	1877–1912 (4)
New York (1685)	Baltimore (1797)	Atlanta (1847)	Akron (1865)	Honolulu (1909)
Philadelphia (1701)	Dayton (1805)	Boston (1822)	Birmingham (1871)	Long Beach, California (1888)
	New Orleans (1805)	Buffalo (1832)	Dallas (1856)	Miami (1896)
	Richmond (1782)	Chicago (1837)	Denver (1861)	Oklahoma City (1890)
	San Antonio (1809)	Cincinnati (1819)	Fort Worth (1873)	
		Cleveland (1836)	Indianapolis (1874)	
		Columbus (1834)	Jersey City (1855)	
		Detroit (1824)	Kansas City (1850)	
		Houston (1837)	Los Angeles (1850)	
		Jacksonville (1832)	Minneapolis (1867)	
		Louisville (1828)	Oakland (1854)	
		Memphis (1826)	Omaha (1857)	
		Milwaukee (1846)	Portland (1851)	
		Newark (1836)	St. Paul (1853)	
		Norfolk (1845)	San Diego (1850)	
		Pittsburgh (1816)	San Francisco (1850)	
		Providence (1832)	Seattle (1869)	
		Rochester (1834)		
		St. Louis (1822)		
		Syracuse (1848)		
		Toledo (1837)		
		Worcester (1848)		

Source: Daniel J. Elazar, "Urban Problems and the Federal Government: A Historical Inquiry," in A. B. Callow, Jr., ed., *American Urban History* (New York: Oxford University Press, 1969), p. 451.

sought economic reward through colonization of the New World, so, in turn, did the cities of the East Coast seek to enrich themselves through expansion of trade networks with the West. Pittsburgh, Cincinnati, Louisville, Kansas City, Chicago, and others all attempted to gain *their* share of trade with their region and beyond. This competition and frenetic growth is portrayed in Cityscape 3-1.

The Beginnings of Industrialization

As Jaimie McPheeters' diary makes obvious, as the nineteenth century wore on, in all the nation's cities one heard more and more the sound of machines. Although the major part of the American Industrial Revolution would not occur until the latter part of the century, its beginnings were much earlier.

The Revolutionary War and, later, the War of 1812 had interrupted trade with Europe. During the lean years that these confrontations occasioned, American entrepreneurs began to realize that they would have to produce their goods themselves. Having a country with abundant raw materials before them, they lost no time in adopting the new industrial techniques of Europe. This process, in itself, gave birth to new and important cities inland. One of the major locations was New England. Literary critic Van Wyck Brooks notes that by the 1830s around Boston, factory towns "were rising on every hand, in Eastern Massachusetts and New Hampshire—Lawrence, Lowell, Fitchberg, Manchester, Lynn. Every village with a waterfall set up a textile mill or a paper mill, a shoe factory or an iron foundry" (1936, p. 4). Slowly, industrialization supported by private investment began to transform America, particularly in the North. As it did so, some new tensions began to mount.

Urban-Rural/North-South Tensions

There always has been a streak of antiurbanism in American life. It has been linked to the popular image of America as the "last frontier," the place where the confines of (urban) civilization could be left behind and adequate "space" be found at last. Many of the country's original settlers came here specifically to escape Europe's rapid urbanization and to attain much-desired "room to breathe." As long as the early American settlements remained small and kept their relatively homogeneous character, few tensions existed between urban and rural America. Yet some of America's founders were worried greatly about what larger cities might do to the new nation. Thomas Jefferson was one.

Close to the rural aristocratic tradition of Virginia, Jefferson believed that cities represented "ulcers on the body politic" and saw their growth as an invitation to all the corruption and evil that had befallen the Old World across the Atlantic. Commenting on an outbreak of yellow fever, Jefferson wrote the following to Benjamin Rush in 1800:

> When great evils happen I am in the habit of looking out for what good may arise from them as consolations to us, and Providence has in fact so established the order to things, as that most evils are the means of producing some good. The yellow fever will discourage the growth of great cities in our nation, and I view great cities as pestilential to the morals, the health and the liberties of man. True, they nourish some of the elegant arts, but the useful [arts] can thrive elsewhere . . . with more health, virtue and freedom. . . . (Quoted in Glaab 1963, p. 52)

As if in defiance of Jefferson's wishes, America's cities grew in number and prominence. To escape their influence, some people moved westward. The cities followed and brought with them the more mechanized existence of the industrial age. By 1850 many rural Americans were deeply alarmed. Agrarian periodicals regularly touted the superiority of country life over the perfidiousness of the city. Box 3-3 suggests the tone and substance of this confrontation.

The debate on the pros and cons of city life soon reached a new and powerful dimension on the regional level: hostility between the North and South. This was largely because the unparalleled growth of American cities between 1820 and 1860 was centered in the North. Cities such as New

CITYSCAPE 3-1
A City-Making Mania

Urban historian Richard C. Wade offers a glimpse of the incredible urban growth that characterized the early nineteenth century. Despite the common conception that towns and cities sprang up after land-hungry settlers had filled up a new region, notice Wade's assertion that towns actually preceded much of the westward movement of population. In fact, many who started west during this period went in search of urban—rather than rural— opportunities.

The towns were the spearheads of the American frontier. Planted as forts or trading posts far in advance of the line of settlement, they held the West for the approaching population. . . .

The speed and extent of this expansion startled contemporaries. Joseph Charless, the editor of the *Missouri Gazette*, who had made a trip through the new country in 1795, remembered the banks of the Ohio as "a dreary wilderness, the haunt of ruthless savages," yet twenty years later he found them "sprinkled with towns" boasting "spinning and weaving establishments, steam mills, manufacturers in various metals, leather, wool, cotton and flax," and "seminaries of learning conducted by excellent teachers. . . ."

Not all the towns founded in the trans-Allegheny region in this period fared as well, however. Many never developed much beyond a survey and a newspaper advertisement. Others after promising beginnings, slackened and settled down to slow and unspectacular development. Still others flourished briefly then faded, leaving behind a grim story of deserted mills, broken buildings, and aging people—the West's first harvest

of ghost towns. Most of these were mere eddies in the westward flow of urbanism, but at flood tide it was often hard to distinguish the eddies from the main stream. Indeed, at one time Wheeling, Virginia, St. Genevieve, Missouri, New Albany, Indiana, and Zanesville, Ohio were considered serious challengers to the supremacy of their now more famous neighbors.

Other places such as Rising Sun, Town of America, or New Athens, were almost wholly speculative ventures. Eastern investors scanned maps looking for likely spots to establish a city, usually at the junction of two rivers, or sometimes at the center of fertile farm districts. They bought up land, laid it out in lots, gave the place a name, and waited for the development of the region to appreciate its value. Looking back over this period one editor called it a "city-making mania," when everyone went about "anticipating flourishing cities in vision, at the mouth of every creek and bayou. . . ."

Louisville, 1849

As evidence of the portrait just painted here is a section from the diary of Jaimie McPheeters, a 15-year-old boy. In 1849, after hearing stories of the gold rush in California, Jaimie and his dad decided to leave Louisville, Kentucky, and head west. Just before leaving, Jaimie's mother told him that when he returned, he could take his rightful place in "the cultural life of Louisville, and share in the city's advancement." This possibility prompted the following ruminations in Jaimie's diary. Clearly, even in 1849, Louisville was no "hick town."

Well, I thought, if you ask me, they've gone too far with this

Louisville already. It was overdeveloped and blown up with commerce and business so you could hardly get across the streets any more without being run down by teamsters. Why, they had eight brickyards in Louisville in 1849—I saw it in a bragging pamphlet that was got up by some merchant or other that seemed to have a good deal of time on his hands. There were three pianoforte manufactures, too, and three breweries, two tallow-rendering houses, an ivory-black maker—for use in refining sugar, you know—eight soap and candle factories; three shipyards; two glue factories; and four pork houses that slaughtered upwards of seventy thousand hogs a year.

And if you were looking for steam machinery, they had twelve foundries that made the best on the river, or so the pamphlet claimed. There were rope factories, flouring mills, oilcloth factories, three potteries; six tobacco stemmeries, a paper mill, and a new gas works that lit 461 street lamps over sixteen miles of main. Not only that, it had a gas holder measuring sixty feet in diameter and twenty-two feet high. People used to ride out Sundays to look at it, but the superintendent said it was a nuisance because he couldn't keep the children off. In the end, they were obliged to hire a watchman, but he was bully-ragged so steady that he sort of went out of his head, so to speak, and they had to place him in a hospital that made a specialty of such cases.

Source: Richard C. Wade, "Urban Life in Western America, 1790–1830," in *American Historical Review* (Oct. 1958), pp. 14–30.

Source: Robert Lewis Taylor, *The Travels of Jaimie McPheeters* (New York: Arbor House, 1985), p. 22.

York, Philadelphia, and Baltimore simply outdistanced the conservative, slowly growing cities like Charleston and Savannah. The northern cities had the canal routes and the bulk of the railroad ties to the West, which produced tremendous increases in wealth and population. Moreover, they were getting ever further ahead, dominating greater shares of regional and national markets and beginning to outstrip the South in overall efficiency in production as industrialization spread. The West, observed Schlesinger,

> . . . was becoming steadily more like the Northeast, whereas the South, chained by slavery to agriculture, contained few sizable cities and those mostly at its edges. . . . Every year sharpened the contrast between the urban spirit of progress animating the one section and the static, rural life of the other. Few important industries existed below the Mason and Dixon line. . . . [The] Southerners, lacking the nerve centers for creative cultural achievement, fell behind in arts, letters and science. "It would have been surprising had they not desired secession," remarked Anthony Trollope, in America shortly after [the attack on] Fort Sumter. "Secession of a kind, a very practical secession, had already [taken place]." (1969, pp. 33–34)

The Civil War broke out in 1861. Although its causes were numerous, many historians believe that it was, in a very fundamental sense, a confrontation between urban and rural, industrial and agricultural values. The North's victory was a symbolic turning point. The world of Jefferson was dying. America's commitment to urban industrial expansion was thenceforth unchallenged. Between 1870 and 1950 an urban explosion comparable to that which had shaken Europe a century before took place.

The Era of the Great Metropolis: 1870–1940

The record number of cities incorporated in the United States during the 50-year period that ended in 1870 had yet to acquire many of the urban characteristics most familiar to us: towering buildings, populations in the millions, and blazing lights downtown. Two historical events would provide the impetus for this transformation: (1) the technological advance of *industrialization* and (2) the *migration* of millions of people to urban America.

Technological Advance

Industrialization involved much more than simply a proliferation of factories in and around the enlarging urban areas. Several inventions emerged that changed the face of the American city. The construction of buildings with iron, and then steel, pushed the city skyward. In 1848 a five-story factory built with an iron frame had made news in New York; by 1884 a ten-story steel structure in Chicago had ushered in the era of urban skyscrapers (Glaab and Brown 1967). The success of these taller buildings was further ensured as another invention, the Otis elevator (devised in the 1850s), became widespread in the 1880s. By the end of the century, some buildings reached 30 stories; by 1910 a few were as high as 50. By 1913 New York had 61 buildings above 20 stories, and the famous city skyline was beginning to take form (Armstrong 1972).

As cities grew upward, they also pushed outward, aided by a new technology in street-level transportation. Prior to the Civil War pedestrians had to contend only with horse-drawn vehicles. By the 1870s steam-powered trains were running on elevated tracks in New York. Soon after, the "els" were added to other large cities. People's ability to move about certainly was enhancd, but the thunderous noise, billowing smoke, and cascading sparks and cinders of these trains surely did little to enhance the peace and quiet of local neighborhoods or the quality of the environment.

In the 1880s the electric street trolley came into use. Still in operation in Philadelphia, Boston, and New Orleans, these devices also helped make mass transit a reality. Indeed, streetcars and the subways that followed were primarily responsible for making suburban life possible for millions. They allowed fast and inexpensive transportation beyond the city limits. Quick to see the possibilities of such transportation, real-estate speculators built housing tracts by the dozens. For example, in the suburbs of Roxbury, West Roxbury, and Dorchester, immediately surrounding Boston, over 23,000 new houses were built between 1870 and 1890 (Warner 1962). To the burgeoning middle class, an escape from the city's dirt and din was at last possible:

> The . . . general satisfaction with suburbs came from their ability to answer some of the major needs of the day. . . . To middle class families [they] gave a safe, sanitary environment, new houses in styles somewhat in keeping with their conception of family life, and temporary neighborhoods of people with similar outlook. . . . In addition to benefitting [the middle class] the suburbs [also served that portion of the city's] population which could not afford them. The apparent openness of the new residential quarters, their ethnic variety, their extensive growth, and their wide range of prices from fairly inexpensive rental suites to expensive single-family houses—these visible characteristics of the new suburbs gave aspiring low-income families the certainty that should they earn enough money they too could possess the comforts and symbols of success. (Warner 1962, p. 157)

Thus did technology spawn the suburban dream in the late 1800s. The attempt to realize this dream has been one of the most powerful motivating factors in American urban history.

Technological advance via the streetcar not only allowed cities to sprout suburbs, it also linked cities to one another with cheap transportation. At one time in the mid–nineteenth century, for example, it was possible to travel from Boston all the way to New York and beyond simply by transferring from streetcar line to streetcar line. Such a system greatly stimulated interurban migration.

The Great Migration

The growing suburbs proved important in yet another way: they helped siphon off the incredible population growth of the era. The expanding industrial economy created opportunities for millions. Between 1870 and 1920, urban places (over 2,500 persons) in the United States increased their populations from a total of just under 10 million to over 54 million. The country became, for the first time, a *predominantly* urban nation. (The country passed the 50 percent urban population mark in 1913.) The rate of growth for many of the largest cities was nothing short of astonishing. By 1920 Chicago had over *12 times* its 1870 population and was fast approaching the 3 million mark. New York, not yet a city of 1 million in 1870, was by 1920 approaching the 6 million mark.

Two demographic trends were primarily responsible for this striking increase in city dwellers: (1) depopulation of rural areas as people moved into cities and (2) immigration to the United States from abroad. The movement from the countryside to the city was occasioned by automation—machinery was making old forms of hand-powered labor obsolete—and the possibility of greater wealth in the city. Between 1880 and 1890, nearly 40 percent of the nation's 25,746 townships actually *lost* population (Glaab 1963, p. 176). Shannon's observation that "between 1860 and 1900 for every urban dweller who moved to a farm there were 20 farmers who moved to a city" (as quoted in Holt 1969, p. 43) cannot be very far from the truth. Perhaps most remarkable is the fact that thousands of farms simply were abandoned as population was drawn

The growth of the great metropolis reflected both changing technology and a high level of migration to cities. This wood engraving shows the first train on the elevated railroad in New York City in 1878. (Library of Congress)

toward the cities (Glaab 1963, p. 176). As might be expected, migration was most intense in the Northeast and Midwest, where the largest cities were.

The absolute number of foreign immigrants to the United States was a bit smaller than the number of city-bound Americans who left rural areas during this period, but the changes wrought by immigrants from abroad were far greater. Representing dozens of different nationalities and ethnicities, they introduced staggering cultural diversity to the large cities of the United States. Glaab and Brown give some hint of the transformation:

> The influx of immigrants to the cities, particularly during the decade of the 1880's when over five million arrived in the United States, produced some striking statistics for individual cities. In 1890, New York . . . contained more foreign born residents than any city in the world. The city had half as many Italians as Naples, as many Germans as Hamburg, twice as many Irish as Dublin, and two and a

half times the number of Jews in Warsaw. In 1893, Chicago contained the third largest Bohemian community in the world; by the time of the First World War, Chicago ranked only behind Warsaw and Lodz as a city of Poles. (1967, pp. 138–139)

One important effect of all this in-migration was the clustering together of cultural groups in distinctive city districts. The tremendous variety of these groups gave cities of the late nineteenth century a degree of diversity and excitement that was quite new in the United States—and would affect the character of the city from that time on. To travel the breadth of Chicago, Cleveland, Pittsburgh or New York was—and still is today— to experience a succession of differing worlds, each characterized by its own shops and products, its own sounds and smells, its own language. Hence, in addition to upward and outward expansion and raw population growth, cultural heterogeneity became a third major characteristic of the new American metropolis.

Politics and Problems

With the enormous changes that reshaped cities in this period came commensurate problems. How were the incoming millions to be fed, provided water, jobs, electricity, and some protection against unscrupulous exploitation? Only the city government was empowered to cope with these issues; however, the pressures *against* coping fairly and in the public interest were great, as Blake McKelvey notes:

> [The] water and gas companies needed franchises permitting them to lay pipes through the streets; the telephone and electric companies required authorization for the erection of poles; and successive transit companies sought public consent for an extension of the grid of iron rails. Local or out-of-town promoters were ready to pay huge sums for these often lucrative franchises, and the conflicting pressures sometimes corrupted the part-time councilmen empowered to govern the city. (1969, p. 60)

Because action on the city's problems was essential (else the city would begin to fall apart at the seams), certain dictatorial political figures—"the bosses"—began to take control of many city governments. They got the job done, but in the process they usually lined their pockets liberally with graft and kickbacks. By the turn of the century many American city officials were as corrupt as any organized crime figure in the modern era.

Outraged, citizens' groups in a few cities demanded reform. In 1880 the Committee of One Hundred organized against a natural-gas monopoly and its illicit connection to Philadelphia's government. Other reform movements—in St. Louis, Milwaukee, Cincinnati and New York—got under way. Progress was slow, however, for the bosses had developed an efficient "machine" with tentacles into all layers of government and neighborhood life (see Chapter 12).

While immigration to the United States was hardly new, reaction against immigrants became increasingly bitter after the turn of the century. This was due in large part to who the immigrants were. By 1900 immigrants were increasingly from southern and eastern Europe, more likely to be Roman Catholic, or Jewish than Protestant, and more likely of darker skin. They often had man-

---

BOX 3-4
The Wealthy Suburb: New Rochelle, 1902

In 1902 father built a house at the crest of the Broadview Avenue hill in New Rochelle, New York. It was a three-story brown shingle with dormers, bay windows and a screened porch. Striped awnings shaded the windows . . . Teddy Roosevelt was President. The population customarily gathered in great numbers either out of doors for parades, public concerts, fish fries, political picnics, social outings, or indoors in meeting halls, vaudeville theatres, operas, ballrooms. . . . Everyone wore white in summer. Tennis racquets were hefty and the racquet faces elliptical. There was a lot of sexual fainting. There were no Negroes. There were no immigrants.

Source: E. L. Doctorow, *Ragtime* (New York: Bantam, 1976), pp. 3–4.

---

ners and dress that made them stand out all the more as newcomers who were "different." These "less desirable" immigrants added significantly to anti-city sentiment because, even more than earlier immigrants, they were overwhelmingly urban settlers. By 1910, in fact, over one-third of the inhabitants of the eight largest United States cities had been born abroad; another one-third were first-generation Americans. In sharp contrast, fewer than one in ten rural Americans were foreign born at this time (Glaab 1963, p. 176).

Within the city, people from "good stock" tried valiantly to get away from the newcomers. The wealthier suburbs often had a decided anti-ethnic or racist tinge to them (see Box 3-4).

The Quality of Life of the New Metropolis

The industrialization of the city began anew the antiurbanism debate. Detractors saw life in cities as simply horrendous—not only was the physical environment being destroyed, but humane social arrangements were being replaced by more "mechanistic" alternatives. Take Willard Glazier's impressions of Pittsburgh in 1884, presented in Box 3-5. Glazier finds Pittsburgh so pernicious he likens it to hell itself.

BOX 3-5
Industrial Pittsburgh, 1884

By all means make your first approach to Pittsburgh in the night time, and you will behold a spectacle which has not a parallel on this continent. Darkness gives the city and its surroundings a picturesqueness which they wholly lack by daylight. It lies low down in a hollow of encompassing hills, gleaming with a thousand points of light, which are reflected from the rivers, whose waters glimmer in the faint moonlight. . . . Around the city's edge, and on the sides of the hills which encircle it like a gloomy amphitheatre, their outlines rising dark against the sky, through numberless apertures, fiery lights stream forth, looking angrily and fiercely up toward the heavens, while over all these settles a heavy pall of smoke. It is as though one had reached the outer edge of the infernal regions, and saw before him the great furnace of Pandemonium with all the lids lifted. The scene is so strange and weird that it will live in the memory forever. One pictures, as he beholds it, the tortured spirits writhing in agony, their sinewy limbs convulsed, and the very air oppressive with pain and rage. . . .

. . . Failing a night approach, the traveler should reach the Iron City on a dismal day in autumn, when the air is heavy with moisture, and the very atmosphere looks dark. All romance has disappeared. . . . There is only a very busy city shrouded in gloom. The buildings, whatever their original material and color, are smoked to a uniform, dirty drab; their smoke sinks, and mingling with the moisture in the air, becomes of a consistency which may almost be felt as well as seen. Under a drab sky a drab twilight hangs over the town, and the gas-lights, which are left burning at midday, shine out of the murkiness with a dull, reddish glare.

In truth, Pittsburgh is a smoky, dismal city, at her best. At her worst, nothing darker, dingier or more dispiriting can be imagined. The city is in the heart of the soft coal region; and the smoke from her dwellings, stores, factories, foundries and steamboats, uniting, settles in a cloud over the narrow valley in which she is built, until the very sun looks coppery through the sooty haze. Her inhabitants are all too busy to reflect upon the inconvenience or uncomeliness of this smoke. Work is the object of life with them. It occupies them from morning until night, from the cradle to the grave, [except] on Sundays, when, for the most part, the furnaces are idle, and the forges are silent.

Source: Willard Glazier, *Peculiarities of American Cities* (1884), quoted in Charles N. Glaab, *The American City: A Documentary History* (Homewood, Ill.: Dorsey, 1963).

Some profited greatly in this age of great economic expansion. Tremendous fortunes were made and urban industrial empires became established. In 1892 the *New York Times* published a list of 4,047 American millionaires; in 1901 J. P. Morgan founded U.S. Steel, the first billion-dollar corporation; and "by 1910 there were more millionaires in the United States Senate alone than there were in the whole nation before the Civil War" (Baltzell 1964, p. 110).

But times were not equally good for all. As the enormous mansion-retreats of the "robber-baron" industrialists rose across the urban fringe, the blight of the inner-city tenement became more and more conspicuous. With a steady stream of people entering the large cities of the North, property owners responded to the rising demand for housing by making the most profitable use of building space. When introduced in the 1850s, the New York tenement (originally meaning a rented, multifamily living quarter) was "hailed by civic leaders as a 'praise-worthy enterprise'" (Glaab and Brown 1967, p. 161). Before long, however, the tenements' quality became worse as designs cheapened and more and more people moved into them. As it did, the word "tenement" assumed its present connotation of "slum." By the turn of the century, perhaps 35 percent of New York City's population lived in such quarters, although the situation in most other industrial cities was somewhat more favorable. Despite periodic attempts at reform through legislation, the urban housing problem remains a controversial issue to the present (see Chapter 13).

Quality-of-life problems in the rapidly expanding industrial cities, unfortunately, were not limited to housing. Health hazards were great where high-density living was combined with inadequate sewerage and generally unsanitary conditions. Through the end of the nineteenth century, toilet facilities were grossly inadequate for immigrant tenement dwellers. Moreover, until the 1880s most Philadelphians drank water from the Delaware River, into which some 13 million gallons of sewage were being dumped weekly (Marshall 1969, p. 150). The frequency of epidemics was high. The *Chicago Times* summed up the problem with appropriate bluntness:

> The river stinks. The air stinks. Peoples' clothing, permeated by the foul atmosphere, stinks. . . . No other word expresses it so well as stink. A stench means something finite. Stink reaches the infinite and becomes sublime in the magnitude of odiousness. (Cited in Glaab and Brown 1967, p. 165)

Of course, attempts were made to remove many of these problems. Urban activists such as Jane Addams, awarded a Nobel Prize for the founding of Hull House (a settlement house) in Chicago (1889), attempted to help the situation of immigrants and improve living conditions. But for decades the battle was uphill. The cities were growing uncontrollably.

Trends Through 1940

Between 1870 and the start of World War I, over 20 million foreign immigrants disembarked on American shores. The vast majority of them became city dwellers. When one adds to this the in-migration from the rural hinterland and natural population increase by births, the shift is dramatic. The following statistic indicates the magnitude of the change: in 1870 only 25 percent of America's population resided in cities; by 1920 the census reported that, for the first time, the urban way of life was the most common—51.2 percent were urban dwellers.

The rush to cities slowed down considerably during World War I but began to leap upwards again immediately after. One source of the new influx was returning soldiers who, after "seeing the world," no longer were content to stay at home. As a humorous popular song of the times argued: "How ya gonna keep 'em down on the farm after they've seen Paree?"

The other source was renewed immigration. From a low of 110,000 in 1918 (the next-to-last year of the war), other countries increased their American-bound human "exports" to 805,000 in 1921, over 222,000 of whom came from Italy alone (McKelvey 1969, p. 86). But it was not to go on forever. All around the country people began to be concerned about the ability of the United States to continually absorb the "tired, hungry, and poor" of foreign states. Such reservations were laced with a considerable degree of ethnic prejudice as well. By lobbying hard, a group of anti-immigrationists was able to press the U.S. Congress in 1921 into passing a law limiting the foreign influx. This was followed by the adoption of a full-fledged immigration quota system in 1924.

The ultimate irony of the quota system, however, was that it did *not* stop migration to the cities, and perhaps set the stage for even greater urban difficulties in the future. The industrial machine that had been building since the late nineteenth century simply looked elsewhere for cheap labor and found that southern blacks were all too eager to find a better way of life. Between 1920 and 1929, over 600,000 southern blacks migrated to northern cities. By the end of the decade, Chicago's South Side and New York's Harlem had the largest concentrated black populations anywhere in the world. In Hartford, Baltimore, Washington, Philadelphia, Cincinnati, and Detroit, the black population grew enormously. The influx in Detroit "was so rapid that the competition for housing and other accommodations became acute and erupted in violence" in the riots of 1925 (McKelvey 1969, p. 87). Major racial tensions thus became part and parcel of the industrial urban scene.

The next crisis happened when the Stock Market Crash of 1929, which wiped out huge municipal investments, threw millions into destitution, and made local public projects virtually impossible to implement. Many cities became financially strapped to the point of bankruptcy. Seeing possible salvation in Franklin Roosevelt, 23 major cities supported the Democratic Party in the 1932 election and ensured his election. The next year the mayors of 50 cities met in Washington to found the U.S. Conference of Mayors and began lobbying efforts in their own behalf. They were not disappointed. The National Industrial Recovery Act appropriated $3.3 billion for much-needed public works and housing operations, and subsequent bills pumped billions more into housing construction, highway construction, and other relief for the cities (McKelvey 1969, pp. 92–95). A fateful corner had been turned: as the thirties progressed into the forties, fifties, and sixties, cities became more and more dependent on the federal government. Although the positive benefits of this connection were multiple, it was also to have major drawbacks.

The American City Today: 1940 to the Present

Just as each previous era in American urban history provided dramatic changes from the era before it, so too have major changes occurred recently. In addition to the trends just mentioned, today's American city is in the process of three major changes: (1) people are abandoning the central cities in record numbers, continuing a suburbanization trend that began nearly 100 years ago, a process aptly called *decentralization*; (2) major population growth has occurred in cities in the South and West, the so-called *Sunbelt phenomenon*; and (3) the work typically performed in the center city has become more and more oriented to white-collar jobs, high technology, and services, as cities enter what appears to be a *postindustrial* era. We shall examine each of these changes.

Decentralization

If the first three eras of American urban history can be characterized as a time of urban "implosion," of ever-greater numbers of people converging on the central city itself, then the period since 1940 has seen the beginnings of a major "urban explosion," of people moving out in droves from the core to the surrounding regions. One indication of this decentralization can be seen in the census data, shown in Table 3-4, for major northern cities between 1910 and 1985. Notice that all the cities in this table had become large metropolises by 1910 and that each grew rapidly in the following few decades. However, by 1950 that growth was slowing. By 1960 there was an actual *decline* in center-city populations and by 1985 what could only be characterized as a full-scale center-city retreat was under way.

Many of these people, however, are not leaving the metropolitan region. They are moving to the suburbs. Table 3-5 makes this clear by examining suburban populations for the cities we examined in Table 3-4 and selected other cities across the country. With few exceptions, suburbs are growing everywhere and have been doing so for over 30 years. Why?

Economic Considerations. By about 1950, more and more businesses, particularly industry and manufacturing, were moving away from the industrial districts of central cities. The costs of refurbishing older buildings were high, and, given high rents, expansion wasn't always possible. Further, some new assembly line procedures required large, low-level structures rather than the multistory buildings characteristic of an earlier era. Concerns over rising crime rates, taxes, and traffic congestion also played their part in a proliferation of new "industrial parks" in the outer urban areas. Workers often moved from the center city to be near their relocated jobs (Hall 1979). The result was a growth in suburban population and a decline in center-city population.

Technology. As noted earlier, technological changes in energy (steam power) and building techniques (steel frame skyscrapers) were important in the creation of a centralized metropolis in the nineteenth century. During the twentieth century the development of electric power, the widespread use of cars and trucks, the all-but-universal telephone, and—most recently—computer technology have been equally important in the decentralization of the urban area.

TABLE 3-4
Population of Selected U.S. Cities, 1910–1985

	1910	1930	1950	1960	1970	1985
Baltimore	588	805	950	939	906	787
Boston	671	781	801	697	641	563
Chicago	2,185	3,376	3,621	3,550	3,367	3,005
Cleveland	561	900	915	876	751	574
Detroit	466	1,569	1,850	1,670	1,511	1,203
Philadelphia	1,549	1,951	2,072	2,003	1,949	1,688
New York	4,767	6,930	7,892	7,782	7,895	7,072

Note: Population in thousands.

Source: *Statistical Abstract of the United States*, U.S. Bureau of the Census, 1960, pp. 20–21; 1976, pp. 24–25; 1986, pp. 23–24.

TABLE 3-5
Population of Suburban Areas for Selected U.S. Cities, 1970–1980

Northern Industrial Cities	1980 Population (in thousands)	Change Since 1970 (in thousands)	Percent Change Since 1970*
Baltimore	1,380	+ 215	+ 16
Boston	2,197	− 61	− 3
Chicago	4,071	+ 466	+ 11
Cleveland	1,323	+ 10	+ 1
Detroit	3,146	+ 226	+ 7
Philadelphia	3,019	+ 146	+ 5
New York	2,045	− 33	+ 2
Southern Cities			
Atlanta	1,588	+ 398	+ 25
Birmingham	552	+ 86	+ 16
Dallas-Fort Worth	1,680	+ 540	+ 32
Houston	1,317	+ 552	+ 42
Miami	1,238	+ 305	+ 25
New Orleans	626	+ 173	+ 28
Orlando	567	+ 213	+ 38
Tampa-St. Petersburg	1,048	+ 453	+ 43
Western Cities			
Los Angeles-Long Beach	4,136	+ 265	+ 6
Phoenix	739	+ 352	+ 48
Portland	871	+ 244	+ 28
Salt Lake City	707	+ 248	+ 35
San Francisco-Oakland	2,213	+ 182	+ 8
Seattle-Everett	1,055	+ 215	+ 20

*Percentages are rounded.

Source: U.S. Department of Commerce.

Unlike steam power, which must be used within the immediate area of its production, electric power can be transmitted over long distances. This makes it possible for both industries and residential areas to spread widely across the metropolitan area. Similarly, cars and trucks provide far greater flexibility in mobility and location than the rail transportation system that dominated the late nineteenth century. This has been especially true since the 1950s with the development of the interstate highway system and the ubiquitous outer-city "loops" (such as those surrounding Washington, Baltimore, and Columbus, Ohio). As rail lines pushed out of the cities in earlier decades, the first suburbs clustered around the stations. But motor vehicles made living possible in a far wider area while still providing access to the urban area as a whole. As late as 1920, the average commute was still only about 1.5 miles (Duncan 1956). By 1960, however, this distance had grown to almost 5 miles (Hawley 1971, p. 191), and it is not uncommon today to travel 20 miles or more. An estimated 15 percent of the work force does so (Blumenfeld 1969, p. 169).

Taken together, these technological changes have changed the meaning of urban space. Because we move more easily across space—in minutes by car or milliseconds by telephone—physical proximity is not as necessary to tie together all the activities within the urban area. In fact, most of us who live in cities routinely think in terms of *time* ("We live about 40 minutes from the airport . . .") rather than *distance*; we may not even know how many miles away the airport is.

Suburban Housing. Any consideration of urban decentralization during the last 50 years must include recognition of the tremendous proliferation of new housing, which is typically being constructed farther from central cities. This process is linked to transportation options and began in the late nineteenth century, but got perhaps its greatest push after World War II. At that time, millions of Americans returned from overseas to find their old neighborhoods in increasing disrepair (in the war effort many neighborhood maintenance projects had been shelved and the ability of private homeowners to maintain full upkeep was cur-

tailed). In many instances, returning white soldiers also found minority groups, especially blacks, living in or close to their previous homes. (Many blacks had migrated north during the war to work the industrial machinery vacated by whites.) Finally, like almost all Americans, these men wanted their own place out of the congested city, a place with a little more room where they could raise their kids in clean air and send them to good schools, without fear of crime and other urban ills. This was, of course, the classic suburban dream.

What made its realization possible for millions was the federal government. The Federal Housing Authority and the Veteran's Administration made low-interest loans for construction available to veterans or to anyone else who could supply some assurance of their ability to repay. Millions of veterans took the FHA and the VA up on their offer and elected to build or buy their new homes outside the center city, in suburban tracts.

The irony of this was that, like the immigration quota system, a well-meaning federal policy once again created major problems for cities down the line. As the white middle class moved out in droves to the separately incorporated suburbs, the cities lost more and more of the tax base that departing industry was already eroding. They became even more strapped financially.

To add to the problem, the population that was left behind in the city core was composed more and more of minorities and the poor. As industry abandoned the center city, many of these people were unable to find jobs and went on public relief. Thus the city was faced with an *increasing* demand for services and a *shrinking* ability to provide them. By the mid-1960s a true urban crisis—largely created by the decentralization phenomenon—was upon the country as a whole. Urban poverty was on the increase, minorities were justifiably angry over their standard of living, services were getting worse, and many cities were facing bankruptcy.

The Metropolitan Statistical Area (MSA). As we mentioned earlier, by 1910 decentralization was well under way in the United States. Cities were growing beyond their traditional boundaries by leaps and bounds. In the cities of the North, for example, workers, unable to find adequate housing in the center city, spilled over into the surrounding towns and small cities. To take a single case, Boston's workers began to settle in Wakefield and Lynn to the north, in Wellesley and Natick to the west, and in Quincy and Braintree to the south, among other communities. While technically these people were residents of their newly adopted local communities, on another level they were still clearly linked to Boston and its larger process.

Noticing this phenomenon, the U.S. Bureau of the Census was faced with a problem: how to count these people to get an idea of how cities were really growing. If they merely counted the residents of the center city—in this case, Boston—they would get a relatively small population count that would not reflect the fact that many of the people who lived in Braintree and Wakefield were really tied to Boston in a fundamental way. Consequently, they decided to count not only the center city and its population in their surveys, but the surrounding towns and cities that were obviously tied to that center city as well. Thus was born the idea of the metropolitan area.

Since 1910 a series of terms have been used to designate such sprawling urban regions. From 1959 until 1983, the term *standard metropolitan statistical area* (or SMSA) was employed. In mid-1983, however, the Census Bureau introduced the concept *metropolitan statistical area* (or MSA). An MSA is currently defined as including at least one city with 50,000 or more inhabitants, the county or counties containing the city, and any surrounding counties that have a high population density and a large proportion of inhabitants commuting to and from the central city. As of mid-1984 the Census Bureau recognized 277 MSAs within the United States, containing roughly three-fourths of the total population.

Megalopolis and the Consolidated Metropolitan Statistical Area (CMSA). The French geographer Jean Gottmann was one of the first urbanists to look closely at the sprawling urban region and to note the linkages between many independent urban municipalities. The first such area, which he called "Megalopolis," was the unbroken urban region that emerged along the eastern seaboard of the United States. It was dubbed the "Bos-Wash corridor" by Gottmann. In Cityscape 3-2 he describes the phenomenon.

The Bos-Wash corridor was the first American megalopolis, but it wasn't the last. Since 1961, when Gottmann's seminal book was published, other megalopoli have emerged in southern California and across the northern Midwest from Chicago to Cleveland.

Once again, such growth has not gone unnoticed by the Census Bureau. To cope with the phenomenon, the bureau coined the term *consolidated metropolitan statistical area* (or CMSA). By 1984, 21 CMSAs were recognized as part of the urban landscape, including Miami–Fort Lauderdale, Houston-Galveston-Brazoria, Portland-Seattle, Milwaukee-Racine, and Cleveland-Akron-Lorain.

Rural Growth. The decentralization of the American population has done more than spread urban settlement outward from central cities, however. Small towns and rural areas are experiencing a precipitous boom as well. During the 1960s rural America lost 2.8 million people, but during the 1970s the trend changed sharply: rural areas gained 8.4 million people, up some 15.4 percent (Fuguitt 1984). No doubt new forms of transportation and communication are an important foundation of this change. Yet Americans moving to small towns or rural areas also may be reacting to the problems of cities in the same way that those moving to the suburbs have done for decades, looking for a greater sense of security and reaffirming the value of simpler living. Still, the people moving to these areas are in no way traditionally rural. Most are well educated, have sophisticated tastes, and often work in nearby cities. Local stores spring up supplying French wines and the *New York Times Book Review*.

It is not clear whether this rural renaissance has abated. In the early 1980s an economic recession slowed the process down. No doubt about it, says U.S. Census official Calvin Beale, the "recession hit the rural areas and small towns harder than the metropolitan areas" (cited

---

CITYSCAPE 3-2
Megalopolis: The Bos-Wash Corridor

The Northeastern seaboard of the United States is today the site of a remarkable development—an almost continuous stretch of urban and suburban areas from southern New Hampshire to northern Virginia and from the Atlantic shore to the Appalachian foothills. . . .

. . . As one follows the main highways or railroads between Boston and Washington, D.C., one hardly loses sight of built-up areas, tightly woven residential communities, or powerful concentrations of manufacturing plants. Flying this same route one discovers, on the other hand, that behind the ribbons of densely occupied land along the principal arteries of traffic, and in between the clusters of suburbs around the old urban centers, there still remain large areas covered with woods and brush alternating with some carefully cultivated patches of farmland. These green spaces, however, when inspected at closer range, appear stuffed with a loose but immense scattering of buildings, most of them residential but some of industrial character. That is, many of these sections that look rural actually function largely as suburbs in the orbit of some city's downtown. . . .

Thus the old distinctions between rural and urban do not apply here any more. Even a quick look at the vast area of Megalopolis reveals a revolution in land use. Most of the people living in the so-called rural areas, and still classified as "rural population" by recent censuses, have very little, if anything, to do with agriculture. In terms of their interests and work they are what used to be classified as "city folks," but their way of life and the landscapes around their residences do not fit the old meaning of urban.

In this area, then, we must abandon the idea of the city as a tightly settled and organized unit in which people, activities, and riches are crowded into a very small area clearly separated from its nonurban surroundings. Every city in this region spreads out far and wide around its original nucleus; it grows amidst an irregularly colloidal mixture of rural and suburban landscapes; it melts on broad fronts with other mixtures, of somewhat similar though different texture, belonging to the suburban neighborhoods of other cities. Such coalescence can be observed, for example, along the main lines of traffic that link New York City and Philadelphia. Here there are many communities that might be classified as belonging to more than one orbit. It is hard to say whether they are suburbs, or "satellites," of Philadelphia or New York, Newark, New Brunswick, or Trenton. The latter three cities themselves have been reduced to the role of suburbs of New York City in many respects, although Trenton belongs also to the orbit of Philadelphia. . . .

This region indeed reminds one of Aristotle's saying that cities such as Babylon had "the compass of a nation rather than a city. . . ."

Source: Jean Gottmann, *Megalopolis* (New York: Twentieth Century Fund, 1961), pp. 3, 5–7.

---

in Schreiner 1984, p. 24). As we approach the 1990s, however, the "invasion of the city slickers" (look ahead to Cityscape 7-2) seems to be underway again.

Mark and Linda Murphy are a case in point. Recently they moved to the little town of Chester, New York, about 55 miles from Manhattan. They are but one family of more than 300 that have settled into Chester (1980 population: 7,000) since 1984. In addition, 400 more homes currently are under construction and officials see the town as possibly doubling or tripling in population by 1990. "It's happening almost overnight," said John Collins, the Town Supervisor. "People are nervous and scared about it. And so am I."

Strangely enough, it was not the rustic life that attracted the Murpheys and others, but the town's affordable housing. To live in Manhattan, the Murphys found, was astonishingly expensive. So, too, was housing in the prestigious suburbs near the city. Hence, to have the home they wanted, they felt they had only one choice, to move still farther out—into the countryside. Of course, there is a price to pay for such a choice: unusually long commuting. Many of the town's new residents wake up long before daybreak, pile sleepily into their cars, and make the long trek to New York or a close-in suburb where their job is. "It's a horror show," says Gregory Bellafiore, who recently bought a home in Yaphank, Long Island,

TABLE 3-6

The Ten Largest American Cities, 1984 and 1950

	1984		1950	
	Population	Rank	Population	Rank
New York	7,165	(1)	7,892	(1)
Los Angeles	3,097	(2)	1,970	(4)
Chicago	2,992	(3)	3,621	(2)
Houston	1,706	(4)	596	(14)
Philadelphia	1,647	(5)	2,072	(3)
Detroit	1,089	(6)	1,850	(5)
Dallas	974	(7)	434	(21)
San Diego	960	(8)	334	(28)
Phoenix	853	(9)	107	(96)
San Antonio	843	(10)	408	(24)

Note: Population in thousands; center city data only.

Source: U.S. Bureau of the Census.

some 50 miles from his job at Kennedy International Airport. With luck, he says, he can make the commute in two hours; if it rains, it can last as long as four (Johnson 1986, pp. B1, B5). Nor are the Murpheys and Mr. Bellafiore alone. All over the nation, it appears that the suburbanization of the countryside is on the upsurge once more, as the American city continues its process of sprawling ever farther outward.

The Sunbelt Phenomenon

A glance back to Table 3-5 will suggest the other main trend that is affecting contemporary American cities. Although suburban population is growing everywhere, the table shows that it is growing fastest in the South and West. Figure 3-1 drives home the point even more effectively. Based on the 1980 census, it shows that every state below the Mason-Dixon Line and west of the Rocky Mountains has shown considerable growth between 1970 and 1980.

Throughout American history the Northeast and Midwest regions and their cities have dominated national affairs. No more. There is an immense power shift under way (Sale 1976); the South is rising again and the West is also coming to preeminence. Table 3-6 illustrates just how dra-

matic the change has been by comparing the raw population figures and national rankings for the ten largest American cities of 1984. Although New York, Chicago, Philadelphia, and Detroit have managed to stay in the top ten, all have lost significant amounts of their population since 1950. If present trends continue, only New York and Chicago are likely to appear on the 1990 list. In contrast, Los Angeles has continued to grow and, by the year 2000, it is expected to be the nation's largest city according to a 1985 study done by the Commerce Department's Bureau of Economic Analysis (AP, Dec. 4, 1985). In addition, "from nowhere," Houston, Dallas, San Diego, San Antonio and, especially, Phoenix have leaped onto the top ten list. Why has the change occurred?

Northern Debits/Sunbelt Assets. To begin with, the northern cities are experiencing the strains of age and find costs and taxes rising to the point where many businesses are not willing to stay. Built around the cruder industrial machinery of the nineteenth century, these cities are finding their physical plants outmoded by newer, and, particularly, "high-tech" industry. Renovation is exorbitantly costly. City streets are in disrepair. Services are declining. Because of their financial

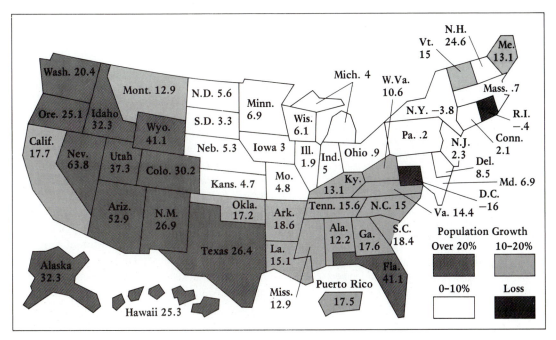

Figure 3-1 *State population changes (in percentages), 1970–1980.*

burden, these cities cannot offer tax breaks as liberally to businesses as they did before. Energy costs are skyrocketing. Superhighways (so vital to modern commerce) typically do not terminate conveniently in the industrial area. Union pay scales make labor very expensive.

The Sunbelt has few of these problems. With many cities industrialized only recently, they have been able to build modern, efficient plants linked easily to superhighways. With stronger economies than their northern counterparts due to booming population growth, they can offer substantial tax breaks to businesses. Energy costs are also much lower. A less-unionized labor force is an added attraction to businesses. The result: businesses by the thousands are deserting the North and heading for the cities of the South and West.

Many benefits are also enjoyed by private citizens living in the South or West. Sunbelt cities are warmer, cheaper, and offer more jobs. For example, in 1979 it cost the average resident of Houston $420 for home heating and $550 for

electricity for the year: Total, $970. In Boston the same costs were $1,052 (heat) and $934 (electricity) for a total of $1,986, over twice as much (Stevens 1979). Not oblivious to such differences, people are heading South or West (see Box 3-6).

The movement out of the North and Midwest is not only affecting whites. The 1980 census showed that from Virginia to Texas, the states of the Old Confederacy, the black population increased 19 percent between 1970 and 1980. This is the first major reversal of the northward black migration pattern since it began after the Civil War. But there is a difference. In the earlier, northward migrations, most blacks were unskilled. They were looking for any type of employment that would pay better than the bare subsistence income they had endured in southern rural areas or cities. As John Herbers reports, many blacks heading the *southward* migration are

professionals or skilled workers who received their education elsewhere and are now part of an emerging middle class in areas where blacks have long been unskilled and heavily dependent on welfare.

BOX 3-6
Why They Escape to the Sunbelt: Joe Delbova's Experience

Laid-off rubberworker Joe Delbova will soon leave his home town to seek a new job in the booming Southwest. Making the move may involve giving up a special education program for a handicapped daughter, but with local unemployment now at 9.3 percent, he believes he has no choice. "I'm pretty much against the wall," says Delbova, who has been out of work for a year. "I've no buying power, and I feel I've been abused. I'm an optimistic person, but I can't make it in Akron, Ohio."

Folks in Detroit, Cleveland and other once burly centers of production in the industrial Midwest feel much the same way. . . . That's hardly surprising: while more than half a million people are out of work in Michigan, Houston has relied on Northern emigres to fill many of the 70,000 new jobs that have opened each year for the past five years. "At least here you have a chance," says V. J. Clay, a former Michigander now living in the nation's energy capital.

In large measure, the loss of jobs from the old industrial states stems from the sickness of the auto business and its ripple effects in steel, rubber, and other supplier industries. Making matters worse, however, is the flight of healthier companies unwilling to pay the region's high tax and wage rates. . . . Small firms have even more reason to move. "It's got to the point where a small business cannot survive in Michigan," says Lewis Snook, who moved his tool-and-die company from Livonia, Michigan, to Dallas last year. "Here we can pay $2 to $2.50 less per hour and get the same quality work, if not better."

Source: *Newsweek*, April 27, 1981, p. 67.

---

cities, becoming urban regions unto themselves. In contrast, most northeastern cities have the same boundaries that they had half a century ago and are surrounded by legally independent suburbs that wish no part of the problems of the old central cities.

The Sunbelt cities are on a growth spurt that resembles that which the great northern metropolises underwent in the period between 1870 and 1940. They are reshaping the face of urban America. The process is feeding upon itself. Business follows people, people follow business.

California provides just one example. For decades, people moving to the so-called golden land at the western edge of the continent tended to settle in that state's coastal cities—San Diego, Los Angeles, Santa Barbara, San Francisco—or their suburbs. Many are still doing so. However, in the last few years the growth of California's inland cities has been nothing short of astounding. Growing like there is no tomorrow are cities like Stockton, Bakersfield, Fresno, San Bernardino, Modesto, and Sacramento. Once again, it is quality-of-life issues that seem behind the change. Housing costs in coastal cities are astronomical, jobs are scarce (especially those that pay well), smog and congestion are omnipresent. Inland, all those problems are less intense for the moment (Lindsey 1986).

Portents of Major Problems. Already there are signs of strain (once again, not unlike those suffered by northern cities in the previous century). A 1985 FBI report indicated reported crime in the Sunbelt region was up some 6 percent over 1984. Pollution is increasing, water is running short (particularly in the Southwest), and the population growth is just too much to absorb in many areas.

Augmenting the population pressure is the influx of hundreds of thousands of Hispanic people from Mexico and other Latin American countries. San Antonio, now the nation's tenth largest city, is the first with a Hispanic majority, but major Hispanic enclaves exist in every major city from Houston to Los Angeles. Many of the immigrants cross into the United States illegally in

And they are settling not on farms, where most of them had lived, but largely in the towns and cities. (1981, p. 1)

One other factor gives the advantage to the Sunbelt cities. Many have been permitted, by law, to annex new territory as they've increased in population. Because of this, their economic and political boundaries are more congruent (Gluck and Meister 1979), and so far they have been able to avoid the financial straits of northern

The spectacular growth of Phoenix has led to a sprawling city quite unlike the more centralized metropolis of an earlier era. The central business district (upper right) seems almost insignificant, for such Sunbelt cities spawn multiple shopping districts throughout their length and breadth. (Georg Gerster/Photo Researchers)

an attempt to escape the extreme poverty of their homeland (Chapter 8) and to take part in the rich American dream. A 1983 estimate put the number of illegal aliens—the vast majority in the Southwest—at 12 million (Gallows 1983). Typically, these immigrants, many of whom are unable to speak English, have taken or have been forced into the worst jobs in the urban economy, the jobs that "involve dirty, physically punishing tasks, low wages, long hours, generally poor working conditions, low job security, and little chance for advancement" (Butterworth and Chance 1981, p. 187).

On another level, there are mounting cultural and racial tensions between Hispanics and white Americans in the Sunbelt. Hispanics often are subjected to the same abusive treatment visited on blacks in many cities and, in an earlier era, on Irish, Italian, and Jewish immigrants in the North. Housing problems also have become acute. Many Hispanic *barrios* in southwestern cities are beginning to resemble the impoverished slums of the Third World (Chapters 8 through 10).

Other difficulties are developing. In the inland California cities mentioned earlier the effects of too rapid change and overcrowding are already beginning to be felt. New, good-paying jobs are being created too slowly to keep up with the number of people seeking them. The welfare roles are swelling with unemployed and disgruntled citizens. Traffic congestion is up; and, with the great increase in automobile and industrial exhaust, so too is the smog level. In Stockton, Fresno, and other inland cities there have been an ever-increasing barrage of calls to city officials from residents encouraging these cities to put limits on growth so that they do not become "another San Jose or another L.A." (Lindsey 1986, p. A14).

The pattern is nothing new. Throughout American history people have come to cities for the amenities they offered—jobs, education, the arts, and so on. When the cities have become too crowded, a large percentage of people have moved on to what they perceive as greener pastures—the suburbs, the Sunbelt, anyplace where the streets are safer, the smog less, the cost of living lower, the jobs more plentiful. In time, these areas too begin to deteriorate as the "secret" of more commodious living gets around and others descend. California and other Sunbelt states are now beginning to experience this declining quality-of-life problem. The question is, where will we go now, now that our older inner suburbs and our Sunbelt cities are experiencing the same deterioration and overload that the Snowbelt cities experienced not so very long ago?

Perhaps the answer is not to move at all but, rather, to attend to the problems of the city as they arise, before these problems get out of hand. Perhaps the urban situation is made *worse* by abandoning cities when they develop problems. Perhaps the urban core and all the amenities it has to offer could be salvaged if we were more attentive and less willing to pick up stakes the moment difficulties arise. Interestingly, there are indications that this regeneration of downtown is beginning to happen.

The Coming of the Postindustrial City

Only 20 years ago, it looked like our center cities were in an irreversible process of self-destruction. One of the enduring images of the mid-1960s was presented one evening on the television news. The White House appeared on the screen behind CBS reporter Walter Cronkite. Swirling all around it was thick black smoke. Washington was in the throes of a major riot, as thousands of minority group members, reacting in desperation to their hopeless poverty, lashed out at their white-dominated society.

The turmoil was being repeated all over America: the center city was in astonishing disrepair, and whites and the affluent were leaving for the suburbs. Industry was following suit as old factories became obsolete. Left behind were those who had little choice—the trapped, the poor, and the minorities, increasingly embittered as the American Dream passed them by. It looked like the end of the city as we knew it. Many doubted that urban America would ever rise again.

Today, in many cities the contrast with the above description is nothing short of amazing. All over America new urban construction is in progress—from Pittsburgh to Seattle, from New York to Phoenix. Office towers are multiplying almost as fast as contractors can build them (Herbers 1985). Many residential areas of the city are being totally transformed as young urban professionals, the "yuppies," move in, renovate old buildings or settle into new apartment complexes. The urban economy is alive once more. In every area of the country, a true urban renaissance seems to be under way.

What appears to have happened is this: the American city is in the process of completing a shift to a *postindustrial economy*. In retrospect, the causes of this shift are discernible in the processes we have already described in this chapter.

Deterioration. Since the mid–nineteenth century, the American city has been an industrial machine. It was the location of factories and their associated support industries. By and large, the people who worked in those industries lived in the city. But all that has changed. As cities became more congested and people became more affluent, they moved to the suburbs, leaving dilapidated housing in their wake. With time, factories too fell into disrepair. Equally important, in the last few decades transportation services improved, making it more efficient for industries to locate outside of the center city on the interstate loops. This left yet another body of building stock deteriorating. Together, these processes created the scene of desolation described above: a city apparently rotting at the core, populated less and less by the affluent and more and more by minorities, the impoverished and the indignant.

Regeneration. But, as these last two chapters have shown, cities are remarkably resilient human creations. Many have a sort of "built-in" facility for regeneration because they are so vital to human life. Probably the city's most important trait, as we will note in detail in Chapter 6, is their ability to *centralize* and *concentrate* human affairs. They allow more efficient communication in all areas of social existence: politics, religion, the arts and sciences, and most important in this case, the economy.

As center cities deteriorated or, worse, went up

in smoke in the late 1960s, scholars, politicians, and nearly everyone else wrung their hands and wondered what could be done about it. How could the city be saved? One voice suggested that *nothing* need be done: with time the city would save itself. That voice belonged to Edward C. Banfield, whose book *The Unheavenly City* (an obvious reference to Cotton Mather's wish for a "heavenly city" in America in the seventeenth century), created an enormous stir. The book, published in 1970, was controversial because of its basically conservative stance: Banfield argued that the poor and minorities rioted because of their fundamentally "antisocial nature" (a claim that we, the present authors, dispute and take up in detail in Chapter 13), and he argued that the city was so powerful as an economic machine that the deteriorated areas would not remain for long. Allow enough time and new businesses and people would see that they could get back into the center city and its great communicative advantages cheaply. They could buy up that land, renovate those deteriorated factories, houses, and apartment complexes, and thus avail themselves of the city's benefits.

Banfield's "do nothing" approach to urban destitution seemed so callous, so mean-spirited at the time, that he was roundly criticized by other urbanists. And yet, two decades later, many of his predictions appear borne out: cities across the nation are in the midst of a major boom. The postindustrial city has arrived, and recent research (DiGiovanni 1984) suggests strongly that general economic revitalization is under way.

The crucial links in this process appear to have been two: (1) the growth of white-collar businesses tied to new technology, especially the use of microcomputers; and (2) a major shift in the way many American industries do business. Regarding the growth of high-technology businesses, such organizations were more than happy to take over, renovate, or rebuild the structures left by departing heavy industry. They *needed* the center city location to maximize their work.

Regarding the changing nature of some American corporations, we are in the midst of a radical transformation. In the nineteenth century major industries believed in a "beginning-to-end" process. That is, they oversaw and controlled their product from raw material to finished marketable item. This was true of most of the "giants," such as the Carnegie Corporation (steel) and the Ford Motor Company (which even went so far as to raise sheep for its car's upholstery!).

Now all that is changing. Big industries are divesting themselves of parts of their operation that no longer are profitable and are contracting out important products to other firms or to foreign companies. Thus, General Electric no longer makes microwave ovens or the ice makers that go in its refrigerators; these are being made by Korean, Japanese, and other American firms. The idea behind all this is flexibility. Firms decide which parts of the production process they can perform profitably themselves and which would be more profitably done by others (Prokesch 1985).

But such changes, which are happening all over the country, have important implications for the city: on the one hand, many U.S. firms are no longer requiring as much blue-collar work or the use of buildings geared to heavy industrial production. On the other hand, these corporations, which play so large a role in our urban scene, have created more white-collar jobs—jobs whose primary reason for being is to make contacts with other corporations, whether in the U.S. or abroad. This is the very heart of a postindustrial economy—the shift to a predominantly white-collar mode of operation.

Naturally, many of the people employed by these newly changed corporations and high-tech industries want to live near their work, and, while some continue to commute from the suburbs (particularly those with families), many have opted to live in the center city. Thus, as the 1970s progressed, the process of *gentrification* began as white-collar professionals bought up and transformed older, decaying neighborhoods of many cities.

Future. Is the postindustrial city the city of America's future? It is still too early to say. The shift in this direction is little more than a decade old. Nevertheless, it is significant and shows no sign of stopping. More people, rather than fewer, are taking on the "yuppie life-style" as the 1980s move inexorably toward the 1990s. In addition, despite relatively high vacancy rates, the office building boom in many cities continues to accelerate.

Cleveland is as good an example as any. In the late 1960s the city was a symbol of urban despair. The river that flows through the city, the Cuyahoga, actually caught fire in 1969 and burned for days because of the pollutants it contained. In the early 1970s the city was on the verge of financial collapse because of the exodus to the suburbs by the middle classes.

Now, Cleveland is beginning to come alive again. Trendy restaurants

> are opening up along the banks of the river and young people are turning abandoned warehouses into lofts and apartments. Cleveland has discovered its waterfronts, and community leaders are counting on waterside amenities to help take the place of its fading economic base in heavy industry.
>
> "Cleveland is a microcosm of a nation that is going through an economic change of life," said George Voinovich, the city's mayor since 1980. "We are becoming a service organization, offering amenities like our orchestra, our museums and playhouses, medical facilities and ball teams that newer cities can never afford to match. Our waterfront development is an important part of our economic strategy." (Holusha 1985)

Strategy is exactly the right word. As the nation's center cities regenerate, many are engaging in a type of competition with other cities that is reminiscent of the interurban competition of the mid-1800s, when American cities were growing by leaps and bounds. In an increasing number of cities, governments are hiring marketing professionals whose job it is to spiff up the city's image so that it can attract more businesses, tourists, and industries. Recently Pittsburgh, a city much-maligned in the popular mind because of its history of pollution (recall Box 3-5), was ranked as "the most livable city in the United States" by Rand McNally's annual *Places Rated Almanac*. Atlanta had won the ranking the year before. To needle the southern city, a Pittsburgh businessman had billboards placed all around Atlanta that read: "Greetings from Pittsburgh—The Nation's Most Livable City, Y'all come." As if to counter,

San Diego placed billboards in Pittsburgh that pictured the surf and sun and bathing beauties. These had the message: "It's the Pitts if you're not in San Diego in the Winter" (Oldenburg 1985, p. 17A).

On the other hand, it is not all so pleasant. It is quite clear that the postindustrial process is not benefiting all of the city's residents equally. DiGiovanni (1984) reports that as gentrification progresses, the poorer residents of many city neighborhoods are simply being displaced. They, quite literally, cannot pay the new rents. They have to find somewhere else to live, presumably somewhere less pleasing. Similarly, the fact that a few areas of our cities have become havens for the affluent has done nothing to change the very poorest areas of those cities: New York still has its Harlem and South Bronx; Chicago, its South Side; Los Angeles, its Watts. Even more worrisome, it may be that the postindustrial economy is *exacerbating* the plight of the city's poor and unskilled.

John Kasarda (1983) reports that as our cities become ever more white collar, unemployment rates among the unskilled are rising along with welfare dependency. Brian Berry (1985) agrees. He sees postindustrial cities as ever more characterized by two labor markets, which, in turn, foster two separate and unequal life-styles—that of the well-paid white collar and professional worker and that of the low-paid service worker. Berry sees little reason for optimism in the near future because he believes that the inequities that exist between the two life-styles will not be eradicated. Instead, they will become worse. Less optimistic still is Anthony Downs (1985). After undertaking a study with Katherine Bradbury and Kenneth Small (1982), which concluded that the decline of the American city was all but irreversible for the foreseeable future, Downs and his associates designed a computer simulation that theoretically pumped into Cleveland everything it seemed to need to really reverse its inner-city problems—more jobs, better housing, improved transportation, the merging of city and county governments, and the restraint of suburban growth. Such improvements were much more than Cleveland could ever hope for realistically. Even so, all the simulated improvements only *slowed* the process of center city decay. In other words, as Berry (1985) phrases it, the postindustrial city has "islands of renewal in seas of decay." Postindustrialism and the windfall of the urban upper classes may be flashy and hopeful on the surface but, in reality, these "improvements" may not penetrate far beyond a very small circle of friends and business associates.

In conclusion, it is important to put the postindustrial phenomenon in perspective. As the above account makes clear, it is essentially the product of economic forces. When the center city decayed, savvy businesspeople and a few wealthy residents took notice and refurbished part of it for their own benefit. This may be all well and good as far as it goes, but it is decidedly *not* the same thing as having the citizens of the city, *as a group*, actively thinking about their city and deciding that some policies are better to implement than others. Until that happens, until we take the city itself as a problem to be studied and worked on, until we see that the city is the home of all its citizens, we will continue to have serious difficulties in America's cities.

In the end, then, the American city has to be seen as a *dynamic process* that extends from its origins—those five communities "hacked out of the wilderness" in the seventeenth century—to the present configuration—much larger and still embroiled in rapid and significant change as decentralization, the growth of the Sunbelt, and postindustrialization unfold. All these changes can be seen in the case study that closes this chapter, an analysis of America's world city, New York.

CASE STUDY 3-1
New York

Jim said everything was in New York. Jim said that he was happy, just standing in Grand Central Station, catching scraps of people's conversations. Jim said he would not mind standing all day on Sixth Avenue where they had the joke shops and the Orange Drinks, just watching the crowds go by. Jim said he would not mind standing all day in Radio City, where the French and British shops and the travel offices were, and the evergreens at Christmas and the tulips in the spring and where the fountains sprayed ceaselessly around Mr. Manship's golden boy and where exhibition fancy skaters salved their egos in the winter. If he grew tired of skaters, Jim said he would not mind standing and staring up and up, watching the mass of buildings cut into the sky.

John P. Marquand, *So Little Time* (1943)

Through almost all American history, New York has been *the* Great American City. It symbolizes the United States to the world and, in many ways, reveals the rest of the world to the United States. New York not only represents the distinctive course of our urban history, it is a timeless display of what urban life is all about. Here are just a few of the features that make it so outstanding.

First, it is huge, an enormous concentration of population. Over 7 million people live within the city limits, and more than twice that many reside in the urban region that has grown outward around the city. Second, it has the nation's greatest concentration of business and finance: more than one-third of the largest American corporations have headquarters in Manhattan, and a huge percentage of all stocks and bonds are traded there. It is also a major location for most international businesses located in this country. Third, it is the largest U.S. port and has dominated American commerce since the early 1800s. Fourth, it is a mosaic of virtually every race and ethnic group in the world—over 50 different foreign-language newspapers are published in the city. Many of these groups have clustered together in such well-known districts as Chinatown, Harlem, Spanish Harlem, Little Italy, and the Lower East Side. In addition, other New York districts are world-famous: Wall Street (finance), Madison Avenue (advertising), the garment district (center of the nation's clothing industry), Central Park (arguably the greatest urban park in the world), Fifth Avenue (for fashionable shopping and living), Greenwich Village (a longtime Bohemian, student, and counterculture enclave), and Broadway (center of the most vibrant theater district in the world). Fifth, New York is also the center of the arts, music, and publishing for the United States.

At street level New York abounds with crowds, traffic, street musicians, panhandlers—every sight and sound bombards the senses. Indeed, the first experience of New York City is one many of us carry with us all our lives (recall Cityscape 1-2, "New York! New York!"). On another level the city is deceptive. Its very size tricks us into thinking things are other than they are, something that Box 3-7 reveals about that grandest of illusion makers, Radio City Music Hall.

One cannot escape, however, the great contradictions, contrasts, and inconsistencies of New York life. The city is home to the richest and poorest of Americans. Some of the worst social problems stand, literally, in the shadow of the proudest cultural achievements. Wealthy beyond belief in the private sectors, New York was on the verge of bankruptcy in the 1970s. Inevitably, perhaps, New York is the most loved and most hated city in America. Say outsiders, "A nice place to visit, but . . . I wouldn't want to live there." Even New Yorkers boast about how awful it is—but most probably would never live anywhere else. In short, if it is to be found at all, it is to be found in New York. It is the world city par excellence.

New York, always at the center of American life, has a varied history. Since its changes serve to illustrate the themes of American urban history generally, we shall look briefly at its development during each of the four phases discussed in this chapter.

The Colonial Era

New York was the earliest of the five major colonial settlements. Henry Hudson entered the river later named for him in the early autumn of 1609 on an expedition financed by the Dutch East India Company. Other explorers skirted the area in subsequent years, and by 1624 a small settlement, based primarily on the fur trade, was permanently in place on the southern tip of Manhattan island.

Peter Minuit arrived from Holland in 1626 as the settlement's first governor. In the same year

---

BOX 3-7
All New York's a Stage

I'll tell you an old joke that will sum up Radio City Music Hall for you.

It seems a man and his wife went to the Music Hall one Sunday afternoon, arriving toward the end of the film. When it ended, the house lights came up for a few minutes before the stage show and the man rose, murmuring to his wife:

"I'm going to the men's room."

He located an exit on his floor—orchestra, loge, mezzanine, balcony or second balcony—but he couldn't find a men's room on it. He descended a staircase and looked on the next floor and couldn't find a men's room and descended another staircase. He walked along corridors and pushed open doors, he went along dark passages and up and down steps, getting more and more lost and more and more frantic. Just as his need became intolerably urgent, he pushed open a heavy door and found himself on a small street lined with houses, trees and shrubs. There was no one in sight and the man relieved himself in the bushes.

All this had taken time, and it took him additional time to work his way back up to his own floor and locate his own aisle and section. By the time he finally reached his seat, the stage show had ended and the movie had begun again. The man slid into his seat whispering to his wife:

"How was the stage show?"

To which his wife replied:

"You ought to know. You were in it."

Source: Helene Hanff, *Apple of My Eye* (New York: Doubleday, 1978), p. 129.

Peter Stuyvesant reached the world-famous agreement with the resident Indians to trade ownership of the island for $24 worth of trinkets.

New Amsterdam, the center of the Dutch New Netherlands, prospered in the decades that followed: houses were built and farmland was cultivated (see Box 3-1). A row of logs erected as a type of protection along the northern edge of the settlement later became known as Wall Street. In 1638 a ferry service to Bruckelin (later: Brooklyn) was begun, and settlement started on Staten Island. A weekly market was held beginning in 1648, and the first lawyer began practice in 1650.

The Dutch Fort New Amsterdam of the Manhattans about 1626. This line drawing is the earliest known view of New York. (Bettmann)

In 1653 a charter granted by Holland allowed the town to organize a local government centered around a mayor and a city council. When the first survey was completed in 1656, the "city" had 120 houses on 17 irregularly placed streets and about 1,000 people. Within a few years, some of the streets were stone covered and a greater measure of security was provided by a town-watch (the earliest direct ancestor of New York's police force). Outside of town to the north were farms the Dutch called "boweries." This area is the point at which the irregular streets end (at about Houston Street today) and is still known as "The Bowery." A farming village called Haarlem was established much further up the peninsula in 1658, at the terminus of a long dirt road known as "Broadway."

The first Jews arrived in the 1650s, establishing a long tradition that was to influence the city's history, and the first Quakers settled in the city in 1657. Not too pleased about this influx of religious diversity, the Dutch outlawed all religions except their Dutch Reformed Church.

An English fleet arrived in 1664 and gained control of the town, renaming the settlement New York in honor of Charles II's brother, James, the Duke of York. The English commander granted religious freedom to all groups. A major tradition was thus begun. New Yorkers thenceforth cherished their independence in matters religious and otherwise. Millions in later years would be drawn to this city where it was possible to express oneself as one chose.

Further conflicts between the Dutch and the English led to a Dutch reoccupation in 1672, but in 1674 the city was returned once more to England, in the Treaty of Westminster. In 1680 it began its climb to economic preeminence. It was given a monopoly on the East Coast in the sifting of flour for export. Docks were built, trade prospered, and support businesses of all sorts became established.

The population grew steadily: from 4,000 in 1703 to 7,000 in 1723; in 1737 it reached the 10,000 mark. The first newspaper appeared in 1725; a stagecoach link to Philadelphia started up in 1730; and the first version of the New York Public Library opened in 1731.

As this growth occurred, New York, like the other colonies, was beginning to resent ever more sharply the British impositions on trade. In 1765 the English government instituted the

Stamp Act, placing a levy on all transactions. The colonists bitterly opposed it. Swayed, Parliament repealed the act in 1766, causing a New York group dubbed the "Sons of Liberty" to build a "Liberty Pole" in the city. The British took strong offense, an altercation followed, and some of the Sons of Liberty were killed. This was the first blood of the American Revolution.

When the revolution began, New York was occupied by the British for seven years. The war drove many New Yorkers temporarily out of the city. In 1776 the population had dropped back substantially, from a 1771 high of 21,500. With the end of the war, the city leaped once more to life. George Washington was inaugurated as the first president of the United States in the Federal Hall at the corner of Wall and Nassau Streets, and for a year thereafter (1790) New York served as the nation's capital.

Growth and Expansion

In 1800 the city's population stood in excess of 60,000. The growth of New York during this second period was nothing short of spectacular. The population soared, exceeding 96,000 by 1810 and 202,000 by 1830—and this was only a hint of things to come. Earlier, in 1792 a group of traders had met in the Wall Street area and planned what was to become the New York Stock Exchange. In 1807 the city's famous grid plan for street development was approved. In 1825 the Erie Canal was completed, linking the Hudson with the Great Lakes region, and giving New York a long-sought trade advantage over its other East-Coast urban competitors. With direct access to the American heartland in the next few decades, the city became the economic center of the United States.

In 1838 overseas steamship service began, establishing a connection with Europe that truly opened immigration. For example, in 1840 over 50,000 people arrived at New York harbor from abroad and most settled in the city (Peterson 1965). In 1846 the first telegraph line between New York and Philadelphia began operation. In 1848 a five-story factory (also a sign of things to come) opened. Urban transportation improved with the introduction of the rail-mounted horse-car in 1850. This made "suburbanization" of the upper island more feasible by establishing a fare—a nickel—within financial reach of most New Yorkers (Glaab and Brown 1967). In 1853 New York hosted the nation's first "expo," symbolic of the grand optimism that by now was part of the city's character. In 1858 one of the greatest of urban landmarks—Central Park—was completed. In 1860 the city, still officially only Manhattan Island, had a population of 814,000, with another 250,000 nearby in Brooklyn, Staten Island, and Jersey City.

The Great Metropolis Emerges

After the Civil War, which temporarily slowed the growth, New York became a great metropolis. A tremendous increase in the city's population occurred between 1870 and 1930, dwarfing all previous gains. Table 3-7 provides some evidence of the change (and includes 1982 data for comparison). Until 1898 the five boroughs were legally separate municipalities; on the first of January of that year they were joined as one city. Table 3-7 shows that New York City as a whole more than *quintupled* its population in the six decades after 1870.

The period between 1870 and 1920 was a time of extensive foreign immigration to the United States, and New York was the major port of disembarkation for the entire country. Some nationalities arrived in huge numbers. For example, Chinatown began to take form in 1884; Italian immigration intensified after 1885; and Jews began to make their way through the Ellis Island immigration facility to the Lower East Side in large numbers after 1890. Many of these new urbanites went directly to work in the industries producing products such as garments and shoes. The excitement of arrival in New York is revealed in this comment by David Quizano, a Russian Jewish immigrant:

> . . . America is God's Crucible, the great Melting Pot where all the races of Europe are melting and reforming. Here you stand, good folk, think I, when I see them at Ellis Island, here you stand in your fifty groups with your fifty languages and histories, and your fifty blood hatreds and rivalries, but you won't be long like that brothers, for these

TABLE 3-7
Population of New York City, by Borough, 1870–1982

	1870	1890	1910	1930	1982
New York City	1,476	2,505	4,764	6,929	7,090
Borough					
Manhattan	942	1,441	2,331	1,867	1,423
Bronx	37	88	430	1,265	1,163
Brooklyn	419	838	1,634	2,560	2,214
Queens	45	87	284	1,079	1,900
Richmond (Staten Island)	33	51	85	158	360

Note: Population in thousands; Boroughs not officially incorporated as New York City until 1898.

Source: Bureau of the Census, *Statistical Abstracts of the United States* (1912); *Historical Abstracts* (1960); *Statistical Abstracts of the United States* (1985).

are the fires of God you've come to . . . German and Frenchman, Irishman and Englishman, Jews and Russians—into the Crucible with you all! God is making the American. (Quoted in Glazer and Moynihan 1969, p. 226)

As amazing as it sounds, by 1890 four out of five people living in the New York area were either born abroad or had foreign-born parents (Glaab and Brown 1967). New York, like other American metropolises of the era, began to take on a characteristic "ethnic mosaic" pattern of settlement as described by social reformer Jacob Riis in Box 3-8.

This process of racial and ethnic mixture, however, has produced as much of a "pressure cooker" as a "melting pot." Indeed, the general economic opportunity New York provided during this period must be contrasted to the tensions that turned groups against each other, wages that were often appallingly low, and living conditions that were highly unfavorable to generations of immigrants. Although citywide residential density in 1890 was about 60 people to an acre, in immigrant areas densities reached alarming levels—as much as seven times greater. This frightful concentration continued to increase to almost 750 persons per acre—about 12 times the city average—in 1898 (Glaab and Brown 1967). Today, the density of central Manhattan is about 106 persons per acre.

Sometimes, when immigrants mixed, the results were explosive. In one area of Midtown,

BOX 3-8
The Crazy-Quilt Pattern of New York

A map of [New York], colored to designate nationalities, would show more stripes than the skin of a zebra, and more colors than any rainbow. . . . [G]reen for the Irish prevailing in the West Side tenement districts, and blue for the Germans on the East Side. . . . [I]ntermingled . . . would be an odd variety of tints that would give the whole the appearance of an extraordinary crazy-quilt. From down in the Sixth Ward . . . the red of the Italian would be seen forcing its way northward along the line of Mulberry Street to the quarter of the French purple on Bleecker Street and South Fifth Avenue. . . . On the West, the red would be seen overrunning the old Africa of Thompson Street pushing the black of the negro rapidly uptown. . . .

Source: Jacob Riis, *How the Other Half Lives*, cited in Charles N. Glaab and A. Theodore Brown, *A History of Urban America* (New York: Macmillan, 1967), pp. 139–140.

from about West 15th Street to West 50th Street along Eighth, Ninth, and Tenth Avenues, blacks and whites of different ethnic groups lived together. During the working week trouble was minimal, but on weekends in the summer, when much drinking and carousing occurred, violent fighting often broke out between groups. So intense were the confrontations that police nicknamed the area "Hell's Kitchen."

Governing this incredible and growing mass of people was difficult, at best. City Hall became increasingly corrupt as interest groups vied with one another for contracts, favors, and patronage. The greatest symbol of corruption in New York's history was the administration of William "Boss" Tweed. In 1870, by means of $1 million in bribes to the New York State Legislature and other groups, Tweed and his gang were able to gain complete political control over the city. It is estimated that they stole nearly $200 million in funds from the city treasury and garnered even more from kickbacks and payoffs. Finally exposed by the *New York Times* in 1871, Tweed was arrested and brought to trial. So confident was he that he would be acquitted, he haughtily said, in response to an allegation about his misappropriation of funds, "What are ya' gonna do about it?" His confidence was misplaced: he went to jail in 1872. Nevertheless, extensive graft in city government continued to plague the city until well into this century.

Certain physical changes linked to technology contributed to the growth of the city during this period as well. In 1881 the Brooklyn Bridge opened. (Along with the Golden Gate in San Francisco, it is considered one of the world's most beautiful.) It was followed in 1903 by the Williamsburg Bridge and in 1904 by the first tunnel under the Hudson connecting the city to the New Jersey shore. In 1906 the Pennsylvania Railroad also tunneled under the Hudson, establishing major rail transport in the heart of Manhattan at Penn Station. The subways opened during this period. All such changes allowed suburban growth to proliferate. People now could live even farther from Midtown and still reach it cheaply and quickly.

At the lower end of Manhattan, the dazzling New York skyline began to take shape. Now, it is difficult to imagine New York without a forest of skyscrapers. Yet, before 1890, Manhattan below Central Park was completely covered by structures under five floors. The first steel structure in New York appeared in 1889 and reached a "towering" 11 floors. From this point, New York grew upward as if the clouds had become great magnets. The number of buildings with 20 or more floors grew from 61 in 1913 to 188 in 1929. Indeed, half of all such buildings in the country were in New York (Armstrong 1972).

Before the Depression stalled construction of office buildings, the city witnessed the completion of three famous architectural innovations that survive to the present day. The Chrysler Building, opened in 1930, is a marvelous 77-story example of Art Deco architecture— topped with six stories of controversial stainless-steel arches. The following year marked the opening of the Empire State Building, which, at 102 floors, has symbolized New York ever since. Rockefeller Center was begun in the same year. It was designed to include "everything" in one place, as urban critic Paul Goldberger observes:

> . . . skyscrapers, plazas, movement, detail, views, stores, cafes. It is all of a piece, yet it is able to appear possessed of infinite variety at the same time. . . . It was conceived as a place in which monumental architecture would spur both business and culture to new heights, and it has come remarkably close to fulfilling that somewhat naive goal. It is surely the parent of every large scale urban complex every American downtown has built since—from Atlanta's Peachtree Center to Hartford's Constitution Center to San Francisco's Embarcadero Center—and it is no insult to say that Rockefeller Center still remains far and away the finest such development ever built. (1979, pp. 168–169)

New York Today

> New York? It'll be a great place if they ever finish it.
>
> SHORT STORY WRITER O. HENRY

By the 1950s New York had grown from being a metropolis to being the center of that vast urban region that Jean Gottmann has called a megalopolis. The United States census places the city at the heart of a vast metropolitan statistical area covering some 4,000 square miles and about 17 million people. To illustrate the point another way, nearly one American in every fifteen lives in the New York MSA.

From another perspective, however, this incredible region is a product of the decentralization trend that has affected so many cities in contemporary America. Bridges, highways, tunnels, cars, costs, congestion—all have led to a rapid move away from the city. Between 1970 and 1980 New York lost over 860,000 people (consider that this loss is more than the entire center-city population of San Francisco!).

Not only have residents disappeared, businesses have too. Changing technology and costs have been primarily responsible. For example, during the nineteenth century, the greatest concentration of commercial activity was at the southern end of Manhattan, in the area called the Battery. The industrial production that started toward the end of the century moved the commercial center somewhat farther uptown, and by the turn of the century many administrative headquarters were locating in the Midtown area north of 34th Street. This spread of business to Midtown was the result of congestion and high land costs in older downtown areas. These same concerns have resulted in the transfer of many businesses—especially those engaged in manufacturing—to the outer reaches of the New York region. Midtown is just too inconvenient and expensive. Nevertheless, Midtown still thrives because it remains a white-collar service center in which executives are able to remain in close, personal contact with one another (Hall 1979).

The exodus of people and firms has had a marked effect on the city's character and fortunes. Most of the outward movement has been by whites and the more affluent (although many of the *most* affluent seem to remain ensconced in their wealthy enclaves on Central Park West, Fifth Avenue, Park Avenue, and the Upper East Side). Since the end of World War II, over 2 million whites have left the center-city area. They have been replaced to some degree by many blacks and Hispanics moving from the South. In 1950 the population of the five boroughs was 87 percent white, 9 percent black, and 3 percent Hispanic. By 1980 that had shifted to about 50 percent white, 20 percent black, and 15 percent Hispanic.

With the exodus of business and of the more affluent members of the population has come a massive decline in revenue. Imagine the effects of the loss of *half a million* jobs between 1969 and 1975 and of *$1.5 billion* in yearly tax revenues! The problem has been made even worse for the city's leadership by mounting costs, including higher city payroll expenses, and also by social service programs made necessary by the presence of large numbers of poor and unemployed people. Taken together, these factors brought New York to the brink of bankruptcy in the famous financial crisis of 1975. Simply put, the city could not pay for its employees and programs any longer.

Although we shall examine the financial crisis of American cities (and particularly that of New York) in detail in Chapter 13, suffice it to say that this crisis was in many ways precipitated by the effects of decentralization, which have been rampant across the nation. Older industrial cities with limited territorial jurisdiction, such as New York, Cleveland, and Detroit, have watched in near helplessness as their financial base has moved away.

Still, New York has survived and has wended its way back to financial solvency. Construction is omnipresent; in various blighted neighborhoods like the South Bronx, a few signs of rejuvenation are appearing: here a house, there a block (see Cityscape 13-2). It seems, as René Dubos (1972) observed in a paraphrase of Mark Twain, the reports of the death of New York are greatly exaggerated. As posters and the city's irrepressible Mayor Ed Koch proclaim: "New York is back!"

Partially back at least. And, the city is back for many of the same reasons that Boston, Baltimore and other cities are coming back: The postindustrial phenomenon has come to New York. Indeed, the 1984 census figures for the city show an *increase* of population from 1980. To be sure, the increase is small—on the order of 90,000— but it is the first increase in the city's population in decades and just may portend the slowing of the city's continuing decentralization.

A symbol of this change is the new Battery Park City project. Located at the southern tip of Manhattan, this new $1.5-billion complex is intended to be a world-class financial center. Built

The suburban decentralization of population that has brought new life to outlying areas of the urban region has brought devastation to many older inner-city districts, such as the South Bronx in New York. (Marcia Weinstein)

by the city in an attempt to keep New York attractive to major investment firms, the project is the future home of such prestigious companies as Merrill Lynch, Sherson Lehman/American Express, Dow Jones, and Oppenheimer and Company. Complementing the office towers will be luxury housing. Said New York Governor Mario Cuomo at ceremonies dedicating the complex in late 1985, Battery Park City is "a soaring triumph." Said Mayor Koch at the same gathering, it will be known as "Wall Street II!" (Gottlieb 1985) As if in echo, Donald Trump, the New York financier responsible for building the famous Trump Tower in Midtown Manhattan in the early 1980s, announced plans to build a new "Television World" complex in lower Manhattan near Battery Park City. In addition to creating the space needed to make New York once again the media center of the world (a title it has partially lost to Los Angeles in the last two decades), the Trump complex would contain the world's tallest building, outstripping Chicago's Sears

Tower (now the world's tallest) by some three hundred feet or more.

All this building and change in the city's economy has generated jobs—upwards of a *quarter million* in the period from 1977 to 1985 (Gottlieb 1985). While the bulk of the construction jobs are blue-collar, these are greatly outnumbered by the white-collar jobs taken by the people who work in the office complexes after completion.

As a result, parts of the city now seem alive with "yuppies," the young urban professionals who herald postindustrial business and services. To chronicle the growth of this group of people, *New York Magazine* recently devoted an entire issue to describing the new Upper West Side, or, as they dubbed it, the "Yupper West Side." Here is part of the description:

> [They] live in yuppie housing projects, and, if they're parents, [they] congregate with their babies on Columbus Avenue every weekend. Says one father, "All the young couples are out there with

their babies, and you feel you're part of a trend."
. . . [Says another area resident,] "All of a sudden,
your neighborhood's a Perrier highway." (*New York
Magazine*, May 13, 1985, p. 3)

As in other cities, the proportion of people
who are participating fully in the postindustrial
phenomenon is small—perhaps on the order of
10 percent. Nevertheless, their impact is considerable, especially in economic terms. Rental
housing is scarce and dear. For example, Carmody (1984) reports that it is almost impossible
to find a multiroom apartment in the city for less
than $1,000 per month. To this frequently is
added a "finder's fee"—usually two or three
months' rent paid to the person who procured
the apartment.

Not surprisingly, such high costs are driving
out poorer residents. Small businesses, some of
them in the same city location for decades, cannot afford to compete with their high-tech, chic,
and wealthy counterparts. Many are closing their
doors. Some middle-class residents are in danger
of losing their apartments as white-collar demand forces housing prices ever higher (Hopkins
1985). In many apartment blocks, residents are
paid large sums to move out. In others, when
residents balk at the idea of leaving, landlords
hire thugs to harass the recalcitrants until they
decide that discretion is the better part of valor
and "voluntarily" leave (Shenon 1984).

As worrisome, the gap between the city's rich
and poor is widening. In a 1986 report prepared
by the Regional Plan Association of Connecticut, it was suggested that in "an era of new-found
prosperity . . . the economic outlook for
hundreds of thousands of poorly educated, low-
income residents throughout the New York area
. . . is growing more bleak." Said report chairman William S. Woodside, "More than anywhere else in the country, we are creating a two-
tier society of the haves and the have nots." Data
from the 1980 Census tell the story. In 1980,
42 percent of the New York MSA's households
had incomes below $15,000 per year. This group
accounted for only *14 percent* of all the income
paid in the region. In contrast, 17 percent of the
households made $35,000 per year or more.

This much smaller group accounted for fully
40 percent of the area's total income. Increasingly this wealthy group is white and the poorer
group is of minority background—black,
Hispanic, Asian. By the year 2000, it is expected
that these minority groups will comprise 60 percent of the city's population and 45 percent of
the MSA's. (The figures now are 48 percent for
the city and 23 percent for the MSA.) It is not a
hopeful state of affairs (Lueck 1986, p. B1).

Federal attempts to cut back on social service
programs also are hurting the city. Cuts that were
scheduled to take effect by 1987 in only three
areas—mass transportation, housing, and education—would reduce the city's coffers by nearly
$400 million, enough to supply about 800 new
buses, rehabilitate nearly 5,000 apartments, and
educate nearly 16,000 college students, most of
whom come from low-income backgrounds
(Green 1985).

In the midst of the difficulties some continue
to try and help themselves. In May 1986, George
Forestal, a black city cabdriver, stood on the
front steps of a two-story house on Creston Avenue in the Bronx. On a cinderblock that had
sealed the entrance was a sign that read: "Owned
by the City of New York." Mr. Forestal looked at
the delapidated structure and said: "It's beautiful.
The pipes are good. The plumbing is not bad."
He was about to begin one of the greatest adventures of his life, refurbishing the abandoned
house he had bought at auction from the city. He
is one of many, a kind of new-style New York
homesteader—of lower-middle income and
deeply frustrated by having to pay exorbitant
rents for few services to landlords for many years.
Finally, he went to the city's auction and in-
vested his life savings in this run-down house in
a run-down neighborhood. Although the road to
making his house livable again is long and ar-
duous, a surprising number of lower-income
New Yorkers have been successful in similar efforts. As they are, they are revitalizing parts of
neighborhoods that, only a year or so ago,
seemed hopelessly lost (James 1986). It isn't
much, only a small ripple in a big pond, but it
is something.

And so New York goes on, with its successes and failures, its ability to symbolize simultaneously all that is great and tragic about the city generally. To many, New York is *the* quintessential city. Peter Berger gives us a sense of this in Box 3-9. If New York fails, in some sense cities everywhere fail.

Conclusion

The development of American cities has been, in its own way, as dynamic and varied as that of European cities. We did not begin as an urban nation; in fact, that idea would have been anathema to many of the country's founders. Nevertheless, in three and a half centuries that is what we have become.

The process of American urbanization began just as European feudalism was breathing its last. Begun as a place of religious and political freedom, the new colonies rapidly established themselves as major trading centers. By 1700 coastal villages were becoming bustling cities.

A century later, after the Revolutionary War had procured American independence, these small cities began to develop into major urban areas. They traded up and down the coast and with Europe and became rich by establishing links with the vast and rich heartland of the country. Inland cities appeared. By the middle of the nineteenth century, industrialization was transforming the cities of the North and, to some degree, their newer Midwestern counterparts into manufacturing centers. The South, still operating on the "small city" pattern associated with agriculture, fell behind. With victory for the North, the Civil War effectively ended the small- versus large-city "debate."

After 1870, American cities, particularly in the North and Midwest, exploded into metropolises of millions. Trade and the industrial process were the driving wheels behind this development. More and more jobs and wealth were created. To absorb them, millions came from abroad, resulting in the incredible ethnic-racial-religious mo-

---

BOX 3-9
In Praise of New York

Much of the rest of the country sees New York as one gigantic agglomeration of social ills: crime, poverty, racial hatred, mismanaged and corrupt government—not to mention dirt, pollution, and traffic congestion of virtually metaphysical dimensions. . . . And yet, despite all this, New York City continues to be a magnet and even an object of love, sometimes fierce love. People, especially young people, continue to come in large numbers, irresistibly drawn to the city by expectations of success and excitement. And New Yorkers themselves, although they, too, frequently share the negative views of their own city, nevertheless continue to be inexplicably, perhaps dementedly, attached to that putative cesspool of perdition in which they reside. Such ambivalence suggests that the reality of New York is more complicated than its symbolic imagery. . . .

. . . New York . . . is not only a vast and vastly important city, but the city par excellence, the prototypical cosmopolis of our age. . . . Every urban experience [that people] have had before has been, in a way, an anticipation of New York. . . . Wherever skyscrapers reach upwards toward the clouds, wherever masses of cars stream back and forth over steel-girded bridges, wherever heterogenous crowds pour through subways, underground concourses, or cavernous lobbies encased in glass—there is a bit of New York. . . . The mystique of New York City is, above all, the mystique of modern urban life, concentrated there more massively than anywhere else.

Source: Peter Berger, "In Praise of New York," *Commentary*, February 1977.

---

saic that characterizes so many American cities. With this influx came great problems. Quality of life began to deteriorate, and poverty and exploitation became rampant. New technological advances made escape to the suburbs possible for many; consequently, cities began to spread over the countryside. Losing revenue because of this exodus and being greatly hampered by the Depression, cities began to depend on federal assistance.

Since World War II the decentralization phenomenon has continued. More and more people and businesses have left the old center city, leaving the innermost area populated increasingly by the poor and minorities (unable to escape because of poverty or prejudice) and by service-oriented or professional businesses. Huge metropolitan regions have become more the norm than dominant center-city cores.

In the North this process has had particularly disastrous results. With the fleeing people and businesses have gone billions in tax and sales revenues and hundreds of thousands of jobs. Many cities face a continual threat of bankruptcy.

The South and West, however, continue to experience an urban boom. First, Sunbelt cities have been the direct beneficiaries of northern cities' problems. Northern cities characteristically have old industrial systems, poor inner-city transportation for products, deteriorating services, and skyrocketing costs. The Sunbelt cities build new plants, are surrounded by efficient superhighways, have good or brand-new service systems, and offer lower costs—particularly for energy and labor. Second, some Sunbelt cities have been better able to flex their physical boundaries. For example, in Texas, one of the states with greatest urban expansion, suburbs have been annexed as fast as they have appeared, thus keeping the tax and business base within the city jurisdiction.

The third contemporary trend may turn out to be the most important of all. American cities are rapidly developing a postindustrial economy, an economy based on high technology, white-collar jobs, and services. Since the mid-1970s, this phenomenon has grown in importance: cities rebuild the deteriorating office and housing stock left from earlier decades, and young, relatively affluent (mostly white) professionals move in.

The evidence suggests that all three trends— decentralization, the move to the Sunbelt, and the growth of a postindustrial economy—will continue in force into the 1990s. Northern cities such as New York will continue, as a result, to try to adapt to a changing economic structure and a new population. Meanwhile, the Sunbelt picture

is not as rosy as it was only a half decade ago. The population boom, in many instances, has been too much to cope with, and racial tensions are on the rise as Hispanics move up from Mexico and Latin America and blacks move back to the South. Furthermore, even in cities where postindustrialization is in full sway, there is no indication that the new-found wealth of the few who are participating in this life-style will spread to the urban population as a whole. On the contrary, it appears that the gap between the urban rich and poor is widening, not lessening.

It seems evident that, in the three centuries since the urban process took hold in the New World, Americans have not built Cotton Mather's hoped for "Heavenly City." Nevertheless, there are signs that American cities are rejuvenating, if only partially, as we make our way toward the twenty-first century. Whether this rebuilding process will continue or whether the American version of the urban experiment will come, as it did in the late 1960s and early 1970s, to resemble Edward Banfield's "Unheavenly City," more than likely will depend on the decisions made by the people living in these cities in the next decade. If Americans continue to see the city as something to "use," but not something to collectively be concerned about, the outlook probably will not be very bright. Cities, like children, need *care* if they are to prosper on all levels. If, on the other hand, Americans begin to see the city as an environment that is a human creation and thus subject to understanding and human control, then we might be justified in being more sanguine about the outcome.

In Chapters 2 and 3 we have provided an overview of the long path that cities have followed from their origins thousands of years ago to the present. But that is only part of our task. In the next four chapters we shall examine how social scientists have come to analyze cities as living entities. As we do so, we shall see that the urban story gets even more interesting.

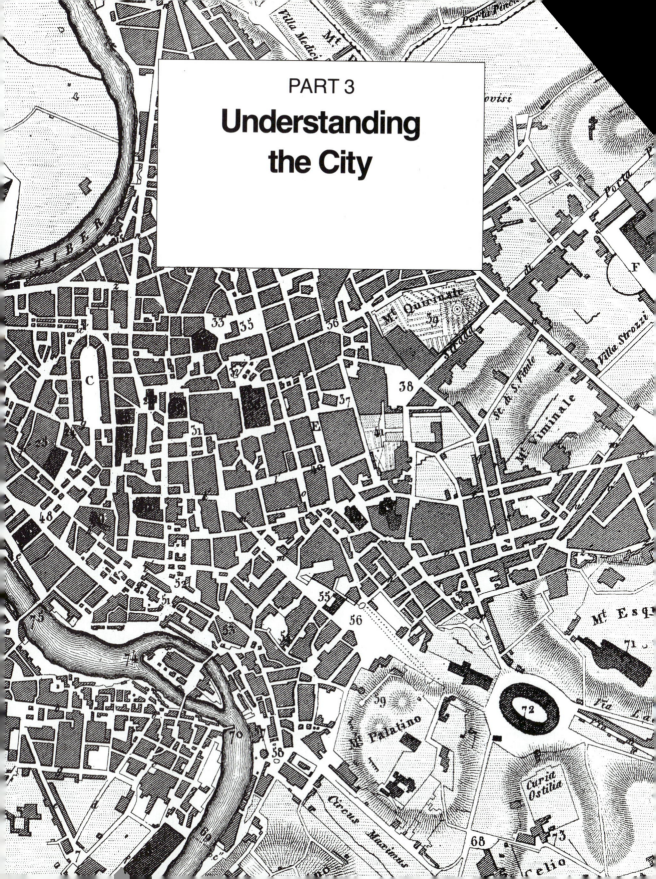

PART 3
Understanding the City

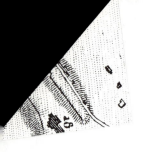

CHAPTER 4

The Emergence
of Urban Sociology

Eva, beware of the city
It's hungry and cold, can't be controlled—it is
* mad*
Those who are fools are swallowed up whole
And those who are not become
What they should not become
Changed—in short they go bad.

TIM RICE, *EVITA*

The nineteenth century was a time of massive urban upheaval in Europe. In 1816 the population of German cities was slightly over 2.5 million. By 1895 it was 13 million. In 1846 France had 8.5 million urban dwellers. By 1891 14.5 million lived in cities. Paris itself had a population of 2.5 million, five times that of 1800 (Weber 1899; 1963, Chap. 2).[1]

The major cause of this striking change was the industrial revolution. Located primarily in cities, the emerging factory system, with its attendant increases in housing, shops, and transportation, drew people in unheard-of numbers. Imagine what such a radical change was like:

a smaller population of older cities, well-entrenched in tradition, was inundated by new arrivals. Old neighborhood ways of life were shattered. Unable to keep up with the incoming people, many cities simply couldn't provide adequate food, shelter, sanitary facilities, medical care, and jobs. As a result, frustration, disease, malnutrition, and crime increased. The streets themselves no doubt seemed chaotic. In Box 4-1, Charles Dickens describes the coming of the railroad to nineteenth-century London. This was the context in which urban sociology emerged.

The European Tradition: 1887–1921

Most of the great European universities are located in cities. Consequently, many practitioners of the fledgling discipline of sociology watched the city's changes with concern. Most were worried deeply about what they saw; a few were more hopeful.

Toennies: *Gemeinschaft* and *Gesellschaft*

One of the most concerned was a German, Ferdinand Toennies (1855–1936). His masterwork,

---

[1]The date of original publication is shown first. The second date identifies a later edition.

BOX 4-1
The City in Upheaval

The [railroad] rent the whole neighbourhood to its centre. Traces of its course were visible on every side. Houses were knocked down; streets broken through and stopped; deep pits and trenches dug in the ground; enormous heaps of earth and clay thrown up; buildings . . . were undermined and shaking, propped by great beams of wood. . . . Everywhere were bridges that led nowhere; thoroughfares that were wholly impassable; Babel towers of chimneys . . . temporary wooden houses and enclosures, in the most unlikely situations; carcasses of ragged tenements, and fragments of unfinished walls and arches, and piles of scaffolding, and wildernesses of bricks, and giant forms of cranes, and tripods straddling above nothing. There were a hundred thousand shapes and substances of incompleteness, wildly mingled out of their places, upside down burrowing in the earth, aspiring in the air, mouldering in the water, and unintelligible as any dream.

Source: Charles Dickens, *Dombey and Son* (London: Chapman and Hall, 1853), p. 53.

Gemeinschaft and Gesellschaft, was published in 1887. In it, Toennies described two contrasting types of human social life: *gemeinschaft*, or "community," which characterized the small country village; and *gesellschaft*, or "association," which characterized the large city. Within the village, Toennies maintained, social life forms a "living organism" in which people have an essential unity of purpose, work together for the common good, and are united by ties of family and neighborhood. Such is not the case in the city, in which social life is a "mechanical aggregate" characterized by disunity, rampant individualism and selfishness, even hostility. In the city a belief in the common good is rare; ties of family and neighborhood are of little significance. As suggested by the lines that opened this chapter, Toennies thought that people could "go bad" in the city.

The typology of *gemeinschaft* and *gesellschaft* was to have a lasting influence on urban sociology because it was one of the first theories to understand human settlements by means of a continuum. At each "pole" of the continuum was a specific, "pure" type of settlement. Using such a

formulation, one could classify any actual settlement at some point along the continuum as having a certain measure of *gemeinschaft* qualities and a certain degree of *gesellschaft* qualities.

Gemeinschaft. Toennies used the concept of *gemeinschaft* to characterize the rural village and surrounding land worked communally by its inhabitants. Social life was characterized by "intimate, private, and exclusive living together," and members were bound by common language and traditions. They recognized "common goods— common evils; common friends—common enemies" and carried within them a sense of "we-ness," of "our-ness." This sense of village togetherness has been expressed eloquently by playwright Thornton Wilder in *Our Town*, excerpted in Cityscape 4-1.

Gesellschaft. In the character of the modern city, Toennies saw a wholly different style of life, in which the meaning of existence shifted from the group to the individual. Where *gemeinschaft* expresses a sense of "we-ness," *gesellschaft* is more rational, more calculating. By its very nature, *gesellschaft* conditions people to be primarily concerned with their own self-interest, to "look out for Number One," in contemporary terms. In *gemeinschaft* the "natural" social institutions of kinship, neighborhood, and friendship are predominant; in *gesellschaft* these forms of association tend to decline. Englishman Robert Crowley's sixteenth-century poem conveys Toennies's sense of what *gesellschaft* is like (see Box 4-2).

One way to readily appreciate the difference between *gemeinschaft* and *gessellschaft* is to consider, when another person asks "How are you?", does she or he *really want to know*? Toennies's communal relation—*gemeinschaft*—is built on broad concern for the other as a person and such a question has significance beyond convention, beyond politeness. In the contrasting case—*gesellschaft*—each person is understood in terms of a particular role and service provided (teacher, TV repairperson, or butcher). In the city the question "How are you?" is usually asked only out of politeness: we don't know other persons well, and, what's more, we usually don't *want* to know them well.

CITYSCAPE 4-1
Our Town: An Example of *Gemeinschaft*

Wilder's play opens with the "Stage Manager" telling the audience about "our town," Grover's Corners, a small village in New Hampshire. He asks the audience to imagine the layout of the town and the life of its inhabitants.

The first act shows a day in our town. The date is May 7, 1901, just before dawn. . . . Sky is beginnin' to show some streaks of light over in the East there, back of our mountain. . . . Well, now I'll show you how our town lies. Up here is Main Street. Cuttin' across it over there on the left is the railroad tracks. Across the tracks is—Polish Town. You know, foreign people that come here to work in the mill, coupla Canuck families, and the Catholic Church. [*points in another direction*] The Congregational Church is over there, the Presbyterian's across the street. Methodist and Unitarian are over there. Baptist is down in the holla—by the river. Next to the Post Office there is the Town Hall; jail is in the basement. . . .

Along Main Street there's a row of stores. Hitchin' posts and horse-blocks in front of 'em. . . . Here's the grocery store and Mr. Morgan's drug store. Most everybody in town manages to look into these stores once a day. . . .

Nice town, y'know what I mean? Nobody remarkable ever come out of it, s'far as we know. The earliest dates on the tombstones up there in the cemetery say 1670. They're Grovers and Cartwrights and Gibbses and Herseys—same names as around here now. . . . Strong-minded people that come a long way to be independent . . . [*points again*] . . . Over there—are some Civil War veterans. Iron flags on their graves—New Hampshire boys—had a notion that the Union ought to be kept together, though they'd never seen more than fifty miles of it themselves. All they knew was the name, friends—the United States of America. The United States of America. And they went and died about it. . . .

Ain't been any burglars in town yet, but everybody's heard about

'em. You'd be surprised though—on the whole, things don't change much around here. This is certainly an important part of Grover's Corners. . . . [Over there is] a hilltop—a windy hilltop—lots of sky, lots of clouds—often lots of sun and moon and stars. You come up here on a fine afternoon and you can see range on range of hills—awful blue they are—up there by Lake Sunapee and Lake Winnipesaukee—and if you go way up, you can see the White Mountains and Mount Washington. . . . And, of course, our favorite mountain, Mount Monadnock's right here—and all around it lies these towns—Jaffrey 'n North Jaffrey, 'n Peterborough, 'n Dublin and there, quite a ways down, is Grover's Corners. Yes, beautiful place up here. . . . I often wonder why people like to be buried in Woodlawn and Brooklyn when they might pass the same time up here in New Hampshire.

Source: Thornton Wilder, *Our Town* (New York: Coward-McCann, 1939), pp. 2–3, 66–67.

Gemeinschaft and *Gesellschaft* in History. Toennies believed that the study of European history revealed a gradual, and generally irreversible, displacement of *gemeinschaft* by *gesellschaft*. He saw the rapid rise of cities in Europe during the nineteenth century as the inevitable emergence of *gesellschaft* as the dominant form of social life. Although he thought it inevitable, Toennies obviously did not think this transformation altogether good: the unity and human concern of *gemeinschaft* was gradually lost in *gesellschaft*.

Toennies's ideas contain the beginning of a sociology of the city. He was among the first to see urban life as distinctive and worthy of study. Moreover, his use of contrasting pure types is a

pattern that numerous other sociologists concerned with the city followed.

Durkheim: Mechanical and Organic Solidarity

The French sociologist Emile Durkheim (1858–1917), like Toennies, witnessed the urban transformation of the nineteenth century. Also like Toennies, Durkheim developed a model of contrasting types. His concepts of *mechanical solidarity* and *organic solidarity* are analogous to Toennies's *gemeinschaft* and *gesellschaft*.

Mechanical solidarity refers to social bonds that are constructed on likeness, on common belief and custom, on common ritual and symbol. Such solidarity is "mechanical" because the

---

> BOX 4-2
> ## The City as *Gesellschaft*
>
> And this a city
>   In name but in deed
> It is a pack of people
>   That seek after meed [profit].
> For officers and all
>   Do seek their own gain
> But for the wealth of the Commons
>   No one taketh pain.
> And hell without order
>   I may it well call
> Where every man is for himself
>   And no man for all.
>
> Robert Crowley

---

people who participate in it—people living in family units, tribes, or small towns—are almost identical in major respects and are united almost automatically, without thinking. Each family, tribe, or town is relatively self-sufficient and able to meet all life needs without dependence on other groups.

In contrast, organic solidarity describes a social order based on individual differences. Characteristic of modern societies, particularly cities, organic solidarity rests on a complex division of labor, in which people specialize in many different occupations. Like the organs of a body, people depend more on one another to meet their needs. A lawyer depends on other people—restaurant owners and grocers, say—to supply the food she needs. By not having to worry about where her next meal is coming from, she can engage in specialized legal activity. Similarly, the restaurant owner need not study law. Knowing there are legal specialists, he can call on a lawyer when necessary.

In this complex division of labor, Durkheim saw the possibility of greater *freedom* for all of society's inhabitants: an ability to make more choices in their lives. Although Durkheim acknowledged the problems that cities might create—impersonality, alienation, disagreement, and conflict—he argued for the ultimate superiority of organic over mechanical solidarity: "[The]

yoke that we submit to [in modern society] is much less heavy than when society completely controls us [as it does in rural society], and it leaves much more place open for the free play of our initiative . . ." (1893; 1964, p. 131).

Durkheim and Toennies: A Comparison

While Durkheim agreed with Toennies's conclusion that history was characterized by a movement from an emphasis on one type of social order to another—in his case, from mechanical to organic solidarity—there are important differences in their ideas. For instance, Durkheim took exception to labeling the tribal or rural environment alone as "natural." Rather, he asserted that "the life of large social agglomerations is just as natural as that of small groupings."

No doubt it was because of this belief that Durkheim did not share Toennies's negative view of modern society. Durkheim reversed Toennies's terminology and called *gemeinschaft* "mechanical" and *gesellschaft* "organic." Although Toennies saw little hope for truly humane life in the city (he cited parents' admonition to their city-bound children to beware of "bad *gesellschaft*"), Durkheim was more optimistic. Durkheim saw the increasing division of labor characteristic of modern urban societies as undermining traditional social integration and creating a new form of social cohesion based upon mutual interdependence. This interdependence is expressed most clearly by contractual agreements among individuals or groups. Still, Durkheim observed, no society can exist *entirely* on the basis of contract: at the very least, a normative foundation is required on which we agree how to enter into and execute fairly all contracts.

Durkheim thus provides an important contrast to Toennies. Although both theorists recognized that cities were associated with the growth of social differentiation and individuality, Toennies feared the undermining of the very fabric of social life, while Durkheim saw the possibility of continuing social cohesion and greater human development. But the city is more complex than either of these visions admits.

Simmel: The Mental Life of the Metropolis

Both Toennies and Durkheim described the broad societal processes out of which the modern city evolved. Although they made passing reference to the mental characteristics of city dwellers—the city dweller was more impersonal, rational, freer—they did not look systematically at the *social psychology* of city life. One who did was the German, Georg Simmel (1858–1918).

Like his contemporaries, Simmel saw in the rise of the modern world a cause for concern: how was the individual to maintain a spirit of freedom and creativity in the midst of "overwhelming social forces"? In his famous essay "The Metropolis and Mental Life," Simmel suggested that the personality would learn to "accommodate itself" to the city (Simmel 1905; 1964).

The City's Characteristics. The unique element of the modern city that sets this accommodation in operation is the *intensification of nervous stimuli* with which the city dweller must cope. Unlike the rural setting, where "the rhythm of life and sensory imagery flows more slowly, more habitually, more evenly," the city constantly bombards the individual with an enormous kaleidoscope of sights, sounds, and smells. In order to cope, the individual learns to discriminate carefully—to tune in what is important and tune out what is irrelevant. In time, urban people become more "sophisticated," more "intellectual" than their rural counterparts.

As a result of this discriminative process, the city's people, as a whole, become more rational, more calculating. They plan and organize their daily lives to achieve more efficiency. Take, for example, the intricate organization of time in the city, symbolized by the ever-present clock and wristwatch. Simmel wrote, "If all the clocks and watches in Berlin would suddenly go wrong in different ways, even if only by one hour, all economic life and communication of the city would be disrupted for a long time" (1964, p. 413). In addition to the rational organization of time, Simmel saw the rationality of the city expressed in its advanced economic division of labor (here he echoed Durkheim). Social life in the city is the interplay of *specialists*.

But perhaps the most powerful means of conveying the message of urban rationality was Simmel's discussion of the importance of money. "The metropolis," he stated, "has always been the seat of a money economy." Why is money so important in urban life? One reason is that the advanced division of labor requires a universal means of exchange. Money performs this critical function. As Simmel wrote (1964, p. 414), "Money is concerned only with what is common to all: it asks for the exchange value, it reduces all quality and individuality to the question: How much?"

The Individual's Response. How, asks Simmel, is the urbanite to behave in the midst of such overwhelming stimulation and unending demand for rational response? Can you *really* stop to help everyone you see in some sort of trouble on the street? Simmel believed not. Consequently, he argued, the urbanite adapts to city life by developing what he called a "blasé" attitude, a social reserve, a detachment. Put simply, in the city we respond with our head rather than our heart. We learn to take on a matter-of-fact attitude about the world around us. We simply don't care; we don't want to "get involved," as is shown dramatically in the examples in Box 4-3.

Even worse, Simmel speculated that the cultivated indifference necessary to living in the city may harden into a measured antagonism. "Indeed, if I do not deceive myself," he wrote, "the inner aspect of this outer reserve is not only indifference, but, more often than we are aware, it is a slight aversion, a mutual strangeness and repulsion, which will break into hatred and fight at the moment of a closer contact, however caused" (1964, pp 415–416). (Recall Mr. Gawber's attitude toward his neighbors in Cityscape 1-3.) Perhaps each of us can recall feeling some anger about the way someone unknown to us was behaving in a city—someone who broke into line ahead of us, for example, or someone who approached us in a city park, demanding some personal response.

Like Durkheim, Simmel saw in the separate-

BOX 4-3

Urban Apathy: The Death of Kitty Genovese and Other Rather Unnerving Events

On March 14, 1964, a grim item appeared on page 26 of the *New York Times*. It reported the murder of Kitty Genovese near her home in the Kew Gardens section of New York's Borough of Queens. What seemed at first to be a report of a crime without particular public significance exploded into a major controversy when the *Times* reported two weeks later that *dozens of Ms. Genovese's "neighbors" had observed her attacker stab her repeatedly during a period of half an hour without coming to her aid or even calling the police until after she was dead!* In an editorial the following day, the *Times* posed a frightening question: "Does residence in a great city destroy all sense of personal responsibility for one's neighbors?" The death of Kitty Genovese thus became symbolic of the argument that the city was an unhealthy setting that

lacked even a rudimentary sense of human community.

But it didn't stop with Kitty Genovese. Hers is only the most celebrated case. On the night of November 30, 1984, the same thing happened in Brooklyn. A woman was attacked in the Gowanus Apartments, a New York City housing project. As she was beaten, she began screaming and continued her cries for 20 minutes. Many heard her—no one came to her rescue. Finally, her assailants dragged her into the lobby of a building and shot her dead. It was only then that someone deigned to call the police. (*New York Times*, Dec. 2, 1984)

Nor is it fair to single out New York. During three weeks in 1984, the same indifference to the victims of urban crime surfaced again, this time in St. Louis. In one case a man was robbed at gunpoint while dozens of people

looked on. When the man approached the onlookers afterwards and asked why they didn't help him, they replied that they just "didn't want to get involved." In another incident a woman was attacked by three men at Busch Memorial Stadium during a Cardinals baseball game. She screamed for help. None was offered. She said later: "I was shocked more than hurt. I just sat there and screamed and not one soul stopped. I saw all these legs going by, and I thought about reaching out and grabbing somebody." Said Sgt. Frank Baricevic of the St. Louis Police after these disturbing incidents: "Police departments are only as good as the people they protect. If [people] don't want to get involved, if they don't want to cooperate, then we're in trouble" (*New York Times*, Aug. 18, 1984).

---

ness fostered by the city a certain freedom. It was possible, he thought, for the urban dweller to transcend the pettiness of daily routine and reach a new height of personal and spiritual development. But, unlike his French colleague, Simmel saw in the city's freedom a haunting specter. "It is obviously only the obverse of this freedom," he wrote, "if, under certain circumstances one nowhere feels as lonely and lost as in the metropolitan crowd."

Feeling like a cog in a giant machine, some people maintain their sense of individuality in a city by doing something "odd," by "being different," and thereby standing out. It is this sense of alienation that Simmel would use to explain the motivation of New York City's recent graffiti madness, a process that in less than a decade has defaced nearly every subway train and public mon-

ument in the city. One graffitist named ALI offered this explanation for his activity: "I'm not just another face in the project among a million others. I exist. I was there" (*New York Times Magazine*, Aug. 21, 1980, p. 45).

Thus, in the end, Simmel appears to side more with Toennies than Durkheim in his evaluation of the city. Although he saw the city as the setting where the great historical contest between true human liberation and alienation would occur, his analysis left little doubt as to which of these options was likely to be victorious.

Weber: The Historical and Comparative Study of Cities

Toennies, Durkheim, and Simmel all approached the analysis of the city abstractly; that is,

Do we want to get involved in the lives of unknown people in the city?
(Jan Lukas/Photo Researchers)

they developed their theories by a general "reading" of what they saw as the main trends of European urban history and the main elements of life in the cities they knew.

German sociologist Max Weber (1864–1920) believed that any theory that did not take account of cities in different parts of the world at different times in history would be of limited value. This concern proved to be a major methodological contribution to urban sociology.

Die Stadt. Weber demonstrated his approach in his famous essay, *"Die Stadt"* ("The City"), which first appeared in 1921. Surveying cities of Europe, the Middle East, India, and China, Weber developed a definition of what he called the *full urban community*:

> To constitute a full urban community a settlement must display a relative predominance of trade-com-

mercial relations, with the settlement as a whole displaying the following features: 1. a fortification; 2. a market; 3. a court of its own and at least partially autonomous law; 4. a related form of association; and 5. at least partial political autonomy. . . . (1966, pp. 80–81)

This definition is an excellent example of what Weber called an *ideal type*, a model of the crucial elements of a social phenomenon constructed from real-world observation. Weber was well aware that some cities would not contain all of the elements in his definition. In such cases, the city simply would not be a "full urban community" in his sense. We shall examine the characteristics of such a community in more detail.

First, Weber's urban community is based on trade or commercial relations. In rural areas, people are more or less self-sufficient, growing their own food, providing their own clothing, and so

Urban graffiti is not simply an act of vandalism; it is a way of saying, perhaps in some desperation, "Hey, world, I exist!" (Jeroboam/Kent Reno)

on. Trade and commerce are of limited importance. Not so in the city. Weber clearly agreed with Toennies, Durkheim, and Simmel that economic self-sufficiency is nearly impossible; people are economically interdependent in the sense of Durkheim's organic solidarity. Indeed, the economic aspects of city life are so important that a distinct mechanism of exchange—the market—evolved to facilitate them.

Second, an urban community is relatively autonomous. Weber specified that a true city has a court and law of its own and at least partial political autonomy. It also must be militarily self-sufficient, having a fortification system and army for self-defense if and when necessary. Such autonomy is absolutely essential if urban dwellers are to identify the city as theirs, as a place demanding their allegiance in the way that the small town receives the allegiance of its inhabitants.

Third, Weber said that the urban community must have "a related form of association." By this he meant that city living must involve social relationships and organizations through which urbanites gain a sense of meaningful participation in the life of their city.

The "Full Urban Community" in History. Like Durkheim, Weber believed that cities could be positive and liberating forces in human life. Unlike Durkheim, however, Weber did not see much hope for twentieth-century cities. Indeed, he thought only the fortified, self-sufficient cities of the medieval period deserved the title of "full urban community." Only in these cities had there existed the commercial relations, autonomy, and social participation that he believed to be of crucial importance.

With the rise to preeminence of the nation in the seventeenth, eighteenth, and nineteenth centuries, Weber claimed, cities had lost their military, and, to a large extent, their legal and political, autonomy—necessary elements for identifying with the city as a psychological "home." People came to identify with other units of society—the nation, country, business, or, as recognized by Toennies and Simmel, with themselves alone. Other reasons for the failure of modern cities were their excessive rationality and reliance on capitalism, the latter with its emphasis on personal profit.

By recognizing medieval cities as examples of the full urban community, Weber hoped to show that "the good life" had existed in cities and might again if those conditions could be recreated. Equally important, by suggesting that a pinnacle of urban culture had been realized *before* in history, Weber implied that history might not necessarily be progressive (Sennett 1969, pp. 6–10).

The City and Culture. Weber stood apart from his colleagues who tended to see the city itself as the sole cause of urban life. In contrast, Weber's analysis, fueled by his deep understanding of other cities in other cultures and at different points in history, suggested that cities are intimately linked to processes larger than themselves, to particular economic or political orientations, for example. If these processes were different, the nature of city life would be different. Thus, feudal or Chinese societies would not produce exactly the same type of urban life that industrial-capitalist European society does.

The European Tradition: An Evaluation

The ideas of Toennies, Durkheim, Simmel, and Weber have formed the core of classical urban sociology and have had an enormous impact on the field ever since. It is important, however, to note their limitations as well as their contributions.

Limitations. More than three-quarters of a century later, it is easy to see how the central ideas of these theorists were an outgrowth of the times and cities in which they lived. Cities were rapidly replacing villages and countryside as the main arena of life. For all their excitement, one hardly could argue that these rapidly growing cities provided a good life for many of their inhabitants. Little wonder then that three of these four theorists—Durkheim is the partial exception—saw the cities of their day as threats to long-cherished human values. Although no one would deny that the cities of today also have their problems, one can only speculate how the theories of these men would have changed had they been able to witness the growth of suburbs, major efforts at urban planning, reforms in many of the most overtly exploitative practices of turn-of-the-century cities (such as child labor), and the rise of socialist cities.

Second, the theorists show some disagreement in their interpretations. The contrast between Toennies and Durkheim is most instructive. Toennies saw *gemeinschaft* as humane and *gesellschaft* as highly problematical. Using his terms of mechanical and organic solidarity, Durkheim reversed the interpretation: the tribal or country life was cloying, undeveloped; the life of the city, in contrast, was liberating and full of potential for development.

On another level, Simmel thought the social-psychological adaptations he studied were a product of the great city itself. He implied that all metropolises would produce similar mental processes. Weber disagreed. He argued that only certain historical and cultural conditions produced the type of city that Simmel observed (modern capitalist cities, for example) and that other historical and cultural conditions would produce very different types of urban social-psychological adaptation. With the evidence available at the time, it was impossible to judge such contradictory claims, although in later chapters we will see that Weber's position on this issue was closer to the truth.

Contributions. Perhaps the most important contribution of the classical theorists was their insistence that *the city is a proper object of sociological study*. Although Toennies and Durkheim did not work out theories of the city as such, their typologies clearly analyzed the contrasts between rural and urban life. Simmel and Weber went a step further by actually developing theories of how cities worked. Urban sociology has grown directly out of these efforts.

Second, all four theorists recognized that there is *something distinctive about the city and the way of life it creates*. They all saw the city as increasing human choice, emphasizing rationality, being characterized by a complex division of labor, and creating a unique experience for its inhabitants. This concern with the city's unique qualities has been, as the next section will demonstrate clearly, a major focus of the discipline ever since.

Third, taken together, these theorists suggested *the main concerns of the discipline*. Toennies, Durkheim, and Weber all considered the social structure of the city. Simmel suggested the importance of the urban experience. In addition, all four stressed the importance of the comparative approach. Toennies and Durkheim, and to a certain extent Simmel, compared cities and non-urban environments to elucidate the distinctive characteristics of each. Weber added to this focus an insistence that urban analysis must compare cities historically and crossculturally if an adequate urban theory is to develop. Finally, all four urbanists made the *evaluation* of cities a fundamental element in their work. Each made quite clear what he thought beneficial and detrimental to the city's ability to produce a humane life for its population.

Urban Sociology in America: 1915–1938

We now turn to the development of urban sociology in the United States, beginning at the time of World War I. The character of this work is somewhat different from the European, particularly in its greater concern with actually going out and exploring the city. At the same time, many of the themes of the European tradition were carried into American sociology.

Again we should take note of the times in which this sociology developed. As in Europe, the turn of the century in America was a period of both rapid industrialization and fast city growth. Although America was still primarily a rural society, the mounting flow of immigrants—most of whom settled in cities—was rapidly altering this condition. It was a world in which the Grover's Corners of America (Cityscape 4-1) were rapidly giving way to the expanding industrial metropolis.

Perhaps no city typified this pattern more clearly than Chicago. Barely a settlement and not yet legally organized as a city in 1830, Chicago was approaching a population of 2 million by 1900. As the city grew in population, it also grew upward and outward. The first steel-frame building—a marvel of the age—was constructed in Chicago in 1884, towering an incredible ten stories above the ground! By the close of World War I, Chicago was entering the Roaring Twenties with a population of almost 3 million. Immigrants and migrants were everywhere (Jurgis and Ona Rudkis, described in Cityscape 1-4, had been among the arrivals in 1900). Like hundreds of exploding American cities, Chicago was billowing the black, smoky flag of prosperity, creating its share of severe problems as it went. It was in Chicago that the main elements of American urban sociology first appeared.

Robert Park and Sociology at the University of Chicago

American sociology came of age in the twentieth century. Although courses in "social science" had been offered as far back as 1865, the subject first gained intellectual respectability when the University of Chicago invited Albion W. Small (then President of Colby College) to found a sociology department in 1892 (Faris 1967). Within the next 30 years the department attracted several prominent scholars. One of the most outstanding was Robert Ezra Park (1864–1944).

Leaving a newspaper job in 1915 to join the department, Park established the first urban studies center in the United States. His interest in urban matters had both European and American roots. In his early years he had studied with the Russian sociologist Kistiakowski (a scholar sharing much the same view of social change as Toennies) and with Georg Simmel. In his own country he was deeply influenced by Lincoln Steffens's *The Shame of the Cities*, a book that suggested that the malaise of the modern city was everyone's responsibility. An excerpt from this critique appears in Box 4-4.

Although aware of the bad and the good, there can be no question that Park had an almost unbounded fascination with the city. Not only did he guide several generations of students in explorations of all aspects of Chicago, but he served as first president of the Chicago Urban League. He dedicated himself to relentless personal exploration of the city and later wrote:

> I expect that I have actually covered more ground, tramping about in cities in different parts of the world, than any other living man. Out of all this I gained, among other things, a conception of the city, the community, and the region, not as geographical phenomenon merely, but as a kind of social organism. (1950, p. viii)

A Systematic Urban Sociology. The program that Park used to guide urban sociology at Chicago was presented in 1916 in his classic article, "The City: Suggestions for the Investigation of Human Behavior in the Urban Environment" (1967). He argued that urban research had to be conducted by disciplined *observation*, in much the same way that anthropologists studied other cultures. Second, he conceived of the city as a social organism with distinct constituent parts bound together by internal processes. The city was not chaos and disorder (stereotypes of Chicago during the era of the Roaring Twenties notwithstanding)

BOX 4-4

The Shame of the Cities: Who's to Blame?

When I set out on my travels, an honest New Yorker told me honestly that I would find that the Irish, the Catholic Irish, were at the bottom of it all everywhere. The first city I went to was St. Louis, a German city. The next was Minneapolis, a Scandinavian city, with a leadership of New Englanders. Then came Pittsburgh, Scotch Presbyterian, and that was what my New York friend was. "Ah, but they are all foreign populations," I heard. The next city was Philadelphia, the purest American community of all, and the most hopeless. And after that came Chicago and New York, both mongrelbred, but the one a triumph of reform, the other the best example of good government that I had seen. The "foreign element" excuse is one of the hypocritical lies that save us from the clear sight of ourselves. . . .

When I set out to describe the corrupt systems of certain typical cities, I meant to show simply how the people were deceived and betrayed. But in the very first study—St. Louis—the startling truth lay bare that corruption was not merely political; it was financial, commercial, social; the ramifications of boodle were so complex, various, and far-reaching, that one mind could hardly grasp them. . . .

And it's all a moral weakness; a weakness right where we think we are strongest. Oh, we are good—on Sunday, and we are "fearfully patriotic" on the Fourth of July. But the bribe we pay to the janitor to prefer our interests to the landlord's, is the little brother of the bribe passed to the alderman to sell a city street, and the father of the air-brake stock assigned to the president of the railroad to

have this life-saving invention adopted on his road. We are pathetically proud of our democratic institutions and our republican form of government, of our grand Constitution and our just laws. We are a free and sovereign people, we govern ourselves and the government is ours. But that is the point. We are responsible, not our leaders, since we follow them. We *let* them divert our loyalty from the United States to some "party"; we *let* them boss the party and turn our municipal democracies into autocracies and our republican nation into a plutocracy. We cheat our government and we let our leaders loot it, and we let them wheedle and bribe our sovereignty from us. . . . The people are not innocent.

Source: Lincoln Steffens, *The Shame of the Cities* (New York: McClure, Phillips, 1904), pp. 2–3, 7–9.

---

but, rather, tended toward an "orderly and typical grouping of its population and institutions" (1967, p. 1). He wrote:

> Every great city has its racial colonies, like the Chinatowns of San Francisco and New York, the Little Sicily of Chicago, and the various other less pronounced types. In addition to these, most cities have their segregated vice districts . . . their rendezvous for criminals of various sorts. Every large city has its occupational suburbs, like the stockyards in Chicago, and its residential enclaves, like Brookline in Boston, the so-called "Gold Coast" in Chicago, Greenwich Village in New York, each of which has a size and character of a complete separate town, village, or city, except that its population is a select one. (1967, p. 10)

There is no doubt that this insight into the city's orderliness was responsible for Park's urging his students to develop detailed studies of all parts of the city. Not only industrial workers, real-estate

officials, and VIPs were studied, but migrants, hobos, musicians, prostitutes, and dancehall workers as well. The conviction that these "parts and processes" of the city were intricately linked was at the heart of his new social science, what he termed "human, as distinguished from plant and animal, ecology." Finally, Park was far from insensitive to the issue of human values in his approach to the city. He saw the city as a "moral as well as a physical organization" and carried evaluative judgments of urban living deep into his sociology.

Park's Image of the City. With some idea of Park's approach to the task of *studying* the city, let us now explore what Park actually observed the city to be. What was it about the city that so fascinated him?

First, like Weber, Park saw in the modern city a *commercial structure* that owed "its existence to the market place around which it sprang up." Like Durkheim, he believed that modern city life was characterized by a complex division of labor driven on by industrial competition. With Toennies, Park believed that this market dominance would result in the steady erosion of more traditional ways of life. The past emphasis upon "family ties, local associations . . . caste, and status" would yield inevitably to a *Gesellschaft*-like system "based on occupation and vocational interests."

Second, Park perceived the city as increasingly characterized by *formal social structures*, best exemplified by large-scale bureaucracies. In time, these would take the place of the more "informal" means by which people had historically organized their everyday lives. Bureaucracies such as the police, courts, and welfare agencies would play an increasing role in urban settings. Similarly, politics would develop a more formalized tone. Park contended that

> the form of government which had its origin in the town meetings and was well suited to the needs of the small community based on primary relations is not suitable to the government of the changing and heterogeneous populations of cities of three or four millions. (1967, p. 33)

The city dweller, unable to understand all the issues at stake in the operation of a complex city, would have to rely upon "the organization represented by the political boss and the political machine or other civic organizations such as voter leagues."

As an ex-newspaper man, Park hardly could have been expected to omit the media from his description of the formalization of city life. The face-to-face oral network by which information flowed in the village ("gossip" is the more precise, if less scholarly, term) would be replaced by reliance on mass media. Information would be conveyed more and more impersonally and routinely to a mass of information consumers. Such was the significance of the city newspaper to Park. Of course, the newspaper was soon to be augmented by radio and, later, by the omnipresent TV set.

The third dimension of Park's image of the city, showing the effects of his studies with Simmel, was his emphasis on the psychosocial dimension of urban life. Park suggested that life within the city would become *less sentimental* and *more rational* than life elsewhere. Deep-seated sentiments and prejudices would give way to calculation based on self-interest. At the same time, however, Park appeared to be aware that the erosion of traditional sentimental ties in the city might give rise to new social bonds—bonds based on interest groups. In this, there is a clear Durkheimian quality to his argument: solidarity based on likenesses (mechanical solidarity) is replaced by solidarity based on the interdependence of differentiated parts (organic solidarity).

Freedom and Tolerance in the City. As a social reformer, Park recognized that the modern city revealed problem upon problem, but he also was fascinated with what he saw to be the possibilities for freedom and tolerance in the city. He wrote:

> The attraction of the metropolis is due in part to the fact that in the long run every individual finds somewhere among the varied manifestations of city life the sort of environment in which he expands and feels at ease; he finds, in short, the moral climate in which his peculiar nature obtains the stimulations that bring his innate dispositions to full and free expression. It is, I suspect, motives of this kind which have their basis, not in interest or even in sentiment, but in something more fundamental and primitive which drove many, if not most, of the young men and young women from the security of their homes in the country into the big, booming confusion and excitement of city life. (1967, p. 41)

What marvelous images! What Toennies saw only as forces of disorganization, Park saw as potential for greater human experience. He continued:

> In a small community it is the normal man, the man without eccentricity or genius who seems most likely to succeed. The small community often tolerates eccentricity. The city rewards it. Neither the criminal, the defective, nor the genius has the same opportunity to develop his innate disposition in a small town that he invariably finds in a great city. (1967, p. 41)

Summing up, we see in the ideas of Robert Park a new emphasis upon the *doing* of urban research and on-site investigation of the city quite unlike the more abstract theorizing of Toennies, Durkheim, and Simmel, and unlike the historical work of Weber. Park's main contribution was his demand that we get out there and see how the city actually works.

Louis Wirth and Urban Theory

If the European theorists had a tendency to err on the side of producing a great deal of theory based on little research, the fusion of the theoretical and empirical was not to be found immediately at the University of Chicago, either. During the 20 years that followed the publication of Park's urban studies program in 1916, Chicago sociologists produced a wealth of primarily descriptive studies. It was not until 1938 that this situation began to be rectified, when Louis Wirth (1897–1952) published his famous essay, "Urbanism as a Way of Life."

Wirth's great contribution to urban sociology was the patient and systematic organization of the insights of previous urban sociologists into the first truly sociological theory of the city. By a *theory* of the city, we mean that Wirth began his analysis by isolating several factors that he argued were *universal social characteristics* of the city; he then proceeded to systematically deduce what implications these factors would have for determining the character of urban social life. He said, in effect (as all good theorists do), *if* this condition is present, *then* that condition will result.

"Urbanism" is what Wirth called the distinctive way of life of the city. This refers to "the forms of social action and organization that typically emerge in relatively permanent compact settlements of large numbers of heterogeneous individuals" (1964, p. 68).

Wirth began with a definition of the city as a (1) large, (2) dense, permanent settlement with (3) socially and culturally heterogeneous people. Let us examine how each of these elements creates certain conditions of urban life.

Population Size. Wirth believed that large population size alone would produce great diversity in the cultural and occupational characteristics of the city. This was partly due to the simple fact that

---

BOX 4-5
The City—A Song of Myself

The pure contralto sings in the organ loft . . .
The married and unmarried children ride home to their Thanksgiving dinner . . .
The deacons are ordain'd with cross'd hands at the altar;
The spinning-girl retreats and advances to the hum of the big wheel . . .
The lunatic is carried at last to the asylum, a confirm'd case . . .
The jour printer with gray head and gaunt jaws works at his case . . .
The machinist rolls up his sleeves—the policeman travels his beat—the gate-keeper marks who pass . . .
The opium-eater reclines with rigid head and just-open'd lips;
The prostitute draggles her shawl, her bonnet bobs on her tipsy and pimpled neck;
The crowd laugh at her blackguard oaths, the men jeer and wink to each other . .
The President, holding a cabinet council, is surrounded by the Great Secretaries;
On the piazza walk three matrons stately and friendly with twined arms . . .
Patriarchs sit at supper with sons and grandsons and great-grandsons around them . . .
The city sleeps . . .
The old husband sleeps by his wife, and the young husband sleeps by his wife;
And these one and all tend inward to me, and I tend outward to them,
And such as it is to be of these, more or less, I am.

Source: Walt Whitman, "Song of Myself," in *Leaves of Grass*, 1855.

---

greater numbers of people in one place logically increase the potential differentiation among them, and partly due to the migration of diverse groups to the city (a major factor in Chicago, where Wirth was writing). This sense of urban diversity probably has never been captured better than in Walt Whitman's 1855 poem, "Song of Myself," from which an excerpt appears in Box 4-5.

Second, the condition of cultural diversity would have the subsequent effect of creating a need for formal control structures (such as a legal system) in city life. Third, a large, differentiated population would support the proliferation of specialization, and an occupational structure based upon differing professions (artist, politician, cabdriver) would emerge.

Fourth, specialization would organize human relationships more on an "interest-specific" basis that Wirth described as "social segmentalization":

> Characteristically, urbanites meet one another in highly segmental roles. They are, to be sure, dependent on more people for the satisfactions of their life needs than are rural people . . . but they are less dependent upon particular persons, and their dependence upon others is confined to a highly fractionalized aspect of the other's round of activity. This is essentially what is meant by saying that the city is characterized by secondary rather than primary contacts. The contacts of the city may indeed be face-to-face but they are nevertheless impersonal, superficial, transitory, and segmental. (1964, p. 71)

In other words, rather than understanding others in terms of *who* they are, the urbanite typically conceives of others in terms of *what* they do, in terms of their roles and what they can do to advance one's own ends. The urban qualities of rationality and sophistication are simply additional ways of suggesting that urban ties become, in essence, relationships of utility. Lastly, even with the stabilizing constraint provided by formal controls and professional codes of conduct, Wirth could not escape the conclusion that large population size carried with it the possibility of disorganization and disintegration, a situation feared by all the European theorists.

Population Density. The consequence of population density was to *intensify* the effects of large population size upon social life. Rather than manifesting the quality of sameness one might associate with the countryside, the city became separated into a mosaic of readily identifiable regions or districts. (Here we can see the direct influence of Wirth's teacher, Park.) Both economic forces (such as differing land values) and social processes (such as racial or ethnic differences) tended to produce fairly distinct neighborhoods and districts.

For example, many American cities have a predominantly Italian area (Boston's North End), a Chinatown (such as San Francisco's), or a skid row (New York's Bowery). Similarly, major cities frequently have a garment district and a financial district, such as New York's Wall Street. Wirth called this process of separating the city into districts "ecological specialization." Some of these districts are portrayed vividly in Cityscape 4-2, in another passage from Charles Dickens.

On the social-psychological level, density also had its effects. Exposed to "glaring contrasts . . . splendor and squalor . . . riches and poverty," Wirth argued, city dwellers develop a mental shorthand, a mental mapping of the city, its regions, and its inhabitants. This insight (an extension of Simmel's) helps us understand the urbanite's tendency to stereotypical and categorical thinking, and the reliance on grasping the city through visible symbols and uniforms (clothing, cars, fashionable street addresses). The implication is clear—population density fosters a loss of sensitivity to the "more personal aspects" of others—and suggests why people in the city often seem "cold and heartless."

As suggested earlier by Durkheim and Simmel, Wirth contended that the "juxtaposition of divergent personalities and modes of life" would result in a greater *toleration of differences* among urbanites. Along with this, physical closeness tended to increase *social distance* among people. Forced into physical proximity, urbanites characteristically close off or tune out those around them. (Sometimes this happens as people, chatting busily, enter a crowded elevator and abruptly become silent, staring up at the numbers on the elevator wall.)

Taking the argument another step, Wirth suggested that high density may cause an increase in antisocial behavior. (Again, Simmel's influence is evident.) Wirth wrote that "the necessary movement of great numbers of individuals in a congested habitat causes friction and irritation."

Heterogeneity. In completing his theory of urbanism, Wirth suggested several consequences of social difference, or heterogeneity. First, "social interaction among such a variety of personality types

CITYSCAPE 4-2
The Streets of London

In this scene from The Old Curiosity Shop, *Dickens describes walking through London one morning in 1840.*

The town was glad with morning light; places that had shown ugly and distrustful all night long, now wore a smile; and sparkling sunbeams dancing on chamber windows, and twinkling through blind and curtain before sleeper's eyes, shed light even into dreams, and chased away the shadows of the night. . . . Bright and happy as it was, there was something solemn in the long, deserted streets, from which like bodies without souls all habitual character and expression had departed, leaving but one dead uniform repose, that made them all alike. All was so still at that early hour, that the few pale people whom they met seemed as much unsuited to the scene, as the sickly lamp which had been here and there left burning was powerless and faint in the full glory of the sun.

Before they had penetrated very far into the labyrinth of men's abodes which yet lay between them and the outskirts, this aspect began to melt away, and noise and bustle to usurp its place. Some straggling carts and coaches rumbling by first broke the charm, then others came, then others yet more active, then a crowd. The wonder was at first to see a tradesman's window open, but it was a rare thing soon to see one closed; then smoke rose slowly from the chimneys, and sashes were thrown up to let in air, and doors were opened, and servantgirls, looking lazily in all directions but their brooms, scattered brown clouds of dust into the eyes of shrinking passengers, or listened disconsolately to milkmen who spoke of country fairs, and told of waggons in the mews, with awnings and all the things complete and gallant swains to boot, which another hour would see upon their journey.

This quarter passed, they came upon the haunts of commerce and great traffic, where many people were resorting, and business was already rife. . . .

The throng of people hurried by, in two opposite streams, with no symptom of cessation or exhaustion; intent upon their own affairs; and undisturbed in their business speculations, by the roar of carts and waggons laden with clashing wares, the slipping of horses' feet upon the wet and greasy pavement, the jostling of the more impatient passengers, and all the noise and tumult of a crowded street in the high tide of its occupation. . . .

They withdrew into a low arch-

---

in the urban milieu tends to break down the rigidity of caste lines and to complicate the class structure." Consequently, there tends to be a heightened social mobility in the city as stabilizing factors such as family social position weaken in the face of greater personal achievements.

Second, social mobility may be accompanied by physical movement. "Overwhelmingly the city dweller is not a homeowner and since a transitory habitat does not generate binding traditions and sentiments, only rarely is he a true neighbor." Remember Kitty Genovese (Box 4-3)?

Finally, the concentration of diverse people leads inevitably to further depersonalization. Against a background of commercial mass production and consumption, personal relations may be displaced by an emphasis on money. Thus, Wirth echoed Simmel's earlier regard for the heightened importance of money, and described the city as a "pecuniary nexus."

These three dimensions of Wirth's theory—size, density, and heterogeneity of population—interact with each other to produce the unique way of life he termed "urbanism." Wirth was clearly pessimistic about urbanism as a way of life. He saw the city as an acid that, in time, ate away traditional values and undermined the formation of meaningful institutions and relationships. Like Park, he saw the possibilities for greater freedom in the city, but he also worried that any such positive aspects would be inevitably compromised by the disorganization he saw in turbulent Chicago. Only by massive attempts at controlling the city—urban planning—did he think that truly humane urban environments could be created.

The American Tradition: An Evaluation

We must not be too quick to accept these judgments. Like their European colleagues, the Chi-

way for shelter and watched the faces of those who passed, to find in one among them a ray of encouragement or hope. Some frowned, some smiled, some muttered to themselves, some made slight gestures, as if anticipating the conversation in which they would shortly be engaged, some wore the cunning look of bargaining and plotting, some were anxious and eager, some slow and dull; in some countenances were written gain; in others loss. . . .

Again this quarter passed, they came upon a straggling neighbourhood, where the mean houses parcelled off in rooms, and windows patched with rags and paper, told of the populous poverty that sheltered there. The shops sold goods that only poverty could buy, and sellers and buyers were pinched and griped alike. Here were poor streets where faded gentility essayed

with scanty space and shipwrecked means to make its last feeble stand, but tax-gatherer and creditor came there as elsewhere, and the poverty that yet faintly struggled, was hardly less squalid and manifest than that which had long ago submitted and given up the same. . . . [Here were] children, scantily fed and clothed, spread over every street, and sprawling in the dust—scolding mothers, stamping their slipshod feet with noisy threats upon the pavement—shabby fathers, hurrying with dispirited looks to the occupation which brought them "daily bread" and little more. . . .

At length these streets, becoming more straggling yet, dwindled and dwindled away. . . . [Then] pert cottages, two and two with plots of ground in front, laid out in angular beds with stiff box borders and narrow paths between, where footstep never strayed to

make the gravel rough . . . then fields; and then some houses, one by one, of goodly size with lawns, some even with a lodge where dwelt a porter and his wife. Then came a turnpike; then fields again with trees and haystacks; then a hill; and on top of that the traveller might stop, and—looking back at old Saint Paul's [Cathedral] looming through the smoke, its cross peeping above the cloud (if the day were clear), and glittering in the sun; and casting his eyes upon the Babel out of which it grew until he traced it down to the furthest outposts of the invading army of bricks and mortar whose station lay for the present nearly at his feet—might feel at last that he was clear of London.

---

cago sociologists were responding to a particular kind of city, a Western capitalist city moving into the high gear of advanced industrialization. This narrow focus limited the significance of their work. For example, the Chicago school neglected any historical or comparative analysis. How would their evaluations of the urban environment have changed had they, like Weber, looked at cities in history or in cross-cultural perspective? What would have happened if they had not based their theories almost exclusively on large, dense, ethnic Chicago?

Their work may be skewed for yet another reason. Park's great insistence on on-site study, coupled with his interest in urban disorganization and problems, led him and his colleagues to concentrate more on the "seamy side" of city life than other aspects. A partial list of the group's classic publications, brilliant though many of them are, reveals this bias: Nels Anderson, *The Hobo* (1923);

Ernest Mowner, *Family Disorganization* (1927); Harvey Zorbaugh, *The Gold Coast and the Slum* (1928); Frederich Thrasher, *The Gang* (1929); Clifford Shaw and Henry McKay, *Social Factors in Juvenile Delinquency* (1931); John Landesco, *Organized Crime in Chicago* (1929); Paul Cressey, *The Taxi Dance Hall* (1932); Norman Hayner, *Hotel Life* (1936); and Edwin H. Sutherland, *The Professional Thief* (1937). It is not that these aspects of city life are unimportant; it is simply that they are not all there is to city life. Yet Wirth based his theory heavily on the evidence supplied by such studies.

Even so, we must not forget the Chicago group's great contributions. Park deserves continuing credit for his dedication to studying the city firsthand. He argued that armchair theories of the city could never be sufficient. The urban sociologist actually had to go out and directly observe the life of the city. The second main contribution was Wirth's theory, which became a persuasive, almost mesmerizing document that would dominate the field for the next 20 years. Tying the main insights of the European tradition to the observational studies of the Chicago group, Wirth showed for the first time that a true urban theory was possible. All in all, the Chicago group was almost solely responsible for the early growth of urban sociology in America (Thomas 1983; Lofland 1983).

The Classic Theories and Modern Research: Myths and Realities

Is the city a heaven or a hell; is it a place where all the best attributes of human life will emerge or a place where people inevitably, despite their best efforts, "go bad"? The seventeenth-century English poet Abraham Cowley thought he knew the answer when he wrote: "God the first garden made, and the first city, Cain." But was he right? The weight of the classic tradition—European and American—is on Cowley's side. Despite qualifiers and hopeful aisdes, only Durkheim is guardedly optimistic. Wirth's theory symbolizes this verdict. On the one hand, he suggested that people in the city are more tolerant. But on the other hand, the more negative side, he hypothesized that city people are impersonal and detached from meaningful relationships. He suggested that the city creates a tendency toward social pathology (crime, violence, mental illness), a tendency only made worse as urban density increases.

Are these observations correct? More than 40 years have passed since the publication of Wirth's urban theory. Only now are we beginning to have the evidence necessary to answer this question.

Tolerance in the City

Early urban theory contended that the characteristic aloofness and social diversity of the city produced an atmosphere of tolerance that contrasted with the jealous parochialism of the village and small town. Indeed, for most of us, our urban experiences are linked somehow to the unusual and the unexpected, which we take in stride because, well, because we're in the city!

Researchers who have taken a close look at the relationship between urban life and tolerance tend to conclude that this contention is only partially valid. Although greater tolerance of others' life-styles and attitudes is more prevalent in cities (in comparison with rural areas, for example), recent work suggests that factors other than living in the city may account for this difference. For example, sociologists have known for some time that higher levels of wealth and education are associated with higher levels of tolerance. If greater percentages of wealthy and highly educated people live in the city than in other environments, as is generally known to be the case, then the tolerance that exists in the city may be as much a product of these factors as it is of any uniquely urban trait. This "importation" idea (Fischer 1971) suggests that the city may be tolerant for reasons quite different from those advanced by the classic theorists. In addition, it has been suggested (Karp, Stone, and Yoels 1977) that young people who are single or married without children may further advance tolerance in urban areas where they are numerous.

Moreover, the difference in tolerance attitudes that does exist between the city and the countryside has declined over time. Not so long ago, it *was* true that cities, generally, were areas of greater tolerance than towns, villages, and rural areas. But, as modern technology has spread, particularly television, noncity dwellers have been exposed, if only vicariously, to all the different types of people that live in cities. As a result, people who live in noncity environments have increased their levels of tolerance (Willets, Bealer, and Crider 1973).

Much more important than the city in predicting people's levels of tolerance, Abrahamson and Carter (1986) found, was the region of the country in which they lived. Thus, people who lived in the East and West, whether they lived in cities or not, were more tolerant of others than people who lived in the Midwest or South. In other words, it seems that subcultural beliefs (such as the general attitude of Californians that almost any life-style, providing it does not impinge on the life-style of others, is acceptable) are more important in determining tolerance levels than the mere fact that people live in a city.

In summary, it seems that Wirth was only minimally correct when he suggested that cities generate tolerant attitudes. While it is true that people in cities have more tolerant attitudes than people who live in other environments, that difference appears to be declining as time passes and to be much more a product of other factors, like wealth and regional differences, than the city itself.

Impersonality in the City

The dominant character of urban relationships suggested by most of the classical theorists was that urbanites would be part of a vast, lonely crowd, anonymous and essentially indifferent to one another. At its most basic level, this argument is built on numerical logic. As the number of people in social contact becomes larger, relationships become "distributed" more broadly; thus, greater impersonality inevitably must follow. Wirth summarized this argument by saying: "Increase in the number of inhabitants of a community beyond a few hundred is bound to limit the possibility of each member of the community knowing all the others personally" (1964, p. 70).

For some time, however, the "urban anonymity" thesis has been subject to widespread criticism based on evidence that many urbanites do not seem to be a lonely lot living the way Wirth and others implied. For example, as early as the 1940s, William F. Whyte's *Street Corner Society* (1943), a study of an Italian immigrant area in an eastern city, revealed the existence of strong family, neighborhood, and friendship ties. A large number of other studies (Bell and Boat 1957; Greer 1962; Bruce 1970) also found that primary ties were not incompatible with city living. Indeed, in some areas of the city—ethnic neighborhoods, for example—such ties appear to be as intense and intimate as any ever uncovered in rural areas.

But perhaps these are the exceptions. What of the lonely crowd living in all those high rises, the people who don't know any of their neighbors?

Doesn't Wirth's theory accurately describe them? Recent research suggests that this idea also may be greatly exaggerated. While it may be true that one does not necessarily know one's urban neighbors, and that one may make considerable effort to maintain personal privacy, this does not mean that the urban dweller has no personal relationships. Indeed, what seems to be significant about the urban environment is not the lack of ties of attachment but how these ties *vary*. That is, cities seem to encourage *alternative* types of relationships more than other environments do.

Harvey Cox (1965) provided some insight into this by recounting the activity of several ministers who undertook a survey of urban high-rise apartment residents. Cox reported that the ministers were "shocked" to learn that these urbanites "whom they expected to be lonely and desperate for relationships did not want to meet their neighbors socially. . . ." Indeed, Cox explained that one of the main reasons people had for moving to high-rise apartments in the first place was "to escape the relationships forced on them by the lack of anonymity in the village."

The implication is clear. The city can provide an opportunity for people, should they *choose* to do so, to avoid the often stifling intensity of less dense settings. This is an exercise in the positive freedom Durkheim saw in the city.

Even the most "private" urban dwellers usually have meaningful personal relationships. Think of urban people you know. Most have friends and relatives, but not always in the same building or neighborhood. To expect urban friendship and intimacy to be local, as they usually are in the village, is a fundamental mistake (Macionis 1978; Wellman 1979).

Other examples of urban connectedness abound. The telephone makes extensive contact possible without actual face-to-face interaction; the specialized groups to which a person may belong provide a distinct set of interpersonal contacts. Consider the proliferation in recent years of voluntary associations in cities, such as film societies, singles' bars, health and natural food centers, karate clubs, meditation and yoga centers, "stop smoking" groups, and physical fitness centers. People come to these organizations, often from all over the urban area, to establish primary relationships.

Suzanne Keller, in *The Urban Neighborhood* (1968), suggested that urban "neighboring" varies markedly—from active and intense relationships to impersonal nods. What pattern neighboring assumes seems to be a matter of group social position (working-class neighborhoods are often "tighter" than those of the upper middle class), stage of life (single people "on the move" typically have fewer personal ties than do families), or personal choice. Such was the argument of Herbert Gans (1962), who, in a stinging critique, concludes that the "impersonality" that Wirth saw in the city *as a whole* characterizes, at best, only the most poverty-stricken and down-and-out of the city's residents.

Wirth's mistake, and that of other classic theorists, was to allow the more visible aspects of city life, its *public* demeanor, to become the basis of his theory about urban living *in general*. Although, following Park, he did acknowledge the neighborhood element in city life, he tended to focus his attention on "street behavior." He saw, of course, the hustling, competing, apparently lonely crowd. By not examining more closely the *private* lives of the city's citizens, he inadvertently distorted urban life into a stereotype of impersonality.

The case has been made most recently by Claude Fischer (1981). In a study of over 1,000 people living in cities and towns in northern California, Fischer found that in the private sphere—that is, with their neighbors, friends, and relatives—urbanites are not the least bit impersonal. They act as one would expect intimates to act: intimately. However, in the public sphere, when urbanites encountered people and groups they did not know, they adopted an aura of impersonality and reserve. Perhaps this is one reason that some city residents do not help other urbanites in trouble—in the Kitty Genovese case, for example. They simply do not know them, and, having their own intimate commitments, their own trials and tribulations, they do not wish to know them. However, if they *did* know the person in trouble, they might readily intervene.

In the same way we must be careful not to accept an exaggerated view of *rural* public life. For example, contentions about the supposed harmony of village existence (Toennies's *gemeinschaft*) have been shaken by the discovery of deeply rooted conflict and distrust. In his study of Tepoztlán, a village in Mexico, Oscar Lewis (1960) described village life as fraught with tensions and feuds, and interpersonal relations as commonly distrustful. Similarly, other research in small towns and local neighborhoods casts doubt on the idealized, *gemeinschaft* view of such areas (Vidich and Bensman 1968; Lee 1985).

We are led, then, to the conclusion that the early study of both rural and urban places suffered somewhat from what might be called a "misplaced concreteness" (Cahnman and Heberle 1971). It is vital not to make the mistake of taking such polarized constructions as *gemeinschaft* and *gesellschaft*, or mechanical and organic solidarity, as synonymous with such real, concrete settings as actual villages and cities. While the overall social order of the city may place greater emphasis upon *gesellschaft* characteristics, and while the village may tend more toward *gemeinschaft* characteristics, it is incorrect to assume that either *gemeinschaft* or *gesellschaft* exists in any absolute, concrete sense. There is an important difference between the statements that one commonly sees more strangers in cities and that cities are impersonal. In some ways they are; in other ways, they most certainly are not.

Density and Urban Pathology

Perhaps the most provocative idea put forth by the classical theorists—particularly Simmel, Park, and Wirth—was that human beings react to increasing population density with psychological disorder (such as mental illness) or antisocial behavior (crime or aggression, for instance). Such suggestions were extremely influential in the field for a generation and, on the face of it, appear to be reasonable.

One source of support for this hypothesis is our own common sense. Probably all of us have experienced some measure of frustration and aggression in crowded settings: trying to push our way through a turnstile at a football stadium or fuming as thousands of cars coalesce in a massive traffic jam. It is easy to assume that the place where this occurs—the city—is responsible for our feeling. But is this correct? Is our response really a reaction to the condition of urban crowding, or are we merely experiencing a sense of frustration, much the same as we might feel if our car broke down along a lonely country road?

This common-sense conclusion that the city is somehow at fault also is linked to our experience on the city streets. We see a drunk lying in the gutter, a patently mentally ill man panhandling for quarters (a dime will no longer do), and the occasional argument or fight in the city streets. "It's the city," we say. And, it is true, in terms of absolute numbers there are more of these events in cities. But there are drunks in suburbs and rural areas, too, as well as fisticuffs and mentally ill people. The only difference may be that in the city these experiences are often more public. Where only a few knew "crazy Uncle Jethro" in the small town, thousands of people know such urban "characters" as the "Duck Lady" of Philadelphia. Common sense, in other words, may not always be as reasonable as it appears.

A second source of the alleged linkage between density and pathology is research that appears to have some bearing on the quality of urban life. For example, Calhoun (1962, p. 139) found that high density in rat populations produced a reaction he termed a "behavioral sink"—an environment where pathologies such as aborted pregnancies, sexual deviation, and cannibalism abounded. Although Calhoun made no attempt to suggest human beings would respond in similar fashion to conditions of crowding, Edward Hall argued that such a connection is not only plausible but is accurately descriptive of urban life. "The implosion of the world population into cities everywhere," Hall wrote, "is creating a series of destructive behavioral sinks more lethal than the hydrogen bomb" (1966, p. 155). Hall warned that if no corrective measures were taken, people in densely crowded areas could "destroy the city." Very scary stuff, indeed. This idea is elaborated in Cityscape 4-3.

Hall realized that different groups of people—whites and blacks, for example—might have different cultural expectations about spatial behavior. Yet, he appeared to believe that all of these different reactions have a *biological* basis, and the human species, like rats and other animals, has a genetically given need for a certain amount of space. If that built-in barrier is transgressed, he asserted, pathology inevitably would result; hence, the "sink."

There are at least two problems with this argument. First, no one yet has been able to locate any genetic code for spatial behavior (or any other pattern of behavior) in humans. Until such a linkage can be demonstrated, projecting onto human beings living in cities what we know about animal pathology and overcrowding is highly questionable. It may well be, for example, that people's perceived needs for space are entirely *learned* and that they react negatively to violations of their learned spatial expectations much as they would to an insult to their learned religious beliefs.

Second, as evidence for his thesis, Hall points to the high incidence of "social problems" (illness, crime) in densely settled areas of the city. Frequently, those cited are lower-class and ethnic areas. But such associations may be spurious rather than causal. By this, we mean that illness, crime, and crowding may appear together because all are caused by some other factor(s), such as racial discrimination, massive unemployment, or widespread poverty (Fischer 1984).

Whatever the difficulties with Hall's thesis, the idea of a linkage between pathology and density has proved intriguing. Other sociologists have tried to determine the effects of crowding on people in two ways: (1) by undertaking controlled laboratory studies where density is increased and the reaction observed and (2) by studying crowding levels in an entire city. In the laboratory studies (Griffitt and Veitch 1971; Freedman, Klevansky, and Ehrlich 1971; Stokols, Rall, Pinner, and Schopler 1973) the results are mixed. Some studies note increases in anxiety and hostility (among men but apparently not women) as density conditions are increased; others note neither pattern.

CITYSCAPE 4-3

O Rotten Gotham! Sliding into the Behavioral Sink

Journalist Tom Wolfe spent some time with Edward Hall in the late 1960s. He put his impressions of Hall's thesis into his own inimitable style.

I just spent two days with Edward T. Hall, an anthropologist, watching thousands of my fellow New Yorkers short-circuiting themselves into hot little twitching death balls with jolts of their own adrenalin. Dr. Hall says it is overcrowding that does it. Overcrowding gets the adrenalin going, and the adrenalin gets them hyped up. And here they are, hyped up, turning bilious, nephritic, queer, autistic, sadistic, barren, batty, sloppy, hot-in-the-pants, chancred-on-the-flankers, leering, puling, numb—the usual in New York, in other words, and God knows what else. Dr. Hall has the theory that overcrowding has already thrown New York into a state of behavioral sink. . . . Among animals, the sink winds up with a "population collapse" or "massive die off." O rotten Gotham. . . .

It got to be easy to look at New Yorkers as animals, especially looking down from some place like a balcony at Grand Central at the Rush Hour Friday afternoon. The floor was filled with the poor white humans, running around, dodging, blinking their eyes, making a sound like a pen full of starling rats or something. . . .

"If it weren't for this ceiling"— [Dr. Hall] is referring to the very high ceiling in Grand Central— "this place would be unbearable with this kind of crowding. And yet they'll probably never 'waste' space like this again."

They screech! And the adrenal glands in all those poor white animals enlarge, micrometer by micrometer, to the size of cantalopes. Dr. Hall pulls a Minox camera out of a holster he has on his belt and starts shooting away at the human scurry. The Sink! . . .

We really got down in there by walking down into the Lexington Avenue line subway stop under Grand Central. We inhaled those nice fluffy fumes of human sweat, urine, effluvia, and sebaceous secretions. One old female human was already stroked out on the upper level, on a stretcher, with two policemen standing by. The other humans barely looked at her. They rushed into line. They bellied each other, haunch to paunch, down the stairs. Human heads showed through the gratings. The species North American tried to create bubbles of space around themselves, about a foot and a half in diameter—

"See, he's reacting against the line," says Dr. Hall.

—but the species Mediterranean presses on in. The hell with the bubbles of space. The species North American resents that, this male human behind him presses forward toward the booth . . . *breathing* on him, he's disgusted, he pulls out of the line entirely, the species Mediterranean resents him for resenting it, and neither of them realizes what the hell they are getting irritable about exactly. And in all of them the old adrenals grow another micrometer.

Dr. Hall whips out the Minox. Too perfect! The bottom of The Sink!

Source: Tom Wolfe, *The Pump House Gang* (New York: Bantam, 1969), pp. 233–235.

No study, however, notes any decreased ability to complete tasks with increased crowding.

The difficulty with such studies is twofold. On the one hand, they are artificial. Even if consistent results had been observed, could we safely assume that laboratory conditions parallel the conditions of the city as a whole? On the other hand, the results observed still may be as much a product of learned expectations about how to react to crowding as they are a product of any intrinsic reaction to crowding itself.

In the studies that deal with entire cities and crowding, a controversy rages. In a recent review of all studies in the area, Choldin concluded generally that "the density-pathology hypothesis fails to be confirmed in urban areas" (1978, p. 109; *cf.* Baldassare, 1979, pp. 191–194). A year later, that conclusion was challenged by the publication of evidence supporting the conclusion that crowding *does* cause both psychological and social problems. Based on a sample of Chicago residents, who were selected to minimize the effects of such social conditions as age, sex, and race, Gove, Hughes, and Galle (1979) reported that crowding measured objectively (number of persons per room) and subjectively (extent of social demands

*A close look at the lives of urbanites reveals they have no greater prob-
lems of psychological distress than people in other types of settlement.
Most city dwellers cope and cope well. (© Marcia Weinstein 1976)*

and lack of privacy) was related to poor mental health and poor social relationships, both in and, to a lesser extent, outside the home. Further, they advanced the conclusion that quality of child care and even physical health may be diminished by crowding.

Disagreeing entirely, Booth, Johnson, and Edwards (1980), authors of a Toronto study that showed no effects of crowding on pathology, reanalyzed the Chicago data and argued that Gove and his associates had seriously misinterpreted their evidence. Gove and Hughes (1980) retorted (not surprisingly) that it was actually Booth and *his* team who were woefully misinterpreting the evidence. The issue continues to be hotly debated (Gove and Hughes 1983; Choldin 1985).

Urban Malaise

A last hypothesis put forth by most of the classical theorists concerned "urban malaise." It suggested that, conditions of density aside, the urban environment created a mental "sickness"—loneliness, depression, anxiety—much more frequently than did any other type of settlement. This has not been demonstrated either.

In a fairly early study of the malaise hypothesis, Claude Fischer found that, regardless of place of residence (rural area, village, city), people seem to demonstrate about the same quality of mental health (Fischer 1973). Indeed, if any trend was observed, it was for the city dweller to be more content than the country resident. (Fischer was quick to note, however, that this is not necessarily a result of the city as such, but may be a product of the generally greater affluence that urban residents enjoy.) These findings were preceded by an in-depth study of Manhattan residents by Leo Srole (1972). Questioning 1,660 New Yorkers in the 1950s and 695 of the same group again in the 1970s, Srole found that the mental health of New Yorkers was slightly better than that of rural residents. He also found that mental health, especially of women, had improved dramatically over the interval between the two samples (Hackler 1979). Similar results have been reported more recently (Freedman 1978; Kadushin 1983).

Making the point even more strongly, Weisner (1981), in a review of studies of the effects of cities on children in many different countries, concluded that the case of the classic theorists was undemonstrated. Cities apparently do not make children any more stressed and neurotic than other types of environments. In addition, the stress that was observed in some urban children seemed to be more the product of rapid change in their lives than the city itself. For example, children moving to the city from the country experienced some increase in stress. However, such an increase in stress is regularly observed in people who have had other major changes in their lives—such as the death of a loved one, loss of employment, or being in a catastrophe (like a fire or hurricane).

Apparently, then, the city doesn't create greater psychological distress. In fact, the higher population density of urban places has positive effects—for example, making more people socially accessible to each other (Verbrugge and Taylor 1980). We can conclude that the vast majority of city dwellers seem to deal quite well with their environment; see Box 4-6.

Overall, the research evidence that relates to the specific claims of the classic theorists about the nature of city life does not strongly bear them out. We have seen that although the city is clearly not a heaven, neither is it the hell some thought it to be. The city is more tolerant than other types of settlement, it is not as impersonal as many thought, and it apparently does not produce greater rates of malaise. Finally, the claim that its density increases pathology has not yet been settled conclusively, but on balance the evidence seems to favor the conclusion that it does not. On the basis of what we now know, there is reason for more optimism than is shown by most classic theorists. People don't inevitably "go bad" in the city. The reality, in other words, is both more complex and more hopeful than the myths.

The New Urban Sociology

All this research has produced a shift in the way many urbanists approach their subject matter. As we have just seen, the classical hypotheses about the city advanced by Simmel, Wirth, and others have not stood the test of careful scrutiny. Some have been shown to be false; others require serious

---

> ### BOX 4-6
> ### How City Dwellers Cope— and Cope Well
>
> How is it possible, given the fast pace and obvious stresses of urban life, that city residents can maintain mental health comparable to that of country folks? One explanation offered by experts: the relationship between stress and mental and physical pathology is dependent not so much on the nature of the stress as on the individual's perception of it. The brain has been called a stimulus-reduction system, a means to reduce, in order to comprehend, the nearly infinite number of stimuli that reach the senses at any given moment. It is an aspect of the brain that seems tailor made for life in the city.
>
> An out-of-towner caught in midtown Manhattan at rush hour, for example, may feel under enormous pressure and strain. But the New Yorker, with his stimulus-reduction mechanism operating at full steam, hardly feels any special stress at all. By the same token, the big-city residents may ignore the loud, the profane, the drunk and the demented—phenomena that might compromise the mental equilibrium of the uninitiated.
>
> And there are statistics to back up such theories. A survey of the National Center for Health Statistics sought to find the incidence of stress-related, chronic health problems, such as hypertension and heart disease, among those over 65 years of age. The results: 47.8 per 100 farm residents; 47.5 for small-town residents; 40.5 for city residents.
>
> Source: Tim Hackler, "The Big City Has No Corner on Mental Illness," *New York Times Magazine*, Dec. 19, 1979, pp. 136, 138.

---

modification. Such findings have occasioned the creation of what John Walton (1981) calls "the new urban sociology."

The hallmark of this approach is that urbanists are no longer as quick to believe that the city itself dramatically affects social life. Rather, the city is an environment in which important social processes occur—politics, religion, interpersonal relations, economic activity. We shall investigate the details of how all these processes (and others) work in an urban setting.

Indeed, if the studies of the past two decades have taught us anything, it is that all of these processes are intertwined in a complex web of relationships. For example, at the end of his study of the city's supposed negative effects on mental health, Charles Kadushin (1983) concludes that one of the reasons we have had difficulty researching this hypothesis is that many variables intervene between the hypothesized cause—the city—and the hypothesized effect—poorer mental health. This is not to say that the task of the urban researcher is impossible—far from it. Progress, as we have just seen, has been made. However, the task is certainly more difficult than the early urbanists realized.

In addition, the new urban researchers emphasize an important fact: The city *never* exists in a "pure" state. It is always shaped by a historical, cultural, and physical setting. For example, the capitalist city has very different characteristics from the socialist city; the Greek cities of the fifth century B.C. had very different characteristics from the Greek cities of today.

All this is a way of coming around, once again, to Max Weber's approach to city studies. As you will recall, Weber stressed the need to study the city as a phenomenon situated in space and time. But Weber's approach, for a long period, was passé in urban sociology. Excited by the hypotheses of Wirth and others, urbanists forgot his cautioning words. Now, nearly seven decades later, we are beginning to see the wisdom of his vision.

Finally, the new approach to urban studies is committed to an evaluative dimension. Like the classical theorists, most contemporary urbanists are concerned with how urban existence affects quality of life. Thus, one of the main objectives of the new urban sociology is to come up with policy recommendations about how the cities of the future might be structured differently to make people's lives more enjoyable.

Conclusion

The context in which urban sociology emerged was one of incredible urban change. Indeed, it was probably that ferment which was responsible for sociologists noticing the city as an object of study in the first place. What have we learned from them?

In essence, they did two things. They suggested what aspects of the city urban sociologists should focus on; and they attempted specific analyses of the nature of the city.

In the latter instance, they had successes and failures. On the positive side they correctly saw in the city elements of social life not prominent elsewhere. They saw the city as having a more complex division of labor, specialized occupations, more formalized interaction patterns, more rationality, and a distinctive tempo of life having social-psychological consequences. On the negative side, they erred rather markedly in some of their specific claims about the nature of the city. They were right about greater tolerance, but exaggerated the city's impersonality, and seem on the whole to have been wrong about urban pathology. The context in which they wrote played a significant role in these misperceptions. Seeing cities growing by the millions with seemingly unconquerable problems, they reasoned that the city itself must be the cause of these ills.

A second cause of their erroneous hypotheses about the city is contained in the limitations of their individual perspectives. Not one of the classical theorists utilized the full complement of perspectives reflected in their work collectively. Toennies and Durkheim employed the comparison of oppositional types but did not consider the city in concrete historical settings. Simmel added the social-psychological dimension, although he too considered only cities of one time and place. Weber argued for the importance of exploring cities in cross-cultural and historical perspective. Alas, Weber wrote little about the modern city, perhaps a subtle way of indicating that he—like all his colleagues except Durkheim—also saw it in a negative light.

Park and Wirth both provided breakthroughs. Park demanded that on-site city research be an integral part of urban sociology, thereby providing the mechanism for getting behind the surface impressions of the urban environment. Ironically, his focus on urban problems and his lack of a comparative historical frame led him to the same negative conclusions about the city as others.

Wirth then tried to build a theory of the city. He tried to put together the suggestions of his colleagues and explain how the city worked. A major difficulty was that he built his theory on Park's skewed data base and on the somewhat misleading evaluations of the European tradition.

Recent research has shown that the specific claims made by Wirth and his colleagues were largely incorrect. Such claims saw the city as the *cause* of greater impersonality, poorer mental health, and the like. The new urban sociology, which has emerged in the wake of the classical urbanists' failing theories, sees the city as existing in a complex historical, cultural, and physical setting. All these elements play a role in how the city operates, and all must be carefully examined by systematic research.

Thus, in the end, what we take from the classical tradition is its interest in urban studies per se and its combined model of urban analysis. We must have a sociology that (1) examines the city on both its social-structural and psychosocial dimensions, (2) studies actual cities in historical and comparative perspective, (3) attempts to build an overarching theory of the city, and (4) evaluates cities in terms of the quality of human life. It will be the task of the remaining chapters to do justice to this legacy.

CHAPTER 5
The Urban Experience

Why are cities so stimulating? Why do they almost demand from us reactions of admiration or aversion? Georg Simmel, whom we discussed in the last chapter, suggested this answer: The city is a place of tremendous concentration of buildings, images, and people. As such it creates an "intensification of nervous stimulation" characteristic of no other form of human settlement. Everywhere you turn, something demands response, as Box 5-1, depicting a scene from turn-of-the-century New York, illustrates.

How do we make sense of this higgledy-piggledy, chockablock creation that is the city? Simmel's answer was that we quickly learn to categorize the city's diversity. We decide what to pay attention to and what to ignore. His American colleague, Louis Wirth, concurred by suggesting that we develop "visual recognition and mental mapping" of the city. Alas, neither theorist provided us with much detail about how this categorization and mapping process worked. It is the purpose of this chapter to fill this gap, to sketch the outlines of the characteristic elements of our social psychology of the city.

The Physical Environment

Kevin Lynch

Essentially, people react to the city as both a physical and a social environment. Intrigued by how people made sense of the city's physical complexity, urbanist Kevin Lynch interviewed people in Boston, Jersey City, and Los Angeles. In each city, Lynch studied a central region approximately 2.5 miles long and 1.5 miles wide. He showed his respondents a map of the region and asked them to describe it. He found first that most had a characteristic *image of the city* that he defined as "the generalized mental picture of the [city's] external physical world" held by an individual (1960, p. 4).

(Before reading the next few paragraphs, take a moment and think of the city you know best. On a piece of paper draw as detailed a map of it as you can, putting in everything of importance you can recall.)

Most of Lynch's respondents developed their image of the city in a similar fashion. First, their

---

BOX 5-1
The Complexity of the City

Upon a wet evening . . . two interminable rows of cars, pulled by slipping horses, jangled along a prominent side street. A dozen cabs, with coat-enshrouded drivers, clattered to and fro. Electric lights, whirring softly, shed a blurred radiance. A flower-dealer, his feet tapping impatiently, his nose and his wares glistening with raindrops, stood behind an array of roses and chrysanthemums. Two or three theatres emptied a crowd upon the storm-swept pavements. Men pulled their hats over their eyebrows and raised their collars to their ears. Women shrugged impatient shoulders in their warm cloaks and stopped to arrange their skirts for a walk through the storm. People who had been constrained to compar-

ative silence for two hours burst into a roar of conversation, their hearts still kindling from the glowings of the stage.

The pavements became tossing seas of umbrellas. Men stepped forth to hail cabs or cars, raising their fingers in varied forms of polite request or imperative demand. An endless procession wended towards elevated stations. An atmosphere of pleasure and prosperity seemed to hang over the throng, born, perhaps, of good clothes and of two hours in a place of forgetfulness.

In the mingled light and gloom of an adjacent park, a handful of wet wanderers, in attitudes of chronic dejection, were scattered among the benches. . . .

The restless doors of saloons,

clashing to and fro, disclosed animated rows of men before bars and hurrying barkeepers.

A concert-hall gave to the street faint sounds of swift, machine-like music, as if a group of phantom musicians were hastening. . . .

The shutters of the tall buildings were closed like grim lips. The structures seemed to have eyes that looked over them, beyond them, at other things. Afar off the lights of the avenues glittered as if from an impossible distance. Streetcar bells jingled with a sound of merriment.

Source: Stephen Crane, *Maggie* (New York: Modern Library, 1937; originally published 1893), pp. 324–328.

---

images emerged as part of a two-way process: (1) the physical environment was constructed in such a way as to suggest distinctions among its various parts, and (2) people, observing these parts, ordered them in a way that was personally meaningful.

For example, in Boston (see Figure 5-1) the large park known as the Boston Common and Public Gardens separates various aspects of downtown from one another. To the west of the park is the residential area known as Back Bay, with its characteristic three- or four-story apartment houses. To the north is the wealthier Beacon Hill district and the State House. To the east and south of the park is most of Boston's central business district, full of high-rise office buildings, stores, and entertainment facilities.

To a person living, shall we say, in a small apartment house just to the west of the Gardens and the Common, the park area may be the dominant element in his image of the city because he goes there every afternoon for walks. He knows every fountain, footpath, and tree. About the rest

of downtown he may know little. In his mind other districts may be indistinct and he may be unsure how to get about in them.

On the other hand, to another Bostonian the park may have little significance in an image of the city. Working in the high-rise offices on the east side of the park, this person may have little desire to use the Garden. For her, the distinct image is of the downtown buildings where she works. She has a detailed knowledge of each building, of where the good restaurants are, and of the quickest way to get from one building or street to another.

Lynch's second discovery was that people tended to use five common categories when describing the city. *Paths* were "channels along which the observer customarily . . . moves. They may be streets, walkways, transit lines, canals, railroads" (1960, p. 47). *Edges* were boundaries between two areas. They might be shores, walls, wide streets, or breaks between buildings and open space. *Districts* were medium-to-large sections of the city. Examples in Boston that people

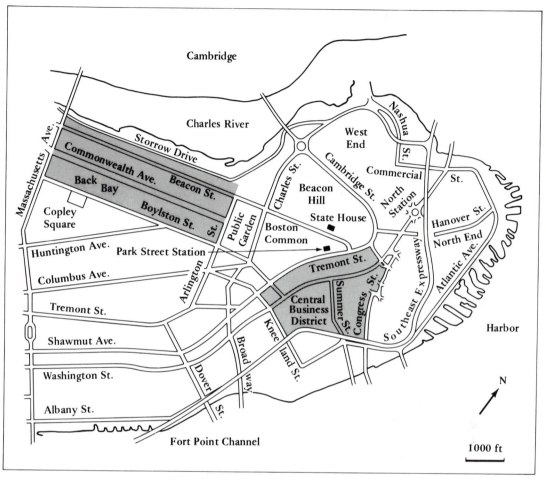

Figure 5-1 *Downtown Boston. Source: Kevin Lynch,* The Image of the
City, *1960. Reprinted by permission of MIT Press, Cambridge, Mass.*

commonly noted were "Back Bay," "Beacon
Hill," "the Common," the "shopping district."
Nodes were intense points of activity, such as a
railroad terminal, a square, or a street-corner
hangout. They were often the place to which
"paths" led. Finally, *landmarks* were physical objects singled out for reference, such as a building,
sign, store, dome, gas station, or hill. Lynch
found that city people used such landmarks continually and employed them, as well as paths, as
primary referencing tools in telling others how to
get around the city (1960, pp. 47–50). (To test
whether Lynch's categories are similar to your
own, refer to the map of the city you drew a few

minutes ago. You should note evidence of thinking in Lynch's categories.)

A third finding was a tendency for people to
have common concepts of at least some paths,
edges, and so forth; that is, what was a path to one
was a path to many. For example, in Boston (Figure 5-1) virtually everyone recognized the Charles
River as a major edge separating one large district
of the city ("downtown") from another (Cambridge). Similarly, most people mentioned "Mass.
Ave." to the west and the Southeast Expressway to
the east as edges. Main paths were Beacon Street,
"Comm. Ave.," and Boylston and Tremont
Streets. Common nodes mentioned were Copley

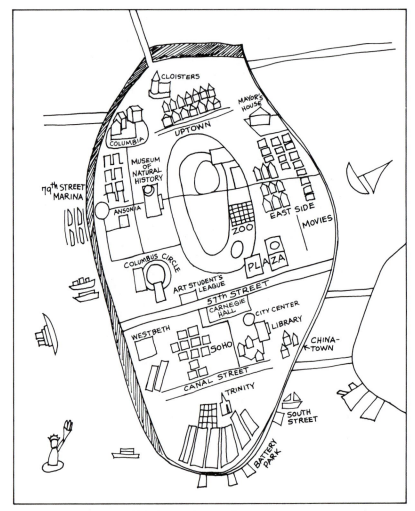

Figure 5-2 Mental maps of Manhattan. Source: Susana Duncan, "Mental Maps of New York," *New York*, Dec. 18, 1977, pp. 52–53. Reprinted by permission of Alexandra Milgram.

Square (site of the "BPL," the Boston Public Library), North Station (a railroad and subway terminal), and Park Street Station. This last was particularly interesting because, located at the southeast corner of the Boston Common, it is quite unprepossessing on the surface. Below ground, however, Park Street Station is a classic example of an urban node: the junction of Boston's three main subway lines, it is constantly abuzz with activity.

Although Lynch found that people in all three cities held many aspects of their image in com-

mon, he also found distinct differences in the complexity and vitality of each city's image. In Boston, virtually everyone interviewed could identify *numerous* paths, edges, nodes, districts and landmarks. In Jersey City, even long-term residents could identify only a few of these elements. Often confused or unsure about what existed in different parts of their city, Lynch found it significant that the landmark most frequently mentioned by Jersey City's residents was the looming, overpowering New York City skyline. (As if in acknowledgment of this weak image, a

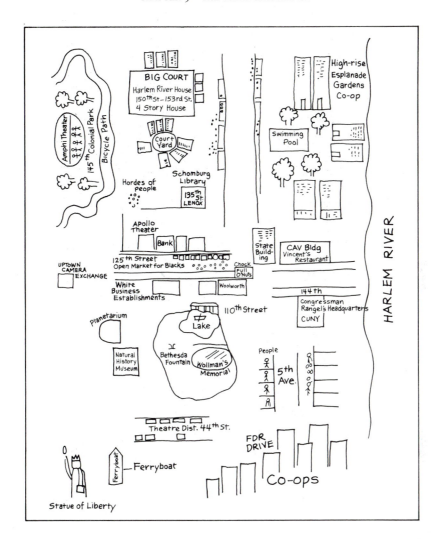

recently successful Jersey City pop group took "The Manhattans" as their name.) This is how Lynch summarizes his findings about Jersey City:

> When asked for a general characterization of the city, one of the most common remarks was that it was not a whole, that it had no center, but was rather a collection of many hamlets. The question: "What first comes to mind with the words 'Jersey City'?," so easy to answer for Bostonians, proved to be a difficult one. Again and again, subjects repeated that "nothing special" came to mind, that the city was hard to [characterize], that it had no
>
> distinctive sections. . . . [T]he general environment was persistently referred to with the words, "old," "dirty," "drab." The streets were repeatedly referred to as "cut up. . . ."
>
> Many remarks came out about the indistinguishability of the physical scene:
>
> "It's much the same all over . . . it's more or less just common to me. I mean, when I go up and down the streets, it's more or less the same thing—Newark Avenue, Jackson Avenue, Bergen Avenue. I mean, sometimes they're more or less just the same; there's nothing to differentiate them." (1960, pp. 29–31)

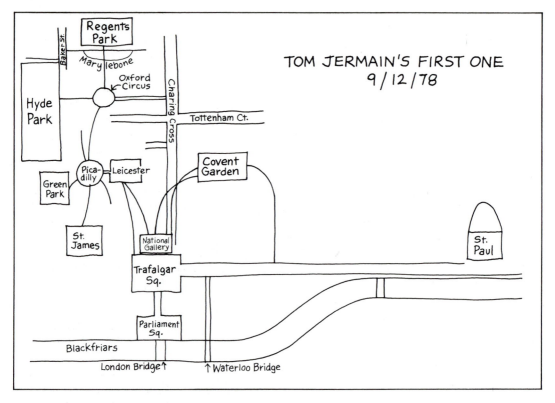

Figure 5-3 Tom Jermain's changing mental maps of London. Source: Tom Jermain. Reproduced with permission.

It was this difference in overall images of the urban environment that led Lynch to a fourth point: Cities differ, sometimes markedly, in *imagability*. A city's imagability is important for two reasons. First, people order the urban environment to give themselves a working knowledge and a kind of emotional security regarding what the city contains. A strong urban image facilitates the relatively easy acquisition of this knowledge and sets people more at east emotionally. Second, a highly legible urban environment "heightens the potential depth and intensity of the human experience" (1960, p. 5). It invites us to experience more, to involve ourselves more in the life of the city. These qualities Lynch believes to be essential aspects of a positive urban environment.

Importantly, although Lynch's original sample of respondents was small, his basic findings have been replicated in further studies of both large and small cities as well as in cities in other societies (Lynch 1984).

Stanley Milgram

One of the most intriguing aspects of Lynch's work was his discovery that when people were asked to draw their city, very different drawings emerged. Individuals' maps frequently showed such distortions as large gaps in or misplacement of districts, landmarks, and paths. (Refer back to the map you drew of your city in the following discussion.)

In an attempt to understand why such oddities should occur, psychologist Stanley Milgram studied how New Yorkers and Parisians constructed mental maps of their cities. In both cases he found similar results. People constructed mental maps based on their *personal experience, their interests,*

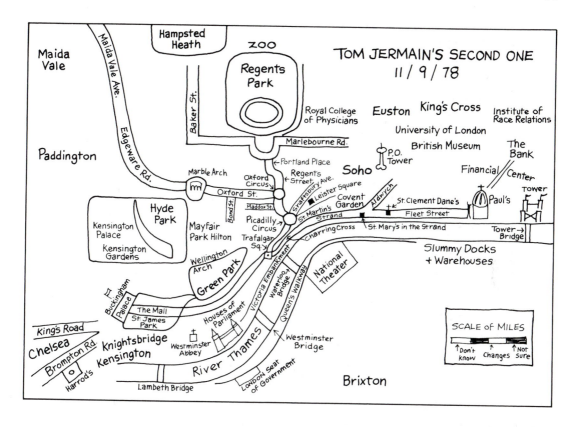

and *their knowledge of the socially recognized "important areas" of the city* (Milgram 1972; Duncan 1977).

In Figure 5-2 you will see drawings of two people's mental maps of Manhattan. Painter Susan Rowland's Manhattan (page 130) emphasizes details of the Upper West Side where she lives, the Upper East Side, and such artistic and cultural centers as the "Cloisters," "SoHo," "movies," the "library." New York's famed Midtown area is virtually absent. In contrast, teacher Cynthia Blanchard's Manhattan (page 131) emphasizes the Harlem district where she lives. Featured prominently are swimming pools, parks, and high-rise apartment buildings. The details of Midtown and lower Manhattan, with one or two exceptions, are absent.

Mental maps, Milgram found, vary from person to person and no one can recreate the com-

plexity of the whole city. Moreover, everyone's image constantly changes as urban experiences deepen or as the city changes. Figure 5-3 illustrates this process with two mental maps of London drawn by Tom Jermain, a student who went there in 1977. In the first map, drawn in the first two weeks of a ten-week stay, London's center city is almost completely lacking in detail and the few areas that are noted are distorted in size and often misplaced. In the second map, drawn eight weeks later, London's details, in more or less their appropriate locations, have slipped into place. The city is clearer and has become a *usable mental space*.

This, of course, is the whole point of mental maps. However partial or distorted the maps may be, people construct their own image from the complex physical reality to make the city comprehensible and useful. As Milgram noted, the city is so varied you can mold it selectively "to your own needs and peculiarities. . . . It is not hard and unyielding but takes on the impress which each individual gives to it" (cited in Duncan 1977, p. 62).

In other words, on one level there are as many Seattles as there are people who have mental maps of Seattle. To each person, this mental map *is* Seattle. On another level each of the active mental maps that Seattle's residents employ helps create the larger urban dynamic that is the real Seattle. For example, using their own maps, some people create street-corner hangouts and back-alley paths and have distinct impressions of certain districts; while other people create other hangouts (a bowling alley, perhaps) and other paths and may have decidedly different preferences about the same districts.

This has been impressively demonstrated by Donald Reitzes (1983) in a recent study of Atlanta's residents. Reitzes found that ethnicity played a large role in how people saw and used the city. Whites preferred quieter, more organized areas of the city, while blacks were more attracted to busy, noisy, and exciting places. Such preferences are probably attributable to the subcultural norms that generally characterize these two racial groups and to social class standing. Whites tend to be middle class in greater proportion than blacks, for instance, and one norm generally associated with the middle class is a quieter, more relaxed environment.

In other words, the city is a dynamic, creative, ongoing admixture of experiences. This has never been expressed more eloquently than by Chicago theorist Robert Park:

> The city . . . is something more than a congeries of individual men and of social conveniences— streets, buildings, electric lights, tramways, and telephones . . . something more, also, than a mere constellation of institutions and administrative devices—courts, hospitals, schools, police, and civil functionaries of various sorts. The city is . . . a state of mind, a body of customs and traditions, and of the organized attitudes and sentiments that inhere in these customs and are transmitted with this tradition. The city is not, in other words, merely a physical mechanism and an artificial construction.

> It is involved in the vital process of the people who compose it; it is a product of nature, and particularly of human nature. (1916; 1967, p. 1)

A final example illustrates what we have been discussing. In Cityscape 5-1 Alfred Kazin describes his return to his old neighborhood in the Brownsville district of New York. Present in his image of the city are all of Lynch's visual categories, complex interpretations of sound and smell, and a working mental map expressed in prose.

The Social Environment: *Gesellschaft*

People have to deal with more than the physical environment if they are to get along in the city. They also have to deal with large numbers of other people, most of whom they don't know and are never likely to know. How do they cope with what Ferdinand Toennies (Chapter 4) would have called the city's *gesellschaft* characteristics—its large numbers and anonymity?

The Pedestrian: Watching Your Step

At the beginning of the film A *Thousand Clowns*, Murray Burns and his nephew Nick are in Manhattan just before rush hour. Murray says, "You're about to see a terrible thing, Nick. People going to work." Suddenly the street is filled with millions of "faceless people" accompanied by marching music. This image of "the urban mass" is very common. It suggests that people on the city's streets are a bit like sheep, an undifferentiated, robotlike herd. Is this so?

Sociologist Erving Goffman (1971, Chap. 1) believed not. Behavior on the street is a very orderly, regulated set of activities that allows people to meet their personal objectives while negotiating a large crowd of unknown others. To begin with, people on the street are there for a purpose. They are going to work, to eat, to meet a friend, to catch a subway, or perhaps just to take a walk. Just because we cannot see these different motives is no reason to think they don't exist. Remember your own experiences as a city pedestrian: were you walking without purpose?

CITYSCAPE 5-1
The Streets of Brownsville

All my early life lies open to my eye within five city blocks. . . . On Belmont Avenue, Brownsville's great open street market, the pushcarts are still lined on each other for blocks, and the din is as deafening, marvelous, and appetizing as ever. . . . When I was a boy, they . . . reached halfway up the curb to the open stands of the stores; walking down the street was like being whirled around and around in a game of blind man's bluff. But Belmont Avenue is still the merriest street in Brownsville. As soon as I walked into it from Rockaway, caught my first whiff of the herrings and pickles in their great black barrels, heard the familiarly harsh, mocking cries and shouts from the market women—*"Oh you darlings! Oh you sweet ones, oh you pretty ones! Storm us! Tear us apart! Devour us!"*—I laughed right out loud, it was so good to be back among them. . . .

Chester Street. . . . The way home.

On my right hand the "Stadium"

movie house—the sanctuary every Saturday afternoon of my childhood, the great dark place of all my dream life. On my left the little wooden synagogue where I learned my duties as a Jew and at thirteen, having reached the moral estate of a man, stood up at the high desk before the Ark *(Blessed Be He, Our Lord and Our Shield!)* and was confirmed in the faith of my fathers. . . .

The block: *my* block. It was on the Chester Street side of our house, between the grocery and the back wall of the old drugstore, that I was hammered into the shape of the streets. Everything beginning at Blake Avenue would always wear for me some delightful strangeness and mildness, simply because it was not of my block, *the* block, where the clang of your head sounded against the pavement when you fell in a fist fight, and the rows of store lights on each side were pitiless, watching you. . . . [I recall] smelling the sweaty sweet dampness from the

pool in summer and the dust on the leaves as I passed under the ailanthus trees. . . .

We worked every inch of it, from the cellars and the backyards to the sickening space between the roofs. Any wall, any stoop, any curving metal edge on a billboard sign made a place against which to knock a ball; any bottom rung of a fire escape ladder a goal in basketball; any sewer cover a base. . . . *Our* life every day was fought out on the pavement and in the gutter, up against the walls of the houses and the glass fronts of the drugstore and the grocery—in and out of the fresh steaming piles of horse manure, the wheels of passing carts and automobiles, along the iron spikes of the stairway to the cellar, the jagged edge of the open garbage cans, the crumbly steps of the old farmhouses still left on one side of the street.

Source: Alfred Kazin, *A Walker in the City* (New York: Harcourt, 1951), pp. 11–12, 17, 25–26, 30–31, 39–40, 83–84.

Next, Goffman suggested that pedestrians follow an intricate set of social rules. There is a tacit traffic code for proper street behavior, just as there is a traffic code for automobiles. Goffman noted that pedestrian traffic in American cities tends to sort itself into two opposing streams, with the dividing line somewhere near the middle of the sidewalk. Within each stream, people "watch their step" in a variety of ways: (1) They keep themselves peripherally aware of obstacles, such as mailboxes, lampposts, or groups stopped on the sidewalk. (2) They subconsciously note the speed of people in front of or behind them, gauging their own speed accordingly to avoid collisions. (3) To move faster or slower than the stream, they move to the outside of the lane. (4) They develop ways of coping with impending collisions. For instance, pedestrians about to be crashed into by

an unwary walker may attempt suddenly to bring their presence to the conscious awareness of the other. (5) Similarly, they evolve ways of coping with actual collisions. A pedestrian collided with may protest, in a miffed voice, "Why don't ya look where you're going?" Such reaction is an indication that people both know the rules for pedestrian behavior and know that if they fail to live up to these rules, they can be called to task for their transgressions.

Rules of pedestrian traffic vary from culture to culture, of course. For example, in American subway stations, passengers all pile onto the escalators together, making passage by anybody behind almost impossible. In London, however, escalator passengers pile to the right side, leaving a lane on the left for anyone wishing to pass. Taking their first ride on London escalators, Americans are often a bit befuddled when, having placed themselves in the left-hand side of a ramp, people behind ask them to "please move over." Conversely, Britons riding an American subway escalator can be quite puzzled at the "rudeness" of Americans who jam up the ramp so no one can pass.

Other research has confirmed the orderliness of much of urban street behavior. To cope with many people wanting a service for which there aren't enough "servers," city dwellers have invented waiting lines (Mann 1973). There frequently are lines in fast-food restaurants, for popular films and art shows, at tollbooths, in banks, in supermarkets, and at airports. As with pedestrian behavior, there is an unspoken norm that governs behavior in lines: "Cutting in" is inappropriate. When this rule is ignored, a quick glance, a mutter, a sharp remonstrance, or even physical violence may be employed to reestablish propriety. For example, in London, a city famed for its long and patient "queue" behavior, one of the authors of this book recently saw an old lady loudly berate a younger woman who had boarded the bus out of order. The older woman then physically dragged the younger onto the sidewalk, leaving the offender in tatters and bewildered as the bus drove off.

Finally, even in that most dense and anonymous of urban worlds, the subway train at rush hour, people have evolved mechanisms for ordering and personalizing the experience. This is illustrated in Box 5-2.

By these examples, we can see that street behavior is not nearly as unsystematic as it might appear at first glance. Despite the fact that the city dweller has to deal with larger numbers of people, often in very crowded conditions, there seems ample evidence that such conditions are not necessarily problematical or dehumanizing.

A World of Strangers

In addition to coping with the city's sheer numbers, urbanites must learn to deal with another particularly urban condition: the fact that, at least when they are in public, they live in "a world of strangers," as sociologist Lyn Lofland (1973) has

---

BOX 5-2
The Subway at Rush Hour

A crowd of people surged into the Eighth Avenue express at 59th Street. By elbowing other passengers in the back, by pushing and heaving, they forced their bodies into the coaches, making room for themselves where no room had existed before. As the train gathered speed for the long run to 125th Street, the passengers settled down into small private worlds, thus creating the illusion of space between them and their fellow passengers. The worlds were built up behind newspapers and magazines, behind closed eyes or while staring at the varicolored show cards that bordered the coaches.

Source: Ann Petry, *The Street* (Boston: Houghton Mifflin, 1946), p. 27.

---

put it. She has argued that we learn to classify these unknown others in the same way that we come to make sense of the city's physical environment and its large population. We tune in to certain things about strangers to get a sense of who they really are, and we use such information to gauge how to behave toward these strangers and to anticipate their behavior toward us.

Appearance and Location. The clues we use are primarily visual. We identify strangers in terms of their *appearance* and where they are *located physically* within the city. Regarding appearance, we continually are giving others "the once-over." We note their clothing, hairstyle, jewelry, and makeup (or lack thereof), as well as what they're carrying and how they are walking. We also characterize others by their location; for example, in a district of office buildings and expensive restaurants, we expect different types of people than in a district full of all-night movie houses or pornographic bookstores.

Lofland has admitted, however, that there is nothing uniquely urban about the use of appearance and location to determine who other people are. In the small town as well, the rich still tend to dress "up," while the poor appear in less elegant clothing. Many small towns also have a clearly demarked "other side of the tracks." In the more populous city, however, Lofland has argued that

BOX 5-3
Clothes Make the Man

To a degree unknown to moderns, the resident of the preindustrial city literally "donned" his identity. The Roman citizen, for example, expressed the fact of his citizenship by wearing as decreed by law, the white toga. A "gentleman" in the Colonial cities of America was known by his "periwig." . . .

Urban elites everywhere struggled to differentiate themselves from their "inferiors" not only by the design of their dress, but by the materials as well. The cap of the medieval Frenchman was made of velvet for the elites, rough cloth for the poor. In Elizabethan England, [Gideon Sjoberg reported that] "Commoners were prohibited by law from wearing clothing fashioned from gold or silver cloth, velvet, furs, and other 'luxury' materials." Hair length also indicated status. Among the Franks, only the elite had long hair. . . .

Occupation, too, was signaled by dress. The lawyers of medieval France, for example, were distinguished by their round caps . . . and the executioners of the period were forced to wear a special coat of red or gold so that they would be readily recognizable in a crowd. . . . Each of the various types of itinerant peddlers of Peking . . . wore a distinctive costume as did the clergy of twelfth century Europe and the members of religious sects in numerous preindustrial cities.

Source: Lyn Lofland, *A World of Strangers* (New York: Basic Books, 1973), pp. 45–46.

reliance on characteristics like appearance and location is more essential. It often is not possible to "check out" a stranger by any other means because nearly everyone is a stranger to everyone else.

Interestingly, Lofland has reported that we who live in modern cities have come to rely more on spatial location for identifying strangers. For comparison, the town square in the preindustrial city often had multiple uses: schooling, religious services, parades, shopping, executions, and general loitering about by people of all classes. Because virtually anybody might be found there, the location provided few clues about who strangers were; thus, citizens learned to put great stock in appearance, as illustrated in Box 5-3.

In modern societies, however, the situation has changed. Although dress is still an important

aspect of stranger identification, it is no longer the central clue it was in preindustrial times. Dress codes have relaxed and people from all walks of life wear, without fear of censure, almost any sort of finery. There are important historical reasons for this change.

In the preindustrial city only the wealthy could afford silks and satins as basic materials or gold and silver as adornments. With the Industrial Revolution, however, the mass production of certain types of dress reduced the cost of previously expensive materials. Further, the rise of a monied (if not truly wealthy) middle class meant that these goods could be bought and worn by a large proportion of an urban population. For example, in the film *Hester Street*, there is a scene in which Jake, a Russian Jewish immigrant to New York in the early 1900s, takes his family to Central Park for an outing. Making more money than he ever did in the old country, Jake has bought himself an inexpensive suit in the best fashion of the day. As he parades around the park, he exclaims proudly: "Look at me! I'm a real American! Who could tell if I was a Jew or a Gentile?"

Unable to rely on dress as the telltale identifying tool, modern city dwellers have learned to focus on what part of the city people are in. This has been made easier by the mechanisms of land use that operate in the industrial city (see Chapter 6). By a complex process, most cities have separated into definable districts. There are usually districts for business, warehousing, residence, and entertainment. Since business people are most likely to frequent business districts, the city dweller can have some expectation that people in such areas will act in a businesslike manner. Once established, expectations about who belongs in each district highly influence who goes there.

To give one example, Huntington Avenue marks the boundary between two major districts of Boston (see Figure 5-1). On the north side of the street, there are the fasionable, upper-middle-class Back Bay and Fenway areas that include Symphony Hall, the Museum of Fine Arts, numerous shops for the rich, and art galleries. On the other side of the street—literally 20 feet away—begins the lower-class, predominantly black, Roxbury district, with severely dilapidated housing and very poor shops.

To stand at the corner of Huntington and Massachusetts avenues near Symphony Hall when the Boston Symphony Orchestra is playing is a remarkable sociological experience. On one side of the street are men in formal black-tie dress and women in ermine and pearls. On the other side are people in informal and often threadbare or tattered clothes. Strangers on both sides of the street are well aware that the appearances are symbolic of two different social worlds. Few people attending the symphony come from or go near the Roxbury side of Huntington Avenue, and few of the people on the Roxbury side cross to mingle with the symphony-goers.

Using "Stranger" Codes Creatively. With a solid knowledge of dress and spatial codes, urban dwellers can use the city more effectively. For instance, what is ostensibly public space can be transformed easily into semiprivate space. A street corner can become a hangout, a bar can develop the exclusive patronage of homosexuals, and a section of a park can be a place where people in their sixties congregate in the afternoons. On a larger scale, whole districts of cities can become home territories, or "turf," to various groups.

If outsiders enter into such spaces—for example, if a heterosexual couple enters a homosexual bar—they soon pick up cues of dress or behavior that indicate they are on semiprivate ground. At that point there are only a few choices open to the interlopers: they can beat a hasty retreat, continue uncomfortably in the strange setting, or make the best of it by becoming a part of the scene. In all cases, however, the in-group controls the situation.

This points up a crucial lesson about how people experience cities. Dress and location codes provide a *context* within which people act. They are not deterministic in a strict sense. They serve as social guidelines, and people exercise considerable choice in deciding whether to follow the codes or not. For example, we all know it is possible for people in cities to pass themselves off as something they are not by manipulating dress, space, and sometimes speech codes. A narcotics

agent may infiltrate a drug ring, and a social scientist may live anonymously in an area in hopes of learning the inside story of people's lives. Other people may "perform": people who aren't blind can hang signs on their chests, don dark eyeglasses, and beg; still others, living sedate, middle-class lives by day, come into the city to "swing" at night, retiring at evening's end to their middle-class routine again. A humorous example of one urban type invading the space of another is presented in Box 5-4.

Other casual meetings reveal that encounters with strangers can be quite pleasant. Standing in line, one may strike up a friendly conversation; or, while walking the dog in the park, one may swap stories with a dog-loving stranger. In a city far from home, people may find "friends" from their home city and pal around with them for a week's vacation. In all such cases city people *decide* how to act toward strangers.

Social Characteristics and the Urban Experience

The foregoing discussions suggest that people have evolved common mechanisms for making sense of the city. Even with such mechanisms, however, we should hardly expect the urban experience to be the same for everyone. Sociologists have known for some time that such social characteristics as class, age, sex, race, and ethnic or religious background affect experience. These factors are as much at work in the city as anywhere.

Alfred Kazin provided us with a young boy's image of the city in Cityscape 5-1. There is no doubt that Kazin's youthful years acted as a particular type of filter on his experience. Cityscape 5-2 provides other examples of the effects of social characteristics on one's awareness of the city.

In the first passage Kathryn Forbes recreates her "Mama's" image of turn-of-the-century San Francisco. Though they were by no means rich, Mama and her family were beginning to succeed in their adopted country. Mama's pride in San Francisco, the geography of which reminded her of Norway, was unbounded.

In the next passage Jonathan Raban speaks

BOX 5-4
Punks, Hippies, and the Middle Class

Picture the following: a bus, at rush hour, laden with passengers going from center-city Vancouver, British Columbia, to the suburbs. On board: various passengers, almost all middle class—neatly dressed businessmen on their way home from work, school kids in nice clothes with nicely combed hair and books under arms, mothers carrying babies in one arm and strollers in the other. In short, what you might expect.

At the back of the bus, however, sit two young people who look like refugees from the 1960s—a man and woman, both with extremely long hair, a bit unkempt, with rather tattered clothes. Everyone is doing what people do in urban *gesellschaft* situations: talking to the people next to them if they know them, looking abstractedly out the window, reading the paper or the latest popular novel.

The bus stops. Enter two other young people—punk rockers— obviously of a later generation than the hippies. A man and woman, they enter the bus and create an enormous stir. He has flaming-blue hair and his head is shaved in a Mohican cut (hair is left only in the center of the head and stands on end from the front to the back). She has flaming-orange hair, some of it teased into long spikes at the front and the sides. Both are wearing leather pants, extremely tight. She has enormous high heels. He is wearing a leather jacket and a tie, but there is no shirt under the tie, only his chest. Because the bus is crowded, they stand and murmur to each other.

The rest of the passengers gape, sneak furtive glances at the newly arrived couple, and look quickly away when one of the punkers looks in their direction. One little girl, about four or so, is flabbergasted, and with the honest-spontaneity of childhood, blurts out very loudly: "Mummy, why does that boy have *blue* hair?" There are chuckles and snickers throughout the bus, behind newspapers, looking out windows. The male punker sneered around the bus. Everyone shuts up and goes back about their business. The mother, embarrassed, whispers something to her little girl. The child, still staring, is quiet.

A couple of stops later, the punk couple gets off the bus. Everyone cranes their neck to watch them head off up the street. The woman punker turns toward the bus and gives another scathing look. People go back, quickly, to their previous routines. The bus goes on.

A moment later, the young hippie man in the back of the bus says out loud: "See. *Long* hair's not so bad, is it?"

Everyone has a good laugh.

Source: James L. Spates

---

about the difficulty he has in keeping from going "soft"—a bit crazy—"in a soft city." Yet much of his vision is shaped by *his* special social characteristics. He is a self-admitted "marginal man"—a free-lance writer, unmarried, living alone, with few friends and no local family.

Raban's experience of just hanging on contrasts sharply with that of Baltzell's typical 1940s "Philadelphia Gentleman," given in the third passage. It is difficult to imagine that such a person, rich and advantaged from birth, *ever* feared "going soft" in the city.

Finally, consider Lutie Johnson's image of New York. A black migrant from the South, Johnson has worked for years to get herself and her son out of the ghetto. Every time she has made some progress, she has seen it disappear in exploitation, robbery, or cruelty. On this particular night she is walking home and sees a robbery.

It symbolizes her inability to escape, despite increasing efforts. She begins to realize that she may *never* get out and that "the street" is part of a much larger social reality that operates along the lines of class and race.

The City as *Gesellschaft*: A Reassessment

Many early urban theorists worried about the ability of people to cope with the city's sheer physical size, its large population, and its anonymity. They feared people would be overwhelmed or become like automatons. This has not happened. People have learned to cope with the city's physical size by creating their own image of the city and by developing mental maps. They have dealt with the complexities of street behavior and the fact that most people are strangers by creating certain flexible codes of behavior. Finally, their urban

CITYSCAPE 5-2
The Varieties of Urban Experience

Mama's San Francisco

In those days, if anyone had asked Mama unexpectedly, "What nationality are you?" I believe she would have answered without hesitation, "I am a San Francis-can."

Then quickly, lest you tease her, she would add, "I mean Norve-gian, American citizen."

But her first statement would be the true one.

Because from the moment she was to step off the ferryboat, con-fused and lonely in a strange land, San Francisco was to become suddenly and uniquely her own.

"Is like Norvay," the Aunts and Mama had declared.

And straightaway she'd taken the city to her heart.

Mama learned so many things about San Francisco. She could tell you how to get to Telegraph Hill; what time the boats came in at Fisherman's Wharf; the names of the young boys who tended the teaming crab kettles along Bay Street; and where to find the blue and yellow lupines at Land's End.

The cable cars were an endless delight, and Mama's idea of a per-fect Sunday afternoon was for Papa to take us riding on them from one transfer point to another.

Papa would tell of the time Mama took out her citizenship pa-pers and astounded the solemn court by suddenly reciting the names of the streets. "Turk, Eddy, Ellis, O'Farrell," Mama had said proudly, "Geary, Post, Sutter, Bush, and Pine."

Papa said the clerk had quite a time making Mama understand that such knowledge was not nec-essary for citizenship.

And if anyone ever asked us where we were born, Mama in-structed us we should say "San Francisco." Didn't copies of our birth certificates, neatly framed and hung on the wall of Papa's and Mama's room, testify to that proud fact?

"After all," Papa used to tease her, "after all, San Francisco isn't the world."

But to Mama it was just that. The world.

The Marginal Man

I live here on a corner of the square in a borrowed flat, without property, at haphazard. By com-parison with the right family and neighborhood life of the small town, I have few attachments or continuities. My existence is lax and unshaven. I have no proper job, just an irregular series of commissions and assignments, the chores and errands of a mid-dle class hobo. . . . Freelance writers . . . tend to drift to the pe-ripheral fringe of things, habitual onlookers and overhearers. My flat is pitched on the western edge of my private version of London, a place to make forays from, scav-enging eastwards for material and odd jobs. I am on the rim, both geographically and socially, and this marginal position suits me very well. . . .

Cities are scary and imper-sonal, and the best most of us can manage is a fragile hold on our route through the streets. We cling to friends and institutions, exaggerate the importance of be-longing, fear being alone too much. The freedom of the city is enormous. Here one can choose and invent one's society, and live more deliberately than anywhere else. Nothing is fixed, the possibil-ities of personal change and re-newal are endless and open. But it is hard to learn to live as gener-ously as real citizenship de-mands. I spot in others the same mouselike caution which keeps me hugging the edge of the pave-ment, running from bolthole to bolthole, unequipped to embrace that spaciousness and privacy of city life which so often presents it-self as mere emptiness and fog.

For me a city day is a succes-sion of guarded moves, as if one was crossing a peat bog. . . . [We] need to hold on tight to avoid going completely soft in a soft city. So much of metropolitan life is just the slowing of symptoms of fright. In the city one clings to nostalgic and unreal signs of community, takes forced refuge in codes, badges and coteries; the city's life, surface and locomotion, usu-ally seems too dangerous and de-manding to live through with any confidence. The mad egotism of the man who stops you in Soho Square to tell you he is John the Baptist, or the weird rural delu-sions of another tramp nearby who fishes hopefully through a grating at the corner of Old Comp-ton Street ("Caught anything?" "I had some good bites"), seem not unlikely consequences of the ex-ercise of the freedom of the city. Its discontinuities give one ver-tigo; few people who aren't crimi-nals or psychopaths will risk themselves on the rollercoaster ride of change and incongruity which the city offers. So much of city life is an elaborate process of building up defenses against the city—the self a fortified town raised against the stranger. We hedge ourselves in behind dreams and illusions, construct make-believe villages and make-believe families.

Philadelphia Gentlemen

In 1940 the Proper Philadelphian at the apex of the pyramid of so-cial prestige and economic power in the city may be said to have had the following attributes:

1. Of English or Welsh descent,

his great-great-great-grandfather would have been a prominent Philadelphian in the great age of the new republic. Somewhere along the line an ancestor would have made money, or married wisely. Along with money and social position, some good Quaker ancestor would have preferred the Episcopal Church, or have been banished from the Society of Friends for marrying "out of meeting."

2. His family would have been listed in the *Social Register* at the turn of the nineteenth century.

3. He would have been born on Walnut Street, facing Rittenhouse Square.

4. After an early education at the Episcopal Academy or some other private school in the city, he would have gone away to one of the fashionable Episcopalian boarding schools in New England.

5. Unless his parents felt an unusual loyalty and pride in local institutions, he would have gone to either Harvard, Yale, or Princeton where he would have belonged to one of the more exclusive clubs.

6. After attending the law school at the University of Pennsylvania, this young Proper Philadelphian would enter one of the fashionable and powerful law firms in the city and eventually become a partner; or enter the field of banking or finance. He would be on the board of directors of several cultural and economic institutions (Pennsylvania Railroad, a bank such as the Girard Trust Company, and perhaps the Fairmount Park Art Association).

7. Finally, the Proper Philadelphian would live either in Chestnut Hill or the Main Line in 1940, attend the Episcopal Church, be married with three or four children, and walk either up or down Walnut Street to lunch with his peers at the Rittenhouse, or preferably the Philadelphia Club.

Lutie Johnson's New York

A man came suddenly out of a hallway just ahead of her—a furtive, darting figure that disappeared rapidly in the darkness of the street. As she reached the doorway from which he had emerged, a woman lurched out, screaming, "Got my pocketbook! The bastard's got my pocketbook!"

Windows were flung open all up and down the street. Heads appeared at the windows—silent, watching heads that formed dark blobs against the dark spaces that were the windows. The woman remained in the middle of the street, bellowing at the top of her voice.

Lutie got a good look at her as she went past her. She had a man's felt hat pulled down almost over her eyes and men's shoes on her feet. Her coat was fastened together with safety pins. She was shaking her fists as she shouted curses after the man who had long since vanished up the street.

Ribald advice issued from the windows:

"Aw, shut up! Folks got to sleep."

"What the hell'd you have in it, your rent money?"

"Go on home, old woman, 'fore I throw somp'n special down on your rusty head."

As the woman's voice died away to a mumble and a mutter, the heads withdrew and the windows were slammed shut. The street was quiet again. And Lutie thought, no one could live on a street like this and stay decent. It would get them sooner or later, for it sucked the humanity out of people—slowly, surely, inevitably.

She glanced up at the gloomy apartments where the heads had been. There were row after row of narrow windows—floor after floor packed tight with people. She looked at the street itself. It was bordered by garbage cans. Half-starved cats prowled through the cans—rustling paper, gnawing on bones. Again she thought that it wasn't just this one block, this particular street. It was like this all over Harlem wherever the rents were low. . . .

Streets like the one she lived on were no accident. They were the North's lynch mobs, she thought bitterly; the method the big cities used to keep Negroes in their place. And she began thinking of Pop unable to get a job; of Jim slowly disintegrating because he, too, couldn't get a job, and of the subsequent wreck of their marriage; of Bub left to his own devices after school. From the time she was born, she had been hemmed into an ever-narrowing space, until now she was very nearly walled in and the wall had been built up brick by brick by eager white hands.

Source: Kathryn Forbes, *Mama's Bank Account* (New York: Harcourt, Brace, 1943), pp. 39–40.

Source: Jonathan Raban, *Soft City* (London: Hamish Hamilton, 1974), pp. 222–227, 230.

Source: E. Digby Baltzell, *Philadelphia Gentlemen* (Philadelphia: University of Pennsylvania Press, 1979), pp. 386–387.

Source: Ann Petry, *The Street* (Boston: Houghton Mifflin, 1946), pp. 228–229, 324–325.

experience is shaped by the social characteristics they possess. All these factors work to provide a *meaningful* (although not always pleasant) urban experience. They are ways of dealing with *gesellschaft*.

The Social Environment: *Gemeinschaft*

Although they have long been ignored by social scientists whose early interest was focused on its qualities of *gesellschaft*, the city abounds with meaningful personal relationships. Only the most extreme of urban isolates—Johnson Raban's "marginal man," perhaps—do not have some intimate ties. Such interpersonal linkages act like the experiential mechanisms we have just discussed: they provide a basis for social and psychological security in the city.

Urban Networks

The study of such interpersonal ties is called *network analysis*. In city settings, network analysis is an attempt to understand the ways in which urban dwellers are linked to one another and to show how these linkages shape the tenor of their experience. Networks may or may not involve organized group relationships. People sometimes are linked together by common membership in a group such as the Elks or the P.T.A., but they can be linked just as easily by childhood friendship, a mutual interest in politics, a chance meeting on the bus.

Urban Marriages. The study of urban networks is not very old. The first analysis, of families in London, was conducted in the 1950s by Elizabeth Bott. Perhaps it is not surprising, given what we have seen about the effects of social characteristics on the urban experience, that the most important of her findings was the discovery that couples from different social classes had very different network relationships. That is to say, working-class couples typically had "segregated" networks, while middle-class marriages had "joint" relationships. This finding is explained further in Box 5-5. Bott's research demonstrated both the existence

---

BOX 5-5
Two Types of Marriage Networks

Segregated Marriage Networks

At one extreme was a family in which the husband and wife carried out as many tasks as possible separately and independently of each other. There was a strict division of labor in the household, in which she had her tasks and he had his. He gave her a set amount of housekeeping money, and she had little idea of how much he earned or how he spent the money he kept for himself. In their leisure time, he went to cricket matches with his friends, whereas she visited her relatives or went to a cinema with a neighbor. With the exception of festivities with relatives, this husband and wife spent very little of their leisure time together. They did not consider that they were unusual in this respect. On the contrary, they felt their behavior was typical of their social circle.

Joint Marriage Networks

At the other extreme was a family in which husband and wife shared as many activities and spent as much time together as possible. They stressed that husband and wife should be equals: all major decisions should be made together, and even in minor household matters they should help one another as much as possible. This norm was carried out in practice. In their division of labor, many tasks were shared or interchangeable. The husband often did the cooking and sometimes the washing and ironing. The wife did the gardening and often the household repairs as well. Much of their leisure time was spent together, and they shared similar interests in politics, music, literature, and in entertaining friends. Like the first couple, this husband and wife felt their behavior was typical of their social circle, except that they felt they carried the interchangeability of household tasks a little further than most people.

Source: Elizabeth Bott, *Family and Social Network* (London: Tavistock, 1957), pp. 52–53.

---

of strong networks among urbanites and the linkage between these networks and characteristics such as social class (Bott 1957).

Tally's Corner. Similar findings came from Eliot Liebow's (1967) participant observation study of poor black men who spent all or part of the day

The myth of urban alienation has been significantly weakened by doctumentation of pervasive social networks among virtually all city dwellers, rich and poor alike. (© Beryl Goldberg 1979)

"hanging out" on a street corner—"Tally's Corner"—in a Washington, D.C., ghetto. Liebow reconstructed the typical history of such men as follows: In their late adolescence most believed—like nearly all American males—that they should be breadwinners as adults. With this ideal in mind, many married and had children. Unfortunately, most had few skills and were poorly educated; hence, the prospect of anything but temporary, menial, or low-status work was slight. This basic situation set up a critical chain of events in the life of each man.

Because his job was poor and often degrading, it was not unusual for a man to come to hate it. In time he lost it. Sometimes he quit, sometimes he was fired. Whether he worked or not, his self-esteem as a successful breadwinner was low and he was unable to provide for his family. His failure was evident to his wife and children and a deep source of personal and familial pain and tension. To make matters worse, he and his wife often realized that she and the children could make

more money by going on welfare. But, government regulations being what they were at the time, this could happen only if he wasn't living at home.

Through all this, street-corner life was a constant source of external support. At Tally's Corner, people commiserated with him and didn't ask embarrassing questions, so, as his problems multiplied, corner life with his buddies became more attractive. He could forget failure, create a world of fantasy, and live from day to day. At some point, a psychological and social transition was made: the man came to identify more with the street corner and its life than he did with the job (if he still had it) or his family.

Life on the corner was not easy. A man had to create plausible stories about why he was there, and he had to support himself by some—often illegal—means. Yet, within this group, strong social networks existed. Liebow noted that each man created his own network and that networks often overlapped or changed. Nevertheless, they were the very heart and soul of street-corner life; indeed, they were what made that life bearable at all. Box 5-6 provides an excerpt from *Tally's Corner*.

Neighborhoods. The most obvious place where we would expect to find personal relationships in the city is in the city's neighborhoods. Distinguished by some sort of physical or social boundaries, neighborhoods contain people who usually share important social characteristics such as social class and ethnic, racial, or religious background.

In his case study of Boston's predominantly Italian West End neighborhood in the 1950s (see Figure 5-1), Herbert Gans (1982) suggested that, despite the many differences that exist among the residents of an urban neighborhood, many *gemeinschaft*-like relations exist.

At the time Gans was writing about, the West End was a low-income, low-rent district adjacent to the city's elite Beacon Hill area. Traditionally a spillover area for immigrants who did not settle in other low-income districts, the area had been dominated by various groups—Jews, Poles, and Italians—over the years. In the 1950s, over 40 percent of the West End's population was Italian, 10 percent was Jewish, 10 percent was Polish, and 5 percent was Irish. The remaining population was composed of other ethnic groups (Albanians, Ukrainians, Greeks) and social groups ("down-and-out" families, "hangers-on" like the street-corner men just discussed, middle-class professionals, students, hospital staff from nearby Massachusetts General Hospital, artists, and bohemians).

A casual observer of the West End would have been very likely to think it a slum and would not have imagined a daily round of urban experiences based on as much *gemeinschaft* as might be found in many nonurban environments. Yet, with some qualifications, such broad personal involvement was exactly what Gans discovered (see Box 5-7). This doesn't mean that everyone experienced personal relationships with everyone else; naturally, the large numbers of the city precluded that. But, for most people in Boston's West End, the urban experience had a significant personal dimension.

BOX 5-6

The Networks of Street-Corner Men

[The most important people in a man's network are those] with whom he is "up tight": His "walking buddies," "good" or "best" friends, girl friends, and sometimes real or putative kinsmen. These are the people with whom he is in more or less daily, face-to-face contact, and whom he turns to for emergency aid, comfort or support in time of need or crisis. He gives them and receives from them goods and services in the name of friendship, ostensibly keeping no reckoning. Routinely, he seeks them out and is sought out by them. They serve his need to be with others of his kind, and to be recognized as a discrete, distinctive personality, and he, in turn, serves them the same way. They are both his audience and his fellow actors.

It is with these men and women that he spends his waking, nonworking hours, drinking, dancing, engaging in sex, playing the fool or the wise man, passing the time at the Carry-out or on the street-corner, talking about nothing and everything, about epistemology or [Mohammed Ali], about the nature of numbers or how he would "have it made" if he could have a steady job that paid him $60 a week with no layoffs.

So important a part of daily life are these relationships that it seems like no life at all without them. Old Mr. Jenkins climbed out of his sickbed to take up a seat on the Coca-Cola case at the Carry-out for a couple of hours. "I can't stay home and play dead," he explained, "I got to get out and see my friends."

Source: Eliot Liebow, *Tally's Corner* (Boston: Little, Brown, 1967), pp. 163–164.

Such neighborhood experiences appear to be common features in many cities. For example, Gerald Suttles (1968) reported strong interpersonal ties among Italians in Chicago's Addams area, and Joseph Howell (1973) provided a similar description of an inner-city neighborhood in Washington, D.C. Finally, a complex study by Fischer, Jackson, Stuere, Gerson, and Jones (1977) found important interpersonal networks for many residents of Detroit's inner-city and suburban neighborhoods.

Such findings, of course, should not delude us into thinking that urban neighborhoods are uto-

BOX 5-7
Boston's Thriving West End

Everyday life in the West End was not much different from that in other neighborhoods, urban or suburban. The men went to work in the morning, and, for most of the day, the area was occupied largely by women and children—just as in the suburbs. . . . In the afternoon, younger women could be seen pushing baby carriages. Children of all ages played on the street, and teenagers would "hang" on the corner, or play ball in the school yard. . . . Many women went shopping every day, partly to meet neighbors and to catch up on area news in the small grocery stores, and partly to buy foods that could not be obtained in the weekly excursion to the supermarket. On Sunday mornings, the streets were filled with people who were visiting with neighbors and friends before and after church. . . .

On the whole . . . the various ethnic groups, the bohemians, transients, and others [lived together] without much difficulty, since each was responsive to totally different reference groups. . . . [For example] as Italians like to stay up late, and to socialize at high decibel levels, the bohemians' loud parties were no problem, at least to them. . . .

Many West Enders had known each other for years, if only as acquaintances who greeted each other on the street. Everyone might not know everyone else; but, as they did know something about everyone, the net effect was the same, especially within each ethnic group. Between groups, common residence and sharing of facilities—as well as the constant struggle against absentee landlords—created enough solidarity to maintain a friendly spirit. Moreover, for many families, problems were never far away. . . . Thus when emergencies occurred, neighbors helped each other readily; other problems were solved within each ethnic group.

For most West Enders, then, life in the area resembled that found in the village or small town, and even in the suburb.

Source: Herbert Gans, *The Urban Villagers* (New York: Free Press, 1982), pp. 14–16.

that, though they may be hidden to the casual observer, personal relationships may be every bit as important to urban neighbors as they are to people living in other types of settlements.

Friendships. Intimate relationships are important to city dwellers who are *not* neighbors as well. As we mentioned in the last chapter, the highly mobile people who live in many of our cities are not linked to neighborhoods in any traditional sense. Yet friends they have. Recent studies have shown that such people have a greater tendency to have friends at work, with whom they have lunch or a drink and dinner, or friends they meet more casually—at a concert, in the park, in a store. Such friendships are often maintained at considerable distance—one partner in the friendship perhaps living across the city from the other. Moreover, these friendships are often maintained by infrequent contacts and by telephone, since time is at a premium in busy schedules. The key point, once again, is that surface impressions of the city may be misleading: all those hurried people don't seem to have close relationships with other folks, but more often than not they most certainly do (Wolfe 1983).

Scenes. One of the city's hallmarks is its diversity of people, but, as we just noted, not all of these people have traditional locations—such as neighborhoods—in which they may develop interpersonal ties. Faced with this fact, such people have no recourse but to invent places where they can get together. Such places, where people from all over the city who are "in the know" go, John Irwin (1977) calls "scenes."

Scenes are expressive and leisure worlds. They can be local bars, bridge clubs, discos, or areas of a city taken over by a group (much as San Francisco's Haight-Ashbury district was inundated by hippies in the 1960s). Most who seriously participate in scenes devote a considerable amount of time and energy to them.

Scenes have a number of characteristics. First, they generally are not full-time. Most occupy the hours between work or after work (a favorite restaurant where taxi drivers go for lunch, or a gymnasium frequented by boxers in the evening).

pian places where true community spirit always flourishes (Hunter 1978). Their interdependency with the larger city and the mobility and mixed social characteristics and interests of their citizenry are all likely to mitigate against that possibility. On the other hand, these findings suggest

Second, the word "scene" itself, coined by participants, suggests the theater, and Irwin suggests that this is no accident. People who "make the scene" are always in some sense "on stage," emphasizing only one particular aspect of themselves—their knowledge of literature or their ability to dance—rather than the whole set of complex elements that make up their personality and life-style.

There are four main types of scenes. The *lifestyle scene* is developed by people who share strong interests or a particular stage in life. For example, most major cities have enclaves of writers, musicians, bohemians or radicals; some have scenes particularly for young people. Toronto has an example of the latter. On summer evenings young people from all over the metropolitan area descend on Yonge Street. They make the scene well into the wee hours of the morning. On foot or in cars, with stereos blaring, they eat, talk, yell, buy records, and generally hang out up and down a dozen city blocks.

The *local scene* is more exclusive. Local bars are a good example. To quote Irwin, "There are 'home territory' bars, which attract a particular crowd of persons who share some characteristic or characteristics (such as living in the same neighborhood, or being gay); in these cases, the clients and management discourage outsiders from using 'their bar'" (1977, p. 33).

The *open scene* is more fluid in terms of clientele, yet it too provides some opportunity for personal relationships. Bars without a well-defined clientele fall into this category. As Sherri Cavan writes:

> Public drinking places are "open regions": those who are present, acquainted or not, have the right to engage others in conversational interaction and the duty to accept the overtures of sociability proffered to them. While many, perhaps the majority, of conventional settings customarily limit the extent of contact among strangers, sociability is the most general rule in the public drinking place. (Quoted in Irwin 1977, p. 35)

Last, *specialized scenes* involve activities such as tennis, juggling, poetry reading, playing chess, cooking, Transcendental Meditation, and countless others. Like the local scene, they provide a sense of "in-group solidarity"—that is, participants share some special interest or experience or knowledge that makes them "members." Yet, because they are not narrowly localized, specialized scenes have a degree of openness and population fluidity that local scenes cannot have.

Perhaps one of the most interesting specialized scenes of recent years is the disco. Many different kinds of people go to discos to dance, to share their inside knowledge (who's the best DJ in the area, the new record), and to establish some type of interpersonal contact.

Scenes, then, offer yet another way in which people can establish personal relationships in the city; they are places where people can respond to the events and conditions they find themselves in; they are a way of making the urban world meaningful. Like neighborhood relations, they are a type of network that mediates the effects of the city as *gesellschaft*. They give the people who participate in them an urban home away from home.

Temporary Networks. A final type of network is used by many urban dwellers to make initial or short-term personal contact in the city. Examples of such networks are "lonely hearts" clubs, dating agencies, public ballrooms, listener-participation radio talk-shows, dial-a-prayer, and suicide hot lines.[1]

Sometimes such networks serve people like Jonathan Raban's "marginal man" (Cityscape 5-2), people who are extremely lonely or desperate. Just as frequently, they serve people whose lives have deep meaning in other contexts. For example, in the film *Marty*, an unmarried man in his thirties visits a public ballroom to find a woman to dance with and talk to. Aside from longing for female companionship, Marty is a successful butcher living in a thriving urban neighborhood where he has many friends. Similarly, people who listen to or participate in late-night talk-shows may not be lonely or alienated at all. They may be working late, or just interested in taking part in public repartée.

---

[1] This category was suggested by Gordon Lewis in personal communication.

Identifying with the City

The ability to know and identify with the city as a whole probably ended in the Middle Ages. With the coming of the Renaissance in Europe, Western cities began an inexorable population growth, a process that resulted in a population and a complexity of social organization impossible for any one person to grasp fully. Stanley Milgram's (1972) finding of the "incompleteness" of modern city dwellers' mental maps attests to this difficulty.

Still, most people have a sense of knowing their city. Such knowledge often is based on clichés and stereotypical images that outsiders also may share. Thus, beer has made Milwaukee famous in the same way that sun and the entertainment industry have created widespread knowledge of Los Angeles and Hollywood. St. Louis has its arch and Toronto its CN Tower ("world's tallest freestanding structure!"). And, while Stratford-on-Avon has its Shakespeare, Rumford, Maine, is proud to be the birthplace of former Senator and Secretary of State Edmund S. Muskie.

On another level, identification with the modern city is fostered by sport teams ("Minneapolis–St. Paul—Home of the Twins, Vikings, and North Stars!") and important local events (St. Patrick's Day in Boston, the Rose Parade in Pasadena, Inauguration Day in Washington, D.C.). One of the most famous of such local events is Mardi Gras in New Orleans. A sense of its vital importance in the experience of residents of the city (not to mention its attraction for a million or so tourists each year) is reflected in Box 5-8.

Historical events—both negative and positive—also lend ambience to the urban experience. The San Francisco earthquake of 1906 and the assassination of President John F. Kennedy in Dallas in 1963 are examples of costly and tragic events, while the ride of Paul Revere through Boston and the First Continental Congress in Philadelphia are Revolutionary War events touted by most of the cities' inhabitants.

To all this is added one's personal, detailed knowledge of the city. People contribute their own images of the city's physical and social aspects, their personal histories (such as Kazin's boyhood in Brownsville), and their knowledge of certain areas or places (the business district, Chinatown, or Zabar's, "absolutely the best deli on the Upper West Side"). Together, these elements create an overall "sense of the city" that enriches (even in its negative aspects) the urban experience.

Gemeinschaft in the City: A Summary

Recent research has suggested that the vast majority of urbanites have clearly defined personal elements as a major aspect of their urban experience. On the one hand, most are engaged in one or even many varieties of networks. Marriages, families, neighborhoods, scenes, and even temporary contacts are examples. Similarly, though it is unavoidably incomplete and can be stereotypical, most city residents have some overall sense of identification with their city. In short, many characteristics of Toennies's *gemeinschaft*—personal relationships, a sense of belonging—do exist in the city, despite the fact that in such a setting they may not be readily apparent.

The Texture of the City

Next let us consider the fact that most cities, if we are familiar with them in any detail, carry with them a kind of individual impression, a uniqueness—what Gerald Suttles (1984) calls a "texture." New York is a city of energy, hustle, fear—the "Big Apple"; Boston is more relaxed, more "cultural," more intellectual; Los Angeles is "laid back," the heart of the "new America." Whether you agree with these stereotypical impressions or not, think of cities you know: more than likely, an image of each city's texture comes easily to your mind.

What accounts for such images? Are they mere figments of the imagination, mere wishes or fears projected by visitors or residents? Suttles argues that such textural qualities of individual cities are eminently real. More specifically, a city's texture is grounded in its history, statues, street names, nicknames for certain parts of town, even in the bumper stickers it produces. All of these

---

BOX 5-8
Mardi Gras: New Orleans' Great Urban Festival

Source: PANA-VUE photo, courtesy John J. Macionis.

It is a state of mind—something that pervades the air and gets into the Orleanians' bloodstreams. The stranger protests, "I don't believe it—but there it is!" And there is not much exaggeration in the saying that the city has just two seasons: Carnival, and after-Carnival. It is not usual nowadays for a mass-scale celebration to be repeated year after year with undiminished success; this one has, in fact, grown with its age. . . .

Christmas is hardly over when Carnival opens, and it goes on for two months, more or less, depending on the date of Lent. During its last week it gathers momentum, with ever grander balls and street parades, shimmering floats in the daytime processions, and night floats whose gold and scarlet hues are caught by flambeaux in the hands of [participants].

Eventually comes Mardi Gras itself—Fat Tuesday, the day be-

---

elements have a certain objectivity, a reality that transcends simple impressions.

Thus, in the Hollywood part of Los Angeles, you can actually *see* the footprints and handprints of the stars in the cement in front of Grauman's Chinese Theater, you can get a map and visit the homes of the stars, you can see the huge "Hollywood" sign on the hills over the city, and, if you are lucky, you might even bump into that famed actor at a luncheon place. All this gives a reality to the Hollywood texture of stars and tinsel and fame and money.

Similarly, for the last two decades Detroit has been battling its image as the "least wonderful town" in the U.S. (Barron 1985). With the decline of the automobile industry in the 1970s, the movement of many of the area's affluent to the suburbs, and the deterioration of its center-city areas, Detroit took on an image of being a grimy,

violent cultural wasteland. The question is How does a city overcome such an image? Mayor Coleman Young argued that the media (TV, newspapers) were somewhat responsible with "sensationalistic reporting." Another cause was the city's reputation as unsafe and crime-riddled. To combat these images, Young tried to persuade the media to be more positive in their reporting; and he put more police on patrol. Still, as we reach the late 1980s, Detroit has not completely shaken off its negative textural image.

Portland, Oregon, has the opposite image (Turner 1985). In the past few years the city has revitalized its downtown housing and businesses, rebuilt its waterfront, and elected a new, energetic mayor, Bud Clark. The city is seen as one of the vibrant, new cities of the West and is capitalizing on that textural quality. Unlike Coleman Young of Detroit, Portland's Clark has an easier

fore Ash Wednesday—the supreme fête celebrated by thousands in costumes ranging from ornate to casual, by "marching clubs," and by truck and wagon parties, with competitions among weirdly masked contestants dancing on the corners. In the midst of all this moves Rex, official King of all the Kings for the day, a crown on his head, a rhinestone-encrusted sceptre in his hand, leading his parade while his Queen waits on a draped reviewing stand. And throughout the day will be heard on every side that foolish but memory-stirring song which is Mardi Gras' theme:

"If ever I cease to love,
If ever I cease to love,
May the fish get legs and the
cows lay eggs—
If ever I cease to love!"

This is a day of gusto and illusion, of buffoonery and satire, of the brilliant and the ridiculous. Fat Tuesday brings the sparkle of delighted eyes, the tap of feet in jazz rhythm, the bubbling of champagne, the magic of the hot-dog (with Creole dressing), the fun of wondering who it is that is talking to you. By and large it is a day marked by pleasant behavior. Obstreperous drunks are few, fisticuffs negligible. Through the decades New Orleans has learned how to have a good time within reasonable bounds. . . .

Bands are blaring along the route. Slowly the floats move along, the path being cleared by police on horses or motorcycles. Mothers hold their children up to see better, or fathers carry them on shoulders or in boxes fixed on the ends of poles. As each float passes, its maskers reach into bags holding the throw-outs: beads, whistles, and other trinkets for the crowd. "Throw me something!" "Gimme something, Mister!"—and the gifts fly in a shower as the float moves by. There is no Carnival excitement to match that of reaching out and catching a gift, no disappointment like that of realizing that the man in front of you has the longer reach. . . .

The day is one of smells—of popcorn, beer, cotton candy, dust stirred by jigging feet, and people. It is a panorama of the life of New Orleans—Creole, American, black, white, brown—compressed into twenty-four hours, with something of everything that the old city has meant. There is French *joie de vivre*, the endless capacity for a good time, the willingness to let others have theirs. To appreciate it requires humor, a relaxed mood, and an aspirin. . . .

Source: Harnett T. Kane, *Queen New Orleans* (New York: Bonanza, 1949), pp. 331–332, 341–342, 346.

time "selling" his city both locally and across the nation.

In other words, your senses are not deceiving you when you get a different feeling from one city than from another. Although urban areas have common elements, their individuality is no less real and important, and no less durable.

Humanizing the City

People have learned to humanize life in the modern urban environment, just as they learned to humanize it in rural areas, villages, and towns in other eras. As Cityscape 5-2 showed, whether one was an immigrant, a "marginal man," or a rich "gentleman," some form of meaningful urban routine appeared.

Even in the face of the most abject poverty, people have found ways of humanizing the city, of coping with problems, and of establishing positive personal contacts. The street-corner men discussed earlier provide one illustration.

A parallel example from Carol Stack's *All Our Kin* (1974) stresses this humanizing aspect of the urban experience. Most of the poverty-stricken blacks in the inner-city area of "Jackson Harbor" (the pseudonym Stack gave to the large midwestern city she studied via participant observation) were recent migrants from the South. Although they traveled north in search of better jobs and living conditions, they found neither in abundance. As a result, most men (the majority of whom were unskilled) were forced into low-paying or menial jobs or became unemployed. Most women were faced with the difficult task of bringing up their children with no predictable income.

Given such conditions, Stack wondered whether she would find families with the features commonly assumed to be characteristic of excessive poverty; that is, families that were "fatherless, matrifocal, unstable, and disorganized" (1974, p. 124). She did not. Instead, she discovered that the poor of Jackson Harbor had responded to the social condition of their own poverty by creating a diffuse family structure that allowed them to maintain a stable community and meet everyone's needs to some degree.

Being poor, families and individuals often found themselves without the financial means to get what they most needed: rent money, clothes, and food. To solve this problem, they set up networks for helping each other over immediate crises. But each time help was given, a debt was incurred. The helping families and individuals, sure to be in need of assistance themselves in time, expected that those they had helped would assist them in turn. As these obligations spread, a massive network of continuing "cooperation and mutual aid" was established among ghetto residents (1974, pp. 28–31). Those people who helped each other out most frequently often developed strong bonds of friendship. The interlocking networks became like large families, a fact acknowledged by ghetto residents when they spoke of their network as "all our kin." Box 5-9 describes how one particular network evolved.

Stack found residents sharing virtually everything, from clothes to food to child care responsibilities. Regarding the latter, sometimes fathers of children lived at home and sometimes they did not. When they did not, it was often because, like the street-corner men discussed previously, they could not bring home enough money to support a family. Even then, fathers frequently contributed what they could to the upbringing of their children. When mothers had to work, their own mothers or neighbors would watch the children. Thus, an informal day-care system evolved that ensured that children always would have the attention of at least one caring adult.

Interestingly, this system of reciprocal aid was not based on the cash value of things. (Most had no cash anyway.) People gave what was needed

---

BOX 5-9
Helping Each Other in the Ghetto

Cecil [age 35] lives in The Flats with his mother Willie Mae, his oldest sister and her two children, and his younger brother. Cecil's younger sister Lily lives with their mother's sister Bessie. Bessie has three children and Lily has two. Cecil and his mother have part-time jobs in a cafe and Lily's children are on aid. In July of 1970 Cecil and his mother had just put together enough money to cover their rent. Lily paid her utilities, but she did not have enough money to buy food stamps for herself and her children. Cecil and Willie Mae knew that after they paid their rent they would not have any money for food for the family. They helped out Lily by buying her food stamps, and then the two households shared meals together until Willie Mae was paid two weeks later. A week later Lily received her second ADC check and Bessie got some spending money from her boyfriend. They gave some of this money to Cecil and Willie Mae to pay their rent, and gave Willie Mae money to cover her insurance and pay a small sum on a living room suite at the local furniture store. Willie Mae reciprocated later on by buying dresses for Bessie and Lily's daughters and by caring for all the children when Bessie got a temporary job.

Source: Carol Stack, *All Our Kin* (New York: Harper & Row, 1974), p. 37.

---

and expected that their kindness would be repaid in time. One woman said:

> My TV's been over to my cousin's house for seven or eight months now. I had a fine couch that she wanted and I gave it to her too. It don't make no difference with me what it is or what I have. I feel free knowing that I done my part in this world. I don't ever expect nothing back right away, but when I've given something to kin or friend, whenever they think about me they'll bring something on around. Even if we don't see each other for two or three months. Soon enough they'll come around and say, "You want this?", if I don't want it my kin will say, "Well, find something else you like and take it on." (1974, pp. 41–42)

Ways of sanctioning people who didn't "play fair" also emerged. Said another woman:

BOX 5-10
All Our Kin

Ruby Banks took a cab to visit Virginia Thomas, her baby's aunt, and they swapped some hot corn bread and greens for diapers and milk. In the cab going home Ruby said to me, "I don't believe in putting myself on nobody, but I know I need help every day. You can't get help just by sitting at home, laying around, house-nasty and everything. You got to get up and go out and meet people, because the very day you go out, that first person you meet may be the person that can help you get the things you want. . . . I used to wish for lots of things like a living room suite, clothes, nice clothes, stylish clothes—I'm sick of wearing the same pieces. But I can't, I can't help myself because I have my children and I love them and I have my mother and all our kin. Sometimes I don't have a damn dime in my pocket, not a crying penny to get a box of paper diapers, milk, a loaf of bread. But you have to have help from everybody and anybody, so don't turn no one down when they come round for help."

Source: Carol Stack, *All Our Kin* (New York: Harper & Row, 1974), p. 32.

Some people like my cousin don't mind borrowing from anybody, but she don't loan you no money, her clothes, nothing. . . . I'll never give her nothing again. One time I went over there after I had given her all these things and I asked her, "How about loaning me an outfit to wear?" She told me, "Girl, I ain't got nothing. I ain't got nothing clean. I just put my clothes in the cleaners, and what I do have you can't wear 'cause it's too small for you." Well, lots of people talks about someone who acts that way. (1974, pp. 34–35)

But, for most, the sense of caring and sharing in a common plight with "kin" predominated, as shown in Box 5-10. There is little chance of the majority of the people of Jackson Harbor climbing out of their poverty: an abundance of decent jobs is not likely to appear, and many will continue to be occupied in simply getting enough to eat or in full-time child care. Nevertheless, in spite of the conditions that hem them in, the people of Jackson Harbor have invented ways to meet at least their basic needs and to soften the blow of their poverty. Such positive adaptation is a prime example of how people can make their urban experience more humane.

Conclusion

Being in cities alters our perceptions. There *is* an urban experience. Basically, this experience has two aspects. First, we react to the city as a physical and social environment. Second, from these reactions we develop a social psychology of the city, a characteristic set of urban reactions.

In both cases we make sense of the city by ordering it. Lynch (1960) observed that we divide the physical landscape into paths, edges, districts, nodes, and landmarks. Such distinctions are suggested partly by the physical form of the city (streets, after all, are "natural" paths) and partly by our personal needs (people invent "back street" paths to get from one place to another more quickly). To this basic insight, Milgram (1972) contributed a deeper understanding of the process of "mental mapping."

A similar ordering occurs as we respond to the city's social aspects. On the one hand, we cope with the city's *gesellschaft* characteristics (large numbers, density) by inventing ways to behave on the street, in the subway, or standing in line. We also have evolved an effective classification system for the world of urban strangers, through which we get a pretty good subjective sense of who all these unknown people really are. Nevertheless, despite a tendency to use common mental categories, we all do not react identically to the city. Our social characteristics—whether we are rich or poor, immigrant or native, mainstream or marginal—have much to do with the tenor of our urban experience.

On another level, we have developed complex ways of establishing meaningful relationships in or with the city. Urban networks are a prime example. Illustrations of personal networks abound:

in marriages and neighborhoods, on street corners, on "the scene," or in temporary contacts like those provided by public dance halls. Most of us also identify with our city as a whole, combining major traits of our particular city (an industry, a sports team, an important historical event) with our own personal urban experience to get an overall sense of our urban environment. All these mechanisms serve to lend *gemeinschaft*-like aspects to the urban experience.

Next, there is the notion of urban texture. Recent research has shown that there is much truth in people's comments that some cities "feel different" from others. Each city has an individual textural quality shaped by its history, location, and people.

Last, in the example from *All Our Kin*, we saw how people can humanize the city and turn it into a meaningful experience even in the most devastating of conditions.

Together, all these elements of the urban experience provide us with a sense of *order* and *security* in this largest of human agglomerations, and they make the city usable.

The city is a big place. It has more people, more buildings, more paths, more nodes, more possibilities for interaction and relationship than any other form of settlement. As Georg Simmel argued 75 years ago, cities demand a lot of mental work from those who wish to make sense of them. In the end, such extra mental effort may be the unique element which creates the sophistication for which urban dwellers are noted.

CHAPTER 6
Urban Geography and Urban Ecology

If you happen to be endowed with topographical curiosity the hills of San Francisco fill you with an irresistible desire to walk to the top of each one of them. Whoever laid the town out took the conventional checkerboard pattern of streets and without the slightest regard for the laws of gravity planked it down blind on an irregular peninsula that was a confusion of steep slopes and sandhills. The result is exhilarating. Wherever you step out on the street there's a hilltop in one direction or the other. From the top of each hill you get a view and the sight of more hills to the right and left and ahead that offer the prospect of still broader views. The process goes on indefinitely. You can't help making your way painfully to the top of each hill just to see what you can see. . . .

This one is Nob Hill, I know that. . . . Ahead of me the hill rises higher and breaks into a bit of blue sky. Sun shines on a block of white houses at the top. Shiny as a toy fresh from a Christmas tree, a little cable car is crawling up it. Back of me under an indigo blur of mist are shadowed roofs and streets and tall buildings with wisps of fog about them,

and beyond, fading off into the foggy sky, stretches the long horizontal of the Bay Bridge.

Better go back now and start about my business. The trouble is that down the hill to the right I've caught sight of accented green roofs and curved gables painted jade green and vermillion. That must be in Chinatown. Of course the thing to do is take a turn through Chinatown on the way down toward the business district. . . .

JOHN DOS PASSOS,
"SAN FRANCISCO LOOKS WEST"

Although they are much more, cities are complex physical entities. They exist within geographic and climatic settings that naturally shape them. But the hands and minds of human beings also play a part. People, reacting to a city's physical setting, in turn shape it. San Francisco is an excellent example—its geography and climate have been interlaced with human creations (cable cars, Chinatown, bridges) to produce a particularly enticing urban experience. It is the purpose of this chapter to explore the interrelationships that exist between a city's setting and the interests of the people who live in that setting.

Automobiles have transformed patterns of access to American cities. Residential patterns have also been changed by the construction of superhighways. (Georg Gerster/Photo Researchers)

Urban Geography

Geography is always important to a city. Some cities, like San Francisco, exist astride hills. Others, like St. Louis, Tucson, or Oklahoma City, are built on flat plains. In any physical setting, however, the city adapts to its physical environment.

Take, for example, Los Angeles, San Francisco's massive neighbor 500 miles to the south. Originally a Spanish mission outpost, Los Angeles did not become a major American city until well into this century. Earlier it was a series of scattered communities surrounded by mountains in the relatively flat, near-desert region of California's southwest.

In the 1920s, however, coincident with the rise of the movie industry, Los Angeles began to grow rapidly and has continued this process ever since. As population within the huge, bowl-shaped re-

gion increased, the number of settlements grew. These settlements had to be linked. The first step in this direction was public transport: electric trains and streetcars. These soon were outmoded. The mass-produced private automobile arrived and, with it, Los Angeles's incredible freeways.

> These remain the city's grandest and most exciting artifacts. Snaky, sinuous, undulating, high on stilts or sunk in cuttings, they are like so many concrete tentacles, winding themselves around each block, each district, burrowing, evading, clambering, clasping every corner of the metropolis as if they are squeezing it all together to make the parts stick. They are inescapable, not just visually, but emotionally. They are always there, generally a few blocks away; they enter everyone's lives, and seem to dominate all arrangements. (Morris 1976, p. 30)

As Los Angeles grew further, the mountains themselves became subject to settlement, with streets "forever ribbing and probing further into [the] perimeter hills, twisting like rising water ever

Figure 6-1 *Geographical location of the 31 most populous American metropolitan areas (1980 census).*

higher, ever deeper into their canyons, and sometimes bursting through to the deserts beyond" (Morris 1976, p. 28).

The city mimicked its geography. "If [Los Angeles] could be pried out of its setting," writes Jan Morris, "one feels it would be like a dried mat of some bacterial mold, every bump, every corner exactly shaped to its landscape" (1976, p. 28). Ironically, the city's increasing population, its near total reliance on the automobile as means of transport, and its geography have combined to produce an unforeseen but nonetheless monumental environmental problem: smog. Although by no means the only city beset by this threat to health, Los Angeles's smog problem is particularly acute because the surrounding hills trap noxious fumes in the bowl-shaped region where the bulk of the city's population lives. Alas, the problem has shown little sign of lessening in recent years, despite California's "toughest in the nation" pollution laws. The reason: the Los Angeles

area continues to grow (by the mid-1980s Los Angeles had become second to New York in population) and the automobile continues to reign supreme.

The Location of Cities

The geographic and climatic characteristics of an urban area, then, provide a set of physical conditions to which people must adapt. Indeed, those physical characteristics usually determine whether an area becomes a city at all.

Take a moment to examine Figure 6-1, which shows the geographical location of the 31 most populous urban areas in the United States. All but one are located on waterways. They are either seaports (New York, Los Angeles), lakeports (Chicago, Buffalo), or on major rivers (Pittsburgh, New Orleans). The advantage of such sites for stimulating trade is enormous. However, even cities on less important waterways (Phoenix,

Dallas, Denver) are where they are because, at least initially, there was enough water to support their populations.

The sole exception to the waterway thesis is Atlanta. Yet its site, too, was determined by a geographical consideration: in the 1840s it was selected as the southern terminus of the Western and Atlantic Railroad because of its centrality to the rest of the South. Atlanta thus also illustrates that environmental advantages play a role in determining city location. With this in mind, we can consider briefly the sites of five other cities: Kansas City; Houston; Miami; Washington, D.C.; and Salt Lake City. What goods or services do you associate with each?

Kansas City. This is one of America's great inland markets. Although, like St. Louis and Denver, it served as a jumping-off point for westward migration in the nineteenth century, its major claim to fame was as a processing and shipping center for cattle and beef produced in the surrounding region. Note, in Figure 6-1, its location relative to Nebraska, Kansas, and Missouri—all major grain-producing states—and its position north of most of Kansas, Oklahoma, and Texas— all major cattle-producing states. Brought to Kansas City, cattle and grain could be processed and shipped farther north and east to the more populous Great Lakes and Eastern Seaboard regions.

Houston. This city has a more recent story. Located near the East-Texas oil fields, it has been booming since the 1950s, but particularly in the last decade. The city increased its population 45 percent between 1970 and 1980, jumping from slightly under 2 million to nearly 3 million. Because of oil—every major company has offices in Houston—and cheap shipping of oil via the Gulf of Mexico, the city has become the second busiest port in the country (after New York), outstripping Chicago and New Orleans for the honor. Although economically suffering with the fall of oil prices in the mid-1980s, many American companies have moved there from Snowbelt cities.

Miami. Although it is a port, Miami's historical raison d'être has been as a tourist and retirement area. The climate in the winter is ideal, with temperatures hovering near the 80s, nearly unlimited sun, and endless beaches offering opportunity for relaxation. "Fun in the Sun" is the city's motto. In the last decade, however, Miami has become a major market for specialized goods. Ousted from Castro's Cuba in the late 1950s and early 1960s, many refugees settled in Miami. For 20 years they built a solid economic base and their population grew. Because of the Cubans' success, the city has become attractive to wealthy Latin Americans. They fly to Miami, stay in or near Little Havana, speak nothing but Spanish, and buy numerous American goods—clothes, TVs, stereos—from Cuban merchants at prices much lower than they can get at home. Their vacations over, they return home, leaving billions of dollars yearly in the city's economy.

Washington, D.C. This city provides a very different case. Its advantages as an economic center (a key consideration in the cities just discussed) were of scant concern to its founders. What did concern them was not being forced to decide between Philadelphia and New York as a permanent capital. Both cities actively sought the honor, given their importance in the American Revolution and as trade centers. In addition, Washington's founders wanted to forge a symbolic link between the North and the South, the two main regions of the country. Hence, the Potomac river basin became America's capital city.

Salt Lake City. Situated at the foot of a mountain range near the forbidding and barren Great Salt Lake in Utah, Salt Lake City can hardly be considered the most auspicious of urban sites. Yet it did not seem so unlikely to the Mormons. Migrating westward in the mid–nineteenth century, looking for a place where they could practice their religious beliefs without censure, the Mormon leaders decided that the Salt Lake region was the place God had set aside for them. In large part, the region's out-of-the-way nature was the key to its founding. As it turned out, the location was more hospitable than it appeared at first glance. Salt Lake City became a point of rest and departure for westward migration, the salt proved to be mineable, and, relative to the surrounding region, it was the only area within hundreds of miles able to support more than a very small population.

Why Cities Are Where They Are

The preceding five examples provide us with the ability to make some generalizations about city locations.[1] They make it clear that both environmental *and* social factors play a role in originating an urban area.

On the environmental side, there are a number of basic conditions that any site must fulfill if it is to become an urban area. First and foremost, it must be a *minimally hospitable environment*. It cannot be infested with disease-producing organisms or have a climate or geography (extreme cold; incessant, massive earthquakes) that makes permanent settlement impossible. In addition, any city has to have *adequate access to food, water, and building materials*, and the larger its population, the greater the need for these goods. This is not to say that cities cannot surmount the problems created if these basic conditions are not met, but settlers' ingenuity and technology must be up to the task. For example, gas and oil heat have made winter survival in northern cities possible for millions, as air conditioning has mitigated the extreme heat of southern urban areas. Similarly, food, water, or building materials can be imported. Las Vegas, in the excessively severe Nevada desert, is perhaps the best modern example of a city without abundant natural resources that is thriving as a result of the applications of modern technology.

Once these basic conditions have been met, other factors, more social in nature, come into play. We will discuss seven such factors, using the five cities just discussed as illustration.

1. Some cities are where they are because they are a *natural crossroads* for a region at a particular point in time. Kansas City, a major rail crossroads in the nineteenth century, is an excellent case in point. Other examples are St. Louis and Chicago, the latter nicknamed "the crossroads of the nation." Such crossroads facilitate the confluence of people, services, and, especially, trade goods.

2. Other cities develop because they are located at what economists call *"break-of-bulk"* points. That is, they are at a point where a good—the "bulk"—has to be transferred to another type of transportation, for example, from truck to ship or vice versa. Houston is a break-of-bulk point for oil. In such places, since the transfer from one carrier to another has to occur anyway, goods often are warehoused for a time or processed in some way to make the next leg of the trip more economical. When this happens, the city grows up around a whole set of subindustries that deal with storing or processing. Again, Houston serves as an example. The oil to be shipped from the city often is stored first in huge tanks and then refined into gasoline or heating oil. James Heilbrun gives another example:

Probably the most often cited case of a city that has attracted industry because it is a transshipment point is Buffalo. An enormous flour-milling industry developed there because grain could be carried inexpensively across the Great Lakes from the grain belt of the North Central States, unloaded at Buffalo, the eastern most port that could be reached before the St. Lawrence Seaway was built, there milled into flour, and then shipped by rail to the large East Coast markets. (1974, p. 65)

Furthermore, the break-of-bulk function of cities is an enduring historical constant. Box 6-1 describes two cases separated in time by a century and a quarter. Note the rather stunning similarities between Charles Dickens's description of 1860 London and Chuck Raasch's comments about 1984 Seattle.

3. Another major reason for a city's location is access to some major *raw material* in demand. Kansas City is also in a grain-producing region of major significance. Houston is also near the East-Texas oil

---

[1]A number of these categories were suggested by Alan Frishman in personal discussion.

BOX 6-1
Break of Bulk in Two Cities

London, 1860

In the following passage Charles Dickens describes London's River Thames in early morning, as seen from a small boat traveling downstream.

Early as it was, there were plenty of scullers going here and there that morning, and plenty of barges . . . and we went ahead among many skiffs and wherries, briskly.

Old London Bridge was soon passed, and old Billingsgate market with its oysterboats and Dutchmen, and the White Tower and Traitor's Gate, and we were in among the tiers of shipping. Here, were the Leith, Aberdeen, and Glasgow steamers, loading and unloading goods, and looking immensely high out of the water as we passed alongside; here, were colliers by the score and score, with the coal-whippers plunging off stages on deck, as counterweights to measures of coal swinging up, which were then rat-

tled over the side into barges; here, at her moorings, was to-morrow's steamer for Rotterdam . . . and here to-morrow's for Hamburg, under whose bowsprit we crossed.

Seattle, 1984

In this passage Chuck Raasch describes a similar morning scene, only this time in a major American port.

SEATTLE—It is early morning at the Port of Seattle, and the imprint of the Orient is distinct, the trade robust.

The Singapore ship Neptune Jasper docks and spills forth canned pineapple, chunk tuna, baby clams, wheelbarrows, artificial flowers, plastic toys, floor tiles, bamboo baskets, baby strollers, shoes, auto-clutch parts, vacuum cleaners and microwave ovens from Taiwan, Singapore and Japan.

"We're getting more tonnage

capacity, more lines coming into service, bigger ships and faster ships, all chasing the same cargo," says shipping agent Bob Fitzgerald as the clanging of 10-story unloading cranes and the growl of trucks reverberate along the waterfront.

Activity like this pushed the Port of Seattle to a record $25 billion in business last year, and other West Coast ports are booming, too. As the USA's trading eyes turn toward the Far East, ports from Seattle to Long Beach are bustling—building new terminals, finding better and faster ways to move goods once off the docks and promoting their ports more than ever.

Source: Charles Dickens, *Great Expectations* (London: Chapman and Hall, 1860), from Chap. 54.

Source: Chuck Raasch, "Sun 'rising' in West for port cities," *USA Today*, Aug. 23, 1984.

---

fields. Similarly, San Francisco boomed in the mid–nineteenth century because it was the closest port to the Sierra Nevada gold mines, and Pittsburgh's greatness is due in large measure to its proximity to coal mines that afforded cheap power for its steel mills.

4. Miami suggests another reason for city location. It is the quintessence of the *amenity city*: a city located in a particular place because it provides a certain type of pleasurable service not easily available elsewhere. Miami provides sea, surf, sand, and sun. In its recent guise as "South America's supermarket," it is a Spanish-speaking city where important American goods are available. But Miami is hardly the only example. Almost all major cities in Florida, including the midpeninsula Orlando (home

of Disney World), are amenity cities. Similarly, Las Vegas is the western gambling city par excellence. On the East Coast, this function is performed by Atlantic City; in Europe, by Monaco's Monte Carlo. Other examples of amenity cities are Hot Springs, Arkansas, and Bath, England (both renowned for their hot mineral waters); and Innsbruck, Austria (a world-class skiing city).

5. Washington, D.C., is an example of an *administrative or political city*, a city established primarily for governmental purposes. Australia has its seat of government in the newly constructed Canberra; Brazil has located its government in Brasilia; and Canada has centered its government in Ottawa.

6. Often closely related historically to the administrative function has been a city's *strategic military location*. Thus, some cities have been situated in easily defensible spots (Athens) and others have been sited because they offered military access into a whole region. The Romans settled London on the Thames because it was the first solid land upriver and thus afforded a point of storage and embarkation for military excursion into England's interior.

7. Finally, cities can be located for *religious or educational reasons*. Salt Lake City was settled as the home of Mormonism. In a similar way, Mecca in Saudi Arabia is the fountainhead of Islam, and Jerusalem is a focal point of no less than three major world religions: Christianity, Judaism, and Islam. University cities, such as Cambridge in England, Ithaca in New York (home of Cornell University), and Berkeley in California (site of one of the main campuses of the University of California) are cities achieving prominence for educational reasons.

Some combination of basic geographic-climatic conditions and social-economic factors is responsible for cities being where they are. In many instances these elements combine to determine the attractiveness of a location. New York City, for example, at the time of its founding was a major port, had access to a huge hinterland's raw materials, was a natural break-of-bulk point, was a crossroads between New England and the more southerly states, and was easily defensible if the necessity arose.

In general, the more of the basic necessities (water, food, raw materials) a region can provide and the more social or economic functions it can serve (trade, defense, administration), the greater its chances for developing into a large city. Thus, New York is probably the American city nonpareil. Comparatively, Salt Lake City, with its disadvantageous location relative to the rest of the country, its lack of abundant basic materials, its less-than-optimal climate, and its concentra-

tion on one major social function—religion—has not grown anywhere near as large as New York City (Salt Lake City had about 175,000 people in 1986).

Should the balance between a city's physical environment and people's social or economic needs and interests change, the city will need to adapt or else it will decline or die. History is strewn with the ruins of cities unable to adapt: the ancient Egyptian capital of Luxor or the recently found Mayan city of El Mirador are but two examples. Just as frequently, cities survive the most calamitous of geographic-economic disasters. San Francisco is America's classic case, having bounced back from one of the great urban disasters of all time (the 1906 earthquake) to become one of America's most vibrant cities.

The Shape of the City

Once cities begin, what determines the form or physical shape they take? The answer seems to depend primarily on the social or economic functions the city's founders wished it to serve—particularly, which of these functions was uppermost in their minds.

To begin with, consider these examples of preindustrial cities: Athens is spread around the natural hilltop of the Acropolis, Edinburgh is sited around a massive outcropping in Scotland, and Paris and Mexico City were situated originally on islands. Although it was by no means the only concern, these examples suggest that defense was one of the prime interests of these city dwellers, as it was for the city of Durham in northern England. Founded around A.D. 1000, Durham is situated atop a high escarpment in the shape of a peninsula that has been cut by the Wear River. The sides of the escarpment would be extremely difficult to scale, even if one could get across the river. Naturally protected on three sides, the founders of Durham only had to work up meaningful defense on the narrow fourth side. It was here that they built their heavily fortified castle.

The Radiocentric City

The importance of the defensive function to preindustrial peoples gave their cities a characteristic form. The city quite literally became a container (Mumford 1961), protected either by naturally occurring geographic features (Durham's escarpment) or, if such features did not exist, by human constructs such as walls, moats, castles, or battlements. Urbanists call cities shaped as containers in this fashion *radiocentric*, suggesting that they radiate outward from a common center.

One of the clearest examples of this type of city is the original layout of preindustrial Baghdad in Iraq (see Figure 6-2). Set up with an outer wall for protection and only four fortified gates for access, the inner core of the city, containing the ruling Caliph's palace and the mosque, was protected further by two rings of densely packed residential quarters where the city's less prestigeful residents lived. From the gates, along the main access roads leading to the core, arcades or shops were set up for easy shopping.

Radiocentric cities did not always assume perfectly radial shapes, however. An example was Ming Peking, a city with which we shall deal extensively in Chapter 7. Take a moment to examine Figure 7-1 on page 195. Ming Peking, heavily walled and moated—thereby indicating its deep concern with defense—took the shape of a series of rectangles and squares attached to and within one another. These shapes are a product of the Chinese cosmology of the 1400s, which saw the cardinal points of the compass—north, south, east, and west—as vital elements necessary to symbolize in a city's shape.

There are, however, other important reasons for the basically radial shape of so many cities. The city is, above all, a center of human activity. This means that, as it grows, people generally will want to be as close to that center as possible for simple reasons of economy, such as cost and time of travel. Because a circle provides the easiest access to a center, as the city grows it will tend to establish subcommunities in a ringlike fashion around its central core. As anyone who has flown above modern cities at night can attest, most appear like huge wheels with central spokes radiat-

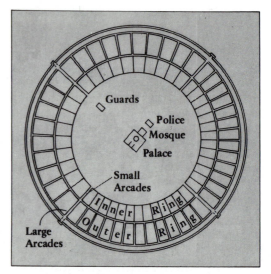

Figure 6-2 *The radiocentric city: Baghdad circa* A.D. *146–762. Source: M. Hugh P. Roberts,* An Urban Profile of the Middle East, *p. 32. © 1979 Hugh Roberts. Reprinted by permission of St. Martin's Press.*

ing outward (Boston's nickname is "The Hub"). The spokes (roads, rail lines) suggest another reason for the city's generally radial form. Because the shortest route to the center of the circle is a straight line, people build their main access roads into the city as directly as possible. Thus originated one of history's best-known aphorisms: "All roads lead to Rome!"

The Gridiron City

Despite the overarching radial pattern of most of the world's cities, the downtown areas of most well-known American cities—Philadelphia, New York, Chicago, Atlanta, Los Angeles—can hardly be described as classic examples of radiocentric design. Indeed, a radiocentric center city is the exception rather than the rule in the United States.

Another shape that characterizes many cities is the *gridiron*, basically composed of straight streets crossing at right angles to create a city of

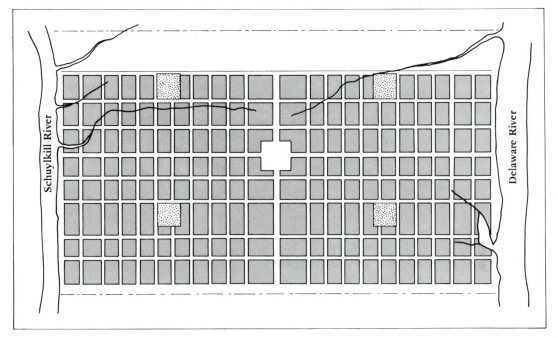

Figure 6-3 *The Gridiron City: William Penn's Philadelphia Plan, 1682*

highly regular blocks. This form is typical of cities built after the rise of capitalism and the Industrial Revolution—cities that placed tremendous importance on the role of economic activity in daily affairs. Evidence of the gridiron pattern is found in a few preindustrial cities, such as those in classical Greece and even earlier in the Indus Valley city of Moenjo-daro. The pattern is also found in the "pomp-and-majesty" areas of many imperial cities such as Rome and the cities of Austria and Hungary, but the gridiron has become a dominant city shape only in the last several centuries.

The benefits of a gridiron begin with its ability to parcel out land efficiently within the city. Figure 6-3 shows William Penn's plan for Philadelphia, conceived in 1682. If land is to be bought and sold as an important economic commodity, regular lots that abut with one another to save every inch of space are far more sensible than irregular, haphazard streets and lots. Similarly, a grid facilitates the quick and easy passage of people and goods through the city.

Finally, it should be noted that grid patterns are not always the result of careful planning. Frequently a settlement would begin and merchants would find it advantageous to set up facing a main street where people could shop, moving from one store to another along the street. Open-ended streets served business better than closed-ended streets because they allowed growth and easy entry and exit to the shopping area. The American Midwest and West are full of such Main Street towns. If, in time, another major street crossed the original street, the beginnings of a gridiron would be created around a "four corners." Once begun, the grid pattern often perpetuated itself due to the economic advantages mentioned previously.

City Growth: Horizontal, Vertical, Interstitial

A final issue related to basic city shape is the directions in which the city can grow as it expands. According to urbanist Hans Blumenfeld, this depends almost entirely on technological know-how. City growth can be of only three types: (1) the city can grow out, that is, expand horizontally; (2) it can grow up, that is, expand vertically; or (3) it can grow denser, that is, expand interstitially. Blumenfeld describes the relation of each of these growth possibilities to technology:

> As long as intracity traffic moved only by foot or hoof, possibilities of horizontal and vertical expansion were strictly limited. Growth was mainly interstitial, filling up every square yard of vacant land left between buildings until the city became a solidly built-up amorphous mass of brick. With the advent of the elevator and the steel frame, the vertical growth of skyscrapers began, leaving interstices of half-developed and vacant lots. Suburbs spread out horizontally along streetcar and bus lines and around suburban railroad stations, surrounded by wide-open spaces. But with the development of the private automobile, these interstices between the suburbs began to be filled in, tending to make the outskirts as amorphous as the central area, though less densely settled. (1964, p. 31)

City Shape and Quality of Life

Some scholars argue that the choices cities make regarding shape are extremely important to the type and quality of urban experience people have. Max Weber, whom we discussed in Chapter 4, was a strong proponent of the type of urban experience afforded by medieval cities. Enclosed within their walls in an organically created, irregular city center, people of the Middle Ages knew where they belonged and what life was about, and they could identify with the entire city as home. The contemporary gridiron and vertical-horizontal city works assiduously against such positive identification by interpreting the city primarily as a scene of economic activity. The most important consideration for modern city dwellers becomes "How much is it (the street, the house, the job) worth?" Other human concerns—the tradition of the old neighborhood, religious ties, identification with the city as a whole—have fallen by the wayside.

The Economics of Urban Land Use

Listen to the music of the traffic in the city
Linger on the sidewalks where the neon lights
*   are pretty*
The lights are much brighter there . . .
Downtown!

TONY HATCH, "DOWNTOWN" (POPULAR SONG)

Those of us who know cities usually have an image of a vibrant downtown, a place where the action is, where the buildings are taller, the lights brighter. When we are thinking about American or European cities, this image usually is correct. Consider the approach to a major city at night along a dark highway: what one sees first is the distant glow of the city lights. Consider also that barring an electrical blackout, there are large areas of the center city that are never dark. Why should this be so? Why shouldn't the "action" be everywhere? Why should most of the tall buildings be concentrated in a single area? Why isn't the Great White Way all over the city?

Central Place Theory[2]

The important thing to realize is that the city is the only place where everything human comes together. Compared to the rural area or the town, the city's possibilities are legion. Indeed, the city is the place where, because of the mix of people and ideas, new things, not thought of before or possible without the mix, can be created for the first time. The city, by its very nature, promotes "interaction and fusion" (Mumford 1961, p. 568).

Moreover, as one approaches the center of the city, the interaction of people and ideas becomes greater. The greatest action is, literally, in the center, where people contact each other most frequently. There—"downtown"—the benefits are greatest.

---

[2]What follows is a distillation of Ullman 1941 and Berry and Horton 1970, pp. 169–175.

Economists have developed a theory explaining the vital economic advantages that, historically, have been so important to the development of cities.

The Economic Advantages of Cities. As we have seen already, cities tend to be located where important goods or services are available in abundance (Winston-Salem, Raleigh, and Durham, North Carolina, are in the heart of tobacco-producing country) or where those goods and services can be obtained easily (New Orleans is near the mouth of the Mississippi River). In either case, such a location allows cities to get or produce their goods or offer their services more cheaply than other areas. To ship heating oil to Boston costs a certain amount, but to get that oil to the small town of Tilton, New Hampshire, over a hundred miles away, entails additional transportation costs from Boston to Tilton.

Second, cities are places where what economists call *agglomeration industries* spring up. Take Detroit, home of the automobile industry. Because the major American car manufacturers have their home base there, they attract various subindustries to serve them—companies specializing in car paints or piston making, for example. The Big Three automakers share these subindustries. This large demand for the subindustries' products allows them to sell more of their particular product more cheaply to all three car manufacturers, thereby keeping down the final cost of the automobile. (Other examples of famous agglomeration industries are the entertainment industry in Los Angeles and Hollywood, meat packing in Chicago, and the fashion industry in New York.) If agglomeration industries aren't around, as they aren't in many small towns or rural areas, it will cost more to make a movie or build a car than it would in Hollywood or Detroit.

Another economic advantage of cities, particularly Western cities grounded in a capitalist free-enterprise system, is that *competition* tends to keep cost down and quality up for many important goods and services. Because so many businesses of the same type exist in cities, any given business cannot charge a great deal more for the same product than any other. If it does, word soon gets around among customers that someone down the street is offering the product more cheaply. In the same way, if one business offers a patently shoddier version of some good at the same price as another, customers are soon likely to ferret out the truth and take their business to the competitor. In comparison, without a great deal of competition, businesses in nonurban areas can charge more for their goods. It's just too inconvenient and expensive for most local people to go to the city to get the lower price.

Competition also explains why so many businesses of the same type tend to locate near one another in a city. There are often entire stereo, camera, fashion, baking, or entertainment districts. The reasons for such proximity are easy to discern. Businesses of the same type located near one another can (1) know what their competitors are up to by simply walking across the street; (2) provide a single locale where customers can do comparison shopping easily, making it as likely they'll buy from one business as another; and (3) share agglomeration services, thereby making the products cheaper for everyone.

Finally, cities can offer higher quality and cheaper products because of the *greater population* they are linked to. For instance, urban businesses have a greater supply of workers available than country areas and thus, other things being equal, can hire the most qualified people. This ensures higher quality work. Furthermore, because people want to take advantage of the amenities offered by cities, they are drawn to them in large numbers, thereby greatly increasing the local demand for goods and services. Greater demand allows business organizations to offer their wares more cheaply because they can reduce production costs by ordering raw materials in greater quantity.

For all these reasons, the city has marked economic advantages over the hinterland. Once begun, cities may become a "magnet" (Mumford 1961) or a "growth machine" (Molotch 1976), drawing raw materials and people in abundance from all around.

Because the economic advantages tend to increase as one gets closer to the city center, most people who stand to benefit from those advantages want to be at or near the center. Thus, many cities are characterized by what is called a *central business district* (CBD). Here the action truly is greater, the buildings taller, and the lights, if not brighter, are at least more numerous.

The Urban Hierarchy. These basic economic advantages also help explain why some cities grow much larger than others. Some are just more centrally located relative to important goods or services. Chicago provides an excellent illustration. It is important not merely because of its location at the southern end of Lake Michigan, but because of its centrality to the nation's population in the nineteenth century. At that time the great bulk of Americans lived in the Northeast. Thus, Chicago was a perfect location for all types of producers who wished to ship goods to the North, West, and South. Similarly, for northeastern travelers going west, Chicago was a natural point of stopover. In comparison, Milwaukee, another major Great Lakes port, did not have such a great degree of geographic centrality. Therefore, Chicago developed into a "higher order" city, while Milwaukee evolved into a somewhat "lower order" urban area.

That cities should arrange themselves into a pattern of dominance of hierarchical order should come as no surprise. We implicitly know that this is the case—all Iowans know, for example, that Des Moines is a more important city than the college town of Fairfield. It was not until the 1930s, however, that this intuition was incorporated into urban theory by the German geographer Walter Christaller (1966; originally published 1933). Christaller suggested that the more important a city's economic function to a region, the larger its population would become. Because all cities specialize in providing goods and services to a region, the larger cities would have, correspondingly, *more* goods and services to distribute. The city's hinterland—smaller cities, towns, rural areas—would become dependent on the large city for many goods and services that their smaller populations could not support.

Christaller also suggested that, all else being equal, cities of similar population and economic power would tend not to impinge on one another. That is, they would be set up at "distance intervals," which would allow each to perform functions for its hinterland without severe competition from the others. The upstate New York area provides an example: Stretched along the New York Thruway, at least 75 miles apart, are the major urban areas of Buffalo (1984 population: 1,002,000), Rochester (1984 population: 714,000), Syracuse (1984 population: 650,000), Utica-Rome (1984 population: 321,000) and Albany-Schenectady-Troy (1984 population: 841,000). Each of these areas serves a distinctive hinterland and series of smaller cities.

All of this means that over a fairly large geographical region we can expect cities to be distributed by size and function. There will be lots of smaller, *local* cities (Geneva, New York, for example), fewer but larger *regional* cities (such as Rochester), still fewer but even larger *national* (Washington, D.C.) cities, and, finally, a very few, but very large *world* cities like New York, Paris, and Tokyo (Hall 1979). These cities offer just about everything imaginable for human consumption. Thus, America's world city, New York—being centrally located within the populous Northeast and having easy shipping access to the entire United States and Western Europe—can support everything from Indonesian restaurants to dozens of Broadway, off-Broadway, off-off-Broadway, and local theater groups. In most other cities, Indonesian restaurants are nowhere to be found and theatergoers must be content with pre-Broadway trial runs, post-Broadway tours, or small local theater offerings. This is why, when they are compared with highest order cities in common parlance, lower order cities often are referred to disparagingly as "one-horse towns." Such a condescending attitude was also in essayist Alexander Woolcott's mind when he wrote in the 1930s: "A hick town is one where there is no place to go you shouldn't be."

The General Pattern of Urban Land Use.

This vertical place is no more an accident than the Himalayas are. The city needs all those tall buildings to contain the tremendous energy there.

EDWARD FIELD

Economists argue that the consequences for urban land use of these economic advantages of cities are enormous. Imagine a typical trip from the countryside into any American city. At the beginning of the trip, there are fields and perhaps some scattered farms or houses. As the city approaches, built-up residential areas appear, often increasing in density as one gets nearer to the city. Finally there comes the central city itself, complete with huge buildings and businesses: the CBD.

Is this pattern typical of other American cities you know? If you think it is, economist William Alonso (1971) would say that this perception is no accident. Cities *do* use their land similarly. In order to explain this pattern, Alonso developed a theoretical model of urban land use.

In constructing his model, Alonso described the ideal case. In order to do so he made a number of assumptions: (1) the city existed on a completely flat, featureless place; (2) it had a single CBD; (3) efficient transportation existed in all directions; and (4) every person in the city was motivated by economic self-interest.

Alonso was well aware that in real life many of these assumptions might not hold. For example, San Francisco exists on hills, the Minneapolis-St. Paul metropolis has two CBDs, Philadelphia's subway system runs only to certain parts of the city, and the Mormons who founded Salt Lake City were hardly motivated by purely economic interests. Similarly, Alonso knew that other factors such as ethnic relationships, politics, and history play roles in shaping cities. Nevertheless, dispensing for the moment with such particulars, one can see how economic concerns shape city land use.

To illustrate Alonso's model, let's examine a typical person, "Susan," who is involved in business. We know Susan can engage in the most trade, maximize her access to goods and services, and draw on the largest labor pool if she locates her business in the center of the city. Of course, all other business people and private citizens also are aware of the benefits to be gained by such a location. This sets up a basic competition between these people for the scarce center-city land. Aware of this competition, those who rent or want to sell land downtown try to get as high a price for it as they can. Hence, for Susan to be sure of getting office space downtown, she has to be willing to outbid other competitors. In her favor is the fact that she is trying to get the land for her business, so she has all the financial assets of her successful organization at her command. She can pay quite a high rent, more than many other competitors, particularly private citizens who have only their personal incomes at their disposal.

To Alonso, this is the key point: only those who can pay the most are likely to get center-city land. Since businesses like Susan's typically have the ability to pay more, downtown becomes predominantly occupied by businesses. In this way a CBD is created, and in some cases it is a rather incredible human artifact (see Box 6-2).

But, wearing another hat, Susan is a private citizen. She has to live somewhere. She doesn't need much space—three rooms perhaps—but, given the fact that CBD rents are so high and that she has only her salary with which to pay the rent she has no choice but to live outside the CBD. Of course, for convenience (to be near the theaters, for example), Susan will want to live as close to the CBD as possible. Luckily, the terrific advantages of the CBD begin to decrease rapidly as the distance from the core increases. It simply costs most businesses too much in terms of transportation, time, and lost contact with competitors and customers to locate farther out. So, away from the CBD, rents drop off, making it possible for Susan to rent an apartment within her salary's possibilities.

Overall, Alonso's model suggests a city with two major districts: (1) a CBD in the middle occupied by businesses of various types (offices, industries, warehouses) and (2) the surrounding residential areas. Circling the inner residential district would be yet other rings, which require even more land. In the fringe area, where residences begin to get less dense, we might expect to find such things as drive-in theaters, junkyards, cemeteries, and golf courses. Farther out, as population dwindles away, we would begin to find

---

BOX 6-2
The New York City Skyline—A Cast of Thousands

No one could look at [the New York City skyline] without asking: "Who built it?" If you consult the library books, you'll be told that the Empire State Building was designed by Shreve, Lane & Harmon, and that Rockefeller Center was created by Corbet, Harrison & MacMurray, Hood & Foulhoux, Reinhard & Hofmeister. Yes, but who? What senior member of the firm drafting plans for the Lever Building said, "Suppose we used green glass?" . . . Who of the Seagram architects first said tentatively: "What about bronze?" . . . Whose pencil drew the spectacular sweeping curve of 9 West Fifty-seventh Street? Who built it? Anon., that's who. Nobody built the New York skyline. Nobody by the thousands.

Source: Helen Hanff, *Apple of My Eye* (Garden City, N.Y.: Doubleday, 1978), p. 54.

Source: American Airlines.

---

farm land. Although the owners of many of these businesses might like to be closer to the CBD, the larger amount of land they require makes it unfeasible because of the higher rents they would have to pay. If one ever found a CBD golf course, however, one could bet that the cost of going nine holes would be expensive, indeed!

Figure 6-4 summarizes Alonso's model of urban land use. As it shows, businesses pay the highest rents to be near the CBD. As the distance from the CBD grows, the number of businesses declines until, at some point, they cease altogether. This means that, despite the lower rents, it would no longer be economically feasible to operate a business because the trade advantages of being in or near the CBD would be lost.

Many residents, on the other hand, cannot afford the high rents of the CBD, so, like Susan, they live some distance away from it. As distance increases, rents continue to drop, but, at some point, no matter how low the rent, transportation problems in terms of time and money become so

great that virtually no city workers choose to live that far from the CBD.

People engaged in agriculture and other land-intensive pursuits can least afford to pay CBD rentals; hence their businesses are not seen often until the distance from the CBD becomes considerable.

Figure 6-4 also reflects the ring effect that Alonso's model described. In the area closest to the CBD—points CBD to (a) on the horizontal axis—businesses predominate; from (a) to (b), residences predominate; finally, from (b) to (c), agriculture and other land-intensive uses are most apparent. As the word "predominate" suggests, this does not mean that the CBD has *no* residents or activities requiring large amounts of land; however, for the economic reasons we've noted, there are *fewer* of these activities. With this in mind, take a moment to think of cities that you know, or refer back to what you know about the cities in Figure 6-1, and consider how well this model explains their land use.

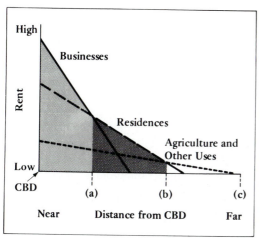

Figure 6-4 *The economics of urban land use.*

The Case of the Inner-City Poor. At this point you may be thinking that while Alonso's model may be generally true, the great majority of cities you know have lots of poor people living near the CBD and a great many wealthier people—middle-and upper-class people, for example—living at greater distances from the CBD (in the suburbs). If Alonso is correct, the poor, unable to afford rents near the CBD, should be living a relatively long distance from the CBD. Alonso attempts to address this problem by analyzing the differences in the income levels of poorer and wealthier urban residents.

Poor families have little disposable income. As a result, they must be very careful how they spend their money. Although land near the CBD is expensive, as one gets farther out from the CBD, transportation costs and the inconvenience of getting to work increase markedly. Consequently, many poor people are willing to pay the higher rents charged for living near the CBD. Moreover, the burden of high rent can become somewhat less onerous if poor families live with other poor families and pool their meager resources. A more affluent family may be willing, for other economic reasons, to put up with the economic and personal inconveniences of living at some distance from the CBD. First, their greater income means that increased commuting costs aren't as much of a problem to them as they would be to a

poor family, and, second, a suburban location offers them a great deal of space—a whole house with a large lawn, say—at prices much lower than similar accommodations would cost in or near the CBD. While poor families might like to have the extra land and amenities of a house in the suburbs, they simply cannot afford the luxury. In a very real sense they are economically trapped in the center city.

There is little doubt that the basic theory of the economic determinants of urban land use is helpful in understanding land use in many cities. But is it descriptive of land use in *all* cities?

Criticisms of the Basic Theory

Some scholars, like M. P. Todaro, question whether free enterprise, in the sense assumed by the proponents of the economic theory we have just discussed, ever exists at all. This question is examined in Box 6-3.

An example will illustrate what Todaro is talking about. "Blackston" is a pseudonym for a poor black area of a major eastern city. Betty Lou Valentine (1978) did a survey of supermarket prices in Blackston and in surrounding, higher income white neighborhoods. She found that poor blacks pay *significantly higher prices* for their groceries in Blackston than do the more affluent whites nearby. For example, in the white areas the price of chicken averaged $.39 a pound, rice was $.26 a pound, apples were $.14 a pound, and soft drinks were $.95 for a six-pack. The same items in Blackston: chicken, $.53; rice, $.42; apples, $.25; and soft drinks, $1. This is typical of ghetto areas nationwide. The reason? Supermarket owners in Blackston know the blacks are "captured customers." Because of the expense and inconvenience of going to white neighborhoods (most black families in Blackston do not own cars) and because of the overt prejudice they encounter when they do, most blacks do their shopping locally. Knowing this, supermarket owners set their prices higher in Blackston than in the more affluent white neighborhoods where residents have more mobility and hence could choose to shop elsewhere. In other words, the poor are exploited because of their inability to compete equally in

BOX 6-3
Does *Free* Enterprise Exist?

In economic theory, the basic questions of what and how much to produce are assumed to be determined by the aggregate preferences of all consumers as revealed by their market demand for different goods and services. Producers are assumed simply to respond to these "sovereign" consumer preferences and, motivated by the desire to maximize profits, they are assumed to compete with each other *on equal terms* in the purchase of resources and the sale of their products. . . . The ultimate rationale for the efficacy of this theory or model of economic activity is Adam Smith's famous notion of the "invisible hand" of capitalism which postulates that if each individual consumer, producer and supplier of resources pursues his or her own self-interest, they will, "as if by an invisible hand," be promoting the overall interests of society as a whole.

Unfortunately, the facts of economic life in *both* the developed and the less developed nations of the world are such as to render much of [this] theory of negligible importance. . . . Consumers as a whole are rarely sovereign about anything, let alone with regard to questions of what goods and services are to be produced, in what quantities and for whom. Producers, whether private or public, have great power in determining market prices and quantities sold. The ideal of competition is typically just that—an "ideal" with little relation to reality. Finally, the so-called "invisible hand" often acts not to promote the general welfare of all, but to lift up those already well-off while pushing down that vast majority of the population which is striving to free itself from poverty, malnutrition, and illiteracy.

Source: M. P. Todaro, *Economic Development in the Third World* (New York: Longman, 1977), pp. 11–12.

economic factors may influence urban land use patterns decidedly. For example, there is often a tendency for people in affluent suburbs to resist strongly the encroachment of the poor upon their residential areas. This resistance may go beyond negative attitudes. Actual zoning laws and the practices of real-estate agents may work to exclude poor people, even from housing they might afford. In an examination of the affluent suburb of Brookhaven on Long Island, Roger Williams reported widespread resistance to a proposed low-income housing project that would allow some poor families to live in Brookhaven. This resistance soon surfaced in local politics:

> In a local election campaign last fall, Bob Hughes, the Republican candidate for town supervisor, warned against the "teeming hordes" who would descend on Brookhaven if it provided low-income housing. "It's the pull-up-the-gang-plank syndrome," says [a] county official. "'I'm here, so don't let anybody else in—especially any of *those* people.'" (Williams 1978, p. 18)

Resistance was decidedly tinged with racism:

> "I used to live in New York City," [said] Walter Beck, the Brookhaven town attorney, "and I know I like cleaner air, the lower population density, and especially the feeling of space you find in the suburbs. . . . I've noticed that poor blacks, for instance, bump shoulders all day and don't mind it." (Williams 1978, p. 18)

The third area of criticism is the most devastating of all. Many scholars argue that the economic theory of urban land use is not meaningfully applicable to many cities in history or in other cultures. For example, anthropologist Richard Fox (1977) argues that the capitalist-industrial city (on which the economic theory is based) is only *one* of at least five major city types that have existed historically. The other types are what Fox terms regal-ritual cities, administrative cities, colonial cities, and mercantile cities. Of these, only the last operates on similar economic principles to the modern Western city. The others, as their names imply, have central concerns very different from the rational economic processes assumed by Alonso's theory. Regal-ritual cities, for example, have political or religious ac-

the free-enterprise system. Worse, Valentine's data show that because of this price differential, the poor have no choice but to become *poorer* as they make their food purchases. Not only are they paying more for their goods, they are spending more of their limited income than are whites.

Valentine's observation that blacks often are treated with overt prejudice when they shop in white neighborhoods illustrates a second problem with the economic model of urban land use: people do not live by bread alone. Important non-

tivities at their core. Thus, in the Egyptian Kingdom of the Pharaohs (2600–2100 B.C.), major cities, such as Memphis, were organized around the political power and interests of the Pharaoh and his court. Beyond this small, favored elite, the population of the city was little more than a large "supporting cast." People worked for the court for whatever pittance they were given and lived where the court decreed. If their land was needed by the Pharaoh, it was taken, not bargained for at the going rate. Clearly, in understanding a city of this kind, the economic processes described by Alonso have little usefulness. One would be much better served by looking at the sociological concept of power and its uses.

Why have we spent so much time examining the economic theory of urban land use if it is beset with such major problems? First, it is not *wrong*; it is just *limited*. It helps us to understand how many Western, and particularly American, cities have organized their land. Second, whatever its limitations, it does underscore the need for keeping the economic concerns of city life in mind when analyzing urban land use. Free enterprise may not characterize all cities, but city people always have to have *some* way of getting enough food, clothing, and shelter.

Thus, economic forces are important considerations, but they are only a part of the story of urban land use.

Urban Ecology: The Chicago School

There are forces at work within the limits of the urban community . . . which tend to bring about an orderly and typical grouping of its population and institutions. The science which seeks to isolate these factors and to describe the typical constellations of persons and institutions which the co-operation of these forces produce is what we call human, as distinguished from plant and animal, ecology. (Park 1916)

Robert Park, dean of the Chicago sociologists we discussed in Chapter 4, wanted nothing less than to comprehend all the forces that shaped human social life. To achieve that end, he used cities as his laboratory and created what he called the science of human ecology.

The Ecological Theory of Urban Development

Although Park was very careful to distinguish his science from the study of plant or animal ecology (the study of the relationship between living things and their environment), he saw many of the same forces at work in the human arena as existed in the biological world. For instance, he believed human life always was motivated by the evolutionary principle of the struggle for existence. This always surfaced as *competition*. In the effort to satisfy their needs, people competed with each other for scarce resources—food, clothes, shelter, and valued land. Inevitably, some people won favored resources and others lost. As a result of this competition, the city took on a characteristic form, dividing itself into "natural" areas (so called because they weren't consciously planned): business districts, ethnic neighborhoods, skid rows, and rooming-house areas.

In this part of his theory, Park was making many of the same assumptions about competition that characterized the economic theory of urban land use. On another level, however, Park saw a distinctly social element in competition. People didn't just compete for economic gain, they also competed for power—for the control of parks, streets, and ethnic districts—and prestige—the right to live in a more respected neighborhood or to have a fashionable business address.

In addition, living in early twentieth-century Chicago, Park became convinced that large-scale *population movements* strongly influenced urban development. Most of the immigrants who came to the growing American cities in the late nineteenth and early twentieth centuries had little education and few skills to sell and were exceedingly poor. As a result, they poured into the center-city area, took low-paying jobs in factories, and were forced to live in overcrowded housing. Marie Jastrow, recalling her father's arrival in New York, gives an illustration in Cityscape 6-1.

Jastrow's father and his family did not stay on Lower Manhattan's Hester Street forever, however. With time most immigrants became skilled,

CITYSCAPE 6-1
The New World—New York, 1905

My father crossed the Atlantic and landed on Ellis Island at the beginning of October 1905, well aware of the ordeal that awaited him. He had heard stories. The threat of deportation haunted every [poor] immigrant. . . .

Eyes, ears, chest—the entire person was scrutinized by doctors. Some were rejected. Those who were turned away fell into the depths of despair, waiting, without hope, for the first ship to take them back.

Hour after hour the examination went on. At last my father found himself on American soil, a silent, solitary figure. He had passed the inspection. Now, for the first time, he was alone, separated from his fellow travellers. It was a painful aloneness. . . .

A policeman walked by and stopped. What was this lonely figure doing in the cold afternoon, sitting in the park? An immigrant, no doubt, just off the ship. . . .

"Are you expecting anyone?" The officer spoke some German. My father shook his head. No, he expected no one, he knew no one. But he would appreciate help

in locating a room. "Can you pay." "Yes," Papa again shook his head. "But not much." He hesitated a moment. "The room has to be cheap."

The policeman smiled, writing something on a slip of paper.

"Go to this address. Tell them that Officer Schmidt gave you this." My father looked at the address he had just received. . . . He wondered how to get to the address he was holding in hand, but dared not ask.

Officer Schmidt was becoming impatient. "What is it? Can't you read?"

"Yes, I can read," said my father, "but, if you would be so kind to give me directions, I do not know this city."

"Of course, you just got in," laughed the officer. "I'll take you to the streetcar on that corner. You give this address to the conductor, he will let you off on the right street."

"Thank you," said my grateful father. "I shall never forget this— how you helped me on my first day in America."

. . . The Hester Street tenement

where my father lived for the first few months stood in the midst of a heavily populated immigrant area. It was the first stopover for many Jewish families. No one arrived here with more than token funds. They had nothing, these people, but dreams and hopes for the better future this new land could offer. None spoke English, very few spoke any language but Yiddish. It is easy to see why they clustered together and found comfort in the nearness of their countrymen.

The six-story structures in that street were planned for thirty-six tenants, six to a floor. Actually, counting the boarders that were crowded into every available corner "to help pay the rent," no landlord knew how many people lived in his building. But no one counted, as long as the rent was ready on the first of every month.

Source: Marie Jastrow, *A Time to Remember* (New York: Norton, 1979), pp. 21–24, 27, 36.

---

made money, and moved to better housing. (Jastrow's family moved to Yorkville in New York's East 80s.) As they did so in cities all over the country, they left their original housing to the next poor group to enter the city. The Chicago sociologists called such population movements *invasion and succession.*

The Concentric Zone Hypothesis

In the processes of competition and population movement, then, Park saw cities being shaped and reshaped. Although local change was virtually omnipresent, Park saw the city as a whole evolving a larger, characteristic pattern. This pattern was illustrated most succinctly by one of his

students, Ernest W. Burgess, in the mid-1920s, who suggested that the city develops something like the interior of a tree. It evolves a series of concentric rings or zones that are added to as the city grows. What makes Burgess's model readily understandable is its similarity to Alonso's model of the city's business, residential, and agricultural rings (Figure 6-4).

However, while Burgess assumed economic competition was vital to the city, he, like Park, saw other social forces at work. In his view, moving to a suburb is more than a purely economic consideration. It also is related to prestige seeking. Living in a prominent suburb often is thought to demonstrate, to ourselves and to others, that we have made it in terms of the American success

New York's Lower East Side at the end of the last century. A street such as this was home to Marie Jastrow's father when he arrived in the United States (Cityscape 6-1.) (Library of Congress)

ethic: we are not only wealthier than we once were, we are respectable as well.

Burgess's model has five main zones (see Figure 6-5, right side). He describes them as follows:

> This chart represents an ideal construction of the tendencies of any town or city to expand radically from its central business district—on the map "The Loop" (I). Encircling the downtown area there is normally an area in transition, which is being invaded by business and light manufacture (II). A third area (III) is inhabited by the workers in industries who have escaped from the area of deterioration (II) but who desire to live within easy access of their work. Beyond this zone is the "residential area" (IV) of high-class apartment buildings or of exclusive "restricted" districts of single family dwellings. Still farther, out beyond the city limits, is the commuters' zone—suburban areas, or satellite cities—within a thirty- to sixty-minute ride of the central business district. (1967, p. 50; originally published 1925)

Burgess illustrated his model by applying it directly to the Chicago of his day (Figure 6-5, left

side). Once the "halving effect" of Lake Michigan was taken into account, Burgess's theory proved to do a creditable job at explaining the location of the city's districts. The most valuable land (Zone I) was contained within "The Loop" downtown and was the exclusive preserve of business. In Zone II, the "zone in transition," were factories and slums, the latter filled to overflowing with bohemians, down-and-out roomers, and ethnic groups of various sorts including Italians (Little Sicily) and Chinese (Chinatown). The third zone, the "zone of workingmen's homes," was predominantly inhabited by second-generation migrants, the descendants of earlier Chicago immigrants who had taken the first step in escaping the inner city by moving out of the slums. Here, too, was the "two-flat" area, where duplex houses actually were occupied by two families, instead of by four or more as was so often the case in the slums. Zone IV was the "residential zone," dominated by residential hotels, apartment areas, and, most important, single-family residences. In this zone as well existed a relatively wealthy

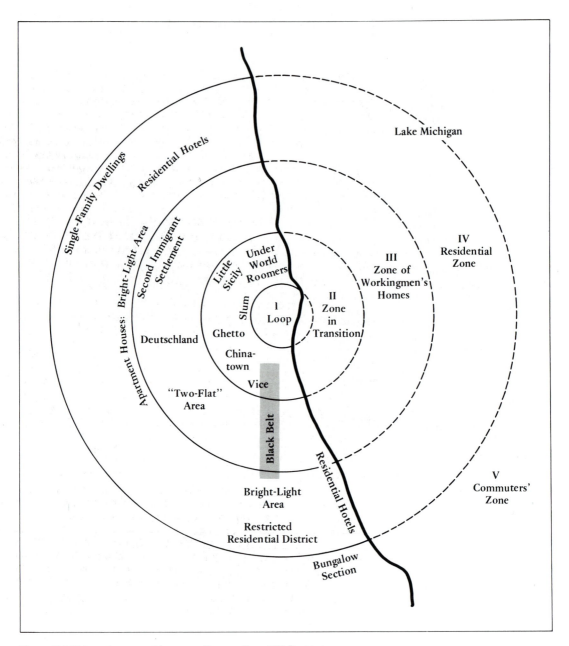

Figure 6-5 *Chicago's concentric zones. Source: Ernest W. Burgess,*
"The Growth of the City," in Robert E. Park and Ernest W. Burgess,
eds., The City *(Chicago: University of Chicago Press, 1967; orig.*
1925), p. 55, chart II. Reprinted by permission of the University of Chi-
cago Press.

"restricted residential district," an area that excluded those with "undesirable" ethnic or racial characteristics.

Criticisms of the Chicago School

Although he used Chicago as the basis of his model, Burgess believed that his zonal hypothesis could describe any city. But do all cities and towns conform to the concentric zone pattern? Certainly some do. Chicago does, as, to a large degree, do Cleveland, Minneapolis, St. Louis, and Milwaukee (Faris 1967, p. 61). Except for these older American cities, however, it is difficult to find overwhelmingly convincing examples.

In addition, criticisms have been raised about the reliance of Park's ecological theory on the concepts of unrestrained competition and population movements (Berry and Kasarda 1977, p. 6). Although there is some strong indication that these forces play a powerful role in how groups "settle out" in American cities—as La Gory and his associates (1980) recently found in a study of 70 urban areas—it seems that these forces are more powerful in some cultures and some periods of history than in others. For example, as we have seen, competition, even in the broader Park-Burgess sense, is not always at the center of urban life, and important periods of population movement come and go. In America the period between 1880 and 1960 stands out, while in modernizing countries like Mexico, now is the time of greatest population movement.

A third criticism is that Burgess's model implicitly assumes that cities everywhere are based on transportation systems like the railroad, something that is patently not the case.

> The discrepancies between [Burgess's] conception and reality (which are always considerable) undoubtedly are augmented by U.S. cities changing from the relatively compact type concentrated around the railroad, which served Burgess as an empirical model, to the dispersed form, broadly organized, which has been produced under the influence of the automobile. When as many empirical studies of the U.S. are accumulated as are available from other countries, it will be clearly seen that Burgess's conception, instead of having the degree of universality he seemed to give it originally, ac-

tually fits only U.S. commercial and industrial cities, and—even more—fits these only in a limited period of development. (Dotson and Dotson, quoted in Schnore 1965, p. 372)

Another major criticism wonders whether zones in the sense suggested by Burgess ever really existed. Alihan (1938) argued that there is no neat transition from one zone to another, but rather an imperfect gradation. Others have challenged the idea of zonal homogeneity, pointing to case after case of high- and low-income people living within one zone (Davie 1937; Firey 1947).

Finally, the ecological theory has been criticized as being "too biological." That is, its use of the principles of plant and animal ecology to explain human processes is seen as potentially distortive. While people surely are subject to the pressures of such large forces as population movements, they are not just swept along with the tide. They are thinking beings who can act creatively on their urban environment. The ecological theory downplays the role of choice in the evolution of the urban environment (Berry and Kasarda 1977).

As a result of such criticisms, Park's ecological theory and Burgess's concentric zone model have assumed positions of less importance in contemporary urban ecology than they had originally. In their stead have appeared a host of alternative theories and models, all of which suggest that the determining forces in land use are much more complex than Park or Burgess ever suspected.

Urban Ecology: Other Theories

The Sector Theory

The first major attempt at modifying the zonal hypothesis was made by Homer Hoyt, who noticed that a fair number of city districts did not conform to the purely concentric model suggested by Burgess. Even in Burgess's Chicago (Figure 6-5), anomalous areas like the "Deutschland Ghetto" (the home of German immigrants) and the "Black Belt" could be seen to cross-cut zones.

To find out why, Hoyt (1939) studied, block by

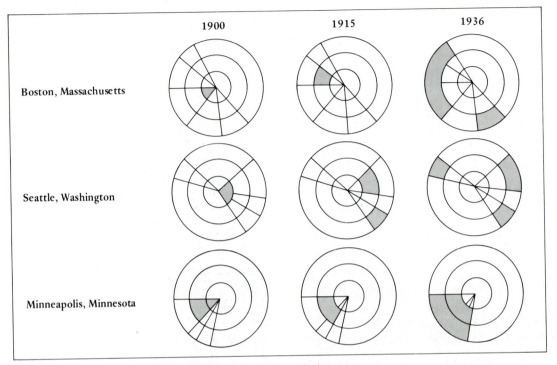

Figure 6-6 *Shifts in the location of fashionable residential areas in three American cities, 1900–1936. Fashionable areas are indicated by shading. Source: Adapted from Homer Hoyt,* The Structure and Growth of Residential Neighborhoods in American Cities *(Washington, D.C.: Federal Housing Administration, 1939), p. 115, figure 40.*

block, the residential patterns of high-rent districts in 142 cities. The scope of this study was a major advance over Burgess's work, which was based almost exclusively on Chicago and selected examples of other cities that fit his theory. Hoyt's study gave him a diversified, *comparative* base on which to draw his conclusions. Hoyt also examined his cities in three different time periods: 1900, 1915, and 1936. This added an important *historical* dimension. Figure 6-6 graphically presents Hoyt's findings concerning high-prestige, fashionable areas in three of his cities.

A number of things are of note. First, Hoyt discovered that most of these areas formed districts or sectors of varying size. Second, although there was evidence of a concentric shape in some sectors, many sectors often took a pie-shaped form; in no case did they take up an entire ring, as Burgess's model suggested. Third, as frequently as

not, fashionable districts abutted and were sometimes even surrounded by lower income districts. (A classic example is Harlem's "Striver's Row," a wealthy, two-block oasis of pristine houses surrounded by buildings approaching utter collapse.) Fourth, as time passed, Hoyt found a tendency for sectors to move out of the city radially, along a path begun by the sector in earlier years (Seattle provides a good example).

Fifth, in the later periods, fashionable areas seldom were found in only a single city location; rather, they commonly occupied two or even three areas. Importantly, Hoyt also discovered that such locations were chosen for reasons well beyond the pressures of competition and population movevment. For example, in many cities Hoyt found fashionable districts on the "high ground" (Boston's Beacon Hill for instance), indicating a preference by the wealthy to be "above"

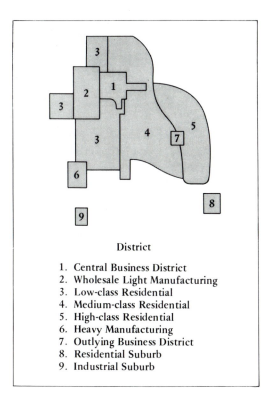

District

1. **Central Business District**
2. **Wholesale Light Manufacturing**
3. **Low-class Residential**
4. **Medium-class Residential**
5. **High-class Residential**
6. **Heavy Manufacturing**
7. **Outlying Business District**
8. **Residential Suburb**
9. **Industrial Suburb**

Figure 6-7 *The multiple nuclei theory. Source: Chauncy O. Harris and Edward L. Ullman, "The Nature of Cities,"* The Annals, *242 (Nov. 1945). Reprinted by permission of the AAPSS.*

the city's other residents. Elsewhere, he found high-prestige sectors located for aesthetic reasons—on waterfronts, for example. In still other cities, he found such districts located along main transportation lines that facilitated easy access to the center city.

The Multiple Nuclei Theory

Although Hoyt's study was a major advance over the work of the Chicago ecologists, it was limited by its focus on residential sectors. Hoyt noted that industry also showed a tendency to move radially outward from the center city—upriver, or along railroad lines, for instance—but he did not spend a great deal of time developing this observation.

In 1945 Chauncey Harris and Edward Ullman developed another theory of urban land use in an attempt to broaden Hoyt's findings. They argued

that as the contemporary city grew, it diversified, developing in the process many sectors of activity. This *multiple nuclei* theory is represented graphically in Figure 6-7.

While Harris and Ullman agreed that modern cities are likely to have a major CBD (sector 1 in Figure 6-7), they suggested that specific historical, cultural, or economic factors fostered the location of other urban districts in places that neither the zonal nor sector theories could explain. For example, while wholesale light manufacturing (2) might be near the CBD, low-income residences (3) might be in various separate districts around it. A medium-income residential district (4) might abut the CBD and be bordered on its outer edge by a high-income residential area (5). Between the two might exist a secondary business district (7), and farther out might exist a completely separate residential suburb (8). Heavy manufacturing (6) might be a relatively large distance from the CBD and evolve an industrial-residential suburb (9) near it.

Why do these nuclei develop? First, certain types of activities require certain types of facilities to operate at highest productivity. For example, heavy manufacturing requires a lot of acreage. In the formative days of American cities, such acreage was available downtown, near the CBD. In recent years, however, space near the CBD has become highly limited because of competition and rising rents. As a result, much heavy manufacturing has moved out of the CBD to places where the needed land is available and where firms can reduce expenditures for rent and taxation. In Chicago, for example, heavy manufacturing that used to be located in the CBD is now on the south side of the city, in or around Gary, Indiana.

A second reason for multiple nuclei is the fact that some types of activity are disadvantageous to one another; therefore, they separate into nuclei some distance apart. For example, districts that feature X-rated movies and peep shows may be distasteful to the properties of more "respectable" businesses. The result is that "porno" areas (such as Boston's "Combat Zone" and New York's 42nd Street) typically exist as distinctive, highly centralized districts with few businesses of any other kind nearby. To preserve this separation of incompatible districts, most contemporary cities have zoning laws—legal restrictions designed to keep some land uses separated.

Third, for some urban activities, a CBD location may not be desirable for social or economic reasons. As we have seen, the desire of many city residents to escape to the suburbs often is motivated by such social considerations as prestige. Similarly, some land-intensive activities, such as automobile salvage, cannot afford a CBD site; hence, they locate at some distance from it. Additionally, many city firms have relocated near the beltways that surround so many American cities because, with trucking assuming a more and more important role in interstate shipping, such locations become the most sensible.

Perhaps the most important contribution of Harris and Ullman's theory was that it seriously questioned the idea that urban land use is strictly predictable. Burgess's zonal hypothesis and, to a lesser extent, Hoyt's sector theory both suggested certain inevitable patterns of land use. Harris and Ullman's multiple nuclei theory suggested that specific historical, cultural, or economic situations would shape each city. As these situations changed over time, the arrangement of the city's districts also would change. Even the supposedly inevitable CBD might disappear or weaken, as it has in the last few decades (Ullman 1962).

Social Area Analysis

Up to this point we have considered a number of urban land use theories: the traditional economic theory, Burgess's concentric zone hypothesis, Hoyt's sector theory, and Harris and Ullman's multiple nuclei theory. The first three have been criticized for being too simplistic, and the fourth has raised the question of whether valid generalizations about urban land use can be made at all. In light of such difficulties, it is not surprising that other urbanists have tried to formulate yet another approach.

In studies of Los Angeles and San Francisco, Eshref Shevky and Marilyn Williams (1949) and, later, Shevky and Wendell Bell (1955) attempted

to describe urban land use by focusing on only the social characteristics of a city's population. The social characteristics they examined were *social rank* (roughly, amount of prestige), *family status* (number of children, type of house, whether mother worked or not), and *ethnicity*. By examining official census tracts for all parts of the city, they tried to determine to what degree a tract's population shared these characteristics. If a fairly large proportion did share these characteristics, they called that district a *social area*. For example, in San Francisco, they found that groups in some areas measured low on social rank and family status but high on ethnicity. That is, people in this area tended to have low prestige, have large families in multiple-dwelling houses, and be of identifiable ethnic or racial background. Conversely, people in other areas measured high on social rank and low on family status and ethnicity. By combining these social characteristics in every possible manner, Shevky, Bell, and Williams argued that fully 32 distinct social areas might be found in cities. Furthermore, they suggested that such social characteristics played an extremely important role in the urban dweller's mind. They were a "language" that everyone understood:

> In the impersonal setting of the city . . . social standing does not rest on any intimate evaluation of persons nor any discriminating appraisal of differences within groups. Instead, certain easily recognizable traits, such as houses and possessions, become symbolic of rank. . . . As every occupation is evaluated and generally accorded honor and esteem on a scale of prestige in society, so every residential section has a status value which is easily recognized by everyone in the city. Even a casual visitor in Los Angeles could name a half dozen places representative of the exclusive sections on the westside and along the foothills of the Santa Monica and San Gabriel Mountains. (Shevky and Williams 1949, pp. 61–62)

This certainly is true enough, as demonstrated by Jan Morris's observations about Hollywood in Box 6-4.

Even if the person on the street easily understands these social characteristics, however, the

---

BOX 6-4
Hollywood—Home of the Stars

Nostalgia blurs the realities of Hollywood, the Versailles of Los Angeles, and peoples it forever with the royalty of another era, the Astaires, the Tracys, the Garbos, and nobles of even earlier vintage. Now as always the tourist buses circumnavigate the Homes of the Stars, and the tours peddle their street plans on Sunset Strip. Now as always Hollywood feeds upon narcissism, cosseted in sycophancy and sustained by snobbery. Scattered over the Hollywood Hills, and over the Santa Monica Mountains into the San Fernando Valley, the houses of the movie people stand sealed and suspicious in the morning, the only sounds the swishing of their sprinklers, the snarling of their guard dogs, or perhaps the labored breathing of their gardeners: and in their garages the cars are profligately stacked, Jag beside Merc, Rolls upstaging BMW.

Source: Jan Morris, "Entering L.A.: Historical Monument," *Rolling Stone*, July 1, 1976, p. 32.

---

movements forced concentric rings to develop. Even for Harris and Ullman, who saw no general pattern of land use, the reasons for the location of an urban nucleus could be understood by looking at the historical, cultural, or economic pressures that existed in that city.

Other detractors have worried about the social characteristics chosen by Shevky, Bell, and Williams. Otis Dudley Duncan (1955) suggested that there was no particular reason for choosing those variables as opposed to others, and, in a review of social area analysis, Janet Abu-Lughod (1969) suggested that, of the three characteristics, social rank seemed to explain the most about how groups in cities are organized. As for family status and ethnicity, she argued that in non-industrial settings such as Cairo these characteristics were of little or no use.

Thus, social area analysis also has had its difficulties in fully explaining urban land use. As a result, in recent years an even more sophisticated technique has been developed, based on the idea of social area analysis. Its results have been surprising.

Factorial Ecology

The Basic Findings. Factorial ecology uses computer technology to analyze the social characteristics of an urban population. It differs from social area analysis because, rather than beginning with a few preselected social characteristics (such as social rank), *all* characteristics thought to be potentially important in a city are analyzed. The computer then compares all these characteristics with one another to see if any characteristics are linked together. As linked characteristics are found, they are called *factors* and are given descriptive names. When the analysis is complete, the city's land use pattern as a whole can be described. Let's turn to an example.

R. J. Johnston (1976) used factorial ecology to examine Whangarei, a city in New Zealand. He took eight social characteristics he thought might be important and instructed the computer to use them in an analysis of each of Whangarei's 22 census-tract areas. His results indicated that some

real question is whether they are truly useful in helping us to understand urban land use. In an attempt to find out, Van Arsdol, Camilleri, and Schmid (1958a, 1958b, 1961) examined ten American cities. While they found the characteristics of social rank, family status, and ethnicity useful in identifying social areas in six of the cities, they also found them of extremely limited use in the others. They suggested that other characteristics also would have to be measured if social area analysis were to prove widely useful in understanding city form.

Like all the approaches we've discussed, social area analysis has been strongly criticized. One argument is that it is not theoretical. It merely provides a description of the social characteristics of an urban area (Hawley and Duncan 1957). Consequently, it cannot be used either to predict where groups will settle or to explain why groups have settled where they have. Whatever their shortcomings, all previous explanations of urban land use did attempt to explain why cities developed as they did. For Park and Burgess, the ecological forces of competition and population

areas of the city had high concentrations of male workers who were in professional or managerial occupations, who earned over $6,000 a year, and who held a university degree. These characteristics were so strongly linked to one another that Johnston combined them into a single factor called *socioeconomic status*. (For all intents and purposes, this factor corresponds to Shevky, Bell, and Williams's social rank.) Johnston also found that other residential areas of the city had many people over 16 who were unmarried and lived in rented housing. Once again, the correlation among these variables was so high that Johnston designated *family status* as a second important factor. Although the correlation was weaker, there was also some evidence that *ethnic* factors were of some importance in determining residence in Whangarei. Interestingly, when taken together, these three factors—socioeconomic status, family status, and ethnicity—could account for over 86 percent of the residential patterning of Whangarei.

Johnston's findings are important particularly because they have been replicated by other people using factorial ecology in other cities. For example, in a study of Copenhagen, Denmark, Pedersen (1967) found socioeconomic status, family status, and population mobility to be key factors that characterized city residence; and, in a study comparing Helsinki, Finland, and Boston, Sweetser (1965) identified socioeconomic status and family status as major factors in both cities and ethnicity as important in Boston.

All this provided verification from an unexpected direction of the apparent correctness of Shevky, Bell, and Williams's original choice of the key social characteristics that play a crucial role in people's minds when they are deciding where to live in an urban area.

A Synthetic Theory: Berry and Rees. Do these findings mean that we have to abandon entirely the earlier theories that suggested the importance of economics, concentric circles, sectors, and multiple nuclei? No, say sociologists Brian Berry and Phillip Rees (1969). In an attempt to tie together the findings of factorial ecology with the earlier theories, they have suggested that all these interpretations have been partially correct. The difficulty was that no earlier theory captured the full complexity of what was going on with urban land use, a complexity Berry and Rees attempt to describe in Figure 6-8.

They began by asking what would happen if each of the major social characteristics uncovered by factorial ecology—socioeconomic status, family status, and ethnicity—were the only force at work in the city, independent from the other factors and from other variables such as time and technological improvement. They reasoned that, if socioeconomic status were the sole determinant of urban location, cities would tend to divide themselves into *sectors* (Figure 6-8A). That is, people would tend to settle where a combination of preferences and finances would allow them. This process is what Homer Hoyt observed in his study as the pie-shaped outward movement of elite groups. But, while Hoyt restricted his observations primarily to wealthy groups, Berry and Rees contended that this outward sectoring would characterize all status groups in the city, whether high, middle, or low.

Second, if family status were the dominant social characteristic, given demands for living space, city groups would tend to arrange themselves in *concentric zones* (Figure 6-8B), as Park and Burgess suggested. Groups with the fewest children and the most working adults would tend to be located in the innermost circle, to be near their work and the advantages of the CBD (I). Groups with more children and fewer working adults would characterize the second circle (II), and groups with the most children and fewest working adults would settle in the outermost circle (III).

Third, were ethnicity the predominant characteristic, minority groups (the shaded areas of Figure 6-8C) would tend to be segregated in various ethnic communities throughout the city, for example, in Chicago's South Side, New York's Harlem, and San Francisco's Fillmore.

Of course, these social characteristics never do operate in isolation. They always influence one another and thus produce a much more complex land use pattern. In Figure 6-8D, Berry and Rees show what might occur if the effects of socioeco-

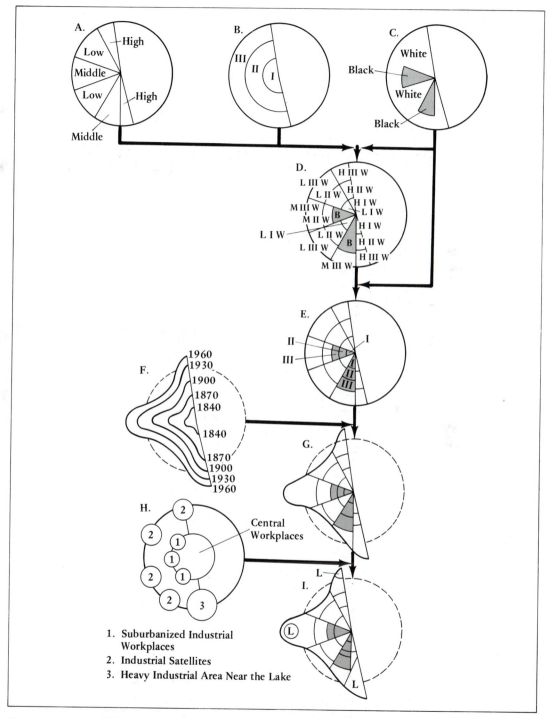

Figure 6-8 *An integrated model of urban land use. Source: Adapted from Brian J. L. Berry and P. H. Rees, "The Factorial Ecology of Calcutta," American Journal of Sociology, 74 (March 1969), figure 13. Reprinted by permission of the University of Chicago Press.*

nomic status, family status, and ethnicity were superimposed on one another. To take a few examples, beginning at the bottom right, you would be likely to find in the outermost area of an American city white people of high socioeconomic status with a lot of children and families with few working adults. (Thus the shorthand of "H III W," where "H" stands for a high income, "III" for numerous children, and "W" for white racial background.) In the next area, closer to the CBD, you also would be likely to find white people of high socioeconomic status, but this group probably would have fewer children and more working adults (H II W) than the previous area. Moving to the sector on the left, you would be likely to find, in the outermost district, white people of middle socioeconomic status with many children and few working adults (M III W). Moving toward the center-city area on the same sector, however, the next group encountered might be a segregated black group of low socioeconomic status (B). The rest of Figure 6-8D can be interpreted similarly.

Berry and Rees knew, however, that the forces that shape urban land use patterning are still more complex. For example, particular ethnic or minority groups frequently are restricted from participating in the general ecological patterns of the rest of the city; hence, within their segregated areas, they often evolve subsectors of their own, "reproducing in miniature the metropolitanwide pattern" (Berry and Rees 1969, p. 459). Figure 6-8E illustrates this by showing, within the segregated area, the subgroups with low fertility and high number of working adults nearest the center city (I) and the subgroups with high fertility and fewest working adults farthest out (III).

The city also may change with time, as shown in Figure 6-8F. As it grows (the diagram uses the years 1840–1960 as an example), what Berry and Rees call *tear faults* develop. Given existing districts and neighborhoods within the city, however, the tear faults are not always symmetrical in their configuration. The result is a pattern exemplified in Figure 6-8G.

Finally, in time, technological development and competition for valuable CBD space produce the multiple nucleation of industry and shopping districts away from the original CBD, as suggested by Harris and Ullman (Figure 6-8H). These develop suburbanized industrial work places (1), industrial satellites (2), and separate heavy industrial areas (3).

The end-result of all these forces is illustrated in Figure 6-8I. In it are seen sectors, inner circles, segregated areas (with their own inner circles), the tear faulting process occasioned by city growth, and the effect of the decentralization of industry (symbolized by the "L" areas that indicate lower socioeconomic groups "pulled out" from the center-city area to be near the industries for which they work).

Obviously, even Figure 6-8I is an *idealized* portrait. It fits no actual city. Yet Berry and Rees contend that, once the additional effects of local geography (a mountain or lake may limit development in some direction) or history (a government grant may fund a low-income housing project in a place not accounted for by the model) have been taken into account, the model could be applied to any city and provide an explanation for where any group or business activity is located.

Still one question remains: *why* do groups choose these locations? What motivates people to live at point X or Y in the city? Berry and Rees suggest that here is where considerations of socioeconomic status, family status, and ethnicity come in. Most residents of Western cities, they argue, base their decisions on three factors: (1) the price of the house, (2) the type of dwelling it is (single- or multiple-family, apartment or house, number of rooms), and (3) the location of the dwelling (social characteristics of the neighborhood, distance from work). Of these, they say,

> . . . [the] most important determinant is undoubtedly income. A large family with many children may need a large single-family home, but unless family income is above that minimum threshold required by the mortgage company, purchase of this type of home will not be possible. Similarly, low wages may make it essential for a worker to live near his place of employment in order to minimize the costs of the journey to work. He may therefore be unable to satisfy his preferences as to type of neighborhood. (Berry and Rees 1969, p. 461)

In the end, like Alonso, Berry and Rees stress the central importance of economics in determining land use in Western cities. How much money you have and how much money a particular location is going to cost is some kind of bottom line for determining where you live or site your business.

Still, Berry and Rees know that economics are not all of the story—social issues play a vital role as well:

> The age structure of the population, average family size, and female labor force participation change as distance from the city center increases: young families locate farther from the center than do older families. This pattern is a response to the change in house age and type as distance from the center becomes greater—the houses are newer, and single-family homes predominate as the city center is left behind. It is the lower land values toward the urban periphery that make possible this land-voracious construction, and the increasing . . . income of home buyers makes possible their purchase. Finally, minority groups find themselves segregated from the rest of the population to a greater or lesser degree as a result of recent arrival in the city, discrimination in the housing market, or through choice of home in congenial communities. (Berry and Rees 1969, p. 463)

Berry and Rees seem to believe that with this model at last we are beginning to find the answer to the complex riddle of urban land use. Although they admit that cultural differences would have to be taken into account, they hope it is possible to explain the where and why of city land use anywhere. Certainly that was the thrust of their comparative factorial ecology of Chicago and Calcutta, India, an analysis that demonstrated that socioeconomic status, family status, and ethnicity explained the bulk of both cities' patterning. Importantly, Berry and Rees's claims have been supported—most recently in a study of 38 American cities by Ervin (1984). Basing his conclusions on a detailed analysis of 1970 census data, Ervin concluded that American cities, in general, shape themselves in zones, sectors, and nuclei depending on the variables of socioeconomic class, family status, and ethnicity.

Criticisms of Factorial Ecology

Yet we must not be too quick here. Important as factorial ecology has been for the advancement of our knowledge of how some cities are arranged spatially, the technique is not without its problems. Critics have essentially taken two tacks: The first criticizes the method itself, the second questions whether the findings are generalizable to cities in other times and non-industrial settings.

Among those who criticize the method is one who has used it extensively himself, R. J. Johnston (1976). In the first place, Johnston argues that because the computer technique employed by factorial ecology is of a particular type, it often forces the complex world of the city into rigid, and possibly distorted, categories. For example, in one study of Detroit, in order to get the information to compute, an average was created to describe a certain area's residential pattern. The average made it appear that the people living in that area were much more concentrated in a particular space than they actually were. Second, factorial ecology usually employs census tract data. But census tracts often do not conform accurately to the areas where particular groups live. People with particular characteristics in common (for example, ethnicity), who see themselves as living in a single area, often are classified as living in *different* census tracts simply because the census tract, defined by a governmental agency, has been constructed for another purpose: counting the city's population. Third, there is the question of whether census tract information is all that accurate anyway. Certainly it is the best thing we have, but it has been known for some time that poor people, migrants, and other groups are often inaccurately counted in such surveys. In short, the method needs to work out some significant problems if it is to become completely acceptable to urban researchers.

Next there is the question of whether the findings of factorial ecology research are descriptive of anything beyond contemporary cities. Consider Berry and Rees's analysis of Chicago and Calcutta. It could be argued that this study is really an analysis of two cities ultimately involved in the same process: modernization along technological and economic lines. True, Chicago and Calcutta, as Berry and Rees admit, are at different stages of that process. Chicago has a highly advanced technology and economy, while Calcutta is just beginning to develop sophistication in these areas.

It is too easy, however, to be seduced by such comparisons into thinking that cities like Calcutta and Chicago illustrate an inevitable developmental pattern for *all* cities. Fortunately or not, most cities in today's world have been or are being "Westernized." That is, they have been deeply influenced by Western values, especially those of technological advance and economic success. Once cities go down this road, it may very well be that the Berry and Rees model may be able to characterize them; that is, they will develop some version of concentric circles, sectors, and multiple nuclei and have populations motivated by considerations of economic benefit and social prestige. Recall, too, that Ervin's supporting findings were drawn from a sample of 38 *American* cities.

But it was not always thus. Cities in history and in different cultures, as we shall see in the next chapters, indicate that some very different values concerned them. In the cities of the Middle Ages, for example, technological development was hardly ever of concern; religious values were predominant. It may be that in different cultural settings socioeconomic status, family status, and ethnicity may play very different roles, or even no role at all.

In other words, different cultural values may produce different urban land use patterns. To assume that such patterns develop on their own in all cities, regardless of cultural influences, may be a major mistake (London and Flanagan 1976, pp. 58–61). For example, in her recent factor analysis of Rabat-Sale, a principal metropolitan area of Morocco, Janet Abu-Lughod (1980, Chaps. 14–15) found that "social caste," a combination of ethnicity and social class characteristics, played the dominant role in determining where everyone lived in the city. Socioeconomic status, while by no means unimportant, was much less significant than it is in American and European cities. Similarly, in a study of Tel Aviv, one of Israel's principal cities, Borukhov and his associates (1979) found that in addition to socioeconomic and family status "religious orthodoxy" was associated with the shape of the city.

The Rise of Radical Urban Geography

Criticisms and findings such as these have become more common in recent years, and, perhaps not surprisingly, an approach that tries to embody them has developed. This is the school of "radical urban geographers," a group of scholars who subscribe, more or less strongly, to the theories of Karl Marx and believe that the city is *always* a product of a certain society at a particular moment in history (Hall 1984). These urbanists claim that to pretend otherwise, to pretend that urban geography is somehow uncovering the eternal truth about cities is delusion, ignorance, or, worse, the product of some urban geographers' own unacknowedged political persuasions.

The radical approach to urban geography began in the early 1970s, not only as a response to what its proponents saw as the deficiencies of urban geography as it was currently practiced (zonal theory, factorial ecology, etc.), but also as a response to the turmoil of the times—recall that the late 1960s and early 1970s were a period of significant upheaval in both the United States and Europe. These geographers began by studying the distribution of wealth and political power in a city and noted that the wealthiest people lived on the most desirable land with the greatest access to the city's valued services. Is it any accident, they asked, that the city's best schools are often situated in the city's richest neighborhoods? Is it any accident that the superhighways, which rip through old urban neighborhoods with patent unconcern for that neighborhood's present residents, lead to and serve the wealthy suburbs?

Among the theorists who subscribe to this position are David Harvey (1973), Manuel Castells (1978), and Michael Dear and Alan Scott (1981). All believe that "the structure of the city is to be explained by the pursuit of profit, which is the *raison d'etre* of capitalist society, modified by the actions of the State, which has the functions of preserving and legitimizing this society" (Hall 1984, p. 32).

At the heart of all contemporary urban land use, then, is an abiding concern for the most profitable use of materials and labor. The question asked by the city's powerful business interests is simply: "If we do this, will we make money at it?" Concerns for the welfare of the worker, the neighborhood, and the city's poor simply do not exist. This "profit-bias" has international roots and consequences, as Hall explains:

> In the modern world, newly industrializing countries undermine the traditional economic bases of older nations and regions. In the latter, skilled workers in declining industries lose their jobs and end up in unskilled service occupations. Entrepreneurs react to the threat of competition by closing older inner city plants and concentrating production in rural areas, where unionization is weaker and wages are lower. Multinational enterprises centralize their control functions in a few of the world's cities, where they can displace other functions to other cities and suburbs. Because profit seeking and competition are inherent and incessant, this process of change is neverending. (1984, p. 33)

In other words, radical urban geography is intended as an alternative to what its proponents see as an inordinately biased approach to the study of land use in cities—a bias that assumes that profit making and capitalism are the natural forces that shape cities.

But this new approach also has its problems. Peter Hall (1984, p. 34) suggests that radical urban geography is as much defined by what it omits as by what it stresses. On the one hand, there is much to be recommended in the radicals' critique of the cultural bias of much of urban geography. On the other hand, the approach does not deal very extensively or very deeply with the cases where capitalist cities have been successful at raising the general standard of living of the city as a whole. In the future, Hall sees both approaches existing side by side, in a continuing and critical dialogue that focuses on each other's excesses. In such a dialogue each approach will push the other to refine its concepts and claims until, one hopes, we get to an even more sophisticated understanding of urban land use.

Conclusion

We have come a long way in our consideration of the uses a city makes of its physical environment.

We began with the simple observation that people founded cities at particular geographical sites because these sites had particular advantages. At a bare minimum, they had to support a population's physical needs locally or provide adequate import facilities. Once people's basic needs were met, however, we found that other human needs—political, religious, educational, and economic—frequently played a role in locating cities.

Indeed, these other needs were so important that they helped determine the two basic city shapes. Radiocentric cities had a tendency to emerge in urban areas where religious and political forces were the central interest of the population; gridiron cities sprang up when economic concerns predominated. The same issues also determined whether city growth patterns were likely to be horizontal, vertical, or interstitial.

We next considered location and the economic advantages of cities. Living in cities allowed people to get more goods of higher quality more cheaply. These economic advantages, economists like Alonso argued, produced certain recurrent patterns in urban land use. Businesses were likely to be at the center (the CBD), surrounded by residential areas and, farther out, agricultural areas. However, this theory was criticized for being descriptive of only Western (primarily American) cities and, even in that instance, for not being complex enough. For example, it left out the crucial role played by various social forces in determining urban land use.

Next we turned to sociological theories. We began with the Chicago School and the work of Robert Park and Ernest W. Burgess. These people saw competition (in the social as well as the economic sense) and population movements as responsible for producing certain urban forms. Their theory was summarized in Burgess's concentric zone model. But critics raised questions as to whether a biologically determined competition could explain people's behavior and pointed out numerous exceptions to the zonal hypothesis.

Recognizing the difficulties of the Chicago theory, Homer Hoyt suggested that many cities were organized in sectors and that the prime determinant of such sectoring was socioeconomic status and income. This was a helpful contribution but, like the Chicago model, it ultimately appeared to be too simple to account for what was actually going on.

Pushing our understanding further were Harris and Ullman, with their theory of multiple urban nuclei. This model abandoned any idea of a deterministic pattern of urban development. Zones, sectors, and even the CBD were seen as variable. The city's land use changed as advantages or disadvantages for its groups changed.

This set the stage for social area analysis, an approach distinguished by its lack of theory. Its originators, Shevky, Bell, and Williams, simply examined the major social characteristics of different residential groups in the city. While their technique produced accurate descriptions of who lived where in cities, it had no ability to explain *why* people lived where they did. With earlier explanations of urban land use (the economic, concentric zone, sector, and multiple nuclei theories) esssentially discredited for being too simplistic, urban ecology was at an impasse.

This impasse was breached by the arrival of factorial ecology. This technique analyzes the significance of all factors that researchers think might be influential in urban land use choices. Its major finding has been that the social characteristics initially examined by social area analysis—socioeconomic status, family status, and ethnicity—do seem to account for most of the residential land uses in cities studied thus far.

This discovery led Berry and Rees to hypothesize that the earlier theories all held a part of the truth. If their essential insights of cities arranging themselves into concentric zones, sectors, and multiple nuclei were combined, and the resulting model combined with the findings of factorial ecology (namely, that socioeconomic status, family status, and ethnic considerations were the dominant factors in people's minds in deciding where to locate in cities), then an overall explanation of urban land use might be possible.

Yet, at present even this model may not be enough to account for the complexities of urban land. The method itself is far from perfect and there is some doubt that its findings can be used to describe cities in all cultures and at all times. The Berry and Rees model does seem to apply to most cities in the contemporary world; however, this is probably because these cities are deeply under the influence of the values of technological advance and economic success, values imported from Western cities. Many cities in other cultures and at other points in history show less concern with such values.

Rising to this critique has been the school of radical urban geography grounded in the Marxist tradition. These geographers believe that urban land use patterns in the modern era are solely the result of capitalist market forces and that to pretend otherwise is folly. This school has added an important dimension to the current debate and it is likely that the radical approach will continue to coexist with the more traditional urban geography for the foreseeable future.

Urban land use, thus, is an extremely complex affair. What we have seen in this chapter is the development of an increasingly sophisticated attempt to capture that multifaceted reality. Major advances have been made, particularly in the understanding of how cities in the Western or Westernizing world organize their space, but more needs to be done. While, as Hawley (1984) has recently argued, we certainly need to pursue all the leads of the theory of urban human ecology, urbanists still need to understand more accurately the powerful influence that different cultural traditions and values have on city life. It is to this topic that we will turn in the next chapter.

CHAPTER 7
The City and Culture

Prologue: Six Months in Ibadan

All her life Dorothy McAllister had lived in Boston. As her plane rose over Logan Airport, she glanced back at the city, marveling at what she saw—a thriving downtown with skyscrapers, interlocking highways and bridges overflowing with cars, factories coughing refuse into the air, and endless crowding of building upon building, from harbor to horizon, some ten miles in all directions. In most of the housing below lived families much like her own—Dad off to work on the subway or in the car in the morning, Mom taking care of the kids and working part time. Across town there were relatives—aunts, cousins, and grandparents—whom she saw occasionally. Whatever awaited her, she thought as the plane banked out over the Atlantic and Boston disappeared from view, would be only a variation on this common theme, for Boston was the very model of the great city.

She was wrong. Four days later, after delays and frustrating airline inefficiency and bureaucratic rigamarole, she arrived in Ibadan for six months in the Peace Corps. A major city of Nigeria with a population of over 1 million, Ibadan was not like Boston at all. As her plane approached, she saw no skyscrapers, no network of superhighways, no clusters of factories, and, beyond the central city itself, nothing like Boston's residential suburbs. In their place were endless cultivated fields containing produce she hardly knew: yams, maize, cassavas, plantains, and cocoyams.

After Dorothy landed, the shock was even greater: this city's daily routines were so unlike those she knew as to be nearly incomprehensible. For instance, she found out that few men worked in offices. Over half went instead to work the farms outside the city. (She knew no one in Boston who was a farmer!) And they didn't ride, they walked. While some returned at night, many stayed away for days, even weeks. Men who were not farmers typically engaged in a trade, such as blacksmithing.

Most women worked at handicrafts, such as pottery or weaving. Heavy machinery was conspicuously absent, and, except for one or two small firms, factories simply did not exist.

Intimate open-air markets are common in Nigerian cities. Much more than in urban America, Nigerian city life is based on kinship and ethnic
(Thomas D. Friedman/Photo Researchers)

Family life, too, had little resemblance to what Dorothy knew in Boston. Mothers, fathers, and children lived together with relatives and tribal allies, often numbering over a thousand and linked by their land holdings, ancestry, and common religious heritage. Power and prestige within this "family" was distributed by age and sex. Some men were deemed more important than others, not as a result of being successful in business, but simply by virtue of being older. Wives (a man could have as many as he could support) held status according to whether they had been married first, second, or later.

Finally, among these people there was a stronger identification with the city itself than was true in Boston. The king was the center of city life and, over the generations, all of Ibadan's descent groups had made pacts with the royal family. Every descent group had access to the king through local meetings and representatives on the king's council. Little distinction was made among descent groups in terms of prestige.

Months later, as her plane rose over Ibadan's central district and market and the city's fields came into view for the last time, Dorothy thought back about her earlier departure from Boston. She could not have imagined, then, a city as different as Ibadan; and yet, there it was, thriving and alive in the 1980s. She had learned that cities are not necessarily all variations on a single theme. They can be as different as night and day.

The City and Culture

The main market of the city, where the farm produce and crafts were traded, was run predominantly by women, and the businesses of Ibadan in no way resembled the competitive free-enterprise system of Boston. Women traditionally traded in only one product, rarely branching out or expanding. Furthermore, vendors seemed to know just about everyone with whom they traded, and their success was as dependent on their personal relations with customers as on their business sense. This city didn't seem as cold and impersonal as those Dorothy had known before.

Louis Wirth, whose urban theory we considered in Chapter 4, argued that cities were dominated by offices and factories and had a characteristically weak family structure. Such cities also tended to create an urban experience dominated by impersonality, transiency, superficiality, and anonymity.

Our portrait of Ibadan contradicts Wirth's characterization on virtually every count. Based on the work of Peter Lloyd (1973), it suggests rather that Wirth's three factors: large population, density, and heterogeneity—Ibadan has all three—cannot be expected to necessarily produce the type of urbanism that Wirth described. Some other factor must be at work.

That factor is *culture*, the shared ideas and patterns of behavior that characterize any social group of long duration. Whenever human beings come together, they construct interpretations of the world, including values, goals, and daily routines. To the extent that people believe in this constructed reality, they think and act in a distinctive way. To the extent that other peoples, in other places and times, believe in different interpretations of the world, they will think and act in their distinctive ways. Hence, we cannot expect the city in different cultural settings to always be the same.

The importance of culture in urban life is what Wirth overlooked. *The city is not an entity unto itself.* It reflects the larger culture of which it is a part. American culture, with its emphasis on free enterprise and the nuclear family, creates cities such as Boston with skyscrapers downtown (which maximize trade advantages) and single-family dwellings all around the city. The culture of the Yoruba (the people that comprise the bulk of Ibadan's population) emphasizes personalized trade relations, handicrafts, and an extended family and generates cities that are quite different.

This chapter is about the all-important link between the city and culture. A city can be fully understood only by exploring the cultural patterns found throughout the larger society.

The City and The Hinterland

Those that are good manners at the court are as ridiculous in the country as the behavior of the country is most mockable at the court.

SHAKESPEARE, *AS YOU LIKE IT, III, 2*

Interdependencies

Shakespeare has noted here something that everyone knows: country and city ways are often quite different. Yet we must be wary of overgeneralization. For example, in Ibadan, with the city's fields so close by and farmers a large part of the city's population, it is virtually impossible to distinguish between city and country ways (Lloyd 1973). Indeed, in any location, city and country are not independent of each other at all, but rather have a symbiotic relationship.

Consider this oft-forgotten connection: *much of the population of the city initially came from the hinterland.* Throughout history, the migration of people seeking a better life has transformed city and country alike. To take but one example, during the great expansion of European cities in the nineteenth century, England changed from an almost completely rural society to a nation in which over 60 percent of the population lived in cities. Table 7-1 presents the population shifts in England and Wales during the second half of that century. In 40 years, the number of towns nearly doubled, the town population more than doubled, and the rural population noticeably decreased.

The relationship between the city and its hinterland involves much more than just the dynamics of migration, however. There is also a reciprocal dependence on the resources each supplies. Because a large proportion of city dwellers (even in Ibadan) engage in specialized occupations other than agriculture, the hinterland must supply the city's food. Many of the specialty occupations of the city—weaving or steel manufacturing—depend on the hinterland's raw materials. Conversely, the hinterland obtains many of its goods—the clothes made by weavers, tractors made with the steel—from the city.

But perhaps the most important link between city and hinterland (Shakespeare notwithstanding) is the reciprocal shaping of life-styles. Migrants who swell the city's ranks bring to the city their cultural traditions. The result is a living kaleidoscope of human behavior, ranging all the way from groups who devotedly try to keep living as they did in the "old country" (New York's Hasidic Jews, for example) to the various "hyphenated" Americans (Italian-Americans, Hispanic-Americans) who maintain only some of the old ways in their new urban setting.

TABLE 7-1

Urban and Rural Population in England and Wales, 1851–1891

	Urban		Rural
	Number of Towns	Total Population	Total Population
1851	580	8,990,809	8,936,800
1861	781	10,960,998	9,105,225
1871	938	14,041,404	8,670,862
1881	967	17,636,646	8,337,793
1891	1,011	20,895,504	8,107,021

Source: Adapted from Adna Weber, *The Growth of Cities* (New York: Columbia University Press, 1899), Table XVIII.

At the same time, other rural influences including traditional folk music, art, and literature are constantly altering the city's character. Country music, in fact, is exclusively played on at least one radio station in nearly every major American city, and "country rock" is a peculiar rural-urban musical confluence.

Very common in American and European cities (less so in African cities like Ibadan) is the human cultural hybrid—the urban person who takes a little bit from many of the originally rural life-styles that exist in the city and integrates them into a new life-style altogether. Such a person was Mayor Fiorello La Guardia of New York, as described in Box 7-1. Perhaps it would be fair to say that a little bit of La Guardia exists in most city dwellers.

This influence works in two ways, however. Just as the city has received much from the countryside, it has typically returned the favor, radiating outward an influence far beyond its borders. Many sociologists think that this influence, in modern times, has far outstripped the hinterland's effect on urban affairs.

Urban Dominance

"I cannot see that London has any great advantage over the country," said Mrs. Bennett, "except the shops and public places. The country is a vast deal pleasanter, is it not . . . ?"

JANE AUSTIN, *PRIDE AND PREJUDICE,* 1813

Thus Mrs. Bennett, engaged in a verbal duel with some of London's high society, defended her rural environment in the early part of the nineteenth century. Her championing of the country was not well received. She was subsequently told by everyone present—her own daughters included—that, like it or not, London had numerous advantages over the countryside, among them a greater diversity of people and, well, there was just so much more to *do* in London.

Right or wrong, Mrs. Bennett was wiser than she knew, for her allusion to what she saw as the city's one advantage—its shops and public places—suggests why the city's influence has spread so far beyond its physical boundaries. As Louis Wirth argued, the city's importance

. . . may be regarded as a consequence of the concentration in [it] of industrial, commercial, financial, and administrative facilities and activities, transportation and communication lines, and cultural and recreational equipment such as the press, radio stations, theaters, libraries, museums, concert halls, operas, hospitals, colleges, research and publishing centers, professional organizations, and religion and welfare institutions. (1964, p. 63)

Thus cities have been in a position of cultural dominance in American society (far beyond that corresponding to the proportion of city dwellers) since the coming of European settlers in the seventeenth century. Moreover, as we described in Chapter 3, the importance of early eastern settlements, most notably Boston, Newport (Rhode Is-

BOX 7-1
Mayor Fiorello La Guardia of New York

To put it sociologically, La Guardia was a marginal man who lived in the edge of many cultures. . . . Tammany Hall may have been the first to exploit the vote-getting value of eating gefullte fish with the Jews, goulash with the Hungarians, sauerbraten with Germans, spaghetti with Italians, and so on indefinitely, but this unorthodox Republican not only dined every bit as shrewdly but also spoke, according to the occasion, in Yiddish, Hungarian, German, Serbian-Croatian, or plain New York English. Half Jewish and half Italian, born in Greenwich Village yet raised in Arizona, married first to a Catholic and then to a Lutheran but himself a Mason and an Episcopalian, Fiorello La Guardia was a Mr. Brotherhood Week all by himself.

Source: Arthur Mann, cited in E. Digby Baltzell, *The Protestant Establishment* (New York: Vintage, 1964), p. 29.

land), New York, Philadelphia, and Charleston was supplemented by newer cities as the population moved westward to such places as Chicago, St. Louis, and Kansas City. In the far West, especially following the completion of the transcontinental railroad to San Francisco in 1869, towns and cities continued to stand at the center of social life. This fact was observed by Josiah Strong, who commented in 1885, "It is the cities and towns which frame state constitutions, make laws, create public opinion, establish social usages and fix standards of morals in the West" (p. 206).

American growth is thus very much the story of the development of cities. Consistently the centers of an expanding market, the loci of advances in communication, and the sources of leadership in politics, fashion, and the arts, cities long have been associated with cultural firsts: the first daily newspaper (Philadelphia, 1784), the first stock exchange (New York, 1792), and the first telephone system (Boston, 1877; linked to New York in 1884 to Denver in 1911, and to San Francisco in 1915).

Such a pattern of urban dominance over the broader society is hardly limited to the United States. A description of the same phenomenon

can be drawn from Alexis de Tocqueville's historical account (1955; originally published 1856) of the French Revolution of 1789, which was hastened by the increasing centralization of French life in Paris, a process that began in the 1600s as the feudal system weakened. Because of this centralization, when the Revolution surfaced in Paris, it quickly carried the rest of French society along with it.

Tocqueville noted that Paris in times past had been "no more than the largest town in France . . . [but by] 1789 things were very different; it [was] no exaggeration to say that Paris *was* France" (1955, p. 72). The city controlled the nation's economic, intellectual, and political lifeblood. This urban dominance was also evident as one left Paris for the countryside. Inquiring as to the political climate of the outlying areas, English observer Arthur Young heard time and again: "We are only a provincial town; we must wait till Paris gives us a lead" (Tocqueville, 1955, p. 74).

That is exactly what Paris did. It is one of the remarkable facts of history that the cultural ideas ("Liberty! Equality! Brotherhood!") that were to transform France and much of Western civilization, in conjunction with the American Revolution a decade earlier, were largely city born.

Urban dominance is thus a central pattern of the modern and historical world. Sometimes, however, urban influence is not so welcome, as the people of Grafton County, New Hampshire, have decided. Their views are described in Cityscape 7-1.

In other instances urban dominance is more subtle. "Springdale" is a pseudonym for a small town in upstate New York. With its quiet streets and surrounding rural countryside, it would seem a world apart from the city. The appearance is deceiving.

While residents of the town display a great deal of pride in their traditions of independence and self-sufficiency—values they associate with small-town life—they also have come to recognize that these sentiments are beginning to ebb away. The average Springdaler, wrote sociologists Arthur Vidich and Joseph Bensman, who studied the town in the late 1950s,

CITYSCAPE 7-1

The Invasion of the City Slickers

[What city people who move to the country] bring along is a series of unconscious assumptions. It might be better for rural America if they brought a few sticks of dynamite, or a can of arsenic.

Take a typical example. Mr. and Mrs. Nice are Bostonians. They live a couple of miles off Route 128 in a four-bedroom house. He's a partner in an ad agency; she has considerable talent as an artist. For some years they've had a second home in northern New Hampshire. The kids love it up there in Grafton County.

For some years, too, both Nices have been feeling they'd like to simplify their lives. They look with increasing envy on their New Hampshire neighbors, who never face a morning traffic jam, or an evening one, either; who don't have a long drive to the country

on Friday night and a long drive back on Sunday; who aren't cramped into a suburban lot; who live in harmony with the natural rhythm of the year; who think the rat race is probably some minor event at a county fair.

One Thursday evening Don Nice says to Sue that he's been talking to the other partners, and they've agreed there's no reason he can't do some of his work at home. If he's in the office Wednesday and Thursday every week, why the rest of the time he can stay in touch by telephone. Sue, who has been trapped all year as a Brownie Scout leader and who has recently had the aerial snapped off her car in Boston, is delighted. She reflects happily that in their little mountain village you don't even need to lock your house, and there is no Brownie

troop. "You're wonderful," she tells Don.

So the move occurs. In most ways Don and Sue are very happy. They raise practically all their own vegetables the first year; Sue takes up cross-country skiing. Don personally splits some of the wood they burn in their new woodstove.

But there are some problems. The first one Sue is conscious of is the school. It's just not very good. It's clear to Sue almost immediately that the town desperately needs a new school building—and also modern playground equipment, new school buses, more and better art instruction at the high school, a different principal. Don is as upset as Sue when they discover that only about 40 per cent of the kids who graduate from that high school go on to any

. . . sees that the urban and metropolitan society is technically and culturally superior to his own community. He sees this in his everyday life when he confronts the fact that his community cannot provide him with everything he needs: almost everyone goes to the city for shopping and entertainment; large numbers of people are dependent on the radio and television; and everyone realizes that rural life would be drastically altered without cars and refrigerators (1968, p. 79)

Nor are these the only links that bind the residents of Springdale to the larger urban society. Their lives are influenced by outside specialists from organizations such as the state agricultural extension service, as well as their own college-trained professionals. Additional organizations that serve to "import" the culture of the urban society include such national organizations as the Odd Fellows and the American Legion. Perhaps more important, the economic and political life of the town is not in local hands; rather, it is shaped by state and federal agencies. Taxes, education for

the town's children, and the price of local farmers' milk are all increasingly subject to outside forces that are mostly city based. Vidich and Bensman concluded that, despite the desires and pretensions of the townspeople, most "plans and decisions that refer directly to the community are made from a distance by invisible agents and institutions" (1968, p. 81). Thus, just as Springdalers now go periodically to the world of the city, the world of the city has subtly transformed, for better or for worse, Springdale and communities like it.

The City and Civilization

Cities have always been the fireplaces of civilization, whence light and heat radiated out into the dark, cold world.

THEODORE PARKER, NINETEENTH-CENTURY AMERICAN PREACHER

form of college. The rest do native things like becoming farmers, and mechanics, and joining the Air Force. An appalling number of the girls marry within twelve months after graduation. How are Jeanie and Don, Jr., going to get into school colleges from this school? . . .

Pretty soon Sue and Don join an informal group of newcomers in town who are working to upgrade education. All they want for starters is the new building ($2.8 million) and a majority of their kind on the school board.

As for Don, though he really enjoys splitting the wood—in fact, next year he's planning to get a chainsaw and start cutting a few trees of his own—he also likes to play golf. There's no course within twenty miles. Some of the nice people he's met in the education lobby feel just as he does. They begin to discuss the possibility of a nine-hole course. The old farmer who owns the land they have in mind seems to be keeping only four or five cows on it, anyway. Besides, taxes are going up, and the old fellow is going to have to sell, sooner or later. (Which is too bad, of course. Don and Sue both admire the local farmers, and they're sincerely sorry whenever one has to quit.)

Over the next several years, Don and Sue get more and more adjusted to rural living—and they also gradually discover more things that need changing. For example, the area needs a good French restaurant. And it needs a *much* better airport. At present there are only two flights a day to Boston, and because of the lack of sophisticated equipment, even they are quite often canceled. If Don wants to be sure of getting down for an important meeting, he has to drive. Sue would be glad of more organized activities for the kids. There's even talk of starting a Brownie troop.

In short, if enough upper-middle-class people move to a rural town, they are naturally going to turn it into a suburb of the nearest city. For one generation it will be a nice and truly rustic suburb, with real farms dotted around it, and real natives speaking their minds at town meeting. Then as the local people are gradually taxed out of existence (or at least out of town), one more piece of rural America has died.

Source: Noel Perrin, "Rural Area: Permit Required," *Country Journal* (April 1980), pp. 34–35.

The reason for the city's increasing dominance in modern affairs, as we have hinted already, is that everything human—art, music, business, traditions, what we love and hate—converges there. The city does not create a way of life all its own but rather provides the setting where any way of life, any cultural tradition, can intensify and recreate itself in a manner not possible in other settings. For example, Socrates, Plato, and Aristotle all lived in Hellenic Athens, sharing ideas and challenging each other. This simply would not have occurred had they all lived in rural hamlets, cut off from one another.

Nowhere is this process of intensification represented more clearly than in the suggestion that the city encapsulates a whole culture. For nearly all of written history, the city has been seen as capturing the essence of human civilization. As Euripides, a playwright in classical Greece, opined: "The first requisite to happiness is birth in a great city." To make the point even more strongly, consider the connection between our most common words about cities and civilization (Box 7-2). Consider as well the linkage between city and civilization as it has been expressed in the writings of some of history's most important urbanists (Box 7-3).

Is the city synonymous with civilization? To find out, let's examine in more detail the ideas of Oswald Spengler and Lewis Mumford.

Oswald Spengler

Oswald Spengler (1880–1936) was a German philosopher who saw in cities the drama of the rise and fall of civilization. He contended that cities developed, ultimately came to dominate a society, and then declined, carrying with them the culture built over generations and centuries. We will be less concerned with the cyclical element in Spengler's theory (generally considered too simplistic by contemporary social scientists) than with his belief that "all great cultures are town-cultures" and that "world history is city history."

BOX 7-2
City Words

Those of us who live in the city should be grateful to our language, because the words that have to do with the city are usually flattering. We city-dwellers, at least in ancient days, were supposed to be more *civil* in our manners and more *civilized* in our ways than others, for both of these words *civil* and *civilized* are the eventual children of the Latin term *civis* which meant "one who lives in a city." All city folks, you see, were regarded as automatically cultured and well housebroken. And from ancient Latin we have borrowed the word *urbs* which also meant city, and we used it to create the word *urbane* which describes the smooth manners that were presumed to be characteristic of *metropolitan* society. The Greek parts of the word *metropolitan* are *metro-*, "mother," and *polis*, "city," so a *metropolis* is the "mother city" or the chief or capital city of a country, and he who lives in a *metropolis* is supposed to inherit the sophisticated ideas and manners that go with such a center. And from the Greek *polis*, "city," we inherited our word *politic*. If you are *politic*, you are expedient, shrewd, discreet, and artful in your address and your procedure which sounds dangerously like a city slicker!

Source: Wilfred Funk, *Word Origins* (New York: Bell, 1978), pp. 97–98.

BOX 7-3
The City and Civilization

Just as the beginning of Western Civilization is marked by permanent settlement of formerly nomadic peoples . . . so the beginning of what is distinctly modern in our civilization is best signalized by the growth of great cities. (Louis Wirth 1938)

The city is . . . the natural habitat of civilized man. (Robert Park 1916)

[The city is] the most precious invention of civilization, second only to language itself in the transmission of culture. (Lewis Mumford 1961)

All great Cultures are town-Cultures. . . . World history is city history. Peoples, states, politics, religion, all arts, and all sciences rest upon one phenomenon . . . the town. (Oswald Spengler 1928)

Spengler was convinced that in the city human civilization takes on distinctive qualities. At some point in its development, the "soul" of the city is created: "Out of the rustic group of farms and cottages . . . arises a totality. And the whole lives, breathes, grows, and acquires a face and inner form and history" (1928; 1969, pp. 65–66). Spengler believed that the countryside never has a soul in this sense; it is a "landscape" at most, never a "world."

Moreover, the city senses its own power and uniqueness:

> . . . it is a place from which the countryside is henceforth regarded, felt, and experienced as "environs," as something different and subordinate. From now on there are two lives, that of the inside and that of the outside, and the peasant understands this just as clearly as the townsman. . . . The new Soul of the City speaks a new language, which soon becomes tantamount to the language of the culture itself. (1969, pp. 66, 68)

Thus, the essence of ancient Egypt was symbolized by Thebes, ancient Greece by Athens, the Roman Empire by Rome, Islam by Baghdad, and prerevolutionary France by Paris. Indeed, Spengler believed that whole periods of European civilization were manifest only in cities. Is it not true, he asked, "that the Renaissance style flourished only in the Renaissance *city*, the Baroque only in the Baroque *city*?" (1969, p. 68).

Because Spengler's cyclical ideas of historical change are not accepted widely today, his contribution to urban sociology generally is regarded as modest. Yet he correctly sensed the connection between city and civilization, an idea that has been developed extensively by an American urbanist whose work we will discuss next.

Lewis Mumford

Lewis Mumford (b. 1895) traces the cultural importance of cities through Western history. He presents the case, based on historical and comparative evidence, that the city has indeed been at the very center of Western civilization from its beginnings.

Mumford believes that of all creatures only human beings seem to be aware of themselves as

---

CITYSCAPE 7-2
The Crystallization of the City

This new urban mixture resulted in an enormous expansion of human capabilities in every direction. The city effected a mobilization of manpower, a command over long-distance transportation, an intensification of communication over long distances in space and time, an outburst of invention along with a large-scale development of civil engineering, and, not least, it promoted a tremendous further rise in agricultural productivity. . . .

When all this happened, the archaic village culture yielded to urban "civilization," that peculiar combination of creativity and control, of expression and repression, of tension and release, whose outward manifestation has been the historic city. From its origins onward, indeed, the city may be described as a structure specially equipped to store and transmit the goods of civilization, sufficiently condensed to afford the maximum amount of facilities in a minimum space, but also capable of structural enlargement to enable it to find a place for the changing needs and the more complex forms of a growing society and its cumulative social heritage. The invention of such forms as the written record, the library, the archive, the school, and the university is one of the earliest and most characteristic achievements of the city. . . .

What happened . . . with the rise of cities, was that many functions that had heretofore been scattered and unorganized were brought together within a limited area, and the components of the community were kept in a state of dynamic tension and interaction. In this union, made almost compulsory by the strict enclosure of the city wall, the already well-established parts of the proto-city—shrine, spring, village, market stronghold—participated in the general enlargement and concentration of numbers, and underwent a structural differentiation that gave them forms recognizable in every subsequent phase of urban culture. The city proved not merely a means of expressing in concrete terms the magnification of sacred and secular power, but in a manner that went far beyond any conscious intention it also enlarged all the dimensions of life. Beginning as a representation of the cosmos, a means of bringing heaven down to earth, the city became a symbol of the possible.

Source: Lewis Mumford, *The City in History* (New York: Harcourt, Brace and World, 1961), pp. 29–31.

---

fundamentally distinctive. We can think, invent, and wonder about such things as life, death, sex, and God(s). In the course of human evolution, Mumford reasons, people attached these thoughts to places. The earliest centers of this kind were probably caves and places of burial. These sites were symbolic centers to which wandering groups could return periodically to ponder the mysteries they wished to understand. Thus began civilization. "In the earliest gathering about a grave or a painted symbol, a great stone or a sacred grove, one has the beginning of a succession of civic institutions that range from the temple to the astronomical observatory, from the theater to the university" (Mumford 1961, p. 9).

As time passed and technology improved, some people began living at these places permanently: the shrine became a camp, then a village, and finally a town. Mumford (like Spengler) suggests that at a certain point the cultural ideas, the people, and the place all jelled as the city emerged (Cityscape 7-2).

Thenceforth, the story of civilization became the story of urban history. Yet we must be careful here. We often impute to civilization the assumption of progress, that what exists today is somehow a better form of what went before. Neither Spengler nor Mumford meant to suggest this notion of cultural evolution; rather, their idea was that the city was culture "writ large," the living embodiment of a society's or epoch's ideas. Cities did not inevitably progress. In them, as already mentioned, Spengler saw the rise *and* fall of civilization; and, like Max Weber before him (Chapter 4), Mumford believes that cities better than today's existed in the past—in Hellenic Athens, for example.

Similarly, despite Spengler's and Mumford's claims, we should not link *all* of civilization to cities, powerful as they may be in concentrating culture. For decades anthropologists have argued that we must look carefully at the lives of all of a society's people. Culture and civilization are just as real in the countryside and the small village, although they may be in other forms.

From Mumford and Spengler, then, we learn that, although the city and civilization are not precisely synonymous, the city has a unique power to intensify and symbolize culture. Any city will dynamically and intensely reflect the characteristics of its surrounding culture; however, because cultural patterns vary so widely, cities may be markedly different from one another. In the following case studies we will read of two cities, Peking during the Ming Dynasty and Hellenic Athens, capitals of vastly different civilizations and separated by some 1500 years.

CASE STUDY 7-1
Ming Peking

Peking (today called Beijing) is a city of about 9 million people (roughly the population of New York or London) and is the capital of the People's Republic of China. Established in the northeast of China to protect the country from invaders from the north, the city has been in existence since at least several centuries before the birth of Christ. During the thirteenth century, when China was ruled by the Yüan (Mongol) emperors, Peking was transformed into a capital city by Kublai Khan.

Soon after the overthrow of the Yüan by the Ming Dynasty in 1368, the Emperor Yung Lo spared no expense in turning the city into a monument to all of Chinese culture and, as we shall see, to himself as symbolic head of that culture (Wright 1977). It was a massive job. Wagonloads "of a specially chosen marble were brought a distance of 1500 miles from Uyn-nan and this precious material was used to renew and extend the palace and to clothe the city's roads and bridges with fresh dignity and beauty" (Loewe 1964, p. 241).

Physical Structure

The entire city was designed as a symbol of everything vital to Chinese life. Perhaps no better example exists of Mumford's idea of the city as a physical container. Ming Peking literally revealed city within city, surrounding the all-important core where the emperor lived (see Figure 7-1).

It was about 25 square miles in size and composed of two major sections, each roughly rectangular in shape. Peking's southern section, known as the Outer City or Chinese City, contained most of the city's population, probably about 320,000 people at the end of the thirteenth century (Chandler and Fox 1974, p. 356).

The northern section, however, was of quite another character. Known by the name Tartar City or Inner City, this area was surrounded by a massive wall about 50 feet in height and just as thick. Indeed, unlike in the West where the words for city are linked to the words for civilization and politics (Box 7-2), in Chinese the word for city literally means "wall," indicating in yet another way that the city was a container of major cultural significance (Murphy 1984, p. 189). All city streets were arranged in a gridiron with gates through the wall arranged symmetrically.

Centrally located within the walls of the Tartar City was another area, called the Imperial City. Protected by yet another wall, and including about 5 square miles of parklike land complete with artifically constructed lakes and hills, this was the focus of the political and religious power and splendor of Ming civilization.

In the midst of this constructed urban tranquility, and surrounded by a moat and yet another defensive wall, were the palaces and residences—facing south—of the emperor. This was called the Purple City by the Chinese and later dubbed the Forbidden City by Europeans upon their realization that access was gained only by the emperor's personal decree. Just to the north was a large, artificially constructed mound of earth, Coal Hill, on which stood temples prominently visible above the city.

The whole city was arranged on a perfect north-south axis, around which were temples

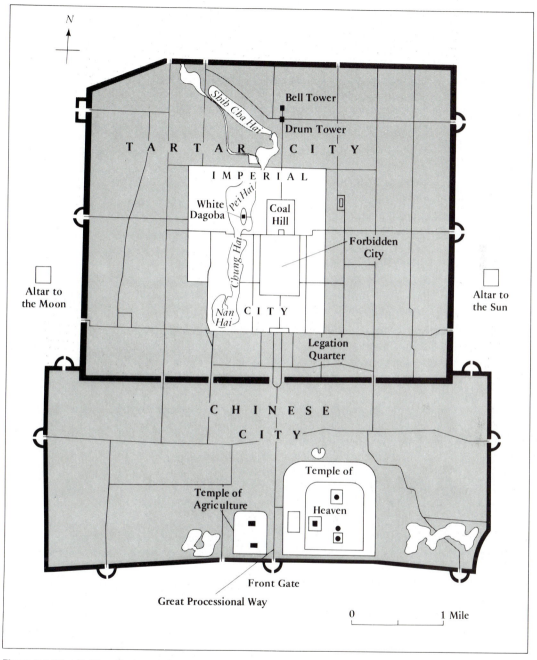

Figure 7-1 *Ming Peking. Source: Adapted from Roderick Mac-Farquhar,* The Forbidden City *(New York: Newsweek, 1972), p. 46. Reprinted by permission of Newsweek Books.*

and altars. On the east was the Altar to the Sun; on the west, the Altar to the Moon; to the south were the Temple of Agriculture and the enormous Temple of Heaven. Between these last two temples passed the Great Processional Way, a magnificent boulevard used only on formal occasions, leading through each defensive wall to the steps of the Emperor's palace. All of this had profound meaning to the Chinese.

Symbolism

Ming Peking was based on elaborate Chinese cosmology (Wright 1977). The temples and altars were religious symbols of the sun, earth, and, most important, heaven.

Chinese astronomers had discovered long before Peking was built that the center of the heavens was the North Star, around which everything revolved. On earth—the human universe—the Chinese believed that everything revolved around the "Son of Heaven," the emperor. Peking was selected as the emperor's capital because it was the northernmost major city of China. The importance of the north was also evident in the city's location on a north-south axis and by the fact that the emperor could be reached only by traveling north along the Great Processional Way. Even the name of the emperor's city, the Purple City, was chosen because the North Star gave off a purple hue in the night sky.

The symbolism did not stop there, however. The colors and height of all buildings had cultural meaning. Peasants, lowly and unimportant, were allowed only houses of one story and could paint their roofs only a dull gray. In the Imperial City various functionaries couldn't have houses of more than one story either, but to signify their higher status they were allowed roofs painted green, red, or purple, depending on their role. Only in the Forbidden City itself were buildings allowed to be more than one story. Their roofs were painted a bright gold-yellow, symbolizing the life-giving (sunlike) qualities of the emperor's rule. As an ancient Chinese text proclaimed, the emperor's role was "to stand in the center of the earth and stabilize people within the four seas." He did this within the Forbidden City, "the place where earth and sky met, where the four seasons merge, where wind and rain are gathered in, and where *yin* and *yang*[1] are in harmony" (MacFarquhar 1972, p. 79).

Given his importance, it is little wonder that the emperor had everything for the "good life" within a stone's throw. The construction of the Forbidden City was a marvel of urban design, as can be seen by carefully examining the buildings shown in Figure 7-2. Note especially the buildings in the center—the emperor's sole preserve. The first group, the buildings immediately to the north of the Supreme Imperial Gate, are buildings of state: the Hall of Supreme Harmony was for special state occasions only, such as the New Year's ceremony and the emperor's birthday; the smaller Hall of Central Harmony was the place where the emperor prepared himself and waited for functions; the Hall of Protecting Harmony was for the reception of visitors and for day-to-day governance. The second group of central buildings, to the north of these state buildings, were the emperor's residences. Entering by the Gate of Heavenly Purity, one found the Palace of Heavenly Purity, the emperor's quarters; next was the Hall of Vigorous Fertility, which, its name notwithstanding, was where official seals were stored; finally, the Palace of Earthly Tranquility, where the empress lived (MacFarquhar 1972).

Ming Peking is a striking example of the city's ability to intensify culture. Peking was a symbolic world, a whole city built upon the cultural themes of harmony with nature, security (city within city), and power. Each "layer of the onion" reemphasized the whole and led to the vital, omnipotent center, the emperor.

This particular symbolism probably means little to us, but we can imagine what it meant to the Pekinese. In a similar manner, our cities transmit and magnify our culture. What is important in our culture is "writ large" in Boston, Birmingham, and Boise. We don't have cities within cities or predominant religious symbolism, like Peking. We have, as Dorothy McAllister saw as she flew over Boston on her way to

---

[1] The two competing forces of nature in Chinese philosophy.

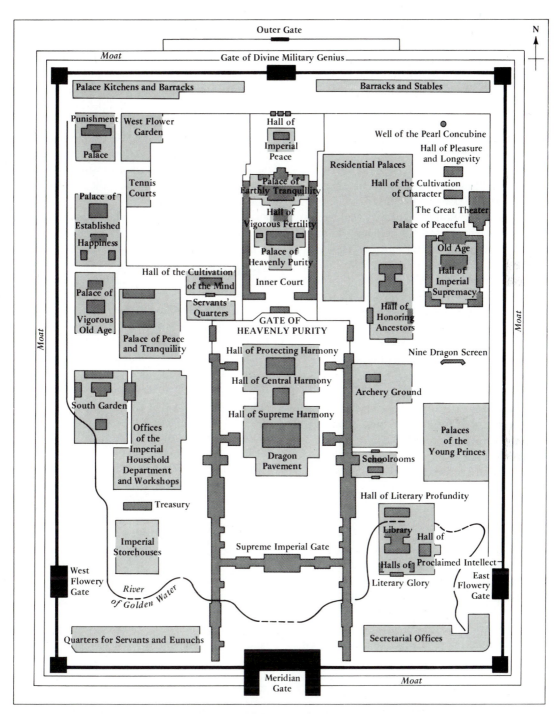

Figure 7-2 *The forbidden city. Source: Roderick MacFarquhar,* The Forbidden City *(New York, Newsweek, 1972), p. 73. Reprinted by permission of Newsweek Books.*

Ibadan, commercial skyscrapers, fast-moving automobiles on superhighways, and private single-family houses. What might such constructions say about what is culturally important to us?

CASE STUDY 7-2
Hellenic Athens

There is small risk of exaggerating the differences between Ming Peking and Hellenic Athens, situated on the rocky northern coast of the Mediterranean. During a period of barely two generations in the fifth century B.C., between about 480 and the start of the Peloponnesian Wars in 431, a civilization took form which Mumford has described as "a far richer efflorescence of human genius than history anywhere else records, except perhaps for Renaissance Florence" (1961, p. 167). Imagine an almost simultaneous development of the arts of painting, sculpture, and architecture; the realization of a rationally structured democracy; and the birth of a body of philosophy that remains at the center of Western thinking today. At the heart of this Golden Age was the city of Athens. "Justly or not," wrote Eric Carlton (1977, p. 77), "Athenian culture has become almost synonymous with the Greek achievement."

The Preclassical Period

Athens was settled as early as 2000 B.C. by four migrating tribes; the Greek peninsula came under the control of feudal overlords who called themselves, perhaps with not the greatest modesty, the *aristoi* (or aristocracy; literally, "the best people"). By the eighth century B.C. these overlords were in charge of several hundred independent Greek city-states, or *poli* (the source of our contemporary word *political* and the urban suffix *-polis*). Over the next two centuries the city-states grew rich, as technology and overseas trade improved and military conquests multiplied.

Ironically, it was this very success that led to the aristocrats' downfall. The improvement of trade created a wealthy middle class that began to demand participation in city rule, and the mar-

tial victories evolved a warrior class with both the skills and arms to take over the city-states. In a series of coups d'état between 660 and 550 B.C., they did just that in many trade and maritime city-states, earning in the process the name *tyrannos* (Burn 1970).

Tyrants or not, the preeminence of warriors during this period was to prove fortuitous. Early in the fifth century B.C. a series of Persian invasions threatened the Greek peninsula. Together, Athens and her rival city-state, the more militaristic Sparta, finally routed the invaders in 479 B.C., setting the stage for what many regard as the city's—and perhaps even Western history's—greatest moment.

The Golden Age

In the fifth century B.C. the city had a population of roughly 300,000 (Mumford 1961) and was not much more than 1 square mile in size. Athenian life in the Golden Age is best understood as the celebration of human possibilities. "Men come together in the city to live," exclaimed Aristotle in a timeless salute to the human possibilities of city life, and "they remain there in order to live the good life." What was this "good life"? In his famous funeral oration in honor of Athenian victims of the Peloponnesian Wars, Athenian statesman Pericles conveyed its essence: the Greek ideal, he said, began with the principle of democracy "which favors the many instead of the few."

The Athenian belief in democracy was grounded historically. Recall that the city-states that preceded the Golden Age were independent units. Indeed, so independent were they that one cannot speak of one "nation," even at the apex of Greek culture. Each city-state pursued its own ends and believed no one had the right to dictate otherwise.

This fierce sense of independence also characterized the Greek citizen. In 600 B.C., with dissatisfaction rife, Athens was on the verge of revolution. To avert this, Solon, an aristocrat, was chosen as arbitrator. He immediately proposed a reorganization of the Athenian constitution that allowed all "free citizens" (excluding women, slaves, and foreigners) a place in the

In the shadow of the Acropolis, Athens today is strongly shaped by its culture and its history. (Nat Norman/Photo Researchers)

city's governing body, the Assembly. He established the People's Council, numbering some 400, with the charge of preparing the Assembly's agenda. Members were chosen from the four main Athenian tribes (a hundred each), thereby preventing dominance by any one group. Finally, government officials were made accountable to the Assembly for their work each year. Political participation was mandatory for all citizens; without regard to "obscurity of conditions," each was required to take part in the public life of the city.

Athenian democracy was a brilliant innovation, affording all free citizens participation in government. It also allowed the citizen the right to live as he chose within that overarching system. Classical Athens did not stand as a monument to an all-powerful god or a ruling family, but rather to all free citizens. In one of the great dramas of the age, Sophocles' *Antigone*, we find this statement (which could well serve as a cri-

tique of Ming Peking): "A city that is of one man is no city."

The ideals of human development and versatility were vital to Hellenic civilization. It was thought that all citizens should strive for refinement, although without extravagance, and pursue individual well being—a fusion of the well-tutored body, mind, and spirit. Athenians developed the body through constant work, exercise, and sport, including the Olympic Games, in which individuals from different city-states competed for the glory of their state. The mind was provoked by continual dialogue. In their leisurely society citizens often spent much of the day talking about the deeper matters of life. Plato's dialogues between the great philosopher Socrates and his friends are the best example. One such dialogue is summarized beautifully by Edith Hamilton in Box 7-4.

Even the life of the spirit was managed differently in Athens. There was, for example, no sys-

---

BOX 7-4
An Afternoon with Socrates

The most charmingly leisured of Plato's dialogues is, perhaps, the Phaedrus. "Where are you bound?" Socrates asks Phaedrus, to which the young man answers that he is going for a walk outside the wall to refresh himself after a morning spent in talk with a great rhetorician: "You shall hear about it if you can spare time to accompany me." Well, Socrates says, he so longs to hear it that he would go all the way to Megara and back rather than miss it. With this, Phaedrus begins to be doubtful if he can do justice to the great man: "Believe me, Socrates, I did not learn his very words—oh, no. Still, I have a general notion of what he said and can give you a summary." "Yes, dear lad," replies Socrates, "but

you must first of all show what you have under your cloak—for that roll I suspect is the actual discourse, and much as I love you, I am not going to have you exercise your memory at my expense." Phaedrus gives in—he will read the whole essay; but where shall they sit? Oh, yes, under "that tallest plane-tree, where there is shade and gentle breezes and grass on which to sit or lie." "Yes," Socrates answers, "a fair resting place, full of summer sounds and scents, the stream deliciously cool to the feet, and the grass like a pillow gently sloping to the head. I shall lie down and do you choose the position you can best read in. Begin." A number of hours are spent under that plane-tree, discussing "the nature of the

soul—though her true form be ever a theme of large and more than mortal discourse"; and "beauty shining in company with celestial forms"; and "the soul of the lover that follows the beloved in modesty and holy fear"; and "the heavenly blessings of friendship"; and "all the great arts, which require high speculation about the truths of nature"; and men who "are worthy of a proud name befitting their serious pursuit of life. Wise, I may not call them, for that is a great name which belongs to God alone—lovers of wisdom is their fitting title." That is the way two gentlemen would while away a summer morning in the Athens of Plato.

Source: Edith Hamilton, *The Greek Way* (New York: Norton, 1942), pp. 114–115.

---

tem of formal or mystical religion that placed the gods at great distance from the people of the city. In Peking the priests were "specialists" sequestered within the walls of the Forbidden City, but in Athens the "priest was just another conscientious layman whose amateurism was not even dignified by prophetic presumptions; his religious duties were simply his civic duties" (Carlton, 1977, p. 226). This ideal of participation meant that temples such as the Parthenon were always open to people, and religious observance typically was carried on informally, frequently outdoors.

Indeed, as Greek civilization entered the Golden Age, the gods themselves became less abstract and more like human beings. They were the objects of jokes, criticism, and bargains, but—all the same—they were used as models for human development. As William Chase Greene (1923, p. 226) has argued, the Olympian gods "became the symbol of something nobler in human nature," something within the reach of human endeavor.

A tripartite focus on body, mind, and spirit:

this unique combination was the crux of Athens's success. By developing serious interests in all three areas, the Athenian indirectly kept any one area from becoming all-absorbing. This focus kept more practical areas of life—politics or economics, for example—in check. Too much politics breeds overconcern with power and control; too much economics cultivates obsession with wealth and material goods. For a brief period, the citizens of Athens avoided these pitfalls.

Behind the Glory

Athens's moment at the pinnacle of urban history was not to last, eventually being undermined by the culture's own egocentrism and exploitative practices. The wealth and leisurely pace of Athens in its Golden Age were built in large measure on the goods and services of others. During its successful expansion before the fifth century B.C., Athens had conquered many other city-states and regions. From them Athens extracted tribute in materials, taxes, and people. Many of the human tributes became slaves;

Mumford (1961) has estimated that one-third of the city's population held this unhappy status. Women, too, were excluded from citizenship and were relegated to household duties. Themselves hesitant to enter into the service of another, the elite Athenian citizens found benefit in the widespread use of such human servants (Gouldner 1965).

Elitism reared its head in yet another, more immediately destructive, way. The Athenians refused citizenship to foreigners, many of whom, as traders, had become permanent residents. This robbed the citizenry of potentially invigorating new ideas, forcing the foreign population into an exclusive concern with economic matters. Demoralized, these traders devoted their energies to money making and material consumption. In time, they became indifferent to government so long as they were free to make a profit. By the end of the fourth century B.C., profit making had become the center of city life, and the older idea that economic activity was simply a means to a more holistic life—so central to the health of the city—began to wane (Mumford 1961, pp. 150–155).

Finally, as the Golden Age reached its climax, Athenians came to see their city as the most civilized in the world and themselves as the apotheosis of humanity. They believed they could learn from no one. The city became static, and demoralization spread further (Mumford 1961).

Into this setting came the Peloponnesian Wars, begun in 431 B.C. between Athens and Sparta. Soundly defeated, Athens surrendered in 404 B.C. In total confusion and in public contradiction of all their democratic ideals, in 399 B.C. the Athenians tried and condemned Socrates to death for "undermining the state by his endless public questionings."

The handwriting was on the wall. In 338 B.C. the Athenians put up belated opposition to an invasion force led by Philip of Macedon. Their defeat at the Battle of Chaeronea has been called "the death of the free polis." After that, Athens became a satellite in the Macedonian Empire until the Roman overlords arrived in 148 B.C.

Ming Peking and Athens: A Comparison

The culture that was magnified in classical Athens was of a radically different character from that of Ming Peking. Without doubt, the cities had certain parallels: substantial inequality; large areas of poor housing; crowded, winding streets; and important central monuments and public buildings. There were all-important differences, however. Chinese civilization was built upon a fundamental cultural belief in a godlike emperor that gave an unmistakable stamp to Peking. Monuments and buildings dwarfed the common individual as they simultaneously magnified the pomp and majesty of the emperor and his elite. Indeed, what could be a clearer indication of a distant, exclusive power structure than a citadel in the form of Peking's Forbidden City?

Athens seems, overall, more humane in character. The Greek cultural ideals of citizen participation stamped that city with a human scale, encouraging openness, communication, and development among its free citizens. Such ideals can be seen in all Athens's public buildings—in the theaters (where, not by accident, the audience sat above the performers, not the other way around), in the public forums, in the temples, in the gymnasia, in the market place. These buildings were not monuments to an absolute emperor; rather, Athens was much more a celebration of the "good life," an ideal that was evident in spite of important failings in practice.

In comparing Hellenic Athens and Ming Peking, we see just how different cities in different cultures can be. But this comparison shows us more: Athenian success at encouraging citizen participation and in developing the very best in human nature by a process of dialogue and growth shows us what the city *can* be. We are prompted to ask, in other words, how or why one city might be better than another. If we agree, for example, that democracy, equality, and continual mental, bodily, and spiritual development are ideals for which human beings should strive, Athens provides us with a real-life case where those ideals were encouraged. What, then,

CITYSCAPE 7-3
The Capitalist City: 1850

London is unique, because it is a city in which one can roam for hours without leaving the built-up area and without seeing the slightest sign of the approach of open country. This enormous agglomeration of population on a single spot has multiplied a hundred-fold the economic strength of the two and a half million inhabitants concentrated there. This great population has made London the commercial capital of the world and has created the gigantic docks in which are assembled the thousands of ships which always cover the River Thames. . . . All this is so magnificent and impressive that one is lost in admiration. The traveller has good reason to marvel at England's greatness even before he steps on English soil.

It is only later that the traveller appreciates the human suffering which has made all this possible. . . . It is only when he has visited the slums of this great city that it dawns upon him that the inhabitants of modern London have had to sacrifice so much that is best in human nature in order to create those wonders of civilisation with which their city teems. The vast majority of Londoners have had to let so many of their potential creative faculties lie dormant, stunted and unused in order that a small, closely-knit group of their fellow citizens could develop to the full the qualities with which nature has endowed them. . . . Hundreds of thousands of men and women drawn from all classes and ranks of society pack the streets of London. Are they not all human beings with the same innate characteristics and potentialities? Are they not all equally interested in the pursuit of happiness? And do they not all aim at happiness by following similar methods? Yet they rush past each other as if they had nothing in common. . . .

No one even thinks of sparing a glance for his neighbor in the streets. . . . We know well enough that this isolation of the individual—this narrow-minded egotism—is everywhere the fundamental principle of modern society. But nowhere is this selfish egotism so blatantly evident as in the frantic bustle of the great city. The disintegration of society into individuals, each guided by his private principles and each pursuing his own aims has been pushed to its furthest limits in London. [emphasis added]

. . . Here men regard their fellows not as human beings, but as pawns in the struggle for existence. Everyone exploits his neighbor with the result that the stronger tramples the weaker under foot. The strongest of all, a tiny group of capitalists, monopolise everything, while the weakest, who are in the vast majority, succumb to the most abject poverty.

What is true of London, is true also of all the great towns, such as Manchester, Birmingham and Leeds. . . . The observer of such an appalling state of affairs must shudder at the consequences of such feverish activity and can only marvel that so crazy a social and economic structure should survive at all.

Source: Friedrich Engels, *The Condition of the Working Class in England*, trans. by W. O. Henderson and W. H. Chaloner (New York: Macmillan, 1958), pp. 30–31.

---

might *we* do to encourage the further manifestation of positive cultural values in our own modern-day cities? (Look now to Cityscape 7-3.)

The Culture of Capitalism and The City

Nineteenth-century London certainly was not like either Ming Peking or Hellenic Athens. Dominated by feverish economic activity, it was the forerunner of the modern city described by American urbanist Louis Wirth in Chapter 4.

But Friedrich Engels, who first saw London in 1842, the year he met Karl Marx and began their long collaboration, made an interpretation radically different from that of Wirth. Whereas the Chicago urbanist imagined he was describing the essential characteristics of all large, modern cities, Engels was aware that he was looking only at a certain cultural setting, a city intensifying the tremendous power of Western industrial capitalism. Note especially the passage in italics in Cityscape 7-3: what Wirth saw as a consequence of a large, differentiated population, Engels interpreted as cultural forces at work.

Engels was mightily disturbed by what he saw. If Hellenic Athens with its cultural ideas of developing the whole person was the city's zenith, surely Engels believed nineteenth-century London to be its nadir. The characteristics of both cities reflect the dominant ideals and activities of the larger culture. In the same way that Greek culture produced cities in which economic activity was regarded as of decidedly secondary importance, Western culture under the influence of capitalism spawned cities where economic gain was an unrestrained obsession.

The Capitalist City

As a means of livelihood, capitalism is very old. A rich capitalist life flourished in the fifth century B.C. in Athens, and no doubt such activity is centuries older. Significant commercial activity aimed at the accumulation of profit also took place on an increasing scale in medieval Europe, especially after the eleventh century. Mumford noted that "so marked was this influence that . . . Alain of Lille could say: 'Not caesar now, but money, is all'" (1961, p. 411).

If capitalism itself was not new, the unparalleled energy with which the spirit of commerce and profit began to assert itself in the sixteenth century A.D. certainly was. There appear to have been various spurs to this change. First, the feudal order of the Middle Ages began to erode as merchants, primarily in cities, gained power. Desiring to broaden their market, these merchants established trade routes among cities all over Europe in the period between 1200 and 1500. Goods began to pour into these cities and people in the countryside began to get wind that a better life—or at least a life with more material amenities—could be had in cities. Major urban population growth ensued and fueled economic vitality further (Heilbroner 1975).

Gradually, from the sixteenth century onward the economic interests of life came to dominate western European cities and capitalism set the principal cultural theme. The new order was organized around a rather different set of economic relationships than its feudal predecessor, however. In the first place, individual workers no longer were bound to lords and manors. They were able to sell their labor to whoever would pay the highest wages. Second, under these conditions economic activity became increasingly competitive. Because everyone was striving for profits, workers had to outdo each other in some way to get the greatest economic benefits. When industrialization arrived in the mid-eighteenth century, capitalism's hold over Western cities was enhanced manyfold.

The Industrial Revolution

Like capitalism, industrialism—the process of manufacturing goods in large quantities for mass consumption—had existed in Western society to a limited degree before the eighteenth century. However, it was only after capitalism had been adopted on a large scale that the influence of industrialism began to grow. For all intents and purposes, large-scale industrialism began in England about 1750.

One important reason that English society proved so amenable to industrialism was the penchant, particularly evident in the upper middle classes, for engineering and guiding economic activities by the most scientific methods available. If efficient methods were not available, the innovative British invented them. Perhaps the most famous example of an invention that changed the economic order was James Watt's steam engine. This machine, perfected by 1775, had literally hundreds of applications, from textile manufacturing to flour mills to the mass production of the common pin. Its ability to save hand labor and contribute to the mass production of items was nothing short of remarkable, and in very little time entrepreneurs put this invention into widespread use. By 1781, Matthew Boulton, Watt's partner in a steam-engine manufacturing company, was claiming that "the people of London, Birmingham, and Manchester [are] all 'steam mill mad'" (Heilbroner 1975, pp. 76–77). From then on, the industrial revolution was in full force. Other inventions, such as Arkwright's spinning jenny and Maudslay's automatic screw machine, revolutionized other areas of production. "The Revolution . . . fed upon itself. The new techniques . . . simply destroyed their handicraft competition around the world and thus enormously increased their own markets" (Heilbroner 1975, p. 75).

For the city dweller, the most important change was the invention of the factory.

> The factory may be singled out as the agent which gives [the industrial-capitalist] city its structural form and social purpose. By the word "factory" I mean more than an industrial enterprise: the factory is the locus of mobilized abstract labor, of labor power as a commodity, placed in the service of commerce as well as production. Accordingly, the term applies as much to an office building and a supermarket as to a mill and a plant. Once the factory becomes an element of urban life, it takes over the city almost completely. (Bookchin 1975, p. 51)

With the domination of the factory, the very symbolism of the city changed. The city in feudal Europe had been, above all, a Christian city, symbolically dominating the region with its Gothic cathedral. (A striking example is Venice, spread about St. Mark's Cathedral, built in 1176.) The capitalist era, as Mumford remarked, turned the culture of feudalism on its head, transforming "six of the seven deadly sins [gluttony, pride, covetousness, envy, lust, and anger] into cardinal virtues [sloth became perhaps an even greater sin]" (1961, p. 346). The church declined as the focal institution of society; in the place of spires appeared smokestacks and the public plaza became a growing central business district.

> If capitalism tended to expand the market and turn every part of the city into a negotiable commodity, the change from [small-scale handicraft] to large-scale factory production transformed the industrial towns into dark hives, busily puffing, clanking, screeching, smoking for twelve and fourteen hours a day, sometimes going around the clock. The slavish routine . . . became the normal environment of the new industrial workers. None of these towns heeded the old saw, "All work and no play makes Jack a dull boy." [They] specialized in producing dull boys. (Mumford 1961, p. 446)

In short, the dominant capitalist cultural theme, in conjunction with industrial mechanization, created a new emphasis in urban consciousness. In describing a typical schoolroom in "Coketown," a fictionalized English factory city

New York's modern St. Peter's Church (foreground) is completely dwarfed by the bulk of the Citicorp building, headquarters of one of the world's largest banks. The size and positioning of both these buildings suggest the relative importance of economics and religion in contemporary Western society. (Menschenfreund)

of the nineteenth century, Charles Dickens explained the main ingredient of this consciousness, presented here in Cityscape 7-4.

Urban Life as Economics

"You are never to fancy!" With this phrase Dickens summarized what so worried Engels about the capitalist city: it reduced everything in life to objective facts and quantity. Other aspects of life—subjectivity, quality, art, music, politics, religion, and creative thought—were downplayed or consciously eradicated.

CITYSCAPE 7-4
"Nothing but the Facts, Ma'm"—Capitalist-Industrialist Consciousness

"Now, what I want is, Facts. Teach these boys and girls nothing but Facts. Facts alone are wanted in life. Plant nothing else, and root out everything else. You can only form the minds of reasoning animals upon Facts: nothing else will ever be of any service to them. This is the principle on which I bring up my own children, and this is the principle on which I bring up these children. Stick to Facts, Sir!"

The scene was a plain, bare, monotonous vault of a schoolroom, and the speaker's square forefinger emphasized his observations by underscoring every sentence with a line on the schoolmaster's sleeve. The emphasis was helped by the speaker's square wall of a forehead, which had his eyebrows for its base, while his eyes found commodious cellerage in two dark caves, overshadowed by the wall. The emphasis was helped by the speaker's mouth, which was wide, thin, and hard set. . . .

Thomas Gradgrind, Sir. A man of realities. A man of facts and calculations. A man who proceeds upon the principle that two

and two are four, and nothing over, and who is not to be talked into allowing for anything over. Thomas Gradgrind, Sir—peremptorily Thomas—Thomas Gradgrind. With a rule and a pair of scales, and the multiplication table always in his pocket, Sir, ready to weigh and measure any parcel of human nature, and tell you exactly what it comes to. It is a mere question of figures, a case of simple arithmetic. . . .

"Girl number twenty," said Mr. Gradgrind, squarely pointing with his square forefinger, "I don't know that girl. Who is that girl?"

"Sissy Jupe, Sir," explained number twenty, blushing, standing up, and curtseying.

"Sissy is not a name," said Mr. Gradgrind. "Don't call yourself Sissy. Call yourself Cecilia."

"It's father as calls me Sissy, Sir," returned the young girl in a trembling voice, and with another curtsey.

"Then he has no business to do it," said Mr. Gradgrind. "Tell him he mustn't. Cecilia Jupe. Let me see. . . ."

"Give me your definition of a horse."

(Sissy Jupe thrown into the greatest alarm by this demand.)

"Girl number twenty unable to define a horse!" said Mr. Gradgrind, for the general behoof of all the little pitchers. "Girl number twenty possessed of no facts, in reference to one of the commonest of animals! Some boy's definition of a horse. Bitzer, yours. . . ."

"Quadruped. Graminivorous. Forty teeth, namely twenty-four grinders, four eye-teeth, and twelve incisive. Sheds coat in the spring; in marshy countries, sheds hoofs, too. Hoofs hard, but requiring to be shod with iron. Age known by marks in mouth." Thus (and much more) Bitzer.

"Now girl number twenty," said Mr. Gradgrind. "You know what a horse is. . . ."

["But Sir," said Cecilia Jupe, blushing] . . . "I fancy . . ."

"Ay, ay, ay! But you mustn't fancy," cried the gentleman, quite elated by coming so happily to his point. "That's it! You are never to fancy!"

Source: Charles Dickens, *Hard Times* (London: Oxford University Press, 1955; originally published 1854), pp. 1, 3–5, 7.

This new consciousness not only transformed how city people acted, it transformed the physical structure of the city itself, thereby intensifying the capitalist theme even further. Land, once merely a place to live, became *real estate*:

If the layout of a town has no relation to human needs and activities other than business, the pattern of the city may be simplified: the ideal layout for the business [person] is that which can be most swiftly reduced to standard monetary units for purchase and sale. The fundamental [urban] unit is no longer the neighborhood . . . but the individual building lot, whose value can be gauged in terms of front feet: this favors an oblong with narrow frontage and great depth, which provides a minimum amount of light and air to the buildings, particularly the dwellings, that conform to it. Such units turned out equally advantageous for the land surveyor, the real estate speculator, the commercial builder, and the lawyer who drew up the deed of sale. In turn, the lots favored the rectangular building block, which again became the standard unit for extending the city (Mumford 1961, pp. 421–422)

So strong was this pattern in the physical form of the city after the sixteenth century that even cities with mountainous geography (such as San Francisco), which might have benefited from a switch-back pattern to facilitate moving up and down the terrain, were subjected to a grid pattern.

Murray Bookchin used even stronger language to suggest the extent to which the modern Western city has been shaped by the industrial-capitalist system:

> Every esthetic urban pattern inherited from the past tends to be sacrificed to the grid system (in modern times, the factory pattern par excellence), which facilitates the most efficient transportation of goods and people. Streams are obliterated, variations in the landscape effaced without the least sensitivity to natural beauty, magnificent stands of trees removed, even treasured architectural and historical monuments demolished, and wherever possible, the terrain is leveled to resemble a factory floor. The angular and curved streets of the medieval city which at every turn delighted the eye with a new and scenic tableau, are replaced by straight monotonous vistas of the same featureless buildings and shops. Lovely squares inherited from the past are reduced to nodal points for traffic, and highways are wantonly carved into vital neighborhoods, dividing and finally subverting them. (1974, pp. 90–91)

Assets and Debits

On one level, there can be no doubt that the capitalist city has been successful: it has generated a higher material standard of living for a larger proportion of its population than any other urban system in history. For example, only about 10 percent of the population of metropolitan America is below the poverty line. Useful material goods and technological innovations are omnipresent, and, given the "hands-off-the-individual" value that is so central to capitalism, there is a very real degree of political and other freedom for residents of such cities. They can vote, come and go as they please, and (if they have the money and the right color skin) live where they like.

But there are debits as well: millions of poor families live in urban America, and districts that are unprofitable (such as New York's South Bronx) have fallen into shocking decay. Within such areas, as we shall see in later chapters, people suffer incredibly. Similarly, the dominant focus on material goods and technological innovations often means that many people are preoccupied with the newest laser disk player or the new car, and less mindful of social and environmental needs that are being compromised.

Pollution is one example. Although attempts to control human waste data from at least 1388 when the English parliament enacted an urban pollution law (Mumford 1961, p. 290), the problem has grown to massive proportion within the capitalist city. While some abuses have been curbed, the problem has continued, tragically illustrated by the smog-related deaths of 5,000 people in London during one week of 1952, the burning of the sludge-filled Cuyahoga River near Cleveland in 1968, and the cancer-inducing chemical dump at the Love Canal near Niagara Falls in 1980. City dwellers even have adjusted to smog reports and—if they live in Los Angeles—to ever-more-serious smog alerts warning that to venture out of the house may be a threat to life.

Finally, even freedoms have their problematical side. The freedom to accumulate wealth, prestige, and power has meant, over the years, that some individuals in our cities have much more of these scarce resources than others. With wealth primarily in the hands of a few (the richest 5 percent of the American population controls a full 54 percent of the wealth; see Table 12-3), there is a tendency for these people to control both the economic and political spheres of life to such a degree that others are effectively cut off from any true success or representation.

Problems such as these have led to a reaction: a second type of modern city, established around and intensifying yet another set of cultural themes, those of communism.

CASE STUDY 7-3
Communist Beijing

To get a sense of the contemporary communist city, we return to Peking. Box 7-5 gets us acclimated. It records the first visit to the city by Liang Heng, a young Red Guard supporter of Chairman Mao Ze-dong, during the turmoil of the Cultural Revolution of the 1960s.

Standing on the Meridian Gate of the old Ming Imperial City (Figures 7-1, 7-2), looking out over the millions assembled in Tian An Men Square, Mao established the People's Republic of China on October 1, 1949. It was on this historic spot that Liang Heng gazed in rapture as a dedicated revolutionary in the late 1960s.

Today, nearly four decades since Mao made that fateful pronouncement, Peking has been transformed. Its feudal, imperial, capitalist past has been almost completely eradicated. Even its name has been changed—to Beijing (the old name, Peking, was a Western transcription of Beijing). On the site of the old dynasties has grown one of the two most important communist cities (the other is Moscow) in the world.

Although not typical of communist cities outside China, modern Beijing provides us with a final illustration of the consequences of different cultural themes in urban places. The great walls that protected the city and the emperor in the Ming period have been destroyed. In their place

is a city-encircling highway. Below them, the city's modern subway system is being built. The Forbidden City is now a museum open to all, surrounded by great new buildings of state: the Great Hall of the People, the Historical Museum, and the Mausoleum that holds Mao's remains. There is also the Peking Hotel which, even at a modest 17 stories, is well able to dominate the old buildings of the emperor. Replaced, too, are many of the old, sonorous names of the imperial years: the Pavillion of Pleasant Sounds has given way to People's Road and Anti-Imperialist Street.

The contrast is jarring on yet another level, especially when seen in comparison to capitalist cities. Beijing has no extreme poverty, no seedy sections of town, no prostitutes, no beggars, no crime, very little pollution, and nearly pristine streets. What makes all this possible is a modern cultural tradition that sees political control of almost all aspects of life by the state, as well as political responsibility of the individual to others, as the cornerstones of the good life.

The Emergence of Modern Beijing

A Communist-controlled China was not won easily. Ironically, it was the expansion of capitalist nations and their cities in the nineteenth century that made it possible.

In 1644 the Ming rulers who had built Imperial Peking were replaced by the Ch'ing Dynasty. Like their Ming predecessors, the Ch'ing emperors were not interested in contact with the outside world; but it did not follow that the world was disinterested in China. In the late 1700s and early 1800s—not coincidentally the time of the industrial-capitalist revolution—various European countries made overtures to China in hopes of finding yet another trade market. Covetous of China's silk, tea, and silver, they were rebuked by the emperor. Tension grew; the Europeans became determined to find a way to open China to trade, and the Chinese were just as determined to keep them out.

The denouement came in the mid–nineteenth century. For many years the British had been smuggling India-grown poppies into

China. Converted into opium and mixed with tobacco for smoking, the poppies gave rise to China's infamous opium dens, which served an estimated 2 million addicts by 1835. Finally enraged, an imperial commissioner from Peking seized and destroyed over 2.8 million pounds of opium in Canton in 1839. It was a fateful decision. Later the same year the English launched the so-called Opium War as a punitive action. They won hands down; the resulting treaty opened five Chinese ports to unrestricted trade and established the British colony of Hong Kong. In 1860 another war and treaty forcibly opened more Chinese ports to European trade.

Severely weakened, the ruling dynasty lost the Sino-Japanese War in 1895 and, during the anti-foreigner Boxer Rebellion of 1900, fled Peking. Chinese insurgents held Peking for 55 days against an eight-nation "relief force." The insurgents' inevitable defeat placed China almost completely under foreign domination. In 1911, Dr. Sun Yat-sen overthrew the remnants of the dynasty and proclaimed a Chinese Republic. He was succeeded by Chiang Kai-shek in 1927, but power struggles throughout the country meant that the government remained ineffectual.

Angered by the disadvantageous trade relations that the republic still tolerated with foreign countries, in 1934 China's fledgling Communist party under Mao Ze-dong undertook the 6,000-mile Long March to China's hinterlands to escape Chiang Kai-shek's army. The Communists returned in 1948 and, after a six-week siege, occupied Peking. The People's Republic was proclaimed the following year.

Urban Life as Politics

The Communists vowed to free China from centuries of domination of the many by the few and from exploitation by foreign countries. To do this they transformed nearly all of Chinese life into an expression of the new political ideas. The job of the state was to provide equally for everyone; the job of the individual was to contribute to the state's success by contributing unselfishly to the state-linked neighborhood units, school classes, factories, and party committees (Bonavia 1978).

Only by collectivizing everything, the Communists believed, and by constantly reminding everyone of the dangers of backsliding into individualism, was true progress to be attained.

The key concept in all this was *tzu-li keng-sheng*, "self-reliance" or "regeneration through one's own efforts." In developing this concept, the party divided each city into districts (Beijing has nine), each district into neighborhoods, and each neighborhood into smaller residential areas. Each residential area developed its own "residents' committee," designed to link each individual with the city authorities and vice versa. It became the job of these committees to oversee local services—security, fire, sanitation—and to keep political responsibility uppermost in peoples' minds (Sidel 1974).

Unceasing political awareness was developed by study groups in which all neighborhood residents participated (there also were study groups in schools and factories). The tasks of these groups were three: (1) to communicate to all citizens the importance of participation in all areas of life; (2) to chastise political troublemakers of all kinds, such as "revisionists," "factionalists," "ultra-Leftists," "capitalists," and "imperialists;" and (3) to examine constantly through group self-criticism each individual's performance (Sidel 1974; Bonavia 1978). As one influential Chinese citizen put it:

> If a person truly loves his neighbor or truly is his brother's keeper, then he has a moral and social duty to correct his brother's shortcomings. If truly no man is an island and the actions of each person directly affect the lives of all others, then the "group," however defined, has a real and direct stake in controlling the actions of its members. (Victor H. Li, quoted in Sidel 1974, p. 59)

Thus, any form of extreme individualism in the Western sense would be seen as a selfish act. In modern China, says a Beijing scholar,

> [a] student may express his individual personality to the full, yet still study for the sake of the revolution. But a student in the grip of [Western-style] individualism studies only to build up his own career. "Individual interest" is respected in China, but an individualistic outlook, which leads a person to exploit others for his own benefit, is not

proper. (Chou I-Liang, paraphrased in Terrill 1975, p. 386)

It is difficult to imagine more contrasting views of city life than those outlined above and those held by people of contemporary Western cities.

The Difficulties of Urban Life

Despite enormous success in correcting the urban ills of the past, Chinese cities haven't yet attained nirvana. With their exploding populations they are bursting at the seams. Beijing's population in 1949, the year of the declaration of the People's Republic, was less than 2.5 million; today it is over 9.5 million. Moreover, with a primitive industrial system, China may have succeeded in feeding and housing its own people, but the standing of a world-class economic power remains elusive. Its educational system likewise lags far behind that of other nations. In desperate need of trained personnel (China was an almost entirely peasant society until the 1950s), the nation has not been able to provide the widespread high-quality education that is necessary.

To curb these problems, in 1959 Mao initiated the "Great Leap Forward," an unsuccessful crash program aimed at improving industry and production. He also launched the "Great Proletarian Cultural Revolution" in 1966 to eliminate "revisionism." Ironically, the overzealous youth movement associated with the Cultural Revolution, the Red Guards (of which Liang Heng was a passionate member) closed the universities, impaired production, and brought many Chinese cities to an almost dead stop. They finally had to be brought under control by the army.

With Mao's death in 1976, a great power struggle emerged in Beijing for the control of the party—a struggle won by Deng Xiaoping and his followers. The new leaders have downplayed the extreme elements of Maoism and in the late 1970s opened China more and more to outside contact by allowing large foreign investments and sending students to Western schools. In recent years the new leadership has attempted to boost economic production by providing personal incentives and allowing privately owned businesses to appear. This is an astonishing change from Mao's policies. No less remarkable have been the results. Agricultural and industrial productivity roughly doubled between 1978 and 1983.

On a recent visit to Beijing, author Spates saw a city alive with energy. In one section of the city—just south of the old Forbidden City—is a shopping section for the capital's citizens. Underneath billboards advertising Toshiba TV sets, there are department stores full of goods. To be sure, they are goods of lesser quality than those found in the West and many are more expensive than their counterparts in capitalist countries. Nevertheless, the stores are filled with lookers and at least some buyers. Most Chinese seem delighted with the availability of such items.

The reason for this overt consumerism is the surplus money that the new policies are generating. For example, in another part of the city, there is a farmers' market where workers from a local commune sell the portion of their vegetables that is not needed for the commune or for state consumption. They are allowed to keep the profits of such transactions.

Another example is Spates's guide. A lifelong resident of Beijing, this young man recently was selected by his government to teach Chinese in an American college. He taught for three years and received a Western salary—astronomical by Chinese standards. When he returned to Beijing, he was allowed to keep the money he had saved. As a result, he has been able to afford a better apartment in a new section of the city and to keep his family in better clothes. He has also been able to live comfortably while looking for work he enjoys.

All this change—a movement "from Marxism to Mastercard" (National Public Radio 1985)—has its critics. Many powerful Communist party members see the revolution of Mao being "sold out," and, as indication that the policies of Deng are not all positive, they cite extensive evidence that corruption is now beginning to appear in many areas of Chinese life as people scramble for the accoutrements of a consumer society. They charge that Deng's policies are generating self-centeredness and a kind of Western decadence. Nonetheless, Deng continues his open-door policy, and China and its cities, once again, are in the throes of major social change.

Conclusion

Ramona thought about the city.
—I have to admit we are locked in the most exquisite, mysterious muck. This muck heaves and palpitates. It is multidirectional and has a mayor. . . . Our muck is only a part of a much greater muck—the nation-state—which is itself the creation of that muck of mucks, human consciousness.

DONALD BARTHELME, *CITY LIFE,* 1970

As we can now see, the city does not exist by itself, but is linked intricately to the broader society of which it is a part. Any city's physical and social forms are shaped by the cultural values of that society and its historical epoch. For example, although there is some truth in the old idea that the ways of the country and the city are distinct and "ne'er the twain shall meet," recent research has shown that cities and their hinterlands are bound together in a complex interdependence that allows each significant influence over the other.

We also have argued that, while cities are not entirely synonymous with civilization, they are symbolic centers that concentrate, intensify, and re-create the cultural forces found throughout the society. Consider again the cities we compared and contrasted in this chapter: Boston and Ibadan, Ming Peking and Hellenic Athens, and the nineteenth-century industrial-capitalist city and contemporary industrial-communist Beijing. How different they are! These differences attest to the importance of culture in shaping the social and physical environment of the city. Only by studying cities in a comparative manner can this urban variability be understood. As Brian Berry has recently said: "The most fundamental axiom of . . . urban sociology is that the urban landscape is a mirror reflecting the society that maintains it." (1984, p. 96)

If urban variety is so marked, what is left as distinctively urban? What do all the cities we've considered in this chapter have in common? To answer this question, we certainly must go beyond the factors of size, density, and heterogeneity proposed by Louis Wirth. We shall propose a new definition of the city, one that acknowledges the importance of the cultural dimension that Wirth neglected: *In comparison to other types of permanent human settlement, a city is a relatively large, dense settlement that has a complex social structure that greatly reflects, intensifies, and re-creates cultural values and forms.*

A few comments are necessary to clarify this definition. The first set of characteristics—"a large, dense settlement"—are Wirth's; he seems quite right about them. The next characteristic—"a complex social structure"—is from V. Gordon Childe (1950). You may recall that Wirth also suggested that the city is composed of "socially heterogeneous individuals." By this he meant that people of different racial, ethnic, or religious backgrounds tend to mingle in the city. Anthropological research has shown that this is much more true of modern Western cities (to which people of different countries migrated) than it is of their non-industrial counterparts (such as Ibadan and Beijing). Yet, even if social heterogeneity is not characteristic of all cities, nearly every urbanist has noted that the city has a more complex division of labor and a more sophisticated political system (if only to handle the large numbers and density) than other forms of human settlement. Such complexities are what we mean by "a complex social structure."

Finally, the idea that any city is a reflector, intensifier, and re-creator of cultural values and forms is a direct outgrowth of this chapter. In the final analysis, the nature of any city lies in its unique ability to interpret a particular set of cultural values into a distinctive form. By "cultural values" we mean those shared beliefs and ideas that characterize any social group of long duration. By "form" we mean the typical round of everyday activities and arrangement of urban space that characterize any city. Thus, because the cultural values of the Greeks during Athens's Golden Era (the fifth century B.C.) regarded money making as secondary and a holistic life as primary, we found that the daily life of the city was dominated by dialogue, politics, recreation, and ritual. While the Greeks surely went to the Agora (the market) to trade, they just as frequently went there to talk and relax. Even their buildings reflected this cultural emphasis. The Acropolis, where the most important buildings of Greek civilization were located (the Parthenon, the Erechtheum, the Propylea, the Temple of Athena Nike), sits on a hill overlooking the rest of the city. The Agora, lesser in importance, lies at the bottom of the hill. All this appears reversed when we consider the form of contemporary capitalist cities such as those of North America. Here the round of daily activities focuses on the economic. Most people spend the bulk of their day getting and spending and planning for more of the same. Dialogue, politics, recreation, and ritual come later—in the evenings, on the weekends, during the two-week vacation. The city's physical layout reflects this cultural priority. Streets are arranged in a grid for easy movement and buying and selling, and the most important buildings—at least those that dominate the skyline of any major American city—are those of commerce.

In such comparative observations lies a crucial lesson about studying cities: Quite simply, if we don't understand the relationship between the city and culture, we can't properly understand the city. The next few chapters will reaffirm this conclusion, as we examine cities in cross-cultural context in much greater detail. As we shall see, cities exhibit tremendous diversity and cannot be easily classified as variations on a single theme. After her trip to Ibadan, Dorothy McAllister, that intrepid traveler whom we introduced at the beginning of this chapter, wouldn't be surprised at the great differences that exist between cities in different parts of our contemporary world.

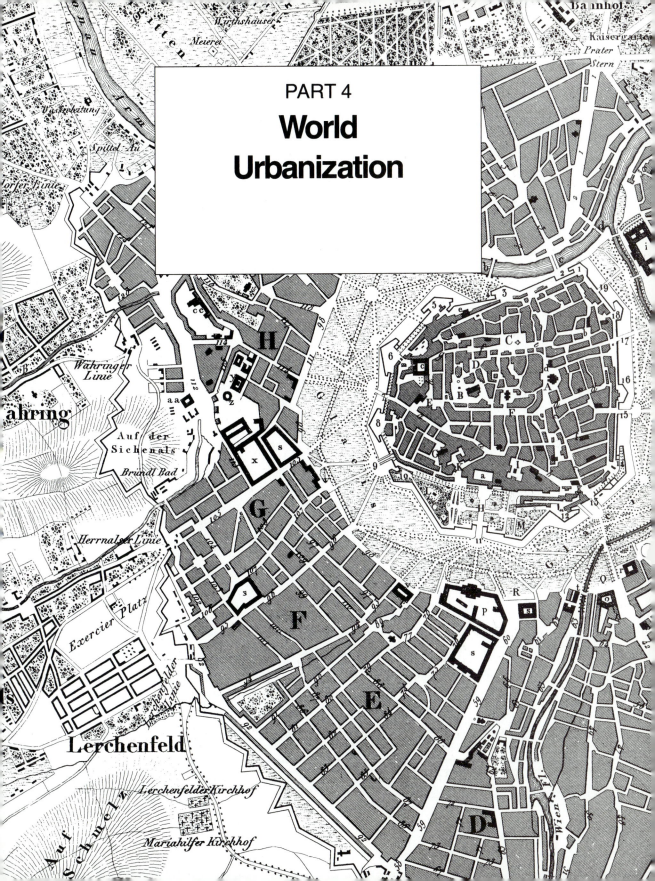

PART 4
World
Urbanization

CHAPTER 8

Latin American Cities

You have to live among our families to see what we suffer from and how it can be cured. They haven't made a thorough study of the problem. Those gentlemen who rule over us have expensive cars and many millions in the bank, but they don't see what is underneath where the poor people live. . . . They disregard the fact that right here in [Mexico City] there are lots of people who eat only one or two meals a day.

There is not enough money, not enough work and everything is so expensive; prices went up again today. . . .

I am not an educated man but I see that before the workers were exploited in one way and now they are exploited in another way, and will go on being exploited. Naturally, Mexico has progressed, but the worker continues to be a worker and continues to be poor, and will be until he dies, because when he gets a raise of fifty *centavos*, food goes up one, two, five *pesos*. So the raise doesn't help the worker, it only hurts him because there is no effective control. . . . [I]n the thirty years I've been in Mexico City, the life of the poor people has changed very little, very little. . . . Why do thousands and thousands of farm hands leave Mexico? Here you have proof you can put your fingers on. Because there's no security here, because wages are terribly low, miserable wages which aren't enough to support any family. (Jesus Sanchez, in Oscar Lewis, *The Children of Sanchez*, 1961)

For most of us, to think of really large cities is to imagine towering New York or sprawling Los Angeles; however, in this century Mexico City has grown from a population of 350,000 to some 11.3 million (1985), and if present trends continue, by the end of this century the population will reach 31 million, making it perhaps the largest city in world history.

In this chapter, we shall explore the development of the cities of Latin America, which, together with much of Africa, the Middle East, and Asia, comprise what often is called the "Third World." Typically lacking the technological and industrial capacity of the other two "worlds"—the capitalist and communist countries—the Third World has an urban history quite unlike that of western Europe (Chapter 2) and the United States (Chapter 3).

Although Mexico City is somewhat atypical in the magnitude of its growth rate, it symbolizes in many ways the current state of Third World cities around the globe: into each are pouring hundreds of thousands of people who must compete for extremely limited resources. Not surprisingly, those meager resources have not been shared very equally. Jesus Sanchez, whose words so eloquently express this struggle, is representative of the many poor who live in the cities of Latin America: despite the efforts of 30 years, he cannot make ends meet. The result of this massive growth has been the evolution of urban problems on a colossal scale: pollution, poverty, ethnic and racial conflict, political repression, and sometimes endless political instability.

Although the crisis is very real, the portrait is not one of complete hopelessness. As we look at the daily lives of even the poorest city dwellers, we shall see that some survive and some manage to build a better life despite overwhelming odds.

Latin American Cities in History

Latin America is composed of three subregions (see the world cities map after the Preface at the beginning of the book): the Caribbean Islands, Mexico and Central America, and South America. To understand Latin American cities today we must look at their past. We begin with the pre-Columbian period, the years before Christopher Columbus's initial, and fateful, westward voyage in 1492.

Pre-Columbian Cities

Most of the cities we readily identify as Latin American—Rio de Janeiro, Buenos Aires, Bogotá, Santiago, Lima, La Paz—did not exist before the sixteenth century. They, and many others, are the product of colonization by Spanish and Portuguese conquerors. Before the founding of such cities, however, other urban centers existed, the most outstanding examples being the capitals of the Mayan and Aztec civilizations in Central America and Mexico and the Inca Empire on the western coast of South America.

The Mayan capital of Teotihuacán in central Mexico was primarily a religious center. Teotihuacán reached the peak of its development between A.D. 450 and 650, when its population was about 200,000. For reasons still un-

clear, it was almost completely abandoned about A.D. 750.

The Inca Empire reached its greatest development somewhat later, between 1430 and 1525, in Peru. Containing a population of over 6 million and stretching from Ecuador into northern Argentina, a land area of over a million square miles, its center was the city of Cuzco, home of "the Inca," absolute ruler of the civilization.

During the same period in Mexico, a comparable yet completely independent empire existed. In 1325 the Mexica, one of several tribes now known as the Aztecs, settled in the Texcoco Lake basin and, on an island, established the city of Tenochtitlán, 30 miles southwest of the old city of Teotihuacán. The site was remarkably favorable, being easily defensible in war and a center for trade with the surrounding region. Within 100 years, bolstered by conquests and commercial dominance, the city controlled a population of between 5 and 6 million and was thriving. Box 8-1 describes the scene.

The Aztec rulers built Tenochtitlán into a city of incredible magnificence. While London was still a backwater of Europe and New York unthought of, Tenochtitlán was probably, after Rome, the world's greatest city. Here are two brief accounts:

> Half city and half floating garden, its profile etched by dozens of temples dominated by the Pyramid dedicated to the worship of Huitzilopochtli and Tlaloc, [Tenochtitlán] rose majestically above the lake and green groves of trees. The setting was imposing: snow-covered peaks, cultivated slopes, and the densely populated fertile valley. (Hardoy 1975, p. 12)
>
> An island-metropolis, Tenochtitlán was set like a radiant jewel amid the clear, calm turquoise of saline Lake Texcoco, linked to mainland suburbs by three great paved causeways. Elegant palaces and pyramid temples, interspersed with broad plazas and exotic gardens, gleamed spotless white in the brilliant crystalline air more than 7,000 feet above sea-level. (Cottrell et al. 1979, p. 37)

It was on this city that the Spaniard, Hernán Cortés, and his 500 men gazed in 1519. They were incredulous. Cortés later wrote that it was "the most beautiful city in the world," and one of

BOX 8-1
The Thriving Metropolis of Tenochtitlán

[In Tenochtitlán, bearers] and canoes overcame the lack of beasts of burden in transporting the merchandise that filled their markets and supplied the needs of their artisans. Arriving continually in the markets of Tenochtitlán and Tlatelolco were green Quetzal plumes and turquoise and yellow feathers from Coayztlahuaca and Soconochco to be made into symbolic headdresses and shields; deerskins from Tepeacac; ready-made clothing from Xilotepec, Axopoacan, Tlapan, and other provinces; cotton and hempen blankets from Cihuatlan, Cuetlaxtlan, Tepequacuilco, and other provinces; cacao from Ahuatlan and Techtepec; dried chile peppers from Tuchpa and Oxitpan; packages of paper from Huaxtepec and Quauhnahuac; balls of rubber from Tochtepec; amber, seashells, and copal; copper and gold objects; and precious stones from Yealtepec, Tuchpa, and Quiauhteopan for mosaics adorning temples and houses. Everything consumed by the Aztec capital was imported daily by bearers who traveled the highways linking the city and the lake's edge, or was unloaded from canoes. Tenochtitlán and Tlatelolco procured goods from the provinces by means of tribute imposed after successful military campaigns or the threat of military occupation. Their artisans, among them specialists in luxury articles, found sure buyers for their work in the city and among the local merchants who controlled regional trade. Tenochtitlán based a large part of its economic strength, which was unrivaled in Mesoamerica after the mid-fifteenth century, upon commerce and tribute.

Source: Jorge E. Hardoy, "The Background of Latin American Urbanization," in Jorge E. Hardoy, ed., *Urbanization in Latin America* (Garden City, N.Y.: Anchor, 1975), pp. 11–12.

Before the destruction: This drawing from a codex of the period shows Hernán Cortés and his soldiers meeting with emissaries of Montezuma. Shortly after this encounter, the seige of Tenochtitlán began. (Bettmann)

over Italy, and in Rome, said that so large a market and so full of people and so well-regulated and arranged, they had never beheld before. . . . (1956, pp. 218–219)

Tragically for Tenochtitlán, Cortés was thought by some Aztecs to be the fair-skinned and bearded God, Quetzalcoatl, who had been prophesied to return in the Aztec 1-Reed Year (1519). Although he no longer believed in Cortés's divinity by the time the explorer and his men reached Tenochtitlán, the Aztec king, Montezuma, approached the Spaniard with fawning and some caution. He invited the Europeans into the city, housed them in a great palace, and gave them gifts of gold—a serious mistake. As Miguel Leon-Portilla, who was present, later wrote: the Spaniards "picked up the gold and fingered it like monkeys: they seemed transported with joy, as if their hearts were illuminated and made new . . . they hungered like pigs for that gold" (quoted in Cottrell et al. 1979, p. 46). This experience foreshadowed what was about to happen in all of Latin America. Cortés and other European explorers did not come to live in peaceful coexistence with the indigenous populations. They came to conquer and become rich. They were about to destroy pre-Columbian civilization.

his soldiers, Bernal Diaz, described the Spanish reaction this way:

We were amazed. . . . [I]t was like the enchantments they tell of in the legend of Amadis, on account of the great towers and [temples] and buildings rising from the water, and all built of masonry. And some of our soldiers even asked whether the things that we saw were not a dream. . . . I do not know how to describe it, seeing things as we did that had never been heard of or seen before, not even dreamed about. Some . . . among us who had been in many parts of the world, in Constantinople, all

Conquest and Colonization

Before long, the Aztecs saw the Spaniards for what they were: enemies bent on the complete control of the Aztec Empire and its riches. Although Cortés increased his forces to nearly 1,200, he was no match for hundreds of thousands of Mexica in their own city. In a night attack, 100 of his men were massacred or dragged out for sacrifice to the Aztec gods. In disarray, Cortés fled to a safe distance where he joined with Spanish reinforcements and over 90,000 Indians wishing the defeat of their overlords. Thus bolstered, in April 1521 he returned, encircled Tenochtitlán, cut off its food and water, and let the inhabitants starve for three months. In August, overcoming the last resistance, he entered the city victorious.

To ensure that the remnants of the proud Aztec Empire never rose again, Cortés demolished Tenochtitlán utterly and on its rubble erected a city focused around a completely alien (European) culture. He called it *Ciudad Imperial de Mexico*—Mexico City. To complete his domination, the surviving Mexicans were made to serve their conquerors.

In the conquest of the Inca Empire about a decade later, Francisco Pizarro followed the same pattern. He conquered and destroyed the Inca cities and replaced them with Spanish cities. Although a pre-Columbian urban civilization did not exist in Brazil, the Portuguese invaders established cities up and down that country's coast (Hardoy 1975, pp. 19–44).

Exploitation and Domination. All over Latin America, the new colonial cities were constructed as administrative centers for local domination and export-oriented trade. Inland cities such as Mexico City were linked with port cities such as Vera Cruz. Where no important port existed before, the Europeans built one; Lima (Peru), Valparaiso (Chile), Buenos Aires (Argentina) and Rio de Janeiro (Brazil) are examples. But the trade these cities were interested in was of a decidedly one-way character. Out of the New World went incredible amounts of precious materials: gold, silver, tobacco, coffee. Into it went little: exploitation of the crudest sort. The colonial cities' main reason for existence was to supply Spain and Portugal—relatively poor and weak nations in Europe—with the goods they needed to become rich and powerful.

The strategic location of most of these cities in relation to the hinterland was important in maintaining the dominance of the colonists over the native population. Ensconced in fortifications on the coast, the Europeans could defend themselves from internal attack and ship in what they needed virtually at will. Such battlements also protected them from an external enemy—the pirate—who became more than a little covetous of the wealth these cities harbored.

European dominance of the new cities and their hinterland was not ensured merely by military might, however. One of the most tragic aftermaths of the conquest was the literal decimation of the indigenous population. Between 1500 and 1600 the loss of native human life in Central America alone has been estimated at no less than 95 percent (Cottrell et al. 1979, p. 48). In terms of raw numbers, other estimates suggest that the Indian population decreased from more than 25 million to perhaps 1 million in this period. The causes of these grim statistics are varied, but paramount among them were the brutal wars with the colonists and the toll taken by European diseases, such as measles and smallpox, against which native Latin Americans had no biological defense (Hardoy 1975, p. 22).

Added to this was the effect that the imposition of European culture had on Latin America. Decreeing a set of principles called the "Laws of the Indies," the Spanish constructed their new cities along very similar patterns, which resulted in the breakdown or severe weakening of local cultural patterns. Although some variations existed that took into account local geography and earlier customs, most colonial cities were constructed around a grid plan with a central plaza—the *plaza mayor*—at the center. At one end of the plaza was an imposing Catholic church. On the other three sides were government offices, residences of the wealthy, and some stores. Such a design established the dominant institutions of European culture—the church, the state, the

The central plaza dominated by the church is typical of the cities created after the Spanish Conquest of Latin America. Shown here is Gua-
dalupe, Mexico. (© Stan Wayman/Photo Researchers)

power of the elite, and commerce—at the very
heart of the city.

Around the city center, in a second district,
were the residences of the city's middle class: artisans, government clerks, and small merchants.
Further out still, in a third zone, were the much
more dilapidated residences of the city's poor. Finally, on the outskirts, were large parcels of land
originally called *encomiendas*, given in trust to
the local elite by the Spanish government. After
independence in the nineteenth century, many of
these large parcels of land became part of the
equally exclusive *hacienda* system: large farms or
ranches run by elites and worked by serfs.

Although these preindustrial colonial cities
were physically similar to cities in Europe, they
were even more exclusive, favoring only a small
and extremely powerful elite of European descent. Under normal circumstances there was no
way native Latin Americans could become elites
(Portes 1977, pp. 64–67). Although remnants of
pre-Columbian culture remained alive—particularly in rural communities—the dominance of
colonial cities in Latin America ensured the dom-

inance of European culture in most areas of life
(Butterworth and Chance 1981, p. 1).

Consequences. The "extraction and domination"
policy meant four things in terms of the early
development of colonial Latin American cities.
First, they did not have true economic independence. The policies of the colonizing country
required that trade could be carried out only
with the colonizer or its satellite countries. As a
result, Latin American cities could establish only
limited economic vitality and remained relatively
small. For example, in 1780, a full two centuries
after its founding, Buenos Aires was a city of only
25,000 with few roads and virtually no contact
with other cities. Compare this to the postcolonial
cities of the United States. Freed of their ties with
England, they exploded in population and wealth
as they forged links with each other and the westward frontier.

Second, politically speaking, early Latin
American cities were dominated by complex bureaucracies oriented toward a government thousands of miles away. To get anything done re-

quired great wealth, influence, or patience. Hardoy (1975, p. 31) reports that in many colonial cities "Spanish centralism reached such a degree that permission was required from the central administration [in Madrid] even to move a small settlement, permission that could be delayed three years or more."

A third consequence was how little the national boundaries established by the European colonizers had to do with the territorial boundaries of indigenous populations. The Spanish and Portuguese carved up Latin America in terms of what they were able to conquer, without concern for any native group's natural homeland. Thus the newly constructed nations often made citizens of the same country of peoples who had been separated by political, linguistic, and other cultural factors for centuries. In the same way the new national boundaries arbitrarily separated some groups who, traditionally occupying a given territory, now found their lands split by the European conquerers. (A similar, but much more severe carving-up process was to be perpetrated by European powers in Africa, as we will see in Chapter 9.) When political independence came, as it did for most Latin American countries in the 1800s, many nations had yet one more barrier to rapid entry into the modern world: a local citizenry divided against itself to a greater or lesser extent by an artificial historical boundary. This situation is seen by many observers as contributing significantly to the political instability of many Latin American nations today.

Fourth, colonization created major distinctions of race and class. As might be expected, the European overlords saw themselves as superior to the groups they had conquered. Consequently, they constructed a social structure that rewarded them—*Latinos*—and gave less favored status to everyone else. In some cities, such as Oaxaca in Mexico, these distinctions became so complex that many levels could be recognized. At the top were the *peninsulares*, people born in Spain. They were followed by the upper-middle-class *criollos*, people of European descent born in the New World. The middle classes were composed of, in descending rank, *castizos* (people with mixed *criolla* and *mestizo* blood), *mestizos* (some mixture of Spanish and Indian blood), and *mulattoes* (people with some discernible negroid features). The lowest rungs were occupied by blacks (imported from Africa as slaves, particularly to coastal cities) and *Indios* (native Latin Americans). Although this system was not completely rigid—people could move upward by getting rich or by marrying carefully—and was officially repudiated after independence was won in the nineteenth century, its residues still are very much alive in most Latin American cities today (Butterworth and Chance 1981).

The Republican Period

By the early 1800s the willingness and ability of the European colonists to maintain Latin American outposts was waning. Many of the raw materials that could be extracted easily had long since been removed. In addition, harassment by local insurgents, such as Simon Bolivar, made colonial governance increasingly difficult. Hence, after a series of wars of independence (1816–1825), most Latin American nations gained their freedom.

With trade restrictions removed, many Latin American cities began to grow, first in terms of economic vitality—trade began with cities in England, France, and the United States (Hardoy 1975, p. 45)—then in terms of population. For example, between 1797 and 1914 the population of Buenos Aires grew from 30,000 to 1.5 million; between 1800 and 1900 Rio de Janeiro's population jumped from 43,000 to 800,000 (Boyer and Davies 1973, pp. 5–33). Similar patterns appeared in Mexico City, Montevideo, Caracas, Santiago, Lima, and Havana. Indeed, by the early twentieth century, these few cities had grown so much they dominated all other cities in their respective countries, becoming what urbanists call *primate* cities (see Cityscape 8-1).

Much of the growth of these primate cities was the result of rural migrants seeking greater economic opportunity in the city, but much of it also was attributable to foreign immigration. Between 1860 and 1930, Latin America absorbed millions

CITYSCAPE 8-1
The Evolution of Primate Cities

A *primate city* is one that grows in population and influence far beyond the other cities in a nation or region. In many countries of the Third World the largest city may have several times the combined population of the next largest two or three cities. Primate cities thus resemble, to use Alejandro Portes's metaphor, "gigantic heads of dwarfish bodies" (1977, p. 68), absorbing an enormous portion of the available labor, trade, and population.

The extent of the dominance of a primate city in its own country can be shown by a *primacy ratio*, computed by dividing the primate city's population by the population of the second largest city in the country. In the table below are some examples.

Note that with the exception of Paris the primary ratios for the largest Western cities (New York, Moscow, Rome) is relatively low. This suggests that primacy is linked to more than a good location and established trade patterns. Recent research suggests that it develops more frequently (1) in small countries—Copenhagen and Vienna are clear examples; (2) in countries that, for historical reasons, have only one or a few cities with anything approaching modern facilities—certainly true of Third World countries around the world; and (3) in countries that were once or still are under foreign control either politically or economically—colonial cities, for example (Berry 1961; Linsky 1965).

Some urbanists argue that primate cities are positive phenomena in a region's urban history. They speed up the evolution of a modern urban facility, which, in time, makes possible the "trickling down" of advanced urban technology and economic vitality to smaller cities. These urbanists point to this process in the developed countries. Historically, for example, London was England's primate city. With the advent of industrialization, however, large numbers of modern middle-level cities emerged in England: Birmingham, Manchester, Leeds, and Sheffield.

Other theorists are much less sanguine. They argue that highly industrialized nations' cities and those of the Third World are not comparable. Developed countries, like the United States or Britain, were, at the time of the emergence of their middle-level cities, much more economically advanced and politically stable than most Third World countries today. In the Third World, because the rest of the country is so poor, the primate city offers people the only chance to better their lives; hence, they flock to it. This hampers the development of a series of middle-level cities and ensures, if growth goes unchecked, that the primate city itself will become so overpopulated that its own vital functioning will be hampered severely. Such theorists argue that the only way to reduce the human suffering that such overgrowth produces is to strictly limit further population growth in the primate city and to plan and build middle-level cities that will drain off some of the population (Berry and Kasarda 1977, pp. 399–400).

Selected Latin American Cities*		Other Selected Cities*	
Lima	13.1	Bangkok	33.0
Buenos Aires	11.5	Manila	11.6
Santiago	8.6	Copenhagen	7.7
Mexico City	6.1	Vienna	7.4
Havana	6.0	Paris	7.1
Sao Paulo	1.2	New York	1.7
		Moscow	1.7
		Rome	1.6

*All ratios are from Robert A. Wilson and David A. Schultz, *Urban Sociology* (Englewood Cliffs, N.J.: Prentice-Hall, 1978), Table 15.2; except Mexico City, taken from Gustavo Garza and Martha Schteingart, "Mexico City: The Emerging Metropolis," in Wayne Cornelius and Robert Kemper, eds., *Latin American Urban Research*, Vol. 6 (Beverly Hills, Calif.: Sage, 1974), Table 2; and Bangkok, from Ralph Thomlinson, "Bangkok: 'Beau Ideal' of a Primate City," *Population Review*, 16 (Jan. 1972), pp. 32–38.

upon millions of Jews, Russians, Poles, Italians, Swiss, and Germans. Because of their generally higher level of education and greater familiarity with business, these immigrants soon came to control much of the medium-scale commerce of Latin America's primate cities, dominating such areas as construction, small industry, workshops, and artisan and craft activities (Hardoy 1975, pp. 49–50). As a result, immigrants occupied many middle-class jobs at the expense of the impoverished indigenous population that also was streaming into the cities.

In addition, most Latin American cities have not followed the pattern of rapid industrialization typical of Europe (Chapter 2) and the United States (Chapter 3). Despite a century and a half of independence, in terms of wealth and productive capacity Latin American cities lag far behind the cities of these other nations. Many urbanists believe this lack of development is a legacy of the colonial era on the one hand, and a result of the needs of modern industrialized nations on the other.

First, from their moments of origin, most Latin American cities were export oriented. Their valued products or raw materials—gold, silver, cattle, coal, oil, grains, coffee, fruits, wool—always have been sent to other countries, not used for their own populations. The demand by other nations for these goods did not change after independence, and Latin American cities continued trading in them. The problem was, they had to sell the goods at the cheapest point in the production-consumption chain. As a result the amount of wealth Latin American cities generated was much lower than that generated by cities that also specialized in processing or manufacturing and distributing those goods to a complex network of consumers.

Second, by depending on raw material exports for their primary source of wealth, most Latin American cities never developed much in the way of an industrial base. Modern cities without major industries not only lose a major employment area for their population, they also cannot compete on numerous levels (skilled labor, investment opportunities) with cities that have such sectors. Consequently, export-oriented cities begin to fall further behind their industrialized counterparts. This pattern is what Barbara Ward (1962) had in mind when she wrote as early as 1962 of the inevitable and ever worsening gap between "the rich nations" and "the poor nations."

This very disadvantageous situation is not solely the result of poor investment policies and lack of foresight by Latin Americans. Many urbanists argue that the developed nations and their corporations have contributed significantly to the problem (Petras and Zeitlin 1968; Portes and Walton 1976). Wanting the raw materials and cheap labor of Latin America, these countries and corporations have tried to ensure that their needs would continue to be met by giving aid and political support to Latin American governments and businesses that favored export over local development. Many Latin American business and government elites, quick to sense that supporting these outside interests would be a very profitable endeavor, have worked actively in their service, thus helping very little the overall development of their country, city, and local population. As Bunker (1984, p. 1055) has recently argued: "Extractive economies geared to world trade tend to impoverish themselves."

The end result is that the old colonial pattern of external domination has been preserved in another guise. Surveying the history of Latin American cities, Portes concludes:

> The economic and social evolution of Latin American cities never deviated markedly from the general directions set in colonial days. It is this inertial force of early events that permitted the natural acceptance of the subsequent chains of events, an almost imperceptible evolution that led, by gradual steps, to present patterns of massive poverty and . . . polarization. (1977, p. 70)

Modern Latin American Cities

The Burgeoning Cities

The crisis of modern Latin American cities goes beyond their link to other nations. All over the globe, Third World nations are experiencing the same phenomenon: their death rates are declining while their birth rates are soaring. The result is a demographic transition of unprecedented proportions (Petersen 1969, Chaps. 13, 16).

As the discussion of primate cities intimated, the great bulk of this population increase has been in cities. Kingsley Davis reports that in 171 Third World countries cities of over 100,000 increased their population by 67 percent in the decade between 1960 and 1970, a rate that would double these cities' populations every 10.3 years[1] if nothing happened to check it (1973, p. 220). Another way of grasping this astonishing growth is to realize that between 1950 and 1970 the 171 Third World nations added over 260 million people to their cities' populations. "There are now more city inhabitants in these countries than there were in the entire world in 1950" (Davis 1973, p. 220).

The reasons behind this population increase are complex. First, the general demographic transition is augmented by two factors. Like the more industrialized countries before them, Third World nations have been making some economic progress. This means more money is available for at least some people in the population and that more children can be supported by a given household. Perhaps more important, major technological improvements solving problems of health have been made (vaccinations, better sewage systems, and the like). The wider distribution of such life-saving services in these nations fosters population growth (Davis 1973, p. 221).

But these advantages are available most prominently in cities, not in the hinterland. Thus, to take advantage of them, people are migrating from rural areas in staggering numbers.

Los Villas Miserias: City Slums and Squatter Settlements

People migrate to cities for a variety of reasons, but prominent among them is their perception that the city offers economic opportunities and various freedoms simply unavailable in the countryside. In their original rural area or village, because of long-standing traditions or limited resources and technology, jobs may be scarce and possibilities for increasing one's standard of living almost nonexistent. Worse, if the rural population begins to increase, as it has in most areas of the Third World, a severe tax on the limited local resources begins to develop (Firebaugh 1979). To try to solve their predicament, many pack up and head for the city.

Taken together, such pressures are commonly called the "push-pull" factors of migration:

migrants are pushed from their original environment by unfavorable conditions and are pulled to the next environment—the city—by the promise of a better life. The life of Jesus Sanchez, whose words opened this chapter, provides an illustration.

As a young boy, Sanchez lived an impoverished life in the rural state of Vera Cruz. When his father died, with few prospects for employment, 12-year-old Jesus set out for Mexico City on the promise of a job from a fellow traveler. The job didn't work out, nor did others, but eventually Jesus found a steady job in a restaurant. He worked in the restaurant for 30 years, never making more than the minimum wage. He married and had four children. In order to support his family, he always had to work at extra jobs or his wife had to work. They lived in a slum, called Casa Grande, near the heart of Mexico City. As Oscar Lewis described it, Casa Grande was

> . . . a poor area with a few small factories and warehouses, public baths, run-down third-class movie theatres, overcrowded schools, saloons . . . and many small shops. . . . This area ranks high in the incidence of homicide, drunkenness, and delinquency. It is a densely populated neighborhood. . . . The streets and sidewalks are broad and paved but are without trees, grass, or gardens. Most of the people live in rows of one-room dwellings in inside courtyards shut off from view of the street by shops (1961, pp. xiii–xiv)

Things have not become any better since this description was written. At present, over 400,000 migrants a year flood into Mexico City, and it is estimated that over 30 percent of the city's families (which average five people) continue to live in one-room dwellings (McDowell 1984).

Not all migrants move to the inner-city slums, however. Millions of others live on the outskirts of the city, in another type of settlement—in shantytowns that have sprung up, primarily in the last three decades, as a response to the scarcity and expense of housing in the center city. Together, the inner-city slums and the peripheral squatter settlements frequently have been called *los villas miserias*—"cities of the miserable"—because they are home to so many desperately poor people.

---

[1]Compounded growth rate.

Among the most prevalent and distressing characteristics of modern Latin American cities is the shantytown slum inhabited by the city's poor. This one—in Caracas, Venezuela—is typical of the hundreds that exist throughout the region. (Bettmann/UPI)

The squatter settlements, illegally established by the poor, are common throughout Latin America. Occupied by different groups—rural or small-town migrants or inner-city poor who have moved out—the squatter settlements are usually without public services, unsanitary, and often physically insecure (on slopes with a large possibility of landslides, for example). They are seen by many wealthier city residents as a social disease of the worst kind, and in many countries force has been used in an attempt to expel their inhabitants. Yet, as Mangin observes, "the tide has been too much. . . . The squatter settlements give every sign of becoming permanent" (1973, p. 233).

Hope and Survival in the Squatter Settlement. Life in a squatter settlement is not at all pleasant. Yet, in comparison to life in an inner-city slum, there are a few advantages. In his study of squatters in Lima, Peru, Mangin concluded that the families of squatters are

. . . relatively stable compared with those in the city slums or rural provinces. Delinquency and prostitution, which are common in the city slums, are rare in the *barriadas*. The family incomes are low, but most of them are substantially higher than the poorest slum level. . . . [The people] are well organized, politically sophisticated, strongly patriotic and comparatively conservative in their sociopolitical views. (1973, p. 233)

In studying these squatter settlements, Mangin and other anthropologists (Peattie 1974; Kemper 1977) have been impressed by a single fact: the creative adaptability and willingness of these urban poor to work hard. We have seen already that Jesus Sanchez worked extremely hard to support himself and his family: "In thirty years I've rarely missed a day of work. Even when I'm sick I go. It seems like work is medicine for me. It makes me forget my troubles" (Lewis 1961, p. 9). In the same way, Mangin describes the residents of the *barriadas* of Lima:

[These people] have shown a really remarkable capacity for initiative, self-help and community organization. Visitors to the *barriadas*, many of them trained observers, remark on the accomplishments of the residents in home and community construction, on the small businesses they have created, on the degree of community organization, on how much the people have achieved without government help and on their friendliness. Most of the residents are neither resentful or alienated; they are understandably cynical yet hopeful. (1973, p. 238)

None of this industriousness in the face of adversity surprises urbanists who have studied carefully the social characteristics of urban migrants. In complete opposition to the stereotyped image of the urban poor as lazy and unconcerned, anthropologists found that many who moved to Latin American cities were from the middle class in their original rural environment, were confident of their ability to deal with the world, were unwilling to accept authority figures unquestioningly, and were filled with ambition rather than resignation (Wilkie 1968).

The observations of a priest from Mexico City provide a sense of the survival instinct that distinguishes many of these slum dwellers:

> To understand the city you must study our countryside. People come here from farms, knowing nothing about city life. In five days they're so miserable that we [the church] have to give them help. But soon they are doing the hard work of the city. The second generation feels more at home, and the third generation is completely used to the city. (McDowell 1984, p. 164)

Even more impressive is this story reported by McDowell:

> I recall a dismal community of shacks at the bottom of a ravine [near Mexico City]. Living there were 87 families, some with as many as 14 children. By stairsteps carved into the clay, I descended their hill in the dry season, marveling that anyone could manage that slope carrying bundles and babies in the rain.
>
> Once there, I talked with the residents. "We used to live up there," Señora Gonzalez gestured toward some mountaintop quarries, "in those caves. Our only hope was one day to have a place to live. And now we do!" She smiled with pride at

the jerry-built shacks. They stood in neat rows . . . and each one had a collection of flowers planted in tin cans. "One day, we hope to extend the water pipes and drainage—perhaps even pave. . . ."

> And what was the name of her community? Señora Gonzalez beamed: "Esperanza!" The name means hope. (1984, p. 172)

To most Westerners this story may seem a bit overdone, to take pride in what seems so little. Yet note the progress Señora Gonzalez remembers, and recall the sense of progress that many of our own relatives must have felt after a generation or so in America.

But is there a reality behind the *esperanza* that Señora Gonzalez feels? Has any progress really occurred?

Urban vs. Rural Poverty. There is convincing evidence that for most migrants life in Latin American cities *is* somewhat better in economic terms than it was in the town or rural area they left. Table 8-1 makes this clear by comparing the income levels of Mexicans as a whole with residents of the rural area known as Michoacan (from which many migrate) and with people in Mexico City. For example, over 70 percent of the population of rural Michoacan has a monthly income in the lowest three income levels. Comparatively, only 45 percent of the population falls into these categories in Mexico City. Moreover, this economic advantage persists even after the higher cost of living in the city is taken into account. While this means that there are still a very great many poor people in Mexico City, and that many who were in the poorest groups in Michoacan still will be in the poorest groups in the city, with the improvement that does occur, "it is not surprising that . . . migrants to Mexico City experience a feeling of 'relative affluence,' no matter how poor their objective living conditions appear to an outside observer" (Kemper 1977, p. 83).

Indeed, the "affluence" of the city is so pronounced for many of these migrants that they can send a good portion of their surplus earnings back to their poorer relatives who remained in the countryside. Such a caring gesture, of course, makes true economic advancement even harder to attain for the new urban migrants.

TABLE 8-1

Income Distribution in Mexico, Michoacan Province, and Mexico City

Monthly Income Levels	Nation	Michoacan	Mexico City
0– 199 pesos	17%	22%	3%
200– 499 pesos	24	31	12
500– 999 pesos	24	20	30
1,000– 1,499 pesos	11	5	22
1,500– 2,499 pesos	7	3	15
2,500– 4,999 pesos	4	2	9
5,000– 9,000 pesos	2	1	4
Above 10,000 pesos	1	1	2
No data	10	16	3
Totals (rounded)	100%	101%	100%

Source: Adapted from Censo General de Poblacion (1970), Resumen General 1971:XXI, pp. 117, 215; cited in Robert V. Kemper, *Migration and Adaptation* (Beverly Hills, Calif.: Sage, 1977), Table 3-3. Used by permission of Robert V. Kemper.

So the fact is that Latin American cities have helped a few of their citizens increase their standard of living. Nevertheless, the deeper truth is, they haven't helped all that much, because whatever advantages they provide and whatever the industriousness of the existing or incoming populations, the burden of population growth in Third World countries as a whole ensures that jobs, goods, services, housing, and health care cannot possibly keep up with the demand.

An Insoluble Problem?

The problem is this: Latin American countries are exploding not only in urban population but rural population as well (Davis 1974). Figure 8-1 compares the population growth patterns of several Third World countries and the population growth patterns of some highly industrialized countries during the period of their greatest urbanization. As it demonstrates, during the period of maximum urban expansion, the highly industrialized countries had negative or very low rural growth rates. Over time, the expanding cities reduced the poverty level of the country as a whole by providing more people with the increased standard of living possible in the city. They also were able to reduce whatever population pressure they were experiencing, through emigration (for example, to North America, Latin America, and other colonial outposts for European countries)

or internal migration (westward in the case of North America).

Such is not the case in the Third World. Although it is clear that Third World cities are increasing their population faster than the rural areas, the rural population is increasing as well. Of the nations shown in Figure 8-1, only Venezuela exhibits a rural growth rate as low as some of the industrialized countries in their prime growth periods. Furthermore, motivated by their own economic pressures or racial prejudice, the highly industrialized nations often refuse entry to the people of the Third World. This policy is at least partially responsible for the illegal immigration problem faced in the southern United States. Thus, nearly all the increase in population has to be absorbed by the Third World country.

This pattern of rural and urban population growth means that every person who gains in real standard of living in Third World countries is replaced in the population by more than one other poor person; hence, no overall progress is made. Seen in this light, it is easy to understand Jesus Sanchez's comment: "In the thirty years I've been in Mexico City, the life of the poor has changed very little, very little" (Lewis 1961, p. 495).

Worsening rural and urban poverty therefore is likely to be a part of the Latin American urban situation for the foreseeable future. Kingsley Davis sums it up thus: "The rapid expansion of

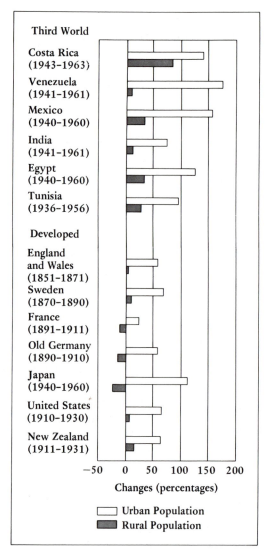

Third World

Costa Rica
(1943-1963)
Venezuela
(1941-1961)
Mexico
(1940-1960)
India
(1941-1961)
Egypt
(1940-1960)
Tunisia
(1936-1956)

Developed

England
and Wales
(1851-1871)
Sweden
(1870-1890)
France
(1891-1911)
Old Germany
(1890-1910)
Japan
(1940-1960)
United States
(1910-1930)
New Zealand
(1911-1931)

-50   0   50   100   150   200
Changes (percentages)

☐ Urban Population
▩ Rural Population

Figure 8-1 *Urban and rural population growth in selected Third World and highly industrialized nations during periods of maximum expansion. Source: Adapted from Kingsley Davis, "The Urbanization of the Human Population," p. 48. Copyright © 1965 by Scientific American, Inc. All rights reserved. Used by permission.*

cities in the underdeveloped world is being largely wasted. It is not buying commensurate development, much less commensurate human benefit. It is buying urban congestion and pollution mainly for the sake of more urban congestion and pollution" (1974, pp. 222–223).

Mexico City is only the worst case in this mas-

sive overgrowth. One urban planner called Mexico's capital a "case study in urban disaster," and novelist Carlos Fuentes describes his home as "the great flat-snouted and suffocating city, the city forever spreading like a creeping blot" (McDowell 1984, p. 144). Despite the accomplishments of the little community called "Esperanza" that we described above, the human tragedy of Latin America continues to grow: there are simply *too many people* for the cities of this region to cope.

Nothing brings home the horror more than the sight of these cities' legions of lost children, children given up by parents who could not support them, and who now roam the streets eking out an existence as best they can—by begging, shining shoes, selling candy, shoplifting, mugging passersby. Estimates put their number at close to *40 million* in Latin America. They are a direct product of the move to the cities described in this chapter. Says Cesare La Rocca, a director of the UNICEF program based in Rio de Janeiro: "Families are disintegrating in Latin America under the pressure of poverty, and what's happening with the children comes from the families' simple incapacity to resist." Of course, many cities try to alleviate the problem with programs like that headed by La Rocca, but, according to Peter Tacon, coordinator of another UNICEF project in Bogota, Colombia, "We know that for every one child we reach, there are 1,000 we don't touch" (Hoge 1983).

In the history and in the lives of the people of La Paz, Bolivia, we shall see at work all the forces we have just been describing.

CASE STUDY 8-1
La Paz, Bolivia[2]

The City

La Paz is the highest capital in the world. Located in a deeply eroded canyon 35 miles long, it

---

[2]This section was prepared by JUDITH-MARIA BUECHLER, Department of Anthropology and Sociology, Hobart

is 12,400 feet above sea level. Even at this height, it is 1,300 feet below the level of the surrounding *altiplano*, the high plateau of Bolivia, and still further below the magnificent snow-capped Andes Mountains.

Viewed from the plateau's rim, the canyon seems at first bare, chilled, and airless; however, if one looks more closely, one sees, clinging precariously to the precipice and endangered by wind and rainy-season landslides, thousands of gaily painted adobe or mud brick huts with their corrugated tin roofs glinting in the brilliant sun. Below them, more closely packed two-story adobe structures appear. Finally, in the middle of the canyon, one sees the *Centro*, the relatively small downtown section that encompasses the two main plazas of San Francisco and Murillo. These are surrounded by Victorian and modern hotels, restaurants, businesses, government offices, shops, boutiques, and recently erected high-rise buildings of glass and concrete.

La Paz is the center of a system of roads, railroads, and telegraph and airline systems that connect the city to other major Bolivian cities, as well as to cities in Chile, Peru, and Argentina. This communications network facilitates trade more with the countries outside Bolivia than with the hinterland surrounding La Paz. Not surprisingly, this network is a remnant of long-past Spanish colonization and its export-oriented policies. As we shall see, the colonial legacy is felt palpably nearly everywhere in modern La Paz.

History

The city's history really begins in the latter part of the twelfth century, when the site became the last refuge of a group of Aymara Indians trying to escape Inca domination. Finally subjugated, the Aymara and the area they defended were incorporated into the Inca Empire in 1185. The Incas built a fort on the site and linked it to Cuzco, their capital, by a system of mountain roads.

Although colonization of South America be-

gan in the early sixteenth century, not until 1548 did the old Inca stronghold become an outpost in the Spanish system. In that year Alonzo de Mendoza established a small crossroads garrison 20 miles from the present city on the trade route from Potosi, a silver-mining city, to Lima in Peru. The settlement was given the name *Nuestra Señora de La Paz*—"Old Lady of Peace"—to celebrate the conclusion of the Spanish Conquest in South America.

Ironically, this "city of peace" has been the center of much discord over the centuries. Periodic Indian raids characterized much of its colonial history, and, late in the eighteenth century, it became one of the centers of the abortive two-year revolt bent on reestablishing the Inca Empire. Reports have it that in the final battle, which took place in La Paz in 1783, more than 40,000 Indians besieged the city for more than 100 days, only to be suppressed brutally by the Spaniards in the end.

Even in this century the city has not been peaceful. As the capital of the country and center of the region's wealthy mining industry, La Paz has been a much-coveted prize. Like many Latin American countries, Bolivia has experienced the rise and fall of many military regimes—the latest coup was in 1980. Also, resistance to the established order is never far below the surface. Resentment centers on the state of the urban poor, the inability of the city to use efficiently the resources it has, and the continuing economic dependence of Bolivia on the United States and Europe.

La Paz thus provides a specific illustration of the more general Latin American pattern. It emerged as a colonial outpost, an administrative center and military enclave for the political and economic control of an undeveloped hinterland. A foreign elite used the city and its resources—material and human—primarily as a means to acquire wealth in their own interests. Even after Bolivians won their independence, this legacy—the export-oriented economy and a class structure favoring the few as opposed to the many—remains. To this must be added the stress of rapid population growth, mostly the product of in-migration. In recent years La Paz has become

---

and William Smith Colleges. It has been adapted by the authors for use in this chapter.

a near-perfect example of a primate city, its population of nearly three-quarters of a million people being greater than that of Bolivia's next three largest cities combined (Portes and Walton 1976).

Ethnicity and Land Use

The racial composition of La Paz reflects the city's long history of intermarriage between persons of Spanish descent and those of Indian heritage, or between members of those groups and *mestizos* or *cholos* (mixed bloods). However, in contrast to the situation in many other Latin American cities, race and ethnicity in La Paz always have been indicated less by overt physical differences than by cultural differences. Thus, in addition to whatever physical attributes they may have, individuals are classified by language, dress, occupation, and place of residence. This allows for the possibility of upward mobility: "An individual who comes from a family known as Indian but who speaks Spanish, obtains an education and, most importantly, ceases to be a peasant [and] will come to be considered mestizo even though [complete transition to that lifestyle] may take a generation or two to complete" (Leons 1978, p. 487).

The city's land use mirrors its concern with ethnicity as well as its colonial history and unique geography. Until its population spurt at the end of the nineteenth century, La Paz corresponded to the typical Spanish colonial model: a basic grid pattern with church, state, elites, and markets concentrated around the central squares. With the great in-migration of this century, however, this has begun to change. Impoverished *mestizo* and Indian populations have spread up the ravines that surround the city and have established squatter settlements, while the lower middle class has settled in a steep section, called Miraflores, close to downtown. In reaction to this change, many wealthier people have moved away from their traditional center-city location to the affluent suburbs of Obrajes and Calacoto. In contrast to most other Latin and North American cities where such an exodus of the elite has occurred, the central areas of La Paz have not been

replaced with slums such as those in which Jesus Sanchez lived in Mexico City; rather, the center city continues to house people of the middle and upper-middle social classes.

The People: Three Families

Throughout this chapter we have emphasized the sharp contrast between social groups in Latin American cities. Few are rich, a greater percentage are moderately well off, but the vast majority are poor. The following composite portraits of three La Paz families show how differences in social background, wealth, power, and prestige translate into very different daily routines. We begin, because of their importance to the whole of Latin American history, with a portrait of an elite family.

The *Criolla* Life: The Quiroz Family. *Criollas* are the Latin American elite. They assumed the mantle of upper-class standing in the early 1800s after the exodus of the Spanish colonizers. At the core of elite status is a genealogy or pedigree of "distinction": an aristocratic background, extensive education, significant political power, and wealth derived from others' poverty.

Don German Quiroz, his wife Maria Elena, their unmarried daughter Maria Christina, and their son Andres live in a two-story house with their maiden aunt, Carlota, an old family cook, a maid, and a steward. They are a short walk from the Prado, a cypress-lined, Spanish-style mall. Their plastered adobe mansion has a tiled roof, iron-grilled windows and doors, and narrow balconies. A wall hides a formal patio with sculptured hedges and tree roses.

If a visitor were to call on the Quiroz family, a servant would usher the visitor through massive, double, brass-studded doors, up a winding staircase, and down a darkened hall to the parlor. Surrounded by heavy, gilt-framed, Spanish-colonial paintings of somber saints and ancestors, one would find in the parlor heavy Spanish furniture interspersed with more delicate French chairs and tables and glowing oriental rugs. The filtered light would illuminate the room's decorative china: pastel French-porcelain nymphs, delicate dishes, and silver colonial candlesticks.

If the visit were formal, the visitor would be served a demitasse of strong coffee and a glass of sherry or brandy, while conversation would linger on the general health and well-being of the family. Then, without unseemly haste, the visitor would be taken into a formal dining room to savor a five-course meal consisting of such delicacies as beef bouillon, *humintas* (cheese and ground corn baked in leaves), chili-spiced chicken accompanied by *tunta* (freeze-dried potatoes), a caramel custard, fruit and coffee, and wine and liqueurs.

In La Paz the Quiroz family is considered *gente muy gente*, a family that can trace its ancestry to members of the Spanish nobility who received an *encomienda* from the Crown during the sixteenth century. Although they pride themselves on the purity of their blood, they are in fact of mixed descent.

Until recently their privileged position was based on wealth derived primarily from large estates (some 1,235 acres) worked by Indians. In 1952, however, Bolivia's land reform act was passed, divesting elites like the Quiroz family of their land. Nevertheless, the family was able to maintain its vaunted position because of the value of its urban land holdings, which also had been in the family for generations. Because of the duration of its elite status, the Quiroz family has a tendency to look down upon newer city elites who have made their fortunes in tin mining or the professions.

The family has been able to maintain substantial power as well. They have a long tradition of government service. They always have educated their sons abroad in such fields as law and medicine and have brought them back to La Paz for careers in the national or city government, the army, and, to a lesser extent, the church. Given such high-ranking positions, the family always is knowledgeable of and influential in political and economic decisions that affect the country, city, or themselves. As a result, with few exceptions, they have been able to protect and strengthen their interests.

Any late morning, Don German Quiroz, a trim, dark-suited, mustachioed, elderly gentleman, can be seen sitting with his cronies, Doctor Mendez and lawyer Barrientos, in the Club La Paz, drinking coffee, playing cards, and discussing the last elections, the traffic in coca, the price of tin and real estate, or the future of oil exploration.

On the same morning, Señora Maria Elena Quiroz, a genteel, maternal figure in black, would be found at home supervising household affairs. On this particular day, she sends the cook to the Camacho market to shop for a special lunch she's giving for her daughter, daughter-in-law, and some grandchildren. All morning she has been concerned about her 20-year-old son, who wants to write, and her teenage daughter, who is bent on a European university education. She makes a mental note to arrange for the chauffeur to drive her to the cathedral so that she can take up these vexing concerns with Padre Leon. She plans to devote the afternoon to bridge with her sister-in-law, a convent school friend, and her second cousin. During the game they are likely to discuss the benefit they are planning to raise money for a playground for children in one of the poorer *barrios* of the city.

Señora Elena always looks forward to the visits of friends and kin and remembers when family *fiestas* and dances were really grand. She used to accompany her family on excursions to their *finca* (country estate) in the balmy valley below the city. She reminisces: "How close families were when they all lived next to each other. How times have changed."

Suddenly she perks up, thinking of her sister in New York. The sister's husband was closing a big business deal, and, while he was doing this, the sister had promised to do some Fifth Avenue shopping for Señora Maria Elena.

The Quiroz are similar to many of La Paz's elite families. They are wealthy, powerful, and at the peak of the city's prestige hierarchy. They are politically conservative, traditional, and very attached to kin and friends. As Arguedes (1920) noted in his novel *Vida Criolla (The Criolla Life)*, La Paz's elites "confine their activities either to the center of the city or to the relatively isolated residential suburbs in which many of them now live and to special exclusive clubs and restaurants. They shop in fashionable commercial areas and use private transportation. The city is seen as the last vestige of Spanish civilization. A place from which free spirits might occasionally flee to the pure air of the country, the controlled nature of an estate." Malloy (1970, p. 3) puts it even more succinctly, arguing that modern-day *criollas* still behave essentially "as European conquerors ruling the savages of a new world and looking to Mother Europe for spiritual and cultural sustenance." Their great lament is that they no longer control the political and economic machinery of the country as tightly as they once did.

La Gente Decente (*"The Decent People"*): *The Romeros.* The middle class in La Paz is of extremely varied background. It includes foreigners, downwardly mobile elites, professionals, white-collar workers, civil servants, as well as successful merchants.

Some authorities (Whiteford 1977) trace the origins of *la gente decente* to the offspring of Spanish captains and their Indian wives, and to the descendants of colonial clerks, priests, and artisans. Others attribute the growth of this class to the development of mining and manufacturing in La Paz. Whatever their origin, they are politically diverse, security minded, unadventuresome economically, and very prestige conscious (Malloy 1970, p. 42).

The Romero family—Alberto, Teresa, and their four children—own a modest two-story adobe house with a small cement patio near the Miraflores section. The house is sparsely but comfortably furnished with plump modern upholstered furniture and decorated with artificial flowers and modern prints of saints. The Romeros pride themselves on their electric kitchen, bathroom, telephone (often in disrepair), and economy-size car, luxuries that most of La Paz's residents do not share.

Alberto Romero is an officer in a foreign bank. He values his career, income, and reputation. To protect all three he makes sure he takes active part in the Rotary Club and the monthly businessmen's luncheon. Still, he is hardly rich. To help with the family's considerable expenses, his wife Teresa is thinking of returning to the secretarial job at a large commercial firm, which she left when the children were born. It seems that what with inflation, new clothes, birthday celebrations, school and university fees, and other social obligations, it is almost impossible to keep up anymore.

Their two younger children attend private schools. Their older son is a university student interested in an engineering degree, and their 18-year-old daughter has just completed her secretarial training. With Alberto's contacts, she recently has landed one of the scarce jobs at the city hall, but her salary barely covers her expenses and pocket money, so she contributes only a small share to the family budget. When she marries her young lieutenant this spring, this contribution will end too.

Similar to the *criolla* elites, the Romeros' extended family is the focus of much of their interaction. There is a constant round of visiting and attendance at the cycle of family *fiestas*: baptisms, first communions, saint's day celebrations, weddings, and funerals. They also are involved in numerous friendships that tie them to others in a complex web of mutual aid, advice, and exchange of gifts. For example, Teresa was involved in helping a woman with a nagging digestive illness. After consulting with two Western-trained doctors, they decided to consult a folk curer, who diagnosed the illness as soul loss due to fear. He recommended herbal tea and the purchase of ingredients for a *mesa*, a spirit offering. Whatever the outcome of this remedy, Teresa knew that her help would be returned at a later date by this woman.

Alberto and his sons are avid fans of the local soccer team and contribute considerable time, energy, and resources to it. Soccer is the Bolivian national sport, and two professional leagues play matches regularly in La Paz. The boys belong to a neighborhood soccer team, which also has a club where the members can drink and play

These women in their bowler hats are selling their wares in the free market in La Paz. The portrait of Petrona Mamanis (Case Study 8-1) is drawn from the lives of these people. (© Beryl Goldberg)

cards. The boys recently persuaded their father to help sponsor a *fiesta* to raise funds for new uniforms.

This family is rather different from the Quiroz family. They have a fair amount of money but must struggle to keep up with their own aspirations. Their prestige is hard-won and their power small; hence, they take very seriously the city's economic and political concerns, knowing that a radical change in either would alter their precarious position. In some sense they are "nervous in all directions." They worry lest those with more power and wealth (like the Quirozes) make decisions that undercut their stability. Likewise, they worry about the city's overpopulation, lack of jobs, and inability to provide services for the poor. They believe that if something is not done to alleviate the worsening situation, the city eventually may be unable to cope and its economy—including the Romero family— will collapse.

The Migrants' Life: The Mamanis. The Mamanis are part of the swelling tide that worries

the Romeros. Recent migrants to La Paz, Juan, his wife, Petrona, and their infant son all were born on a former hacienda on Lake Titicaca, two hours from the city by truck. Because their families were large, the couple did not have access to much land, nor were they able to look forward to any sizable inheritance. Given their rather bleak prospects, Juan and Petrona began thinking about migrating.

With urban experience from the army and knowledge of trucking, Juan was confident that he could make a go of it in the city. Petrona was also familiar with the capital. Since the age of 13, she had accompanied her aunt to the city on weekends to sell crops such as onions in the free market. She hoped to establish herself in that market and inquired about the possibilities of sharing a stall with a cousin.

Upon their arrival in La Paz, the Mamanis's first concern was lodging. Petrona's cousin's father-in-law owned a four-room adobe brick house in one of the *barrios*. Because they were relatives, they were given a room with two straw mattresses, an old chest of drawers, a small table, two rickety straight-backed chairs, and a bare lightbulb. The pair considered themselves lucky because their room had a window, the patio outside had a water faucet and sink and a one-burner kerosene stove to cook meals. Down the alley was a small general store for staples, notions, hardware, and some clothes and furnishings. Buses ran by regularly. On the whole, despite the fact that all 15 members of the household had to use a single outhouse, the Mamanis felt fortunate.

But things were not all *that* good. Migrants from their *altiplano* home had complained bitterly about the lack of jobs, housing, and public services in La Paz. Worse, during the last rainy season one family had lost their shack and all their possessions during a landslide.

Nevertheless, Juan believed he would become a successful trucker and already saw himself as a brave navigator of treacherous single-lane gravel highways. He hoped to work his way up, eventually even owning his own truck. He knew it would be unpredictable work: easy one moment, horribly exacting the next. He might go out daily or only twice a month. He might work only two hours a day; just as easily, he could be on 20-hour shifts.

Petrona had other dreams. By establishing herself at the free market, she hoped to initiate a wide circle of connections with clients. If she was successful, she thought she might eventually try to buy a stall in a central market from which she could, in turn, go on to buy a small store or even set up a small restaurant. Ultimately, she yearned to be a Spanish-speaking *chola decente*, clothed in several layers of expensive taffeta skirts, a silk-fringed shawl, a felt bowler hat, and fine jewelry. But that was in the future.

She knew she would have to begin by selling produce from her *altiplano* home and then add to her wares when she made friends in the market who had access to produce from other regions. Her mother had given her some capital with which to begin her enterprise, but she realized that she would have to work on her credit rating. At first, she knew she could borrow money from relatives for her weekly supplies,

but after a period of time when she had bought regularly from a supplier, she might be able to buy on credit.

In order to take advantage of every opportunity, Petrona entered into a complex network of mutual-aid friendships and business deals. She promised to become the godmother of her landlady's daughter in hopes that this woman would return the favor by becoming the godmother or sponsor of her own son's first haircutting ceremony. At the market she was undecided as to whether she should sponsor part of the upcoming *fiesta*. She feared the expense of the dancers, the renting of costumes and instruments, the food, and the transportation. On the other hand, if she didn't take on the responsibility, someone else would, and they would reap the benefits of prestige and connections. The traditional market leader would sponsor the mass, pay for the rental of the lights, hire the band, and provide for the alcohol, so perhaps it wouldn't be all that expensive.

In any event, the *fiestas* were wonderful affairs and a very important part of the migrants' lives. One, called "Trinidad," had expanded greatly in recent years. Centered on the church, it was a three-day celebration with masses, a procession, and the participation of up to 58 different dance groups. Each dance group was composed of 30 to 100 persons who worked together and who all had migrated from the same place. They performed elaborate traditional costumed dances to traditional tunes.

Since the coup d'état in 1980, which abolished the market unions, Petrona had tried to avoid politics. High taxes, shortages, contraband, harassment in the form of curfews, fines, beatings, confiscation of stalls, and price fixing had become daily occurrences. She earnestly hoped that the new government would lead eventually to greater market autonomy, the return of unions, and more opportunities. Yet, if it did not, she felt confident that there always would be the need for cheap labor and the inexpensive goods her family could provide for the growing city.

Conclusion

Despite differences, La Paz has been much affected by the historical and cultural forces that have been at work in most Latin American cities. Like those cities, La Paz has experienced the decimation and degradation of its indigenous population, colonialism, independence, the effects of an all-pervasive class system, dependency on foreign powers, and a recent population explosion of unprecedented proportions. The day-to-day lives of its people are influenced strongly by these forces.

The Quiroz family lives a life of decided advantage. Their worries are few and minor. Their wealth, power, and prestige assure them, barring the worst disaster, of a secure future. A century and a half later they are near-replicas of the Spanish overlords they replaced.

The Romero family, on the other hand, lives a less sumptuous life. They have worked hard to establish their middle-class standing and are proud of their achievements. Yet they cannot be improvident. Their wealth, power, and prestige are limited. At any point those above—in government, finance, or industry—could make decisions that would alter their delicate "means-ends" situation. Similarly, they fear the city's huge incoming migrant population. Its members eventually may compete for their jobs and houses and even now are taxing the city's ability to cope. The Romeros have to work hard and be continually watchful to protect their interests.

Finally, the Mamanis represent the vast majority of La Paz's population. Migrants from an overpopulated hinterland, they have virtually no wealth, power, or prestige and, as a result, the least ability to control threatening outside forces. They must work extremely hard to maintain even minimal financial security. The likelihood of reaching their dream status—an independent trucker in Juan's case; a self-sufficient vendor or restaurant owner in Petrona's—is not very high. More realistically, they shall spend the bulk of their lives, like their neighbors in the *barrio* and like Jesus Sanchez in Mexico City, working to

improve their own lot and that of their children a little. The ideal of improving the conditions of life for the next generation is a common one. As Jesus Sanchez put it:

> I want to leave [my grandchildren] a room, that's my ambition; to build [a] little house, one or two rooms or three so that each child will have a home and so that they can live together. . . . I asked God to give me the strength to keep struggling so I won't go under soon and maybe finish that little house. Just a modest place that they can't be thrown out of. I'll put a fence around it and no one will bother them. It will be protection for them when I fall down and don't get up again. (Lewis 1961, p. 499)

BOX 8-2
The Pope and the Poor

On several occasions in the 1980s, Pope John Paul II traveled to Third World countries around the world in an effort to dramatize the plight of their poor. On one of his trips he visited Rio de Janeiro.

At Rio's Vidigal favela (slum), [the Pope] climbed a steep hill to where the shanties of some 20,000 squatters command a spectacular view of the sea—prize property that real-estate developers covet. Just days earlier, the reluctant government had installed previously denied utilities—running water, sewers, and power lines—but only for a handful of shanties in the area the Pope was to visit. Moved by the poverty, John Paul II abruptly removed his gold ring and gave it to the local priest as a sign of solidarity with the favelados. The slumdwellers were thrilled by the gesture. But many were aware that his impact on their lives was only fleeting. "The next time a Pope comes here," one of them remarked, "maybe the government will get around to the rest of us."

There was a final, ironic twist to the Pope's gesture. So honored were religious officials and residents of the favela by the fact that it was the Pope himself who gave the ring, they decided to immortalize the gesture by building a shrine to house it. Thus, not only was the ring not sold and the proceeds used to alleviate the plight of the local poor, the shantytown's residents have become a bit more impoverished by contributions for the shrine.

Source: *Newsweek*, July 14, 1980, p. 83.

But even if Sanchez and the Mamanis are successful in their efforts, behind them will be millions of other Latin American poor—unable to advance greatly because, given the ever-increasing population, there simply will not be enough jobs, houses, or health services to go around.

The development of Latin American cities thus provides a marked contrast to that of European and American cities. Perhaps the most remarkable aspect has been the speed at which their modern development has taken place.

Most of us probably still have images of a basically rural Latin America, but in the wake of the recent urban explosion, Latin America's earlier rural character is disappearing, probably forever. The region is rapidly overtaking the highly industrialized areas of the world in terms of urban population (refer back to Table 1-1 to see this trend). As this growth continues in cities that lack the level of industrialization and resources characteristic of more developed areas, we can expect continued political crises (as the current unrest in El Salvador and Nicaragua suggests) and widespread suffering (see Box 8-2).

Latin America's urban situation is not unique, however. As we shall see in the next chapter, similar processes have been at work in Africa.

CHAPTER 9
African Cities

L-A-G-O-S. Lagos! The magic name. She had heard of Lagos where the girls were glossy, worked in offices like the men, danced, smoked, wore high-heeled shoes and narrow slacks, and were "free" and "fast" with their favors.

CYPRIAN EKWENSI, JAGUA NANA, 1972

After our consideration of Latin American cities, the fantasy that a character in Cyprian Ekwensi's novel has about the free and happy life that supposedly exists in Lagos, Nigeria's capital, is a familiar theme. Like much of the Third World, Africa is in the midst of rapid and far-reaching urban transformation. All over the continent people are pouring into African cities at enormous rates.

There are distinct parallels with Latin America. Africa also began with indigenous cities, experienced the political control and economic exploitation of colonizers, and like its counterpart in the Western Hemisphere, is now mainly independent.

There are important differences, however. For instance, colonization in Africa began when colonization in Latin America was over. Although initial contact by the Portuguese occurred in the fifteenth century, full-scale colonies did not appear in Africa until three centuries later. Second, independence for most African nations has been very recent. The Gold Coast was ceded its independence from Britain as the sovereign state of Ghana in March 1957. This opened the gates. In the time since, country after country has gained its freedom, the most recent being Zimbabwe (formerly Rhodesia) in 1980.

Only after the independence movement took hold did Africa's current urban explosion begin. A glance back at Table 1-1 will reveal that of the continent's 475 million people, only 20 percent were urban in 1980, making Africa one of the least urbanized major areas of the world. At the same time, the rate of urban growth in Africa is the highest of all continents.

This growth rate is due partly to in-migration from the hinterland. All over the continent people like the woman portrayed by Cyprian Ekwensi at the beginning of the chapter are seeing greater opportunity and excitement in the "magic" city. Also contributing to the growth are improvements in health services. As in Latin America, Africa's average life expectancy has increased while its birth rate (one of the highest in the world) has leaped ahead. Fully one-half of its population

TABLE 9-1

Urban Population Growth of African and Selected Industrialized Countries

African countries	Urban Population as Percentage of Total Population		Average Annual Urban Population Growth Rate (%)	
	1960	1980	1960–70	1970–82
Angola	10	22	5.7	5.8
Algeria	30	45	3.5	5.4
Benin	10	15	5.4	4.4
Burundi	2	2	1.3	2.5
Cameroon	14	37	5.8	8.0
Central African Rep.	23	37	4.7	3.5
Chad	7	19	6.8	6.4
Congo, People's Rep.	30	46	5.0	4.4
Egypt, Arab Rep.	38	45	3.5	2.9
Ethopia	6	15	6.5	5.6
Ghana	23	37	4.6	5.0
Guinea	10	20	4.9	5.2
Ivory Coast	19	42	7.3	8.2
Kenya	7	15	6.4	7.3
Lesotho	2	13	7.5	15.4
Liberia	21	34	5.6	5.7
Libya	23	58	8.4	8.0
Madagascar	11	20	5.0	5.2
Malawi	4	10	6.6	6.4
Mali	11	19	5.4	4.7
Mauritania	3	26	15.5	8.1
Morocco	29	42	4.2	4.1
Mozambique	4	9	6.5	8.1
Niger	6	14	7.0	7.2

is now below the age of 15 (Best and Blig 1977, p. 130).

Together these factors help account for the rather terrifying reality of today's headlines. Africa is a continent in severe crisis. Much of its population is starving. As an indication, consider this: of the 25 poorest countries in the world, no fewer than 17 are in Africa. Chad, in central Africa, is the world's most destitute nation—the average income per person per year is only about $80 (U.S.). Ghana, on the west coast, is the 25th poorest country in the world, but its average per capita income is only $360. Imagine what that means for a moment and the magnitude of Africa's crisis becomes apparent. Many of us in the West easily spend $80 for a single dinner for

two, and $360 is gone for a single decent piece of stereo equipment.

Although the bulk of Africa's rural population is abysmally poor, as highlighted by the 1985 "We Are the World" recording session and the "Live Aid" concerts, the crisis hardly stops there. Africa's cities, in most countries, are in great disarray as well. This is suggested in Table 9-1, which compares urban population percentages and urbanization rates in the African nations with a few countries of the industrialized world. The key to the table lies in the urbanization rates. A glance at the African nations indicates that their cities have recently been growing at rates ranging from 2.5 percent to 15.4 percent. In comparison, since 1970 no industrialized country listed has had a

African countries	Urban Population as Percentage of Total Population		Average Annual Urban Population Growth Rate (%)	
	1960	1980	1960–70	1970–82
Nigeria	13	21	4.7	4.9
Rwanda	2	5	5.4	6.4
Senegal	23	34	4.9	3.7
Sierra Leone	13	23	4.9	3.9
Somalia	17	32	5.7	5.4
South Africa	47	50	2.6	3.2
Sudan	10	23	6.8	5.8
Tanzania	5	13	6.3	8.5
Togo	10	21	5.8	6.6
Uganda	5	9	7.1	3.4
Upper Volta	5	11	5.7	6.0
Zaire	16	38	5.2	7.6
Zambia	23	45	5.2	6.5
Zimbabwe	13	24	6.7	6.0
Selected industrialized countries				
Canada	69	76	2.7	1.2
Japan	63	78	2.4	1.8
United States	70	78	1.8	1.5
USSR	49	63	2.7	1.8

Source: Adapted from *World Development Report 1984* (Fairfield, N.J.: Oxford University Press), Table 27.

growth rate higher than 1.8 percent. This means that for the bulk of Africa's cities we have a repeat of the Latin American pattern we saw in Chapter 8: continuing and massive urban overload not likely to improve in the foreseeable future. To better understand the complexities of all this, let us look at the continent as a whole.

African Urbanization: A Complex Pattern

It is an immense continent, covering almost 5,000 miles north to south and nearly 4,500 miles at its widest east-west point. Three countries the size of the continental United States could settle comfortably into it. Given such size, Africa is a place of tremendous geographic and cultural variation (over 1,000 languages are spoken). These factors, in conjunction with its history, have influenced considerably Africa's pattern of urbanization.

That pattern is uneven. Most contemporary cities, and the cities with the greatest population, are located on or near the continent's coast. The reasons are not hard to uncover. In the first century A.D. the Roman scholar Pliny the Younger wrote, "There is always something new out of Africa." Although he had more than material goods in mind, it was primarily for such goods that Africa was prized for nearly two millennia. Thus, the greater urbanization on Africa's north coast is a historical legacy of trade, both with Europe and the Islamic countries of the Middle East. For the European trade, goods were brought from the interior, usually over the forbidding Sahara desert, and shipped across the Mediterranean or up Europe's west coast. The many cities on Africa's west and east coasts were established during nineteenth-century European colonization to facilitate exports (including slaves) and shortly became the most technologically and economically sophisticated cities on the continent. When independence came, these cities, many of which were also colonial administrative centers of their countries, had a tremendous advantage over urban centers in the interior.

Second, with few exceptions, the sub-Saharan region (the area south of the Sahara) is less urbanized than that to the north. In most central and western African nations, under 20 percent of the population lives in cities, and in East Africa the figure is 15 percent. Within these areas, however, the pattern just mentioned still persists: the coastal nations, such as Ghana (38%) and Senegal (34%) are more urbanized than their inland counterparts such as Upper Volta (11%) and Chad (19%).

Third, although no sub-Saharan African nation has cities approaching the size of Cairo (the continent's megacity, with a population of over 8 million), a few, such as Nigeria and the Union of South Africa, have cities of considerable size. Moreover, virtually all African countries are dominated by primate cities that have appeared in the last half of this century. As we found in Latin America, such cities concentrate an enormously disproportionate amount of their country's population, economic, and technological resources in a small area.

With these factors in mind, we now turn to a brief consideration of the history of African cities.

African Cities in History

Indigenous Cities

In the popular literature of the last century, Africa was referred to often as the "Dark Continent." Although this term surely had racial undertones

to most Europeans and North Americans, it also referred to the unknown interior south of the Sahara. For centuries this area had been isolated almost completely from the rest of the world by the great width and breadth of the Sahara, a virtually impenetrable wasteland traveled only by local traders and nomads with knowledge of desert survival.

Whether known by other people on other continents or not, however, complex civilizations, complete with highly developed urban centers, existed in Africa as early as 3000 B.C. One such civilization, Kush, with its core cities of Meroe, Musawarat, and Naga, was centered about 100 miles north of the modern city of Khartoum. Recent archaeological evidence has determined that these Kushite cities, originally imitators of the pharaonic cities of Egypt, were highly sophisticated. By 590 B.C. Meroe traded extensively with Saharan and Mediterranean peoples in slaves, gold, ivory, iron, and copper (Wenke 1980, pp. 492–493). In fact, Meroe's trade in copper was so extensive that great slag heaps from the manufacturing process still can be found in the city's ruins.

Throughout Africa many other cities came and went. Some, particularly those in North Africa, were tied directly to Greece and Rome when those civilizations were at their height. For example, Alexandria, at the head of the Nile in Egypt, was originally a key city in the Egyptian empire. In 332 B.C., however, it was made a Greek outpost by Alexander the Great (hence its name). By the first century B.C., the city had between 20,000 and 30,000 inhabitants (Hance 1970). Roman cities in North Africa included Tangiers, Algiers, Tunis, and Carthage. After Rome's demise as a world power in the fifth century A.D., many of these cities remained as trade outposts for European and Islamic nations.

Other early African cities, particularly those in the sub-Saharan region, established themselves independently of Mediterranean peoples or cultures. Such cities served as capitals of indigenous African empires, as craft or manufacturing centers, or as break-of-bulk points on major trade routes. Gao, in present-day Mali, was built in the seventh century A.D. as the capital of the Songhai empire. More impressive was Kumbi, capital of the empire of Ghana around A.D. 1000:

> [Ghana] was a powerful state with a large army equipped with iron weapons. The capital, at Kumbi, is estimated to have had a population of 30,000 and the rulers could apparently call on the services of a rural population numbering in the hundreds of thousands. The economic basis of the state was principally trade in gold and ivory, as well as in salt, kola nuts, slaves, and iron weapons. (Wenke 1980, p. 497)

As Wenke suggests, trade was crucial to these cities. In the eighth century, shortly after the establishment of Islam as a major religion, cities based on trade with Arab countries and the East began to appear throughout Africa, two examples being Mogadishu in Somalia and Mombassa in Kenya. As exchange became more lucrative, the Muslim traders first conquered the cities of North Africa in the name of Islam, developing them into major shipping centers to Europe. To get goods to these cities, they established or had agreements with inland sub-Saharan cities. Kano in Nigeria (the focus of Case Study 9-1) and the legendary Timbuktu, founded in 999 and 1100 respectively, were cities that specialized in this trans-Saharan trade.

All these early African cities shared the main characteristics of the preindustrial city (see Chapters 2 and 7). They were walled, had narrow and winding streets, had all land controlled by the government, and organized their daily life around religion, craft, and the crown. Residence was determined by various factors. Some people lived with others of their craft—for example, with other blacksmiths—while others set up residence by tribal or religious affiliation. There was nothing approaching the modern Western pattern of a CBD surrounded by residential rings determined by income. Rich and poor, commercial and residential uses—all intermingled.

As in Latin America, however, the isolation of African cities would not continue forever. Although this period of empire building, trade, and urbanization (from approximately 500 B.C. to A.D. 1500) was "the formative period of modern Africa" possessing "its own dynamic of growth and change" and producing "its own cultures and civilizations, uniquely African" (Davidson 1959, p. 21), all would be progressively submerged in the coming centuries. Looking for an easy passage to the East, the Portuguese arrived in the late 1400s. Other European colonists—the French, British, Danish, and Dutch—were not far behind.

Colonization

The Europeans came and assumed command of African history; and the solutions they found were solutions for themselves, not for Africans.

BASIL DAVIDSON, *THE LOST CITIES OF AFRICA*

First Attempts. In some sense, the first European colonization attempts in Africa failed. The Portuguese had initial success in Ethiopia but were expelled later by local resistance. Ports they established disappeared or became merely backwaters of European trade. Nor, despite some success (see Box 9-1), were they able to maintain their military dominance of the interior.

Nonetheless, this initial opening of Africa by Europeans stimulated one of history's most wretched and grisly practices: slavery. Although the use of slaves has a long history—Egyptians, Greeks, and Romans regularly subjugated those they conquered—the slave trade between 1500 and 1850 is second to no era in barbarity and inhumanity. The Spanish and Portuguese imported slaves to Latin America to replace the decimated Indian population; the English and Americans shipped slaves in vast numbers to the New World to do the backbreaking work of building a new country. Other European countries participated as well. All enlisted the aid of a cadre of professional slave traders—Europeans, Muslims, Africans—whose job it was to bring the "black gold" to market at Dakar in Senegal, Elmina on the coast of Ghana, Zanzibar in Tanzania and other slave-trade towns established up and down the continent's coasts.

The first European foray also upset many of the delicate economic, political, and interpersonal linkages of precolonial Africa. The Portu-

---

BOX 9-1
The Ceding of Africa

The following poignant excerpt from a 1607 document describes the complete surrender of all local riches to Portuguese conquerors by an African emperor. This pattern was typical of Africa's colonization.

I, the emperor Monomotapa, think fit and am pleased to give to his Majesty [of Portugal] all the mines of gold, copper, iron, lead, and pewter which may be in my empire, so long as the king of Portugal, to whom I give said mines, shall maintain me in my position, that I may have power to order and dispose therein in the same manner as my predecessors . . . and shall give me forces with which to go and take possession of my court and destroy a rebellious robber named Matuzuanba, who has pillaged some of the lands in which there is gold and prevents merchants trading with their goods.

BOX 9-2
The Plum Pudding in Danger

The cartoon below depicts the colony-mad spirit that obsessed industrializing Europe in the nineteenth century. Drawn in 1805 by Gillray, one of the most famous satirists of the day, it shows William Pitt, England's prime minister, and Napoleon carving up slices of the world for consumption. The caption reads, "Too small for such insatiable appetites."

---

guese destroyed the east-coast cities and sundered the vital trade alliances that had been built up over centuries between these cities, the Persian Gulf, India, and the Far East. In other parts of Africa, Europeans destroyed many of the political allegiances that had kept African tribes and empires in balance with one another. Added to this was the incalculable confusion and suffering brought about by the slave trade, which forcibly separated husband from wife, brother from sister, mother from child. In the wake of such practices, much of Africa was left in an eminently exploitable condition.

The Second Wave. The character of urban Africa was to change radically in the nineteenth century when the Europeans arrived in force. No longer looking for a passage east, and with slave trade waning, the rapidly industrializing colonizers now eyed Africa with much the same rapacity as Cortés and Pizarro had eyed Latin America more than three centuries before: it was a source of almost incalculable raw materials and wealth. Like locusts, they swarmed over the continent trying to claim as much valuable land as quickly as possible (see Box 9-2).

Between 1862 and 1915, Europeans established city after city. Where no previous cities existed, they built them. Where indigenous urban centers were in place, they "Europeanized" them. Among those established or transformed during this period—some easily betraying their colonial origin by their European names—were Dar es Salaam (1862), Accra (1876), Kinshasa—originally Leopoldville (1881), Brazzaville (1883), Johannesburg (1886), Harare—formerly Salisbury (1890), Kampala (1890), Nairobi (1899), Kisangani—formerly Stanleyville (c. 1900), Jos (1903), Lubumbashi—formerly Elisabethville (1910), and Kalima—formerly Albertville (1915).

Unlike Latin America, where the "Laws of the Indies" resulted in a continent of similar cities, the presence of many European nations in Africa resulted in various different policies for urban areas. The British, for example, subscribed to a policy of indirect rule, generally content to let local African rulers maintain their position if they would be subservient to the colonial government.

The French, on the other hand, believed in the eventual assimilation of Africans into the French way of life. To promote this they dismantled indigenous governments, taught only French in public schools, and encouraged total identification with French culture on the part of the local population.

In still other instances, where prominent African cities existed prior to the coming of the colonizers, dual cities appeared. In cities like Kano (Case Study 9-1), Ibadan (Chapter 7), and Kampala, the Europeans, allowing the already extant African city to continue to exist, erected a city of their own next to it. The contrast was striking: an African city constructed of mud bricks and organized around its religious life and craft associations would coexist with a European city built of stone and organized around a growing CBD.

Whatever the particular variation, however, the results were the same: European domination and local subjugation. Instrumental in achieving this end in all cities was a policy of racial segregation. The official rationales developed for the implementation of such policies are instructive because they illustrate the racial and paternalistic attitudes on which the segregation system was based. Not accidentally, it also was a system that resulted in tremendous economic, political, and social advantage for Europeans at the expense of Africans. Here is an excerpt from an official Rhodesian government publication:

> The whole [segregation] system rested on the assumption, well justified at the time [the late nineteenth century], that there was a wide gap between European and African modes of life, and that the African would not wish to live permanently in the town. All he needed therefore was a place of temporary residence, where his doings might be supervised and where some minimum standards of health might be enforced. (Brelsford 1960, p. 72)

The effect of such segregation was observable to any visitor to African cities in the period between 1900 and the end of World War II. The Union of South Africa, with its doctrine of *apartheid* (total separation of white and nonwhite races by law), provides the most glaring continuing case. As anthropologist Marvin Harris describes it, racial segregation in colonial cities was ensured as frequently by subtle realities as it was by overt apartheid-type policies:

> In Mozambique "Europeans Only" notices are not needed in order to maintain an almost perfect separation between the African mass and the Europeans. For example, a bus ride in [the city of] Lourenzo Marques costs the equivalent of one-fourth of the average African's daily wage. Whites transact their business at the post office and bank through African runners and servants. At the movies, soccer games, restaurants and hotels and other semi-public places, prices and clothing act as efficient color filters. There is no need for establishing native "locations" as in the Union [of South Africa]. Perfect residential segregation follows automatically from urban zoning laws and rents. Whites can indeed walk safely in Lourenzo Marques' African quarter in the dead of the night, but this is because the Africans who live there are forbidden to step out of their houses after nine o'clock. (1958, p. 4)

Racism was at its worst in southern Africa. In more northerly parts of the continent it was mitigated somewhat by different colonizers and by urban traditions that allowed the races some contact. This has had important consequences for modern Africa. Although racial tensions still exist in West, East, and North Africa, in the south the Union of South Africa and Namibia (administered by the Union of South Africa)—racial differences have threatened to erupt into bloody confrontation. Indeed, if the bloody confrontations of the summer of 1985 in South Africa are any foreshadowing, the racist policies of that country are going to be challenged again and again until the black majority gains its long-denied rights.

The Modern Era

During the period of colonization, most African cities grew slowly, hampered as their Latin American counterparts had been by the disadvantageous trade policies they had to bear as colonial outposts (exporting at low prices to a single buyer or a few at most). Some cities—coastal ports or mining cities, for example—grew somewhat more swiftly because of their location or because of the product they offered.

Independence. A major change was ushered in after World War II, however. Four factors coincided, leading to the independence of virtually all African nations. First, the oppressive systems of racial segregation and political and economic inequality began to spawn nationalist movements. Second, such movements encouraged the revival of each country's precolonial heritage, long-suppressed by colonial policies. Third, Africa became a confrontation site for world ideologies. Siding with the Africans in most cases were leftist or Communist countries, prominent among them the USSR, China, and, later, Cuba. Such countries often equipped insurgent local groups with the arms necessary to resist the colonizers. Finally, colonies became increasingly disadvantageous, both economically and politically, for European countries to maintain.

To take a single example, England was a crippled nation after World War II. With London and many other cities bombed, with an industrial system in disarray, and with an economy wholly unable to keep up with the needs of the local population, maintaining colonies thousands of miles away became a tremendous expense. When they added to this the likelihood of fighting lengthy wars of independence against dogged insurgents in each colony, the British began to seriously reconsider the wisdom of maintaining their African holdings. Although in some cases the British fought hard to prevent independence, as in their attempt to hold on to Malaya, such efforts became more and more futile.

In the 1960s, 32 former colonies became sovereign nations. Indeed, in the "African Year" of 1960 (so called because of the large number of colonies that won freedom), over 3 million square miles and 53 million of Africa's people gained independence (Herskovits 1962, p. 303). Independence movements spread like wildfire. As they did, the retreating colonizers made more frequent and less carefully considered concessions. As a result, "later states in the race for independence had a much shorter and smoother passage in the bargaining process with the [colonizing] power" (Lloyd 1967, p. 63). The result of this rapid change in at least a few cases, however, was debilitating political disorder. Wanting to maintain their colonies, the Europeans often did little to train native Africans to govern. For example, after the hurried Belgian retreat from the Congo in 1960, that country (now Zaire) endured five years of bloody civil war as faction warred with faction for control.

As in Latin America over a century before, the freeing from colonial overlords led to major growth in the cities. This growth was spurred by various conditions. Most important among them were (1) the ability of the newly independent nation to trade with whomever it chose and (2) the attractiveness of the city as a place to live for impoverished rural people. Regarding the latter, Schapera reports that, in a study of 297 men who had migrated to cities in the Union of South Africa, all but six gave economic reasons for doing so: they wished money to pay their taxes; to buy cattle, clothing, other goods; or for their families (cited in Herskovits 1962, p. 267).

Problems. With the benefits of such growth—an increased standard of living for some, international eminence, and self-governance—have come problems. One of the greatest has been the growth of city slums and shantytowns. The latter, called *bidonvilles* ("tin-can cities") in former French colonies and other names in other countries, are comparable to the squatter settlements we have encountered already in Latin American cities.

In Cityscape 9-1 Henry Kamm and Franz Fanon contrast these slums and *bidonvilles* with the European sectors of a number of African cities. With such conditions directly connected to colonialism and its legacy, it is no wonder that many Africans regard Westerners with distrust and rage (Abu-Lughod 1980). Furthermore, there is increasing evidence that the contemporary form of "colonialism"—the allegiance between multinational corporations and government elites—continues to exploit the mass of Africa's people (Bradshaw 1985).

Other problems of urban Africa also remind us of Latin America:

1. Some African governments are still unstable. Most scholars think there are two primary reasons. First, independence came so

---

CITYSCAPE 9-1
Africa: The Colonial Legacy

Henry Kamm

Luanda in Angola, Lourenco Marques and Beira in Mozambique are white man's cities—with downtowns of pleasant, Portuguese-style colonial houses of commerce of the last century, surrounded by the pompous public buildings of the authoritarian Government of Salazar Portugal and enveloped by the massive, shapeless concrete blocks of today's men of business. At the edges are housing developments for the "poor whites" and villas on tree-lined streets for those less poor. One wonders how cities so seemingly small can have population figures as large as the 475,000 given for Luanda, 355,000 for Lourenco Marques and 114,000 for Beira. The answer lies beyond, in endless, warrenlike shantytowns of surpassing wretchedness. There the African population lives, and there it becomes quite obvious that the population figures are, if anything, understated and, more likely, guesswork.

Shack next to shack of the most disparate bits of wood, tin or anything else that will offer shade and shelter but uniform in their shabby inadequacy are crowded into the plains of beaten dirt. It must have been savanna country before, with grass, bushes and some trees, but only at the edges do flashes of green relieve the dun barrenness now. The houses are arranged, if the word is not too strong for such unplanned mazes, to resemble the homesteads of families in the bush, with the shacks of the different members facing onto small patches of ground on which children play without toys and often without clothes and women cook over scraps of wood or charcoal.

Franz Fanon

The settler's town is a strongly built town, all made of stone and steel. It is a brightly lit town; the streets are covered with asphalt, and the garbage cans swallow all the leavings, unseen, unknown and hardly thought about. The settler's feet are never visible, except perhaps in the sea; but there you're never close enough to see them. His feet are protected by strong shoes although the streets of his town are clean and even, with no holes or stones. The settler's town is a town of white people, of foreigners.

The town that belongs to the colonized people, or at least the native town, the negro village, the medina, the reservation, is a place of ill fame, peopled by men of evil repute. They are born there, it matters little where or how; they die there, it matters not where, nor how. It is a world without spaciousness; men live there on top of each other, and their huts are built one on top of the other. The native town is a hungry town, starved of bread, of meat, of shoes, of coal, of light. The native town is a crouching village, a town on its knees, a town wallowing in the mire.

Source: Henry Kamm, "The Last Days of Empire," *New York Times Sunday Magazine*, Aug. 18, 1974, p. 58.

Source: Franz Fanon, *The Wretched of the Earth* (New York: Grove, 1963), p. 32.

---

quickly and still is so new for most African nations that an established leadership has not yet emerged. Second, many Africans are still united by tribal, more than national, ties. Colonies were formed by European land claims that made no effort to conform to local territorial allegiances. Hence, many contemporary African nations are composed of tribes (Nigeria has more than 200) that, historically, have not been the best of friends. National politics, as a result, is often a process of vying for power, frequently with bloody results.

2. Even when their governments are stable, African countries are extremely poor—so much so they simply cannot generate the wealth to solve their cities' problems at this time.

3. Most African nations usually are dominated by a primate city so preeminent in national affairs that other cities fail to draw significant migration. This exacerbates the overpopulation that already exists in the primate city and simultaneously saps the strength of other cities and rural areas.

4. Many cities are beset by chronic underemployment and unemployment. Historical and colonial dependency on one or two trade goods and the lack of a generalized industrial base are key causal factors here. One way many African nations have tried

Children in front of their home in the tin-roofed shantytown of Cape Town, South Africa. Such structures are typical of black townships, segregated residential areas for black Africans that are part of the white government's policy of apartheid. (Woodfin Camp/Alon Reininger)

to improve this situation is by encouraging tourism. A mixed blessing, tourism brings the world's richest citizens into contact with its poorest. The contrast and clash are poignantly portrayed in Box 9-3, which describes a visit by European tourists to the fabled North African city of Marrakech.

5. Finally, political corruption, crime, and urban violence are everywhere on the rise (Hance, 1970, pp. 265–292). Nigeria, one of Africa's most economically and technologically advanced countries, serves as an example.

The streets of Lagos have become so dangerous that few honest residents go out at night. . . . Bribery— or "dash" as it is known in Nigeria—also is a big problem. "Kickbacks start at a minimum of 15 percent and usually go to 50 percent," admits a Nigerian businessman. The government says that it was impatient international businessmen who brought bribery to Nigeria in the first place and insists that it is carrying out a campaign to eliminate the practice. There have been scores of dismissals for corruption and a sign outside the office of [President] Shagari's top aide could hardly be more explicit:

"Bribery is a crime. Bribery is a sin. Do not give it. Do not take it." (*Newsweek*, March 30, 1981, p. 43)

Daily Life. Despite such disquieting problems, most Africans have found ways to survive. They have found or created some type of livelihood and are supported by intricate links with friends, relatives, and members of their tribes. Together, these elements produce an urban life-style that combines elements of both European and indigenous traditions. Azuka A. Dike calls this the "binary nature" of African cities (1979, p. 19). He argues that it is a fundamental mistake to see African cities moving relentlessly toward being like their European or North American counterparts. While some such movement is evident, African cities will never become mirrors of cities elsewhere; rather, they will continue to absorb and transform Western urban characteristics while at the same time retaining and transforming parts of their African tradition. Thus,

[the] Ghanaian national dress known to the outside world is as much part of modern Ghana as the skirt of leaf of the Kusasi woman. An Ashanti medical doctor is as much an Ashanti as he is a doctor and a

BOX 9-3
Rich Meet Poor

In the accompanying passage, Elizabeth War-
noch Furnea and her daughter Laila are out for
a walk in Marrakech when they are accosted
by a beggar.

"Baksheesh!" A beggar boy with a twisted arm
stuck his dirty hand, extending from a ragged
piece of sleeve, under Laila's elbow. She recoiled
as if struck. Pressing his advantage, the boy followed on. We were tourists; he was shameless.
"Baksheesh," he hissed. I stopped and took a
coin out of my purse while Laila avoided looking
at the boy's eyes as though her own might be
burned on contact. I dropped the money into his
dirty palm. The eyes stared at me, at Laila, went
blank. He was gone.

"Mama, why did you do that?" Laila looked
sick, and I reflected, after consoling her and
pointing out that the child was hungry, that she
was, after all, only experiencing what many well-
brought-up Westerners, not so young as Laila,
experience the first time they have personal contact with poverty, disease, the horror of destitution, of deformity. Most Western cities manage
very neatly to bundle up all of those troublesome
sights and put them into institutions called old
people's homes and prisons, orphanages and
correctional centers, or into sections of town and
country not frequented by our middle classes.
The law-abiding, affluent citizen does not need to
be bothered by such sights, to constantly be reminded of the impermanence of health, affluence,
the shortness of life, the uncertainty of good fortune. In Marrakech, rich and poor, healthy and
sick were not so neatly separated.

Source: Elizabeth Warnoch Furnea, *A Street in Marrakech* (Garden City, N.Y.: Doubleday, 1975), pp. 51–52.

Kano, Nigeria[1]

Situated in northern Nigeria, Kano is a city of
over 1 million people. It has experienced a long
and tumultuous history. Founded over 1,000
years ago, it has exhibited remarkable tenacity:
most of its early West African urban counterparts
are gone. It continues, a product of a unique set
of historical and cultural forces.

Precolonial History

Kano the city began in A.D. 999 as a center for
local clans interested in dominating the region,
but its origins as a settlement are at least 300
years older. By the seventh century blacksmiths
were smelting iron at Dalla Hill, an ironstone
outcrop (Willett 1971, p. 368). The land immediately surrounding the outcrop was fertile. As a
result, the settlement flourished, and in the early
1100s Kano became the capital of the region. For
protection clan leaders erected a huge, 40-foot
mud wall nearly 12 miles long (see photo). Expanded and reconstructed many times, this wall
still outlines the original city.

Given the independence of the clans, unified
control of Kano and its surrounding hinterland
did not occur until the mid–fifteenth century,
when Islam became the dominant religion, sup-
planting the earlier spirit-possession religion of
Bori. By the late 1500s Kano had become a true
city-state similar in many respects to those of
Medieval Europe.

After unification the city prospered. A rival
city-state was conquered, and a large region was
incorporated into the kingdom. Trade expanded in all directions, most importantly across the
desert on the trans-Saharan trade routes (see
Figure 9-1).

Geographical location is the most important
reason for the city's historical endurance. Situated at the very northernmost part of tropical Africa, Kano had access to tropically produced

---

Ghanaian. The Igbo college professor who takes his
village "title" is no less modern than he is Igbo.
(Uchendu, as quoted in Dike 1979, p. 24)

If such observations are correct—and we have
every reason to believe that they are—we must
expect that African cities of the future, products
of a unique coming together of cultural and historical forces, will bring about their own blend
of urban life and structure. Case Study 9-1, an
examination of Kano, Nigeria's third largest
city, suggests that this process already is well
under way.

---

[1]This section was prepared by ALAN FRISHMAN, Department of Economics, Hobart and William Smith Colleges. It
has been adapted by the authors for use in this chapter.

Modern Kano, still appearing today as it did to centuries of travelers who arrived at its mud-walled gates. (Alan Frishman)

goods—for example, kola nuts and hides—and easily could produce other goods itself, either directly (grains) or by manufacture (leather items, cotton, cloth, dyes). Second, the city was a perfect break-of-bulk point, gathering goods from all directions, warehousing them, and sending them on the long journey to and from Europe via desert caravans. Third, the city was far enough north that it could raise cattle and horses without threat from the devastating Tsetse fly that makes such herding impossible in tropical Africa. At the same time, it was not so far south that the camel, the major beast of burden in the trans-Saharan trade, could not be used effectively.

People drawn to the city throughout the precolonial period were mostly artisans, who came to join the city's thriving crafts market, or traders who came to Kano to represent their families, tribes, or kings. Many present-day districts in Kano derive their names from these original settlers: Lokon Makera is, literally, "the area of blacksmiths," and Soron Dinki is the area of "the houses of tailors." Similarly, Durimin Turawa is the "field where the Arabs live," and Tudun Nufawa is the "hill where the Nupe tribe resides."

Due to rivalry with other city-states over resources and trade, early Kano was not peaceful.

At the end of the fifteenth century, war broke out between Katsina and Kano for control of the trans-Saharan trade, local territory, and population. The conflict lasted for a decade with no clear victor. This was merely the first of many wars between Kano and Katsina and other city-states, wars that, over the next four centuries, were to result in Kano's losing and regaining regional dominance several times.

Not until the early 1800s did Europeans first look upon the city. Their reports indicate a powerful, well-organized, prosperous trading center. Paul Staudinger, a German, visited Kano in 1885 and reported, "Kano is the capital of the richest and most flourishing province of present-day Hausaland" (as cited in Moody 1967, p. 47). A decade later, C. H. Robinson wrote, "The market of Kano is the most important in the whole of tropical Africa and its manufactures are to be met with from the Gulf of Guinea on the south to the Mediterranean on the north and from the Atlantic on the west to the Nile or even the Red Sea on the east" (1897, p. 111). Such glowing reports only increased the desire of the colonizing British to capture and control all of Nigeria. With the French laying claim to neighboring territory, the British moved on the city

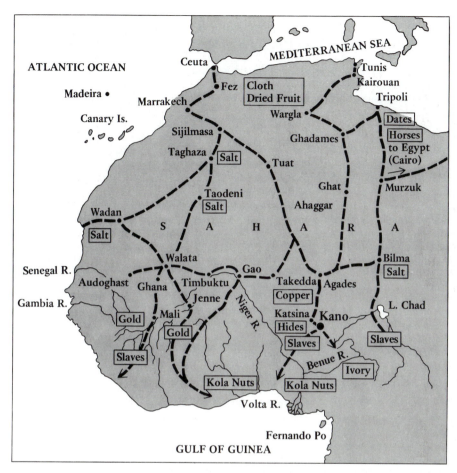

Figure 9-1 *Kano and the Trans-Saharan Trade. Source: L. H. Gunn and P. Duigan,* Africa and the World *(San Francisco: Chandler, 1972), p. 162. Copyright © 1972 by Harper & Row, Publishers, Inc. Reprinted by permission.*

in 1903. A fictionalized account of the encounter, based on the actual events, is recorded in Cityscape 9-2.

British Rule

The British colonists, holding to their policy of indirect rule, recognized that city-states like Kano had elaborate governments already in place. If these governments could be controlled and scrutinized, they could administer their respective provinces better than any British substitute. Thus, the British issued a dual mandate: they would directly administer their own inter-

ests and the local emir would be allowed to control the indigenous population as long as he complied with British demands.

To protect their interests, however, one of the first official acts of the colonists was to segregate the races. They began a township of their own, east of the old city wall, and restricted this new area to Europeans. Not surprisingly, the European Township soon became the focus of lucrative trade. By 1911 a railroad linking Kano with the coast was terminated there and several large European trading companies requested sites near the station. Business boomed. Before long the

CITYSCAPE 9-2
The Capture of Kano, 1903

Yusufu, a portly Hausa whose modest compound lay within a stone's throw of the massive Nasarawa Gate, emerged from his mud hut, cleared his throat and listened to the medley of sounds—cocks crowing, braying donkeys, the first assiduous pestles in mortars—that heralded the day. He had overslept and missed the first prayer.

Scratching thoughtfully, he remembered that he had an appointment to buy cotton thread in the market. He (and his father and his father's father before him) belonged to a weaver's guild. No member of the family had ever followed any other trade.

Sitting at the entrance to his compound and pulling on his sandals, Yusufu reflected on the strange rumors that were circulating the night before—that Bebeji, one of the stronger towns to the south, had been taken without a struggle by an army commanded by a handful of Turawa ("pale-faces") armed with weapons never before seen in Hausaland. There were rumored to be incredible machines: one that poured out a stream of lead pellets and another capable of firing a metal shell of great weight a long distance. Rumor had it that such a shell had actually killed the District Head of Bebeji and impressed upon the townspeople the futility of further resistance. It was now being said that the Turawa and their troops were advancing on Kano itself. But Yusufu was unconcerned. It mattered little, even if the stories were true. The people of Kano would teach these infidels a chastening lesson. Kano was no Bebeji. With its great thick wall, its moat filled with sharp thorns and branches, and its tortuous towers that dominated each of the city's main gates, it was impregnable.

Yusufu walked briskly towards the market. He had barely drawn even with the Emir's (king's) palace when the way was suddenly cleared for horsemen galloping from the Zaria Gate. They shouted that, at that very moment, the infidels were storming the southern walls of the city. Yusufu immediately forgot his cotton thread and ran with many others to the Zaria Gate, one of the strongest of the city's bastions.

When Yusufu and the others arrived on top of the city wall the battle was beginning to reach its height. Explosions were landing everywhere. Everyone seemed terrified. The attackers breached a smaller, less fortified gate. The breach was so small that only one man at a time could force his way through but, because of their confusion and fear, the Emir's soldiers began to beat a rapid retreat. To the astonishment of Yusufu and his fellows, the storming party streamed through the breach and straggling defenders were mercilessly cut down. Within a matter of minutes the main body

of the invading army, few of whom appeared to be even wounded, followed the remnants of the Emir's army into the very heart of the city.

Yusufu learned later that the Emir and a few of his followers had fled. The Turawa who commanded the invaders sent a party to take over the arsenal and treasury. There was some resistance. One of the Emir's slaves attacked a white officer. He was killed.

By the afternoon, Kano had capitulated to the foreign army in the same manner as all the other cities further south. But strangely, instead of looting and burning the city, the Turawa commander gave orders that he did not in any way wish to interfere with the ordinary life of the civilian population. As a result, the market was soon at its height, as it always was at that time of day, and Yusufu was able to find the man with whom he had arranged to buy the cotton thread. Before nightfall, some of the foreign soldiers even visited the market.

As the sun set and Yusufu returned home, he reflected upon the day's events. How had his impregnable city fallen so easily? And just what was it that these new pale-face rulers had in mind for the future?

Source: Adapted from R. L. B. Maiden, "The Nasarawa Gate," in *The Nasarawa Gate and Other Stories* (London: Brown, Knight and Truscott, n.d.), pp. 1–5.

Europeans were profitably exporting cotton, leather, and peanuts and importing salt, cloth, sugar, and manufactured items.

As a result of this prosperity and growth, additional segregation of Kano's population developed. The new businesses wanted Western-educated African clerks, but the only schools in Nigeria were run by Christian missionaries, and the local Islamic tradition (which the colonists respected) would not allow their people to be trained by Christians. Thus the British encouraged the migration of southern Nigerians—primarily members of the Ibo and Yoruba tribes. These Africans were unwelcome in the Old City because they were Christian, and they were excluded from the Township because they were African. Out of necessity, a second African residential area called Sabon Gari (literally, "New Town" in Hausa) was established to the north of the Township.

There were also Arabs. Considered by the British to be non-Africans, they were allowed more leeway. Many asked for and were given living space near the railroad yard, where they established another area known as the Syrian-Lebanese quarter.

From 1920 to 1945 the Old City was virtually ignored. In the minds of the colonists the Township *was* Kano. Ironically, such an ostrichlike attitude was, in many respects, benign neglect. Throughout the colonial period the Old City maintained much of its previous economic vitality, despite the loss of the trans-Saharan trade occasioned by the railroad and the unsettling presence of a powerful European force literally a few yards away.

Independence: Modern Kano

One City. The first crack in the wall of British domination of the city came in 1959 when Kano's town planner, D. Ball, began work on a ten-year development plan. The significant feature of this plan was the recognition, for the first time in its colonial history, of Kano as a single urban area. After independence was achieved in 1960, Ball's reports were expanded into a 20-year plan that recognized the fact that Kano was likely to become one of Northern Nigeria's main cities. In order to handle the expected growth and consequent strains that would be put upon the urban area and its facilities, the plan called for a permanent planning board that would oversee the unified urban area.

Statehood and Growth. In May 1967, Nigeria was divided by federal decree into 12 states. Kano Province became a state and Kano its capital. This had a striking effect on the city. Before the twentieth century it probably had never been home to more than 40,000 people. From the time of the British occupation in 1903 to the end of World War II, the population was about 100,000. Even after the war, the city grew only at a modest rate of about 5 percent a year. After statehood in 1968, however, the growth rate soared, resulting in a population of nearly 1 million by 1980. The city still is growing by about 12 percent annually.

Two factors seem responsible. First, statehood created a large number of government jobs. Second, a severe West African drought began in 1968 and lasted for six years. Many crops failed and destitute farmers flocked to the city for potential employment.

The Economy. This incredible influx has had predictable results: many people in Kano are either underemployed or unemployed. However, as in La Paz, Bolivia (Chapter 8) and Jackson Heights in the United States (Chapter 5), the poor are kept from destitution by their extended-family network. This private welfare system extends to relatives and beyond to people of the same tribe or ethnic group. Those with some income feel obligated to provide others who are less fortunate with food, a place to sleep, clothing, and contacts for work. Unlike the situation in Latin or North America, however, the Islamic religion stresses that it is the obligation of wealthy people to help the poor. This directive is taken seriously; as a result, the effects of extreme poverty are mitigated for many.

Even with this support, however, there are wide income differentials in Kano. Not surprisingly, these differences favor Europeans who still work there and well-educated Nigerians. In 1973 the average income level of Old City households was $1,373 per year, while it was $2,859 in Sabon Gari and $4,808 in the Township. This difference is attributable mainly to the employment available and products sold in each area. In the Township jobs are principally white-collar and industrial. In contrast, in the Old City and Sabon Gari there is a continuing reliance on cottage industries (the production of items in one's home, such as shoes, mats, and tools) and what can be sold each day.

But, also in contrast to the more modern areas where trade tends to be of the impersonal variety found in many Western cities, the Old

City and Sabon Gari are dominated by thriving markets, which are the focus of much social as well as economic activity. These markets contain thousands of small shops and open-air stalls. Competition is intense; items sold are not standardized, so constant bargaining is necessary. This process, however, allows both buyer and seller to feel out the market and to get to know one another. Conversation often drifts to other subjects during the course of their haggling and often a personal relationship is established, which brings the customer back to the seller. There are also innumerable hawkers and peddlers in the densely populated areas, who carry wares directly to customers. Selling everything from food to clothing, these people work on small profit margins and are willing to divide products into very small quantities (for example, a pack into single cigarettes).

Religious and Social Life. One major influence upon the bulk of Kano's population is Islam. There are five prayers a day, which take from five to ten minutes. Work often stops so that people can pray. On Friday afternoon, the major prayer time of the week, most people attempt to go to a mosque, although this is not obligatory. Most children attend Koranic school to learn to read and write Arabic and to understand Moslem prayers and the Koran (the holy book).

By Islamic law, men are allowed to have up to four wives if they can support them. Women are kept in seclusion (*purdah*) from the age of marriage (often 14 or 15) until old age. Thus family and home life become very important for women since they cannot move about freely. They are allowed to visit friends at night and can attend festivals and ceremonies. For the most part, however, they stay within the compound walls, take care of the household duties, and in some cases engage in cottage industries such as cooking, sewing, or preparing food that is sold in other places. Children are used as messengers and hawkers of wares and act as a distribution network in such trade. Hawking also allows young girls to come into contact with young men who are potential suitors.

To marry and have children is expected, and

any nonconformity is considered to be gravely deviant. The family is patriarchal, and the male head of the household is treated with great respect. Sons are given a portion of their father's compound. Sometimes, however, a family with many sons is forced either to expand its compound or to have some sons live nearby. Sons who are forced to live elsewhere almost always attempt to live in the same neighborhood, due to vital services the family provides.

Problems and the Future. Although on many levels Kano works, it has severe problems as well. Housing is one. When the great migration wave came after statehood in 1968, the city was simply unable to cope with the growing number of migrants. There were three major effects: (1) the scarcity of land and homes intensified and drove up prices; (2) unable to afford the increased prices, poorer migrants had to crowd into existing structures, thus increasing density; and (3) squatter settlements began to appear. Large sections on the periphery of the city began to expand as people quietly, and illegally, seized or bought farmland in order to build homes. Thus, Kano too has its *bidonville*.

In 1973, a report estimated that 284 acres of center-city housing was needed immediately to eliminate overcrowding. The cost of this housing, together with the necessary amenities (electricity, water, sewage, drainage, roads, and health services) would be $146 million, a figure totally impossible for the government to achieve. By 1980 it was further estimated that an additional 23,000 houses would be necessary to handle the city's needs (Doxiadis 1973, pp. 85–90). Although many new houses have been built, they do not come close to meeting these demands.

Lack of adequate employment opportunity continues to plague the city. Industrial expansion has not taken place at a rapid enough pace to keep up with the growth of the labor force. The result is unemployment and increased competition in trades and services that demand few skills.

Summary

All cities are exceedingly complex affairs—an interplay of individuals, interests, cultures, and

CITYSCAPE 9-3
Mohammed Sokoto: A Day in the Life

Mohammed Sokoto wakes up at 5 A.M. in the room that he shares with his wife and three children. His family is one of five that share the compound, a housing unit of rooms surrounding an open courtyard with a common bath, latrine, and cooking area. Mohammed washes with water carried the night before from the public tap located 100 yards down the street. After, he prays the first of his five daily prayers. While the rest of his family and neighbors arise, he eats his breakfast, a thick porridge prepared by his wife.

Mohammed comes from Sokoto, a city of the Hausa tribe several hundred miles away, but he has lived in Kano for over 15 years. Since he was not born in Kano he claims he is not a real Kanoman, yet he shares the same Hausa language, culture, and religion of his neighbors and clearly is accepted by them.

Mohammed left Sokoto as a teenager when it became apparent that his older brothers would take over his father's cloth-trading business. When he arrived in Kano, he found a job as a laborer for the government and also learned gardening. Years later he found friends who were willing to teach him to drive. After passing his road test about five years ago, he became a driver for the Kano Urban Development Board, an organization that plans and partially administers the city.

As he leaves his compound in the congested Old City, he greets his friends and neighbors. Many are off to work in the government and commercial offices and factories located in the new part of the city. Others sit and chat before going to the Old City Market to hawk their wares. Still others, all men, sit at home all day hoping to be called for an odd job in the neighborhood. Mohammed walks a quarter of a mile along the dusty, unpaved road, which is lined with an open sewer. At the Dan Agundi Gate he leaves the Old City to find a taxi on the new four-lane road that runs beside the Old City wall.

His job begins at 7:30 A.M., and it is about 4 miles from home to work, so, despite the expense, he must use the taxi or public transport. His first responsibility is to check the car he drives. Then he spends his day running errands, driving officials to sites for inspections, and carrying employees to various meetings.

During the day Mohammed usually finds time to have a light lunch and pray again around 2 P.M. By 3:30 his workday has ended. Home once more, he washes and sits outside his compound with his neighbors, listening to the radio and discussing politics, family affairs, and general gossip. At 4 P.M. and again at sunset there are prayers and then a big meal.

Mohammed's compound has electricity, but it is used only for lighting. The families are too poor to afford any other electrical appliances such as fans, refrigerators, or televisions. The cooking, done in the open courtyard with a wood fire, is in his wife's hands and she generally is responsible for all food and family welfare. Although usually confined to the house by the Moslem custom of *purdah*, she manages to run the house quite well. Hawkers bring wares and her children run errands to buy food and other household goods. At night, she visits friends. Sometimes they come to spend time with her.

Mohammed ends his day chatting with friends and saying his fifth prayer around 10 P.M. The routine of the following day will be a repetition of this one. Saturday and Sunday are exceptions. On those days he will do the washing and ironing, and he will visit friends.

His income is barely sufficient to cover the family's needs for food, clothing, and shelter; thus, life is simple and they enjoy no luxuries. Nevertheless, Mohammed is content in his job and prefers to work for the government because of the security of the position. He enjoys his comfortable neighborhood and would rather travel the long distance to work than move closer so that he could walk to his job and save the travel money. His fulfillment in life comes from his family, friends, and religion. His concerns are based upon his lack of wealth— he will never be rich—and the state of his family's health.

---

history. Kano is no exception. The modern city has arisen out of its particular interplay of these forces. In Cityscape 9-3, we see all these forces at work in the daily life of a single individual, Mohammed Sokoto, who is a contemporary embodiment of Nigeria's and Kano's past and present.

Note how his religion, his native African background, his job, and the contemporary state of the city itself all play a role in shaping his day and his concerns.

Conclusion

African cities provide yet another contrast to the familiar Western pattern of urbanization we discussed in Chapters 6 and 7. Recall that Chicago theorist Louis Wirth (Chapter 4) suggested that the experience of modern urbanites everywhere would be likely to show a breakdown of tradition, ancient loyalties, and a weakening of family ties. Certainly such a characterization does not apply very accurately to Mohammed Sokoto of Kano.

Horace Miner (1953) and William Bascom (1955; 1963) were among the first to argue that Wirth's urbanism hypothesis did not apply to African cities. The key reason for its inapplicability, suggested Bascom in his study of Yoruba tribal cities in southern Nigeria, was that the cities Wirth had in mind when developing his theory were those that emerged within a very different cultural and historical framework, a framework emphasizing industrialization, capitalism, and technological advance. All these forces have been weaker, even nonexistent, in many parts of Africa until recently, and there is doubt whether they will ever come to characterize African cities in the way they have their Western counterparts. African cities have their own, often multiple, cultural traditions and a different history. Such forces are shaping different cities and different urban experiences.

The story of African cities bears some resemblance to that of the cities of Latin America. Africa, too, was characterized by indigenous cities and empires before the coming of the colonists, suffered many of the indignities resulting from external control of its affairs, gained independence (for the most part), and now finds itself undergoing breakneck population growth and its consequent problems.

Yet, in contrast to Latin America, the residual effects of colonization do not seem, at this point, as deleterious in Africa. European domination lasted less than 100 years in most parts of the continent, a far cry from the three centuries of Spanish and Portuguese rule in Latin America. Moreover, given its own complexity and the presence of *many* colonial policies, Africa was not

The mix of traditional culture and twentieth-century urban growth is a distinctive mark of cities across Africa. This is Addis Ababa in Ethiopia. (Georg Gerster/Photo Researchers)

stamped as indelibly as Latin America. In Spanish Latin America (the vast majority of the region) the "Laws of the Indies" prevailed, Catholicism became the main religion, and indigenous cities and cultural traits were crushed callously. Cultural domination was less lopsided in Africa. Some European colonists, like the British, allowed indigenous cities and cultural traditions to exist alongside the colonial culture. Other colonists, like the French, were more imposing but still less domineering than the Spanish and Portuguese in Latin America. Already assured of their status in the European hierarchy of nations, wealthy, powerful countries like England, France, and Germany were primarily interested in Africa as a source of raw materials and as a potential market. As long as they got what they wanted, they were willing to be somewhat less dictatorial in their control. In addition, the decimation of the indigenous population which occurred in Latin America never came about in Africa. Many areas in the African interior had little contact with Europeans until very late in the nineteenth century. The result of these crucial differences was that, when independence came for African nations and cities, the older cultural traditions reasserted themselves.

This in no way implies that Africa and African cities are free of problems. On the contrary, sometimes the results of the ensuing conflicts of interest and competition for power between rival cultural groups create enormous difficulties (Gugler and Flanagan 1977, Chap. 1). In addition, African cities (Kano is a single example among hundreds) are likely to experience major shortages of such basic necessities as water, electricity, housing, and jobs for decades. This lack of "fit" between things needed and number of people in a city is called by some urbanists "overurbanization" (Davis and Golden 1954). There is no doubt that the overurbanization of African cities will get a good deal worse before it gets better.

Moreover, this overurbanization is just part of a larger pattern of troubles that beset this huge and energetic continent. Hilary Ng'Weno, editor in chief of the *Weekly Review*, published in Nairobi, Kenya, sums up:

> A most disturbing aspect of Africa's current crisis is its pervasiveness. It has affected nations regardless of their political or ethnic complexion. Poverty, famine, pestilence and civil strife are now the lot of numerous African nations, a far cry from the dream of African leaders at the time their nations gained their independence. The goal of most of the new nations was to catch up with the rest of the world by the end of the century. Instead of catching up, Africa is fast falling behind. (1984, p. 27)

But these problems are not unique to Latin America and Africa. Although we will see a much more varied pattern, the same issues will be raised again in the next chapter, where we complete our analysis of the non-industrial world by considering the cities of the Middle East and Asia.

CHAPTER 10
Middle Eastern and Asian Cities

In this chapter we complete our survey of urban development outside the more familiar Western setting. The Middle East and Asia cover an enormous portion of the world. Although these areas vary markedly in their cultural and historical traditions, there are similarities nevertheless. We will examine the cities of these regions to determine how they parallel or diverge from the cases we have considered already: Latin America (Chapter 8) and Africa (Chapter 9). This done, we conclude this chapter with some general comments about the problems and likely future of non-industrial cities.

The Middle East

Journal Entry
Date: *Mid-November, 1984*
Place: *Cairo, Egypt*
Personnel: *Author Spates, Professor David Eaton, and members of an American student group*
Time: *4 A.M.*

It is pitch black. The headlights of our minibus only begin to illuminate the road. After traveling through deserted streets for what seems hours, we reach our destination. The bus grinds to a halt at the bottom of a hill and can go no farther. All 20 of us pile out, immediately overwhelmed by a God-awful, indescribable smell that assaults the nose from all sides. The stench seeps into our clothes, making them feel somehow heavier. Grumbling, the driver tries to maneuver his shiny new vehicle over the slimy ground. Having finally turned around, he drives off cursing in a language we do not understand. The darkness returns and envelops us almost completely.

Now what? In time, we decide to climb the hill. We stumble through the darkness, joking with each other to mask our nervousness. At what seems to be the top, we see a few lights of the city twinkling in the distance and, eerily in the blackness of the night, smoldering fires all around us. The stench continues unabated. It seems to settle on our skin like fine dirt, encrusting itself bit by bit in our very souls.

The dawn creeps in. The first thing we see, silhouetted on the hills all around us, are the dogs. They are routing and scrounging about. Every now and then they stop, look up, howl at the sky, sending shivers down our spines. Then they go about their business. Here's one! Right beside me! Gaunt and dirty, he looks warily at me. This dog has not seen my like before, nor I his. I am afraid. He knows it. He glances, growls, moves off.

The dawn continues. As it proceeds, we see, all around us, more smoldering fires. There must be 50 of them. Their smoke engulfs and gags us and I think of the poet Shelley's line about London, that hell is a smoky, populous city. If there is an urban hell on earth in this century, *this* must be it. For now we are beginning to see clearly: we are not on a true hill at all. This is not terra firma. We are on an enormous pile of refuse, paper, wire, scraps of clothing, partially eaten food, excrement. For this is the Cairo dump, the place where most of the garbage of a city of nearly 12 million comes to rest. It is an unbelievable sight. The "hill" we are on is some 60 to 70 feet high and it is solid garbage!

Suddenly, from below us comes an odd creaking sound, moving up the "road" (itself nothing but refuse) we had earlier struggled up. Slowly, out of the gloom, comes a tired, small, broken-down wagon, pulled by the saddest creatures I have ever seen—two mules, filthy, tattered, thin beyond all comprehension, looking as if all the world were on their shoulders.

My mind rebels. This place is not possible. This *is* something out of Charles Dickens or Shelley, something out of the horrors of nineteenth-century London. But I know I am engaging in a fantasy. I cannot wish this place away. This is today and this is Cairo, the largest city on the African continent. And driving that wagon are the very denizens of this hell—a man and two children, both boys apparently about six years of age. They are all wearing the traditional Egyptian dress, the galabea, but they appear as dirty, tattered and world-weary as those sad, sad mules. As they approach, they look at us and smile. But they also have a quizzical look about them, for, like the dogs, it is doubtful that they have seen our like *here* before. The contrast is striking, embarrassing: they, as just described; we, quintessentially American, with our clean clothes, our nice sneakers, our $500 camera systems. Although we are professors and students, we are essentially tourists. But *they* are not tourists! They *live* here amid the fires and the smell. And with only that one, quizzical glance, they go about their business.

And what is that business? These people are the Zebaleen, Cairo's coptic Christians, and they make their living by gathering up the trash of this smoky, overpopulated, overstrained Third World city. In a passionately Muslim nation, Christians are not accepted easily into the city's life. It is difficult for them to get jobs. So, many Zebaleen have chosen to work and live in the dump. After all, as we shall see in a moment, it is *better* than going back to the little village most of them came from.

Their business? Specifically, this: up the hill behind the wagon now come others, a dozen or more, children, women. In the smoke and stench and filth they set to work, sorting through the trash that has been brought from the city the previous day by the men, on wagons just a little better than the one we see before us now. They sort for anything that might be of value, that they might sell to someone in the city. Two little girls are gathering bits of red ribbon and putting it in a basket, two boys are getting tin cans, others are gathering bits of wood for the fire in their village below the hills of garbage, and—most horrifying of all—as we watch, one woman is going through the fly-infested refuse and pulling out half-eaten pieces of pita bread, much of which is covered with the remnants of other pieces of food—who can tell what? This woman sees us watching and, knowing that we have no language in common, she shows us in gestures—and she looks proud!—that she is going to take the bread back to the village for something or someone *to eat*—her pigs? her children?

This is their business—trying to stay alive in a city that cannot keep them alive by any decent means of work. Further we must remember this: the Zebaleen are not *paid* for their work. Cairo, an urban area of nearly 12 million people, larger than New York by 2 million, larger than all but four or five other cities in the whole world, has no organized garbage removal. So the Zebaleen have found a niche, horrifying as it might be. Cairo desperately needs its trash removed. They, as desperate, do it. And, wondrous to tell, they survive. Not well, or with any sense of opulence, but they survive. They gather their bits and pieces of trash, bag them, sell them, and, then, burn the rest in the fires. And slowly, but inexorably, as they go about their business, the pile grows higher. Then there are two piles, then three, then four, as the millions continue to pour into Cairo. No one knows when the piles will stop.

Perhaps most interesting of all, most frightening of all, is that the story of the Zebaleen is *not* atypical. This is not how a *few* live, this is quite literally how "the other half" of humanity lives. The Third World currently is home to about 48 percent of the world's people. Most of them live, in one way or another, like the Zebaleen, on the edge of starvation, without job security, in places like the Cairo dump, all over the globe.

Why They Come to the City. Obviously, the life just described is not a pleasant one. The Zebaleen who live in the Cairo dump have to scramble for a living every day. At any moment their land can be confiscated by the authorities as Cairo grows ever outward. They are despised by much of the population because of the job they do.

Why then do they do it? While other jobs may be difficult for Christians to get in a Muslim society, why don't they go elsewhere or return to the villages they came from? Indeed, why don't millions of other Cairenes who live on the edge of subsistence do the same?

A chance to experience where these migrants lived before the trek to Cairo provides the answer. Our student group had such an experience the day before the journey to the dump. Traveling from Alexandria to Cairo, we had come up the delta road to the point where the life-giving Nile broadens into alluvial tributaries approaching the sea. All along the delta road are small villages, occupied by people who work the farms in the area. Arbitrarily, we stopped at one village.

Around two in the afternoon, we walked in from the road, once again carrying all the accoutrements of Western civilization—our Betamaxes, cameras, fine clothes. At first, the village of about 30 buildings seemed deserted. Then, as we walked further we saw a few children playing and women in doorways. They shied away from

us—bizarre invaders. Then a few men appeared. They were very friendly, inviting us into the village proper. What we saw there was unforgettable.

All the one-story buildings were made of mud brick. They were hardly furnished at all: a semblance of a bed, a few pots, cold, dirty, earthen floors. There was no running water, no electricity. On the floors or in the doorways of most houses were small children, most of them dirty, in even dirtier clothes, and almost all of them covered with flies, especially on their faces. The babies were too small to brush the flies away; the older children paid little attention to them. On the roofs of most of the houses were mounds of hay, put there out of reach of rats and other vermin.

We walked to the back of the village. Here we found more people, working. Some women were washing in a little irrigation ditch. Others were sifting grain through hand-held wire containers. The older women seemed to be watching the children. A few men appeared, some carrying primitive spades and other instruments used in the fields. We were astounded at the extreme poverty. Clothes were tattered. Many villagers were obviously ill. A large number of the children had a skin disease, a kind of blotchy encrustation on parts of the face over which the flies climbed. Most of the villagers had very bad teeth. There was not an ounce of extra flesh on anyone. The temperature was close to 100 degrees, and yet they had no choice but to work outside in the broiling sun.

The comparison with the dump was striking. Although certainly bad, the dump was clearly better than this. A few indicators: the Zebaleen village at the dump had electricity; there were trucks, some machines; the houses had some furnishings. But perhaps most impressive of all were the children. Before we left the dump that morning, we walked through the village and saw the children getting ready to go to school. After doing their early morning work on the hill of refuse, the older children had come back to the village, had their breakfast, and then changed for school. As they proudly lined up for a picture, we noticed that they were clean and had clean clothes. As impressive was their attitude: they were smiling, laughing, joking as they posed for us. In contrast, there were virtually no smiles to be found on the faces of the rural village's children. Life was hard for them and it already seemed to have made an indelible negative impression.

People are intelligent. News of the contrast between life in the city and life in the rural areas travels quickly. Although to most Westerners the differences seem minor (who, among us, would care to live in *either* place?), to people living in such poverty the differences are most significant. The city offers a chance to move up a step materially, for children to go to school, to get better water and medical care. And, if one dreams (and these people surely do), the city offers the *chance* of even greater advantages—perhaps, if they work extremely hard or are lucky, true wealth, perhaps a life with some real leisure time. Certainly, at the very least, things can't be any worse in the city. So, given the chance, people pick up stakes and go—by the millions.

The Third Urban Revolution

This story is being repeated all over the Third World, as we have already seen in considering the cities of Latin America and Africa. In essence, it has been repeated throughout the history of cities. And, although now familiar, the story bears repeating because it tells, once again, of the power of the city to attract people, and helps explain the massive transformation that is altering the nonindustrial world—the third urban revolution.

We described two earlier urban revolutions in Chapter 2. The first occurred after the end of the last Ice Age, when cities first flourished and drew people in large numbers. The second occurred after the Middle Ages, when industrialism and capitalism became vital components of the urban scene. Most of the Western nations—the United States, the countries of western Europe—became dominant urban centers at that time, roughly from the sixteenth to the mid–twentieth centuries. Now, urban growth in these areas of the world is slowing considerably. But this is patently *not* true of the rest of the world, where urban growth is unprecedented, virtually out of control.

Two Zebaleen children pick up ribbon from the huge mounds of garbage at the Cairo dump, 5 A.M. (James L. Spates)

Unless this growth is checked, we may experience in the decades ahead unprecedented urban disasters. Cities may collapse under their own weight, simply unable to function.

Already this seems true of Cairo on some days. The city is growing at the rate of 1 million people a year by some estimates. Its housing is already overburdened beyond belief. Yet people continue to move in with one another and share the already overcrowded space. Or they move to the Cairo dump. Or they move into the city's cemeteries and take up residence in the mausoleums. Or they sleep on the streets, anywhere. The city's phone system is a disaster; you call one number and frequently are connected with another; or you are not get connected at all. The streets are so filled with traffic that "gridlock"—where cars

---

CITYSCAPE 10-1
The Islamic City

In this description of the typical Islamic city, notice how the environmental and cultural elements dominant in the Middle East combine to produce a unique urban place.

The surrounding wall is the most obvious feature, usually seen on first entry to an Islamic town. Apart from the defence requirements of the population, such structures represented barriers to dust-laden winds coming from a variety of directions depending on the time of day or season of the year. When planted with bush shrubs, the effect on wind and dust was that of an almost total barrier, and with strategic planting of vegetation within the settlement, wind and dust could be kept aloft and away from inhabited

areas across the whole extent of the settlement. . . .

The bustle and intensity of activity on the main thoroughfares were a notable feature of the Islamic town. The animated nature of its commercial sections and the awareness of a rich texture of human contact and activity were, and in some cases still are, the very life force of Islamic urbanism. In sharp contrast to the harsh desolation and silence of the desert, the sugs or bazaars provided access to a multitude of goods and services. . . .

Turning away from the main thoroughfares, a further contrast was encountered as the traveller ventured into the residential quarters on either side. Here the streets were much narrower, with walls often within touching dis-

tance on either side. The intimacy and semi-private atmosphere of these streets were borne in on the visitor as the shade provided by the dense building pattern created cool conditions in which to linger. The noise of the main streets was quickly cut to a distant murmur as the traveller moved further into the quarter. . . .

On gaining entry to a private house, yet another contrast was unveiled as the anonymous faces of the outsides of houses presented to the street were transformed by the wealth of detailed internal decoration, apparent in even quite modest homes. Houses were usually built on the courtyard principle with rooms opening onto a central space, often embellished with a fountain. This space provided the chief

---

converge on a spot from many directions so that none can move—is a daily phenomenon. Quite simply, the city cannot cope. The situation appears likely to get worse.

And Cairo is only one Middle Eastern city among many that is undergoing this transformation. Take a moment to think of the Middle Eastern cities most prominently in the news in the last half decade: Cairo, Jerusalem, Beirut, Kabul, Tehran. Now think of the Middle Eastern cities of legend: Damascus, Baghdad, Mecca, Isfahan, Istanbul. Despite their currently less publicized status, most of these cities also are undergoing rapid transformation. Indeed, from Egypt on Africa's north coast to Pakistan thousands of miles away, over the whole length and breadth of the Middle East, change is the characteristic urban experience.

It was not always thus. Before waves of modernization, Middle Eastern cities, in all their variegated forms, experienced a millennium of Islamic culture relatively free from outside interference. Before that, indigenous cities and thriv-

ing empires dominated various parts of the region. Thus, to understand the current state of Middle Eastern urbanization we must look to its past.

Pre-Islamic Urbanization

In Chapter 2 we discussed at length the most famous early Middle Eastern cities. In this region the world's first known city—Jericho—developed nearly 10,000 years ago. It was followed by other early cities such as Catal Hüyük and Eridu and, beginning in the fourth millennium B.C., by the domination of the Persian and Egyptian empires (refer to Figures 2-1 and 2-2). As these empires faded—a process hastened by the invasions of Philip of Macedon, Alexander the Great, and the Romans in the last four centuries before Christ—they left behind the residue of urban greatness. Although many of these cities would never rise again, they established sites on which more modern cities would flourish.

A second period of city building occurred on the heels of Alexander's conquest in 334 B.C.

communal living area for the family. In keeping with the modesty of Islamic tradition, rooms of one part of the house were used only by women and the overall layout catered for the entertaining of guests without their need to encounter all members of the household.

The courtyard principle provided the ultimate achievable protection of private open space from the extremes of temperature, dust and wind outside the settlement. In an almost cell-like structure the town was set within its walls as a first line of protection from the environment. The residential quarters, often within their own walls, were then located close together in a pattern which afforded mutual protection of each building by all the others. The building density

did nothing to compromise the privacy of individual houses orientated inwards as they were, so that a third and final line of protection between courtyard and residential street was afforded by the house itself. . . .

Moving finally towards the centre of the town, the traveller was confronted with the mosque. These were originally built not so much as houses of God but as a means by which to exclude unbelievers from regular prayer ceremonies. The addition of minarets, though partly only ornamental, was made to project the muezzin's call to prayer, with other mosques built once the call was out of earshot in an expanding city.

There can be little doubt that Islamic towns and their specific fea-

tures which still exist today reveal a high degree of unity and atmosphere which is often lacking in more recent urban settlements in the Middle East. As complete contrasts to the desolation of much of the region, the flavour of the urban communities was at once intimate, intricate and intense. In one of the harshest environments in the world, Islamic towns were capable of furnishing comfortable living conditions for populations which in many cases such as Fez, Cairo, Baghdad or Tehran ran into hundreds of thousands.

Source: M. Hugh P. Roberts, *An Urban Profile of the Middle East* (New York: St. Martin's, 1979), pp. 37–41.

Seeking trade for his growing empire, Alexander established a string of colonies from present-day Syria all along the coast of northern Africa. As Romans followed Greeks, additional cities, primarily military outposts, were established. After A.D. 300 the declining fortunes of Rome, plus soil erosion and overgrazing, led to the eclipse of most coastal and trade cities. Some of these ruins still remain, stark reminders that the Middle East has had its share of foreign overlords.

Islamic Urbanization

The prophet Muhammad died in 632, unleashing a religious movement that was to sweep over the entire Middle East, into Europe via Spain and the Balkan states, across much of sub-Saharan Africa, and, eventually, as far east as Pakistan, India, Indonesia, and the southern Philippine islands. As it spread, Muslim culture built an impressive array of cities. While Europe's preindustrial cities were contracting during the Middle Ages, the Islamic peoples expanded the coastal

cities of North Africa and built or rebuilt impressive regional centers inland throughout the Middle East. The success of these cities was assured by the Muslims' status as among history's greatest "middlemen." The Middle East's geographical location made it possible for Muslim traders to be the link between Europe and the Far East and, in the case of North Africa, between Europe and the sub-Saharan region.

Perhaps the inland cities were Islam's greatest triumph. For centuries, as nomads and overland traders, the people of the Middle East had learned how to live in desert conditions and how to trade across vast distances of inhospitable terrain. Needing centers for this trade, they established Mecca, Riyadh, Baghdad, Tehran, and Kabul among others.

All the Islamic cities had a similar cast to them, as described in Cityscape 10-1. By and large, the layout of the traditional Muslim city was a product of decisions made by the city's royal and religious elites. There is little doubt that they often created a city that was remarkably beautiful.

The following passage, excerpted from Robert Bryon's writings of his travels in the Middle East in the 1930s, describes Isfahan in Iran.

> The beauty of Isfahan steals on the mind unawares. You drive about, under avenues of white tree-trunks and canopies of shining twigs; past domes of turquoise and spring yellow in a sky of liquid violet-blue; along the river patched with twisting shoals, catching that blue in its muddy silver, and lined with feathery groves where the sap calls; across bridges of pale toffee brick, tier on tier of arches breaking into piled pavilions, overlooked by lilac mountains, by the Kuh-i-Sufi shaped like Punch's hump and by other ranges receding to a line of snowy surf; and before you know how, Isfahan has become indelible, has insinuated its image into that gallery of places which everyone privately treasures. (1950, p. 174)

But this image is misleading, for Islamic cities often were characterized by enduring internal conflict. Given the division of the city into multiple residential quarters—Costello (1977, pp. 14–15) reports that sixteenth-century Damascus listed no fewer than 70 quarters in the city itself and another 30 in the suburb of al-Salihiyyah—in-group solidarity often led to virulent out-group hostility, particularly when religious or other central values were at stake:

> So intense was neighborhood communal solidarity that at times faction fights broke out between quarters. . . . [It was] a society where economic grievances could seldom be articulated without group violence. Political communication with the ruling . . . caste was limited. Food shortages or abusive taxation provoked street demonstrations, assaults on officials, pillage of shops and the closure of markets. . . . [Youth gangs, associated with different quarters] preyed upon the quarters, running protection rackets, pillaging, and murdering. (Costello 1977, pp. 15–16)

These Islamic cities were at their zenith in the Middle Ages. After that, like their Persian, Egyptian, Greek, and Roman predecessors, they began to slide into decline. Once more the land in and near the cities, probably because of overpopulation and poor planning, became overgrazed, the valuable topsoil depleted, facilitating evaporation

of precious water supplies and increasing dust and erosion. Timber, the most important raw material in any preindustrial city because it was used for heat, cooking, artifacts, houses, ships, and tools, began to disappear (Costello 1977, p. 18).

The spread of the Turkish Ottoman Empire in the late fifteenth and early sixteenth centuries only hastened the process. As the Turks gained more and more control of the Middle East, the trade guilds, the earlier lifeblood of these cities, became more restricted in their activities by the government. The result was economic stagnation. "The initiative allowed to [the guilds] was small: the number of shops was limited for each guild and only master craftsmen were allowed without the guild's sanction; and the price of the commodity was fixed by the government" (Costello 1977, p. 17).

City population plummeted. For instance, Baghdad was reduced in the sixteenth century to a population of between 50,000 and 100,000, a tenth of its former size. Cities in Syria, Egypt, Iran, Iraq, and Saudi Arabia were reduced to shadows of what they had been. Even in still-vital cities such as Alexandria and Aleppo (in Syria), trade was reduced to a trickle (Costello 1977).

Nineteenth- and Twentieth-Century Urbanization

Not until the nineteenth century, under direct European influence, did urban growth begin once more. European motivation for such connections was the same as it had been all over the world: the Europeans saw in the Middle East ready-made markets for their goods, a potential source of raw materials, and, in some areas such as Suez, strategic locations for military affairs.

But the Europeans also recognized that the Middle East was not all that valuable a prize; hence, their efforts at direct colonization were limited. Britain administered Egypt as a protectorate from 1882 to 1914; but otherwise the main inroads were made via trade. This was enough, however, to begin to weaken the centuries-long Islamic pattern. In the nineteenth and early twentieth centuries, Muslim attempts to keep nonbelievers and their modern accoutrements—books, telephones, automobiles—out of their cities and countries began to fail.

As European influence spread across the region, new urban patterns were introduced. French efforts to establish a textile industry in Egypt after 1830 sparked urban growth which led to a sharp increase in city population in the latter half of the century. Similar changes, clearly evident in cities such as Cairo, Beirut, and Tehran, introduced swelling suburban districts beyond the quarters of the old cities, and new, wider roads, increasingly clogged with motor vehicles, began to be constructed (Roberts 1979).

The real change, however, went deeper than the physical level. Foreign traders ventured into rural areas to make more advantageous deals for agricultural products, thereby passing up the ancient bazaar tradition. Foreign investors opened businesses and factories in Middle Eastern cities and began selling at lower prices than the guilds, undermining the guilds' exclusive control of the market. Competition altered the face of entire urban and rural economies. Whereas before, local sheikhs had administered land communally and restricted the open-market sale of goods, now people began to sell land, goods, and skills to the highest bidder. The effect was the weakening of traditional authority and the community-oriented system. Before long, Middle Eastern cities had begun to alter their earlier self-sufficient, subsistence economies, becoming export-oriented and dependent on the economies and needs of Europe and the United States (Costello 1977). This process was accelerated by the discovery of the new "black gold" of the region: oil.

The main effects of this transformation have been (1) to emphasize the development of coastal cities and to downplay the significance of inland urban areas and (2) to set off major migration to all cities. This latter phenomenon, as we have seen in Latin America and Africa, further upset the basic social structure of the traditional Muslim city. First, the in-migration of people looking for the better life began to swell many Middle Eastern cities beyond the point of coping. Turkey's urban population, for example, increased

138 percent—from 5.4 million to 9.3 million—between 1950 and 1965, while Saudi Arabia's cities increased over 400 percent from 1932 to 1970—from 300,000 to 1.3 million (Costello, 1977, pp. 30–32).

Political conflicts in the region also have augmented the population problem. The most prominent example is the plight of the Palestinian Arab refugees, nearly a million of whom set up temporary "homelands" in the cities of Lebanon, Kuwait, Saudi Arabia, and Jordan after the establishment of the state of Israel in the late 1940s. The vast majority of these refugees live in the destitution of the shantytowns we have encountered in other areas of the Third World.

A second change has been that capitalist markets have created, as they have everywhere, a relatively large middle class of affluent entrepreneurs. By and large, this middle class has settled in new and exclusive suburbs outside the old cities.

Finally, rapid urban growth has established a primate-city pattern for the entire region. Tehran, for instance, has outdistanced all other Iranian urban centers in size, market strength, and problems. In similar fashion, Baghdad, Kuwait, Damascus, Beirut, Amman, and Cairo dominate their countries. As elsewhere in the Third World, the existence of such primate cities is seen by some urbanists to be "parasitic," simultaneously curbing the growth of other cities and creating virtually insoluble problems (Costello 1977, pp. 35–37).

In short, contemporary Middle Eastern cities are in a period of intense social change. They are no longer the pure Islamic cities of the past millenium, nor are they likely to become fully Westernized. Like the cities of Latin America and Africa, these cities are in the process of forging a new and complex urban tradition. The emphasis here is on the word *complex*. As Janet Abu-Lughod has recently argued: "If, at some previous point in time, it was possible to generalize about cities in the wide region encompassed by Arab-Islamic culture, it is clear that such generalizations are no longer realistic" (1984, p. 116). In fact, Abu-Lughod identifies no fewer than five different patterns of current urbanization in the

Middle East. These she calls (1) "neo-colonial," typified by cities in Tunisia and Morocco; (2) "state socialist," the urban pattern in Algeria, Iraq, and Syria; (3) "charity cases," exemplified by cities in countries that are supported by other countries such as Jordan, Egypt, and Lebanon; (4) "oil and sand," including cities in Libya, Saudi Arabia, and Kuwait; and (5) "fourth world," cities in countries that are astonishingly poor such as the People's Democratic Republic of Yeman and the Sudan. The reason such a varied pattern exists at present, Abu-Lughod contends, is because the countries and cities of the Middle East, unlike many of their counterparts in Latin America, Africa, and Asia, are deeply enmeshed in world economics and politics. In some sense, then, their urban development is not completely of their own making. Abu-Lughod concludes: "It is unlikely that this situation will change drastically in the near future" (1984, p. 117).

Asia

We now look at the nature of cities and urban growth in Asia. As in the Middle East, the richness and complexity of culture in Asia is so vast that we must be highly selective. Indeed, of all areas of the world, Asia provides the most challenging case because within it lies almost 30 percent of the earth's land area and four major cultural traditions. Sharp contrasts will be evident: Japan is a highly industrialized and Westernized nation, has controlled its population growth with relative success, and is one of the richest nations in history. In China we shall find a highly centralized urban policy that manages the largest urban population of any country in the world. Despite successes, urban difficulties in China are rife. Southeast Asia, unlike all the other areas, has no real tradition of indigenous cities at all; yet, despite this, major cities are growing almost uncontrollably. India may be faring even worse. It has urban problems probably unparalleled anywhere in the world and faces an urban future likely to crease with worry the face of the most diehard urban optimist. We begin there.

India

Everywhere I went during my visit to India this year, I did not merely sense, but actually observed the population growing. The sidewalks were tangibly more packed, the buses audibly more overloaded, the trains more alarmingly scrambled over by desperate commuters, the country roads more jammed with carts and bicycles, and half-derelict trucks and knots of women with pots on their heads and cows and ruminative goats and swarms of naked children and old men asleep in the shade of banyan trees and beggars apparently dead, their sticks still in their hands, flat on their backs in the gutter. (Jan Morris 1980b)

The above is not a very enticing portrait. Unfortunately it *is* an accurate description of most major Indian cities. This is the state into which Indian cities have fallen after a long, often glorious, history.

Chapter 2 revealed that the India-Pakistan region had thriving cities such as Moenjo-Daro and Harrappa in the Indus Valley as early as 2500 B.C. Indeed, for centuries, the fabled opulence and beauty of early India and China held nearly mythical fascination for the West. These myths induced that most famous of world travelers, Marco Polo, to set out from Venice in 1271 to find an easy route to the East (see Box 10-1).

Tales such as Polo's only fired the European imagination further. Yet his stories also chronicled the enormous difficulties of reaching India and China via an overland route. So the Europeans had no recourse but to take to the sea. Beginning in the early 1400s, the Portuguese began moving down the west coast of Africa, establishing outposts as they went. By 1460 they had reached Sierra Leone; by 1488, the Cape of Good Hope. Eleven years later, Vasco da Gama, first moving up the east coast of Africa, made the leap across the Indian Ocean and arrived in India. By 1534 the Portuguese had outposts at Goa and Diu along India's west coast. The passage, however, was hardly easy. Between India and Europe lay over 10,000 miles of ocean. Hence, when the riches of the New World were discovered in the early 1500s (Chapter 8), Portugal quite naturally turned much of its attention to the considerably nearer continent of South America.

BOX 10-1
Marco Polo's India: The Cities of Malabar and Guzzarat

After three years of extremely difficult travel, Polo and his two brothers finally found themselves deep in Asia at the capital of the great Kublai Khan in Peking. The Khan took a liking to the Polos, gave them every comfort, and over the next 20 years they toured extensively in China. Finally, they convinced the Khan, who had grown very attached to them, to allow them to go home. En route they visited two thriving cities on the western coast of India. Note the quality of Polo's description: he sees the Indian cities primarily in terms of wealth and objects. Although he described the culture of India as well, it was such passages that fueled European interest in opening these areas to trade.

Malabar

Malabar is an extensive kingdom of the Greater India, situated toward the west, concerning which I must not omit to relate some particulars. The people are governed by their own king, who is independent of every state, and they have their proper language. . . .

In this kingdom there is vast abundance of pepper, ginger, cinnamon, and Indian nuts. The finest and most beautiful cottons are manufactured that can be found in any part of the world. The ships from Manji bring copper as ballast. Besides this they bring gold brocades, silks, gauzes, gold and silver bullion, together with many kinds of drugs not produced in Malabar, and these they barter for the commodities of the province. There are merchants on the spot who ship the former for Aden, from whence they are transported to Alexandria. . . .

Guzzarat

The kingdom of Guzzarat, which is bounded on the western side by the Indian Sea, is governed by its own king, and has its peculiar language. The north star appears from hence to have six fathoms of altitude.

Here there is great abundance of ginger, pepper, and indigo. Cotton is produced in large quantities from a tree that is about six yards in height, and bears during twenty years; but the cotton taken from trees of that age is not adapted for spinning, but only for quilting. Such, on the contrary, as is taken from trees of twelve years old, is suitable for muslins and other manufactures of extraordinary fineness.

Great numbers of skins of goats, buffaloes, wild oxen, rhinoceroses, and other beasts are dressed here, and vessels are loaded with them, and bound to different parts of Arabia. Coverlets for beds are made of red and blue leather, extremely delicate and soft, and stitched with gold and silver thread, upon these the Majometans are accustomed to repose. Cushions also, ornamented with gold wire in the form of birds and beasts, are the manufacture of this place; and in some instances their value is so high as six marks of silver. Embroidery is here performed with more delicacy than in any other part of the world.

Source: Manuel Komroff, ed., *The Travels of Marco Polo* (Norwalk, Conn.: Heritage, 1964), pp. 408–411.

A century later, the British began the colonization of India in earnest. In 1639 they established George Town at the mouth of the river Cooums on India's southeast coast. (The settlement later would become the city of Madras.) Shortly thereafter (1661) the British gained control of Bombay Island from the Portuguese. In 1690 they established the city of Calcutta. As in Latin America and Africa, such cities had a dual purpose: the extraction of goods from the region and the subjugation of the region by military might.

Not all of the Indian cities that were dominated by the British were created by them, however. In cases where a city already existed, such as

Delhi, a second, contiguous settlement was begun, in this case New Delhi. This pattern of separation (which we encountered in dual-city African settlements such as Kano) is described by John Brush:

> . . . every city or town with pre-British origins which has grown at all during the last century shows a striking contrast between the indigenous part and the Anglicized part. . . . [The] typical urban center contains a congested old section, adjacent to which may be found *carefully planned* and often spacious sections dating from the British period (1961, pp. 58–59)

The old section (the original city) was very much like the Islamic cities we described earlier.

It contained a central market or bazaar "crowded with numberless small retail shops which dealt in foods or cloth, hardware, jewelry, and other consumer's goods" (Brush 1961, p. 59) and a surrounding residential area strictly separated into quarters with which city residents had high identification. The mix of Muslims and Hindus and the characteristic Indian caste system created a complex pattern of residential segregation:

> Brahmins and other high castes are usually in the best-built residential areas in or near the center of the old cities. Muslims are clearly separate from Hindus and are themselves divided into quasi-castes and economic classes. The laboring castes and the menial outcastes of lowest socioeconomic status occupy the poorest houses and tend to be located in the outskirts rather than the center. (Brush 1961, p. 60)

The British part of the city, on the other hand, was very Western in form, with broad rather than narrow streets, often arranged in a grid pattern, with a central trading and manufacturing area and a railroad.

The British controlled India until 1947. There was noticeable but limited urban growth during their occupation. After independence, urban population skyrocketed. For example, in 1944 India's cities contained 44 million people, almost 14 percent of the entire country's population. By 1971 those figures had risen to 109 million and 20 percent. By the year 2000, slightly more than a decade away, the estimates are for India to have 278 million city dwellers comprising 42 percent of the counry's population (Bose 1976).

As elsewhere in the Third World, this massive city growth is a product of two factors: (1) technological and health improvements that generate wealth and lengthened life and (2) unceasing inmigration by rural people, as described by Jan Morris at the beginning of this section. However, like much of the Third World, India also is experiencing tremendous rural population growth (Bose 1976). The land use techniques available in the countryside, despite improvements, simply cannot cope with the burden of local population increases. Hence, people are "pushed" off the land and "pulled" into cities scarcely better

equipped to cope with them. From this human overload have come the *bustees*, India's version of the shantytowns we have seen throughout the Third World. Conditions in the *bustees* are often horrific, including inadequate protection from the elements and no water, electricity, or other amenities.

In Calcutta these conditions are at their worst. Indeed, with regard to quality of human life, Calcutta, with its ever-increasing population (now at 11 million), may well be the worst city in the world. As Nirmal Kumar Bose has said, "Calcutta has become a metropolis without benefit of the industrial revolution that gave rise to cities in advanced nations" (1973, p. 250). Without the industrial capacity of a London or Chicago, Calcutta cannot generate the jobs and wealth necessary to take care of its population. It is literally being buried alive in people, "more than three-fourths of [whom] live in overcrowded tenement and bustee quarters" (Bose, 1973, p. 251). The poverty experienced by the bulk of the city's inhabitants—70 percent are estimated to be below the government's official poverty line—is spectacular even by Third World standards. The average income of a family of five is $34 a month! (Friedrich 1984, p. 39)

Worse, lacking even shantytown accommodations, hundreds of thousands of Calcutta's people are entirely homeless and sleep on the streets or wherever temporary shelter is available. Into open sewers is dumped all manner of human and other refuse. Transportation is sorely lacking. As one might expect, disease and suffering are omnipresent.

So poor are most people in Calcutta that many actually compete with animals as beasts of burden in an effort to survive. Bose reports, "It is [more expensive] to maintain cattle in Calcutta; one has to pay rent for stabling them, and when they die it is all loss to the owner. But a [human being] can be hired without the charge of stabling him, and when he dies he dies at his own expense" (1973, p. 253).

The short-run prognosis for Indian cities is not good. Not only can the cities not keep up with the legions streaming into them, the rural areas with few exceptions are stagnating because of an ever-

Many of India's largest cities have difficulty meeting the needs of the legions of people streaming into them. Shown here is Benares.
(© 1980 Bernard Pierre Wolff/Photo Researchers)

worsening primate-city phenomenon. Bombay is one example of many: "The Bombay metropolis acts as a magnet for the working manpower and injects directly into the region its commercial wares through wholesale and retail trading: regional stagnation and declining towns and market centers are the visible effects" (Deshpande and Bhat 1975, p. 372). But for migrants from the countryside, things are not much better in the city; the bulk of India's urbanites do not make much progress as years go by. Banerjee concludes his study of Calcutta's poorest laborers this way: "The worker survives from day to day. His future is as uncertain as that of Stone Age man" (1982, p. 185).

Thus the unsanitary conditions and the great suffering affecting much of India's urban population are not likely to disappear soon. Plans have been made by urban officials to deal with the situation, but so far they have proved less than effective. Jan Morris offers this trenchant image of the crisis:

[Setting: Calcutta's] Hooghly Bridge, still the only bridge across the river in a city of 11 million people, at the end of the day. It is a burly bridge, but in the sunset it seems almost to sag with the burden of its traffic. It is a truly tragic spectacle as the darkness falls: it looks as though a broken army is in retreat westward across the river, or a great horde of refugees is streaming they know not where, escaping some threatened catastrophe, a plague perhaps, or a holocaust. (1980b, p. 45)

The long-run picture for India's cities may (but only *may*) be somewhat brighter. Rhodes Murphy (1980, Chap. 7) has noted recently that, since independence, real progress has been made in India. For example, famine has been curtailed (if not completely eliminated), services such as education, transportation, and electricity are more widely available than ever before, some rural areas—notably the Punjab—are beginning to be quite self-sufficient, and smaller cities (under 100,000) seem less afflicted by the problems of major cities like Bombay, Delhi, Calcutta, and

Madras. And even in these seemingly desperate cities, as always people are fueled by the small but significant improvements in their material lives and by the hope for an even better future. Says Ram Kewan, a recent migrant to Bombay, when asked whether life will be better for his children: "Only God knows." But he *is* sure it will be better than anything he experienced in his rural village (Stevens 1984). Whether such trends and hopes can reverse the urban horrors remains to be seen.

China

Like India, China is a land of ancient cities. Cities such as Peking have long existed as magnificent centers of Chinese culture; however, much of that traditional culture is now gone or revamped, altered by more than 100 years of rapid change.

From the mid–nineteenth century until the end of World War II, China was subjected to foreign control, first European and then Japanese. Outside influence was greatest in the cities, particularly in the so-called treaty ports established by the Treaty of Nanking, which ended the Opium Wars in 1843. The treaty allowed European investors free reign in these cities. As might be expected, this had a transformative effect. From Shanghai to Canton, European elements rapidly established themselves. Hotels, parks, tennis courts, and residential areas emerged, all catering to non-Chinese. More important in terms of foreign control of China's economy was the European-style CBD, complete with banks, corporate headquarters, and docks equipped to handle modern Western ships. As always, the Europeans saw themselves as being on a "civilizing" mission. Said J. H. Wilson in 1887: "Progress has planted her foot firmly on the banks of [Shanghai's Wusung River] and from her safe and abiding place in the foreign city is sure, slowly but inevitably, to invade and overcome the whole vast empire."

Despite such pronouncements, European-style "progress" apparently was not much concerned with the Chinese themselves. In one of the most infamous of history's signs, placed at the entrances to Shanghai's foreign-built park separating the Chinese from the European sector, one read, "No Dogs or Chinese Allowed." Similarly, Shanghai's European merchants routinely placed unsuspecting Chinese laborers, without consulting them, on ships bound for far-off ports. So symbolic did this practice become that to be "shanghaied" became one of the most feared of any sailor's experiences.

Not surprisingly, Chinese resentment of such treatment festered for some time. Thus, when the People's Republic was established in 1949, a decided attempt was made by Mao Tse-Tung and his followers to eradicate all aspects of European influence and Western privilege from China's cities. Moreover, believing cities by their very nature to be destructive of revolutionary ideals, Mao encouraged China's citizens to remain in the rural areas or their villages and transform their country from there.

In this he was singularly unsuccessful. Despite an antiurban bias, China's urban population has grown markedly since 1949. Although reliable data are scanty, estimates suggest that while only 11 percent of the Chinese population was urban in 1950, more than one quarter is now (Davis 1969). Aware that overurbanization could undermine the goals of the revolution, the Chinese used their pervasive and highly regimented political system to resettle large numbers of people into rural areas or provincial urban areas. Some estimates suggest that this movement, undertaken largely in the 1970s, affected some 25 million people.

Despite these efforts the urban tide remains undiminished. Nine hundred miles from Beijing, the country's capital, is Chongqing, a city that has grown with such rapidity that it is now the world's largest, at 14 million people. (Greater Mexico City, currently around 18 million, is larger overall, but its central-city area is estimated to be a little more than 11 million.) Not surprisingly, Chongqing has major problems, not the least of which is woefully inadequate transportation. Says Chen Zhihui, the vice president of the city's planning commission: "There are not enough trucks, cars, trains, or taxis. We have to plan to import more." In addition, hotel space is insufficient and air transportation in and out of the city is chancy at best (Davidson 1985, p. 29).

Still, in all cities there have been notable successes. Modern Chinese cities are clean and safe and no one seems to starve. The standard of living is improving steadily, if slowly. The unique Chinese venture into urban communes seems to be doing well (Sidel 1974). All this is in sharp contrast to the situation in the Third World.

Alas, as already indicated, there are severe problems. China lacks the industrial base to generate wealth quickly, and what industry it has still lags behind world standards after years of effort. The cities continue to grow. The reason is not hard to find: the gap between rural and urban wealth is great. Whatever privation the urban Chinese suffer, it is less than their rural counterparts. Nevertheless, as Murphy reports, modern Chinese "urban life is far from easy, affluent, or gracious for almost everyone. Crowding is excessive, housing and basic services seriously inadequate, and work is hard, long, and often tedious" (1980, pp. 146–147).

Whatever China's urban successes may be (it has no Calcutta, for example), Murphy (1980, Chap. 7) argues that, on the whole, the country is not that much better off than modern India. Both have advanced in the more than 30 years since foreign control ended, yet both still are incredibly poor and face severe long-term difficulties.

The main culprit seems to be population growth. Like India, China is experiencing the same demographic transition that we first encountered in Latin America. It is adding people to its urban and rural population faster than it can produce the goods and services necessary to care for them adequately.

In response to this doleful situation, China's party chairman, Deng Xiao-ping, has introduced major reforms. He has repudiated the tight control of Mao's policies and begun to allow China's cities to introduce private enterprise. Such a policy was first successful on China's farms and, encouraged by the enthusiasm generated by such liberalization, Deng is giving urban dwellers the chance to sell their surplus produce for a profit (Wren 1984a; 1984b; Iyer 1984). In the Chinese capital of Beijing in the fall of 1984, author Spates found the city alive with hope that the new plan would be successful. People continually de-

scribed the old system as restrictive, providing no way for the population to express their talents and energies.

Perhaps Deng's most radical innovation is the establishment of so-called "Special Economic Zones." One example is the new city of Xiamen in southern China. Xiamen is so liberalized from the old policies that it seems almost capitalist. The city is a free-trade zone where China's manufacturers can wheel and deal with their Western counterparts without the restrictiveness that characterized the Mao regime (Lu 1984).

Deng's intent is clear. China has made decided progress since the Communist takeover of 1949, but continues to lag far behind the West in productivity. Hence, in an experiment designed to help Chinese cities "catch up quick," Deng is taking the reigns off. He has stated that communism will still be the main orientation of China but that controlled private enterprise is no threat to the goals of the revolution. China, he says, can be one country with two systems (*China Daily*, Oct. 17, 1984: p. 1).

Once again, massive Chongqing serves as an example. The Beijing government has given the city free rein to make deals with foreign companies and has encouraged Chongqing's citizens to use their ingenuity to find ways to make the city more productive. One such citizen is Kang Gomin, a 36-year-old who opened a successful noodle shop near a market where over 1,300 farmers sell their produce. He got the idea, he said, when he realized that the people who sold their goods at the market could not go home for lunch. His efforts were so successful, he shortly opened another shop. This one too was a success. Quite simply, Kang Gomin is getting *rich*, something just not possible in the China of only a few years ago (Davidson 1985).

"If this is Marxism, I must reread Marx," a Russian visitor to the city of Guangzhou (formerly Canton) is said to have remarked recently. Like Chongqing, Guangzhou is alive with Deng's new spirit of "free enterprise." In 1978 the city had *no* private businesses. By 1985 it had an estimated 35,000. In 1978 its largest department store carried about 6,000 varieties of goods. In 1985 it had more than 30,000.

With glittering window displays of cosmetics and fashions and video appliances, major streets like Dongfanglu look more like Nathan Road in Hong Kong than anything previously seen in China. Down side-streets block after block is lined with private stalls selling clothes, stir-fried food and household commodities. [The competition] has cut the profits of the state stores, but Mr. Wang [director of the city reform office] welcomes it.

"The state stores were too lazy," he said. "With the competition, they're getting better day by day." (Burns 1985)

Along with Guangzhou's surging economic energies, however, have come some elements that worry hard-line Maoist conservatives. These "evil winds," as the Maoists call them, include open gambling, pool halls, prostitution, a thriving smuggling operation that deals in China's antiquities, and crime (Burns 1985).

The situation is volatile and by no means is Deng's policy solidly entrenched. Whether his attempt at reforming Chinese cities will be successful in pulling them up by their bootstraps in the next few years is open to much question. Even if significant economic progress is made, will the price be too great? Will China's cities exchange one "evil" for another, gaining wealth at the expense of a citizenry divided against itself—rich against poor, law-abiding against law-breaking— the very divisions the Communist revolution was fought to eliminate? Only time will tell.

Hong Kong

The same problems afflict Hong Kong, the British crown colony on China's coast. Consisting of the only remaining piece of foreign-controlled real estate on the mainland and several islands, the small (403 square miles) trade and manufacturing center has an estimated 5.2 million people. It has had a growth rate of nearly 1 million people a decade since 1950 (Leeming 1977, p. 5), which only recently has shown signs of abating. The growth is caused by refugees from mainland China (over 140,000 in 1979 through 1980) and by natural population increase.

Not surprisingly, overcrowding is omnipresent. Shantytowns, which have virtually disappeared from the People's Republic, house some 15 percent of the city's population, despite determined efforts to provide public housing. Other, particularly older, housing is bursting at the seams. Even the port itself has become a kind of slum, housing hundreds of thousands of the city's poor on Chinese-style boats called junks. In some areas one can literally walk across much of the harbor by simply stepping from one moored junk to another.

Desperate, the Hong Kong government and the people themselves have tried to halt the refugee inflow. Until 1980 migrants who were able to reach the colony were allowed to stay. No more; acceptance has been replaced with icy rejection and deportation.

Cold and starving, a 21-year-old commune worker from China sneaked into town aboard a rickety boat, hoping to find refuge with her relatives. Instead of a joyful welcome, she was given only a hot meal and commands to get out.

A skilled mechanic from Canton took a different route, swimming through shark-infested waters to reach this British colony, his dangerous journey made bearable by expectations of plentiful work and good money.

Desperate and weary after wandering the city for days without finding anyone willing to employ him, he finally walked up to a police officer and asked to be sent back to China. (*Finger Lakes Times*, April 20, 1981)

Even with this immigration policy, Hong Kong's density problems are not likely to abate for some time. Indeed, so great is the space problem that the city's roofs have become among its most prized possessions, as illustrated by Box 10-2.

On one level Hong Kong has been and continues to be very successful. It has become the most important trade port other than Shanghai on the China coast and has generated an industrial machine the envy of much of the world, replacing a number of other major manufacturing points. Ninety percent of its output is exported. Thus, wages have risen, increasing the standard of living of the population as a whole (Leeming 1977).

On another level, however, Hong Kong has problems well beyond density. Many of the city's migrants are extremely poor, and an adequate

BOX 10-2
Hong Kong: Up on the Roof

The roof-tops were a civilisation for themselves, a breath-taking theatre of survival against the raging of the city. Within their barbed-wire compounds, sweat-shops turned out anoraks, religious services were held, mah-jong was played, and fortunetellers burned joss and consulted huge brown volumes. Ahead . . . lay a formal garden made of smuggled earth. Below, three old women fattened chow puppies for the pot. There were schools for dancing, reading, ballet, recreation, and combat; there were schools in culture and the wonders of Mao, and this morning . . . an old man completed his long rigmarole of calisthenics before opening the tiny folding chair, where he performed his daily reading of the great man's Thoughts.

The wealthier poor, if they had no roof, built themselves giddy crow's-nests, two feet by eight, on home-made cantilevers driven into their drawing-room floors.

Source: John Le Carré, *The Honourable Schoolboy* (New York: Bantam, 1978), pp. 115–116.

number of jobs to absorb them is not on the immediate horizon. Perhaps as a result, crime is rampant and growing. Robbery, often accompanied by violence, is commonplace; youth gangs terrorize many of the city's communities; and public and private corruption is rife. If one is not careful to shop in the government-controlled shops, one can easily be sold counterfeit or damaged goods. And an unwary shopper later may find in his package a cheaper item than the one he thought he had bought.

But what the future holds for this vibrant port is unclear. Britain's lease on Hong Kong runs out in 1997, and Communist Chinese government officials clearly stated that they were not about to renew the lease—something they regarded as a last vestige of imperialism. Negotiations between China and Britain were held during 1983 and 1984. In October 1984 the British agreed to surrender their claims to the colony; in return, the Communists guaranteed to maintain Hong Kong's economic system—that is, its free-port status and capitalist orientation—for 50 years.

While this solves the basic problem of who will own Hong Kong after 1997, the question of what will actually happen after the transfer of title takes place remains unanswered. Such uncertainty has made the colony's people—especially its capitalist entrepreneurs—nervous. On the positive side, the residents of Hong Kong are encouraged by China's move toward capitalistic policies in general and, specifically, by the establishment of "Special Economic Zones" such as Xiamen, obviously modeled on Hong Kong. In addition, they are buoyed by the fact that China is in great need of the income that a free port like Hong Kong can generate in trade with the West. On the negative side, however, no one is sure the Chinese will honor their agreement. After all, treaties have been broken in the past. Last and most worrisome, will China's move toward private enterprise last? Chairman Deng is in his eighties and, as we have already suggested, many of Mao's old supporters in China's Communist party think Deng is selling the revolution short. If he cannot consolidate his power base before he dies or steps down, it is possible that this Maoist element will come to power in China once more and Hong Kong as we know it today will become a thing of the past (Sancton 1984).

Southeast Asia: Familiar Themes

Unlike the subcontinents of India and China, Southeast Asia has little tradition of large indigenous cities. Most of its urban areas are the product of Chinese or European influence within the past few centuries. To a greater or lesser degree, the principal cities of the region—Rangoon (Burma), Bangkok (Thailand), Ho Chi Minh City (formerly Saigon, Vietnam), Manila (Philippines), Jakarta (Indonesia), and Singapore (Republic of Singapore)—reflect the themes we have encountered throughout Asia. A few portraits will illustrate.

Singapore. Like Hong Kong, Singapore is a type of city-state. Situated at the southern extremity of the Malay Peninsula, it is the largest port in the region and the fourth largest in the world. Despite a dearth of natural resources, it has prospered economically.

Created in 1819 by the British East India Company, it developed as a center of east-west trade, a status that it maintained following its independence from Britain in 1959. In 1963 the city became part of the Federation of Malaysia. Two years later, ethnic tensions between Malayans (dominant in the Federation) and Chinese (dominant in the city) caused Singapore to become an independent republic. Most recently, the city's success has been made possible by increasing industrialization. Between 1961 and 1971 the number of industrial firms rose from 560 to 1,880, the industrially employed work force from 27,000 to 148,000, and the value of trade goods jumped from under $1 billion to over $7 billion.

In 1981 the city had a population of approximately 2.5 million, about 75 percent Chinese, 15 percent Malayans, and 7 percent Indian. Eighty-five percent of these people live in the city itself, on 28 square miles of land. Density is thus a problem. As population increased throughout this century, shantytowns and squatter settlements began to appear on Singapore's periphery. To alleviate the situation, the government took a novel, if heavy-handed, approach: it ripped up old neighborhoods, constructed thousands of high-rise apartment buildings, and literally forced the city's population into them. The process has transformed an old Asian city into one with a modern guise. From a distance, today's Singapore appears very Western, with a clearly recognizable downtown and apartment high rises almost as far as the eye can see. The high rises have absorbed nearly two-thirds of the city's population at present, and each group of buildings boasts its own school, parking lot, community center, and social facilities center.

On the other hand, the high rises have had their costs. Old neighborhood units were destroyed wantonly by the renewal process, peoples of strikingly different backgrounds have been thrown rapidly together, and the physical size of the high rises themselves has also been disruptive. Living on the twelfth floor, for example, one cannot easily supervise children playing below; living with thousands of others in the same building, separated by floors and doors, neighbors do not readily share a community feeling (Wee 1972).

Yet, there is reason for significant optimism. Singapore's economy continues to thrive, it is still a vital center of East-West trade, and, perhaps most important, the city has been able to bring its population growth almost under control. With a growth rate of about 1.2 percent a year, it falls far behind other Third World cities (whose rates of increase often exceed 10 percent). This last success has been the product of an all-out attack: Singapore's government has made abortions and contraceptives readily available, has decreased taxes for families with fewer children, has increased educational and housing benefits for small families, and has raised hospital costs for families with too many children (each additional child costs more to have).

All of this progress has come at a price: Singapore's highly autocratic government. So strong has been the hold of Prime Minister Lee Kuan Yew's People's Action Party in the past two and a half decades that the Republic's commitment to "democracy" has often seemed a cruel joke. Systematically the government has suppressed political opposition and squelched any reporting in the press deemed "misrepresentational." But there is a crack in the ice. In early 1985 Prime Minister Lee called an election prior to stepping down after one more term in office. The PAP actually lost two of the city-state's 81 parliament seats. This was a stunning defeat for Lee, and in the aftermath, vocal opposition from the two newly elected non-PAP parliamentarians, the press, and people on the street was rife (Crossette 1985). Whether this means a significant change in Singapore's future only time will tell.

Jarkarta. Indonesia won independence after World War II, ending three centuries of colonial influence. Before it was occupied by the Japanese during the war, it had been under Dutch control since 1618.

Indonesia has valuable resources, including large oil reserves, but these have paid small dividends for the majority of the country's citizens. Business and industry are controlled by the few, and a rapidly increasing rural and urban population has resulted in cities racked with overpopulation and underemployment.

CITYSCAPE 10-2
Ibu Bud: A Jakarta Street Trader

Jakarta has thousands of small food traders, all of them fighting for survival. . . . Ibu Bud is but one of these food sellers and in many ways an atypical one. She survived and thrived where others became destitute. This . . . conveys something of the vitality of a remarkable woman and gives some insight into the problems facing the poor people of Jakarta.

Ibu Bud provided an unusual service. No other food seller had the audacity to sell where she set up her stall each night. It was on one of Jakarta's main roads near a complex of army and government offices. And it was there late one evening—for she was a night trader—that I bought a hot lemon juice and subsequently returned again and again until I became a regular customer. I am sure I returned for the same reason as many of her other customers. She sold good food cheaply at a place and time when it was wanted.

To be precise she was breaking the law, for hawkers were not allowed to trade where she did. But in Indonesia, as elsewhere, one must distinguish between what is legal and what is permissible— and her activities were evidently permissible. For Bud that was all that mattered. . . .

Ibu Bud had a river-side house, less than five minutes' walk from a road lined by modern buildings, banks and hotels. . . . Bud's house, like her food stall, was illegally situated. . . . But there was no prospect of Ibu Bud moving to legal ground. How could she compete with the businesses, embas-

sies and the rich who all vie for what little land is available? . . .

Each morning at eight from Monday to Saturday Bud set off for market. She was the center of the household, handled all the money, did all the buying of raw materials and selling of food. Like most Indonesians she shopped daily, for she lacked the money to buy for more than a day at a time and had neither the storage space nor refrigeration required. . . .

Cooking began when Bud returned with the food from the market. The chickens were slaughtered and plucked, the bananas peeled, the vegetables diced and the rice cooked. . . . By five in the afternoon the food was ready. It was neatly packed into saucepans and bamboo baskets or wrapped in cloth and then carried over the rickety bridge to Bud's mobile stall. . . . From five to ten in the evening she traded in [a] side street where she was less likely to encounter difficulties with the authorities. Experience had taught her that by 10 P.M. it was safe to venture into a more important thoroughfare. . . .

. . . She was insistent that food be served politely and elegantly and reprimanded any of her assistants who failed to keep the standards she set. . . . She tried to keep her prices stable, for she feared variation would drive her customers away. As the cost of raw materials fluctuated she adjusted the size of the portion she served. She would fill a plate with rice at the expense of the quantity of the vegetables or mix Indone-

sian rice with a cheaper but less tasteful American variety. She did this so cunningly that few of her customers noticed. . . .

The trading usually continued until three or four in the morning, by which time most of the perishable food had been sold. Then the stall had to be cleaned and pushed home and the valuable pots and pans, kerosene stoves, cigarettes and beer carried back across the rickety bridge into Ibu Bud's house. . . .

Her success came only with great effort. She worked eighteen or nineteen hours a day six days a week. . . . She knew her survival depended as much on good luck as hard work. Perhaps one day someone will forget to warn her [of a crackdown on traders] and she will lose everything. . . .

Even if she avoids such a catastrophe . . . her prospects look grim. She will find it increasingly hard to compete with shops as her cheap source of supply, the "poor man's markets," are progressively eliminated. Her patrons are fickle. If, through illness, Bud fails to appear for more than a few days another trader could rapidly take her place and be at least as eager to please Bud's former patrons.

Yet for all this Bud feels more prosperous than she has ever been. . . .

Source: Lea Jellinek, "The Life of a Jakarta Street Trader," in Janet Abu-Lughod and Richard Hag, Jr., eds., *Third World Urbanization* (Chicago: Maaroufa, 1977), pp. 244–256.

Until the usurpation of the title by Singapore in the nineteenth century, the Indonesian capital, Jakarta, was unquestionably the most important city in Southeast Asia. Today, it is a primate city par excellence, replete with shantytowns, terrible living conditions, and massive poverty. Its population in 1930 was 533,000; now it is over 7 million and there is little relief in sight. By the year 2005, the city is expected to have over 17 million people (Crossette 1986). All attempts at population control (such as making city residents carry identification cards) have failed.

People migrate to Jakarta for the same reasons they trek to all cities: they want a better life. Most are doomed to disappointment. A few struggle to limited success. One such is Ibu Bud, profiled in Cityscape 10-2. Note the similarities between her life and that of Petrona Mamani, the woman who struggled to make a go of it in La Paz, Bolivia, half a world away (Chapter 8).

Bangkok. Jakarta, unlike Singapore, is relatively typical of Southeast Asia's cities. Also typical is Bangkok, the capital of Thailand, a country never colonized. Currently with a population close to 5.5 million, the city has more people than all 118 other Thai municipal areas combined. It is also over 33 times as large as the country's second largest city, making Bangkok the premier primate city of the world (Thomlinson 1972).

The overdominance that such primacy causes in Thai affairs can be illustrated by a few figures. In the early 1970s Bangkok contained 77 percent of the nation's telephones and half its cars, consumed 82 percent of its electricity, held 72 percent of all commercial bank deposits, and generated 65 percent of its construction (Romm 1972, p. 7). All automobile roads, railroads, and airplane routes converge on the city (so much so that to go from one place to another you have to go through Bangkok, even if it is out of your way); most Thai universities are in Bangkok, as are all the country's television stations; the city has about 20 daily newspapers (a few other cities have one); and it is the seat of the federal government (Thomlinson 1972).

All these advantages continue to draw people to the city by the millions, strapping its meager resources still further. A massive "riverboat culture," much like that in Hong Kong, houses many of the city's poor. If the current growth continues, the city will contain an estimated 10 million people by 1990 (Yeung 1976). If so, the quality of urban life, already in severe decline, will have nowhere to go but down, making Ralph Thomlinson's description of the current city, given in Box 10-3, seem optimistic by contrast.

BOX 10-3
Bangkok: Primacy Beyond Reason

Bangkok's . . . megalomaniac rate of metropolitan growth . . . must be recognized as a potential hazard of the first magnitude. Enlargement of the already-insufficient consumer services in time to meet the strains imposed by doubling the population in a decade may demand greater technical skill and political initiative than municipal officials can call forth. . . .

Greater Bangkok [is not] a pleasant city in which to live. . . . [T]raffic jams choke daily transportation, water shortages and stoppages develop frequently during the dry season, electricity failures black out sections of the city, both the air and the water are polluted, the housing industry is unable to provide enough satisfactory homes for the influx of migrants. . . .

Source: Ralph Thomlinson, "Bangkok: 'Beau Ideal' of a Primate City," *Population Review*, 16 (1972), p. 37.

Summary. Southeast Asia remains one of the least urbanized areas of the world (see Table 1-1), yet its urban growth rate is incredible. Between 1950 and 1970 Jakarta, Kuala Lumpur (Malaysia), and Hanoi (Vietnam) tripled their populations. In the same period Surabaja (Indonesia), Rangoon, Manila, and Ho Chi Minh City doubled theirs (Yeung 1976, p. 285). This pattern of overurbanization is not likely to stop. Natural population increase and in-migration will be unceasing for the foreseeable future. As Norton Ginsburg has written of Southeast Asia, apparently nothing

> will keep them down on the farm—not better roads, not higher literacy, not improved sanitation, not farmers' cooperatives, not even higher incomes or other consequences of governmental welfare policies. All of these will stimulate, rather than retard, migration. (1972, p. 277)

Only Singapore seems an exception, both in terms of population growth and economic self-sufficiency. But this exceptional status can be fairly easily explained: Singapore is a city-state, a very small area (238 square miles) located at the end of the Malay Peninsula. It draws population only from its own very limited hinterland. In all other cases primate cities cannot keep up with staggering growth and cannot meet obvious needs. Unlike Singapore, they draw population from the whole geographical spans of their countries. For example, people from all over Thailand (almost 200,000 square miles) flock to Bangkok. As a result, overurbanization is rampant. There aren't enough jobs; there aren't enough services. This condition of urban growth without commensurate expansion of economic opportunity and services has been called "static expansion" (Wertheim 1964, pp. 216–217). This is typical of Southeast Asia and the Third World generally.

With this in mind, we now turn to Japan, a nation that provides a sharp contrast to the rest of Asia.

Japan

Japan is about the size of Montana, and its population has more than tripled in 100 years. By 1980, with a population close to 115 million, Japan had become the most densely populated country in the world (Vogel 1979). By 2000, the population is expected to reach 135 million (Kuroda 1976). About 76 percent of the present population is urban, and the Tokyo-Yokohama urban complex, one of the world's largest, contains nearly 15 million people. But that is only part of the story. If one boards a westbound train in Toyko, one can go all the way to Shimonoseki on the far tip of Honshu island, over 400 miles away, and never completely leave an urban setting!

The urban roots of the country extend back at least to the eighth century A.D., when a series of provincial capitals was established by ruling elites. These capitals were protected by a warrior caste (the samurai) and were weakly linked to an emperor living in the capital city of Kyoto (Yazaki 1973, pp. 141–142). Within this feudal structure, local elites kept the citizenry in subjugation while they warred with each other for control of various regions over the next few centuries.

At the end of the sixteenth century, a samurai named Ieyasu emerged victorious over the warring elements. The emperor named Ieyasu shogun (leader and protector of Japan), and Ieyasu established his capital at the city of Edo (now Tokyo).

Ieyasu and his successors set about reorganizing the administrative system of Japan, putting greater emphasis on cities. Hall (1979, p. 221) reports that by the eighteenth century Edo had a population of nearly 1.5 million, making it the largest city in the world (London at the time had a population of 900,000). Osaka and Kyoto had populations of over half a million (Yazaki 1973, p. 144).

Over the centuries the growth of Japanese cities produced, as it had in Europe and North America, a wealthy and powerful middle class. By the mid-1800s, these merchants had come to control the purse strings of the country and the power of the shogun had declined considerably. When America's Commodore Perry and various European interests (British, French, Russian, Dutch) arrived in the 1850s, intent on opening Japan to Western trade, the shogun had little power to resist.

Amid cries for revolution, the shogun stepped down in 1868. The new 16-year-old emperor, Meiji, urged his country to end centuries of economic isolation and become a modern nation strong enough to resist attempts at colonization. The Japanese responded. In less than half a century, Japan became a world power economically, technologically, and militarily. People flocked to the cities, which began to transform themselves. This change is expressed in the following passage from an 1881 guide book to Tokyo:

A great change has taken place since 1868 in the outward appearance of many parts of the city which were formerly covered with the *ya-shiki* or mansions of the territorial nobility. Many of these have been pulled down to make room for new official buildings. At the same time the disappearance of the two-sworded men [samurai], the displacement of the palanquin [an enclosed carriage, carried by people] by the *jin-riki-sha*, the adoption of foreign dress . . . and the European style of wearing the hair, now almost universal, have robbed the streets of the picturesque aspect which was formerly so great an attraction to the foreign visitor. (Quoted in Maraini 1976, p. 84)

Industrialization proceeded throughout the twentieth century. Japan's lack of the natural resources needed to run its industrial machine, as well as its own imperialistic ambitions, led the country into foreign expansion and finally into the disaster of World War II.

As has happened so often in the history of cities, however, the war produced an unforeseen effect. By destroying many of the nation's urban areas, it necessitated rebuilding most of the industrial system from the ground up. By the early 1960s Japan was outfitted with completely new and efficient production machinery. This proved an incredible advantage in capturing world markets.

The war loss also cast doubt on the old way of doing things. Earlier patterns of work—its mandated link to family, for example—no longer seemed efficient. People streamed into Japan's cities in huge numbers, enticed by employment opportunities and the chance for upward mobility that a more open system promised.

The economic success of contemporary Japanese cities is remarkable. In the 1950s Americans looked with disdain on Japanese products. They were thought to be cheaply made and prone to breakage. Today, the same critics shun American products in favor of Japanese watches, TVs, stereos, radios, cars, motorcycles, and cameras. Fosco Maraini suggests that one of the reasons for Japan's success lies in its unique combination of the spirit of free enterprise with a collective orientation.

> Industrial enterprise, whether in the small workshop or gigantic factory, is typical of Tokyo, something deeply engrained in the character of the *Edokko*, the true Tokyoite. An *Edokko* likes to start in business on his own, adventurously, perhaps opening a small workshop in his backyard, helped at first by his immediate family and later taking on additional employees who become no less members of his "family." . . . Tokyo . . . has many thousands of [such] small firms with only a [few] employees, and such businesses continue to make an extremely important contribution to the national economy.
>
> The other, more familiar, side of Tokyo industry is the larger scale *kaisha*. The dictionary defines

kaisha as a company, corporation, firm or concern, but it is really much more than that. It is a whole way of life. Whereas a Western company "engages" an employee, a *kaisha* "envelops" him. The individual gives his *kaisha* a life of devotion in exchange for life-long security. . . . The system derives from [a combination of] both the feudal *han* (clan) and from the family unit, the *ie* (house). . . . A good employer is expected to have the responsible attitude of a good parent—a kind of "uncle" figure who advises his workers on their personal problems, helps them with their housing arrangements. . . . In return, the employee gives maximum loyalty and effort, takes the attitude of a good team player that does not wish to let his side down. (1976, pp. 157–159)

To this portrait Richard Meier and J. M. Richards would add the crucial role that the Japanese city itself has played in facilitating such interactions. Meier suggests that "the cities of Japan, particularly Tokyo, [have] made the difference between rapid growth and ordinary growth." Cities, he says, "nurture institutions, public, private, cooperative, and hybrid," and Japanese cities have been particularly good at facilitating such interactions (1972, p. 559). Richards suggests that the reason for this facilitation lies in the way Japanese view their cities—as places for experimentation and freedom within a framework of basic restraints. Only such a framework, he contends, can allow the vitality and spontaneity necessary for growth and life satisfaction and keep humane "social priorities" as a central concern (1972, pp. 590–594).

With such growth, however, as we might expect, have come some problems. Housing is very expensive in Japanese cities, and clean water, adequate sanitation, and effective public transportation are not available to many city residents. The country is also coping with a severe pollution problem brought on by its rapid industrial development amidst a densely packed population. Perhaps more worrisome, with economic success have come signs of a breakdown of traditional Japanese decorum, especially in public. The subways of Tokyo are often an exercise in pushing, shoving, and general rudeness (Haberman 1984); muggings and assaults are on the rise

(Haberman 1985); and many urban Japanese youth are quite openly antiwork and pro-hedonism (Smolowe 1984).

Even with these difficulties, the Japanese enjoy a standard of living comparable to many other highly industrialized nations. They have established an exemplary health care system and Japanese life expectancy (74 years) is among the world's longest. They have made great gains in reducing crime, unemployment, and slums, have set the strictest air pollution standards in the world and, perhaps most importantly, have controlled their population growth (Vogel 1979). The success of the Japanese in establishing a high-quality urban life is also impressive to Westerners who "express amazement at the tidiness of urban facilities, the reliability of public transportation, the courtesy of commercial personnel, the affluence of department stores, [and] the quality of restaurants" (Vogel 1979, p. 22).

Thus, the cities and urban life of Japan stand in marked distinction to most of Asia. Their familiar neon lights and thriving central business districts place Japanese cities solidly in the frame of the industrial nation. Indeed, the first-time visitor to Japan, even a visitor from the United States or western Europe, is bedazzled: Tokyo's Ginza district alight at night makes New York's Great White Way and London's Piccadilly Circus seem tawdry in comparison. In Asia, only Hong Kong and Singapore provide partial parallels.

What makes Japan such an exception to the overurbanization-underdevelopment pattern so common elsewhere in the non-industrial world? At least four factors seem crucial. First, Japan was never colonized. It was thus spared the social indignities and exploitation-oriented urban economy characteristic of so many other regions.

Second, without colonization, it was able to generate, maintain, and revitalize numerous urban centers (controlled by different warlords) over the centuries. Although Tokyo-Yokohama is a major primate city, it is only twice the size of the Osaka-Kobe-Kyoto complex (Hall 1979, p. 5), and other vital urban centers (Hiroshima, Nagasaki, for example) are found throughout Japan. All have been able to industrialize effectively,

spreading wealth and opportunity throughout the country. This has kept "overload" on a single city to a minimum.

Third, as already mentioned, there is encouragement of and opportunity for individual and collective advancement within the Japanese social structure. Although not everyone is rich, through hard work most Japanese can better their lives economically and socially. This is not the case in urban areas and countries still regulated by caste (India, for example) or by rigid ethnic boundaries. Nor do elites so tightly control access to the higher reaches of the status system that the less fortunate can never hope to better their situation.

Finally, fourth, despite major population increases, Japan is in possession of a much more favorable demographic pattern than the rest of the world. It has moved even closer to zero population growth by continuing publicity campaigns and widespread dissemination of birth-control information. Because of this, Japan has been able to provide jobs and keep the lid on the massive shortage and pollution problems that bedevil many other cities throughout the world.

In the next section we shall take up these factors in more detail as we pull together the main issues raised in this chapter, as well as Chapters 8 and 9, concerning non-industrial cities.

World Urbanization in Perspective

We have now completed our examination of cities and urban life in those areas in which most of the world's urban population lives. Perhaps the first lesson of this comparison is that these cities vary enormously from the Western cities with which we are most familiar. The diversity of history, cultural traditions, religion, and politics account for these differences. Thus, Islamic cities of the Middle East are in many respects radically unlike cities of the United States. Equally important, the cities of the non-industrial world—Latin America, Africa, the Middle East, and Asia—vary tremendously among themselves. No brief formula can ever hope to grasp the diversities that exist among La Paz, Kano, Calcutta, and Tokyo.

While cities everywhere seem to be relatively large, dense agglomerations of socially heterogeneous people characterized by a complex division of labor and a multifaceted set of interactions and experiences, little more can be said about their universal characteristics. Beyond this, we must *examine cities in their cultural and historical context* (see the conclusion of Chapter 7). Each of the cities covered in these last three chapters is working out its own version of the urban story; nevertheless, there are a few common themes that emerge when these areas of the world are compared.

Common Elements

Colonization, Economic Underdevelopment, and Political Instability. With the exception of some parts of the Middle East, Southeast Asia, and Japan, all of the regions covered in Part 4, "World Urbanization," have been colonized. Although the specifics of such colonial control varied (it was longer in Latin America than Africa; it destroyed indigenous culture more thoroughly in Latin America than in Asia), its legacy has been much the same.

One consequence is that colonization left behind an urban system with an underdeveloped economy. As we have seen, it was a process that in most instances was established for the benefit of a ruling elite and the citizenry of the mother country. Most colonial cities specialized in exports and showed little interest in generating wealth or opportunities for the bulk of the local population or in developing industrial capabilities. Thus, when independence came, colonial countries found their cities well behind Western cities in competitive advantage and without the technical know-how or capability to catch up. Despite efforts, most are still unable to provide enough jobs or wealth for their populations.

Colonization also left political instability in its wake in many areas of the non-industrial world. The leadership vacuum left by departing elites left rule of the country either to a foreign-trained native elite or simply "up for grabs" between competing factions. Foreign-trained elites (as in much of Latin America) have typically recreated the limited-opportunity social structure of colonial days—advantageous to the few, difficult for the many. Competing-factions (in much of Africa) have typically generated continued violence and unrest in urban areas. All these conditions have further retarded economic growth. What business corporation wants to invest heavily in a city where a coup may cause the loss or nationalization of the entire investment?

Even in areas of the non-industrial world that never were colonized directly, economic underdevelopment remains the rule rather than the exception. In non-colonial Southeast Asia (Thailand, for example), urban industrial capacities lag far behind those of the West primarily because there is no tradition of vital indigenous cities and because of disadvantageous export-oriented trade agreements with Western countries. In the non-colonial Middle East, the situation is much the same. Although indigenous cities have long existed, the insular policies of Islam and foreign domination of trade in the last century have formed cities unable to provide for the needs of their growing populations. (This situation may change as oil money continues to pour into the region.)

The only other exceptions to this pattern are Singapore, Hong Kong, and Japan. Singapore, via rigid politics, has been able to control its population growth and maintain a slow but steadily growing standard of living. Hong Kong, still a British colony, has been able to accomplish the latter goal (though not for all of its people by any means) but not the former. Japan has done both. This makes Japan unique among the countries discussed in Part 4. Yet Japan's history is markedly different: with a tradition of vital indigenous cities, no colonization, strong commitment to industrialization a century ago, a basically stable political system, and a social structure flexible enough to allow most of its people the chance to improve their standard of living.

Once Again: Demographic Transition. In decades past, social scientists debated whether economic growth was preferable to the preservation

TABLE 10-1

World Population, Population Growth Rate, Percent Urban, and Urban Population Growth Rate by Major Geographical Area

Area	Population 1985[1]	Growth Rate 1975–80 (% per year)[2]	Percent Urban 1980[3]	Urban Growth Rate 1970–80 (% per year)[4]
World	4,900,000,000[5]	1.7	41	2.8
North America	254,000,000	0.7	72	2.2
Europe	406,000,000	0.4	71	1.2
USSR	268,000,000	0.8	62	1.8
Latin America	366,000,000	2.3	67	3.4
Africa	406,000,000	2.9	27	4.6
Asia	2,608,000,000	1.8	28	3.4
Oceania	23,000,000	1.3	73	2.2

Sources: [1]*U.N. Demographic Yearbook 1985*
[2]*U.N. Demographic Yearbook 1985*
[3]*World Bank Atlas* (1985)
[4]*World Bank World Development Report* (1985)
[5]Werner Fornos, "Growth of Cities Is Major Crisis," *Popline* 8 (March 1986), p. 8.

of local urban traditions. People taking the latter position usually argued, quite convincingly, that "creeping Westernization" by way of industrialization and foreign-oriented trade was rapidly obliterating ancient urban traditions, valuable not only to their peoples but to the world as examples of the alternative forms that the urban process could take.

Although the preservation argument has lost none of its appeal today, the simple fact is that most cities in the non-industrial world are being inundated with so many people that they cannot hope to provide adequately for their populations without major advances in economic vitality and technological efficiency. Already—as we have seen perhaps most dramatically in Calcutta—millions upon millions of the world's urban dwellers are suffering tremendous deprivation. As Daniel Vining has succinctly stated, "Some of the large cities in developing nations are so crowded and polluted that it appears they have reached the limit of the carrying capacity of their environment" (1985, p. 42).

Once again, the city is literally transforming our world, as it has twice before. In Chapter 2 we spoke of the first and second urban revolutions—the first occurred when people moved into cities

in large numbers for the first time, approximately from 8000 to 2000 B.C.; the second occurred during the capitalist and industrial revolutions, which began around A.D. 1700 and continued through the first half of this century. This second urban revolution was responsible for a demographic transition, an unprecedented growth in population, made possible by the city's ability to provide greater income, technological efficiency, and health care than rural areas. Now, once again, the city is fostering a demographic transition, only this time with two differences: (1) the greatest population growth is not in the First (capitalist) and Second (communist) worlds but in the Third World, and (2) the magnitude of the change makes the demographic transition of the 1700–1950 period look meager by comparison. This is the *third* urban revolution, which we spoke of at the beginning of this chapter. No one ever expected the kind of growth we are seeing now.

Table 10-1 tells the tale. It indicates that population (column 1) continues to grow throughout the world's regions. Note, however, where the world population growth rates (column 2) are most pronounced: in Latin America (2.3%), Africa (2.9%), and Asia (1.8%)—the Middle East is

TABLE 10-2
The World's Ten Largest Urban Areas, 1981 and 2000

1981		2000*	
Urban Area	Population	Urban Area	Population
New York	16,485,000	Mexico City	31,616,000
Tokyo	14,377,000	Tokyo	26,128,000
Mexico City	13,993,000	Sao Paulo	26,045,000
Los Angeles	10,605,000	New York	22,212,000
Shanghai	10,000,000	Calcutta	19,663,000
Buenos Aires	9,749,000	Rio de Janeiro	19,383,000
Paris	8,547,000	Shanghai	19,155,000
Moscow	8,011,000	Bombay	19,065,000
Beijing (Peking)	8,000,000	Beijing (Peking)	19,064,000
Chicago	7,661,000	Seoul	18,711,000

*Estimates based on current (1984) rate of growth.

Source: United Nations *Demographic Yearbook 1978; World Almanac and Book of Facts 1981* (New York: Newspaper Editors Association, 1981); *The New Book of World Rankings* (New York: Facts on File, Inc., 1984).

combined in the latter two areas—the areas we have just been considering. More important, though, is a comparison of urban growth rates by region. Going down column 4, we see that city growth rates are *below* the world average (2.8%) in North America (2.2%), Europe (1.2%), the USSR (1.8%), and Oceania (2.2%). However, urban growth rates are *above* the world average in Latin America (3.4%), Africa (4.6%), and Asia (3.4%). What these figures suggest is what we have been encountering in our analysis in the last three chapters: Massive overurbanization is occurring in these parts of the globe. Werner Fornos, President of the Population Institute, put it starkly in a recent address to the United Nations Conference on Urban Planning in Mexico City: "While populations in developing countries are doubling every 25 to 30 years, their large cities are doubling every 10 to 15 years. And the urban slums and shantytowns in these cities are doubling every 5 to 7 years" (1986, p. 4). To put it in a slightly different perspective, by the year 2025 the world's population is expected to pass the 8 billion mark. In that year it is estimated that nearly 7 billion of these people will be residents of the undercapitalized, undernourished Third World (Russell 1984, p. 24). If present trends continue nearly 5 *billion* of these people will live in the cities of this struggling part of the world.

Alternatively, consider this: a generation or two ago, one correctly thought of the developed world as the locus of the world's largest urban areas. No more: rapid growth and urban migration already have moved several Third World cities into this category, as the 1981 column of Table 10-2 shows. The shift to Third World dominance becomes even more pronounced when we consider the longer term (Table 10-2, right-hand columns). By the year 2000, only two First World urban areas, New York and Tokyo, are expected to be in the top ten. Next, look at the magnitude of the urban areas in the 2000 column: the *smallest* one is over 2 million larger than the *largest* one in the 1981 column. These will truly be *megacities*, unprecedented in human history. Given what we already know about the inability of the Third World to cope with its urban problems, the concerned question has to be Can anything be done to reduce the ever-increasing difficulties and suffering that appear to lie ahead? Everyone recognizes that there is an unparalleled problem in most non-industrial cities. The trouble is, there are extremely different opinions as to what is responsible. Hence there are radically different suggestions about what should be done to make the problem disappear.

The Future: Theories and Possible Solutions

Modernization Theory. One theory suggests that Third World cities and countries everywhere are going through an inevitable process of modernization and economic development. This process is quite similar to that undergone by European and North American cities in the past few centuries. These now-developed areas of the world once experienced the growth of primate cities and severe poverty; however, modern industrial technology was responsible for greater productivity than ever before. At the same time, as people throughout the population adopted modern attitudes—an openness to change, a willingness to work for the future, a value on technical skills and education, a tolerance for others (Inkeles and Smith 1974, Chap. 2)—they began to increase substantially their standard of living. Wealth grew in all sectors of the population; other cities evolved, reducing the primacy problem; and eventually population growth itself declined. Modernization theorists such as Walt W. Rostow (1978) have argued that although some intervention might be helpful in alleviating the most immediate and severe of the non-industrial world's urban problems, time is the main factor. In time, the modernization process itself will solve the problem. Fifteen years ago, probably most urbanists agreed with this assessment (Berger 1967).

The difficulty with this position, critics respond, is that Third World cities and countries simply are not developing *in the same way* as other areas of the world. For one thing, the developed countries had declining rural population growth patterns as their cities grew (see Figure 8-2). The long-term production of wealth in cities thus was able to catch up with population growth.

This has not been the case in most contemporary Third World cities. As more and more people have continued to swell their ranks, the low level of technology and economic growth has not been able to cope with the overload. Worse, the overload cannot be dispersed. Conditions in the overpopulated countryside are worse and there are no frontier countries left to absorb the overflow. (For example, recall the American resistance to immigrating Mexicans discussed earlier.) As a result, no matter what has been done, conditions in many non-industrial cities have gotten only worse. As Deshpande and Bhat say about India:

> Though urbanization is necessary for improving the economic and social condition of the people and is a process associated with economic development, the magnitude of the problems created by urbanization in India . . . would seem to suggest that the present pattern and trends of urbanization could hamper the basic strategy of economic development itself. (1975, p. 373)

Jan Morris has put it even more succinctly: "India struggles, [but] India sinks" (1980b, pp. 42–43).

A second criticism of modernization theory is that non-industrial areas of the world are making economic progress only very slowly. Meanwhile, the West continues to increase its standard of living by leaps and bounds. In other words, non-industrial nations continue to fall further behind despite modest gains.

Dependency Theory. A second interpretation of the world urban crisis suggests that full modernization never will occur in most non-industrial cities and nations because Western nations are continuing to siphon off the valued products of such cities and nations. Without the technology or diversified industrial base to generate their own wealth internally, non-industrial areas of the world have had no choice but to rely on the wants of Western nations; hence, they are dependent. Butterworth and Chance summarize dependency theory as it applies to Latin America:

> The process [of dependency] began with the centuries-long exploitation of Latin America by the Iberian colonial powers and continues today through dominance by neocolonial industrial powers, especially the United States. . . . Foreign investors and multinational corporations have siphoned off a large proportion of the profits generated in the Latin American economies, leaving the countries themselves with an insufficient supply of capital, technology, and skilled personnel. . . . Consequently, most nations in the region continue to rely heavily on exports of a small number of . . . commodities [oil, sugar, rubber, cocoa, and so on]. This has had

two results: (1) Latin American nations are dependent for their foreign earnings on goods whose prices are notoriously unstable; and (2) the overall terms of trade have moved against their interests, for while the price of raw commodities fluctuates both upward and downward, the prices of manufactured products for which they are exchanged have been moving in only one direction—up. . . . As a result, much of Latin America is dependent on crucial economic and political decisions that are being made far beyond its borders in cities such as London, New York, Washington, Paris, Moscow, and Tokyo. (1981, pp. 199–200)

Recently considerable evidence has appeared that supports this argument. Evans and Timberlake (1980) studied 50 countries around the world in an attempt to determine whether dependence on foreign investment had major internal consequences for the dependent country. By means of a sophisticated computer analysis they found that dependency was strongly associated with greater levels of income inequality. That is, dependent countries when compared with other countries tended to have a wider gap between the very rich and the very poor and to have fewer people in the middle income brackets. More important, Evans and Timberlake argue that greater modernization will not decrease this inequality; rather, it will exacerbate it. The few rich will get richer while the many poor get poorer. The poor cannot rise higher on the income ladder because (1) there are so many of them and (2) access to the well-paid jobs is strictly controlled by the elite. The same argument has been made by Nolan, who, in a study of worldwide data, concludes that "dependency does increase income inequality and retards per capita economic growth" (1983a; 1983b, p. 410). In a more complex set of findings, Jaffe (1985) found that while export dependence did stimulate economic growth, that growth was *least* when foreign investors controlled the local economy.

Many who support dependency theory also argue that the only way to right the injustices of such a system is to have a revolution that will facilitate the establishment of a socialist or communist government committed to the redistribution of wealth to all people in the urban area and

the nation (Gilbert and Gugler 1983). Such revolutions have occurred already (in Cuba and China) and are likely to continue in coming years as some poverty-stricken peoples react against neo-colonial domination and repressive local elites.

They are not likely to be widespread, however. Recent research indicates that most of the world's urban poor are either so poor or so committed to their own personal or familial advancement that they are patently uninterested in revolution. In a study of the urban poor of six communities on the outskirts of Mexico City, Cornelius (1975) reports that half saw their chief concerns as increasing income and obtaining steady work. Ownership of one's home dominated the concerns of another 14.8 percent of his respondents, and gaining an education for self or for one's children was paramount for 15.2 percent. Still others cited better service (electricity, sewage) or improved health as their main interest. Less than 1 percent saw community or political issues as their primary concern. Similarly, in her study of the poor of Rio de Janeiro's shantytown, Perlman reports that these people "have the aspirations of the bourgeoisie, the perseverance of pioneers, and the values of patriots" (1976, p. 243; italics deleted).

This lack of revolutionary fervor among the urban poor is probably a reaction to being positioned at the bottom of the city's hierarchical structure. They have little of life's most valued possessions: land, wealth, power, security, and prestige. Seeing the benefits these accoutrements have produced in the lives of higher ups, even those slightly above them in the social structure, the urban poor naturally want such advantages and compete for them. Unfortunately, in the eyes of some urbanists, such an individualistic orientation may keep the poor from seeing that the individualistic system is itself responsible for their situation. Thus, people are unlikely to collectively seek to improve their situation.

On the other hand, in non-industrial countries where a socialist or communist revolution has occurred, major urban problems still exist. Michael Lewis-Beck (1979) has noted the lack of spectacular progress in Cuba, and Walton (1979, p. 3), in a study of revolutionary regimes, has concluded that while "redressing many of the characteristic features of urban underdevelopment in the Third World, revolutionary regimes may introduce new forms of inequality."

In short, the solution may not be as simple as choosing between capitalist or socialist alternatives. Capitalism's great strength historically has been its ability to produce individual initiative. Its great weakness has been the production of an inegalitarian social structure that actively suppresses some people and creates widespread suffering at the bottom. Communism's great strength has been its overarching commitment to the welfare of everyone in society. Its great weakness has been the restriction—in the name of the common good—of individual desires and, thus, of vital energy. Murphy (1980) suggests that what might be preferable to either extreme is some type of system that joins the benefits of each: a social order that provides for individual and small-group initiative within a broader, society-wide commitment to the basic welfare of everyone. It remains to be seen whether such a social order is possible, given the political rhetoric and orthodoxy that surround the current capitalism-versus-communism debate.

The only place where such an experiment seems to be in its beginning stages at present is the People's Republic of China. Slowly, tentatively, Chairman Deng is allowing individual striving for profit to appear in China's cities. But these are halting and small steps. Whether this experiment of capitalist-style initiative within a Communist system can survive is a most intriguing question.

Urban Overpopulation. Nevertheless, non-industrial cities, capitalist and Communist alike, continue to face the grim prospects of continuing overpopulation. It is this phenomenon that a third group of urbanists suggests is the root cause of the non-industrial urban crisis. Without control of this problem, the modernization-versus-dependency and capitalism-versus-communism debates are moot.

Frederich Turner (1976) suggests that government intervention is the best way to begin to stem the tide. First, governments could attack urban overgrowth directly by limiting population increases. This could be done by providing free contraceptives and birth-control information, by postponing legal marriage until a later date (thereby decreasing the number of fertile years for a couple), by providing benefits for families or communities that show lower birth rates, by rewarding voluntary sterilization, or even by forcing sterilization.

A second possibility is that governments could support smaller cities, hence helping solve the primate-city problem. Of course, this is difficult to do because the primate city is seen by virtually everyone in these countries as the place where the action is and where the opportunities are greatest (usually not a misplaced evaluation). Because of this, Turner suggests that governments must actively establish or benefit smaller cities by governmental investment or by giving major breaks—by taxes or incomes—to industry or workers.

Fiscal policies provide a third option. Governments could tax city dwellers substantially, or they could lower taxes on nonurban dwellers, thereby making life in the city less desirable and life outside more attractive.

Fourth, if such benign measures fail, more authoritarian policies could be instituted. Residence permits might be required of city dwellers, with new arrivals immediately deported back to the countryside or imprisoned. This would, however, demand strict record keeping and unbribable officials. (Both Jakarta and China have failed in their attempts along these lines.) Couples having more than a specified number of children could be denied social services, housing loans, or jobs in government. A policy like this has worked in Singapore but has not had much success elsewhere.

Finally, systematic planning for the whole society could be undertaken. Cities do not exist in isolation, and planning the entire settlement continuum—from rural area to village to small city to metropolis—could have substantial benefits. One such plan is the Plan of Economic and Social Development of Colombia, devised in 1973. Envisioning both continued population growth and urbanization, the plan "called for the development of cities of between 30,000 and 200,000 people, emigration of the unemployed to selected zones for resettlement, and provision of agricultural credit, health, education, and recreation services in the countryside" (Turner 1976, p. 960). Alas, the plan was shelved after a change in government.

This failure to institute a plan with a real possibility of solving urban overpopulation problems symbolizes to Turner the great difficulty of curbing the current urban crisis. Ideas are one thing; implementing them in a complex cultural, economic, and political setting is quite another.

All the measures just discussed have their costs and benefits, considered simply in their own right; however, if one adds the issues raised by considering them in a specific setting, the waters get much murkier. Can free contraceptive information ever be a viable possibility in Catholic Latin America? Can economically strapped and politically unstable governments in Africa effectively subsidize smaller cities? Will people take happily to enforced sterilization or mandated moves to the countryside? Recent experiments in India and China have suggested such policies have their limitations.

The City Is Not the Problem: Jane Jacobs's Theory. Many people, looking at the overgrowth of Third World cities and the suffering rampant within them, believe, like those just cited above, that the solution to the urban problems of the world is to get city growth under control. But this is to miss the forest for the trees, argues urban economist Jane Jacobs (1984). The city is *not* the problem. On the contrary, the city has been, and continues to be, the most important generator of wealth in human history. If poverty is part of the *world's* problem—and we have seen in these three chapters that it most assuredly *is*—then, if we wish to eliminate poverty, we should hardly consider dismantling or crippling the economic mechanisms of the very thing that has shown itself capable, historically, of decreasing poverty!

The problem, suggests Jacobs, is not the basic idea of modernization either. Modernization can work (we have lots of evidence of this), but only under certain conditions. Rather the problem is dependency, but not merely the type that dependency theorists talk about. Dependency cripples a city *only* when that dependency is on a city or cities much more complex and sophisticated than

itself. Thus, while it is undesirable that weak Third World cities be dependent for trade on strong First World cities (as most dependency theorists suggest), the institution of a communist system is no panacea either, especially if it results in weaker communist cities being forced into unequal trade arrangements with stronger communist cities. That too is dependency, simply another sort.

The key, Jacobs insists, is the relationship between trade and the process of urban development. History shows us that cities develop fastest when they trade with other cities that are like them in terms of needs, jobs, and wealth. Such cities pull themselves up by their bootstraps, because what one city needs, the other invents. Here is how Jacobs describes the process:

> What this means is that the trade among vigorously developing cities is volatile, continually changing in content as cities create new kinds of exports for one another, and then in due course repeatedly replace many of them. So it was with the development of the backward cities of Europe. They were forever producing new exports for one another—bells, dyes, buckles, parchment, lace, carding combs, needles, painted cabinetwork, ceramics, brushes, cutlery, paper, sieves and riddles, sweetmeats, elixirs, files, pitchforks, sextants—replacing them . . . [and] becoming customers for still more innovations. . . . They [became] exceptionally good markets for innovations because they [could] afford them. . . . They were developing on one another's shoulders. (1984, p. 144)

In other words, the great problem with Third World urban development *now*, is that most Third World cities trade with cities that are much more complex and wealthy than themselves. They can only give to those cities raw materials or cheap labor or cheaply made goods. In return, they buy from those more sophisticated cities goods they cannot afford—like televisions, John Deere tractors, computers—and get themselves ever deeper into debt and dependency. To solve the problem, Jacobs suggests that such underdeveloped cities have to give up such trade arrangements, realize that the road to modernization cannot be instantaneous, and set about building themselves up, step-by-step, with vigorous trade with cities like themselves. If they do not do so, such cities will continue to languish in the shadow of the developed cities—whether communist or capitalist—for the indefinite future.

If Jacobs's thesis is plausible, is the action she suggests likely? Are Third World cities likely to give up their dreams of being like their more materially developed First and Second World cousins, especially if that means giving up the symbols of that development—the most modern and sophisticated technologies and machinery and fashions? In a trip during 1984 to much of the Third World, author Spates found one attitude characteristic of most of the peoples of Asia and the Middle East: Their desire to be like the people of more affluent countries. They wanted modernization and they wanted it *as soon as possible*. The imported movies and TV programs have done their job only too well. The allure is too great, the neon of those "fancier" cities is too bright, the "life-styles of the rich and famous" who live in those cities are too captivating. Hence, it is likely that, right or wrong, Jacobs's pleas will fall on deaf ears, at least for the present.

Conclusion

Thus we come, at the end of this overview of world urbanization, to no hard-and-fast solution to the problems we have encountered. Scholars themselves are divided about the causes and most efficient solutions.

One conclusion seems certain. Whatever is done, the cities of the non-industrial world are going to continue to grow at enormous rates for the foreseeable future. With this growth will come, inevitably, greater problems. As each country copes with its crises, perhaps one, or a combination of two or more, of the solutions we have discussed will emerge as clearly superior, thereby lightening the load on other overburdened cities some decades hence.

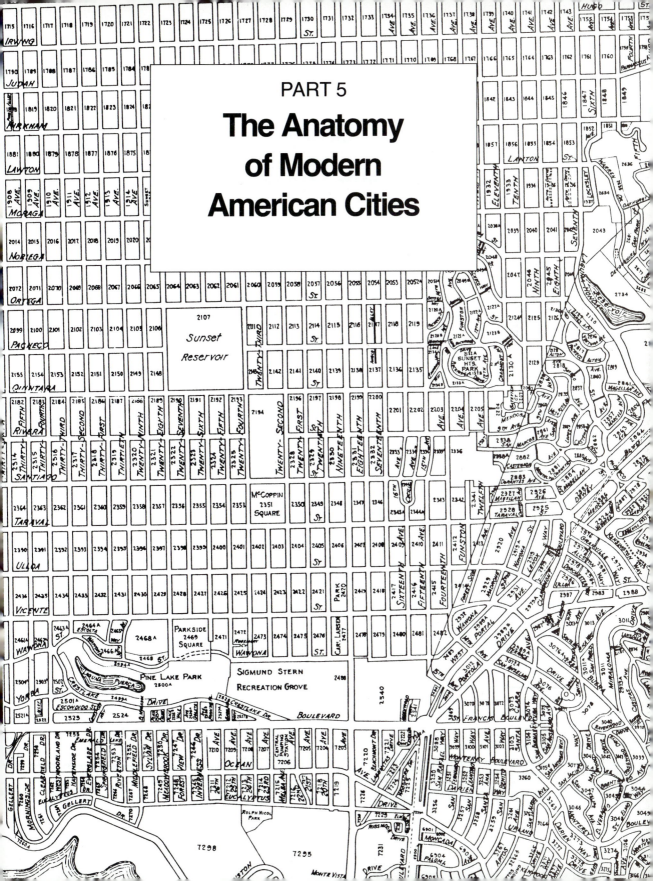

PART 5

The Anatomy
of Modern
American Cities

CHAPTER 11

Urban Life-Styles

Having considered the general patterns of world urbanization in the last three chapters, we now return to more familiar ground. In this and the two chapters to follow we undertake a detailed consideration, an anatomy, of the American city. We shall find that our own cities, like those of the rest of the world, are frequently a study in paradox. While some urbanites clearly have experienced "the good life," others have continually fallen victim to less favorable conditions: poor housing, poverty, unemployment, discrimination, crime. We will consider the causes and consequences of such variations. Finally, we will explore what has been done and what might be done to create a more humane urban environment.

Urban Diversity: Multiple Views

Imagine sitting in Union Square in downtown San Francisco noting social differences in people who walk by. A well-dressed young woman carrying an attaché case hurries past, presumably on her way to her next appointment. An old man, unshaven and in shabby dress, reclines on the grass enjoying the sun; occasionally he takes a brown bag from his coat pocket, unscrews the top of a bottle inside, and has a drink. Four long-haired young men in bright floral shirts and dungarees are engaged in a serious discussion about the state of the nation. A short distance away, a black woman plays a guitar as she offers Christian messages to anyone who will listen. Few do. A group of Chinese children, 10 or 11 years old, playfully skip their way through the square. A middle-class couple emerges from the City of Paris department store carrying a large assortment of packages. They buy an ice cream from a street vendor, stroll into the square, and sit wearily but happily on the grass.

Similar scenes are played out daily in all major American cities. This brief portrait suggests the essence of city life: tremendous human diversity—sometimes worrisome, sometimes exhilarating, always interesting. If we followed any of these people through their day, few professional skills would be required to observe that they live very differently from one another. Although their lives touch for a moment in Union Square, they are shaped by very different interests, experiences, and life circumstances.

This chapter examines various urban life-styles. By *life-style* we mean the patterned ways of living that distinguish people in the urban arena. We shall see that these life-styles are largely a result of people sharing certain social characteristics—such as age, sex, income level, ethnic or racial background, political and religious beliefs. In addition, we shall be curious as to just how much these urban life-styles are shaped by the city itself. For example, does living in a certain location (an in-town residential area versus a suburb) characteristically shape one's life? Indeed, this debate—over whether more general social characteristics or the city itself is the primary cause of urban diversity—lies at the heart of the whole notion of urban life-styles.

Louis Wirth: Urbanism as a Way of Life

The champion of the view that the city itself shapes the life-styles of city dwellers was University of Chicago theorist, Louis Wirth, whom we first encountered in Chapter 4. Said he in his classic 1938 essay, "Urbanism as a Way of Life": "Urbanism" refers to that "distinctive . . . mode of life which is associated with the growth of cities." It is the "changes . . . which are apparent among people . . . who have come under the spell of the city." Clear enough. Wirth went on to say that the city accomplished this shaping of life-styles by forcing people to encounter one another in a unique environment: in the city, *large numbers* of people with *heterogeneous social characteristics* come into contact in settings of *high density*. The result is a new type of awareness, an urban consciousness. City dwellers become rational, self-interested, specialized, somewhat reserved, and highly tolerant.

Harvey Cox captured Wirth's point brilliantly in his description of his own experiences. Of his boyhood days in a village, Cox wrote:

During my boyhood, my parents never referred to "the milkman," "the insurance agent," "the junk collector." These people were respectively, Paul

Weaver, Joe Villanova, and Roxy Barozano. All of our family's market transactions took place within a web of wider and more inclusive friendship and kinship ties with the same people. They were never anonymous. In fact, the occasional salesman or repairman whom we did not know was always viewed with dark suspicion until we could make sure where he came from, who his parents were, and whether his family was "any good." (1965, p. 37)

His later life in the city was, however, quite different:

Now, as an urbanite, my transactions are of a very different sort. If I need to have the transmission on my car repaired, buy a television antenna, or cash a check, I find myself in functional relationships with mechanics, salesmen, and bank clerks whom I see in no other capacity. These contacts are in no sense "mean, nasty, or brutish," though they tend to be short . . . unifaceted and segmental. I meet these people in no other context. To me they remain essentially just as anonymous as I do to them. (1965, pp. 37–38)

As Wirth understood it, the essence of urbanism as a life-style was *cosmopolitanism*, literally, "belonging to all the world." Robert Merton (1968, pp. 447–453) drew a useful distinction between "local" and "cosmopolitan" life-styles. The life of the localite is centered in the immediate area. Typically born in the area in which they live, localites are bound up within the social relations and life commitments that are encapsulated within that specific territory. Cosmopolitans, on the other hand, are more rootless and think in terms of wider possibilities. They are more likely to move on (perhaps to new jobs or a better home). Whether rich or poor, the cosmopolitan displays a degree of detachment, a somewhat blasé attitude toward immediate surroundings, and has a sophistication in matters of taste and friendship not typical of the localite. Although Merton acknowledged that cosmopolitans and localites could exist anywhere, there is little doubt that the cosmopolitan attitude is found more frequently among city dwellers and the localite attitude is more typical of small towns or rural areas. (Keeping in mind these differing modes of consciousness, reexamine Cityscape 4-

l, "Our Town," which depicts localism perfectly, and Box 4-5, "A Song of Myself," Walt Whitman's poem to cosmopolitan cities everywhere.)

But are cosmopolitanism and localism so sharply delimited as Wirth intimates? Perhaps cosmopolitanism is more common in non-city areas than a cursory glance would suggest. Small college towns, such as Gambier, Ohio, often exhibit remarkably high degrees of cosmopolitanism. Conversely, many cities contain residential enclaves where localism abounds—the traditional Jewish Hasidic community of the Williamsburg district of Brooklyn is an example. If this is the case, perhaps the city doesn't produce these distinctive ways of life at all. So argues Herbert Gans, the most outspoken critic of the Wirthian position.

Herbert Gans: Urbanism as Many Ways of Life

Gans (1968) contends that the city is a kalaidescope of *many* life-styles, only some of which bear the stamp of cosmopolitanism described by Wirth. Further, Wirth's key variables—size of population, density, and social heterogeneity—cannot account for many of these life-styles. Rather, Gans suggests, urban diversity is the result of more general *social characteristics*, such as age, sex, income, or educational level. For example, if we find that higher levels of education are associated with a cosmopolitan attitude, we would be able to explain why cosmopolitanism may be found frequently in a nonurban setting, such as a college town.

Using this general orientation, Gans turned to the life-styles typical of the American city. Basically, he found four that, alone or in combination with others, describe the city's people: the cosmopolites, the unmarried or childless, the ethnic villagers, and the deprived or trapped. We'll consider each in turn.

The Cosmopolites. This first life-style bears the greatest resemblance to Wirth's notion of the urban sophisticate. Cosmopolites are people who choose to live in the city because of its human and cultural diversity or because the city offers

them the unique group of experiences, contacts, or friends they need. Usually highly educated and displaying "sophisticated taste," cosmopolites choose a residential area carefully, are detached from most of their neighbors, and value privacy. Most of their contacts are based on shared and specialized interests. Georgia Fideris, an editor for *Woman's Day* magazine who lives in New York's upper Second Avenue district, is one example. In her late twenties, she chose the neighborhood because she believed its residents were "more culturally educated." (Associated Press, Aug. 7, 1984) Gans believed the clearest examples of cosmopolites are intellectuals, artists, musicians, writers, and students. Some are affluent—affluence always increases the range of available choices—but this is by no means always the case. Typically they congregate in certain districts. New York's Upper East Side (where the average per capita income is $32,000 per year) and Greenwich Village (where the average per capita income is around $18,000 per year) are examples of two different types of cosmopolitan area. New Orlean's French Quarter and San Francisco's Nob Hill are other examples.

The Unmarried or Childless. This second urban life-style (which, Gans notes, overlaps frequently with the cosmopolite category) includes single adults or couples without children who live in city apartments rather than the single-family residences found in other areas of the city or the suburbs. Apartments are easier to maintain and more efficient for people who don't need a lot of space. This group typically includes young people out of high school or college and newly married couples with city-centered careers. Also included are people whose children have grown up and left home. Of course, many in this group are transient. They may later marry if they are single or have children if they are married, and either event can precipitate a move to a single-family neighborhood. Others remain, perhaps maintaining a single life-style for their whole lives. In fact, the proportion of singles in the central-city population has been increasing steadily as the decentralization of families to the suburbs has continued

---

BOX 11-1
The Unmarried: "Love Among the Skyscrapers"

Ted, a highly successful management consultant, has lived in Boston, the Far East, San Francisco, Chicago. He is a partner, at the age of 35, in the country's leading consulting firm. Never married, he's come as close as wanting to be, to Caroline, with whom he lived for two years. His life professionally is a highly social one, deeply entwined with business dinners, client entertainment, black-tie celebrations in dark-paneled club rooms.

In this milieu of manners and image, Ted found Caroline to be impeccably appropriate. She was witty, vivacious, and physically stunning. And when their relationship ended, for lots of reasons . . . Ted spoke, far into a drinking night, of lessons learned. He said that, if nothing else, he'd realized that in the future he'd again need someone as socially graceful as

Caroline. "I'll never be satisfied," he said "after her, with someone who I cannot, with full confidence, trust to stand in for me. Caroline was so marvelous in that way and I realize that I need someone who can act as my representative. Whose personality makes people say to themselves, 'This is what Ted is about.'"

Love according to ingredients. Evaluating a partner as one would read on the new car window the list of included options. She has manners, beauty, charm. I'll take her.

[Susan] is 32, and has had several love affairs in the six or seven years we've been friends. She has been involved with an editor who stopped by on Thursdays at ten. (There was this wife and child, you see.) She's loved a gentried Hindu, a Cleveland news director. . . . She's had an affair

with an unemployed locksmith referred to as the Italian Stallion and with her sister's ex-fiance. It's important to understand that Susan has not gone lightly into these affairs. . . .

Now, once again, Susan is in love. She has known her lover for several years, knew him casually when they both worked for a national magazine. . . . "He loves me. And that's nice." . . . She [also] knows the guy's a liar and a thief and will never move from the midwest to New York. . . . So there are no disappointments to creep in. "It's good for now," Susan says.

This may be the cliche of city love, raised to theme: it's good for now.

Source: Doug Bauer, "Love Among the Skyscrapers," *The Real Paper*, Sept. 28, 1979, pp. 37–38.

---

and cities have become progressively more white-collar and service-oriented. According to one study over one-third of all central-city residents in major cities were singles (Long and Glick 1976).

There is no doubt that at least for some people in this group, Wirth's characteristics of high rationality and self-interest predominate. There may be an element of hard-headed consumerism about what's available in the city—sadly enough, even concerning love, as Doug Bauer reports in Box 11-1.

The Ethnic Villagers. Not everyone lives as do Ted and Susan of Box 11-1. Another group shows almost *none* of the so-called typical urban characteristics noted by Wirth. Of these city dwellers, Gans comments, "The 'ethnic villagers' are ethnic groups which are found in such inner-city neighborhoods as New York's Lower East Side,

living in some ways as they did when they were peasants in Europe or Puerto Rican villages" (1968, p. 37). The ethnic villagers sustain many rural life patterns in the city, emphasizing traditional religious beliefs, family ties, and suspicion of outsiders. They build their lives within a local area that is identified traditionally with *their* group. Most of these neighborhoods are old, having been settled for some time by different generations of the same families.

Ethnic villages often reflect moderate or working-class incomes and are characterized by a lack of anonymity. People *know* one another. In addition to New York's Lower East Side, Little Italy, and Chinatown, such "tight" neighborhoods are found in Philadelphia's Kensington (Polish) and "South Philly" (Italian) districts, Cleveland's multi-ethnic West Side, Boston's Irish South Boston area ("Southie"), and Los Angeles's Mexican-

CITYSCAPE 11-1
The Ethnic Villagers

New York: The Jewish Lower East Side

The streets were ours. . . . It was a prospect not always amiable or ever free from terror, but it drew Jewish boys and girls like a magnet, offering them qualities in short supply at home: the charms of the spontaneous and unpredictable. In the streets a boy could encircle himself with the breath of immigrant life, declare his companionship with peddlers, storekeepers, soapboxers. No child raised in the immigrant quarter would lack for moral realism: just to walk through Hester Street was an education in the hardness of life. To go beyond Cherry Street on the south, where the Irish lived, or west of the Bowery, where the Italians were settling, was to explore the world of the gentiles—dangerous, since one risked a punch in the face, but tempting, since for an East Side boy the idea of *the others*, so steadily drilled into his mind by every agency of his culture, was bound to incite curiosity. Venturing into gentile streets became a strategy for testing the reality of the external world and for discovering that it was attractive in ways no Jewish voice had told him. An East Side

boy needed to slip into those gentile streets on his own. He needed to make a foray and then pull back, so that his perception of the outer world would be his own, and not merely that of the old folks, not merely the received bias and visions of the Jews.

When he kept to the Jewish streets, the East Side boy felt at home, free and easy on his own turf. Even if not especially friendly or well mannered, people talked to one another. No one had much reason to suppose that the noisiest quarrel between peddler and purchaser, or parents and children, was anything but a peaceful ritual.

Boston: The Italian West End

To most of the West Enders, the area had been home either since birth or marriage. Some were born in the West End because this was where their parents had settled when they first came to America or where they had moved later in life. Others came as adults in the Italian "invasion" of the West End during the 1930s. Many of them had grown up in the North End and had moved at the time of marriage in order to take advan-

tage of better and larger apartments in the West End. In any case, almost all of the West Enders came to the area as a part of a group. Even their movements within the West End—that is, from the lower end to the upper—had been made together with other Italians at about the same time. . . .

. . . West Enders were in the West End because this is where they "belonged." . . . While they do want to be left alone, they are not averse to the aural or visual closeness of their neighbors. As everyone knows everyone else's activities and problems anyway, they know that it is impossible to hide anything by physical privacy. As one West Ender put it:

I like the noise people make. In summer people have their windows open, and everyone can hear everyone else, but nobody cares what anybody is saying; they leave their neighbors alone. In the suburbs, people are nosier; when a car comes up the street, all the windows go up to see who is visiting whom.

While the image of the suburb is overdrawn, it is true that in the West End, where people knew so

---

American barrio. Cityscape 11-1 provides two firsthand accounts of life in urban ethnic villages.

The Deprived and Trapped. The remaining lifestyles that Gans identified within the central city are distinct in one major way from the others: those that live them usually do so because they have no other choice. This lack of choice extends not only to *ways* of living but to *where* one lives. The cosmopolites and the unmarried or childless by and large choose their locale; ethnic villagers

live in their neighborhoods "partly because of necessity, partly because of tradition." But for those who suffer intense poverty (many of whom face the additional handicap of racial discrimination), there is little opportunity to escape. As Gans puts it, the deprived—the very poor, the handicapped, those in broken family situations, or of nonwhite racial background—"must take the dilapidated housing and blighted neighborhoods to which the housing market relegates them" (1968, pp. 37–38). The plight of such people is described poignantly in Cityscape 11-2, in which Lutie John-

much about each other, there was no need for prying. A feeling of privacy could be maintained in the midst of high density.

In addition, hearing and seeing their neighbor's activities gave the West Enders a share in the life that went on around them, which, in turn, made them feel part of the group. . . . West Enders, living mainly in the group, have an insatiable appetite for group experience. . . .

I was told by one social worker of an experiment some years back to expose West End children to nature by taking them on a trip to Cape Cod. The experiment failed, for the young West Enders found no pleasure in the loneliness of natural surroundings and wanted to get back to the West End as quickly as possible. They were incredulous that anyone could live without people around him.

Source: Irving Howe, *World of Our Fathers* (New York: Harcourt, Brace, Jovanovich, 1976), pp. 256–257.

Source: Herbert Gans, *The Urban Villagers* (New York: Free Press, 1982), pp. 19–23.

In many cities ethnic villages still survive. Shown here is a Jewish delicatessen on New York's Lower East Side. (Jeroboam/Bill Aron)

son, a black woman living in Harlem, has just found out that her son has been arrested for a serious crime.

The trapped, a category of urbanites similar to the deprived, are those who wish to move from deteriorating neighborhoods but lack the financial resources to do so. Often such people have lived in what was a desirable neighborhood, only to be left behind as industry or minorities "invaded" the area. At the extreme, they live a prisonlike existence, trapped both by their fear of a new environment that may seem strange and hos-

tile and by their own limited income. Many are America's rapidly growing population of elderly people. In Box 11-2, Barbara Myerhoff describes the entrapment of a group of elderly Jews living in Venice, California, a Los Angeles beach community that has been undergoing major population transition in the last few decades.

The Disaffiliated. An additional life-style, not specifically considered in Gans's analysis, could be called the disaffiliated. Examples include the

CITYSCAPE 11-2
The Deprived

Bub would go to reform school. She stopped on the fourth-floor landing to look at the thought, to examine it, to get used to it. Bub would go to reform school. And she reached out and touched the wall with her hand, then leaned the weight of her body against it because her legs were trembling, the muscles quivering, knees buckling.

Her thoughts were like a chorus chanting inside her head. The men stood around and the women worked. The men left the women and the women went on working and the kids were left alone. The kids burned lights all night because they were alone in small, dark rooms and they were afraid. Alone. Always alone. They wouldn't stay in the house after school because they were afraid in the empty, silent, dark rooms. And they should have been playing in wide stretches of green park and instead they were in the street. And the street reached out and sucked them up.

Yes. The women worked and the kids go to reform school. Why do the women work? It's such a simple, reasonable reason. And just thinking about it will make your legs stop trembling like the legs of a winded, blown, spent horse.

The women work because the white folks give them jobs— washing dishes and clothes and floors and windows. The women work because for years now the white folks haven't liked to give black men jobs that paid enough for them to support their families. And finally it gets to be too late for some of them. Even wars don't change it. The men get out of the habit of working and the houses are old and gloomy and the walls press in. And the men go off, move on, slip away, find new women. Find younger women.

And what did it add up to? She pressed closer to the wall, ignoring the gray dust, the fringes of cobwebs heavy with grime and soot. Add it up. Bub, your kid— flashing smile, strong, straight back, sturdy legs, even white teeth, young, round face, smooth skin—he ends up in reform school because the women work. . . .

Only you forgot. You forgot you were black and you underestimated the street outside here. And it never occurred to you that Bub might find those small dark rooms just as depressing as you did. And then, of course, there wasn't any other place for you to live except in a house like this one.

Then she was shouting, leaning against the wall, beating against it with her fists, and shouting, "Damn it! Damn it!"

She leaned further against the wall, seemed almost to sink into it, and started to cry. The hall was full of the sound. The thin walls echoed and re-echoed with it, two, three floors below and one floor above.

People coming home from work . . . turned their faces away from the sight of her, walked faster to get away from the sound of her. They hurried to close the doors of their apartments, but her crying came through the flimsy walls, followed them through the tight-shut doors.

Source: Ann Petry, *The Street* (Boston: Houghton Mifflin, 1946), pp. 388–390.

tramp, hobo, wino, or the wandering "bag-lady." They exist in surprisingly large numbers in just about every city. One recent estimate is that 50,000 homeless people live in New York alone (Coleman 1983).

Most of us have encountered members of this group from time to time, perhaps sleeping on benches in parks or bus stations, standing in doorways along skid row streets, or panhandling on busy walkways. It is all too clear that they are at the peripheries of social life, and we usually assume they are cut off from work and family, weeks away from their last job or even their last square meal—a familiar stereotype.

Research that has examined closely the lifestyle of the disaffiliated has challenged some parts of the stereotype, however. A brief profile of the typical skid row dweller, based on the work of Howard Bahr (1973), will illustrate.

True to popular conception, the skid row dweller is typically male. He is almost always single (half have never married) and generally older (the most typical ages were 50 to 54). Appearances often suggest the men to be older still. Contrary

BOX 11-2
The Trapped: "Number Our Days"

Signs of what was once a much larger, more complete Yiddish ghetto remain along the boardwalk. Two storefront synagogues are left, where only a few years ago there were a dozen. There is a delicatessen and a Jewish bakery. Before there were many kosher butcher stores and little markets. Only three Jewish board-and-care homes and four large hotels are left to house the elderly. The four thousand or so elderly Jews in the neighborhood must find accommodations in small, rented rooms and apartments within walking distance of the Center. A belt, roughly five miles long and a mile wide, constitutes the limits of the effective community of these Eastern European immigrants, nearly all of whom are now in their middle eighties and up. . . . Muggings, theft, rape, harassment, and occasional murders make it a perilous neighborhood for the old people after dark.

A decade ago, census figures suggest that as many as ten thousand elderly Eastern European Jews lived in the neighborhood. Then Yiddish culture flourished. . . .

In the late 1950s, an urban development program resulted in the displacement of between four and six thousand of these senior citizens in a very short period. It was a devastating blow to the culture. "A second Holocaust," [one] called it. "We've only got a few more years here, all of us. It would be good if we could stay till the end. We had a protest march the other day, when they took down the old Miramar Hotel. I made up a sign. It said, 'Let my people stay.'"

Source: Barbara Myerhoff, *Number Our Days* (New York: Dutton, 1979), pp. 5–7.

is younger (about three-fourths are under 50) and less likely to have been married (about 75 percent have never married) than their predecessors (Rimer 1984).

Nor is it true that a skid row dweller never works. Bahr's research, based on a sample from Philadelphia, suggests that at any given time up to half of the skid row population is gainfully employed (1973, p. 95), although most work in low-paying jobs in restaurants, in loading or unloading, or in transportation.

A significant proportion of the disaffiliated suffers from illnesses, physical or emotional handicaps, or alcoholism. While alcohol is certainly a major preoccupation for many, Bahr found that outsiders often exaggerate this problem. At least half the people have drunk heavily during some period of their lives, although only one of three is engaged in excessive drinking at any particular time (Bahr 1973, p. 103).

How can a city deal humanely with large numbers of the disaffiliated? New York City has attempted to break up their overconcentration in places like the Bowery and disperse them throughout the city. But dispersion hasn't been easy. For example:

> The [City of New York,] under court order to find more beds for homeless men, approached every community board in the city and could not find a neighborhood in any borough that was willing to accept a new 200-to-300 bed facility for men in its area. . . .
>
> A proposed assessment and referral center for former mental patients scheduled to be opened by the city later this year at 88th Street and Amsterdam Avenue has drawn vehement protests from residents in the immediate area. They say it will endanger the neighborhood. . . . (Carmody 1981, p. 1)

Nor is this just local prejudice and insensitivity. In a letter to New York Mayor Edward Koch, Gertrude Huston, secretary of Community Board 5, complained bitterly about what had happened to her neighborhood since the First Moravian Church at 30th Street and Lexington Avenue had begun a program to provide meals and counseling for the city's homeless. She wrote:

to the stereotype, at least half have had contact with a relative in the past year.

Some social characteristics of the population are changing, however. About 15 years ago Bahr found that about 90 percent of the homeless were white, with the remaining population distributed among other racial groups. But a recent study of New York City's homeless shelters, completed in 1982, found that only 20 to 25 percent were white, 60 percent or more were black, 10 percent Hispanic, and the rest from various other backgrounds. Moreover, the recent homeless urbanite

The disaffiliated live at the peripheries of social life. They may spend their nights on park benches or in doorways, their days in the streets, panhandling or searching through trash cans. (Jeroboam/Karen Preuss)

Since the program opened, this has been a disaster area. Our brownstone steps, doorways, and vestibules have been invaded by derelicts and bag people—and their urine and feces. Some of us have been physically attacked by the more violent of the church's clients. (As quoted in Carmody 1981, p. 34)

Another recent tactic of the Koch administration has been to round up the homeless on nights when the thermometer dips below 32 degrees and take them to city-sponsored shelters or hospitals. This policy was put into place in 1985 after at least one homeless woman had frozen to death in her cardboard box "home" on a city street. But the policy is both controversial and hard to enforce. Most homeless people do not want to leave the streets. After all, what friends they have are there

and they have learned to survive, if barely, in such an environment. Many claim their rights as individuals are being usurped by such a policy. In addition, their admission to hospitals overloads already crowded facilities. Finally, many homeless do not want to go to the city's shelters because there they may be preyed upon by others. They are frequently beaten, their scant belongings stolen. Better, they argue, to take their chances on the mean streets that they know so well (Barbanel 1985).

Urban Characters. Cities contain more than a simple range of life-styles; they also are home to a category of people whose lives are in some way distinctive: the strange people, the ones you can't figure out, the odd balls, the characters. Here is William H. Whyte's recollection of a stroll in Manhattan:

On a stretch of Fifth Avenue recently, the following [street acts] could be caught: steel drum player at 60th Street; flutist at 59th; mime at 58th; two girl folksingers at 54th; the Krishnas at 53rd; a trio playing Bach at 49th. There are [also] acrobats, musicians, one-man bands, violinists, Karate groups [and] animal acts. (1974, p. 27)

And that isn't all. Within a few blocks in any direction New Yorkers would be likely to run across "Preacher Willie," the "Husband-Liberation Man," or "Mr. Magoo," the free-lance traffic director. If you walk along Market Street in San Francisco, over through Union Square, and catch the cable car to Ghiradelli Square and Fisherman's Wharf, in all probability you will see dozens of street acts, sidewalk crusaders, and would-be star entertainers.

It is not that city living makes people strange. Rather, large cities provide a type of environment in which more people with idiosyncrasies are visible (Wilson 1986). The chances of a city dweller encountering a character are much greater than they are for the resident of a small town. And the anonymity of the city can make people "act out" in a way they never would in settings where they are more well known. The city provides a safe haven for people who flout convention or tweak the public's nose.

Wirth and Gans: A Comparison

The preceding discussion of prominent urban "types" as discerned by Gans is only a partial list. Gans would readily acknowledge important variations and subvariations on all of these life-styles. But that is just the point. So *many* general types of urban life-styles exist, it makes little sense to see the city, as Wirth did, as producing a relatively uniform type of human being.

The rather hard-nosed, calculating person Wirth hypothesized as the typical urban dweller does appear—most frequently in the cosmopolite and unmarried or childless categories. Similarly, the lives of those at the very bottom of the urban status hierarchy—the deprived, the trapped, and the disaffiliated—may be shaped by large numbers, density, and heterogeneity, Wirth's key variables. But even among them there are exceptions, and among the other categories these variables appear to have little effect. For instance, the cosmopolites and unmarried or childless usually can buy the space they need to fend off what they believe is excessive density, and many ethnic villagers positively thrive on high-density living.

Thus, Gans sees little value in Wirth's idea that urbanism produces a distinctive way of life based upon large numbers, density, and heterogeneity. Rather, he argues that (1) all the major life-styles found in the city are not limited to the city; that is, they can be found anywhere, and (2) what explains the main characteristics of these life-styles is the general set of social characteristics that their members possess. Thus, cosmopolites tend to live as they do because they are relatively wealthy and highly educated; likewise, the deprived and trapped live as they do because they are poor, unskilled, not well educated, and often the object of racial or ethnic discrimination. Similar arguments could be made for any other life-style on the list.

Wirth's mistake, it might be argued, was that he generalized too quickly from the urban conditions of the time in which he was living. Observing the incredibly rapid growth of American and European cities in the late nineteenth and early twentieth centuries, Wirth saw the city as a powerful force that would increasingly shape human life. Naturally, he was well aware of the great variety of social life that exists in cities. Nevertheless, he apparently believed that the powerful forces of urbanism ultimately would seep into even the most tightly sealed urban village and produce an ever-increasing cosmopolitanism.

A generation later, Gans and others could see that this simply wasn't happening; urban diversity continued to flourish. We therefore conclude that *urbanization*—the process by which an area becomes more citylike—is not necessarily linked to *urbanism*—a distinctive way of life.

Claude Fischer: A Subcultural Theory of Urbanism

Still, doubts persist. Despite Gans's critique, many continue to argue that there is something different about the city and its people. Believing so, Claude Fischer (1975) developed what he calls a "subcultural theory of urbanism." Fischer acknowledges that much urban variety is understandable, as Gans argued, in terms of such factors as age, income level, and family status. Yet Fischer claims that there is a level of *intensity* in the city that simply does not exist elsewhere. That intensity is produced by a unique combination in the city of Wirth's key ecological variables.

The basic idea is this: large numbers, high levels of density, and social heterogeneity *intensify* the subcultural characteristics that people possess, producing the unique variety and dynamism of the urban experience. In using the term "subcultural characteristics," Fischer is referring to the same social characteristics as Gans—that is, level of income, race, sex, age, religious background, and so on. Fischer believes that to imply, as Gans does, that these characteristics produce the same effects in the country or in a city of 10 million is wrong. In the city the effects are magnified in a new way.

On one level the large numbers of the city allow formation of a "critical mass." Once there is a certain number of people of a given type in a city, they find out about one another, establish their own meeting places, create their own rituals, and begin to specialize their activities. An example is the entertainment industry in Hollywood.

BOX 11-3
Chateau Marmont and Schwab's: Showbiz Personified

My hotel was the Chateau Marmont, a monument in itself, built in the French manner half a century ago, and directly overlooking Sunset Boulevard. Everyone in Hollywood knows the place. That's where Bogart proposed to Bacall, they say, that's where Garbo used to stay, Howard Hughes had a suite there, Boris Karloff loved it, Valentino preferred the penthouse. It is impregnated with showbiz, from the gigantic antiques in the downstairs lounge to the strains of the electronic organ from the pop group practicing in the garden bungalow. . . .

Every morning . . . I walked across the boulevard to have my breakfast at Schwab's, "The World's Most Famous Drugstore." Everyone knows Schwab's, too. Schwab's is where Lana Turner was discovered, sitting on a barstool. Hardly a Hollywood memoir is complete without a reference to Schwab's and it is heavy with the old mystique. Elderly widows of emigré directors reminisce about Prague over their cornflakes. Young men in jerkins and expensive shoes ostentatiously read *Variety*, or greet each other with stagey endearments and expletives. Ever and again one hears across the hubbub, in the whining intonations pecular to not very successful actors offstage, an exchange of critiques—"I love her, she's a fine, fine actress, but it just wasn't *her*—"Well, but what can you expect with Philip directing, she needs *definite* direction"—"True, but shit, it just made me *puke*, the way she did that last scene. . . ." Nearly everyone seems to know nearly everyone else at Schwab's: I used to drink my coffee at the counter, until I found this instinct for intimacy too cloying for comfort, and took to sharing a table with the divorced wife of a Mexican set designer who shared my enthusiasm for Abyssinian cats.

Source: Jan Morris, "Entering L.A. Historical Landmark," *Rolling Stone*, July 1, 1976, pp. 32, 77.

In Box 11-3 Jan Morris describes a favorite meeting place for people in show business.

Specialized places like this exist very infrequently in nonurban areas simply because the critical mass of people of any one type simply doesn't exist. (Of course, it is possible that city-people living a particular life-style may "export" themselves to a nonurban area for certain purposes—"the Hamptons" on Long Island is a favorite haunt for New York's wealthy cosmopolites.)

On another level the city's ecological forces make possible the extension and deepening of subcultural characteristics in a way that is not possible in other settings. A historical example will illustrate.

A specialist in the life-style of American urban elites, E. Digby Baltzell (1979) became puzzled that one American colonial city—Boston—had produced so many important figures in our national life while another important city—Philadelphia—had produced so few. The Boston historical register reads like a veritable "who's who" of national prominence—John Adams and John Quincy Adams became presidents; then there were the Cabots, the Lodges, the Lowells, the Lawrences, the Holmeses, all of whom, in one way or another, left a mark in American history. Other than Benjamin Franklin (who actually grew up in Boston), Philadelphia can boast of very few national leaders. Who, outside of Pennsylvania, immediately recognizes these elite names: the Biddles, the Drexels, the Cadwaladers, the Whartons, the Wetherills? Why this difference?

Baltzell answered by suggesting that each city, in Fischer's terms, intensified a very different type of cultural pattern. Early Boston was founded by Puritans, a distinctive religious group that stressed the importance of building a city that would embody their values of publicly recognized excellence. They worked hard to accomplish their task. They established Harvard and ran it, in many respects, not only as *the* place of national intellectual excellence, but as a "local club" where their children could be trained in all the right values. Over the years, many Bostonians rose to national prominence in a wide range of pursuits.

Philadelphia was different. Founded by Quakers, the religious beliefs of the city's people stressed an "egalitarian individualism" wherein hierarchy and social leadership were downplayed. True, the University of Pennsylvania is also a prestigious "ivy league" institution in Philadelphia, but it was never as important in the life of the elite as Harvard was in Boston. Thus, while Philadelphia's elite amassed individual wealth they lacked the impulse to become involved in positions of social responsibility or prominence in state or national affairs. Emphasizing equality and downplaying leadership, is it any wonder, Baltzell asked, that Philadelphia has an "instinct for disparagement?"

Baltzell's study shows us that although subcultural characteristics are magnified by the large numbers, density, and heterogeneity of the city, they do not generate any single type of urban person. Philadelphia's Quakers were, after all, markedly different from Boston's Puritans.

Fischer's ideas balance Wirth's emphasis on the ecological forces of the city with Gans's emphasis on the subcultural characteristics of urban dwellers, claiming—as most of us sense intuitively—that *both* play a role in shaping urban lifestyles. Recently, Fischer's hypothesis has been substantiated. Taking a national sample of city and suburban dwellers, Wilson (1985a) found that a fear of strangers was much more pronounced in some city dwellers than in similar suburbanites. Those found to be more afraid of strangers in the city were the elderly, people with children, and the poor. However, in the suburbs these groups showed no greater concern about "stranger danger" than their fellow suburbanites. Thus, Wilson concludes that the setting—city or suburb—has an effect on some people that is independent of their socioeconomic characteristics.

Life Beyond the City Limits: A Brief History of Suburbs

When a city dweller packs up and moves his family to the suburbs, he usually acquires a mortgage, a power lawn mower, and a backyard grill. Often, although a lifelong Democrat, he also starts voting Republican.

NEWSWEEK, *April 1, 1957, p. 42*

Thus far we have ignored the life-style of the fastest growing urban region of all: the suburbs. The 1980 census showed the United States to have a population of 226.5 million people. That was up some 23 million from the 1970 census, a ten-year increase of 11.4 percent. In contrast, the population of America's suburban areas was some 90 million in 1980 (almost 40 percent of the national total) and reflected an increase of 14.5 million between 1970 and 1980, up some 17.4 percent. Furthermore, having passed the center cities in terms of overall population by 1970, the suburbs are, by far, the preferred type of settlement of Americans. Hence, any understanding of urban life-styles must take this urban region into account.

Yet, like the central cities themselves, we shall hardly find the suburbs monolithic in terms of mores. Although stereotypes of suburban dwellers (like the passage above) were once somewhat truthful, the suburban picture now is much more complex. For one thing, America's suburbs are no longer, as they were only a couple of decades ago, almost exclusively white. Almost every major city outside the South showed an increase in the number of blacks living in its suburbs between 1970 and 1980. The suburban black population of New York went from 5.9 percent to 7.6 percent, Los Angeles from 6.2 percent to 9.6 percent, St. Louis from 7.0 percent to 10.6 percent, and the District of Columbia from 8.3 percent to 16.7 percent. For another thing, as we discussed in Chapter 3, the suburbs are pushing even further out. New, outer suburbs, which some have called the "exurbs" (Spectorsky 1957), are emerging like wildfire, and older, inner suburbs are beginning to decay. Very distinctive populations are emerging in these different types of suburbs.

But that is getting ahead of the story. To understand the suburbs of today, we need a quick look at the suburbs of the past.

Suburbs and the Gilded Age

Most people are vaguely aware of how rapidly suburbs have grown since World War II. It would be a mistake, however, to assume that suburbs are therefore a modern phenomenon. Suburban settlements in the United States have been a continuous part of our history since the seventeenth century, although their significance has grown over time.

In the mid–nineteenth century, as railroads pushed outward from the central city, an increasing number of affluent and fashionable people established summer residences in small outlying settlements (chiefly along the old turnpike routes that connected cities of the Northeast). Of fashionable Philadelphians, Baltzell writes:

> The early suburbanites usually spent only the summer months in the country, the more wealthy in their country houses and their less affluent friends in various popular boarding houses. With the improvement of rail service in the last few decades of the nineteenth century, large suburban estates began to multiply, suburban developments were built, and many families remained the year round. (1979, p. 197)

In the 1870s the Pennsylvania Railroad offered to sell land in the area of the Bryn Mawr Station (about 10 miles west of Philadelphia) and offered it to wealthy prospective suburbanites. In 1881 what was probably the nation's first suburban development was built by George W. Childs (himself owner of a fabulous country estate at Bryn Mawr) and A. J. Drexel in nearby Wayne. Baltzell records that ". . . they erected fifty modern homes which included spacious lawns, ample shade trees, and such conveniences of the city as water, sewer, and gas mains" (1979, p. 204).

Such suburban residence in the United States clearly was limited to the economically privileged. The magnitude of that privilege, however, is not always appreciated today. For instance, one of the most grandiose suburban residences (in Elkins Park, just to the north of Philadelphia) was built in 1900 by Peter Arrell Brown Widener and remains today as a monument to the excesses of the Gilded Age. Built on 300 acres, Lynnewood Hall has 110 rooms, formal French gardens, and, while owned by the Wideners, contained "one of the finest private art collections in the world" (Baltzell 1979, p. 212). The fact that the early suburban residence was associated so closely with the life-style of the well-to-do has remained an important source of suburban prestige to the present time.

Streetcar Suburbs

The research of Sam Bass Warner in the Boston area supports Baltzell's account of the affluence of the mid-nineteenth-century suburbanites. Warner describes the growth of the suburbs of Roxbury, Dorchester, and West Roxbury in the area south of central Boston. From 1850 to 1900 these communities increased in population from 60,000 to about 227,000 (1962, p. 35). Formerly independent settlements beyond the "walking city" of Boston, their growth was greatly stimulated by an innovation in transportation. Once steam locomotives (which stopped infrequently) were supplanted by streetcars, lines of new houses sprang up along track routes. Suburban living and streetcar service "moved together: the more street railway service, the faster the rate of building" (Warner 1962, p. 49). Later, cross-town service filled in the area between the original suburbs and downtown. As this happened, the old "walking city" of several square miles disappeared forever. In its place emerged a vastly larger urban area of streetcar suburbs. By 1900, these suburbs actually contained about half of the population of metropolitan Boston (Warner 1962, p. 3).

The process was repeated throughout the country in cities that had efficient mass transportation. As urban subway and elevated systems pushed ever deeper into the city's hinterland at the beginning of the twentieth century, suburbs appeared everywhere. Today this growth process is still visible. A ride on subway or elevated lines with stops at stations along the way invariably will show major shopping and residential units close by the transit station itself and, as one moves outward on the line, residential tracts of progressively newer design.

The Arrival of the Automobile

Central cities retained about 65 percent of the total urban population in 1910. Suburban growth was rapid, however, surpassing that of the central cities after World War I (Farley 1976, p. 4). Major decentralization had begun, and at its root was the increasingly widespread ownership of automobiles. Before the automobile, early suburban growth was tentaclelike, stretching out along the

The movement of affluent urbanites to suburban areas in the late nineteenth century conferred a quality of prestige upon suburban living that persists today. Here, a New Jersey family plays croquet on the well-mown lawn behind their house. (Bettmann)

tracks that led from the city core. This pattern of the suburb began to change however, as cars made every part of the region accessible to the commuter.

The first automobile (the Duryea) was driven in the United States in 1893. Mass production began soon afterward with Henry Ford's Model T in 1908. In the next two decades, production moved from a few thousand to nearly 4.5 million a year (see Table 11-1). The availability of relatively inexpensive cars—a 1912 Ford runabout sold for $525 (Tobin 1976, p. 102)—increased the mobility of the population and literally changed the face of the nation. Roads were paved, development areas were bought, and the percentage of people living in suburbs moved ever upward. Table 11-2 shows the growth of the suburban population relative to the central cities from 1900 to 1980. From 1900 to 1940, growth was moderate. World War II stalled new construction, but

after the war the nation was seized by a virtual "suburban fever."

1945–1970

With both the Great Depression and the war behind, America's suburbs exploded. Suburban growth had its roots in prosperity, the long-term desire of most middle-class Americans to have a place of their own out of the city's hubbub, the baby boom of the postwar era, and the rush of many whites to escape the deteriorating and increasingly minority-occupied housing of many inner-city areas. Across the country new housing developments appeared—Park Forest near Chicago and Drexelbrook near Philadelphia are two of the more well-known examples. None, however, is more emblematic of the suburban change that swept the country than Levittown on Long Island.

TABLE 11-1
Automobiles Manufactured in the United States (Selected Years)

Year	Number of Vehicles
1905	24,000
1909	120,000
1916	1,500,000
1922	2,270,000
1929	4,455,000
1950	6,666,000
1983	6,739,000

Source: Adapted from Gary A. Tobin, "Suburbanization and the Development of Motor Transportation," in B. Schwartz, ed., *The Changing Face of the Suburbs* (Chicago: University of Chicago Press, 1976), pp. 101–104; and U.S. Bureau of the Census, *Statistical Abstract of the United States 1985.*

Some 30 miles east of Manhattan, Levittown was built on land previously used for growing potatoes. Begun in 1947 by Abraham Levitt and his sons, it was originally planned as 2,000 rental units for veterans. However, the project escalated to 6,000 units within a year, and by 1951, when the last house had been built, 17,447 homes were in place (Wattel 1958, p. 287).

The houses (virtually all of which were sold, not rented) were small and strikingly uniform in appearance:

The original Levittown house was designed in the "Cape Cod" manner, with 720 square feet of space on the first floor. A concrete slab . . . served as the ground floor; there was no cellar. The heating unit (oil) was located in the kitchen. In addition to the kitchen, the first floor contained two bedrooms, a bath, a living room, numerous closets and a stairway which led to the unfinished (expansion) attic. Homes were situated on plots of 6,000 square feet or slightly larger. All interiors were exactly alike, four facades with assorted colors were used to vary the exteriors. (Wattel 1958, pp. 291–292)

Retail businesses were quick to follow the flow of population into these bedroom communities, and local shopping malls increasingly became part of suburban living. Although a suburban shopping center was built as early as 1907 in Baltimore and another shortly afterward in the Coun-

try Club district of Kansas City (Jackson 1973), by 1946 only eight such centers existed. By 1960 the number had soared to some 3,800 (Tobin 1976), by 1970 some 13,000 "malls" existed across the United States (King 1974, p. 102), and the number continues to increase into the 1980s. Moreover, by 1970, with industry moving outward, jobs had become just about evenly distributed throughout the central city and surrounding suburban rings (Rosenthal 1974).

In short, in the 25 years that followed the Second World War, the suburb arrived as a force to be reckoned with on the American urban scene. Although the vast majority of these suburbs were populated by white people who still worked in the center city, such was not to be the case for long.

1970 to the Present

Minorities. Today the suburbs, particularly the innermost ones, are no longer the white, middle-class, family-with-kids bastions they once were. More and more, they are populated by minorities, the working class and poor, and the aged. Table 11-3 illustrates the process by showing the gains made by blacks in the last decade.

Although in many cases the black inroads are minor (for example, in Boston the growth was from 1.0 percent in 1970 to 1.6 percent in 1980), the trend is real and likely will continue. The

TABLE 11-2
Central Cities and Suburbs, 1900–1980 (Percent of United States Population)

Year	Central Cities	Suburbs
1900	21.2%	10.7%
1910	25.0	12.7
1920	28.9	14.8
1930	31.8	18.0
1940	31.6	19.5
1950	32.3	23.8
1960	33.4	33.3
1970	31.4	37.2
1980	29.6	44.1

Source: Adapted from D. Bogue, "Urbanism and Metropolitanism," in W. Dobriner, ed., *The Suburban Community* (New York: G.P. Putnam's, 1958), p. 24. Also calculated from U.S. Bureau of the Census, *Statistical Abstract of the United States 1980*, No. 21, and *1985*, No. 23.

TABLE 11-3
Blacks in the Suburbs of Major Cities, 1970 and 1980

Region and Suburban Area	1970		1980	
	Total Blacks	Black % of Population	Total Blacks	Black % of Population
Northeast				
New York	123,143	5.9	156,291	7.6
Newark	147,447	8.8	225,770	13.8
Philadelphia	191,311	6.7	245,527	8.1
Boston	22,580	1.0	34,205	1.6
Pittsburgh	65,845	3.5	73,790	4.0
Baltimore	69,914	6.0	125,721	9.1
District of Columbia	179,428	8.3	404,814	16.7
Midwest				
Cleveland	44,637	3.4	94,285	7.1
Chicago	129,794	3.6	230,827	5.6
Detroit	99,314	3.4	131,478	4.2
Minneapolis	2,408	0.2	8,308	0.6
South				
Atlanta	92,440	8.4	215,909	13.5
Dallas-Forth Worth	41,032	3.6	65,955	3.9
Houston	73,515	9.6	88,256	6.7
West				
San Diego	9,245	1.4	26,752	2.7
Los Angeles	240,021	6.2	398,069	9.6
Anaheim, Calif.	2,934	0.3	13,455	1.0
San Francisco-Oakland	109,729	5.4	145,566	6.5

Source: U.S. Bureau of the Census.

following sentiments expressed by new minority suburbanities are typical:

> "I got tired of all the winos in my neighborhood," says Ruby Ashby, who lives in a St. Louis suburb. "I always wanted to see my kids play baseball on the grass," says Patricia Harris of Park Forest South, Illinois. "It's the American dream," says Juanita Ashe of Novato, California. "It's what we worked for." (*Newsweek*, Dec. 31, 1979, p. 35)

The movement of these various groups to the suburbs, however, has typically *not* resulted in an integrated community (Logan and Schneider 1984). Rather, as time passes, groups tend to take over whole areas or neighborhoods, either by a process of accretion or, in the case of wealthy developers, by wholesale purchase. Moreover, the rapid growth of the exurbs, the outer ring of the suburbs, has been almost exclusively dominated by whites and the well-to-do. The inner suburbs, in some cases many decades old, are beginning to physically deteriorate, and the costs of keeping them up, as well as taxes, are increasing. Given these problems and suburb-bound minorities and working classes, more affluent members of these older suburbs have simply packed up and moved farther out. In the exurbs they usually can get the newest version of their dream home with a lower tax rate and escape living with what they prejudicially see as undesirable neighbors (Marshall and Stahura 1979). They also can afford the more expensive commute.

In some cases private developers for the elderly or wealthy literally have brought entire tracts of exurban land, built extremely expensive private housing, and set up purchase requirements that all but exclude minorities. For example, near Chicago, the inner industrial suburbs of Evanston, Joliet, and Waukegan showed marked increases in their black populations between 1970 and 1980, while exurban McHenry County, which grew 32 percent in the decade, showed only 108 blacks among a population of 148,000. Similarly, near Atlanta, the inner suburban area of DeKalb County increased its black population from 57,000 in 1970 to 131,000 in 1980. In contrast, exurban Forsythe County counted only one black in a population of 27,958 (*New York Times*,

May 31, 1981). Obviously, serious racial segregation continues in the suburbs. It is not a pattern likely to disappear soon.

Population Trends. After the initial suburban population boom of the postwar era, most analysts thought that "it couldn't go on forever." After all, suburbanization was a decided compromise. People moved to these areas outside the central cities because they wanted bigger houses, lawns, better schools, and the like. The compromise, for most, was commuting. Most wage earners in the suburbs still worked in the center cities, and the need to transport themselves back into the city remained an important limitation on how far out the suburbs could go. In addition, the center cities still had all the commodious elements of urban life—the symphony, the ball parks, the best shopping.

But recent evidence suggests that the trend of increasing suburbanization has not reversed itself as many predicted. Indeed, from 1970 through 1975 the process continued unabated (Edmonston and Guterbock 1984). The reason appears to be related to the fact that the above description of the relationship between the suburbs and the city is no longer fundamentally true. To take a crucial case, the center city no longer is where everybody works. Huge numbers of businesses, as we reported in Chapter 3, have moved out to the suburbs in the past few decades. Obviously, they brought their jobs with them. Hence, for many suburban residents the commute no longer is much of an issue. In fact, it has become possible for many people getting jobs for the first time to take up residence in the suburbs without ever having lived in the center city at all.

In addition, the last few decades have seen the suburbanization of virtually everything that used to be in the purview of the center city. Retail businesses, as we mentioned in the last section, were the first to jump on the bandwagon. With all those people living out of downtown, it made sense to bring the goods to them. Thus began the "malling of America," as suburb after suburb developed centers that were able to challenge the center city for both amount of goods available and dollars spent (Steinnes 1982; Jacobs 1984). The malls, growing rapidly in the 1960s, have ballooned into astonishing "money machines" in the period since 1970. Some, like King of Prussia, some 20 miles from downtown Philadelphia, are so vast it is possible to get *anything* in them. Others, like one near Denver, have days like this:

> To the swelling strains of "Oh What a Beautiful Morning" on the Muzak, a new day [is] breaking at Southwest Plaza, an enormous pentagonal shopping mall that floats above a vast sea of suburban homes like the battleship New Jersey at a convention of canoes.
>
> Before the end of the shopping day 13 hours later, about 30,000 people pass through the Plaza, staying an average of 2.3 hours apiece. They fill all 6,928 spaces in the sprawling asphalt parking lot, drop 150 pounds of pennies into the fountains around the mall's central "performance center," eat 1,000 Super Pretzels and purchase a half million dollars worth of goods and services ranging from diamonds to doorknobs, dental checkups to divorce settlements. (Reid 1985)

But shopping areas are not the only accoutrements of the center city that have moved out to the suburbs. Theaters and musical entertainment of high quality are now common in the suburbs, and the ball parks are beginning to make their shift to where the population is.

In other words, both in terms of work and the amenities of life, for many people there is simply no reason ever to live in the center city. The suburbs, increasingly, are not only where the people are, but where the action is. For all these reasons, suburban growth continues.

Politics. Given this shift of population and economic strength, it should come as no surprise that suburbs have gained considerable political clout in recent years (Slovak 1985). Increasingly, as their populations have become wealthier, suburbs attached to cities via annexation have demanded, and received, more services (often to the detriment of deteriorating or less powerful inner-city neighborhoods).

This battle has intensified under Reagan administration policies that have been dubbed "the New Federalism." Specifically, since it took power in 1981, the Reagan administration, essentially conservative and "states' rights" oriented, has tried to divest the federal government of as many public support programs as possible and return these services to the states (Wade 1982). Such a process of federal divestment, however, would pit cities against suburbs at the state level for available funds, a competition that would decidedly favor the suburbs.

For example, consider various federal antipoverty programs, such as AFDC (Aid to Families with Dependent Children). As the program was set up initially, cities, which have a much higher percentage of poor families with children than suburbs do, were assured of getting a certain amount of money because the federal government administered the funds. If the federal government no longer runs the program, however, the cities will be forced to go to the state government for these funds. However, since suburbs are growing in population, their representation in state governments has increased in recent years. Furthermore, antipoverty programs worked in the past only because they were funded via taxes by the wealthier members of society—to a significant degree, people who live in the suburbs. It is doubtful that suburban representatives will vote to increase taxes on themselves and their constituents to support the inner-city poor, when such taxes, if necessary at all, might be much better spent, in their estimation, on new schools, roads, or sewage systems in the suburbs.

The prospects for the center city, in other words, are not very bright as the New Federalism is instituted. Assuming they lose various financial battles with suburban representatives at the state level, Richard Wade argues that city governments, "already saddled with inordinate financial problems, would be required to raise new revenues or see traditional services curtailed. In the process, ethnic and racial tensions would inevitably heighten, and restless, unemployed youth would turn to crime in even greater numbers" (1982, p. 46).

But the problem is more complex still. Despite their increasing population and political power, the suburbs are hardly all alike. Muller suggests that there now exists in America a "mosaic" of different suburban types, a mosaic that has resulted, as might be expected, in "sharply contrasting life-styles" (1981, pp. 67–68), a topic to which we now turn. To put our discussion in the appropriate context, we will trace suburban life-styles as they evolved throughout the suburban history just presented.

Suburban Life-Styles

The Aristocratic Life

Back in the late nineteenth century, suburban residence symbolized the life-style of the well-to-do and sophisticated; the suburbs were the playground of the nineteenth-century "jet set." Thus, the Country Club (the nation's first), founded in Brookline, Massachusetts in 1882, was frequented by people who took to heart the advice wealthy Bostonians gave their children: "Boston holds nothing for you except heavy taxes and political misrule. When you marry, pick out a suburb to build a house in, join The Country Club, and make your life center about your club, your home and your children" (recalled by Supreme Court Justice Louis Brandeis; Mumford 1961, p. 495).

Fabulous estates such as Widener's Lynnewood Hall—called the Versailles of America—near Philadelphia clearly set off the life-style of early suburbia from that of the central city. The idea was to emulate the country ways of European aristocracy, as the following example makes clear.

In 1886, Pierre Lorillard II (heir to a tobacco fortune) inherited some 600,000 acres and at a cost of $2 million created a millionaires' colony north of New York. Tuxedo Park was "a kind of country club *cum* family resort where some two or three hundred of New York's Best People who were growing tired of resort hotels at Saratoga or Richfield Springs might come to hunt, fish, and skate" (Baltzell 1979, p. 357).

> At Tuxedo Park Lorillard produced almost a caricature of the Victorian millionaire's mania for exclusiveness. In less than a year, he surrounded seven thousand acres with an eight-foot fence, graded some thirty miles of road, built a complete sewage and water system, a gate house which looked like "a frontispiece of an English novel," a clubhouse staffed with imported English servants, and "twenty-two casement dormered English turreted cottages." On Memorial Day, 1886, special trains brought seven hundred highly selected guests from New York to witness the Park's opening. (Baltzell 1964, pp. 122–123)

As he offered his club members property within Tuxedo Park for purchase, Lorillard created, as Baltzell suggests, a sort of Levittown for aristocrats.

Yet, as streetcar lines and then roads dominated by automobiles appeared in the late nineteenth century, new housing rippled outward from cities across the nation. A new image of the suburban life-style began to take hold. Although its roots were the same—the new suburbanites wanted to live "the good life" as much as the aristocrats did—the very magnitude of the change assured the watering down of the elite vision.

The New Suburbia

After World War II, suburban migration for the first time became a mass phenomenon (not for a small elite but for almost anyone of middle-class standing who chose it), and the Tuxedo Parks of America began to give way to the standardized "Cape Cods" of the Levittown variety. By the mid-1950s the picture of the life-style of the new suburbia was not very positive. Most authors seemed to agree with influential sociologist David Riesman, who confessed at the outset of his essay, "The Suburban Sadness," that he was "one who loves city and country, but not the suburbs . . ." (1958, p. 375).

First Impressions. Criticism centered on several supposed characteristics of the middle-class suburban way of life. The most important problem was presumed to be an overbearing conformity. Just as the houses were standardized in appearance, so too, it was said, were the lives within them. Suburbanites were young, had small children, ate crunchy breakfast cereal, socialized with each other relentlessly (coffee klatches in the morning, barbecues in the evening), and obsessively copied each other in tastes and styles in a

BOX 11-4
"Little Boxes on the Hillside"

The image of suburbia began to change after World War II as mass-produced housing replaced the opulence of an earlier era. This neighborhood in Daly City, California (near San Francisco) is typical of the housing developments that inspired Malvina Reynolds's song. (© Robert A. Isaacs/Photo Researchers)

Little boxes on the hillside,
Little boxes made of ticky tacky
Little boxes on the hillside,
Little boxes all the same.
There's a green one and a pink one
And a blue one and a yellow one
And they're all made out of ticky tacky
And they all look just the same.

And the people in the boxes
All went to the university
Where they were put in boxes
And they came out all the same,
And there's doctors and there's lawyers
And there's business executives,
And they're all made out of ticky tacky
And they all look just the same.

And they all play on the golf course
And drink their martinis dry,
And they all have pretty children,
And the children go to school,

And the children go to summer camp
And then to the university,
Where they are put in boxes
And they come out just the same.

And the boys go into business,
And marry and raise a family,
And they all get put in boxes,
Little boxes all the same.

There's a green one and a pink one
And a blue one and a yellow one
And they're all made out of ticky tacky
And they all look just the same.

Source: Malvina Reynolds, 1963

demeaning attempt to "keep up with the Joneses." Always thinking *of* themselves, but rarely *for* themselves, suburbanites constantly turned to each other and relied heavily on experts: Dr. Spock explained child care to mothers; Dale Car-

negie (*How to Win Friends and Influence People*) guided husbands to success within some corporate organization. The Eisenhower landslides of 1952 and 1956 (Ike did extremely well in the suburbs) furthered the assumption that city Democrats tended to become, when they moved, suburban Republicans. If the frenetic activity of the suburban life-style ever did allow one to settle down a bit, it was only for a moment, only until the next move—for families allegedly picked up stakes every few years in their treadmill-like search for success and happiness.

Journalists as well as sociologists were unrelenting in their attack. John Keats blasted suburban developments in his best-selling book *The Crack in the Picture Window* (1956) and named his major characters John and Mary Drone (their neighbors included the Faints and the Amiables) to make it indubitably clear that the people of suburbia were as prefabricated as their two-car garages. Another study (also a best-seller) by Gordon, Gordon, and Gunther, was subtly titled *The Split Level Trap* (1960). The authors provided a data-based report of high stress, anxiety, and related illnesses among residents of "Disturbia." Most influential of all was William H. Whyte's best seller, *The Organization Man* (1956), a study of Park Forest, Illinois, which documented the "wanderings" of the rootless corporate executive. To cap it all off there was folksinger Pete Seeger's popular rendition of Malvina Reynolds's "Little Boxes" (see Box 11-4).

Taking a Closer Look. Was all this banality really the truth of the situation? Many thought not, claiming much of the work on suburbia to be a product of sloppy research and preconceived notions, an overgeneralized attack by intellectuals and journalists on a way of life much more complex than they imagined. Even the solid research—Whyte's *Organization Man*, for example—had been unconscionably overgeneralized by some interpreters to include all of suburbia. Some critics, like Herbert Gans (1968), suggested that the so-called observers of suburbia were much more interested in creating a nasty "suburban myth" than they were in actually *studying* the suburbs.

Yet, for a time, a "suburban myth" was actively embraced by many in this country. The question is, why?

Probably there are three answers. First, many of the suburban developments of the late 1940s and the 1950s *were* populated by whites who were young parents and who had a roughly comparable income level. For example, Wattel (1958) reported that the average age of adult residents of Levittown in 1957 was 35 and that the average household had two or three children.

Second, the intensity of the attack on suburbia also can be seen as a reaction by journalists and intellectuals to the purported emergence of America as a "mass society"—living within the embrace of large bureaucratic organizations and thereby surrendering the American ideal of the rugged, independent, and individualistic pioneer. Surely America has lost some measure of the frontier spirit—although, as Donaldson (1969) correctly points out, the "yeoman farmer" days of America are probably more a romantic ideal than a historical fact—but can one blame the rise of the organizational way of life on the *suburbs*? The target is more properly America taken as a whole.

Third, even the grains of truth in the suburban caricature are decidedly time based. With the influx of subcultural groups of varying racial, occupational, and age composition, the suburbs of the last two decades simply do not support easy generalization. They possess about as much diversity in this regard as do the central cities that we discussed in the first part of this chapter.

Table 11-4 makes this clear by comparing some general social characteristics of a range of contemporary suburban types that had emerged by 1970. As can be easily seen, the suburbs vary widely in terms of income, racial composition, age composition, mobility, education, and occupational characteristics. Naturally, such differences translate into different life-styles.

Contemporary Suburbia: Complexity and Diversity

Middle-Income-Family Suburbs. Of the suburbs listed in Table 11-4, only two, Darien, Connecticut, and Levittown, New York, come close to the stereotype of suburbia discussed in the last section. The needs of the family still shape interaction in these particular communities, but even here there is little evidence of the frantic neigh-

TABLE 11-4
Socioeconomic Characteristics of Selected Suburban Communities, 1970

| | Exclusive Upper-Income (Grosse Pointe Shores, Mich.) | Upper Middle-Income (Darien, Conn.) | Lower Middle-Income (Levittown, N.Y.) | Working Class (Milpitas, Calif.) | Cosmopolitan Suburb (Princeton, N.J.) | Black Suburban types | | |
						Spillover (Glenarden, Md.)	Colony (Kinloch, Mo.)	Satellite City (Chester, Pa.)
Median family income	$32,565	$22,172	$13,083	$11,543	$12,182	$12,544	$5,916	$8,511
% families > $25,000	60.4	41.9	5.7	1.7	18.0	2.2	1.9	1.6
% families < $15,000	19.1	29.6	64.0	75.8	59.8	65.8	91.4	86.4
% families in poverty	2.1	2.4	3.0	5.3	5.2	4.7	32.6	16.2
% black	0.2	0.5	0.1	5.2	10.0	87.2	99.1	45.2
Median age	41.3	32.1	24.0	20.9	28.4	20.8	21.3	28.0
% < 18 years old	30.3	35.5	41.4	46.4	16.3	45.6	44.2	34.0
% > 65 years old	12.4	7.8	3.6	2.1	10.6	2.4	10.5	10.6
% same address, 1965	59.5	60.3	75.1	31.5	34.2	43.0	67.1	62.0
% in school	80.3	71.0	63.0	55.3	67.4	58.9	58.3	33.8
% high school graduates	83.1	83.1	64.2	63.6	76.5	66.7	16.6	10.2
% women in labor force	20.8	34.5	41.9	45.5	49.4	66.0	46.4	43.7
%professional and technical workers	28.3	25.7	13.6	16.9	37.6	25.9	4.5	9.1
% managerial/ administrative workers	31.6	25.2	9.4	5.2	7.5	41.1	0.3	3.5
% operatives	0.8	4.3	7.6	18.5	2.8	3.5	17.0	21.6

Source: Peter O. Muller, *Contemporary Suburban America* (Englewood Cliffs, N.J.: Prentice-Hall, 1981), p. 79.

borhood socializing of the earlier stereotype. As Muller describes them:

> The management of children is a central . . . concern, and most local social contact occurs through such family-oriented formal organizations as the school PTA, Little League, and the Scouts. . . . Neighboring is limited and selective, and even socializing with relatives is infrequent. . . . The insular single-family house and dependence on the automobile for all trip making [accommodate the development of a] network of self-selected friends widely distributed in suburban space. (1981, p. 72)

There are few in poverty, hardly any blacks, and few who have not finished at least high school.

Upper-Income Suburbs. These communities, though more densely settled than their historical antecedents, in many respects resemble the old aristocratic suburbs of yesteryear. In addition to Grosse Pointe Shores near Detroit, Valley Forge in Pennsylvania and Beverly Hills in California are among their ranks. Their populations tend to have an older median age than those of other suburbs, and very few families are below what would be termed "middle income." They have large houses, usually built on large properties, and center their social lives around churches and country clubs. Membership in the latter is usually difficult to obtain and jealously guarded once acquired (Muller 1981, p. 71).

Working-Class Suburbs. Just a few miles to the north of San Jose, California, the suburb of Milpitas stands in stark contrast to suburbs like Darien or Grosse Pointe Shores. In 1960 Bennett Berger published an account of the life-styles of 100 residents of Milpitas, most of whom were employed in blue-collar jobs at a neaby Ford assembly plant. His study revealed that these families were not of very high status, weren't looking to "get ahead," identified themselves as Democrats, didn't in any sense rely on "experts" like Doctor Spock to tell them how to manage their lives, didn't join clubs or organizations, and did spend a good deal of time with their relatives. Perhaps most important, Berger found that the men and women of Milpitas were not transformed by suburban living. They remained generally true to the same patterns of living held by working-class people in the central city.

This isn't surprising when the socioeconomic characteristics of Milpitas residents are examined (Table 11-4). Most families made under $15,000 in 1970, many had small children absorbing a fair amount of that income, and few had high levels of education when compared to Darien or Grosse Pointe Shores.

Such working-class suburbs have multiplied rapidly since World War II. Many were created when working-class families moved out of the center city to be near places of employment as industry decentralized. Muller describes the dominant interests of most:

> [Suburban] working-class ethnic-centered neighborhoods are characterized by a broad social interaction of informal groups congregating at such local meeting places as the church, tavern, street corner, or door stoop. Local group acceptance and integration is the dominant social value, and communal life stresses the availability of a satisfying peer-group society, similar neighborhoods, maintaining easy access among people well-known to each other, and collective defense of neighborhood respectability. (1981, pp. 74–75)

Suburban Cosmopolitan Centers. In marked contrast to Milpitas (and more like Darien and Grosse Pointe Shores) are such communities as Princeton, New Jersey, home of Princeton University. Composed mainly of academics, professionals, writers, actors, artists, and students, these communities are often comparable to university areas, bohemian enclaves, or cosmopolite residential areas in the central cities. Their population is usually deeply interested in "high culture"; thus, theaters, music facilities, and esoteric and elegant restaurants are found in abundance (Muller 1981).

Black Suburbs. A glance at Table 11-4 will show that in none of the suburbs discussed thus far did blacks constitute over 10 percent of the population. Although, as we have noted, the reasons that whites move out of increasingly black suburbs are related to finances and convenience as well as race, the result is still the same. Eventually most whites leave and a segregated black suburban community—analogous in many ways to its center-city counterpart, the black ghetto—is created.

Muller (1981) distinguishes three subtypes of black suburbs. The first is what he calls the "spillover" community—represented in Table 11-4 by Glenarden, Maryland, adjacent to Washington, D.C. These suburbs are direct outgrowths of center-city black ghettos that move, over time, beyond the center-city. Significant spillover suburbs of blacks presently exist in Cleveland, St. Louis, Chicago, Atlanta, Miami, Los Angeles, and New York and are becoming more and more prevalent throughout the country. The income level of spillover communities is high relative to other black suburbs because, like whites departing from the center cities throughout this century, those blacks moving outward tend to be middle class, and wish to leave poorer areas and poorer blacks behind.

"Colonies," such as Kinloch, Missouri, just outside St. Louis, represent a second type. Often these isolated communities originally arose as shantytowns outside the city proper and in recent decades have been literally surrounded by white suburbs. As Kinloch's data in Table 11-4 show, they are poor areas with deteriorating housing and large numbers of people living below the poverty level (almost a third in Kinloch's case). Few members of the population have much education, and most work in non-white-collar jobs. The outlook for these people is as bleak as it is for center-city ghetto residents.

Only somewhat better off than the black suburban colony is the "satellite city," exemplified by Chester, Pennsylvania, in Table 11-4. Originally constructed as an industrial city about 10 miles downriver from Philadelphia, Chester was once a place of thriving shipbuilding and metal fabricating. No more. Both industries have fallen on hard times in the Philadelphia area, leaving Chester and its black population—which makes up about half of the suburb's 56,000 residents—high, dry, and extremely poor. Although their income figures are slightly better than Kinloch's, their outlook isn't all that much brighter.

The Exurbs. One type of suburb remains to be discussed. The 1980 census showed conclusively that all around the country the fastest growing area was the newer, second ring beyond the old suburbs. By and large, the people moving there are white, relatively wealthy, highly educated, and professional. Although it would be misleading to say that this region's residents are all the same, there seems little doubt that, depending on the locale, they are much more likely to resemble the residents of Grosse Pointe Shores, Darien, or Princeton than other suburban groups.

In 1957, A. C. Spectorsky published the first account of these people, based on his observations (none too systematic, it should be noted) of an exclusive residential area on the fringes of the New York City metropolitan area. Spectorsky called this outlying area an "exurb," and the name has stuck. Moreover, his book has proven prophetic, for what was a small trend in 1957 has become a veritable stampede in the 1980s. Then, the exurbanites settled heavily in counties such as Fairfield (Connecticut), Rockland and Westchester (New York), and Bucks (Pennslvania). Today, they are in the counties surrounding every major city—in Marin near San Francisco, in Forsythe near Atlanta.

Spectorsky notes, however, that the populace of the exurbs, despite their relatively long physical distance from the center city, are clearly urbanites at heart. For one thing, their life-style is like that of the cosmopolite—very high-brow—but transplanted into the rustic, rural charm of some outlying nook-of-a-village. When not commuting to and from "The City," exurbanites devour books, theater, and art, and (if they can) they raise horses. They are indeed a curious mix of "high tech" and rustic charm, as Spectorsky noted with characteristic wit:

> Your true exurbanite is gadget happy. He is never so delighted as when he is combining his love for old things and his fascination with new ones. Handhewn oak pegs hold his Leica and Rolleiflex cases; he stores his electric worm-digger in a Hepplewhite chest. (1957, p. 39)

To give an indication of the growth of the exurbs, consider these facts: (1) the nonmetropolitan area of the United States was the fastest growing region during the period between 1970 and 1980, despite the fact that the farm population of the country *decreased* during the same period (Fuguitt 1985); and (2) the area designated as the "urban fringe" by the census bureau increased from 26.8 percent of the total national population to 31.8 percent during the same decade. Why are so many people moving still further out from the center city? Recent research suggests a variety of reasons, but, on the whole, reasons that are not very surprising when we consider the suburban exodus of the early postwar era. When people are asked why they moved to the exurbs, typical responses are "retirement," "because my job is there or nearby," "because I like to live in the country and have some open space around me," "because I have friends or family in the area," and, of course, "because I want to get out of the city" (Fuguitt 1985). In short, the exurb, like the suburb before it, is seemingly another step in the American quest for greener pastures (in this case, perhaps literally), another attempt to find the place where the American Dream will at last come true.

Is exurbia the ideal fusion of rural and urban living? Spectorsky doubted it: the exurbanite, he said was torn by the strain of a double life, trying to live both "in" and "out" of the city. Worse still, Spectorsky believed that most exurbanites carried the competitiveness and anxiety of the job right home with them.

CITYSCAPE 11-3
The Natural History of a Reluctant Suburb

What it means for a long-established village to be suburbanized can be seen from the recent history of a community called here, for reasons of tact, "Old Harbor." It is a real place, in the general New England area, on the Atlantic Coast. Over 300 years old, Old Harbor lies at the foot of a curving valley between two green necks of land stretching into the sea.

In its early years, Old Harbor served as the local nexus of an agrarian and colonial society. Its grist mills ground local grain into flour through the power of the impounded waters of the tide ponds and mill dams. The natural harbor drew shipping from all over the east coast. Whaling ships worked out of the home port, and coastal shipping from ports as far away as the West Indies unloaded hides, rum, cattle, cord-wood, charcoal, etc., on Old Harbor's busy wharfs. Over the [centuries] . . . the village prospered but remained comparatively changeless in some fundamental ways—it continued to be a Yankee village of industrious merchants, seamen, farmers, and craftsmen. . . .

By the middle of the nineteenth century . . . change was imminent. In 1867 the railroad came to the village and became a serious competitor with marine transpor-

tation, and thereafter the harbor declined as a vital force in the village's economy. Even more ominous was the fact that 36.6 miles from the village lay the borders of a city . . . showing a capacity for incredible growth and its influence was extending beyond its borders. . . . In writing to a relative in 1872, one villager noted, "There has been a very curious thing this summer, I must have seen 15 or 20 strangers in town during July and August."

The first invaders of Old Harbor were members of the new industrial aristocracy who emerged in the decades after the Civil War. . . . By the turn of the century, Old Harbor had become their carefully guarded preserve. They bought the old farms and cleared away acres for their summer playgrounds and gigantic estates. They fenced off two- and three-hundred-acre parcels and created separate dukedoms populated by communities of servants and laborers.

By the early 1920's, the township in which Old Harbor is located was undergoing rather intensive immigration from the metropolitan area. The city was going through one of its growth spasms, and the population was spilling over the city limits into the

adjacent counties. Old Harbor was one county removed, but this was the decade in which the automobile drastically changed the character of American society and culture. [Soon] a few miles to the south of the Village, in "Old Harbor Station," the railroad terminus, a new and rather singular figure stood on the platform waiting for the 8:05 to the city: the commuter, the classic suburbanite, with his freshly pressed tight trousers, starched white collar, and morning paper folded neatly under his arm.

After the Second World War, population that had been trapped in the city during the war years exploded into the county neighboring Old Harbor. In ten years, the number of people in this "rural" county passed a million and made it one of the most rapidly growing areas in the United States. . . . In the ten years from 1945 to 1955, Old Harbor Township doubled its population, and the village itself has now absorbed between two and three times the number it had in 1940. In just ten years, a 300-year-old village, with many of the descendants of the original founders still living there, underwent a social shock that wrenched it from whatever remained of the patterns of the past. . . .

Perhaps most worrisome of all, exurbia is radically altering much of what is left of America's small town. William Dobriner saw it coming back in 1963. His description in Cityscape 11-3 of the fate of "Old Harbor" reviews almost all of the suburban story.

Urban Culture and the Suburbs

Finally, what are the effects of Wirth's ecological variables—large numbers, density, and social heterogeneity—in the suburbs? Are suburbanites

forced to deal with these phenomena and adapt their life-styles to them in the same way that Claude Fischer claimed inner-city residents had to?

Obviously not. All these variables, at least at present, generally are much weaker in the suburbs. Although more people live in the suburbs than in the center city, their dispersion over a wide area keeps their contact with one another more limited; housing density is lower, and much more open space exists for daily life; and con-

No longer is there enough space in Old Harbor. You can't park your car on Main Street any more, there may not be room in church if you arrive late on Sunday, classrooms are "overcrowded," and you have to wait your turn for telephones to be installed in your new house. . . . [But] the fundamental schism between the world of the old-timers and the world of the newcomers makes a problem that is less obvious but both more important and harder to cope with.

The temper of the suburbanite "community" may be summarized in the way the suburbanites talk about Old Harbor:

I came to Old Harbor because there is still some green around here and yet I can still get to the airport in 45 minutes. It's a nice place to live—the schools are good. . . . I like being near the water. It is hard to say how long we'll be here. I would like to be based further south, but as a place to live Old Harbor is fine.

I can't think of Old Harbor as my own town or anything like that. Most of my friends live closer to the city and I work there. . . . I guess I sleep more of my time here than anything else, but it's a good place for the kids. I've got a lot of contacts and interests outside.

But an old-timer says:

They [the suburbanites] don't know what's going on around here. They don't care. But I do; this is my town. I used to fish down at the tide basin. Now they're talking of tearing it down. I went to school here. All my friends live around here. It's crazy what's happening. I can look out my shop window and can't recognize 49 out of 50 faces I see. There was a time I knew everybody. It used to be our town. I don't know whose it is any more. . . .

This is the real issue that splits the suburbanite and villager communities apart. For the suburbanites, Old Harbor is another commodity; it is a product that can be rationally consumed; it is a means by which they hope to achieve a complex series of personal goals. For the villagers, on the other hand, Old Harbor is not a means to anything; it is simply an end in itself.

Yet the future lies with the metropolis and not the village. You can see it in the new super expressways that slice through Old Harbor's meadow-lands. You sense the shift in internal balance in the village by the domination of the suburbanites at school board meetings. You know it on an autumn's evening, in the crisp sea air, and in the deepening twilight around the mill pond. The great shuddering bulk of the mill squats in the hollow, intimidated by the headlights of the commuters as they race down and through the valley, dreary from the city and hungry for home. Pencils of light search into the gaping slats and crudely intrude upon the embarrassment of the mill's decay—the rusting gears, the splintered shaft, the rotting timbers, and marsh slop heaped up by the last high tide. . . . Up along the darkening necks the lights are going on in the new split levels and "contemporaries" tucked into the ridges. The lights go on and off as the night rolls in. They seem to be winking at the senile mill as it sits and broods in the gathering darkness.

Source: William M. Dobriner, *Class in Suburbia* (Englewood Cliffs, N.J.: Prentice-Hall, 1963), pp. 128–136, 140.

tact among socially heterogenous people has been restricted by the development of suburban communities based on class, age, or ethnic considerations.

Thus, more than in the center city, in the suburbs we would expect to find sociocultural characteristics like class and race determining lifestyles more directly. We also would expect to find less diversity, intensity, and change in life-style patterns over time. Whereas the inner city produces diversity, intensity, and change automatically because of its unavoidable mix of peoples, the suburbs are more "laid back" and less pressured to adapt in quick or novel ways because the mix is weaker. Because of their somewhat greater numbers, density, and heterogeneity, however, we would expect the inner suburbs to exhibit more diversity, intensity and change than the exurbs.

Nevertheless, it would be a mistake to assume, just because the inner city's ecological characteristics are weaker in the suburbs, that suburbanites are not much affected by the city. On the contrary, as Spectorsky noted, in a fundamental sense all suburbanites are "of" the city. Many work there and "bring the city home" with them. Even if the don't work in the city, even if they hardly ever *go* there, they are affected by the city's media, politics, economy, and problems. In other words, suburbanites are influenced by the city's *culture*—its values, activities, and issues. As Cityscape 11-3 shows so well, Old Harbor's exurbanites are "city-slickers" through and through. Because they orient their lives toward the city (however indirectly or unconsciously), most suburbanites can be accurately said to live urban life-styles.

Conclusion

We find, in the end, that most clichés and stereotypes about urbanites are gross distortions. Research in the past two decades points again and again to the existence of pronounced urban variety—a range of life-styles that defies easy conceptualization. This is as true of the suburbs as it is of the center city.

In center cities, as Herbert Gans analyzed them, there are at least five major life-styles. The cosmopolites, to take just one example, are as different from the disaffiliated as can be imagined. Such diversity significantly weakens Louis Wirth's hypothesis that the city's unique ecological characteristics—large numbers, density, and social heterogeneity—produce a single, characteristic life-style. Refuting Wirth's hypothesis, Gans argues that sociocultural characteristics—such as age, sex, race, and income—and not the city itself are responsible for each group's life-style.

Not content with this claim, Claude Fischer retorted that Wirth was not all wrong. In his view, the city's ecological characteristics *do* affect urban dwellers' lives, but not quite in the way Wirth suggested. Rather than producing a deterministic effect, Fischer argues, large numbers, density, and heterogeneity encourage combinations and intensifications of sociocultural characteristics to produce distinctive urban life-styles. Thus, Fischer argues that to understand life-styles in the

central city, *both* Wirth's ecological characteristics and Gans's sociocultural characteristics have to be considered.

But what of the outer city, the fastest growing urban region? This question led us to the suburbs, in recent years probably the most maligned of urban areas. Until recently, the suburbs have been berated for producing a single life-style: dull, middle-class people, rubber-stamped by a dehumanized physical and social environment of chilling mediocrity and sameness.

A brief review of the history of the suburbs saw them emerge in the late nineteenth century as country estates and small enclaves for the well-to-do, people anxious to escape the pressures of immigration and rapid industrialization in the inner city. With the invention of the automobile in the twentieth century, however, the suburbs were transformed. The middle class moved to them in ever-increasing numbers, and after World War II the process intensified. In two and a half decades (roughly from 1945 to 1970) the population of American suburbs mushroomed from under 30 million to over 75 million.

A closer look showed the suburban life-style stereotype—of white middle-class families with children and white-collar jobs living in "little boxes"—to be decidedly biased. Even in the heyday of the new suburbia, life was never as monochromatic as the critics would have had it. The last two decades have seen a marked increase in suburban diversity as the aged, the working class, and minorities have moved to these outlying areas in large numbers. This migration has produced a life-style complexity in contemporary American suburbs that in many respects rivals that of the inner city. There is every reason to believe that this complexity and diversity will continue to increase into the 1990s as decentralization continues.

The influx of new groups to the outer city usually has not resulted in communities embracing sociocultural diversity. Instead, the typical pattern has been the evolution of distinct types of suburbs. There are middle-income suburbs, exclusive upper-income suburbs, working-class suburbs, black suburbs, and—increasingly in the South, Southwest, and West—Hispanic suburbs.

This demographic pattern, moreover, appears to be getting stronger as the years pass, despite concerted efforts in some parts of the country to open up the suburbs to all people (Downs 1973). One indication of this pattern is the growth in the last two and a half decades of yet another urban ring, the exurbs—the area beyond the original suburban tracts. By and large, this area is being inundated by wealthy white urbanites, looking, as had their parents before them, to leave the problems of the city behind as they search for more living space.

Two other patterns caught our attention. First, it is no longer true that the center city is the place where all the amenities of urban life exist. The suburbs have developed, in some cases, into true "minicities" in their own right. They have all the goods and services and are rapidly developing all the entertainment facilities that the center city used to have the "lock and key" to. The reason is the continuing population shift to the suburbs. Business in America, quite simply, goes where the people are. Second, there is a serious political battle looming between the center cities and the suburbs over monies for programs and services. While the suburbs were small, the center cities held the purse strings. Now, with the growth of the suburbs, political power has shifted, and suburbs are beginning to "feather their own nests" at the expense of the center cities. This confrontation has been augmented by the policies of the Reagan administration and its desire to rid the federal government of programs that it feels can be better handled at the state level. Unfortunately, the true losers in this encounter are most likely to be the inner-city poor, who will find, as funds dry up or are diverted to suburban programs, that center-city governments no longer have the ability to help them.

In the end, then, three distinct sets of variables appear to be responsible for urban life-styles. Wirth's *ecological variables* (large numbers, density, heterogeneity) have their strongest effect in the center city and its residential areas; they get noticeably weaker as one moves out of the city into the inner suburbs and weaker as one moves out of the city into the inner suburbs and weaker still as one gets to the exurbs. Gans's *sociocultural variables* (age, race, and so on) have a major effect in *any* type of settlement; however, in the central city they are intensified and recombined in unique ways because of their "forced contact" with the city's greater numbers, density, and heterogeneity. In the inner suburbs and particularly in the exurbs and beyond, sociocultural variables act more independently to shape life-styles. Finally, there is *urban culture*, which remains in force to the degree that people in any type of settlement orient themselves to a particular city. Usually that extends all the way from the inner city to the exurbs. Beyond the exurbs (or even in them, as the "old timers" of Old Harbor illustrated), lives are much less city focused, the influence of urban culture weakens, and we can speak of truly nonurban life-styles, those of the town or the rural area.

Behind the overarching pattern of urban life-styles, however, lies much more than a preference for living in a certain location. Economic and political factors, not to mention racial and ethnic prejudice, all play major roles. These factors have *always* been crucial in the organization of urban life—so crucial in fact that we will devote the next chapter to a consideration of them.

CHAPTER 12

Stratification, Race, and Power in the City

All the life-styles portrayed in Chapter 11 are certainly not equally attractive to each American. As one black woman said, her move to the suburbs was what she had been waiting for all her life; it was the fulfillment of the American dream.

Various life-styles typically involve more than *difference*; they also represent *social inequality*—the focus of this chapter. We think that this job, this location, those people have *more* of some important resource or quality than others. What do people have in mind when they make such judgments?

Social Stratification

Weber: Dimensions of Social Inequality

One of the most useful attempts at describing patterns of social inequality is that suggested by Max Weber (1946). Weber recognized three distinct dimensions of social inequality. First, people are distinguished from one another by their economic resources. Put simply, this refers to *wealth*. The more one has, the better one is able to satisfy needs, indulge whims, and protect oneself from what Shakespeare called "the slings and arrows of

outrageous fortune." The astonishing economic resources of late-nineteenth-century American entrepreneurs John Jacob Astor and J. P. Morgan (Morgan's opulence was portrayed in Cityscape 1-4) allowed both men to live in luxury and to control the lives of many others. Both Astor and Morgan had mansions, servants by the score, and material comforts that were the envy of their era. Further, with a word or a gesture, each could affect the destiny of thousands, even a nation. In sharp contrast to these "robber-barons," the average unskilled worker in turn-of-the-century America received less than $500 a year in wages (Baltzell 1964, p. 110). Such striking economic differences continue to shape American society, and nowhere is this contrast drawn more intensely than in the city. At the end of the last decade, for example, New York City was reported to contain 16,255 millionaires, more than could be found in most *states* (*Cleveland Plain Dealer*, June 23, 1979). At the same time, however, this city contained over 1 million people living in poverty (Hall 1979, p. 189).

Weber's second dimension of inequality is social honor, or *prestige*. Some people enjoy greater respect and esteem than others based on their occupation, income, family name, ethnicity, or education. For example, research has shown that Americans rank various occupations according to level of prestige and that these evaluations tend to remain remarkably stable over many decades (Counts 1925; N.O.R.C. 1947; Hodge et al. 1964). A recent study of occupational prestige, conducted by the National Opinion Research Center (1983), was based on a sample of average Americans that was intended to represent a broad range of age, sex, race, and economic positions. These people were asked to rank a list of occupations according to the prestige they perceived each to have. The results are contained in Table 12-1.

As the table shows, there is considerable overlapping between blue- and white-collar occupational prestige; nevertheless, the highest prestige rankings are reserved for white-collar jobs and the lowest for blue-collar jobs. In addition, several "pink-collar" positions (marked with an asterisk), mostly held by women, generally receive relatively little occupational prestige. Clearly, all jobs are not equal.

Third, Weber recognized *power*—the ability to achieve ends or goals, even against opposition—as a dimension of social inequality. Within the city—whether we consider Ming Dynasty Peking, La Paz in Bolivia, or contemporary Chicago—differences in power are crucial determinants of social events. Use of political power let the Ming emperors dictate completely the comportment of everyone in Peking; military and political power provided European colonizers and their descendants with the ability to dominate La Paz from the 1500s to the present; and the power of a great political "machine" allowed Mayor Richard J. Daley to control Chicago politics for over 20 years.

Seven Levels of American Urban Stratification

These three dimensions of social inequality—wealth, prestige, and power—are the basis of a system of *social stratification*. Some categories of people are seen as "higher up" and others as "lower down" on a social hierarchy.

Three important studies have uncovered a great deal about how stratification works in the

city. These are W. Lloyd Warner and Paul S. Lunt's (1941, 1942) classic observations of "Yankee City," a pseudonym for a small industrial city near Boston; Richard Coleman and Bernice Neugarten's (1971) study of Kansas City; and Coleman and Lee Rainwater's (1978) comparative study of city dwellers in Kansas City and Boston. All three studies produced much the same findings.

For instance, there was little evidence to suggest that Americans perceived social boundaries as being rigidly drawn. People have relatively higher or lower standing, but their actual social position was often fuzzy in respondents' minds. Further, numerous inconsistencies existed. Although there was a general tendency for people with more wealth and power to be given more prestige, this was not always the case. Thus, a small-business owner might have modest prestige or power but a fairly high income; likewise, an important minister might have high prestige but little power; finally, a gangster might have great wealth and power but very little prestige.

In determining social rank, most people used three variables as the basis of their judgments: level of income, amount of education, and occupational prestige. Putting their data together, Warner and Lunt identified six tiers of social stratification in America. Coleman and Neugarten's Kansas City study essentially used the same framework, while Coleman and Rainwater's Kansas City/Boston study added a seventh category to describe better the changes in the last decade or so.

Before beginning a brief description of each category, we should note three limitations of such a classification system. First, the distribution of each social class may vary from city to city. For example, the number of established, "aristocratic" families is likely to be higher in older East Coast cities than in the newer cities of the West. Second, the same social position may be perceived differently from one city to another. In industry-dominated cities like Pittsburgh, many blue-collar positions may be ranked higher than they would be in more service-oriented cities such as Miami. Third, a person's own social position affects how others are ranked. Thus, to lower-class Americans, the upper levels seem "all of a piece," even though these "upper-crust" people

TABLE 12-1
The Social Prestige Associated with Various Occupations

White-Collar Occupations	Prestige Score	Blue-Collar Occupations
Physician	82	
College/University Professor	78	
Lawyer	76	
Dentist, Physicist/Astronomer	74	
Bank Officer	72	
Architect, Aeronautical/Astronautical Engineer, Psychologist	71	
Airplane Pilot	70	
Clergy, Chemist, Electrical Engineer	69	
Geologist	67	
Sociologist	66	
Secondary School Teacher	63	
Mechanical Engineer, Registered Nurse	62	
Dental Hygienist, Pharmacist, Radiologic Technician	61	
Chiropractor, Elementary School Teacher, Veterinarian	60	
Postmaster, Union Official	58	
Accountant, Economist	57	
Draftsman, Painter/Sculptor	56	
Actor, Librarian, Statistician	55	
Industrial Engineer, Forester/Conservationist	54	
Surveyor	53	
Dietician, Funeral Director, Social Worker	52	
Athlete, Computer Specialist, Editor/Reporter, Radio/TV Announcer	51	Locomotive Engineer
Bank Teller, Sales Manager	50	
	49	Electrician
Bookkeeper	48	Aircraft Mechanic, Machinist, Police Officer
Insurance Agent	47	
Musician/Composer	46	Secretary*
	44	Fireman

may distinguish many sublevels among themselves (Coleman and Rainwater 1978, Chap. 7). Box 12-1 provides an illustration. Helene Hanff explains how two affluent areas of Manhattan are differentiated by those who live there. Would such distinctions about the same areas exist in the minds of a poor family in Harlem?

The Upper-Upper Class. This category is composed only of true "bluebloods." Members of "high society," these families are characterized by inherited wealth and a gracious way of life that reflects generations of affluence. In the Kansas City study, this group has an average income (several hundred thousands dollars a year) three times higher than the next highest stratum. Warner finds this group to be just 1 or 2 percent of Yankee City's population, and Coleman and Neugarten find it to include only 0.5 percent of Kansas City's residents. As was the case with Baltzell's "Philadelphia Gentlemen," profiled in Cityscape 5-2, these people typically have attended private schools and prestigious colleges and universities, are members of respected churches and associa-

White-Collar Occupations	Prestige Score	Blue-Collar Occupations
Adult Education Teacher, Air Traffic Controller	43	
	42	Mail Carrier
Buyer/Shipper, Farm Products, Photographer	41	Apprentice Electrician, Farmer, Tailor
	40	Carpenter, Telephone Operator,* Welder
Restaurant Manager	39	
Building Superintendent	38	
	37	Auto Body Repairperson
Airline Stewardess	36	Brick/Stone Mason
	35	TV Repairperson
	34	Baker
	33	Hairdresser,* Bulldozer Operator
Auctioneer	32	Bus Driver, Truck Driver
Cashier	31	
File Clerk	30	Upholsterer
Retail Salesperson	29	Drill-Press Operator, Furniture Finisher
	23	Midwife
	22	Gas Station Attendant, Security Guard, Taxi Driver
	21	Elevator Operator
	20	Bartender, Waiter/Waitress
	18	Clothing Presser, Farm Laborer, Household Servant
	17	Car Washer, Freight Handler, Garbage Collector
	16	Janitor
	14	Bellhop
	09	Shoeshiner

*So-called pink-collar occupation.

Source: Adapted from National Opinion Research Center, *General Social Surveys, 1972–1983: Cumulative Codebook.* (Chicago, 1983), pp. 338–349. Used by permission.

tions, and usually exert great influence not only in their own cities but across the entire country (Domhoff 1983). They tend to cluster in a particular area of the city—Hill Street in Yankee City and the Ward Parkway in Kansas City. Their counterparts exist on Beacon Hill in Boston, the Gold Coast of Chicago, and in exclusive sections of other cities. Many have extensive exurban estates. Linked by blood, marriage, and shared schools and clubs, this category, of all strata examined, comes closest to being a self-conscious group. Their exclusivity is captured well by the joke about Boston's "Brahmins": "In Boston, the Lodges speak only to Cabots; the Cabots speak only to God."

The Lower-Upper Class. This category also appears at the top of the city's social hierarchy—especially when viewed by lower-status people—but shows important differences from the upper-upper class. Composed of very successful executives or professionals and making up another 1 or 2 percent of the city's population, it represents those who have *achieved* elite status. Their wealth and power are more likely to be earned than inherited; consequently, even individuals and families with higher incomes than members of "society" are likely to be perceived as lower in prestige, as "nouveau riche." Coleman and Neugarten report that this group has few connections with the educational traditions and club memberships that the upper-upper class has established over several generations. Nevertheless, most are well educated and probably earn at least $75,000 a year. They tend to live in exclusive central-city areas like Manhattan's Upper East Side (Box 12-1), in exclusive suburbs like Detroit's Grosse Pointe Shores, or, increasingly, in the new exurban developments like Pittsford, New York, near Rochester.

The Upper-Middle Class. The third level of the urban hierarchy contains professionals and managers who are quite comfortable financially but who lack the greatest wealth (they typically earn between $40,000 and $75,000 a year). A larger group than the upper class—roughly 10 percent of the population in both Yankee City and Kansas City—this group exerts considerable influence in community organizations. Likely to be college graduates with advanced degrees, people in this category commonly reside in "better," but not truly "exclusive," suburban areas (Devon, near Philadelphia) or relatively high-prestige inner-city neighborhoods (Cambridge, near downtown Boston).

Coleman and Rainwater (1978) suggest that there is a "marginal" group within this class—people who don't earn all that much (maybe $30,000 to $50,000) but who are seen as upper-middle class because of their education or relatively prestigeful jobs. Examples include engineers, college teachers, middle-level civil servants, or researchers.

The Middle-Middle Class. This is the additional stratification level suggested by Coleman and Rainwater. These are the typical, "average Americans." Some are "people who didn't finish college but are making good money—maybe certain kinds of small businessmen, craftsmen getting top pay, and salesmen of all sorts" (Coleman and Rainwater 1978, p. 128). Others, slightly less prestigeful, are secure and respected. On the white-

collar side, they are high school or elementary school teachers, accountants, or bank tellers; on the blue-collar side, they tend to be construction foremen, electricians, plumbers, or factory shift supervisors. They tend to earn between $20,000 and $35,000 and live in "respectable" but hardly opulent neighborhoods—parts of San Francisco's Richmond District and New York's Borough of Queens are examples.

The Lower-Middle Class. This group (which in the earlier Yankee City and Kansas City studies contained the middle-middle class just discussed) is composed of lower-level white-collar workers—clerks, bookkeepers, mail carriers—and rank-and-file blue-collar employees—factory workers, truck drivers, automobile mechanics, dockworkers. While incomes vary (a few very successful truck drivers make well over $35,000), the typical salary ranges between $15,000 and $25,000. Depending on how many children are in the family, these people get by, but with not much left over. Satirized in the "Archie Bunker" television series, this group often lives in moderately priced neighborhoods in the central city—the South Side of Kansas City or East Boston—or in working-class suburbs like Milpitas, California (discussed in Chapter 11). Many of their neighborhoods are ethnically based—Boston's Irish "Southie" is an example.

The Upper-Lower Class. Whereas the lower-middle class gets by, this group constantly struggles. Distinguished from the former group by possessing fewer skills and less education, they earn roughly between $8,000 and $15,000 per year, holding jobs such as waiter, factory worker in a nonunionized plant, hospital attendant, airport baggage operator, janitor, or salesclerk in a hardware store. They live in more tattered neighborhoods than the lower-middle class. Frequently, such neighborhoods are composed of ethnic or racial minorities. The black suburb of Glenarden, Maryland, near Washington (Chapter 11) is one example. Nevertheless, as Coleman and Rainwater (1978) suggest, despite their low income, these people are working and proud of it (even if they don't love the job). They are usually indignant about those on welfare.

BOX 12-1
East Side, West Side: Different Parts of Town

The real difference between the East Side and West Side is in the people. They not only think and behave differently from each other; they look different.

Generally speaking, West Siders look dowdy, scholarly and slightly down-at-heel, and the look has nothing to do with money. They look like what a great many of them are: scholars, intellectuals, dedicated professionals, all of whom regard shopping for clothes as a colossal waste of time. East Siders, on the other hand, look chic. Appearances are important to them. From which you'll correctly deduce that East Siders are conventional and proper, part of the Establishment and in awe of it—which God knows, and God be thanked, West Siders are not.

I'll give you an example. Suppose tomorrow's *New York Times* prints that JFK airport is building new runways for supersonic jets. The West Side Democratic clubs will charter buses, ride out to JFK and march around the airport with placards reading "No SST for NYC" and "Save the Environment for our Children." They'll sing fight songs, have a couple of clashes with the police and turn up on the eleven o'clock TV evening news.

The East Side clubs will hold a dignified debate and then send a telegram to the governor telling him they're against air pollution.

Source: Helene Hanff, *Apple of My Eye* (Garden City, N.Y.: Doubleday, 1977), pp. 88–89.

BOX 12-2
White Ethnics: The Forgotten Americans

The stereotypes are familiar: white ethnics are the "racists," "bigots," and "rednecks" who almost 20 years ago cheered when the police arrested Vietnam demonstrators and today want only to keep blacks out of their neighborhood. These stereotypes mask the complexity and struggle of many white ethnics in American society, people—according to Peter Schrag—who are no longer living in poverty, but not yet economically secure. They can be found

. . . between slums and suburbs [in] South Boston and South San Francisco, Bell and Parma, Astoria and Bay Ridge, Newark, Cicero, Downey, Daly City, Charlestown, [and] Flatbush. [In the] union halls, American Legion posts, neighborhood bars and bowling leagues, the Ukranian Club and the Holy Name. . . .

These are the "forgotten Americans," caught between the attention given to the rich and powerful, on the one hand, and the poor on the other. As one man sitting on the stoop in front of his house in South Boston puts it: "I'm working my ass off. My kids don't have a place to swim, my parks are full of glass, and I'm supposed to bleed for a bunch of people on relief."

The problem is simply that the American vision of upward mobility and cultural assimilation has been only partly true:

Somewhere in his gut the man in those communities knows that mobility and choice in this society are limited. He cannot imagine any major change for the better; but he can imagine change for the worse. And yet . . . he is the one who has been asked to carry the burden of social reform, to integrate his schools and his neighborhood, has been asked by comfortable people to pay the social debts due to the poor and the black.

[But] some of the poorest people in America are white . . . and have lived all of their lives in the same place as their fathers and grandfathers. The problems that were presumably solved in some distant past, in that era before the textbooks were written—problems of assimilation, of upward mobility—now turn out to be very much unsolved. The melting pot and all: millions made it, millions moved to the suburbs; several millions—no one knows how many—did not.

Source: Peter Schrag, *Out of Place in America* (New York: Random House, 1969), pp. 15, 22, 25.

This group, and the lower-middle class above them, are the American "working class," a group of "forgotten Americans," people who tend to go unnoticed because of all the publicity given to the very wealthy and the very poor (see Box 12-2).

The Lower-Lower Class. The outstanding characteristic of this category is a lack of regular employment. These people are likely to live in the poorest or most segregated housing in the urban area, not only because their lack of resources prohibits living in better districts, but because they often are shunned by other groups or are kept out of other areas by active discrimination. Lower-lower class neighborhoods include Chicago's South Side, Los Angeles's Watts, and New York's

Bowery. Most people in this group are very poorly educated; a large percentage receive public assistance; and a great many are black, Puerto Rican, or Hispanic. In terms of life-style, they are the "deprived," the "trapped" or the "disaffiliated" (Chapter 11). Still, lower-lower-class respondents in Coleman and Rainwater's study refused to see themselves as a single group. Most made a clear distinction within their ranks between "people who are on welfare but keep themselves clean" and others who are "just dirty—they don't have any pride at all" (1978, p. 130).

Urban Stratification: Visibility and Opportunity

While social stratification is not solely an urban phenomenon, the city does lend it at least two characteristics. First, the city tends to make stratification more visible. Cities characteristically contain people with the greatest affluence, the highest prestige, and the largest measure of "social clout;" simultaneously they are the home of the poorest, the least respected, and the most powerless people. Such contrasts are all the more evident in the city because large numbers of each class live there, often visibly clustered in distinctive communities. Moreover, the city-based mass media publicize the activities of all these groups, making them more aware of themselves and each other.

A second characteristic is that cities, commonly thought to offer greater opportunity, continually draw people of every social stratum. In Cityscape 1-4, for example, we saw Jurgis and Ona Rudkis come to Chicago hoping to find a better life than they had in their native Lithuania. Jesus Sanchez (Chapter 8) had much the same dream when, as a boy of 12, he went to Mexico City.

Is this widely held belief of greater urban opportunity a myth or a reality? Are city people more upwardly mobile than people elsewhere? In a review of research, Lipset and Bendix concluded that, yes, evidence "derived from . . . different countries suggest that the related processes of urbanization and migration are major sources of social mobility" (1967, p. 204). National survey data in one study showed that males who spent

their teens in larger cities were more likely to reach white-collar and executive positions than those reared in smaller cities and on farms, even when their level of education was the same. Twenty-seven percent of males from large cities (over 250,000) with at least one year of higher education (13+) reached high-status occupations, while only 18 percent of those who spent their teens in smaller cities and 15 percent of those raised on farms did so.

The most common pattern related to urban opportunity appears to be this: Many lower-status positions in cities are filled by those who migrate from smaller urban and rural settlements. Over time, a substantial proportion of these people or their descendants reach higher-status positions, probably due to a combination of several factors outlined by Lipset and Bendix (1967, p. 217) and paraphrased as follows:

1. Cities have a greater division of labor. There are many more kinds of jobs to be filled than would be the case in a smaller settlement.

2. The larger the city, the more white-collar jobs tend to exist. This means more jobs are available at higher status levels.

3. If the city is growing economically, it tends to create more jobs, usually at all levels. If jobs are created faster than the population grows, opportunity for migrants or their descendants is increased even more.

In addition, we may note that

4. Many people increase their skills over time, becoming more competitive for higher-level jobs.

5. Also as time passes, many workers increase their level of affluence and provide the opportunity—sometimes for themselves but usually for their children—to get a better education. The higher income and education level make further advancement up the status ladder easier.

Such factors have been particularly characteristic of large industrial cities in the past two centuries and have resulted in a general "pulling up" of

TABLE 12-2
Poverty in America, 1984

	Percent Below Poverty Level
Urban Areas	11.1
Central Cities	16.3
Outside Central Cities	7.8
Rural Areas	14.8
Entire United States	15.2

Source: U.S. Bureau of the Census, *Statistical Abstract of the United States 1985* (Washington, D.C.: U.S. Government Printing Office, 1984), Tables 764, 767.

people along the status continuum over time (Marsh 1963).

This is too rosy a picture, however. As we all know, not everyone "makes it" in cities. Despite the city's historical role as generator of wealth and upward mobility, there continue to be significant limits to urban opportunity.

In 1984 there were over 35 million Americans officially recognized as living in poverty (about 15 percent of the entire population). Because the United States is a predominantly urban society, there is little surprise in the fact that most poor people live in cities. Within urban areas, however, poverty is not evenly distributed, as Table 12-2 shows. Central cities contain the highest proportion of poor people (16.3 percent), while the suburbs—now the home of the majority of American urbanites—have less than half this level of poverty (7.8 percent). Just as important, urban areas as a whole (the center cities plus the suburbs) hvae a considerably *lower* proportion of poor people (11.1 percent) than rural areas (14.8 percent). Thus, we can understand why people have historically been drawn to cities in the hope of a better standard of living. As long as people *think* that the city offers the chance for greater affluence (overall, urbanites *do* have a higher income than their rural counterparts), the rural poor are likely to move to cities seeking a way out of their destitution. The continued presence of millions of poor in American cities, however, belies the notion that urban opportunity—while certainly real—will be able to completely eliminate poverty.

Another problem with the general assertion that cities provide opportunity is that some cities provide more opportunity than others. One reason for this may be certain cycles of growth and decline that favor cities in one region or country over another. Whereas nineteenth-century migrants often found greater opportunity in the cities of the Northeast and Midwest, today many lower-income families are leaving these older, struggling cities for Sunbelt cities where greater economic opportunity may be found (see Chapter 3).

We must also bear in mind that urban opportunity may be more limited in the Third World. As we saw in chapters 8 through 10, many Third World cities, undergoing an incredible demographic transition, are unable to provide the same opportunity as cities of other, more prosperous countries, such as Japan. In many Third World cities, the poor tend to *stay* poor, whatever they do. For this reason, many of Latin America's poor try to migrate to American cities, where they believe opportunity will be greater.

Third, even within the industralized West, some countries seem to provide greater urban opportunity than others. For example, Switzerland's per capita income has risen to be among the highest in the world, recently surpassing both the United States and Sweden. Swiss cities do not reveal the dramatic patterns of inequality we commonly find in New York or other European cities. "Even with the more rapid urbanization of the last decade . . . no typical slum areas have grown up in the large Swiss cities (i.e., Zurich, Basel, and Geneva) as compared . . . to such cities as Hamburg, Munich, Paris, Marseilles, London, or . . . cities in the United States" (Clinard 1978, pp. 105–106). This is due, Clinard says, to a combination of political, economic, and historical factors, including Switzerland's extensive industrial and banking activities coupled to political neutrality.

Fourth, although some Americans experience extensive upward mobility in the course of a lifetime, the vast majority do not. Horatio Alger success stories are mostly myths. For every Henry Ford, there are millions of people who can hardly afford a new car. People who climb the stratification ladder usually do so slowly, over the course of generations. This is demonstrated in Stephen Thernstrom's (1965) work on Yankee City, which showed upward mobility to be very limited.

There are at least two reasons for this: first, gaining the requisite skills for higher-status jobs or the savoir faire for upper-crust living is very difficult, even where the opportunity exists. Professor Henry Higgins in George Bernard Shaw's *Pygmalion* enabled London cockney flower girl Eliza Doolittle to "pass" in high society only after months of intensive efforts to teach her to speak "properly." As Higgins said about Eliza in *My Fair Lady* (the musical version of *Pygmalion*), "It's [expressions like] 'Aaow' and 'Gom' that keep her in her place, not her wretched clothes and dirty face." Social barriers are more than skin deep.

Moreover, those higher up on the status ladder have a much greater chance at maintaining or bettering their position than those lower down. Lipset and Bendix (1967) produced ample evidence to suggest that the upper strata easily perpetuate themselves; William Miller (1962) found that few early-twentieth-century American corporate heads had come from poverty-stricken backgrounds; and Stephen Thernstrom's (1973) study of Boston showed that children of white-collar elites were many times more likely to become white-collar elites than were children from lower-class backgrounds. People on top have the lion's share of the advantages, as Table 12-3 suggests by indicating the percentage of America's wealth controlled by various segments of the population.

Arranged by the social class divisions discussed earlier, Table 12-3 makes it indubitably clear that if wealth (everything that a person owns, including income, durable goods such as houses and land, and financial assets such as stocks and insurance policies) can be translated into certain types of advantages—a superior private school, good food, a healthful environment, travel experience—those advantages are not likely to be equally distributed throughout the population. The upper-upper class, approximately 1 percent of the population, controls almost a third of the nation's wealth. Together, the upper-upper and lower-upper classes (5 percent of the population) control over half the country's private assets, while the middle class (55 percent of the population) is somewhat less well off (it controls 45 percent of the wealth). Nevertheless, the middle classes live in luxury compared to those at the bottom. The upper-lower class (approximately 20 percent of the population) shares only 3 percent of the wealth and the lower-lower class, a full 20 percent of all Americans, controls no wealth at all. They are in debt, bankrupt, or on public assistance.

Finally, in considering the limits of opportunity, we must not forget that movement up the social ladder has not been equal for all groups. Once again, Stephen Thernstrom's (1969) work provides an example. In a study of mobility in Boston between 1890 and 1940, Thernstrom found that native-born whites advanced further than foreign-born immigrants and that some white immigrants—British and Jews—advanced further than some others—Italians and Irish. Whites today have advanced far more than blacks and Hispanics, as can be seen in Table 12-4.

This table shows how great the disparity is between whites, blacks, and Hispanics with regard to poverty. The United States is an overwhelmingly white society and, consequently, most poor people are white—some 24 million of the 35 million total. Yet, proportionately, Hispanics and especially blacks shoulder the greater burden.

TABLE 12-3
Class and the Distribution of American Wealth

Class		Approximate Percent of Population		Approximate Percent of Wealth Controlled	
Upper	{ Upper-Upper	1	} 5	32	} 52
	Lower-Upper	4		20	
Middle	{ Upper-Middle	15		24	
	Middle-Middle	20	} 55	16	} 45
	Lower-Middle	20		5	
Lower	{ Upper-Lower	20	} 40	3	} 3
	Lower-Lower	20		0	
		100		100	

Source: Adapted from Stephen J. Rosen, *Social Stratification in the United States* (Baltimore: Social Graphics, 1979), Table X.

TABLE 12-4
Percentage of Population Below the Poverty Level, 1984

	Whites	Hispanics	Blacks
Urban Areas	8.2	25.8	30.6
Central Cities	10.8	29.5	34.2
Outside Central Cities	6.8	20.7	22.2
Rural Areas	12.5	28.1	38.3
Entire United States	12.1	28.4	35.7

Source: U.S. Bureau of the Census. *Statistical Abstract of the United States 1985* (Washington, D.C.: U.S. Government Printing Office, 1984), Tables 760, 764.

While only 12.1 percent of all whites are poor, the corresponding proportion is 28.4 percent for Hispanics and 35.7 percent for blacks. This pattern holds for all areas of the country—central cities, surrounding suburbs, and rural areas.

These findings suggest that social stratification in the city is strongly shaped by race and ethnicity. Just how deep this influence goes is the topic we will consider in the next section.

Race and Ethnicity

The importance of racial and ethnic characteristics to American cities is evident in the fact that between 1880 and 1910, seven in ten immigrants settled in cities. For most of our nation's history, New York has been the symbol of racial and ethnic diversity. A generation ago, E. Digby Baltzell noted:

> Even today [New York's] citizenry, almost half of whom are foreign born or the children of foreign born, includes more blacks than most cities in Africa, a greater concentration of Jews than at any other time or place. . . . More Puerto Ricans than any other city outside of San Juan, more persons of Italian descent than most cities in Italy, and more [Irish] than Dublin. (Baltzell 1964, p. ix)

From the vantage point of the mid-1980s, Los Angeles stands out as a migratory capital. This city has absorbed some 2 million immigrants since 1970. Today, one in three residents of Los Angeles County is Hispanic—the vast majority

---

TABLE 12-5

Los Angeles: The "New Ellis Island"; Minority-Group Populations, 1970 and 1983

	1970	1983
Mexicans	822,300	2,100,000
Iranians	20,000	200,000
Salvadorans	*	200,000
Japanese	104,000	175,000
Armenians	75,000	175,000
Chinese	41,000	153,000
Koreans	8,900	150,000
Filipinos	33,500	150,000
Arabs	45,000	130,000
Israelis	10,000	90,000
Samoans	22,000	60,000
Guatemalans	*	50,000
Vietnamese	*	40,000

*Fewer than 2,000

Source: *Time*, June 13, 1983, p. 22. Copyright 1983 Time Inc. All rights reserved. Reprinted by permission.

TABLE 12-6

Legal Immigrants to the United States, 1861–1979 (Percent of Total)

Region of Birth	1861–1900	1901–1930	1931–1960	1961–1970	1971–1976	1977–1979
Northern and Western Europe	68	23	41	17	7	5
Southern and Eastern Europe	22	56	17	16	13	8
Canada	7	11	21	12	4	3
Asia	2	3	5	13	32	39
Latin America	0	5	15	39	41	42
Other	1	2	1	3	3	3

Source: Leon F. Bouvier, *Immigration and Its Impact on U.S. Society* (Washington, D.C.: Population Reference Bureau, 1981).

Mexican Americans. As shown in Table 12-5, this represents more than twice the Mexican population in 1970. But the ethnic and racial mix of Los Angeles brought by the "new immigration" is far more complex, as the table indicates: large populations of Iranians, Salvadorans, Guatemalans, and Vietnamese and other Asian groups have come to the city. A century ago, millions of immigrants, mostly from Europe, entered New York through the immigration center on Ellis Island; today, however, Los Angeles justly deserves to be called the "new Ellis Island" (Andersen 1983).

The shifting pattern of ethnic and racial immigration to this country is important to understand if we are to grasp the complexities of today's cities. Table 12-6 gives us a sense of this. From

1861 to 1960 the vast majority of America's legal immigrants were from regions of the world whose populations are mainly white—Europe and Canada. During this period the main differences between immigrants and people already in this country were *ethnic*. The Irish and the Jews, for example, had different cultural traditions, but they were white. Since 1960, however, that pattern has changed radically. Now, the bulk of our legal immigrants are from Asia and Latin America—nonwhite regions of the world (and this says nothing of the millions of *illegal* Latin American immigrants streaming into the American Southwest). In other words, to ethnic differences a distinctly racial element has been added.

As a result of both these factors—racial and ethnic differences from the dominant majority—today, as throughout this country's history, most newcomers experience life in the United States as minorities. In a sociological sense, the term "minority group" implies more than social differences based on race, culture, or nationality. Also involved is social inequality. Minority groups are typically disadvantaged, ranking low in one, two, or even all three of the dimensions that define social stratification: wealth, social prestige, and power.

The Melting Pot

The American city has been described as a "melting pot," a place where, with the passage of time, the immigrant's distinctive cultural characteristics would disappear, creating that unique blend of humanity known as "The American." This was an appropriate industrial metaphor for an incredibly industrial era. That new immigrants wanted to become "American" there is little doubt. For example, in the film *Hester Street*, about immigrant East European Jews in New York at the turn of the century, we find newly arrived and traditionally dressed Gitl amazed and shocked at the American-style dress of Mamie, a woman who had arrived only months before. Gitl's husband, Jake, who also had been in New York a few months and had shed his European garb, chided his wife: "Don't make like a greenhorn, Gitl. In America, *everyone* dresses like that!"

The melting-pot thesis has been the subject of much debate. Some, like Herbert Gans (1962; 1982), have argued that the ethnic identification that fostered strong "ethnic villages" among first-generation immigrants has not always been sustained by second- and third-generation Americans, many of whom have moved from "old neighborhoods" in the inner city to middle-class inner-city and suburban areas with less ethnic character. In contrast, in their study of New York, Glazer and Moynihan categorically asserted that urban ethnicity simply had not dissolved: "The point about the melting pot . . . is that it did not happen. At least not in New York and . . . those parts of America which resemble New York" (1970, p. xcvii). They added that as far as New York was concerned, in 1970 "ethnicity and race [still] dominate the city, more than ever seemed possible" (1970, p. ix).

Whichever position on the melting-pot debate one takes, the general minority-group pattern in American cities seems to have been this: most of the predominantly white ethnic groups of the Great Immigration (Jews, Poles, Italians, Irish, Russians) have, in second, third, and fourth generations, moved to higher rungs on the urban stratification ladder. With the partial exception of some Jews who retain strong religious-ethnic traditions even at the highest stratification levels, most of these groups have "melted" somewhat. Their previously strong ethnic background has weakened over the years, though it probably has not disappeared altogether. Many still celebrate ethnic holidays, visit "the old country," and are proud of their ethnic heritage. (As one Irish urbanist colleague is wont to claim, a bit tongue-in-cheek, "It was the Irish who first discovered New York! They were here before the Vikings!" Of course, there's not a shred of evidence for this claim.) For whites still living in urban "ethnic villages," however, the "melt" has not been as pronounced.

In addition, Americans have generally *wanted* to perceive their country as a great melting pot. Such a belief supports the view of the United States as a society in which talent and ability, rather than race and ethnicity, are what matters— in short, a society in which "anyone can make it." Yet, many minorities have found that race and ethnicity *have* mattered; and assimilation into the social mainstream has been sought actively by many immigrants eager to escape the prejudice and discrimination visited upon them by others. Perhaps, then, the more open discussion of personal ethnicity during the past generation may be an indication that American society has begun to relax traditional hostilities toward at least some people who display social differences (Hirshman 1983).

The "New Minorities": Nonwhites in the City

As the minority groups of the Great Immigration have moved up the stratification ladder in recent years, they have been replaced by blacks (especially in the older cities of the Northeast and Midwest) and Hispanics (especially in the newer Sunbelt cities); millions of Asians have also joined the urban mix across the country in recent years. Especially for blacks, progress up the urban hierarchy has been, with few exceptions, much slower.

Census figures given in Table 12-7 show that nonwhites have increased their numbers in almost all major cities and regions of the country between 1970 and 1980.[1] The most significant feature of this table is not the population growth

---

[1] A warning before proceeding further with this table: People indicated their racial or ethnic background on the 1980 census questionnaire by checking "white," "black," or "other." In the "other" category were subcategories for "American Indian," "Asian or Pacific Islander," or "Other." In another section entirely, they could indicate whether they were of "Hispanic" background or not. But since "Hispanic" was *not* provided as a category in the main racial/ethnic-background question, people who checked "Hispanic" in the later category also could check "white," "black," or "other" if they chose. It is impossible to know how many did this; hence, it is impossible to compute accurate percentages of racial and ethnic groups for these cities in 1980. Finally, the 1970 census provided no question at all on "Hispanic" descent; hence, comparing 1970 and 1980 figures is not possible. New York City, however, conducted its own subcensus on Hispanics in 1970. Because of all this, city population totals derived in this table are subject to distortion and will not necessarily match those of other 1980 census tables in this book.

in the nonwhite categories (although in a few cases that is substantial), but rather the *decline* in the number of whites in these cities. As discussed in chapters 3 and 11, the decade of the 1970s saw a continuing decentralization of the white population. Coupled with the increase in nonwhite population, the result is that many cities have, for the first time in history, nonwhite *majorities*. Atlanta, Gary (Indiana), and the District of Columbia had black majorities in 1970, but since that time, Baltimore, Detroit, New Orleans, and a host of smaller cities including Birmingham (Alabama), Richmond (Virginia), and Savannah have been added to the list. Hispanics also are gaining rapidly, particularly in the South and the West. They outnumber blacks in Los Angeles, San Diego, Phoenix, and Denver; now they also represent a majority of the population of Miami. Let us consider what such figures imply, not only for the city, but for each group.

Blacks. From the time of the first census in 1790 until the beginning of this century, about 90 percent of the black population of the United States lived in the South. Only about one black in four lived in an urban area, and, while a few southern cities had black populations of perhaps 25 to 50 percent in the late 1800s, the black population of northeastern cities had yet to reach even 5 percent.

This situation began to change as World War I and the restrictive legislation that followed put an end to the Great Immigration. Cities such as Chicago, New York, and Boston continued to grow into industrial metropolises, and blacks began to see greater opportunity in the urban North than in the agricultural South. On the one hand, agriculture had declined in the South and machines were replacing human labor. On the other hand, northern industries needed workers so badly some actively recruited black workers from southern states.

During the 1920s the net black out-migration from the South was almost 1 million people. Slowing during the Great Depression of the 1930s, the massive relocation of blacks accelerated once again as industrial production rose during World War II and remained high until the

TABLE 12-7
Ethnic and Racial Composition of Major U.S. Cities, 1970 and 1980

Region	City		White	Black	Hispanic Descent	Other*
Northeast	Boston	1970	524,709	104,707	—	11,555
		1980	393,937	126,229	36,068	42,858
	New York	1970	6,091,503	1,665,470	1,104,327	177,906
		1980	4,293,695	1,784,124	1,405,957	993,211
	Philadelphia	1970	1,278,717	653,791	—	16,101
		1980	983,084	638,878	63,570	66,248
	Baltimore	1970	479,837	420,210	—	5,712
		1980	345,113	431,151	7,641	10,511
	Washington, D.C.	1970	209,272	537,712	15,108	9,526
		1980	171,796	448,229	17,652	17,626
Midwest	Cleveland	1970	458,084	287,841	—	4,978
		1980	307,264	251,347	17,772	15,211
	Detroit	1970	838,877	660,428	—	12,177
		1980	413,730	758,939	28,970	30,670
	Indianapolis	1970	607,902	134,320	—	2,402
		1980	540,294	152,626	6,145	7,887
	Chicago	1970	2,207,767	1,102,620	—	56,570
		1980	1,490,217	1,197,000	442,061	317,855
	Milwaukee	1970	605,372	105,088	—	6,639
		1980	446,620	146,940	26,111	22,652
	St. Louis	1970	364,992	254,191	—	3,053
		1980	242,567	206,386	5,531	4,123
	Kansas City, Mo.	1970	391,496	112,005	—	3,586
		1980	312,836	122,699	14,703	12,624
South	Atlanta	1970	240,503	255,052	—	1,419
		1980	137,878	282,912	5,842	4,232
	Jacksonville, Fla.	1970	407,695	118,158	—	3,012
		1980	394,734	137,324	9,775	8,840
	New Orleans	1970	323,420	267,308	—	2,743
		1980	236,967	308,136	19,219	12,379
	Houston	1970	904,889	316,551	—	11,362
		1980	799,530	440,257	281,224	176,299
	Dallas	1970	626,247	210,238	—	7,916
		1980	555,270	265,594	111,082	83,214
	San Antonio	1970	597,723	50,041	—	6,389
		1980	617,636	57,654	421,774	110,120
West	Denver	1970	458,187	47,011	—	9,480
		1980	367,344	59,252	91,937	64,800
	Phoenix	1970	542,510	27,896	—	11,156
		1980	642,059	37,682	115,572	85,170
	San Diego	1970	619,498	52,961	—	24,310
		1980	666,829	77,700	130,610	130,975
	Los Angeles	1970	2,173,600	503,606	—	138,855
		1980	1,816,683	505,208	815,989	644,872
	San Jose, Calif.	1970	417,013	10,955	—	17,478
		1980	470,013	29,157	140,574	137,380
	San Francisco	1970	511,186	96,078	—	108,410
		1980	395,082	86,414	83,373	197,478
	Seattle	1970	463,870	37,868	—	29,093
		1980	392,766	46,755	12,646	54,325

*Includes all American Indians, Hawaiians, all groups of Asian background, and any "others."

Source: U.S. Bureau of the Census.

1970s, when urban decentralization slowed the process. For example, in Table 12-7, note that only Detroit and a few other cities show a major increase in the number of blacks in the 1970s and that some cities—Philadelphia, Washington, Cleveland, St. Louis, and San Francisco—actually show decreases.

City life was not everything blacks had hoped it would be. For one thing, as Table 12-4 shows, many have remained extremely poor and have little chance of getting ahead.

Another factor affecting population patterns among blacks has been overt racial segregation. All over the country urban blacks have been isolated in racial ghettos. Table 12-8 shows that the continuing white exodus to the suburbs is isolating center-city blacks further, and our discussion in Chapter 11 indicated that despite modest inroads into suburban areas (Table 11-3), blacks remain a small and segregated suburban minority.

The most complete study of racial segregation in urban America is that carried out by Karl and Alma Taeuber in 1965. To measure segregation, the Taeubers developed what they called an "index of dissimilarity," which they applied to each neighborhood. Their index ranged from a low of zero, meaning the neighborhood reflected the same proportion of blacks and whites as the city as a whole, to a high of 100, meaning that no racial mixture was found. Their findings were sobering: in 1960 the average segregation index for 207 large cities was 86.2, with scores ranging from a not-so-low 60.4 (San Jose, California) to 98.1 (Fort Lauderdale, Florida).

Has segregation decreased since the Taeubers' research was completed? Van Valey, Roof, and Wilcox (1977) computed a segregation index (although not exactly comparable to that used by the Taeubers) for 137 large, urban regions in 1960 and the 237 that existed by 1970. Their average segregation score, 75.4 in 1960, had dropped to 69.5 by 1970. Once again, the greatest segregation was found in Fort Lauderdale (94.9), while Manchester, New Hampshire, was the least segregated city (34.0). Thus, it may be that there was an average decrease in segregation in the period studied.

A quite different picture emerges, however, if we look at only the 137 urban regions that existed in *both* 1960 and 1970. As shown in Table 12-8, the segregation index stayed about the same: overall scores were 75.6 in 1960 and 75.1 in 1970. Note that urban segregation overall was highest in the Midwest and lowest in the South (where the proximity of blacks to the homes of their white employers historically produced a superficially integrated "backyard pattern" of black residence [Hirschman 1983]). Note further that the only significant change between 1960 and 1970 was in the western cities. The conclusion is clear: urban America continues to be characterized by high levels of segregation. Furthermore, this pattern persists despite economic and political advances made by some blacks in the past decades.

Such advances have been notable, if not spectacular. For instance, between 1970 and 1982, the proportion of blacks who were high school graduates increased from 53 percent to 79 percent (the white rate was 87 percent), the income level for black married couples rose from $18,370 in 1971 to $19,620 in 1982, and the number of black homeowners jumped from 2.6 million in 1970 to 3.7 million in 1980—a 45 percent increase (*Washington Post*, Aug. 22, 1983). However, such changes seem to have had no effect on segregation.

The main issue seems to be this: *The majority of urban whites do not want to live with blacks in their neighborhoods, whatever attitudes or level of income these blacks may have.* History seems to bear out such an assertion. Between 1870 and 1920 segregation in the cities of the North was slight. However, between 1920 and 1960, the period analyzed by the Taeubers, the segregation index climbed dramatically. The primary reason was not so much the greater number of blacks who came to Northern cities, but the improvements in urban transportation—subway and trolley lines, the automobile. Such improvements allowed whites a chance to move out into the suburbs and escape from neighborhoods in which blacks were settling (Kusner 1983).

The pattern is still repeating itself. Recent studies by Wurdock (1981), Massey and Mullan

TABLE 12-8
Trends in Urban Segregation, 1960 and 1970

Region	Number of SMSAs*	1960 Index	1970 Index	Average Difference	Percent Change
Northeast	24	73.0	74.2	+ 1.2	+ 1.6
Midwest	40	79.3	79.7	+ 0.4	+ 0.5
South	54	73.5	73.3	− 0.2	− 0.3
West	19	77.0	71.4	− 5.6	− 7.3
Nationwide	137	75.6	75.1	− 0.5	− 0.7

*Standard Metropolitan Statistical Areas

Source: T.L. Van Valey, W.C. Roof, and J.E. Wilcox, "Trends in Residential Segregation," *American Journal of Sociology* 82 (Jan. 1977), Table 3. Reprinted by permission of The University of Chicago Press.

(1984), and Hwang et al. (1985) all show the same thing. When blacks move in, whites move out. Indeed, there seems to be an active, if unacknowledged (by the white community at least), attempt to keep blacks from buying housing in white urban neighborhoods. Thus, according to a recent study by the Department of Housing and Urban Development (HUD), if a black couple were to visit any four apartment buildings at random in most large cities, chances would be two to one they would be told no vacancies existed even if some did. Another discriminatory practice is called "steering." Real-estate brokers show housing to blacks, but only in already integrated areas. HUD estimated there were 2.5 million acts of real-estate discrimination in 1977. In 1980 a new set of Fair Housing Act amendments was passed in an attempt to give HUD more ability to control such practices.

When steering and other methods fail, more terrifying tactics can be used. This was illustrated all too clearly in Philadelphia—the "City of Brotherly Love." Southwest Philadelphia is an area of modest row-houses with a working class population containing many poor people. Until 1960, the area was almost all white, by 1970 it was more than half black, and is now about 85 percent black. Still, there is little racial integration as several all-white neighborhoods have strongly resisted racial change. In November, 1985, an interracial couple with two young children bought

a home in an all-white neighborhood. Nearby, a black family did likewise. Trouble was not long in coming.

From the point of view of many of the white residents, the presence of these two couples was perceived as the beginning of a "black invasion" that would inevitably transform their neighborhood into a ghetto. Other white residents thought otherwise and welcomed the newcomers. But vandals destroyed much of the interior of one home shortly after its new owners arrived. For several evenings, a mob of several hundred angry whites formed outside each of the homes. Windows were broken and the crowd chanted: "We want them out!" "Move! Move! Move! We have rights too!" and "Beat it!" Large numbers of police were necessary to restore order and the mayor declared a state of emergency in the area (Infield 1985). One woman screamed at the police: "I have lived in this neighborhood for thirty-one years and I'm not going to see it go downhill and I'm not going to live with niggers!" Although the black couple decided to leave the neighborhood, the interracial couple vowed to stay. As the wife, a white Englishwoman, told reporters: "If they don't like us, fine. Don't talk to us, that's OK. We bought this house, so we're here to stay" (Associated Press, Nov. 22, 1985).

While situations of this kind are unquestionably complex, the violent reaction of many whites is deeply racist. But Philadelphia has no corner

---

BOX 12-3
Voluntary Integration: The Case of Lincoln, Massachusetts

While most suburbs try desperately to prevent the building of low-income housing, Lincoln, Massachusetts, went out of its way to provide it. Lincoln, a small town 20 miles west of Boston, has been an upper-middle-class commuter enclave since the end of World War II; in the ensuing years, it has enacted two-acre zoning and has clamped down on growth.

But some of the town fathers became worried about Lincoln's insularity. They formed a commission to investigate the feasibility of turning a portion of the town's public land into multifamily, mixed-income housing. Three years ago, Lincoln saw the result of that investigation—the opening of Lincoln Woods, a modern, 250-unit complex, half of which is devoted to government-subsidized

apartments for middle- and low-income families. The tenants include a substantial number of blacks and some Hispanics.

"We met plenty of opposition in town," says David Donaldson, a member of the Lincoln planning board. "Some people worried about costs (the town itself had to put up a sizeable portion of the money); some others worried about the building design. And a few came right out and said, 'I moved here to get away from the city, and I don't want those people following me.'" Donaldson readily admits that problems have accompanied the project: "It would've been much better if we could have scattered the units. As it is, we've been accused of building a ghetto. Also, some of the low-income kids have had trouble adjusting in our schools." Overall

social integration has come slowly, despite the efforts of churches and other local institutions: Even after three years, the perceived taint of being "a Lincoln Woods person" is not easy to overcome.

Yet Lincoln is sufficiently pleased with the experiment to consider expanding it. Smaller dwellings would be purchased by a community foundation and rented below cost to families with income similar to those of families that occupy Lincoln Woods. The total scheme, Lincolnians feel, is not so much altruistic as it is practical: to create a community that shares the rich variety of American life.

Source: Roger M. Williams, "How It Played in Lincoln, MA," *Saturday Review*, Feb. 18, 1978, p. 19.

---

on the market. In a study of Detroit inner-city and suburban neighborhoods, Farley et al. (1983) found the same attitudes generally dispersed throughout the white community. Overtly, whites denied that they were prejudiced against blacks and claimed that the reasons their neighborhoods were not more integrated was because "blacks like living together." But whites' hidden attitudes toward integration came out in a more subtle test: Respondents were given fictional neighborhood maps that showed areas as all white, mixed, or mostly black; they were asked which area they wished to live in and why. They were then asked about their willingness to buy a house in a racially mixed neighborhood. Whereas black respondents generally indicated a willingness to live in and to buy houses in mixed neighborhoods (contrary to the whites' claim that blacks "like living together"), white respondents were much more loath to do so.

In a nationwide study of housing turnover, Marullo (1985) found the same pattern: all across

the U.S., whites leave when blacks arrive. The conclusion seems inescapable. All these results "contradict the view that race is declining in importance within U.S. society" (Massey and Mullan 1984, p. 836). Furthermore, this recent evidence suggests that real change is decades away unless more communities follow the practice of the people of Lincoln, Massachusetts, whose story is told in Box 12-3.

Hispanics. By far the fastest growing nonwhite category in America is Hispanics—Mexicans, Puerto Ricans, Cubans, Central and South Americans, and others of Spanish origin. As Table 12-9 shows, these people are overwhelmingly urban and most are concentrated in or below the lower-middle-class income level.

The first group of Hispanics we shall consider here are Puerto Ricans.

If someone had looked around at the potential sources of new [urban] immigration . . . his eye might well have fallen on Puerto Rico . . . in

TABLE 12-9

Hispanic Americans: Percent Urban Dwellers and Income Levels

	All Hispanics	Mexicans	Puerto Ricans	Others*
Total population (1980)	14,634,000	8,740,000	2,014,000	3,880,000
Entire SMSA†	85.1%	80.3%	95.8%	89.7%
Central city	51.0%	45.6%	79.2%	46.2%
Median income (1983)	$16,228	$16,399	$11,148	$18,996
Percent below poverty level (1983)	28.4%	30.0%	46.3%	19.8%

*Cubans, Central and South Americans, and others of Spanish origin.
†These data refer to the population of Standard Metropolitan Statistical Areas (SMSAs) in 1979. SMSA is the designation of large urban regions used by the census bureau prior to 1983.

Source: U.S. Bureau of the Census, *Statistical Abstract of the United States* (Washington, D.C.: U.S. Government Printing Office, 1985).

the middle 1930's [it was] a scene of almost unrelieved misery.

So wrote Glazer and Moynihan (1970, p. 86) in their account of the migration of Puerto Ricans (and others) to the city of New York. Migrate they did: after World War II, postwar prosperity and regular air flights to the mainland brought as many as 50,000 Puerto Ricans per year to the United States. Most came to New York. Why? Anthropologist Elena Padilla explained in 1958:

For years now Puerto Ricans have been hearing about New York City, have read about it in the local papers, heard about it on the radio, and seen some of its scenery in the movies. . . . New York is regarded as a place where many Puerto Ricans live and where they have improved their conditions of life, their health, and their general welfare. Many . . . have known New York migrants who have returned to Puerto Rico and boasted of their "good life" in New York. . . . (1958, pp. 21–22)

By 1960 some 900,000 Puerto Ricans lived within the continental United States; about 600,000 were residents of New York City. Both figures have now more than doubled. The center of Puerto Rican settlement has been East Harlem, or Spanish Harlem, in New York City (97th Street to about 125th Street between Third and Fifth avenues).

Glazer and Moynihan (1970) noted that often

men migrated first, leaving wives and children in Puerto Rico until enough resources were established to support the entire family. (This is a pattern common in the Third World as well, as we saw in Chapters 8 through 10.) In other cases, women, often with children (but unmarried or separated), moved from the island, hoping for work or at least welfare support until employment was found.

Upon a newcomer's arrival, friends and extended kin provided support services to help ease the adjustment to mainland city life. Despite this, life in New York was significantly different from Puerto Rican life and created particular hardships. Padilla (1958) suggests that this "culture shock" involved matters of proper behavior, differing attitudes and values, and, perhaps most significant, a loss of group cohesion. Often expecting others to make sacrifices to aid newcomers, migrants frequently were disappointed at the degree of individualistic self-interest shown in the city. Many encountered a dog-eat-dog world in which only the strongest and most calculating survived. In Cityscape 12-1 Piri Thomas describes his initiation into the street life of Spanish Harlem in the 1950s.

The success that migration has brought Puerto Ricans has been limited. Table 12-9 shows that they are the poorest of Hispanic groups overall: they have the lowest median income of all Hispanics and the highest proportion (46.3 percent)

CITYSCAPE 12-1
Piri Thomas: Down These Mean Streets

We were moving—our new pad was back in Spanish Harlem—to 104th Street between Lex and Park Avenue.

Moving into a new block is a big jump for a Harlem kid. You're torn up from your hard-won turf and brought into an "I don't know you" block where every kid is some kind of enemy. Even when the block belongs to your own people, you are still an outsider who has to prove himself a down stud with heart.

As the moving van rolled to a stop in front of our new building, number 109, we were all standing there, waiting for it—Momma, Poppa, Sis, Paulie, James, José, and myself. I made out like I didn't notice the cats looking us over, especially me—I was gang age. I read their faces and found no trust, plenty of suspicion, and a glint of rising hate. . . . *I'm tough, a voice within said. I hope I'm tough enough, I am tough enough. I've got mucho corazón, I'm king wherever I go. I'm a killer to my heart. I not only can live, I will live, no punk out, no die out, walk bad; be down, cool breeze, smooth. . . .*

The next morning I went to my new school, called Patrick Henry, and strange, mean eyes followed me.

"Say, pops," said a voice belonging to a guy I later came to know as Waneko, "where's your territory?"

In the same tone of voice . . . I answered, "I'm on it, dad, what's shaking?"

"Bad, huh?" He half-smiled.

"No, not all the way. Good when I'm cool breeze and bad when I'm down."

"What your name, kid?"

"That depends. 'Piri' when I'm smooth and 'Johnny Gringo' when stomping time's around."

"What's your name now?" he pushed.

"You name me, man," I answered, playing my role like a champ.

He looked around, and with no kind of words, his boys cruised in. Guys I would come to know, to fight, to hate, to love, to take care of. Little Red, Waneko, Little Louie, Indio, Carlito, Alfredo, Crip, and plenty more. I stiffened and said to myself, *Stomping time, Piri boy, go with heart.*

I fingered the garbage-can handle in my pocket—my homemade brass knuckles. They were great for breaking down large odds into small, chopped-up ones.

Waneko, secure in his grandstand, said, "We'll name you later, *panín.*"

I didn't answer. Scared yeah, but wooden-faced to the end, I thought, *Chevere, panín.*

It wasn't long in coming. Three days later, at about 6 P.M., Waneko and his boys were sitting around the stoop at number 115. I was cut off from my number 109. For an instant I thought, *Make a break for it down the basement steps and through the back yards—get away in one piece!* Then I thought, *Caramba! Live punk, dead hero. I'm no punk kid. I'm not copping any pleas.* I kept walking, hell's a-burning, hell's a-churning, rolling with cheer. *Walk on, baby man, roll on without fear. What's he going to call?*

"Whatta ya say, Mr. Johnny Gringo?" drawled Waneko.

Think, man, I told myself, think your way out of a stomping. . . . "I hear you 104th Street coolies are supposed to have heart," I said. "I don't know this for sure. You know there's a lot of streets where a whole 'click' is made out of punks

---

below the poverty line. Furthermore, there is no doubt that, like blacks, Puerto Ricans have been the object of much racial discrimination. Indeed, when all American urban minorities and considered, Puerto Ricans, after blacks, are the group most segregated from whites. The reason, Massey and Bitterman (1985) argue, once again is white racism. Since a significant percentage of Puerto Ricans are of black descent, there is a tendency for Puerto Rican groups in cities to live near blacks. But we have already seen that whites shun blacks when choosing residences. Then "Puerto Ricans become bystander victims of [whites']

racial prejudice, leading to their residential segregation in society" (Massey and Bitterman 1985, p. 306).

Nonetheless, many Puerto Ricans have persevered: Glazer and Moynihan (1970) reported that significant advances by Puerto Rican workers in New York were becoming evident as early as 1950. Younger men, born in New York, were far more likely to rise into sales and clerical jobs—leaving behind the semiskilled factory jobs more commonly held by new migrants. Women appeared to be moving into higher-status jobs even more rapidly.

who can't fight one guy unless they all jump him for the stomp." I hoped this would push Waneko into giving me a fair one. His expression didn't change.

"Maybe we don't look at it that way."

Crazy, man. I cheer inwardly, the cabrón *is falling into my setup. We'll see who gets messed up first, baby!* "I wasn't talking to you," I said. "Where I come from, the pres is president 'cause he got heart when it comes to dealing."

Waneko was starting to look uneasy. He had bit on my worm and felt like a sucker fish. His boys were now light on me. They were no longer so much interested in stomping me as in seeing the outcome between Waneko and me. "Yeah," was his reply.

I smiled at him. "You trying to dig where I'm at and now you got me interested in you. I'd like to see where you're at."

Waneko hesitated a tiny little second before replying, "Yeah."

I knew I'd won. Sure, I'd have to fight; but one guy, not ten or fifteen. If I lost I might still get stomped, and if I won I might get stomped. I took care of this with

my next sentence. "I don't know you or your boys," I said, "but they look cool to me. They don't feature as punks."

I had left him out purposely when I said "they." Now his boys were in a separate class. I had cut him off. He would have to fight me on his own, to prove his heart to himself, to his boys, and most important, to his turf. He got away from the stoop and asked, "Fair one, Gringo?"

"Uh-uh," I said, "roll all the way—anything goes." I thought, *I've got to beat him bad and yet not bad enough to take his prestige all away.* He had corazón. He came on me. *Let him draw first blood,* I thought, *it's his block.* Smish, my nose began to bleed. His boys cheered, his heart cheered, his turf cheered. "Waste this chump," somebody shouted.

Okay, baby, now it's my turn. He swung. I grabbed innocently, and my forehead smashed his nose. His eyes crossed. His fingernails went for my eye and landed in my mouth—crunch, I bit hard. I punched him in the mouth as he pulled away from me, and he slammed his foot into my chest.

We broke, my nose running red, my chest throbbing, his finger—well, that was his worry. I tied up with body punching and slugging. We rolled into the street. I wrestled for acceptance, he for rejection or, worse yet, acceptance on his terms. It was time to start peace talks. I smiled at him. "You got heart, baby," I said.

He answered with a punch to my head. I grunted and hit back, harder now. I had to back up my overtures of peace with strength. I hit him in the ribs, I rubbed my knuckles in his ear as we clinched. I tried again. "You deal good," I said.

"You, too," he muttered, pressuring out. And just like that, the fight was over. No more words. We just separated, hands half up, half down. My heart pumped out, *You've established your rep. Move over, 104th Street. Lift your wings, I'm one of your baby chicks now.*

Source: Piri Thomas, *Down These Mean Streets* (New York: New American Library, 1967), pp. 55–58.

The second group of Hispanics we shall discuss are Mexican Americans. The 1980 census counted over 14.6 million Hispanics in the United States. Of this total, about 60 percent are Mexican Americans. Moreover, this number is probably greatly underestimated. Given that some are recent illegal immigrants to cities in the South and West, not all Mexican Americans were enthusiastic about being counted by the census, since recognition also may mean deportation. Some estimates suggest as many as 12 million illegal immigrants from Latin America may live in the United States (Fallows 1983, p. 46).

Although most are new arrivals, Mexican Americans, like blacks, have been in this country for well over 100 years. Generally accorded greatest prestige are families who were residents of the Southwest as early as the Mexican-American War in 1848. Immigration of a second group from Mexico began around the turn of the century. The descendants of these more "recent" residents now occupy a middle status level. Below them are the many arrivals of the past three decades (particularly the 1970s). Many of this latter group, struggling for economic and political identity and success, prefer to be called Chicanos, a name that

CITYSCAPE 12-2
Women in the Gangs of East Los Angeles

East Los Angeles—the sunshine ghetto. Seven square miles of street after street of 1920s-style bungalows, *burrito* takeouts, churches, cemeteries, and freeway interchanges. There is barely a concrete surface that does not carry a spray-painted graffito proclaiming some gang's turf; for each *barrio* . . . be it four blocks or a mile long, has its reigning gang and its rains of violence.

For three generations street gangs have been a fact of life for the roughly 130,000 Chicanos of East L.A., although, according to police estimates, only one percent of the community's youth are hard-core members and less than 15 percent of them even identify with the gang image.

Cholos (both male and female gang members) generally range in age from 11 to 25. They are often school dropouts with few job prospects. Without steady incomes or cars, they are isolated from everyone except each other. A few hard-core members are even ready to put their lives on the line for a neighborhood as a soldier would in defense of the homeland. . . .

Women have always been a part of gang life. . . . Nineteen year old Sylvia describes her gang membership: "For me the greatest days were in junior high school when I was fourteen or fif-

teen. I used to sniff paint, take downers, and I was always ditching school. I was a fighter, running the streets, looking for trouble. A group of us would walk down the sidewalk and we wouldn't move for anybody. We were too bad, we were from Primera Flats. The girls hung around in fours and fives for protection. You learn young that you don't be on the streets by yourself, you just don't."

At 36, Ruth has gone through hard times in East L.A. and now reflects on two generations of gang-life:

"I think I was born gang. From eleven on, I identified with *pachucos* and *pachucas* [fifties' slang for gang members]. We drank, we lowrided, and we got into fights with girls from other gangs. Our motto was 'This is the way we're going to live, this is the way we'll die, standing up for our gang's name.'

I saw a lot of stabbings and killings as a kid. I was frightened, but you can't show it. If there was a gang fight, I went to the front even if I felt fear. I would have to down somebody, but inside I felt sorry for them.

I had this image to uphold—and it almost killed me because I carried it for so long.

Little by little, I started to grow into a different person. I haven't had a drink, a fix, pills, anything in

years. I've gotten my kids back. . . . I own my own home.

Now, what I like to do is help kids that feel they have to live up to the gang image or kids who get loaded. My boyfriend tells me I'm becoming a square.

Sure, there are still problems. We had to move out of East L.A. because of the gang scene. Basically the scene is the same as in my day, but now they're playing rougher. You hear of more guns, more killings. It scares me.

Yes, there are gangs where we live now, but I feel the kids are under less pressure. My son has been able to get through school. . . . But my kids have a good chance of making it. They have interest in life, and they've had a chance to go to places outside of East L.A. . . ."

Living surrounded by affluence, the poor of East Los Angeles are keenly aware of their low position in the urban hierarchy. It is not simply a matter of poverty, but of little opportunity linked to being part of a visible urban minority. In Sylvia's words:

"Yeah . . . it's not really that I hate whites, it's just that maybe I'm jealous a little. I mean, why can't I get the chance they get? That's all."

Source: Suzanne Murphy, "A Year with the Gangs of East Los Angeles," *Ms.* (July 1978), pp. 56–64.

---

implies both a sense of political consciousness and strong cultural pride in their Mexican heritage.

Most Mexican Americans live in ghetto-type urban barrios in Texas and California. Poverty is rife, although it is not as bad for Mexican Americans as a group as it is for Puerto Ricans (Table 12-9) or for blacks. As is the case among Puerto Ricans, Mexicans have a strong tradition of family

support, which continues (although somewhat weakened) in large cities. There is also a pronounced pattern of male dominance among the population. Fertility rates are at roughly the same level as for Puerto Ricans—well above the national average. This means Mexican Americans tend to be young—averaging about 21 years of age, compared to 30 for whites in 1979 (Moore and Pachon 1985, p. 62). Large families tend to reduce the standard of living as well.

As do other nonwhites, Mexican Americans face disadvantages common to urbanites at the lower levels of the social stratification hierarchy. There is discrimination in employment and housing and the inability to speak English often limits success in school and in the job market. Many Mexican Americans believe they can never "get out," that is, rise to positions of some comfort. To combat this sense of powerlessness, especially strong in adolescents faced with relatively limited adult opportunities, some young men and women turn to membership in street gangs. In Cityscape 12-1 we saw Piri Thomas joining such a gang in "El Barrio" in New York City. In Cityscape 12-2 we see what gang membership means in terms of belonging, security, and power to Chicano women in East Los Angeles, on the other side of the continent.

Is the outlook for continuing segregation as bleak for America's urban Hispanics as it is for urban blacks? The current evidence suggests not. Massey and Mullan (1984), in a study of southwestern SMSAs, found that when Hispanics gained in socioeconomic status and moved into previously all-white neighborhoods, whites moved out, but not in the numbers that fled when blacks moved in. When blacks moved in, nearly all the whites moved out in relatively short order, creating, once again, a completely segregated black community. However, in most neighborhoods when Hispanics moved in, only about half the whites moved out, creating a truly mixed living area. The implications once again are clear, if disturbing: Many whites, while not enthusiastic about living with people of Hispanic descent, are willing to do so. But they are not willing to make similar "concessions" with blacks.

Asians. Like Hispanics, Asians in America include a wide range of distinctive cultural groups. Most numerous are the Chinese, approaching 1 million. Japanese and Filipinos are also large minorities in the United States, each numbering some 800,000. In addition, during the 1980s a significant number of Vietnamese and Korean

immigrants have entered the urban mix, primarily in larger cities such as Los Angeles and Chicago (described further in Case Study 12-1 at the end of this chapter).

The first Asians to come to the United States were Chinese, who arrived in the San Francisco area about 1850. In the frenzy of the California gold rush (beginning in 1849), Chinese immigrants easily found jobs performing tasks that whites generally sought to avoid, thus living relatively harmoniously—if unequally—with whites for several decades. When the economy turned sour in the 1870s, however, whites felt a growing economic threat from the Chinese and a period of marked hostility ensued. This reaction was exacerbated by the arrival of immigrants from Japan, which had recently undertaken a crash program in Western-style modernization (as described in Chapter 10). During this period many whites complained bitterly about the "Yellow Peril"—a phrase that suggests both the extent of animosity toward Asians and its racist foundation. In 1877, for example, Asians were the target of vicious rioting by whites in San Francisco (described later in Case Study 15-1). As hostility grew, the United States moved to curb the immigration of all Asians in 1882—a restriction that was strengthened in the 1920s and did not completely end until after World War II.

In response to this animosity, many Asians moved eastward; others banded together in urban enclaves—the beginning of the Chinatowns and Little Tokyos that mark many American cities even today. Within these communities, Asians were able to pool their economic resources and establish some semblance of economic and personal security. During much of this century, however, the barriers to social equality for all Asians were considerable indeed. Kept within the limits of racial ghettos by white prejudice and discrimination, many Chinese never learned the English language, further limiting their opportunity to advance. Not until 1943 were immigrants born in China extended the opportunity to become citizens of the United States.

The years of World War II brought special hardship to Japanese in the United States. In the wake of the destruction of Pearl Harbor by the air force of Japan, rampant hostility and fear was directed toward Americans of Japanese descent. Within a year, over 100,000 people of Japanese ancestry—most of whom were United States citizens—were rounded up from the West Coast and moved to military detention centers inland. Beyond the anger and humiliation experienced by these people—not one of whom had been convicted of any anti-American act—America's Japanese suffered a crushing economic setback. Relocation meant that homes, land, and businesses had to be sold; under the circumstances, only rarely did the owners receive a fair market price.

Despite a century of various hardships, Asians in America have a striking record of achievement. Taken together, Asian Americans in 1980 were better educated and enjoyed a higher income than the average American. This has certainly helped the process of assimilation by which many Asians have left traditional neighborhoods in favor of residences throughout the urban area. Yet, the picture is not entirely favorable; in contrast to those who have reached new levels of affluence, many continuing residents of the old neighborhoods hold poorly paying jobs and live in poverty. In New York's Chinatown, for example, poverty is twice as common as in the city as a whole (Sowell 1981).

Asian immigrants figure prominently in the immigration pattern (Table 12-7) that continues to change the face of American cities, especially on the West Coast. In 1965 relaxation of the strict immigration quotas imposed in the 1920s marked the start of a new period of immigration that has continued ever since. After Mexico, the countries from which the greatest number are arriving are the Philippines, South Korea, China, Taiwan, and Vietnam.

Interestingly, of all the minority groups considered thus far, Asians are the most well-off economically. One reason appears to be education: Asians educate themselves and their children more than other minorities and, as a result, have moved higher on the socioeconomic ladder. In comparison, the educational attainment levels for blacks and Hispanics are considerably lower—and so is their income (Hirshman and Wong 1984).

A second reason may be the cultural values that Asian immigrants bring with them—values that are quintessentially "American," stressing competition, unceasing hard work, and unflagging energy. One example is provided by members of North Vietnam's Tai Dam tribe who fled the Communist government in the 1960s and settled in Des Moines, Iowa. "The Tai Dam," says Marvin Weidner, manager of the Iowa Refugee Center, "have a strong sense of how the American game is played—what is expected, what is to be done and not done." For one thing, they join Des Moines's Protestant churches and begin making contacts on various levels—religious, political, economic, and social. For another, they have learned that they can benefit themselves politically if they join agencies dealing with issues that affect their group (*Newsweek*, July 7, 1980, p. 29).

Another example is provided by New York City's Korean population. Koreans have virtually taken over the city's greengrocery (retail produce store) industry (Kim 1984). Observes one veteran produce supplier: "When I first came into this business—that was before the War—to do business here you had to know Jewish phrases. Then, some years later you had to pick up a few Italian words to make it. Now I'm trying for all the Korean words I can. There are that many Korean buyers now." Why have the Koreans gone into greengroceries? The answer is provided by Mr. Chung, a 35-year-old Korean and the holder of two master's degrees in city planning from a school in Korea: "What else can I do?" he asked. "I need money but there are no good jobs for Koreans." So, greengrocering is one anwer. Kim notes that the Korean success depends on three variables: First, the business can be opened with little capital and can be managed without a knowledge of English. Second, Koreans are very aggressive and competitive about their business endeavors. Employing relatives and friends, they have been able to push out older, more sedate Jewish and Italian competitors. Third, they have figured out how to compete with the big supermarket chains as well: they work, for very little pay, the long hours necessary to get their goods to the stores before other distributors.

Finally, there is a third hypothesis about the relative success of Asians on the American urban scene: Not only are their cultural values similar to those of mainstream America, but (like the Hispanics, who, as we saw earlier, are also somewhat better-off) their skin color is not black. Hence, prejudice against Asians, which certainly exists, may not be as unbending as prejudice against blacks.

Natives. The American "Indian" has been in North America since prehistoric times. The history of this group since the arrival of our European forebears, however, has been one of the bleakest chapters in the American saga. By the late nineteenth century, this once proud collection of small societies had been decimated by war and disease and shunted, with virtually no say in the matter, onto barren reservations.

Actually, the widespread use of the single European term "Indian" to characterize these people is highly distortive. In the first place, it is a misnomer. When Columbus discovered America in 1492, he thought he had gone around the world to India—not knowing there was another continent in the way. So he called the people he found in the New World "Indians." In the second place, to categorize such a complex set of societies under a single term of *any* kind is distortive. There were well over a hundred different societies extant on the North American continent in the late 1400s, most with widely varying patterns of belief and social life. Finally, even to call these people "Americans" is problematic. That term, too, is European: the two continents of the hemisphere were named after the Italian discoverer Amerigo Vespucci. So perhaps the best solution is to call these people "natives," as is now being done in parts of Canada. After all, they were here first.

The largest groups of natives still existing are the Navajo (about 100,000) and the Cherokee (about 70,000). According to census data, there were just over 1.4 million natives in 1980, up from just over 800,000 in 1970. About 715,000 reside in the West and another 375,000 in the South.

They are becoming increasingly urban. More than half lived in cities in 1970, and many more are part-time city residents. Still, even in the western cities where they are most prominent, natives comprise a very small percentage of the total urban population (see Table 12-10).

Movement from the reservations to the cities, as we have seen everywhere throughout the world, has been stimulated by the desire for a better life. The tracts of land given to natives by various governments often were selected because they were least desired by local settlers of European descent. Not surprisingly, therefore, most reservations have not become thriving economic centers. Jobs are scarce, education is poor, and most services—many controlled by the notoriously inefficient Bureau of Indian Affairs—are inadequate. The city promises more.

Unfortunately, for most natives the city has not delivered much. Housing discrimination (and other forms) are rampant, and most are forced to live in slums. Further, as Joan Albon's (1971) work demonstrated natives find themselves at a distinct cultural disadvantage in cities because their traditional values stress consensus, equality, and communal use of property. From this point of view, the use of nature or other persons to advance one's own ends is immoral. Laudable as these values may be, to "make it" in the American city with such principles as a guide is difficult, at best. Albon concludes that

> . . . [many] fundamental Indian values not only are incompatible with those of American culture, but work directly in opposition to the principles on which the modern competitive capitalistic order is based. It is this great value disparity that sets Indians apart from other migrants now entering our cities. (1971, p. 387)

Despite a few success stories, the situation of most urban natives is not good. Alan Sorkin summarizes:

> The average income of urban Indians lags far behind that of most city dwellers. An unduly high number of Indians are forced to subsist solely on welfare payments, private charity, or handouts from relatives. Native Americans face nearly overwhelming problems coping with the city school system. Drop out rates are very high (even greater than on

TABLE 12-10
Native American Population, Selected Cities, 1980

Region and City*	Total Population	Native Population	Percentage of Total Population
Northeast			
Boston	646,352	897	0.1
New York (5 boroughs)	7,071,030	11,824	0.2
Washington, D.C.	637,651	1,031	0.2
South			
Atlanta	483,024	347	0.1
New Orleans	557,482	524	0.1
West			
Oklahoma City	403,213	10,405	2.6
Albuquerque	409,589	8,615	2.1
Phoenix	764,911	10,771	1.4
Los Angeles	2,966,763	16,595	0.6
San Francisco	678,974	3,548	0.5
Portland	366,383	3,526	1.0

*Incorporated city only; not SMSA.

Source: Calculated from U.S. Bureau of the Census, *Advance Reports* (Washington, D.C.: U.S. Government Printing Office, 1980).

reservations) and achievement levels are generally low. Indians complain of prejudice and discrimination in the schools and an irrelevant curriculum. . . . Alcoholism is a major problem. Many newly arrived migrants gravitate to skid row and an existence centered around the bottle and the bar. Unfortunately, the bar is often the only place where Indians can go to meet their friends or fellow tribesmen. (1978, p. 139)

Given such grim realities, it may be that as a group, natives are the most disadvantaged of all urban dwellers. In recent years many natives have been involved in political activity with the American Indian Movement, which has attempted to win Indian rights across the country. Others conclude, however, that only massive government changes and intervention can alleviate the situation in the near future (Sorkin 1978).

Diversity Among Urban Minorities

The preceding portraits of urban minorities give only a general picture; we must bear in mind that whole subgroups within each category never

really fit the pattern. The life-styles of urban minorities vary considerably.

For example, while slightly over 30 percent of urban blacks are below the poverty level, the majority are not. Depending on the level of their income and their location within the city, these people live very differently from the poor. Blacks who have white-collar and high-paying blue-collar jobs live nearly identical lives to their white counterparts (Wilson 1980).

Similarly, the Cuban experience in Miami stands in sharp contrast to our discussion of city-dwelling Hispanics generally. In little more than two decades many of Miami's Cubans, middle- and upper-middle-class emigrés from Castro's socialist regime, have become affluent, built a solid community, and increased their control of the city's economic and political apparatus enormously (Wilson and Portes 1980). To cap this success story, in November 1985 Miami elected its first Cuban-born mayor, Xavier Louis Juarez. Moreover, our discussion of Hispanics concentrated on inner-city residents; however, like suburban blacks, suburban Hispanics are becoming even more numerous. The 1980 census showed that, in Los Angeles, 58 percent of the city's Hispanics lived outside the center city; in Chicago the figure was 28 percent; in Philadelphia, 45 percent. As they become more suburban, there is every reason to believe that their lives will reflect their surroundings.

Thus making generalizations that capture even a single city neighborhood is virtually impossible. In a study of a Mexican American barrio in Dallas, Shirley Achor (1978, Chap. 5) found four major life-styles present. There were the *puros mejicanos*, Mexican Americans uninterested in moving out of the barrio into the wider society, even though in many cases their income would have allowed it. A contrasting group were the *anglo sados*, people trying to adapt to the wider white culture and to move up within it. *Chicanos*, a third group, took political mobilization as their main interest and focused their lives on finding ways to combat racial, economic, and political discrimination. Finally, the *pelados* were truly "down and out." Beaten down by discrimination or personal troubles, they had given up and resigned themselves to lives of destitution. On the basis of this evidence, Achor concluded her study with an observation applicable to any urban minority:

> In contrast to some widely held assumptions of cultural homogeneity . . . among Mexican-Americans, these findings show that dynamic variation and ongoing culture change characterize the barrio. They clearly fail to support the belief that there is a "typical" Mexican-American culture. . . .
>
> In the midst of poverty and disease, there is also a full measure of pride and dignity. A devout and supportive religious life, warm and close-knit family relationships, beloved children and honored grandparents . . . all are as real a part of the barrio experience as its crowded housing, blighted alleys, and long-endured episodes of human anguish. No one can deny the thorns . . . but we must also remember the roses. (1978, p. 154)

In sum, then, both the Great Immigration of Europeans (discussed in Chapter 3) and the newer urban immigrants just considered have played a crucial part in shaping the cities of the United States. At one time or another, almost all American minority groups have been concentrated heavily in cities, and the urban racial and ethnic mosaic of a half century ago persists today. The most significant change in recent years, however, has been the declining significance of ethnicity in urban life and the growing significance of race: black, Hispanic, Asian, and native concentrations are coming to characterize more and more the central cities, while whites are moving out to the suburban rings.

This pattern reminds us that cities do not exist in a cultural vacuum. They are shaped by the dominant values, norms, and stratification systems of the broader society. American society is clearly hierarchical and has always generated a segment of population (disproportionately composed of minorities) relatively lacking in wealth, prestige, and power. Furthermore, racial prejudice and discrimination continue to play a prominent role in our society. We could hardly expect our cities to be different, although in cities we are likely to find the systematic distribution of wealth, prestige, and power and the effects of racial discrimination to be reflected with characteristic urban intensity. However, the evidence suggests that racial prejudice and discrimination, historically and in the present, have been most detrimental to blacks and natives. Unlike their Asian and, to a lesser degree, their Hispanic counterparts, these groups have found it exceedingly difficult to "get a leg up" on the American urban scene. There is little evidence that in the future things will be much better for these minorities.

In the next section we will turn to a deeper analysis of how power is (or is not) distributed within urban America.

Power

The element of power—the ability to achieve ends, even over opposition—always exists in social life. In complex settings such as cities power is linked to differences in economic resources and prestige, as well as to control of the city government and its bureaucracies. The patterns of social stratification described by Warner and Lunt in

Yankee City (1941, 1942), Coleman and Neugarten in Kansas City (1971), and by Coleman and Rainwater in Boston (1978) reflect not only the wealth and prestige of various urbanites but also their ability to shape events in the city. Similarly, the urban minorities we discussed in the last section all share a position of relative powerlessness. Given this, several questions will guide the ensuing discussion: Who or what shapes decision making in the city? Do urban political systems reflect the needs and desires of all city residents in a democratic fashion? How have urban politics changed during this century?

Theoretical Perspectives on Urban Power

There is little reason to expect that the political structures of all cities will be the same. A city such as "Middletown," Indiana (which we'll describe shortly), dominated by a single industry in the early part of this century, would differ politically from a complex industrial city such as Chicago in the same era. Similarly, significant historical events can change the shape of urban politics in any city: Detroit's political future was altered by the racial riots of 1967 and the automobile industry recession of 1980, and Atlantic City was transformed by the introduction of gambling casinos in 1978. Even so, several general themes have emerged in studies of urban power in the last half century of research.

The Power Elite. The phrase "power elite" is linked with C. Wright Mills (1956), who believed power to be concentrated in the hands of the upper-upper class: a small number of families who enjoy tremendous wealth, social prestige, and the power to shape the lives of countless others. As Mills suggests in Box 12-4, the "metropolitan 400" are not merely rich and well respected, but exercise power mainly in their own interests, and often over many generations. In this view, the shape of urban power is a pyramid with the few on top and the rest of society—the urban poor, as well as many urban minorities—categorically excluded from the most influential positions.

How does the power of this elite group manifest itself in urban life? Often in the most direct manner. For example, in Case Study 12-1 at the

---

BOX 12-4
"The Metropolitan 400"

In the big cities of America there flourishes a recognizable upper social class, which seems in many ways to be quite compact. In Boston and in New York, in Philadelphia and in Baltimore and in San Francisco, there exists a solid core of older, wealthier families surrounded by looser circles of newer, wealthier families. This older core . . . was once said—by Mrs. Astor's Ward McAllister—to number Four Hundred. . . . There is little doubt, however, that among their small town counterparts, there is an accumulation of advantages in which objective opportunity and psychological readiness interact to maintain for each generation the world of upper social classes.

Source: C. Wright Mills, *The Power Elite* (New York: Oxford University Press, 1956), pp. 47–48.

---

end of this chapter, we shall see how the Chicago area town of Pullman, Illinois, grew under the control of one powerful family. Another example is provided in the study of Middletown, Indiana, conducted by Robert and Helen Lynd (1937). Returning to Middletown several years after an initial study (1929), the Lynds wrote that "one thing struck the returning observer again and again: the increasingly large public benefactions and the increasing pervasiveness of the power of [a] wealthy family of manufacturers . . ." (1937, p. 74). This family (called the "X" family by the Lynds), whose economic fortune was based on a glass-canning-jar industry, was so pervasive in the life of the city that the Lynds opened a chapter devoted to an analysis of this family with a local resident's telling observation:

> If I'm out of work I go to the X plant; if I need money I go to the X bank, and if they don't like me I don't get it; my children go to the X college; when I get sick I go to the X hospital; I buy a building lot or house in an X subdivision; my wife goes downtown to buy clothes at the X department stores; if my dog stays away he is put in the X pound; I buy X milk; I drink X beer, vote for X political parties, and get help from X charities; my boy goes to the X Y.M.C.A. and my girl to their Y.W.C.A.; I listen to the word of God in X-subsidized churches; if I'm

a Mason I go to the X Masonic Temple; I read the news from the X morning newspaper; and, if I am rich enough, I travel via the X airport. (1937, p. 74)

A later study of Regional City (a pseudonym) in Georgia, done by Floyd Hunter (1963), also advanced the power elite orientation. Hunter found Regional City dominated by 40 persons "in top levels of power." These people clustered together in a distinctive residential area and lived similar lives of privilege. In interviews with these elites, Hunter found a dozen were constantly referred to as being at the top of the city's power structure (1963, Chap. 4). All were men, and all formed the core of the "commercial, industrial, financial, and professional positions in Regional City" (1963, p. 74).

A recent survey of Philadelphia, edited by Maury Z. Levy (1979), focused on the power structure of that city. A wide-ranging elite was found to exist, including powerful figures in the media, the sports world, and even organized crime. The survey also discovered that a relatively small number of Philadelphians held multiple positions of power on city boards of directors. Again, all were men, mostly white and from "old families." These are Philadelphia's "power hitters," the study observed, "because they're steady performers, sometimes because they're hot shots, sometimes . . . because they own the ball" (1979, p. 166).

Pluralist Politics. Not everyone agrees with the power elite orientation. A competing analysis holds that *many* centers of power are found in complex social organizations—especially one as complex as a city. The fact that some people are reputed to be powerful doesn't mean that they actually make all the decisions. Pluralists therefore hold that no single person or group (such as the X family in Middletown) or clique of business leaders (as Hunter argued of Regional City) dominates the urban aea. Most pluralist visions of urban power suggest that while some have more power than others, various organizations and groups (composed of working-class and poor people as well) provide input to the system. Also, because leaders compete among themselves for wider support, urban decision making must re-

flect to some degree the wishes of a wide population, rather than the narrow interests of the leaders themselves. An additional difference between the power elite and pluralist orientations is a matter of method: pluralist studies direct attention not to the reputations of leaders but the process of formal decision making itself.

Nelson Polsby (1959) studied New Haven, Connecticut, and focused on three arenas of urban decision making: redevelopment, political nominations, and public education. Polsby's findings simply didn't jibe with the power elite model. The number of people he found to be involved in each of the three areas of decision making was large, and, more importantly, leaders in one area typically did not exert influence in other issue areas. For example, there were 435 persons (the large number itself is significant) in the "leadership pool" in matters of urban redevelopment, and 497 were involved in deciding about political nominations. The overlap between the two (which could have been as high as 435 persons) was only 15, or 3 percent (1959, p. 799). Polsby also challenged the implication of the power elite model that the people with high economic position also would enjoy high social prestige. He identified 239 people who had positions of economic leadership and 231 who were prominent in the New Haven "society." Once again, the overlap was insignificant: only 25 names appeared on both lists (1959, pp. 800–801).

These conclusions were echoed by Robert Dahl (1961) who, along with Raymond Wolfinger, collaborated on the New Haven study. Dahl acknowledged that early in the city's history decision making had been dominated by "Congregational patrician families," but, as have other cities, New Haven "passed through a . . . transformation from a system in which resources of influence were highly concentrated to a system in which they are highly dispersed" (1961, p. 227). Summarizing this pluralist analysis of power in New Haven, Dahl wrote:

This system of dispersed inequalities is, I believe, marked by the following six characteristics:

1. Many different kinds of resources for influencing officials are available to different citizens.

2. With few exceptions, these resources are unequally distributed.

3. Individuals best off in their access to one kind of resource are often badly off with respect to many other resources.

4. No one influence resource dominates all the others in all or even in most key decisions.

5. With some exceptions, an influence resource is effective in some issue-areas or in some specific decisions but not in all.

6. Virtually no one, and certainly no group of more than a few individuals, is entirely lacking in some influence resources. (1961, p. 228)

The City as a Growth Machine. More recent research initiated by Harvey Molotch (1976) and further developed by William Domhoff (1978; 1983; 1984) provides a deeper understanding of how both the power-elite and pluralist models of power can be applied to cities.

In essence, the growth machine theory is based on the following ideas (Domhoff 1983, pp. 166–173). First, the power structure within cities is based in a small number of landowners who seek to increase their own wealth by increasing the value of their holdings. Second, these people typically work in concert, believing that what increases the value of some land in the central city is likely to raise the value of all commercial land. Third, in an effort to increase the value of commercial land, owners attempt to attract economic investment by corporations, governmental agencies, educational facilities, and any other type of organization that will bring more wealth and people to the city, thereby stimulating commercial activity. In other words, increased prosperity for private commercial landowners depends on stimulating the commercial growth of the city—it is on this basis that the city is described as a "growth machine."

The landowning elite that is the basis of this effort at urban expansion finds a number of allies, including bankers, newspaper executives, utility executives, and retail business people. This is simply because all stand to gain from greater economic activity in the city. Thus, cities deliberately "groom" themselves to be as attractive as possible to outside investment (a recent example is the competition among cities in a number of states to attract the new General Motors Saturn automobile plant). At the same time, however, the emphasis in commercial expansion is also likely to spawn opposition—especially from local community groups interested in providing more and better residential housing and environmentalist groups seeking more open public spaces. Domhoff notes, for instance, that a coalition of students (empowered to vote since 1971) and local neighborhood groups has successfully opposed many efforts to develop the central business district in Santa Cruz, California (1984, p. 15).

How does the growth machine theory shed new light on the long-standing debate between the power-elite theorists (such as Mills and Hunter) and the pluralist theorists (such as Polsby and Dahl)? First, turning to Atlanta, in which Hunter (1963) conducted his influential study, we find that the vast majority of the power elite in Atlanta were, indeed, commercial landowners of the kind we have just described. Their influence can be easily seen in efforts to economically revitalize that city during the period of urban renewal that began in the early 1950s (detailed discussion of urban renewal appears in the next chapter). Much of inner-city Atlanta at that time was anything but booming; many dilapidated neighborhoods contained thousands of poor people. Yet, seeking the profits from commercial development rather than providing housing for the poor, landowners directed Atlanta toward a business renaissance that, in the process, pushed one-seventh of the city's residents (who were unable to mount a successful opposition) from their homes between 1956 and 1966 (Stone 1976, cited in Domhoff 1983, p. 183). In short, Domhoff argues that the *national* power elite is concerned primarily with corporate profits and requires a suitable urban environment for its operations; *local* power elites encourage business into their cities as a means of reaping profits for themselves.

The case of Atlanta suggests that the growth machine theory is thus generally consistent with the earlier power elite orientation. But what of New Haven, the city that Polsby and Dahl argued was the classic example of a pluralist power structure? Domhoff (1978, 1983) reports that a reevaluation of the material used by Dahl (1961) casts strong doubts on some earlier conclusions. Dahl reported that no one group appeared to take the lead in various urban issues such as political nominations, school policies, and urban renewal; with regard to the first two of these issues, Dahl's conclusion appears to be fair enough. In the case of political nominations, this is because the landowning elite is apparently less concerned with *who* is nominated or elected than with *what policies* are subsequently implemented. Similarly, as Dahl had noted, with most of their own children enrolled in private schools, the business elite showed limited concern with educational matters. Urban renewal, however, was another matter—it was at the heart of the business elite's economic concerns. In this case, Domhoff presents evidence that contradicts Dahl's earlier conclusion that business leaders played a minor role in New Haven's economic development. In contrast, he concludes that the business elite was very much at the forefront of the renewal program, consistent with the growth machine theory. Finally, Domhoff claims that a more careful examination of New Haven elites reveals that economic power and social prestige overlapped considerably—a strong rebuttal to Polsby's earlier claim that the two spheres were quite distinct.

Summing Up Urban Power. Ideas about urban power structures are likely to remain controversial, not only because the evidence gathered has historically often been contradictory, but also because research of this kind frequently reaches to the heart of social and political beliefs held dear by scholars. On the one hand, the pluralist orientation implies that although some differences in power may exist, American democracy is working rather well. The power elite orientation, on the other hand, does not see America as democratic, believing instead that a small group shapes events to its own liking.

Nonetheless, we are able to reach several conclusions that seem consistent with all the evidence. First, the power elite orientation seems, on balance, to be basically correct. Power *is* very unequally distributed within American society, and this basic fact has obvious consequences for city politics. Second, as Domhoff (1983) points out, the power elite that functions on the national level (largely corporate leaders and other members of the upper-upper class) is not generally interested in the internal politics of cities; rather, it operates in a much larger economic sphere, national (and, indeed, international) in scope. Local elites, however, have economic interests that are more narrow—increasing the value of commercial land in their own cities. To do this, as we have explained, local elites court national elites hoping to attract economic activity to their own city. Third, and finally, local elites are not all-powerful, indicating that there is some truth in the pluralist orientation as well. Local elites are primarily concerned with economic issues; others can and do take the lead in various additional areas. Further, coalitions in opposition to economic elites may form, in some cases successfully, opposing economic development in favor of other priorities such as housing or public recreational facilities. In general, however, the economic power of urban landowners, supported by cultural values that support the "rightness" of seeking to maximize individual profits, suggest that at least much of the urban political scene will remain under the control of a small minority of people. In the next section we shall see, however, that although cities may never have been truly democratic, they were not always controlled by economic elites.

The Urban Political Machine

If we associate power in the city today with business leaders, images of urban politics in years past inevitably seem to include a cigar-chomping "boss" at the head of a not-totally-reputable political organization. The American political "machine" has, in fact, played a central part in the implementation of urban power for well over 100

CITYSCAPE 12-3
George Washington Plunkitt on Honest and Dishonest Graft

Plunkitt was born in an Irish neighborhood on the Upper West Side of Manhattan in 1842. As a boy he worked in a butcher shop, quit school, and began to work his way up the ladder of the Democratic political organization—popularly known as Tammany Hall. Plunkitt was also a true urban "character"—witty and endearing—which perhaps makes him appear to be more of a hero than he really was. With candor not at all typical of his kind, Plunkitt describes how he made his fortune as a political "boss" in New York.

Everybody is talkin' these days about Tammany men growin' rich on graft, but nobody thinks of drawin' the distinction between honest graft and dishonest graft. There's all the difference in the world between the two. Yes, many of our men have grown in politics. I have myself. I've made a big fortune out of the game, and I'm getting richer every day, but I've not gone in for dishonest graft—blackmailin' gamblers, saloon-keepers, disorderly people, etc.—and neither has any of the men who have made big fortunes in politics.

There's an honest graft, and I'm an example of how it works. I might sum up the whole thing by sayin': "I seen my opportunities and I took 'em."

Just let me explain by examples. My party's in power in the city, and its goin' to undertake a lot of public improvements. Well, I'm tipped off, say, that they're going to lay out a new park at a certain place.

I see an opportunity and I take it. I go to that place and I buy up all the land I can get in the neighborhood. Then the board of this or that makes its plan public, and there is a rush to get my land, which nobody cared particular for before.

Ain't it perfectly honest to charge a good price and make a profit on my investment and foresight? Of course, it is. Well, that's honest graft.

Or, supposin' it's a new bridge they're goin' to build. I get tipped off and I buy as much property as I can that has to be taken for approaches. I sell at my own price later on and drop some more money in the bank.

Wouldn't you? It's just like

---

years, although, as we shall see, the machine has weakened considerably in the years since the Depression. There is no better introduction to the machine than the words of George Washington Plunkitt, political leader and outspoken defender of the political machine in New York City in the late 1800s. His ideas are presented in Cityscape 12-3.

The Machine and the Great Migration

Between the Civil War and the Great Depression, nearly every large city in the United States was overwhelmed with massive immigration, mainly from Europe. Mostly poor and unskilled, immigrants came in search of a better life. But lacking the manners, money, and in many cases even the language of the Anglo-Saxon "natives" who had immigrated earlier, they occupied a position at the bottom of the city's social stratification hierarchy (Mann 1963, p. xv). Although numerous, they lacked almost all access to established positions of power.

The machine was a way of gaining some political voice. Local immigrants affiliated with a political party—usually the Democrats—and a few became ward leaders who worked to get out the vote. Successful ward leaders might work their way up in the party organization, much as Plunkitt did. Because election victory meant control of thousands of jobs and other opportunities for party members, the fate of the local population was linked inextricably to the machine's success. In New York, for example, Tammany leaders controlled some 12,000 patronage jobs—more than many "robber-baron" industrialists of the same period (Mann 1963, p. xviii). This alone made the machine an indispensable source of upward social mobility for many immigrants with otherwise limited opportunities. Second, the machine benefited the local citizenry by serving as a source of social services at a time when extensive social

lookin' ahead in Wall Street or in the coffee market. It's honest graft, and I'm lookin' for it every day in the year. I will tell you frankly that I've got a good lot of it, too. . . .

Somehow, I always guessed about right, and shouldn't I enjoy the profit of my foresight? It was rather amusin' when the condemnation commissioners came along and found piece after piece of the land in the name of George Plunkitt of the Fifteenth Assembly District, New York City. They wondered how I knew just what to buy. The answer is—I seen my opportunity and I took it. I haven't confined myself to land; anything that pays is in my line.

I've told you how I got rich by honest graft. Now, let me tell you that most politicians who are ac-cused of robbin' the city get rich the same way.

They didn't steal a dollar from the city treasury. They just seen their opportunities and took them. That is why, when a reform administration comes in and spends a half million dollars in tryin' to find the public robberies they talked about in the campaign, they don't find them.

The books are always all right. The money in the city treasury is all right. Everything is all right. All they can show is that the Tammany heads of departments looked after their friends, within the law, and gave them what opportunities they could to make honest graft. Now, let me tell you that's never goin' to hurt Tammany with the people. Every good man looks after his friends, and any man who doesn't isn't likely to be popular. If I have a good thing to hand out in private life, I give it to a friend. Why shouldn't I do the same in public life? . . .

Now, in conclusion, I want to say that I don't own a dishonest dollar. If my worst enemy was given the job of writin' my epitaph when I'm gone, he couldn't do more than write:

"George W. Plunkitt. He Seen His Opportunities, and He Took 'Em."

Source: As quoted in William L. Riordon, *Plunkitt of Tammany Hall* (New York: Dutton, 1963), pp. 3–6.

---

welfare bureaucracies did not exist (Mann 1963, p. xix). Third, machine politics provided a way for ethnically based power groups to emerge—by intensifying political clout through organization and sheer power of numbers in a given locality.

Machine leaders became important symbols of the dream of mobility that sustained many of the immigrants of this period. Jane Addams, the founder of Hull House (a settlement house in Chicago) and a Nobel Prize winner, noted in 1902 that, while gifts and favors were important, "the machine leader's standard suits his constituents. He exemplifies and exaggerates the popular type of a good man. He has attained what his constituents secretly long for" (as quoted in Banfield and Wilson, 1963, p. 118).

Sociologist Robert Merton (1968) has suggested that the machine also personalized and humanized the large city to the newcomer. Richard Croker (who rose from an unskilled laborer to become head of Tammany Hall) asserted that, when many people wouldn't even shake hands with the immigrant, the machine took "hold of the untrained, friendless man and turned him into a citizen" (Mann 1963, p. xix).

But there were flagrant abuses. First, there was excessive graft—whether "dishonest" or "honest." Second, there was often no pretense at even a semblance of fair voting practices, as Lincoln Steffens noted in his exposé, *The Shame of the Cities* (see Box 12-5). Third, the services provided by the machine may have forestalled more radical political organization by immigrants who were, by and large, receiving more crumbs than cake in their new surroundings (Knauss 1972).

The Decline of the Machine

From the time of its inception, machine politics brought forth reform movements aimed at curbing its favoritism and excesses. Bosses, like New York's Boss Tweed, were tried and convicted.

BOX 12-5
Voting and Corruption in Philadelphia

The machine controls the whole process of voting, and practices fraud at every stage. The assessor's list is the voting list, and the assessor is the machine's man. "The assessor of a division kept a disorderly house; he padded his list with fradulent names registered from his house; two of these names were used by election officers. . . . The constable of the division kept a disreputable house; a policeman was assessed as living there. . . . The election was held in the disorderly house maintained by the assessor. . . . The man named as judge had a criminal charge for a life offense pending against him. . . . Two hundred and fifty-two votes were returned in a division that had less than one hundred legal voters within its boundaries." These extracts from a report of the Municipal League suggest the election methods. The assessor pads the list with the names of dead dogs, children, and non-existent persons. One newspaper printed the picture of a dog, another that of a little four-year-old negro boy, down on such a list. A ring orator in a speech resenting sneers at his ward as "low down" reminded his hearers that that was the ward of Independence Hall, and, naming the signers of the Declaration of Independence, he closed his highest flight of eloquence with the statement that "these men, the fathers of American liberty, voted down here once. And," he added, with a catching grin, "they vote here yet."

Source: Lincoln Steffens, *The Shame of the Cities* (New York: Peter Smith, 1904), pp. 18–19, 199–200.

Deal of the 1930s] were vastly expanded, and *per capita* incomes rose steadily and sharply in war and post-war prosperity. To the voter who in case of need could turn to a professional social worker and receive as a matter of course unemployment compensation, aid to dependent children, old-age assistance, and all the rest, the precinct captain's [bucket] of coal was a joke. (1963, p. 121)

A final factor in the machine's decline was the growth of unions. Although they sometimes were corrupt themselves, unions gave workers assistance directly, through their weekly paychecks and benefits. As their influence spread across the country as the twentieth century progressed, urban workers transferred their allegiance away from the machine.

Although it is true that in some cities—Chicago, for example—machine politics still exist in some form, their heyday is over. The machine's history, however, illustrates the complexity of the urban power story. On the one hand, the machine bosses hardly began as the upper-crust gentry imagined in C. Wright Mill's power elite thesis. Bluebloods they were not. George Washington Plunkitt made no bones about his lowly beginnings, and few would argue that Chicago machine boss and mayor "Big Bill" Thompson's comment about King George V of England in the 1920s—"If that guy ever sets foot in my city, I'm gonna punch him in the nose!"—was the height of gentility. Still, once ensconced on top, the machine leaders did become power elites of a sort, akin in influence if not in breeding to the Astors, the Rockefellers, and the Lodges.

On the other hand, the machine did give power and influence, for a time, to the city's poorest and least skilled citizens. Yet machine politics were hardly pluralistic in the sense described by Polsby (1959) and Dahl (1961) when writing of New Haven. The machine played favorites, worked actively for its own ends, and systematically tried to exclude others.

Gradually, with the growth of unprecedented wealth in the United States, national corporate power supporting local elites in control of commercial land created even greater political power. In some ways, of course, today's business leaders are like the machine politicians of an earlier era—

Civil service regulations were instituted, limiting the ability to hire and fire employees at will. Everywhere the trend was toward a more impersonal style of politics, toward a city run by impersonal laws and professional administrators.

Although these efforts had their effect, the machine really declined because its original reason for being disappeared. The people it served—America's immigrant classes—changed, and the times changed. Banfield and Wilson sum it up:

The petty favors and "friendship" of the precinct captains declined in value as immigrants were assimilated, public welfare programs [after the New

they see their opportunities and take them in classic American style. In sum, we see elements of both the power elite and the pluralist orientation in the history of the urban political machine. The expansion of government social service programs and business helped bring about the machine's ultimate downfall.

Power and Minorities

While there may be spirited debate as to who or what shapes the power structure of urban America, there is perhaps more agreement as to who does not. In the last two decades virtually all minorities within the United States have sought a greater voice in urban decision making.

Women

Although women are actually a slight majority of the American population, they have long been treated as a minority group. For example, Jo Freeman has argued that women and men are affected differently by current urban policies. Take housing: Freeman explains that "central cities have a disproportionate share of women, especially women who are elderly or solely responsible for families" (Freeman 1980, p. 5). Yet in 1977 only 18 percent of owner-occupied homes were owned by women heads-of-households; the majority of women rent. Therein lies the problem. In a hearing on housing-related discrimination against women in San Francisco, one witness observed:

> . . . the woman alone with the child or children really has the worst time of all because of the entanglements of all kinds of discrimination, the layers of discrimination. And if the woman is of a minority group it adds another layer . . . and if she's "on welfare," it adds another layer; if she's got a large family, it adds another; it becomes impossible. (U.S. Dept. of Housing and Urban Development 1975, p. 83)

Because large cities have a disproportionate share of women who make greater use of many urban facilities and services—including transportation and child care—an urban policy responsive to women's needs is imperative. Nonetheless, Freeman concludes, "nothing in our current urban policy is specifically geared to improving women's financial resources" (1980, p. 13).

Such an analysis suggests that although women have gained public attention as mayors of such cities as San Francisco, Chicago, Phoenix, Portland, Oklahoma City, San Antonio, and San Jose, fundamental changes in policies to meet many needs of urban women have yet to be undertaken. As Bachrach and Baratz (1970) might suggest, although many women now participate in decisions in urban America, they have had limited success in putting on the political agenda some key issues that challenge male dominance.

Other Minorities

The same sort of problem, of course, exists for much of black America. As we have seen, the decades since World War II have brought a redistribution of the urban population, which has increased greatly the proportion of blacks in central cities. Many major cities—including Philadelphia, Chicago, Cleveland, Detroit, Gary, Washington, D.C., Richmond, Atlanta, New Orleans, and Los Angeles—have elected black mayors. Indeed, the rise of black mayors nationwide has been nothing short of spectacular. In 1970 there were 48; by 1975 that number had grown to 135, by 1980 to 182, and by 1984 to 286 (Pear 1985). Yet, despite such gains, as we have seen, blacks continue to endure the brunt of many urban ills.

In 1981 the first Mexican-American mayor of a major city was elected, as Henry Cisneros defeated John Steen, "a pillar of old San Antonio society" (*Time*, 1981, p. 59). How much of an impact this will have, however, on the city's 53 percent Hispanic population remains to be seen. As mayor, Cisneros faces problems that affect the entire city. Serving many constituents and in charge of long-term city success, he has argued that growth must occur in all areas of the city, not just in the dilapidated sections of the barrio; that city water rates must be raised so that new water sources can be found to attract industry; and even that property taxes may have to be raised to offset a city budget deficit.

The difficulties Cisneros faces—in spite of his continuing commitment to his minority group—are typical of those faced by all city politicians. The city is a complex network of interrelationships, utilizing limited resources. Thus, all decisions involve trade-offs. By deciding for one course of action, by definition you decide against all others. Few political leaders—whether minorities or not—can therefore easily aid one segment of the population without arousing resistance from others.

In concluding this chapter, we turn to a case study of what was for a century America's "second city," its greatest inland metropolis: Chicago. As we consider Chicago's development, we shall see all the general issues raised in this chapter at work in a particular setting. As Jurgis and Ona Rudkis (Cityscape 1-4) and Robert Park and the University of Chicago sociologists (Chapter 4) found out, Chicago was a city in which matters of stratification, race, ethnicity, and power were of prime importance.

CASE STUDY 12-1
Chicago, City of the Big Shoulders

Hog Butcher for the World,
Tool Maker, Stacker of Wheat,
Player with Railroads
    and the Nation's Freight Handler;
Stormy, husky, brawling,
City of the Big Shoulders:
They tell me you are wicked and I believe them,
    for I have seen your painted women under
    the gas lamps luring the farm boys.
And they tell me you are crooked and I answer:
    Yes, it is true I have seen the gunman kill and
    go free to kill again.
And they tell me you are brutal and my reply is:
    On the faces of women and children I have
    seen the marks of wanton hunger.
And having answered so I turn once more to
    those who sneer at this my city, and I give
    them back the sneer and say to them:
Come and show me another city with lifted head
singing so proud to be alive and coarse and
    strong and cunning.
Flinging magnetic curses amid the toil of piling
    job on job, here is a tall bold slugger set vivid
    against the little soft cities;
Fierce as a dog with tongue lapping for action,
    cunning as a savage pitted against the
    wilderness,
                Bareheaded,
                Shoveling,
                Wrecking,
                Planning,
        Building, breaking, rebuilding,
Under the smoke, dust all over his mouth,
    laughing with white teeth,
Under the terrible burden of destiny laughing as
    a young man laughs,
Laughing even as an ignorant fighter laughs who
    has never lost a battle,
Bragging and laughing that under his wrist is the
    pulse, and under his ribs the heart of the
    people,
                Laughing!
Laughing the stormy, husky, brawling laughter
    of Youth, half-naked, sweating, proud to be
    Hog Butcher, Tool Maker, Stacker of Wheat,
Player with Railroads and Freight Handler to the
    Nation.

CARL SANDBERG, "CHICAGO"

Carl Sandberg captures beautifully some of the flavor of turn-of-the-century Chicago in this poem he wrote in tribute to the city in 1916. Not everyone, of course, shared his enthusiasm. Visiting Chicago in the 1850s, Swedish novelist Frederika Bremer decried "one of the most miserable and ugly cities" of America; a city where people come "to trade, to make money, but not to live" (cited in Glaab and Brown 1967, pp. 85–86). Rudyard Kipling, visiting the Chicago of the Gay Nineties, was more direct: "Having seen it," he wrote, "I urgently desire never to see it again. It is inhabited by savages" (cited in Rokove 1975, p. 22).

What is it about Chicago that draws such wildly divergent responses from observers? Perhaps it is this: some of the most powerful themes in the United States concern wealth, prestige,

(Georg Gerster/Photo Researchers)

power, and the drama by which they are gained or lost. Chicago, which rocketed to prominence in barely 50 years, exhibits these themes more directly than most. This "city of the big shoulders," at once brash and breathtaking, is a magnifier without equal of America's successes and failures in these areas.

Early Chicago

Over a century and a half ago, standing where the Chicago River joins Lake Michigan, one would have felt worlds away from the life of great cities. The site's promise, however, as a water link between Lake Michigan and the Mississippi caught the attention of early European explorers Jacques Marquette and Louis Joliet in 1673.[2]

_____

[2]Much of the history of Chicago that follows is based on Harold M. Mayer and Richard C. Wade, *Chicago: Growth of a Metropolis* (Chicago: University of Chicago Press, 1969).

The area remained under Indian and French control for almost a century. The English took charge of the area in 1763; shortly thereafter, it passed into the hands of the new United States of America. Early in the next century, the Indians relinquished the area where the city would soon be and Fort Dearborn was erected amidst a sprinkling of cabins. Another generation passed before, in the shadow of a new fort, settlement of Chicago began in earnest.

After 1830 the settlement began a century of spectacular growth. Starting with just 50 persons in 1830, the new city (incorporated in 1833) boasted over 4,000 residents by 1837. As the Erie Canal began to stimulate trade in the region, Chicago took on the look of a boom town. A building lot that sold for $100 in 1830 brought $15,000 by 1835. The population also soared—practically tripling for several decades after 1850. So great was the demand for housing that the city emerged as a center for innovative architectural techniques, a tradition it has maintained. "Balloon frame" housing—assembled quickly with machined lumber rather than heavy timbers—was an early Chicago first that provided homes for the waves of new arrivals.

The key to the economic success of the city was its position in the growing urban trade network (Chapter 3). It was linked to the East by the Great Lakes and the Erie Canal; to the South by river and canal to the Mississippi River; and, by midcentury, to the West by the railroad. On November 20, 1848, a locomotive brought the first load of wheat into the city. Although it was a trip of only 10 miles, the significance was clear: with the railroad Chicago became the center for the entire midwestern part of the country—a break-of-bulk point for goods being shipped in all directions.

By 1855, ninety-six trains a day were going in and out of the city. In the 1850s the McCormick Reaper Company made the city a center for farm machinery. The city's famed stockyards began increasing in importance during the Civil War, and with the making of steel rails, Chicago also became a manufacturing center. "Chicago had become Chicago" (Mayer and Wade 1969, p. 24).

In the decades that followed, the wealth and

regional influence of Chicago grew enormously. Railroad lines converged at the city from all directions, and water traffic became continuous, as lumber, grain, and livestock trade increased manyfold. As factories proliferated, new industrial districts of the city were founded. Fortunes were made by Cyrus McCormick with his reaper and other agricultural inventions, by Henry B. Clarke in hardware, and by Archibald Clybourne, Gustavus Swift, and Philip Armour in beef and meat packing. By 1885, Armour employed some 10,000 workers in his meat packing business.

Confirming novelist Frederika Bremer's observation, in the second half of the nineteenth century Chicago was a capitalist's paradise. Mayer and Wade note:

> The old boundaries could no longer contain the burgeoning commerce and industry. . . . Lumber yards, factories, [grain] elevators, warehouses, docks, and depots lined the river and pushed north and south along the banks of both branches; commercial facilities steadily expanded at the city's center, forcing residential construction to move out to the edge of town . . . urban displacement . . . had begun. . . . (1969, p. 54)

Class and Stratification in Nineteenth-Century Chicago

Industrial giants such as McCormick, Clybourne, Clarke, Swift, and Armour became the city's first entrenched elite. As in other cities, their social position was evident not only by the amount of wealth they possessed but by the ostentation of their clothes and residences. While the early poor and working classes of Chicago had to be content with squalid settlements near Packingtown (Cityscape 1-4) and other industrial areas, wealthy Chicagoans showed an immediate inclination to establish elegant and spacious homes apart from the city's busier center. The life-style of more privileged residents was enriched further by the opening of an opera house and art gallery in 1850 and, a decade later, of Marshall Field's, America's first modern department store. State Street, Chicago's famous commercial center, took shape under the guiding hand of the fabulously wealthy merchant, Potter Palmer.

As time passed, new districts of working-class cottages emerged, along with middle-class districts of modest single-family homes occupied by highly skilled workers. Still later, as mass transit facilities made living some distance from work possible, the rich and poor came more and more to inhabit separate and quite distinct areas of the city.

The Burning and Rebuilding of Chicago

According to Chicago lore, on the night of October 8, 1871, near the corner of 12th and Halsted Streets, Mrs. O'Leary left her cottage to milk her cow in the small barn behind. The cantankerous old cow kicked over her lamp, however, and started the fire that burned the city of Chicago. Fanned by a stiff wind from the southwest, the fire swept northward along the lake, consuming some 1,700 acres within 24 hours. As in London in 1666 and Atlanta in 1864, the destruction in the affected area was virtually total. Some 100,000 Chicagoans were rendered homeless, and the heart of the city's business district lay in ashes; however, the forces that had created Chicago—the quest for commercial and industrial success—were very much alive. The "second" Chicago was being born even while the ashes of the old city were yet warm. Surveying the ruins, John Stephen Wright predicted: "Chicago will have more men, more money, more business within five years than she would have had without the fire. . . ." As if in response, the next day one enterprising citizen had opened a fruit and cider stand among the blocks of debris (Mayer and Wade 1969, p. 11).

New Chicago became a "growth machine" more than ever before. In 1884 the city opened the age of the urban skyscraper with the construction of a ten-story steel building. Chicago's population passed the 1 million mark by 1890. Pushing its borders outward, within only a generation the nation's second largest city grew once again to dominate the Midwest.

Social Conflict in the Industrial City

Chicago was truly a dazzling monument to the power of the American economy to shape great cities. But wealth, prestige, and power were not distributed equally. The late 1800s were an era rocked by workers' challenges to the empire built by the industrialists. This confrontation between rich and poor is illustrated by the social conflict in Pullman, Illinois, a company town founded just to the south of Chicago in 1880 and annexed to the city in 1898.

George Mortimer Pullman was one of the most successful Chicago industrialists. Born to a poor family, he went to Chicago to manufacture railroad cars, and his astonishing fortune was matched only by his unyielding opposition to labor organizations. In 1881 he completed construction of a 4,000-acre company-run town that was to be dominated by his organization perhaps even more than Middletown would later be dominated by the "X" family. The Pullman Post Office, Pullman Bank, and the Florence (Pullman's wife) Hotel stood among modest but clean houses for Pullman's employees. By 1893 the population of the town exceeded 12,000.

There can be little doubt that political control of life in the small city was a classic case of the power elite phenomenon discussed earlier. It also is clear that the interests of Pullman himself were at odds with those of his employees. Strikes by workers were frequent but were broken forcefully by management. In 1894 the most violent and far-reaching conflict erupted on the heels of a severe winter amidst general economic depression. Seeking higher wages, Pullman workers began a strike on May 12. By late June some 50,000 men had been fired by the company (most for union activity, which the company prohibited), and a boycott of the company's products was spreading. Then violence escalated as soldiers were ordered to Pullman on the fourth of July by President Grover Cleveland, causing confrontations resulting in injuries and extensive damage to property.

By the end of August the workers found themselves unable to continue their action against the company. Most were rehired—but at the same rates as before the strike. The incident was over, but problems that caused the conflict had not been resolved and bitterness endured.

Chicago in the Early Twentieth Century

Chicago . . . offered a world of hope and opportunity to the beginner. It was so new, so raw; everything was in the making . . . the youth, the illusions, the untrained aspirations of millions of souls . . . Chicago [at the turn of the century] meant eagerness, hope, desire. It was a city that put vitality into almost every wavering heart. It made the beginner dream dreams.

THEODORE DREISER

Chicago plunged into the new century with clear title as the metropolis of the Midwest. The city grew upward: a towering skyline took form. Immigrant groups from Europe swelled the city's population: Germans, Swedes, Irish, Poles, and Italians. For many, such as the Rudkis family (the Lithuanian immigrants who settled near the stockyards as described in Cityscape 1-4), life in Chicago's poorest neighborhoods was brutally hard. Housing often was unsanitary and exceedingly crowded. An estimate at the turn of the century revealed that if all of Chicago "were as densely populated as its worst slums [900 people per acre], the whole of the Western Hemisphere could have been housed in Chicago" (Dr. Frank Felter, as cited in Mayer and Wade 1969, p. 256).

Over time, however, the dream of opportunity became something of a reality for many working-class Chicagoans. More and more people—sons and daughters of immigrants—moved outward from the old crowded neighborhoods into newer middle-class housing. This outward flow spilled into the developing areas that had been annexed to the city since 1889.

Opportunity was not available equally to all, however, and blacks were victims of particularly unfavorable conditions. Drawn to Chicago in ever-increasing numbers after the great immigration subsided in the early 1900s, blacks settled primarily on the South Side. Unlike many other groups, however, blacks did not experience prosperity and outward migration. The black ghetto simply expanded, supplemented by black residential areas on the north and west sides of the city. Periodically, violence linked to racial conflict erupted. On July 27, 1919, after a confrontation on a local beach, a black youth was drowned. This led to five days of rioting in the South Side ghetto. Damage was extensive and many blacks suffered death and injury at the hands of white mobs.

By the 1920s, when the sociologists of the University of Chicago were studying the city intensively, they were confronted by a city shaped by a complex social stratification system based on race and ethnicity, as well as occupation and income. (A glance back to Figure 6-5 shows how Ernest Burgess depicted the spatial segregation of these varying social groups). As group vied with group for political power, the city, long a home of organized crime, found itself virtually at the mercy of gangsters in the 1920s. Nowhere was this more true than in the smaller city of Cicero, adjacent to Chicago, where the mob, headed by Johnny Torrio and Al Capone, had its headquarters. "It was said that the way to determine when one crossed the Chicago line into Cicero was simply to sniff. 'If you smell gunpowder, you're in Cicero'" (Asbury 1940, pp. 260–261).

To consolidate his control of the city, Capone launched a campaign of terror on election day in April 1924. This was the corruption of politics at its height and the mob's victory gave them control of much of the city (see Box 12-6). Still, attempts to curtail crime continued throughout the 1920s. Capone finally was convicted of income-tax evasion in 1931 and sentenced to prison.

Then came the Depression. It struck a deep blow to the economic lifeblood of Chicago. Unemployment soared, construction stalled, and even the city's second World's Fair in 1933 couldn't conceal the widespread social injury. Homeless Chicagoans asleep in public parks or milling about the streetcorners became commonplace. Only with World War II did the economy finally recover.

The Postwar Period

Decentralization. As we found to be the case in most industrial cities of the United States, post–World War II growth took place largely beyond the political limits of the city. The familiar pattern changed the social character of Chicago as the more affluent population moved out, leaving behind a growing number of poor and minorities. Table 12-7 showed that this pattern has continued into the 1980s. This means that Chicago faces high demands for services amidst a contracting economic base. By 1960 the population of the city proper actually began to show a decline, although outer areas continued to grow. Many spoke of the "death of the city." Chicago began trying to recover under the leadership of a new mayor, Richard J. Daley, whose long and controversial record in Chicago politics as mayor and political boss lasted from his election in 1955 until his death in 1976.

The Chicago Machine. An old saying about Chicago is that "the Jews own it, the Irish run it, and the blacks live in it" (Rakove 1975, p. 32). This is partly incorrect—the greatest wealth in the city is controlled by white Anglo-Saxon Protestants—but the Irish have controlled the politics of the city for most of its history, although they now face a growing political challenge from the more than 2.5 million blacks and Hispanics who are becoming an ever-larger proportion of the city's population.

The Chicago machine became strong in the 1930s, later than in many other cities, but did not reach its greatest strength until Richard J. Daley became the undisputed boss. Political life in Chicago under Daley carried the tone of the immigrant political machines of the late nineteenth century. Its leaders, from block captains to the mayor himself, tried to meet the specific needs of their constituents. In return, they expected continuing electoral support. How has the political machine met the fiscal, social, and political challenges of the last 25 years?

Under Daley's leadership, Chicago worked hard to maintain the quality of the central business district, the Loop (Figure 6-5). Centered

---

BOX 12-6
Al Capone's Cicero, 1924

Banks of heavily armed gangsters, commanded by Capone and campaigning for Mayor Klenha and the Democratic ticket, terrorized the city from dawn to dusk. A man was killed in Eddie Tanel's saloon. Two others were shot dead in Twenty-second Street. Another man's throat was slashed. A policeman was blackjacked. Citizens who attempted to vote Republican were slugged and driven from the polls. "Automobiles filled with gunmen paraded the streets," said the Illinois Crime Survey, "slugging and kidnapping election workers. Polling places were raided by armed thugs and ballots taken at the point of the gun from the hands of voters waiting to drop them in the box. Voters and workers were kidnapped, taken to Chicago and held prisoners until the polls closed." Late in the afternoon honest citizens appealed to Chicago for help, and seventy policemen were sworn in as deputy sheriffs by County Judge Edmund K. Jarecki and rushed to Cicero by automobile. A police squad commanded by Detective Sergeant William Cusick came upon Al Capone, his brother Frank, Dave Hedlin, and Charley Fischetti, with pistols in their hands, standing in front of a polling place at Cicero Avenue and Twenty-second Street. Frank Capone shot at Patrolman McGlynn, but missed, and McGlynn killed him. Hedlin was wounded. Fischetti was chased into a field and captured after a gun battle in which no one was hurt. Al Capone fled down Cicero Avenue, encountered another group of policemen, and with a gun blazing in each hand fought them off until darkness came to his aid and he escaped. . . .

Mayor Klenha and his ticket were, not unexpectedly, elected by tremendous majorities, and Al Capone was master of Cicero. Almost overnight the city became one of the toughest in the United States. . . . The one-time peaceful streets of downtown Cicero were filled with arrogant, roistering, swaggering gangsters, and crowded with saloons and gambling-houses. One hundred and sixty of these places ran full blast day and night, with sidewalk barkers urging passers-by to step in. . . . Torrio and Capone owned many of the gambling-houses and had shares in others. In every independent resort was posted an agent of the syndicate; his job was to protect the dive and see that Torrio and Capone received their split, which ranged from twenty-five to fifty percent of the gross receipts. . . .

Source: Herbert Asbury, *The Chicago Underworld* (New York: Ace, 1940), pp. 260–261.

---

along State Street, the Loop is the economic heart of the city, of vital concern to the powerful business interests of Chicago, as the growth machine theory suggests. In addition, the city revitalized the lakefront to make Chicago attractive and exciting both to visitors and to Chicagoans themselves.

The record of improvements is uneven, however. While all residents of the city benefit to some degree from improvements in city services (such as lighting, street cleaning, and snow removal), the poorer areas of the city certainly have not received the attention given the Loop. A political opponent of Mayor Daley observed:

Get off the subway anywhere in the central business area and you won't find a broken city sidewalk. Get off the subway almost anywhere else, and you will. Between the central business area and the outskirts lie large, almost uninterrupted grey areas of urban dry rot. This is where most Chicagoans live. (Leon Despres, cited in Rakove 1975, pp. 78–79)

Chicago also boasts three of the the five tallest buildings in the nation—including the Sears Tower, the tallest in the world—yet commitment to improving housing for the poor has not been dramatic. For blacks especially, segregation remains all too evident.

The fact that the Chicago machine has so unequally distributed city resources has not gone unchallenged, especially by Chicago's black population (now approaching half of the city's population). Over 900,000 Hispanic Americans are also a growing political force. Under Daley's leadership, the machine managed to fend off these groups by meeting some of the needs of minority communities while at the same time actively undermining any effective political opposition. As Sidney Lens, another critic of the Daley machine, remarked:

> Chicago government is of, by, and for the few thousand members of interlocking power elites. It is a government by manipulation rather than participation and its purpose—subtly hidden from public purview—is to preserve the social status quo. (Cited in Rakove 1975, p. 79)

As we approach the 1990s, the fate of the traditional business elite in the face of a growing minority population is a matter of continuing interest.

Ordered Segmentation. Race and ethnicity are thus fundamental parts of the social organization of Chicago. This is made crystal clear by Gerald Suttles (1968) who lived in the Addams area on Chicago's West Side for more than two years. Once part of the main stomping grounds of the Capone mob, this area was commonly believed to be a disorganized slum, filled with "undesirables" of all types and mainly inhabited by blacks and Italians. Suttles's most important finding was that while some housing clearly was dilapidated and many people were poor, the area was hardly disorganized. Indeed, Suttles found a marked social order he termed "ordered segmentation" because it was based on ethnic, racial, and territorial distinctions.

Four groups—blacks, Italians, Puerto Ricans, and Mexican Americans—made up the bulk of the areas's population at that time. Each had its own subcultural way of life, its own clearly delimited "territory," and its own characteristic impressions of and rules for interaction with the other groups. Suttles found the Italians very closely knit and trusting of one another. The blacks, in contrast, were much more alienated from each other, distrustful, and very poor. The Mexican Americans and Puerto Ricans fell somewhere in between. They were somewhat better off than the blacks economically and had more contact with each other outside the home.

Contacts *among* these groups were rare, however. While each group knew that the dominant stereotypes about its own members were over-

drawn, they were not so sure this was the case with the other groups; hence members of different groups tended to avoid each other.

The positive irony was that such divisiveness allowed people living in tenuous city circumstances to establish meaningful relationships with those whom they *did* trust. By omitting blacks, Italians, and Mexican Americans from their "inner circle," Puerto Ricans could form a sense of identity and community among themselves, thereby providing some defense against a hostile outside world. Suttles concluded:

> For all its shortcomings . . . the moral order they have developed includes most, if not all, of their neighbors. Within limits, the residents possess a way of gaining associates, avoiding enemies, and establishing each others' intentions. In view of the difficulties encountered, the [ordered segmentation] of the Addams Area has provided a decent world within which people can live. (1968, p. 234)

Suttles's analysis thus reveals a surprisingly complex social order of racial and ethnic discrimination that confirms an old sociological maxim. Just as the machine did some good for those it served despite its corruption, so too do out-group hostilities like those expressed in the Addams area create in-group solidarities. This would suggest that the real culprit in creating such prejudices in the first place is a larger social order that does not equally parcel out wealth, prestige, and power equally to all groups. Insecure because of their lack of these resources, many groups apparently resort to racial and ethnic prejudice as a means of self-defense (protecting what they do have) and as a means of establishing positive bonds with others.

Post-Daley Chicago

Since Daley's death in 1976, the Irish-dominated machine has continued its hold on Chicago, although with considerably less power. Soon after Daley's death, Jane Byrne became the city's first woman mayor, followed by Harold Washington, Chicago's first black mayor, who was elected in 1983 following a campaign that bitterly divided the city on racial grounds. Furthermore, the new immigration experienced in the 1980s (like that described earlier in Los Angeles) ensures that race and ethnicity will remain important dimensions of social life in Chicago for some time to come.

Across Chicago today, a remarkable change is under way. As we have indicated, the black population of the city continues to increase, but changes are greater still. Immigration is nothing new to Chicago, but today's immigrants are introducing new dimensions of social diversity to the city. During the last century, the vast majority of white immigrants were of European background. During the 1970s, however, the European-born population of Chicago actually declined by about one-fourth to some 300,000. In their place are now Hispanics, whose numbers more than doubled during the 1970s to at least 200,000 (one estimate placed the 1983 Hispanic population at over 500,000), and the Asian-born, who have increased over threefold to some 125,000 (Kiefer 1984).

Consequences of this change are evident everywhere. Neighborhoods that once contained Germans, Poles, and Czechs now bustle with blacks, Mexicans, Puerto Ricans, Koreans, Filipinos, and Vietnamese. Within each category, of course, there is still greater diversity. Some new immigrants have come to Chicago with extensive education, bilingual fluency, and considerable wealth. Others, in contrast, are poor—like immigrants throughout history, they have come with little, seeking something more. As one might expect, those with the greatest social advantages tend to spread most widely throughout the city; most of Chicago's new immigrants from India, for example, are professionals and are widely dispersed. On the other hand, those with the fewest social advantages are recreating the racial and ethnic enclaves that have existed in Chicago throughout its history. Thus, clusters of signs along commercial streets signal the founding of Mexican, Korean, and Chinese neighborhoods. In such cases, social isolation much like that described by Gerald Suttles continues. Notes one observer of Hispanic communities, "There are people who come here and live and die and never learn English" (Kiefer 1984, p. 130).

The certainty that these new minorities will increase their number over time raises fascinating questions about the future of Chicago politics. The election of Harold Washington as mayor, for example, was possible not only due to widespread support among blacks, but also because of strong backing from the city's Hispanics. Asians, too, are becoming a greater political force as more and more become naturalized citizens eager to vote. One new Korean resident remarked about his changing conception of Chicago as a melting pot: "When we came to the United States with only a superficial knowledge of this country, we thought we were going to be assimilated into the white people. But after we came here, we found, especially in the Chicago area, that this is a multiethnic society" (Kiefer 1984, p. 135).

With the recognition that race and ethnicity continue to be important dimensions of social life, new immigrants typically see a need to advance their own interests. Other than blacks and Hispanics, new racial and ethnic groups in Chicago are still too small to make a marked impact on the political scene. Yet, in the heyday of the Irish-dominated political machine, probably few could have imagined its demise; similarly, during the racial unrest of the 1960s, probably few could have foreseen a black Chicago mayor. But no matter who becomes mayor, as Chicago nears the end of its second century, the leaders of this large and complex city will need to have big shoulders indeed.

Conclusion

Cities always have been places where inequality abounds. From their beginnings nearly 10,000 years ago, they have been characterized by a complex division of labor and a hierarchical power structure. The main difference between these two characteristics is that, while a complex division of labor is not inevitably "vertical," a hierarchical power structure is. Some people in a city always have more power than others.

The same may apply to the other major social resources that people use to meet their various needs: wealth and prestige. Either may be awarded differentially for jobs done or because some people meet better than others the expectations of a powerful group. Whenever this happens, a city develops a system of social stratification, a structure that distinguishes residents on the basis of the amount of wealth, prestige, and power they possess. With higher amounts of these resources clearly go more social opportunities. With smaller amounts go clear disadvantages.

This has been a chapter about such urban inequities. Although a stratification system has existed in all cities, its consequences can be exaggerated or downplayed because of the city's link with the larger cultural patterns of the society as a whole. If the society stresses cooperation among individuals and groups and makes a clear commitment to sharing wealth, prestige, and power as widely as possible, the divisions among different urban groups are likely to be more nominal than substantial. If, on the other hand, the society stresses competition among its citizens and groups and allows each to accumulate as much wealth, prestige, or power as it can, then the stratification system is likely to be entrenched with pronounced differences in advantages.

Because American society falls closer to the latter end of this continuum, our analysis found the urban stratification system to be a major feature in Americans' lives. From Warner and Lunt's studies of Yankee City in the 1940s to Coleman and Rainwater's studies of Kansas City and Boston in the 1970s, sociologists have discovered wide-ranging inequality in American cities. This stratification involves not only differential amounts of wealth, power, and prestige, but markedly contrasting abilities to control the quality of life as well. Indeed, the whole range of urban life-styles discussed in Chapter 11 is made possible by each group's possession of varying amounts of wealth, power, and prestige. The upper-upper class, for all intents and purposes, can do pretty much as it pleases. The lower-lower class has little such freedom. These people must live where they can and get by as best they can. Usually, they don't get by very well.

Another characteristic of the city in history has been its ability to generate *more* wealth, power,

and prestige—in short, more opportunity for its citizens—than the rural areas. Seeking this opportunity over the centuries, billions have streamed into cities. Certainly this was the driving wheel behind the Great Migration to American cities that occurred between 1880 and 1920. By and large, the American city provided that opportunity. As generations passed, more and more immigrants and their descendants moved from poverty into relative affluence. For most, the urban dream came true.

This was not true for all, however. American cities always have been characterized by the presence of an underclass. Historically, it has been the city's newest arrivals: various northern European groups until about 1830, then southern and eastern European groups until about 1920. Most recently, it has been the "new minorities," people of nonwhite racial background—blacks, Hispanics, Asians, and natives.

The trouble is, most of the new groups have been less able to make the transition to the more favored, more affluent urban positions now occupied by their predecessors. Many continue to be fixed in the worst inner-city slums, with few skills and terrible prospects. Income differentials between whites and these groups in the 1980s continued to be marked. The average Mexican American earned only 67 percent of what a white counterpart did in 1975, and the figures for the other minorities were even worse. Blacks earned 59 percent of the average white's income, Puerto Ricans earned only 51 percent, and native Americans had to be content with 46 percent (Shaefer 1979).

Further, the continuing exodus to the suburbs by whites in the 1980s is only exacerbating this situation. The center city is occupied more and more by poor minorities, and city governments find themselves ever more bereft of the tax money needed to ease the city out of fiscal crisis. There is little doubt that serious racial prejudice and discrimination play a continuing role in this situation (Frey 1980).

We next turned to the issue of urban power. Who has it? Answers vary. Some, like C. Wright Mills, argue that most urban (and national) power rests in the hands of a power elite, an amalgam of business, "old family," and political leaders. Oth-

357

(Michael Uffer/Photo Researchers)

ers, like Nelson Polsby and Robert Dahl, present a more pluralist interpretation, claiming power to be widely dispersed among many individuals and groups. More recent research by Harvey Molotch and G. William Domhoff sheds new light on both orientations, suggesting the cities be understood as growth machines in which owners of commer- cial land seek to maximize their wealth by stimu- lating economic development of the city.

Finally, our case study of the Windy City, Chicago, illustrated all of these themes. From its beginnings as the Midwest's regional center to its emergence as America's "second city," Chicago (like any other American city we might have studied) exhibited a clear-cut stratification system based on differing amounts of wealth, prestige, and power. At the top were the Armours, the McCormicks, and the Pullmans. At the bottom were first, poor immigrants from Europe; somewhat later, blacks; and most recently, immigrants from Latin America and Asia.

Earlier in this century Chicago's power reins were shared by organized crime (particularly in the 1920s) and the great Democratic Party machine that arose in the Depression and reached its culmination in the 21-year administration (1955–1976) of boss Richard J. Daley. Like machines elsewhere, the Daley version advantaged its friends and disadvantaged its enemies.

Among the latter were various ethnic and minority groups, such as those who lived in the Addams area on Chicago's West Side. In his study of this slum district, Gerald Suttles found racial, ethnic, and territorial divisions between groups the order of the day. His discovery of what he called the "ordered segmentation" of the area showed that slum areas are actually highly organized on the basis of race, ethnicity, and territory. As European immigrants organized themselves within urban neighborhoods in decades past, so many of the "new immigrants" are beginning to do today.

The larger insight from Suttles's work concerned urban racial and ethnic discrimination generally. Intergroup prejudice is always a means of distinguishing an in-group from an out-group. "They," quite literally, don't look (act, think) like "us." Indeed, some sociologists, among them Kenneth Clark (1980), argue that such discrimi-

nation is what explains the continuing position of blacks at the bottom of the urban stratification ladder, despite efforts stretching over years, even generations, to get out. In a hierarchical society, a group on the "bottom rung" is always needed (see next chapter). Whatever else blacks do, they cannot change the color of their skin. The same applies to people with a different language: whatever else they do, as long as their language is not that of the majority, they are clearly identifiable and potential targets for discrimination. By eradicating many of their cultural and linguistic differences from mainstream American society over a few generations, white ethnic groups have been able to "pass," to assimilate into the dominant urban culture. The same opportunity is not afforded others with more clearly identifiable differences. Hence, racial prejudice and discrimination continues to bedevil the American city and is likely to continue to do so for the foreseeable future.

In the final analysis, then, stratification, race, ethnicity, and power in the city all are tied together inextricably. In turn, all are linked deeply to the larger culture and its values and commitments.

Still, as we saw in the case of Mexican American Mayor Henry Cisneros in San Antonio, it is not as simple as just committing oneself to more egalitarian values. The American city of the late twentieth century is an incredibly complex phenomenon in itself. Problems are virtually omnipresent. What the main ones are and what has been done to combat them we shall consider in the next chapter.

CHAPTER 13
Urban Problems

I am an optimist about the possibilities and a pessimist about the probabilities.

LEWIS MUMFORD

We did not all come over in the same ship, but we are all in the same boat.

BERNARD BARUCH

We opened this book by suggesting that whether we want to admit it or not, we are an urban nation. Seventy-six percent of the American population resides in the country's 257 MSAs (1984). Inescapably, therefore, as go our cities, so goes the nation.

Unfortunately, there appear to be major difficulties. Chapter 12 showed cities to be deeply enmeshed in the stratification system of American society as a whole. Wealth, prestige, and power are pursued intensely in our urban areas, with the result that some individuals and groups come to control more of these scarce resources than others. Chapter 12 also demonstrated that the control of these resources often is linked to racial and ethnic prejudice and power politics.

There are more problems, as the drawing in Figure 13-1 somewhat sardonically attests. Urban problems are not new. As America has become an increasingly urban society, many believe that our

cities are falling apart at the seams. In this chapter we will tackle several of the topics most often described as major urban problems: poverty, poor housing, crime and violence, and urban finances. While not exclusively urban phenomena, there is no doubt that each of these issues is intensified and more clearly evident in our cities. Although there are other urban problems that legitimately could command our attention, the issues selected are among the most important that beset the modern American city. We will also review what has been done to combat each problem.

None of these issues is isolated from the others. They are all part of a "package," partially a product of the structure and values of American society, and partially a product of the postindustrial, high-technology city itself. Like it or not, these problems are part of the "boat" our cities are in. The question is, will the city remain a viable center of human life as we move toward the next century? Is the boat sinking?

Poverty

A timeless feature of cities has been the promise of both security and prosperity. Often this promise is realized; yet, as we found in the last chapter, there are limits to opportunity in contemporary American cities, clearly demonstrated by the almost 20 million urban families who continue to live in poverty (see Table 12-3).

While there is no universally accepted definition of being poor, formal discussions of poverty in the United States generally refer to those persons or families with annual income below the so-called "poverty line" or "poverty level." In 1983, the poverty line for a family of four was $10,178. Poverty in the United States can be described further as follows.

1. *The concentration of poverty is greater in metropolitan areas and greatest in the inner cities*. Although nonmetropolitan areas had 8.2 million people below the poverty level in 1983, MSAs contained almost 20 million. Of these, about 9.3 million lived in inner cities—some 16 percent of the inner-city population (see Table 12-3).

2. *Poverty is more concentrated among minority groups than whites*. Although roughly two-thirds of the poor are white, only about 12 percent of the white population is poor. In contrast, over one-third of all blacks are poor. The situation for Asian Americans is much better; for Mexican Americans, slightly better; for Puerto Ricans and natives, somewhat worse (see Tables 12-5 and 12-8).

3. *Over 54 percent of those who suffer from poverty are children, adolescents, and elderly people*. Table 13-1 indicates that for all races, children (under 16 years) and adolescents (16–21 years) make up 40.6 percent of the poor, with the elderly comprising another 14.1 percent. Because their birth rates are higher, the poor often face the burden of more dependent children. The plight of the elderly has improved dramatically in recent decades. But faced with rising health-related expenses and often the costs of maintaining older residences, many elderly on fixed incomes live carefully from month to month. For instance, a recent study by the National Consumer Law Center in Washington, D.C., found

that, on average, in all but three states of the union, elderly citizens had less than $61 left after they paid for their heat. "It becomes very clear that these people are facing an impossible situation," said Carol Werner, a spokeswoman for the law center. "Do they pay for energy or for rent? What do they do for food or transportation?" (*Los Angeles Times*, April 20, 1984).

Table 13-1 also shows once again that minority groups suffer poverty in greater percentages than whites. While 17.8 percent of white children are poor, 47.2 percent of black children and 38.8 percent of Hispanic children fall into this category. The percentages for minority adolescents and elderly show similar imbalances.

4. *The rate of poverty has increased in recent years*. Table 13-2 shows that there were dramatic drops in both the number and percentage of impoverished people in the United States between 1959 and 1969. During the following decade, the decrease—though more modest—continued. In the years between 1979 and 1983, however, poverty levels shot back up to a point last seen in the early 1960s. Although not shown in the table, 1984 saw a slight decline in the rate, to 14.4 percent. Many factors appear responsible for this overall rise, including the period of economic recession in the early 1980s and cuts in social welfare programs carried out by the Reagan admininistration (Morganthau 1982).

Overall, despite fluctuations over the last several decades, we can see that millions of urban Americans have remained poor. In the midst of great affluence, how can this be?

Understanding Urban Poverty

Banfield: The Unheavenly Poor. Edward C. Banfield thinks he has an answer to the question. He begins by noticing that the city has historically attracted the poor:

> The city attracts the poor—especially the poor parents with numerous children—by offering better

TABLE 13-1
Persons Below Poverty Level By Age and Race, 1983

Age	Number below Poverty Level (in thousands)			
	All Races	White	Black	Hispanic
Under 16 years	12,148	7,964	3,928	1,964
16–21 years	4,132	2,611	1,343	516
22–44 years	10,511	7,318	2,735	1,267
45–64 years	4,430	3,220	1,083	353
65 or more years	3,711	2,860	796	149
Total	34,932	23,973	9,885	4,249

Age	Percent of Each Age Group below Poverty Level			
	All Races	White	Black	Hispanic
Under 16 years	22.7	17.8	47.2	38.8
16–21 years	17.9	13.7	40.7	29.9
22–44 years	12.6	10.3	28.4	23.4
45–64 years	10.0	8.2	25.5	17.0
65 or more years	14.1	12.0	36.3	23.1
Total	15.2	12.1	35.7	28.4

Source: U.S. Bureau of the Census, *Statistical Abstract of the United States 1985* (Washington, D.C.: U.S. Government Printing Office, 1984), Table No. 760.

TABLE 13-2
Poverty and Race, 1959–1983

Group	Number below Poverty Level (in millions)					
	1959	1966	1969	1975*	1979*	1983*
All Persons†	39.5	28.5	24.1	25.9	25.2	35.2
Whites	28.5	19.3	16.7	17.8	16.7	23.9
Blacks**	11.0	8.9	7.1	7.5	7.8	9.9

Group	Percent below Poverty Level					
	1959	1966	1969	1975*	1979*	1983*
All Persons†	22.4	14.7	12.1	12.3	11.6	15.2
Whites	18.1	11.3	9.5	9.7	8.9	12.1
Blacks**	56.2	41.8	32.2	31.3	30.9	35.7

*Beginning 1975, not strictly comparable to prior years due to revised procedures.
†Beginning 1966, includes races not shown separately.
**In 1959 includes blacks and other races.

Source: U.S. Bureau of the Census, *Statistical Abstract of the United States 1980* (Washington, D.C.: U.S. Government Printing Office, 1980), Table No. 773; 1984, Table No. 760.

CITYSCAPE 13-1
Banfield on the Poor: Their Own Worst Enemies

The lower-class individual lives from moment to moment. If he has any awareness of a future, it is of something fixed, fates, beyond his control: things happen *to* him, he does not *make* them happen. Impulse governs his behavior, either because he cannot discipline himself to sacrifice a present for a future satisfaction or because he has no sense of the future. He is therefore radically improvident: whatever he cannot use immediately he considers valueless. His bodily needs (especially for sex) and his taste for "action" take precedence over everything else—and certainly over any work routine. He works only as he must to stay alive, and drifts from one unskilled job to another, taking no interest in his work. As compared to the working-class individual, he "doesn't want much success, knows he couldn't get it even if he wanted to, and doesn't want what might help him get success. . . .

The lower-class individual has a feeble, attenuated sense of self; he suffers from feelings of self-contempt and inadequacy, and is often apathetic or dejected. . . . In his relations with others he is suspicious and hostile, aggressive yet dependent. He is unable to maintain a stable relationship with a mate; commonly he does not marry. He feels no attachment to community, neighbors, or friends (he has companions, not friends), resents all authority (for example, that of policemen, social workers, teachers, landlords, employers), and is apt to think that he has been "railroaded" and wants to "get even. . . ."

. . . The lower-class individual lives in the slum, which, to a greater or lesser extent, is an expression of his tastes and style of life. . . . The subcultural norms and values of the slum are reflected in poor sanitation and health practices, deviant behavior, and often a real lack of interest in

formal education. With some exceptions, there is little general desire to engage in personal or community efforts for self-improvement. Slum persons generally are apathetic toward the employment of self-help on a community basis, they are socially isolated, and most sense their powerlessness. This does not mean that they are satisfied with their way of life or do not want a better way to live; it is simply that slum apathy tends to inhibit individuals from putting forth sufficient efforts to change the local community. They may protest and they may blame the slum entirely on the outside world, but at the same time they remain apathetic about what they could themselves do to change their world.

[The slum dweller] is not troubled by dirt and dilapidation and he does not mind the inadequacy of public facilities such as schools, parks, hospitals, and

---

conditions of life—better food, clothing, shelter, health care, schools, treatment from employers and officials; this is why [the city] always has so many poor. The problem of poverty in the city is seldom of the cities' own making. It is essentially a problem made elsewhere and then brought to the city. (1974, p. 128)

So, the poor bring their poverty to the city, hoping for something more. For some, hopes are fulfilled: the city is a stepping-stone to economic well-being. Others—not so lucky—remain mired in destitution. Why?

Banfield believes luck is of little importance. Although he recognizes that poverty may result from complex circumstances including illness, involuntary unemployment, and racial or ethnic discrimination, he believes that the stubborn persistence of the problem is due to another factor: a

deficiency in the poor themselves. The lowest stratum of the urban population—the lower-lower class we described in the last chapter—simply has a "distinct patterning of attitudes, values and modes of behavior" that renders them unable or unwilling to take advantage of urban opportunity. In Cityscape 13-1, Banfield elaborates his position.

The crucial characteristic of Banfield's explanation of urban poverty is the focus upon the personalities and cultural patterns of the poor themselves. The poor are understood to be *different* from the rest of society: they can't or don't want to help themselves and, as a result, create and support the conditions of their own degradation. Some even gain a kind of perverse pleasure from a life-style that flouts conventional norms. Hence, to Banfield, they are hardly objects of

libraries; indeed, where such things exist he may destroy them by carelessness or even by vandalism. Conditions that make the slum repellent to others are serviceable to him in several ways. First, the slum is a place of excitement—"where the aciton is." Nothing happens there by plan and anything may happen by accident—a game, a fight, a tense confrontation with the police; feeling that something exciting is about to happen is highly congenial to people who live for the present and for whom the present . . . is often empty. Second, it is a place of opportunity. Just as some districts of the city are specialized as a market for, say, jewelry or antiques, so the slum is specialized as one for vice and for illicit commodities generally. Dope peddlers, prostitutes, and receivers of stolen goods are all readily available there, within reach of each other and of their customers and victims. For "hustlers," the

slum is the natural headquarters. Third, it is a place of concealment. A criminal is less visible to the police in the slum than elsewhere, and the lower-class individual, who in some parts of the city would attract attention, is one among many there. In the slum one can beat one's children, lie drunk in the gutter, or go to jail without attracting any special notice; these are things that most of the neighbors themselves have done and that they consider quite normal.

So long as the city contains a sizable lower class, nothing basic can be done about its most serious problems. Good jobs may be offered to all, but some will remain chronically unemployed. Slums may be demolished, but if the housing that replaces them is occupied by the lower class it will shortly be turned into new slums. Welfare payments may be doubled or tripled and a negative income tax instituted, but some per-

sons will continue to live in squalor and misery. New schools may be built, new curricula devised, and the teacher-pupil ratio cut in half, but if the children who attend these schools come from lower-class homes, the schools will be turned into blackboard jungles, and those who graduate or drop out from them will, in most cases, be functionally illiterate. The streets may be filled with armies of policemen, but violent crime and civil disorder will decrease very little. If, however, the lower class were to disappear—if, say, its members were overnight to acquire the attitudes, motivations, and habits of the working class—the most serious and intractable problems of the city would all disappear with it.

Source: Edward C. Banfield, *The Unheavenly City Revisited* (Boston: Little, Brown, 1974), pp. 61–62; 63; 71–72; 234–235.

---

pity. They should stop wallowing in their own misery. They should *do* something constructive with their lives, as members of higher social classes do.

Lewis: The Culture of Poverty. Banfield's analysis flows from the widely known "culture of poverty" thesis formulated by anthropologist Oscar Lewis (1961). Lewis's studies of Hispanic families in conditions of poverty—in Mexico City, San Juan, Puerto Rico, and New York—suggested that some poor adapted to their impoverished condition by creating a set of attitudes and behaviors that seemed to perpetuate their own poverty. Here is Lewis's most succinct outline of the idea:

Some of the social and physiological characteristics [of the culture of poverty] include living in crowded quarters, a lack of privacy, gregariousness, a high

incidence of alcoholism, frequent resort to violence in the settlement of quarrels, frequent use of physical violence in the training of children, wife beating, early initiation into sex, free unions or consensual marriages, a relatively high incidence of the abandonment of mothers and children, a trend toward mother-centered families and a much greater knowledge of maternal relatives, the predominance of the nuclear family, a strong predisposition to authoritarianism, and a great emphasis upon family solidarity—an ideal only rarely achieved. Other traits include a strong present time orientation with relatively little ability to defer gratification and plan for the future, a sense of resignation and fatalism based upon the realities of their difficult life situation, a belief in male superiority which reaches its crystallization in machismo or the cult of masculinity, a corresponding martyr complex among women, and finally, a high tolerance for psychological pathology of all sorts. (1961, pp. xxvi–xxvii)

Like Banfield, Lewis acknowledged that particular social conditions such as prejudice and discrimination can serve to perpetuate poverty. His use of the term "culture," however, suggests that poverty is not simply a result of barriers to opportunity but a socially created way of life the poor pass on to their children. By the time poor children reach six or seven years of age, they are likely to have accepted the despair, fatalism, and present-time orientation of their parents. Consequently, change is unlikely as their lives go on (Lewis 1966). This "cultural transmission" argument also explains how particular areas—say, a low-income immigrant district—would, over the years, carry "germs of poverty" or criminality, readily "infecting" each newly arriving population.

Ryan: Blaming the Victim. Criticism of the closely related views of Banfield and Lewis has been strongest from those who insist that the cause of poverty is not the poor themselves but the systematic limitation of opportunity imposed by the wider society. One who takes this position is William Ryan. He argues that because virtually all of society's wealth, prestige, and power are controlled by those higher in the social stratification hierarchy, the poor have few resources for controlling their own fate. Without money or power, the poor cannot insist on greater police protection in their neighborhoods and quality schooling for their children. Similarly, inadequate education limits the ability to compete for jobs with their more affluent counterparts. Moreover, if racial or ethnic barriers are added into the bargain (as they often are), the minority poor find themselves literally trapped in a never-ending cycle of poverty.

Having created such a social structure, which—by its very nature—commits some to the bottom of the heap, Ryan says that wealthier members of society often claim that the person on the bottom is responsible for his or her own condition. By focusing on the poor's "faults," the higher classes fail to see their own complicity in creating the condition of poverty in the first place and are absolved from doing anything about it. "If the poor created their poverty, *they* should do

A look behind the scenes of virtually any city in the United States will reveal thousands of poor for whom the promise of the city has never been fulfilled. (Laurie Cameron/Jeroboam)

something about it." This whole rationale Ryan calls "blaming the victim." By using it, members of higher classes perpetuate their own social advantages. See Box 13-1.

The Inner City: Motivation and Changing Employment Patterns. There can be no doubt that blaming the victims of urban poverty forms the core of many popular stereotypes about the poor. And the same idea is at the heart of the theories of Banfield and Lewis. *Are* the poor unmotivated? Studies of the values of poor people conducted by Leonard Goodwin (1971) in Baltimore, Leonard Reissman (1969) in New Orleans, and Davidson and Gaitz (1974) in Houston suggest that poor urbanites *do* have ambition and a desire to work

---

BOX 13-1
Blaming the Victim

Twenty years ago, Zero Mostel used to do a sketch in which he impersonated a Dixiecrat Senator conducting an investigation of the origins of World War II. At the climax of the sketch, the Senator boomed out, in an excruciating mixture of triumph and suspicion, "What was Pearl Harbor *doing* in the Pacific?" This is an extreme example of Blaming the Victim.

Twenty years ago, we would laugh at Zero Mostel's caricature. In recent years, however, the same process has been going on every day in the arena of social problems, public health, anti-poverty programs, and social welfare.

Consider some victims. One is the miseducated child in the slum school. He is blamed for his own miseducation. He is said to contain within himself the causes of his inability to read and write well. The shorthand phrase is "cultural deprivation," which, to those in the know, conveys what they allege to be inside information: that the poor child carries a scanty

pack of cultural baggage as he enters school. He doesn't know about books and magazines and newspapers, they say. (No books in the home: the mother fails to subscribe to *Reader's Digest*.) They say that if he talks at all—an unlikely event since slum parents don't talk to their children—he certainly doesn't talk correctly. (Lower-class dialect spoken here, or even—God forbid—Southern Negro. *Ici on parle nigra.*) If you can manage to get him to sit in a chair, they say, he squirms and looks out the window. (Impulse-ridden, these kids, motoric rather than verbal.) In a word he is "disadvantaged" and "socially deprived," they say, and this, of course, accounts for his failure (*his* failure, they say) to learn much in school.

Note the similarity to the logic of Zero Mostel's Dixiecrat Senator. What is the culturally deprived child *doing* in the school? What is wrong with the victim? In pursuing this logic, no one remembers to

ask questions about the collapsing buildings and torn textbooks, the frightened, insensitive teachers, the six additional desks in the room, the blustering, frightened principals, the relentless segregation, the callous administrator, the irrelevant curriculum, the bigoted or cowardly members of the school board, the insulting history book, the stingy taxpayers, the fairy-tale readers, or the self-serving faculty of the local teachers' college. We are encouraged to confine our attention to the child and to dwell on all his alleged defects. Cultural deprivation becomes an omnibus explanation for the educational disaster known as the inner-city school. This is Blaming the Victim.

Source: William Ryan, *Blaming the Victim* (New York: Vintage, 1972), pp. 3–4.

---

and succeed—a motivation level not significantly different from those who enjoy geater privileges.

These observations have been underscored recently by the work of Greg Duncan and his associates (1984). In a study of 5,000 American poor families over 15 years, they found that the poor are a changing population. That is, there is no permanent underclass like that suggested by Banfield and Lewis. While a few people never get out of poverty during their whole lives (about 2 percent of the total poor population), most do—at least for a time. Unfortunately, many slip back into poverty because of major life traumas (divorce, for example, usually decreases a person's monetary resources considerably) or the loss of a job. In addition, the researchers found that, on

the whole, most of this nation's impoverished are neither apathetic or averse to advancement.

What this suggests is that people such as Lutie Johnson in New York (Cityscape 5-2), Jesus Sanchez in Mexico City (Chapter 8), or Ibu Bud in Jakarta (Cityscape 10-2) are poor not because they don't desire anything better (and much less because they enjoy it!) but because the *opportunity* to achieve prestigeful skills with secure income is simply not available to them in the same way that it is to many other city dwellers.

Why is this opportunity limited at the present time? One reason is that blue-collar industries, which have traditionally provided jobs to the working class and the poor of the inner-city, have moved out of the inner cities in record numbers in the last decade. A second and related reason is that blue-collar skills are everywhere in less demand as the country moves into a postindustrial era. Table 13-3 shows that since 1960 the percentage of both whites and blacks in blue-collar work has decreased while the percentage employed in white-collar work has risen. Since white-collar jobs demand more general education and specialized training than blue-collar jobs, people with those skills have a better chance at economic success in the city.

Together, such changing employment patterns have left many poor and minorities who have remained in the inner city high and dry when it comes to long-term secure employment. The opportunities for today's lowest classes are not the same as they were for the European immigrants who helped build the American metropolises of an earlier era. More problematical, the burden of this "opportunity gap" has fallen disproportionately on blacks, Hispanics, and other racial minorities, as we saw in the last two chapters. The magnitude of the problem can be illustrated by noticing that the unemployment rate for white teenagers in 1982 was 21 percent, but for black teenagers it was 49.7 percent. The fundamental reasons for the discrepancy, suggested Janet L. Norwood, U.S. Commissioner of Labor Statistics, are the black teenagers' lack of skills and their lack of hope of finding decent, continuing employment (Associated Press, March 23, 1983). Without skills they are less attractive to employers and because so few of them get good paying jobs, many are disheartened and stop looking altogether.

Aldrich and Blauner: Ghetto Colonization. Another factor that has hampered efforts by poor urban blacks to improve their economic power is "colonization"—the ownership of businesses by persons outside the ghetto. In a study of three cities with sizable black ghettos, Aldrich (1973) found that extensive white ownership of business in black areas hindered black economic opportunity. Table 13-4 provides a summary of his findings. In each city, one district (categorized as a ghetto area on the basis of racial composition and income) was compared to a second, nonghetto

district. Although few whites lived in ghetto districts, they retained control of more than half of ghetto businesses in Boston and Chicago. Only in the Washington, D.C., ghetto district did blacks control a slight majority of businesses. Aldrich concluded:

> White owned businesses in black ghettos dominate and affect the local labor market in a variety of ways . . . whites employ the great majority of persons who work in the ghetto . . . are more likely than black owners to hire employees from outside the area and . . . hire white employees in greater proportion than the racial composition of the area would imply. (1973, p. 1422)

Robert Blauner's research, also an examination of white influence in the black ghetto, went a step further. The pattern of white economic dominance, he observed,

> . . . is also true for the other social institutions that operate within the ghetto. The educators, policemen, social workers, politicians, and others who administer the affairs of ghetto residents are typically whites who live outside the black community. (1969, p. 397)

Because of this white dominance, Blauner asserted that ghettos represent a "colonization" of blacks by whites, comparable to the earlier colonization of indigenous populations around the world by European powers (Chapters 8 through 10). Previous ghettos (such as the Lower East Side of New York) were *chosen* by immigrants to a much greater degree than the more forcefully segregated black ghettos. Also, the ethnic immigrants of the nineteenth and early twentieth centuries in American cities eventually gained economic control of their area and usually were able to move on to other areas of the city in a generation or two. In a few continuing cases of nonblack ghettos, such as San Francisco's Chinatown, Blauner suggests that the persistence of segregation is due primarily to choices made by the group itself, *after* they have made enough money to move out if they wish. The outlook for blacks, however, is not at all bright, for, as Aldrich notes, even if they come to exercise increasing economic control over ghetto resources, "the current number of jobs available to black workers in the

TABLE 13-3
Type of Occupation of Whites and Blacks, 1960–1981

Occupation	White (%)			Black (%)		
	1960	1970	1981	1960	1970	1981
White-Collar	46.6	50.8	54.3	16.1	27.9	37.8
Blue-Collar	36.2	34.2	30.7	40.1	42.2	36.5
Service	9.9	10.7	12.2	31.7	26.0	24.2
Farm	7.4	4.0	2.8	12.1	3.9	1.5
Total	100.1	99.7	100.0	100.0	100.0	100.0
Total Number	58,850,000	70,182,000	88,709,000	6,927,000	8,445,000	9,355,000

Source: U.S. Bureau of the Census, *Statistical Abstract of the United States 1982–83* (Washington, D.C.: U.S. Government Printing Office), Table No. 648.

TABLE 13-4
Who Controls Ghetto Business?*

City	White Population (%)	White-Owned Business (%)	Absentee-Owned (%)
Boston			
Ghetto	28	73	86
Nonghetto	79	99	63
Chicago			
Ghetto	10	58	93
Nonghetto	94	100	58
Washington, D.C.			
Ghetto	17	46	72
Nonghetto	19	76	64

*1970 data are used; absentee-owned figures for Boston and Chicago are for 1968.

Source: Compiled from H.E. Aldrich, "Employment Opportunities for Blacks in the Black Ghetto: The Role of White-Owned Business," *American Journal of Sociology*, 78 (May 1973), pp. 1403–1425, Tables 1 and 2. Reprinted by permission of The University of Chicago Press.

ghetto, under either white or black owner-ship, is simply not enough to make a difference in their relations with the white community" (1973, p. 1423).

Gans: The Positive Functions of Poverty. Found on a wall at a well-known college, the graffiti in Box 13-2 suggest that American young people are well aware of the consequences of having—or lacking—wealth, prestige, and power.

Herbert Gans (1972) suggests that we wish not only to keep ourselves out of poverty, but we also benefit from the poverty of others. As a result, we probably don't want to eliminate it. There are, in short, some positive functions (consequences) of poverty—positive not for the people who are im-poverished (we have seen already many of the indignities they suffer), but for those above them in the social hierarchy. Here are some examples.

First, the existence of a poor underclass means that there always will be a pool of people willing (because they aren't wealthy enough to be *un*will-ing) to do the "dirty work" of society. These peo-ple can be counted upon to take the most physically demanding jobs, the temporary jobs, the low-paying jobs, and the menial jobs—like street cleaner, shoe shiner, bus boy (see those listed at the bottom of Table 12-1).

Second, by taking such jobs, the poor subsidize their employers. By paying the poor the lowest wages possible, employers can add the money saved to their own personal wealth. As a French writer put it at the beginning of the Industrial Revolution, "to assure and maintain the prosperities of our industries, it is necessary that the workers should never acquire wealth" (quoted in Gans 1972, p. 279).

Third, many people in our society make their livings directly from the poor. We have just seen the extent of white control of businesses in the black ghetto, and we explained in Chapter 6 how such control can force the poor to pay more for their goods than more affluent people. In addition, various organizations and individuals, such as welfare agencies, the inner-city police, the Salvation Army, Pentecostal ministers, prostitutes, and drug dealers "serve" the poor in one way or another. The poor are thus good business for many others.

Fourth, in poor areas the less-qualified members of certain professions can practice—the doctors, lawyers, and teachers who are unable to succeed in the more competitive, higher echelons of society. In the same way, the poor are more or less forced to "buy goods which others do not want and thus prolong their economic usefulness, such as day-old bread, fruit and vegetables which would otherwise have to be thrown out, second-hand clothes, and deteriorating automobiles and buildings" (Gans 1972, p. 279). Lest anyone think that Gans is stretching his point, examine Box 13-3, in which Ann Petry's protagonist in *The Street*, Lutie Johnson, surveys what is available for her to buy in Harlem's stores.

Finally, the poor serve a "referencing" function, both for social norms and for positioning within the prestige hierarchy. "The defenders of hard work, thrift, honesty, and monogamy need people who can be accused of being lazy, spendthrift, dishonest, and promiscuous to justify these norms" (Gans 1972, p. 280). More-

---

BOX 13-2
The Handwriting on the Wall

[Graffito #1] Take the road less travelled. Find a job you enjoy. If you don't your life will be wasted. Don't *worry* about money!

[Graffito #2] And wind up in the South Bronx or Harlem? You jackass!

---

over, these accusations continue to be made even when the facts do not support them. Similarly, Gans continues,

> . . . [in] a stratified society, where social mobility is an especially important goal and class boundaries are fuzzy, people need to know quite urgently where they stand. As a result, the poor function as a reliable and relatively permanent measuring rod for status comparison, particularly for the working class which must find and maintain status distinctions between itself and the poor, much as the aristocracy must find ways of distinguishing itself from the *nouveau riche*. (1972, p. 281)

No wonder our second graffitist (Box 13-2) was so concerned about the consequences of slipping into poverty. Unfortunately, it is this very attitude that creates poverty all over again. As long as societies are characterized by established systems of social stratification, some categories of people will have considerably more wealth, prestige, and power than others will. This was recognized by the great English poet, William Blake, over two centuries ago: see Box 13-4.

Gans thus clearly sides with William Ryan. Poverty—urban or rural—is the creation of a hierarchical society and its insistence on competition among individuals and groups as the principal mechanism for allocating wealth. Most of the evidence suggests that this is a more accurate interpretation than Banfield's and Lewis's culture of poverty thesis.

Gans believes there are ways to redress the situation, should we choose to do so. The most basic change would be to decide to pay the poor enough so that, whatever job they had, they no longer would be at such a terrible disadvantage. "Dirty

---

BOX 13-3
The Quality of Merchandise in the Ghetto

Eighth Avenue was lined with small stores. And as they walked toward 117th Street, Lutie looked at each store closely, reacting to it as violently as though she had never seen it before. . . .

The windows of the butcher shops were piled high with pigs' feet, hog maw, neck bones, chitterlings, ox tails, tripe—all the parts that didn't cost them because they didn't have much solid meat on them, she thought. The notion stores were a jumble of dark red stockings, imitation leather pocketbooks, gaudy rayon underwear edged with coarse yellow lace, sleazy blouses—most of it good for one wearing and no more, for the underwear would fade and ravel after the first washing and the pocketbooks would begin to disintegrate after they had been opened and closed a few times.

Withered oranges and sweet potatoes, wilting kale and okra, were stacked up on the vegetable stands—the culls, the windfalls, all the bruised rotten fruit and vegetables were here. . . . All of them—the butcher shops, the notion stores, the vegetable stands—all of them sold the leavings, the sweepings, the impossible unsalable merchandise, the dregs and dross that were reserved especially for Harlem.

Source: Ann Petry, *The Street* (Boston: Houghton Mifflin, 1946), pp. 152–153.

BOX 13-4
Blake: The Human Abstract

Pity would be no more
If we did not make somebody poor;
And mercy no more could be
If all were as happy as we.

Source: William Blake, *The Complete Writings of William Blake*, ed. Geoffrey Keynes (New York: Random House, 1957), p. 473.

---

ities, and social commitments. By choosing to organize our social life as we have for the past few centuries, we have ensured that many will succeed in life and that some always will not. We cannot help but ensure the continuing and wrenching juxtaposition of Park Avenue penthouses and South Bronx tenements as long as we maintain such values. Only by changing our priorities toward the creation of a more humane life and environment for all of society's citizens is it possible even to conceive of the elimination of poverty as a real alternative.

Coping with Poverty: The Consequences

How do poor people in the city cope with poverty? Two of the most frequent adaptations were portrayed in Chapter 5 in the discussions of street-corner men (Box 5-6) and ghetto families (Box 5-11). Some poor people, like the men on Tally's Corner, find solace in escape from the system and its demands. Unable to find a meaningful way out, they create a separate world with few real-world obligations. More hopeful is the cooperative self-help system evolved by ghetto "families," where adults and children alike band together to share welfare checks or take-home pay, food, clothes, furniture—virtually everything.

A third adaptation is oriented more toward "getting out." Ghetto residents, says Douglas Glasgow (1980), can attempt to alleviate their situation by competing for jobs in the mainstream society, by working on government anti-poverty programs, or by improving their skills and educa-

work" and some kinds of menial jobs, for example, are probably always going to be present. By paying those who take them more, the job will not be eliminated but the difficulties of trying to subsist on minimal wages will. Of course, higher wages will increase the employer's overhead; hence, the real decision is whether to give up some profit for the benefit of others. Another alternative would be to institute a type of guaranteed income for everyone in society—and thereby eliminate poverty. Such a commitment would raise taxes, however, particularly for the most affluent individuals and businesses, and Gans is not optimistic that the rich would be willing to make this sacrifice, whatever the positive benefits in quality of life for the poor.

Poverty thus becomes an issue of values, prior-

tion. A fourth way of coping is to develop a militant identification with the ghetto, its culture and people, and their needs. People with this outlook view the subculture within which they exist with pride and do whatever they can to further the success of that culture; hence, they work for ghetto improvement or consciousness-raising efforts.

A last adaptation is "hustling." Even a menial job, welfare check, or help from kin is usually not enough to meet people's needs. As a result, Betty Lou Valentine argues, many ghetto poor turn to "a wide variety of unconventional, sometimes extralegal or illegal activities, often frowned upon by the wider community" (1978, p. 23). Hustles include working the numbers game (where people bet some amount in an attempt to guess a three-digit number) and other forms of gambling, buying and selling stolen merchandise, bootlegging liquor on Sundays, stealing cars, stripping abandoned buildings of valuable parts (sinks, pipes), shoplifting, selling narcotics, mugging, burglary, and armed robbery.

In hustling, we see a direct link between urban poverty and urban crime, a topic to which we will return later in the chapter. This link, observers like Gans, Glasgow, and Valentine would say, is no accident. Crime is a way of getting money when other means are not available or are insufficient to meet one's needs. Indeed, Gans, Glasgow, and Valentine all would agree that each adaptation to poverty just described is a survival-oriented response by the poor to larger social-structure situations over which they have little control. Nevertheless, the likelihood of achieving much success through these means is not great. As Glasgow notes:

> Those who seek success in the broader society in the main do not achieve it. Those who identify with [ghetto] life underachieve, because this system is underdeveloped and therefore unable to provide adequate opportunity. And those who seek security through deviant and criminal activity usually end up in jail. . . . [Despite the fact that most ghetto residents] do aspire to success, . . . do seek achievement in the broader society, . . . and are motivated to pursue their objectives, . . . the structural barriers to mainstream entry are formidable. (1980, pp. 157–158)

BOX 13-5
Unsafe Housing in America

In fact, most Americans have no conception of the filth, degradation, squalor, overcrowding, and personal danger and insecurity which millions of inadequate housing units are causing in both our cities and rural areas. Thousands of infants are attacked by rats each year; hundreds die or become mentally retarded from eating lead paint that falls off cracked walls; thousands more are ill because of unsanitary conditions resulting from jamming large families into a single room, continuing failure of landlords to repair plumbing or provide proper heat, and pitifully inadequate storage space. Until you have actually stumbled through the ill-lit and decaying rooms of a slum dwelling, smelled the stench of sewage and garbage and dead rats behind the walls, seen the roaches and crumbling plaster and incredibly filthy bathrooms, and recoiled from exposed wiring and rotting floorboards and staircases, you have no real idea of what bad housing is like. These miserable conditions are not true of all inadequate housing units, but enough Americans are trapped in the hopeless desolation of such surroundings to constitute both a scandal and a serious economic and social drag in our affluent society.

Source: Anthony Downs, *Urban Problems and Prospects* (Chicago: Markham, 1970), p. 116.

Housing

The life-styles of the urban population, as we saw in Chapter 11, are strikingly diverse. Such differences are dramatically reflected in housing preferences. Some urbanites prefer the life of a downtown apartment, others desire the ongoing excitement of row houses in an ethnic neighborhood, still others prefer the more spacious living of a single-family suburban home.

But housing and neighborhood are not simply a matter of choice. Differences in wealth mean that for some the basic concern of where one eats, sleeps, and is sheltered constitutes a serious problem.

Adequate Housing: Who Has It?

To define housing as "adequate" or "substandard" is obviously somewhat arbitrary. It is also cultur-

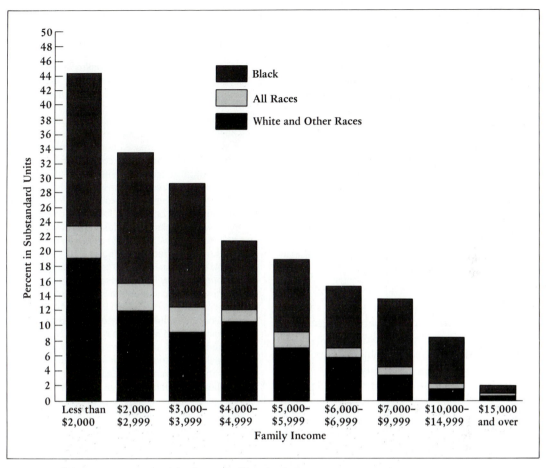

Figure 13-1 *Family Income, race, and substandard housing in the United States. Source: Office of Management and Budget, Social Indicators, 1973* (Washington, D.C.: U.S. Government Printing Office, 1973), p. 193.

ally variable because much of the worst housing in the United States is of a level of quality far better than that which commonly exists in the Third World (Chapters 8 through 10).

Still, there can be little question that housing characterized by structural defects, inadequate plumbing, heating, or sanitation, or lead paint easily ingestible by children poses a threat to the health and safety of those who live there. Although there were over 5.6 million run-down or abandoned houses in the United States in 1977, the great majority of which were in cities, Anthony Downs (1970) points out that most Ameri-

cans have never had any direct experience with such housing. We would be quite shaken, he warns, if confronted with the daily reality of the worst-housed Americans (see Box 13-5).

Like all valued resources, quality housing is distributed very unequally in urban America. Not surprisingly, the worst housing is concentrated more among (1) the poor and (2) minorities subject to discrimination—in short, among people who have "the least social choice" (Greer 1965, p. 143). Figure 13-1 provides a graphic illustration of who these Americans were a decade or so ago. Looking first at the income level reported on the figure's horizontal axis, notice that only a small fraction—about 1 percent—of families ("all races") with incomes over $15,000 in 1973 lived in substandard housing. For those families with only one-third of that income level (that is, below $5,000) the proportion in substandard housing jumps more than tenfold.

Figure 13-1 also shows how significantly the issue of race is related to living in substandard housing. For *every* income level, blacks are more likely than whites to be constrained to poor housing. This reflects the patterns of residential segregation discussed in the last chapter. Because urban America is so highly segregated by race, even blacks with an income adequate to purchase higher quality housing may be limited in their choices by the practices of real-estate personnel ("racial steering") and the response of local residents. Box 13-6 provides a case in point.

In a highly stratified setting such as a large city, the problems of poor housing take on major proportions. Nowhere are such problems more evident than in low-income inner-city areas.

Deterioration and Abandonment in the Inner City

Picture this: block after block of empty, dilapidated buildings, many burned, as if the area had been the object of a full-scale bomb attack. Can such urban "ghost-towns" really exist in the United States? Especially in the older, industrial inner cities of the Midwest and Northeast, the answer is, sadly, yes.

As the economic strength of cities spread outward as part of rapid post–World War II decentralization, the older central cities fell on economic hard times. Without the resources necessary for repairs and improvements, many inner-city neighborhoods deteriorated sharply, in some cases becoming subject to extensive vandalism and arson. Estimates suggest that there were over 2 million abandoned buildings in center cities nationwide in 1977, their numbers growing by some 150,000 yearly (Conway 1977).

While no older city has escaped, the devasta-

BOX 13-6
Racial Discrimination in Housing

Segregation practices of the seventies are subtle but no less effective than those of former years. Sociologist Diana Pearce investigated real estate practices in a 1974–1975 study of the Detroit area. Pearce sent black and white couples posing as buyers to a random sample of about one hundred real estate firms, 87 percent of them in Detroit suburbs. Although the couples gave nearly identical income and family information to the real estate brokers, Pearce found that the salespersons showed homes to three of four white couples, but only one of four black couples. Further, when blacks and whites were taken to see houses, they were taken to different areas. This is known as "racial steering." . . .

I know this from personal experience. In 1963, after completing my Ph.D. and receiving a faculty appointment at Michigan State University, I attempted to buy a home in East Lansing. Although I had a job and an adequate income, I was not able to find anyone willing to sell a home to a black family. It was not until I had filed suit against three realty firms and had received indifferent to hostile treatment from many East Lansing residents that I was finally able to purchase a home.

Source: Robert L. Green, *The Urban Challenge: Poverty and Race* (Chicago: Follett, 1977), pp. 164–165.

---

tion has been unparalleled in New York's South Bronx, an inner-city area where suburb-bound whites have been replaced primarily by blacks and Puerto Ricans (most of them poor). In the South Bronx some 30,000 buildings were subject to abandonment and arson during the 1970s (Hanson 1980). This averages to over eight buildings a day for a decade!

Why would people simply abandon otherwise usable buildings in cities where housing is in short supply? The answer is a complex vicious cycle of decline. Faced with the mounting expenses of taxes, insurance, heating fuel, and repairs for vandalism, not to mention the loss to the suburbs of middle-income renters, some building owners reduce or entirely eliminate routine maintenance and repairs in an effort to retain some profit. Angered tenants often withhold rent until services

In the vicious cycle of deterioration that characterizes many inner-city neighborhoods, landlords of unprofitable buildings shut off services such as heat, leaving residents cold and embittered. If this rent strike does not lead to reconciliation, the landlord may abandon the building and eventually the tenants will leave. Thus are created devastated neighborhoods like the South Bronx. (© 1976 Ray Ellis/Photo Researchers)

are restored, which in turn encourages owners to withhold more services to obtain rents. If a point is reached at which the building represents more costs or trouble than rental income warrants, some owners simply default on their mortgages or cut off all utilities. In some cases buildings are deliberately "torched" in an effort to secure insurance claims. As desperate ex-tenants scatter in search of other housing, vandals and looters seek whatever of value remains (including sinks, bathtubs, and plumbing). First the building, then the block, and then eventually the whole neighborhood succumbs to the process. In the end, just hollow buildings remain: giant headstones marking the grave of a now-dead urban neighborhood.

This part of the urban housing predicament is only the most recent chapter of the story, however. Earlier chapters set the stage.

Housing Problems in Urban America: A Brief History

Nineteenth-Century Housing Problems. Housing problems in America are hardly new; in fact, in the great metropolises of the nineteenth century, housing conditions were far worse than today—recall our discussion of tenement housing in Chapter 3. In an examination of housing conditions in New York in about 1870, James D. McCabe, Jr., recorded the following impressions of life in the cellars of those tenements.

> If the people [housed in tenements] are sufferers, they at least live upon the surface of the earth. But what shall we say of those who pass their lives in the cellars of [these] wretched buildings . . . ?
>
> [Most] have but one entrance and that furnishes the only means of ventilation . . . and . . . the filth of the streets comes washing down the walls into the

room within. The air is always foul. The drains of the houses above pass within a few feet of the floor, and as they are generally in bad condition the filth frequently comes oozing up and poisons the air with its foul odors.

    . . . [T]he poor wretches who seek shelter here are half stupified by it, and pass the night in this condition instead of in a healthful sleep. (McCabe 1970, pp. 405, 406, 409)

Despite the horrors of such poor housing for millions, there was little governmental effort during the 1800s to regulate housing. (Most private builders did little on their own, concerned only with profits.) Indeed, only the crisis occasioned by the collapse of the American economy in the 1930s generated a housing program, associated with President Roosevelt's "New Deal."

A New Deal. Under the Roosevelt administration, the federal government became more involved in American life than ever before. The rationale was twofold: (1) inadequate housing was sufficiently widespread to constitute a serious social problem, and (2) without governmental intervention, the social and economic forces of American society were unlikely to yield an adequate solution.

Federal housing programs under the New Deal had several specific goals. First, funds were made available to encourage the construction of new housing. Second, assistance was given to homeowners faced with foreclosure by banks. Massive foreclosures, a result of people's inability to pay their mortgages because of the Depression, had forced some 500,000 families to lose their homes between 1932 and 1933 (Abrams 1967). Third, guarantees were provided for construction loans under the Federal Housing Administration (FHA), which began operation in 1934. Fourth, to increase the housing supply, the Public Works Administration, begun in 1938, employed people otherwise out of work to construct low-rent public housing in 30 cities.

Taken together, these programs immediately improved urban housing. According to the housing census of 1940, however, about 40 percent of urban housing in the United States still had at least some serious defect (such as a lack of running water or other inadequate plumbing).

Postwar Programs. Housing construction slowed for the duration of World War II. Soon afterward, however, as we discussed in Chapter 11, the United States faced a great housing shortage as military personnel returned home and began having children. This shortage, along with the continued need to improve the overall quality of housing, led to several new government strategies.

One was a broadening of federal mortgage guarantees through the FHA and the Veterans Administration (VA). The latter agency, created under the Serviceman's Readjustment Act of 1944, provided federally backed loans to military personnel and veterans. These programs created "a revolution in home mortgage practices" (Aaron 1972, p. 89) that greatly enhanced the home-buying ability of moderate-income Americans. For example, loans guaranteed by the government allowed new owners to make significantly lower monthly payments (Greer 1965).

Another major initiative was the passage of the Housing Act of 1949. This program provided a two-pronged attack on urban decline by launching major efforts aimed at urban renewal and the construction of more public housing.

The urban renewal program was built on a local city government's ability to claim a decaying area through the right of eminent domain and sell the property to a private developer who would rebuild it. Of course, developers sought *profitable* redevelopment, so the outcome of urban renewal most frequently was not housing for the (usually poor) residents who had previously occupied the area. Instead, many urban renewal projects created housing for the middle class. A classic example is Boston's once-thriving Italian West End (see Box 5-7). Declared in need of renewal in 1953—despite the fact that the outwardly dilapidated buildings were, on the inside, extremely well-kept by residents—the city bought up the area between 1958 and 1960, evicted its residents, and let the developers have a go at renewal. The personal trauma of such relocation was often enormous. Said one evicted West Ender,

I wish the world would end tonight. . . . I wish they'd tear the whole damn town down . . . damn scab town . . . I'm going to be lost without the West End. Where the hell can I go? (Gans 1982, p. 331)

What was built in place of the West End were high-rise luxury apartments, unaffordable to virtually all of the area's previous residents. As this pattern was repeated throughout the 1960s, critics often remarked derisively that urban renewal meant "poor or Negro removal." Many of the displaced poor had no choice but to crowd into other low-grade housing districts, simply because only in such areas could they afford the rents. The resultant overcrowding only hastened the decay of those buildings; thus, ironically, "slum clearance" actually created more slums.

Urban renewal often exacerbated the housing crisis in another way. Redevelopers frequently did not build the same number of units as had been destroyed. Result: fewer homes for city dwellers to choose from and thus more competition and more overcrowding.

This is the point at which public housing entered the picture. There were over 1 million living units in public housing projects by 1973 (McClellan 1974) [and almost 1.5 million in 1984 (U.S. Bureau of the Census)]. The belief was that government-subsidized residential projects would alleviate the housing pressure felt most acutely by the poor. But the idea—let alone the reality—of public housing was never very successful in America. For one thing, private home ownership, throughout our history, has been seen as the foundation of a virtuous life and a stable social order (Bellush and Hausknecht 1967, pp. 453–455). For another, we, as a culture, are quick to suspect those who live in publicly supported rental housing as being somehow deficient. As a result, it is not surprising that public housing has become almost exclusively the preserve of the poor and minorities. For example, between 1974 and 1977, some 514,113 families moved into publicly supported units. Of these, 45 percent were white, 43 percent were black, 10 percent were Hispanic, and the rest were other minorities (U.S. Bureau of the Census 1980). Even more telling are these figures: in 1977, the median an-

---

BOX 13-7
Pruitt-Igoe: A Case of Minimal Charity

It sounded so promising in 1951—a public housing project designed to improve the lives of thousands in a badly run-down area of east St. Louis. Taking advantage of the 1949 Housing Act, local officials sought to break through the "collar of slums which [was] threatening to strangle [the] downtown business section" (*Architectural Forum*, 1951, p. 129).

The project was occupied three years later: 2,762 apartments in 33 innovative high-rise buildings. But by 1959, Pruitt-Igoe "had become a community scandal" (Rainwater 1970, p. 8). Crime, dirt, and accidents were rampant; the project became "a concrete shell where anarchy prevailed" (Green 1977, p. 179). Essentially a concentration of poor, welfare-dependent black families (57 percent were female-headed households with children), the population declined as more and more residents could not bear to remain. The history of Pruitt-Igoe came to a dramatic close in 1973 when the buildings were dynamited by the St. Louis Housing Authority.

---

nual income of new public housing families was $3,651, with 73 percent of all families receiving some form of welfare (U.S. Bureau of the Census 1980).

Although often conceived as exciting housing innovations, too often these projects turn into unmitigated human disasters, plagued by crime, low income, overcrowding, and terrible sanitary conditions. One of the most infamous of cases is St. Louis's Pruitt-Igoe project, described in Box 13-7. Even though many projects have fared better than Pruitt-Igoe, public housing in the United States cannot be considered to be a successful venture. Scott Greer has suggested that, in light of the results, the program can justly be called one of "minimal charity" (1965, p. 16).

Exactly why life in public housing is often so bad is a matter of bitter disagreement. Urban critics such as Banfield point to the people who live in the projects, saying the problems are of the residents' own making. Architectural critics (as we'll discuss shortly) frequently condemn public high-rise structures as open invitations for crime and vandalism (Newman 1972). Others, such as Lee Rainwater (1970), point to poverty—not the people or the projects per se—as the fundamental cause of public housing's rather dismal record.

More Recent Programs. In the climate of criticism and social reform that characterized the late 1960s, the federal government renewed efforts to ensure a "decent home for every American," the elusive goal first put forth in 1937 and reaffirmed in 1949.

The Housing Act of 1968 provided for the construction or rehabilitation of 26 million housing units, 6 million of which were to be targeted for low- and moderate-income families—although even meeting this objective completely would not have ended the housing crisis entirely (Pynoos et al. 1973, p. 7).

An important part of the 1968 legislation was its attempt to place home ownership within reach of more families through loan guarantees and direct subsidies. Ideally, this would have provided an alternative to public housing and helped to improve neighborhoods by increasing the number of families who had a long-term stake in the area because they owned their own home. To succeed, the program depended upon the fair cooperation of real-estate and government personnel. Too often, however, this didn't happen: the program provided unscrupulous real-estate speculators or public officials with the kind of "opportunities" that would have delighted Plunkitt of Tammany Hall.

There was another irony. Once again, government policies assured that the program would run into difficulties. The basic plan was laudable: low-income families were to pay only 20 percent of their income toward the expenses of home ownership, while the government picked up the rest. This was a major step toward providing the lowest income levels with the kind of federal assistance that had been made available to more middle-class Americans at the beginning of the FHA program in the 1930s (Green 1977).

But the government did everything possible to protect the investments of developers and lending banks; hence, when purchasers ended up with a house that was overpriced or in need of extensive repair—a frequent occurrence—they often found themselves unable to meet their payments. The result was foreclosure. The bank was paid off (by the government), the "owners" were back on the street, and the government had on its hands another undesirable house.

By the early 1970s the handwriting was on the wall and the program was cut back. By 1975 over $4 billion had been spent and the government was saddled with 100,000 houses. "With hindsight," Green concluded, "it can safely be said that private concerns [investors, developers, banks] were given too much rope, and with it, they hung the poor" (1977, p. 181).

Evaluation. It is clear even from this brief history that federally supervised urban housing programs did not realize their lofty goals. Some specific criticisms, foreshadowed in the previous discussion, are worth noting more explicitly.

First, who has been helped the most by the urban housing programs of the past three decades? Because private banking and construction industries were involved so deeply in renewal programs, it should be no surprise that, for many, profit overshadowed social responsibility to help the poor. There is also the related matter that some redevelopment has been designed for more affluent buyers, to sell at a price out of the reach of those who lived there originally. Greer suggests that the original intention of urban housing programs of the 1930s—to improve the housing of the poor—has been "slowly transformed into a large-scale program to redevelop the central city" (1965, p. 32), usually with economic interests predominating. It is for this reason that Greer (1965) and Lowe (1967) claim that, while urban renewal created "tall towers and green malls," the total amount of low-cost housing in urban America actually has been *reduced* by these programs.

A second criticism is that, given the tendency of investors and developers to pursue profit rather than assist the poor, local residents usually were not brought into the decision-making process and too often found themselves at the mercy (and

This inner-city housing project, now largely in ruins, is a testimony to the lack of success of much public housing in the United States. (John J. Macionis)

there wasn't a lot of it) of "the powers that be." Herbert Gans, who studied the redevelopment of Boston's West End, claimed that, unorganized and lacking understanding of the programs that "attacked" them, local residents were unable to defend their neighborhood. For many renewal was a bitter experience. Said one resident, "It isn't right to scatter the community to all four winds. It pulls the heart out of a guy to lose all his friends" (Gans 1962, p. 298).

Third, Gans and other critics like Jane Jacobs have argued that many areas subject to redevelopment would have been found to be quite healthy neighborhoods had the redevelopers ever deigned to look more closely. Thus, in addition to being a crass attempt to make money in many cases, development programs often reflected the bias of middle-class planners against the life-style of low-rent areas. Somehow, such areas just weren't what the planners considered "normal."

> Reformers [who] have long observed city people loitering on busy corners, hanging around in candy stores and bars and drinking soda pop on stoops . . . have passed a [class-biased] judgment, the gist of which is: "This is deplorable! If these people had decent homes and a more private . . . outdoor place, they wouldn't be on the street!" [Such a judgment] makes no more sense than to drop in at a testimonial banquet in a hotel and conclude that if these people . . . could cook, they would give their parties at home. (Jacobs, 1961, p. 55)

Lastly, there is the issue of what effects federal housing policies have had on the ecology of the city. Where has the construction of most public housing occurred during the last 40 years? Not surprisingly, it has been where the most inexpensive available land was: outside the central cities. Between 1950 and 1970, two-thirds of the 21 million new housing units constructed were beyond the city limits (Tobin 1976).

This has had two effects. First, within ghettos, the poor have been isolated from the services and life of the city. Two examples will suffice. In Boston, a government-funded housing project known as Columbia Point serves as mute testimony to the insensitivity of urban planners. Built on swampy land on a small peninsula near the first suburbs of Dorchester and Roxbury, Columbia Point consists of a few dozen bland, institutional-style high-rises a full mile from the closest subway stop. Although buses run from the subway station, the project is isolated further because of the water that surrounds it and the few roads that lead into it. Since few significant stores exist in the area, shopping is a major effort, both more expensive and more time-consuming than for other city residents nearer the mainstream of Boston life. In San Francisco, Hunter's Point more or less repeats the Columbia Point story. Isolated on an unwanted peninsula in the southeast corner of the city, the project's quite lovely government-subsidized apartments are miles from San Francisco's thriving downtown. No subway stops are near, so transportation to and fro must be made by car (too expensive for many poor families) or inefficient bus.

Second, as might be guessed, given the high proportion of minorities among the poor, both the Columbia Point and Hunter's Point projects (and others around the country) have become a type of federally sponsored racial ghetto. We have seen already (chapters 3 and 11) how the FHA and VA programs of the 1930s, 1940s, and 1950s aided urban segregation by encouraging loans for suburb-bound whites. Indeed, before the 1960s the government arguably sanctioned such segregation through an FHA warning against guaranteeing loans to "inharmonious racial groups" (Freedman 1969, p. 135). Intended or not, such segregation is often found within newer public housing programs as well.

In all fairness it should be noted that housing in urban America has improved enormously since the days of the nineteenth century tenements, and gains have continued steadily since (or in spite of) the onset of government programs (see Figure 13-2). Still, the housing choices available to the rich or poor or the black or white remain glaringly different. Government programs, with a concern for protecting *both* public and private investments, frequently have aided and abetted the very problems they were seeking to alleviate. Robert

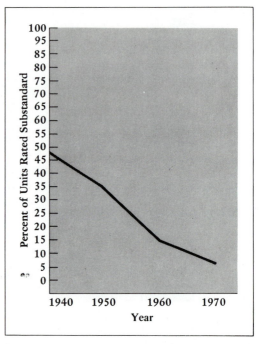

Figure 13-2 *Substandard housing in the United States, 1940–1970. Source: Office of Management and Budget, Social Indicators, 1973* (Washington, D.C.: U.S.Government Printing Office, 1973), Chart 6/1.

Wood, in an assessment of housing programs in the New York City area, put his finger on the real problem:

> [The] public programs [which are] expanding most rapidly . . . are those that exhibit an operating philosophy most clearly akin to a market economy. . . . The final result is that a public sector committed to this ideology by financing and structure offers no countervailing influence against the [discriminatory] trends in the private sector. (Cited in Greer 1965, p. 164)

Inner-City Housing Today: A Revival?

When a city begins to grow and spread outward from the edges, the center which was once its glory . . . goes into a period of desolation, inhabited at night by the vague ruins of men . . . Nearly every city I know has such a dying mother of violence and despair where at

night the brightness of the street lamps is
sucked away and policemen walk in pairs.
And then one day perhaps the city returns
and rips out the sore and builds a monument
to its past.

JOHN STEINBECK,
TRAVELS WITH CHARLIE

Although the success of public programs has surely been limited, efforts by private groups to rebuild certain inner-city areas have gained momentum during the 1970s and 1980s. Two trends deserve our attention: urban homesteading and gentrification.

Urban Homesteading. Recall for a moment our earlier portrait of the abandoned, arson-riddled buildings of many areas in today's cities. Despite the growing number of such buildings across the country, there are a few rays of light visible through the clouds. In 1973 the city of Wilmington, Delaware (burdened with some 1,200 abandoned homes) enacted the Urban Homesteading Ordinance (Conway 1977). Buildings that the city acquired because of default of tax payments simply were given away for people to rehabilitate if they agreed to live in them for three years. Many cities now operate such programs, often transferring houses to people at the top of long waiting lists who become "urban homesteaders"—pioneers in rebuilding an urban area.

In New York's ravaged South Bronx, local citizen groups such as the People's Development Corporation are beginning to stand up against seemingly impossible odds to return deteriorating inner-city buildings to life. With little capital to invest, such groups must rely on their own physical efforts to be successful. Having no collateral, the equity they put up for bank and other loans is their own sweat. Although perhaps only a small back-eddy in a river of decay, the people described in Cityscape 13-2 seem to have spirit enough to take on the whole city if they have to.

Gentrification. Urban homesteading of the type just described seems fairly limited. It is not occurring in all cities by any means, and even in cities where it is relatively prevalent, it is a very limited

phenomenon; few buildings and few blocks are reclaimed. This is not the case with the gentrification movement. Virtually every major city in the country has seen this process begin and quickly spread. The word "gentrification," coined to describe the renovation of run-down London homes by the wealthy "landed gentry" in the nineteenth century, refers to the movement of more affluent Americans back into older, often decaying areas in the city. There is disagreement about the extent and long-range impact of this movement (Laska and Spain 1980), but optimistic analysts see the beginning of a general urban renaissance. Paris and London, as already noted, have had such a revival in effect for some time, and it is gaining momentum in the United States as well.

Today's gentry, like those of the past, are a rather select group of people. They are usually the cosmopolites or unmarried and childless groups we discussed in Chapter 11. Or, to put it another way, they are frequently the "yuppies" we first spoke of at the end of Chapter 3. More to the point, they are people with enough money to buy a brownstone in Manhattan, a Society Hill townhouse in Philadelphia, a brick cottage in the German Village area of Columbus, Ohio, or a Victorian house in San Francisco's Haight-Ashbury district. Most assuredly as well, these gentry are *not* the ethnic working class—a group that was quick to leave the central city when resources allowed them to do so.

Why would people *choose* central-city neighborhoods when the trend for the last century has been to escape the inner city? The reasons are varied but certainly include the following. First, the central city still has the greatest amount of variety and stimulation. Theater, music, the most chic stores—all are found in the greatest concentration downtown. Second, as family size has decreased (a clear trend during the 1970s and 1980s), the desire for single-family suburban housing has dropped (Lipton 1977). Third, as we've discussed in other chapters, the central cities still contain a large proportion of the administrative and professional jobs held by many gentry. Central-city living eases the time and costs of getting to work. Fourth, as more and more women

---

CITYSCAPE 13-2
Sweat Equity in the South Bronx

Talking rapidly and in bursts, Danny Soto Diaz hunkered down amid broken plaster and other products of demolition that littered the South Bronx tenement. . . . Street sounds—portable radios and playing children and laughing adults idle on a midweek afternoon—punctuated the tomblike quiet of the gutted building.

Danny Soto, a 22-year-old Puerto Rican, lives in the South Bronx, so he is certainly familiar with tenements. Yet this one—at 1186 Washington Avenue—is very special to him and unusual to anyone: it has been rehabilitated through the labor of a group of mostly poor young blacks and Puerto Ricans trying to improve

their own neighborhood. This is the process of "sweat equity"— which simply means that people invest their own labor rather than money in a residence. And labor, in the strongest sense of the word, is what is involved. Writer Roger Williams explains:

. . . "Toil" is almost a euphemism for the work involved—exhausting and sometimes dangerous demolition, performed in the extremes of climate and the accumulation of several decades' worth of structural abuse and neglect. . . .

. . . The first requirement was to clean out and gut the rotting six-story structure; it was an exhausting and at times a loathsome task,

performed by the group with no outside financial assistance. Rubble, rats, and feces were everywhere, and dead dogs were commonplace. The basement was the worst: ice-cold mud up to the knees, refuse that defies the imagination, fleas that accompanied the workers home. . . .

Sweat equity is not likely to become popular with people who have the money to buy a home they like, but it is one option for the poor who have the skills and strength to undertake such a monumental task. In some of the poorest neighborhoods of New York City, people like Danny Soto are trying to turn housing that is all but falling down into liveable

---

enter the work force (by the mid-1980s, about two-thirds of women had done so) and two-career couples become common, the greater upkeep involved in a single-family suburban house often looks less and less attractive (Lipton 1977). Fifth, there is the cost of housing itself. Suburban housing is expensive, and, while some central-city housing is extremely costly (brownstones in Manhattan often top $750,000), there still are bargains to be found, particularly in districts where the average income is low. Catherine Van Allen found such a bargain. In 1982 she camped out for eight days on a Baltimore sidewalk to purchase an abandoned building from the city for $200. By 1985 she had put $64,000 into the building and completely renovated it into a modern, efficient home (Hinds, 1986). Sixth, and finally, remember that much central-city housing built from about 1880 to 1910 has a level of craftsmanship and quality—with solid oak floors and stained-glass windows—rarely found in the suburbs. Most of these elements can be seen in Cityscape 13-3, in which Marian Engel describes the gentrification of an older street in Toronto, a major

Canadian city undergoing the same type of investment revival that characterizes many American city neighborhoods.

Indeed, the fact that deteriorating inner-city housing eventually may become a bargain for someone with cash and energy is what causes critics like Edward C. Banfield to be unmoved about inner-city decay. Eventually pure market and locational considerations (Chapter 6) will make the inner city attractive again. But, with the exception of local sweat-equity projects like those in the South Bronx, once again the poor get the short end of the bargain. Gentrification of deteriorating neighborhoods almost always displaces the previous poorer inhabitants by causing tax assessments and rents to rise (DiGiovanni 1984).

An example is lower Lancaster Street in Albany, New York. As portrayed in a 1981 PBS documentary, despite the contribution of the renovated buildings to the city's declining tax base and the added vibrancy it has brought to the area, lower Lancaster Street is rather quickly seeing its original working class pushed out. Profits are the key. Said one real-estate owner to a renter he had

homes for themselves and other local residents. The benefits of sweat equity are very real—this one building became 28 apartments—but, just as important, a project of this kind brings neighborhood residents together with a sense of common purpose.

Urban homesteading projects are still quite rare and hardly likely to eliminate the massive housing problem in the United States. Yet people like Danny Soto are optimistic that they can make a real change in at least a small piece of their city:

. . . "All around this area you see people sleeping in doorways, drinking all day, cleaning a car for three dollars when they can get it.

Their fathers taught 'em nothing, and they don't know nothing. We want to create a village of ten thousand people surviving on their own, with their own firemen, police patrols, schools—people for maybe forty blocks living good, the way everybody else lives good in this country."

This particular building had been seized by New York City for default of taxes. Soto's group, the People's Development Corporation (PDC), bought the building from the city for one dollar. Once they completed the onerous task of cleaning out the building, the group restored the structure, including all the necessary plumbing, wiring, and carpentry. The

work was time consuming and difficult, but, Williams explains, the group had an evident sense of spirit driving them on:

Talking about a forthcoming celebration of the PDC's success at 1186 Washington Avenue, Danny Soto chuckled sardonically and said, "Man, wait till you see the politicians who show up for that party, trying to take credit for what we've done."

Source: Adapted from Roger M. Williams, "The New Urban Pioneers: Homesteading in the Slums," *Saturday Review*, July 23, 1977, pp. 9–14.

---

just evicted, "I'm sorry that something like this has to happen, but it's not my fault. It's economics right now."

Evaluation. It is too early to reach a definitive conclusion about the housing revival in the center cities. Perhaps homesteading and gentrification—as well as recent commercial successes such as New York's South Street Seaport and Baltimore's Inner Harbor—will mark the beginning of a true urban renaissance. Maybe they won't: sweat-equity programs are monumental undertakings for local residents, even when they can get the funds; similarly, gentrification and flashy new malls at present only represent "pockets of plenty" in a languishing center city (Nathan 1979, p. 5). By the mid-1980s, we can see that these changes have become widespread, yet they do not seem destined to help those who need *inexpensive* housing.

Two things, however, do seem clear. First, there is now small slowing of the outward flow that has characterized our cities for decades. Gentrification has also partially reversed the trend for

the wealthy to move ever-outward, as Ernest W. Burgess predicted they would do in the 1920s (Chapter 6). This is elaborated upon in Box 13-8.

Second, without other, much more massive intervention, these trends are likely to have no significant impact on the people who need better housing the most: the poor. As Michael Sterne said of renewal efforts in the South Bronx:

[Nothing] will work . . . unless jobs are provided for the tens of thousands of poor people who live there. Only stable incomes will permit the people to sustain their housing, local services and retail businesses. [But] jobs alone will not solve the huge problems. . . . Unless good schools, efficient health care and attractive housing in safe streets are also provided, the people who get the new jobs will move away, as thousands have before them. (1978, p. 5)

As a real solution to the problem, Sterne suggests giving major tax breaks to business and industry if they relocate in decrepit neighborhoods. Something of the like has been proposed by the Reagan administration in the form of its Urban

CITYSCAPE 13-3
Remaking the City for the Yuppies: Gentrification in Toronto

In 1967, to celebrate Canada's hundredth birthday . . . a broker named Morgan Wickwire bought his wife a street in Toronto.

In terms of the streets other people were buying, it was not a very large one. In terms of the neighborhoods others were choosing, he did not choose well. His "charming cul-de-sac," as it was subsequently called in real-estate advertisements, consisted of a dozen houses facing each other in two rows like broken teeth, bounded on the south by a [water works] substation, on the west by a mattress factory, and on the north by a neighborhood where no one has spoken English since 1926. . . . Three of the houses, already condemned, seemed beyond repair. . . . [Three were unavailable because their present owners would not sell them.] This left Wilma Wickwire six houses to play with, and soon enough she was supervising crews of groggy-eyed dew-worm pickers as they heaved rotten window frames and rusted sash weights into bulk loaders. She had decorated many houses in the past, but never had the satisfaction of starting quite so close to the beginning. . . .

But, as everyone said, you could say a lot about Wilma—she landscaped Number 8 before she brought the bulk loader to sit on the new turf—but you couldn't say she wasn't a worker. . . . She bossed and stripped and plunged; by Christmas she had worked so hard and learned so much about heating, plumbing and electricity that she collapsed in her ski lodge and raved for some time about party walls and by-law restrictions. It was a month before she was on her feet again, shivering in the house she kept for an office, staring at blueprints and samples of wallpaper. . . .

She spent the next two weeks at bankruptcy warehouses and insurance brokers' outlets. She went to wholesale houses and bought enough velvet and braid to please Scarlett O'Hara. She reminded her brother-in-law that he owed her some money and could pay it off in plumbing. She ordered appliances on her credit cards, dug from her basement chiffoniers, escritoires, washstands, dry sinks, breakfronts and kitchen tables, chipped speckled pottery, fern stands, wicker chairs, violin cases, butler's tables, brass hooks, half-broken Tiffany shades, stone crocks, pots and innumerable porcelain door-knobs. . . . With the aid of [her friend] Hal's plans, striped wallpaper, and all the gilt rope she could lay her hands on, Number 11 became a Regency bijou. Number 8 . . . was dusted, sanded, vacuumed . . . and lit so brilliantly that the workmen could not complain about their fear of rats. . . . [While she took care of all this] Hal supervised the conversion of one of the condemned houses into a dream of skylights, catwalks and cathedral ceilings, reducing a six-room house to the size of a very smart bachelor apartment. . . . [And, at last, she was ready to sell.]

It took [until 1979] for the street to reach its full height; first Sylvia had to buy Number 7 in order to install her wheelchair ramp and her aviary; and meet and marry Vinnie at the Bird Fanciers' Association; and, even before that, the trust company fell into receivership so that two houses were sold for the price of one to Harriet, who, to avoid the embarrassment of having two front doors, made a two-storey flat out of Number 8, which she rented then and still does, to cover taxes and utilities, to her friend Marshallene. . . . Bob the Painter bought the corner store when the Italian grocer retired, and kept the Salada tea letters but silvered the inside of the window so he could paint unobserved, which was spiteful but not quite, because he was Bob Robbins whom they [the street's residents] loved. Hal did what he could with the house beside Harriet, but that was resold and resold as well. The new people all seemed to want larger cars and a neighborhood that summered up north instead of noisily under its grape arbors. And the neighborhood lacked, in addition to a library, it is true, a non-ethnic butcher, silence and a mailbox. Some of these difficulties Roger [who had bought Number 9] assuaged by getting them all involved in city politics. A city magazine wrote the place up as "trendy"; Roger said it could hardly be trendy when Harriet's twins went to the bathroom on his lawn. Harriet fired her housekeeper and spent the money she saved on a psychiatrist and a downstairs john.

Source: Marian Engel, *Lunatic Villas* (Toronto: McClelland and Stewart-Bantam, 1981), pp. 7–13.

BOX 13-8

Gentrification and the Burgess Concentric Zone Model

Figure 6-5 shows Burgess's concentric zone theory, which indicated that progressively wealthier residential areas would be located at an increasing distance from the CBD. According to the Burgess model, gentrification— higher-income people seeking residential housing in the central city—shouldn't happen. Urban planner S. Gregory Lipton, in the following, attempts to link gentrification to Burgess's earlier theory of urban ecology.

The apparent contradiction between the Burgess theory and the observations [of gentrification] can possibly be explained by looking at the underlying political, social, and economic differences present at the time of [his] studies. Burgess was observing cities during a major growth period that was characterized by large-scale immigration of poor Europeans

and Americans. Industry was largely labor intensive and the automobile had not yet allowed the blue-collar worker and the factory to be geographically separated to any great extent. Industry was fairly dependent on a limited number of rail and water ways for transportation as trucking had not yet emerged as a long distance hauler. Thus, a centralized location for most activities was the norm. The major public transportation arteries exemplified this by generally intersecting only in the center, making travel between two noncentral locations difficult.

Another assumption, that the well-to-do would continually prefer to move away from the center as the central business district and city grew, was shown not to be universally true. Luxury apartments were being built in the center of New York City. These apartments catered to those with great

mobility who could easily afford to live in the suburbs. An even more interesting development than the fact that these people chose to stay in the city was that in a number of cases, their new luxury buildings were replacing tenements and substandard housing. A reverse succession, not postulated by Burgess, was taking place.

At some point in time, the land occupied by an old slum becomes too valuable to justify its use as an old slum, and its inhabitants become too weak politically to hold on to it. Property is then reacquired, leveled or rehabilitated, and put to more efficient use, such as high income apartments or office buildings or public housing.

Source: S. Gregory Lipton, "Evidence of Central City Revival," *Journal of the American Institute of Planners* (April 1977), p. 137.

Enterprise Zones program. Unfortunately, few investors have leaped to the bait; most appear to feel that such an investment is too risky. Once again, we face a question of priorities: commitment to high profits overrides concern for neighborhoods like the South Bronx.

Crime

They started walking at dusk, two teen-agers casually spreading the message that the streets of West Los Angeles were no longer safe. First they stopped Phillip Lerner and demanded money. Lerner had no cash, only his infant in a stroller. They let him pass and kept walking. They hailed Arkady and Rachel Muskin at a nearby intersection. The couple quickly handed over $8 and two wristwatches, and gratefully fled. Next the boys intercepted two

elderly Chinese women and pulled out a pistol. When one woman tried to push the gun out of her face, ten bullets blazed out, killing both. The boys kept walking. They came upon a trio of friends out for an evening stroll. They took a watch and a few dollars and, without so much as a word, killed one of the three, a Frenchman visiting Los Angeles for the first time. The boys kept walking. At last they reached a drive-in restaurant where they found 76-year-old Leo Ocon walking on the sidewalk. They argued with him for less than a minute and then shot him down. Their evening over, they climbed into an old sedan and then, much as they had started, calmly went off into the night. (*Newsweek*, 1981, p. 46)

So began a recent account of the apparent explosion of street crime in urban America. Crime has always been part of the imagery of urban life, but in recent decades the problem—as well as the fear of it—has assumed major proportions.

Consider, for example, the case of Bernard Goetz, a New York businessman who entered the subway in late 1984 to be confronted by four young men, who demanded his money. Three of the assailants carried sharpened screwdrivers. Like a scene out of Charles Bronson's film *Death Wish*, Goetz suddenly pulled a .38-caliber handgun from his pocket and shot all four of his attackers, leaving them seriously wounded (and one paralyzed) on the floor of the subway car. Goetz was subsequently taken to court for his actions—but in a city riddled by fear of crime he also became something of an instant folk hero to many New Yorkers and urbanites across the country. He was fully acquitted in 1986.

Is crime a necessary way of life within the city? How bad is this problem? Is it getting better or worse? Who commits it? Why? In attempting to answer these questions, we turn first to some facts.

The Data

What we read often leaves the impression that crime is a strictly urban phenomenon. This is not true, as Table 13-5 indicates. Nonetheless, comparing crime rates in metropolitan areas, other cities, and rural areas given in Table 13-5 does reveal that metropolitan areas and other cities have a much higher incidence of crime. The crime index total is more than twice as large for other cities as it is for rural areas, and the metropolitan areas index is nearly three times that of the rural areas. Further, when Table 13-5 is examined in each category of crime, the metropolitan areas and other cities rates are *always higher* than rural areas rates—sometimes spectacularly so (robbery, for example, is more than ten times as frequent in metropolitan as in rural areas).

Table 13-6 goes two steps further, showing, first, that city size is related to the amount of violent crime (murder, forcible rape, robbery, aggravated assault) committed; and, second, that violent crime, despite the exception of individual cities early in the decade, was on the increase throughout the 1970s. This increase in urban crime reached a peak in 1981, but had dropped significantly—back to roughly 1979 levels—by 1983. As Table 13-6 shows, between 1979 and

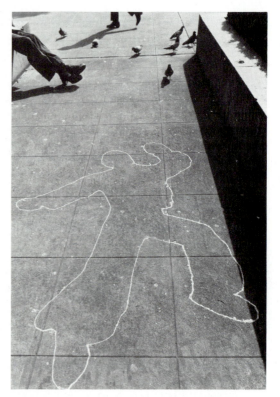

Too often the public response to crime—such as the murder scene shown here—is one of apathy. (Bruce Kliewe/Jeroboam)

1983 crime rates increased only slightly for the largest cities and actually fell for smaller cities.

Before going further, however, we should issue a warning: crime statistics are notoriously imperfect. For example, many crimes are not discovered, not reported to police, or not recorded carefully. All the statistics in Tables 13-5 and 13-6 are compiled from police records of crime. Many criminologists believe that a more accurate portrait of crime is given by the census bureau's semiannual random survey of victims. By questioning people at random, the victimization survey uncovers many unreported crimes missed in the crime index and crime rate calculations. Such studies show that the actual number of crimes is considerably higher than official statistics suggest—taking all types of crime together, perhaps twice as high.

TABLE 13-5
Crime Rate by Locality, 1983

Offense	Total United States	Metropolitan Areas	Other Cities	Rural Areas
Crime Index Total[1]	5,159	5,852	4,629	1,882
Modified Crime Index Total				
Violent	529	627	315	161
Property	4,630	5,225	4,314	1,720
Murder	8.3	9	5	6
Forcible Rape	33.7	39	21	15
Robbery	214	273	49	17
Aggravated Assault	273	306	240	124
Burglary	1,334	1,501	1,039	656
Larceny/Theft	2,866	3,200	3,085	964
Motor Vehicle Theft	429	523	189	100

[1]Crimes per 100,000 population

Source: *Statistical Abstract of the United States, 1985* (Washington, D.C.: U.S. Government Printing Office, 1984), Tables 275, 276.

TABLE 13-6
Violent Crime Rates in Cities, 1970–1983

	1979 Population	Crime Rates (Number Recorded Crimes per 100,000 Population)					Annual Percent Change
		1970	1975	1979	1981	1983	1979–1983
Cities with Population of							
250,000 or more		980	1,159	1,238	1,441	1,294	1.1
100,000–249,999		450	632	702	826	736	1.2
50,000–99,999		274	451	526	584	511	−0.7
25,000–49,999		214	343	420	452	403	−1.0
10,000–24,999		159	268	315	342	403	−1.5
Fewer than 10,000		141	232	279	291	260	−1.8
Selected Cities							
Baltimore	791,000	2,088	1,862	1,963	2,224	2,003	0.5
New York	7,109,000	1,381	1,781	1,862	2,220	1,868	0.1
San Francisco	659,000	1,339	1,364	1,675	1,735	1,403	−4.3
Detroit	1,286,000	1,934	2,121	1,670	1,941	2,169	6.8
Washington, D.C.	656,000	2,227	1,774	1,609	2,275	1,915	4.5
Los Angeles	2,863,000	1,062	1,114	1,515	1,743	1,692	2.8
Chicago	3,061,000	1,101	1,180	909	850	1,317	—
Philadelphia	1,757,000	571	867	827	1,044	1,003	4.9
Indianapolis	514,000	704	925	813	983	893	2.4
San Diego	829,000	285	502	656	734	582	−3.0
San Antonio	889,000	497	549	493	567	609	5.4
Dallas	882,000	966	885	1,298	1,360	1,149	−3.0

Source: U.S. Bureau of the Census, *Statistical Abstract of the United States, 1980* (Washington, D.C.: U.S. Government Printing Office, 1980), Table 305; *Statistical Abstract of the United States, 1985* (U.S. Government Printing Office, 1984), Table 278.

CITYSCAPE 13-4
Guardian Angels: Saviors of the Subways

At the age of eight, Curtis Sliwa of New York's South Bronx received his first stab wound on a subway. In 1979 at 24, he decided that the crime problem had surpassed the resources of police, courts, and prisons. He formed a group of local young people who patrolled the subways, bus lines, and parks of New York, alert for possible crime. Now called the "Guardian Angels," some 1,000 men and women—black, white, Hispanic, and Asian—carry out round-the-clock, eight- to ten-person patrols, dressed in highly visible red berets and white T-shirts. Trained in the martial arts, they are motivated by a genuine philosophy of mutual concern. Says Sliwa:

I look out for you and you look out for me. What the Guardian Angels do is take the attitude that the people are our brothers and sisters, our fathers and mothers. So, to put it in the clearest example, if I'm on a train and across from me is an elderly black woman—I'm white, she's black; I don't know her, she doesn't know me—but as far as I'm concerned she's my mother. As far as I'm concerned, the elderly Hispanic man in the corner is my father—he don't know me, I don't know him. For all I know, I may not like him, he may not like me, but he's my father. And the other people on the train are my brothers and sisters.

For Sliwa and other Guardian Angels—85 percent from New York's worst slums—security patrols involve great personal risk. To date they have made hundreds of citizen's arrests. The work is rewarding, but often dangerous; Sliwa describes an incident that nearly cost his life:

[We] used to have three-man patrols, this was about two months after the formation [of the organization]. This was a late spring night, about 12 o'clock . . . and we were patrolling . . . the Brownsville section of Brooklyn— probably the worst part of the city. [We were on a subway] platform, about 150 feet, the only way you can get from one train to the next. Plus . . . it's the only way to get from one side of Brooklyn to the other side. . . . Now, with all these people going across . . . it became a mugger's delight. Why? Because there was no lighting. On this particular night, the three of us . . . started to walk down the

Nevertheless, even allowing for imperfections in the data, two conclusions are warranted: (1) crime is not distributed evenly throughout the urban area, and (2) fear of crime is widespread. Concerning the first point, as is the case with other urban problems, the greatest concentration of offenses tends to occur in inner-city districts with poverty-stricken minority populations. In 1982, for example, the poorest households in America, with incomes under $3000, were almost 60 percent more likely to experience a burglary than more affluent households, with incomes over $25,000 (U.S. Bureau of the Census 1984). This pattern was recognized by urbanists at the University of Chicago in the 1940s (Shaw and McKay 1969), and is true for both the inner city and the suburbs (Stahura et al. 1979).

As to the second point, *fear* of crime is so widespread that it should be considered a problem unto itself. Evidence suggests that fear of crime

platform. Immediately, one of the guys . . . smelled peppermint . . . and we knew right away somebody was "dusting up." There had been people in that area smoking "angel dust" for a long period of time for it to be that strong a smell. So we were on alert. We move a little bit farther down the platform and see six silhouetted figures in the distance. They have this female on her hands and knees and they're attempting to sodomize her. Immediately, at that point, they saw us. With that red beret and that white T-shirt, boy, we were like neon lights. They immediately came at us 'cause they knew who we were and they knew we were going to stop them and try to arrest them. And then it was a scene out of a Kung-Fu movie, kicks and punches were going in all directions. People were being knocked around as if they were rag-dolls. We were taking it and giving it out. You know, I don't want to give the impression that we were like three Bruce Lee's, knocking everybody out; we were getting beat-up and we were dishing it out. A few minutes into the fight, the female gets up off her hands and knees. She begins to run down the stairs of the platform. . . . 30 feet above the ground. . . . [O]ne of the men steps out of the fray, pulls a

sawed off shot gun out of his army coat and pumps it once aiming at the fleeing woman, and he's ready to blow her up. . . . At that point, I'm being hit in the back of the head with an elbow and I launch a flying jump-kick . . . totally off balance . . . I end up hitting the gun. . . . [T]he shot gun flies up in the air, the man falls down the steps . . . and I end up falling 30 feet to the street below. . . . [E]verybody thought I was dead . . . I would not move and I was in tremendous pain. Luckily, nothing was broken. Showing how dangerous this area is, the police would not respond to the scene until there were three squad cars. Now, I'm not saying they're wrong. . . . There have been cases in that area of police being sniped and there were two police that were killed in that area; there are numerous false-alarm calls, and there is a heavy gun trade. So the police were very cautious, and rightfully so. But by the time they got there, the guys were home sleeping, ya know, and had just finished watching Johnny Carson on TV. I mean, they were *long*-gone. I was . . . hospitalized for two days.

*Similar groups now exist in Springfield, Massachusetts, Boston, Philadelphia, Buffalo, Wash-*ington, D.C., New Orleans, Oakland, Columbus, Ohio, and Chicago. Officials in London, Paris, and Tokyo have contacted Sliwa for help in combatting crime in their subway systems. Sliwa responds by answering that the city is composed of people who can make a difference in the security of their neighborhoods. In his words:*

. . . [W]hile everybody else sits home and belly-aches and watches the five o'clock . . . news and says "Boy, ya know, thirty, forty years ago you never would have seen any of this stuff," and young people will be standing on the corner and drinking a beer or smoking a joint. While they belly-ache about the problems . . . we're riding the trains, we're out in the parks protecting people. Whether you agree with us or not, we're out there putting our butts on the line for what we believe.

It may be a hopeful sign that in the city which stood by and watched the murder of Kitty Genovese (Box 4-3), men and women are indeed standing up for each other once again.

Source: Interview material supplied courtesy of National Public Radio, Washington, D.C., and originally broadcast June 18, 1980, on "Horizons." © National Public Radio, 1980.

Photo from Bettmann/UPI.

may be in fact the single greatest concern of urbanites, particularly women. A 1972 national survey found that two to three times as many women as men expressed fear about walking at night in their neighborhoods. A more recent study of Chicago, Philadelphia, and San Francisco found that "49% of women . . . indicated that they felt 'very unsafe' or 'somewhat unsafe' when out alone in their neighborhoods at night [while] only 7.5% of men responded this way" (Gordon et al. 1980, p.

147). And an Associated Press national poll (broadcast by National Public Radio, July 21, 1981) reported 85 percent of Americans were more afraid of crime than they had been five years earlier. This problem is especially great among the elderly, particularly elderly women (Markson and Hess 1980). Not surprisingly, a recent national survey found that two-thirds of Americans believed more stringent action was necessary to combat crime (NORC 1983, p. 77). Indeed, the fear that local authorities may be unable to control crime has led to some innovative local solutions, none of which has been more astonishing than New York City's "Guardian Angels," profiled in Cityscape 13-4.

Understanding Urban Crime

To some, such as Edward Banfield, crime flourishes in areas of the city where lower-class culture is rooted, a product of the "present-time orientation," low aspirations, and moral irresponsibility that urge the poor to victimize each other and anyone else who seems an easy mark. Since a high proportion of the poorest people in American cities are black, Banfield's view would lead to the expectation that urban ghettos are districts with especially high rates of violent crime. Official records of violent crime suggest that this is the case. One of the most sobering facts is that, within many overwhelmingly black urban ghettos, homicide has reached crisis proportions. Nationwide, the leading cause of death for black males between the ages of 18 and 24 is homicide. In 1981, about 6,000 blacks were killed by other blacks—about the same number that died in the entire Vietnam War (Stengel 1985). A recent government study clearly shows that race—as well as sex—is linked to a person's chances of dying as a result of homicide. The odds of becoming a victim of violent homicide were calculated to be one in 369 for white women and one in 131 for white men. For black Americans, however, the odds are one in 104 for women and, for black men, one in 21 (Langan and Innes 1985)!

On the face of it, Banfield would seem to be correct that the extensive poverty in many predominantly black districts of American cities is an important cause of violent crime. At the same time, however, many sociologists do not agree with Banfield that crime is simply a consequence of "lower class culture," nor that crime is caused simply by poverty.

The most common counterargument is that most crime that is not of the "white-collar" (embezzlement, for example) or "organized" (Mafia-controlled prostitution, for example) variety is a response by society's have-nots to a wider situation that they cannot control. Systematically prevented by lack of training or prejudice from getting a good job and unable to survive on welfare or other aid, many poor or near-poor people seek to supplement their incomes by turning to crime. It is, as Betty Lou Valentine (1978) has argued, an almost necessary form of "hustling," of providing the income necessary to survive. Living in a particular crime-riddled area can place pressures toward crime upon the individual, and also increase the likelihood that he or she *will be perceived as criminal* regardless of actual behavior. Therefore, these theorists argue that the primary problem is one of social structure.

Marxist urban critics such as Manuel Castells (1977) take such a view. The contention is that capitalism, with an unceasing orientation toward profit, defines "crime" and "criminals" largely in terms that protect the interests of the rich. People in such societies do not believe that causing people to suffer a life of poverty is criminal, but rather that taking another's *property* is—especially if the victim is somebody "important." In a society in which wealth and power are largely in the hands of the few, therefore, high rates of criminality among the more deprived are to be expected simply because of how crime is defined and how the law is enforced.

Recent research by Judith Blau and Peter Blau (1982) strongly supports the Marxist explanation of urban crime. Examining the 125 largest metropolitan areas in the United States, they concluded that high rates of urban crime are not caused by race, nor by poverty, but by *income inequality*. Their evidence suggests that, insofar as a city is a concentration of people with highly unequal incomes, those who have less than others are likely to see themselves as relatively deprived. Therefore, even if a city were to have no *absolute poverty* (that is, people with no food, no housing, no work whatsoever), as long as the population still had significant differences of income within the population, *relative poverty* would still breed crime. In other words, Blau and Blau conclude that blacks engage in more crime as offenders—and suffer more as victims—only because they are heavily represented among a group of Americans who are poor relative to others. Thus, in contrast to Banfield's assertion that poor people are *themselves* to blame for criminality, this explanation sees the poor as victims of patterns of social inequality within American society. In other words, violent crime appears to be an inevitable consequence of a society that creates widespread income differentials. They sum up:

> Thus, aggressive acts of violence seem to result not so much from lack of advantages as from being taken advantage of, not so much from absolute deprivation but from relative deprivation. In a society founded on the principle "that all men are created equal" economic inequalities rooted in ascribed positions [such as being born black or impoverished] violate the spirit of democracy and are likely to create alienation, despair, and conflict. (1982, p. 126)

What Is the Solution?

Can high crime rates in urban America be reduced? Is there a way to make our cities safe once again so that a walk through the park in the *daytime* (let alone at night!) can be enjoyed without fear and trembling? Is there a way to make cities secure so that urban parents need not worry when their children play out of eyesight for more than ten seconds?

These are hard but vital questions, and many answers have been proposed. Some are admittedly limited solutions, like that suggested by urban planner Oscar Newman (1972). His idea is that some building and neighborhood designs encourage social participation and, by so doing, inhibit crime, while other buildings and neighborhoods have the opposite effect. High-rise apartment blocks, which Newman believes to be the worst in promoting crime, serve to isolate inhabitants from each other, inhibiting communication and creating many unwatched places where crime can easily occur. Newman argues that crime can be reduced in multifamily housing if

> as low a number of units as possible share a common entry off the street. Designers can position windows, and entries, and prescribe paths of movement and areas of activity so as to provide inhabitants with continuous natural surveillance of the street. . . . [I]nstead of relegating this responsibility to others [police and security guards], it [can be]

assumed by the residents in the natural flow of their everyday activities. (1972, p. 15)

Nowhere is the need to design what Newman calls "defensible space" greater than in the federally subsidized low-income housing that was built during the heyday of urban renewal. Such projects typically have "lobby, stairs, elevator, and corridors . . . open and accessible to everyone . . . interior areas [which] are sparsely used and impossible to survey [and] become a nether world of fear and crime" (Newman 1972, p. 27).

To support his argument, Newman compared crime data from various low-income public housing projects in New York. Some of the findings are as follows:

1. The average crime rate is higher in taller buildings (over six stories) than lower ones. Tall buildings with many (over 1,000) living units are worst of all and appear to "encourage crime by fostering feelings of anonymity, isolation, irresponsibility, [and] lack of identity with surroundings" (1972, p. 28).

2. The larger, taller buildings, which provide less opportunity for residents to know who "belongs" in the building, also have most of their crime in the public areas of buildings themselves (for example, elevators, halls, lobbies, and so on). This pattern does not hold for low-rise buildings, which are supervised more easily by residents.

3. In a comparison of two low-income projects in New York—low-rise Brownsville and high-rise Van Dyke, which are sociologically alike with regard to inhabitants but different architecturally—crime and vandalism were found to be significantly higher in the "less defensible" Van Dyke project. The data used in comparing the Brownsville and Van Dyke projects are presented in Table 13-7. If Newman is right, the physical design of buildings may provide a partial solution to the urban crime problem in the future.

Of course, regardless of architectural design, residents of a building must be motivated to no-

TABLE 13-7
Defensible Space: The Effect of Architecture on Crime

	Brownsville	Van Dyke
	6-Story with Some 3-Story Wings	14-Story (87%) with 3-Story Wings (13%)
Population		
Total Population	5,390	6,420
Average Family Size	4.0	4.0
Percent Minors	57.8	57.5
Percent Black Families	85.0	79.1
Percent Puerto Rican Families	12.4	15.3
Average Annual Income	$5,056	$4,997
Average Number Years There	9.0	8.5
Crime		
Total Crime Incidents	790	1,189
Number of Robberies	24	92
Incidents of Malicious Mischief	28	52

Source: Oscar Newman, *Defensible Space* (New York: Macmillan, 1972), Tables 4, 5, 6. Copyright © 1972, 1973 by Oscar Newman. Adapted by permission of Macmillan Publishing Co., Inc.

tice and respond to potentially criminal situations. There is evidence, for example, that the belief that police will not promptly respond to reported crimes keeps some residents—even in "defensible" buildings—from becoming personally involved in crime prevention (Merry 1981).

Newman's plan, however, is only one that has been proposed as people try to "take back the city" from criminals. Other groups want to proceed differently. Curtis Sliwa of the Guardian Angels thinks street patrols by local citizens is one way to help. Still others, like one neighborhood in New York's Bronx and a town in New Jersey near New York City, have combatted crime through sensitizing all community members to the problem and by having everyone take turns watching for criminal or suspicious behavior. Both have had significant success (Wellisz 1983; Belkin 1983). Yet another approach is suggested by urban critic Roger Starr (1985). He says cities should adopt a "get tough, no nonsense, this has gone far enough!" approach. He lists various strategies, all of which, he claims, will work only if people are thoroughly committed to them. Some of his sug-

gestions: (1) cities need to target special areas— the subways, for example, or an area where numerous robberies take place—and then go all out in an effort to eradicate the problem; (2) mixed racial and ethnic boards need to be established to fight for more jails, more police, and to pressure legislators to reform the laws that let many criminals slip through with little or no punishment; (3) in that regard, we should adopt a policy of punishment that will increase the severity of the jail sentence with each subsequent offense; only this will deter criminals from striking again; and (4) parents and educators must make a commitment, not only to combatting crime directly, but to instilling in their children and students a sense of social responsibility so that they will not be tempted by deviant behavior.

It is difficult to argue with almost any of these plans. Some have already produced important, positive effects. Others promise to do the same. And yet, one wonders if any of them is really anything more than a stopgap, way to put a finger in the dike for a time. They may work, but then another "leak" will spring up somewhere else. In this regard, there is a long history of communities that have attacked certain criminal activities in the city, successfully for a time, only to see those activities reappear later, perhaps in a different location. Drug dealing is a case in point. From time to time a city, understandably fed up with all the consequences of drugs—ruined lives, addicted people, robbed stores—makes an attempt to get the dealers, pushers, and addicts off the streets. Frequently, the effort is successful, and drug dealing is stopped or driven underground for a period. Then, when the vigilance weakens or ceases, drug traffic reappears, with all the same negative consequences.

Is there then no ultimate solution to the problem of urban crime? While no one knows *the* answer, a suggestion, based on the work of Blau and Blau, might be offered. Recall that these researchers saw violent urban crime as an inevitable consequence of a society that produces great disparities in income. These disparities produce similarly great frustration and, in at least some cases, violent reactions. If we want to eliminate violence in our cities, these findings suggest that the only effective and permanent way to do it is to eliminate those great income disparities. If people did not live with the despair and alienation generated by having so much less than others take for granted, we would expect the violence within American society to greatly diminish. Of course, this is a solution that would involve radically reorganizing American society—which wealthier and more powerful Americans would certainly resist.

Herbert Gans suggested that, as a whole, American society really doesn't want to eliminate poverty because the costs to those who are not poor would be too discomforting. Perhaps it is the same with violent urban crime. Naturally we deplore it and are afraid of it (sometimes with good reason). But do we really wish to eliminate the income inequalities that may be its source? Americans have never been too quick to give up what they see as their "fair share," even when that share may be much larger than someone else's. In the end, then, the violence of urban America may be the price that is paid (mostly by the poor) for the "good life" enjoyed by others.

Urban Riots

The summer of 1981 saw dozens of English cities, including London, Manchester, and Liverpool, aflame. Riots that pitted police against white and black attackers and saw widespread looting shook these generally complacent British cities to the core. Although some confrontations between whites and blacks did occur, indicating the presence of deep-rooted racial problems (see Cityscape 1-3 and Case Study 2-2), in most instances the races banded together. The common objectives seemed to be to give the police a drubbing and to make some money in the looting. Said one black participant in the London riots,

> I've been searched every week, man. Stop, search, stop, search. Now I'm getting my own back. I don't care . . . I threw a couple of bricks, hit a couple of policemen. Just getting my revenge back. (*Finger Lakes Times*, 1981, p. 1)

Said a white participant while taking camera equipment from a shattered storefront window,

> It's just a great free-for-all. If you want to know why I'm doing it, I won't give you any of this rubbish about being oppressed. I'm just in it for the money. I'll sell all this stuff . . . I don't think this riot was planned. I happened to be here at the time, so I'm cashing in on it. (*Finger Lakes Times*, 1981, p. 1)

A year earlier a similar scene had been played out in Miami as the predominantly black district of Liberty City erupted into violence in the wake of the acquittal of four police charged with the death of a black businessman. For days, roaming groups of blacks attacked white citizens, ransacked businesses, and traded gunfire with police. Sixteen people died, many more were injured, more still were arrested, and the damage was in the millions of dollars. The unrest spread to Chattanooga, Tennessee, and Orlando, Florida. Blacks clashed with police in Wichita, Kansas, and even in small Wrightsville, Georgia, violence appeared.

A period of far-more-serious rioting began in the mid-1960s. Faced with the failed promise of urban renewal and with continuing limited opportunity, despair and frustration increased among many of the nation's urban poor. On July 18, 1964, the first in a series of riots occurred in the Harlem ghetto of New York. Violence, looting, and burning rocked the area until July 23. A day later, racial violence flared in Rochester, New York. Philadelphia erupted in August, 1964.

In August 1965 the worst riots occurred. The Watts area of Los Angeles endured days of rage in which 34 lives were claimed, injuries climbed to over 1,000, and buildings and businesses by the hundreds were destroyed. Rioting followed in Chicago and San Diego. A year later, violence returned to Los Angeles and Chicago, and riots also took place in Jacksonville, Dayton, San Francisco, and Omaha. Some 40 cities in all had major outbursts of violence.

After the April 1968 assassination of Dr. Martin Luther King, Jr., in Memphis, violence flared once again in over 100 cities in the United States. By the end of the summer, however, an uneasy quiet had settled on urban America.

What Causes Urban Riots?

Riots had occurred many times in American cities before the "long hot summers" of the 1960s. Racial violence directed against blacks occurred, for example, in Atlanta in 1906, Springfield, Illinois, in 1908, St. Louis in 1917, and Washington, D.C., and Chicago in 1919. Other minorities have been victims of rioting as well: in San Francisco anti-Chinese riots took place in the 1870s (see Case Study 15-1). Zane Miller pointed out, however, that the urban riots of the 1960s introduced a new dimension into the matter:

> In previous cases of collective racial violence whites took the initiative, either as a reaction to black competition for jobs and housing or as a response to a black challenge to patterns of racial subordination or segregation in the cities. But in the 1960s blacks struck out first and . . . seemed less interested in attacking white individuals than in flaunting and destroying symbols of white authority and oppression. (1973, p. 58)

But why the pressing need to strike out so violently? To explore this question more deeply, we can reapply the two contrasting theoretical perspectives that we have used throughout the chapter: is the rioter or society responsible?

Rioting Mainly for Fun and Profit. Edward C. Banfield argues that rioting is not caused by any single factor and certainly is not a simple result of poverty and racial tension. He wrote, "If one looks at the facts . . . one sees that race, poverty and injustice, although among the conditions that made the larger riots possible, were not *the causes* of them and had very little to do with many of the lesser ones" (1974, p. 212). Not unexpectedly, Banfield believes the causes of urban rioting are found within the "culture of poverty": restless youth seek excitement and action; others see a chance to profit from looting; some become spontaneously indignant observing an incident (perhaps a police action) on the street. All these rationales—as well as racial hostility—can be seen in the quotes from London rioters given earlier in this section.

Banfield believes that rioting is an ever-present possibility among those who share the lower-class present-time orientation described in Cityscape 13-1. Rioting is not racially based because most blacks report that they are not antiwhite, nor do they see the future as hopeless (Banfield 1974, p. 221). Members of the lower class, black or white, are just more susceptible to rioting than others. The media often make matters worse, Banfield says. Rioting can be triggered easily and spread readily, via television coverage, to lower-class districts of other cities.

Rioting as Urban Conflict. Quite a different analysis follows from a social-conflict perspective. Taking this view, we see the root cause of urban rioting not as a culture of poverty but as economic and racial inequality that exists in American society as a whole.

Looking back over several decades, we recall that cities changed substantially between World War II and the 1960s. For many urbanites these years brought a new suburban home linked by expressways to the downtown. Although largely sharing the same rising expectations, increasing concentrations of urban poor found little cause for optimism. The better schools, better housing, and better jobs were *out there*; the inner city festered with high unemployment and rising crime.

The rage that fueled urban riots, as seen through the social-conflict view, was the result of blocked opportunity for the poor, and especially minorities. Although Banfield is correct in noting that blacks are *hopeful* about the future, this does not mean they *expect* that future to materialize. As Zane Miller puts it, many blacks believe "that even if they somehow managed to secure an education, acquire a decent job, and build a cohesive family, neither they nor their children could escape the ghetto" (1973, p. 58). Young rioters in English cities in the summer of 1981 expressed much the same frustration and hopelessness.

Recent analysis of the state of inner-city ghettos remains pessimistic. As we have seen, there is little evidence that many of the problems we have considered in this chapter have substantially improved. To take a single example, in a survey of the Liberty City riots in Miami, *Time* (1980) reported that blacks in New York continue to occupy over 40 percent of the city's substandard housing, hundreds of thousands remain tied to welfare support (which is falling behind the rapidly rising cost of living), and city services are being cut back. Unemployment among young blacks runs as high as 60 percent, a problem found in many other large cities as well. Similarly, the British economy entered the 1980s with the worst recession since World War II. Worst hit in this crisis were the poor and, especially, the minorities. In the latter group, unemployment among young people approached 75 percent. All these groups (poor, minorities, the young) were predominant in the 1981 riots.

Moreover, research conducted in the wake of urban riots suggests that the disturbances were *not* spontaneous outbursts by a few restless youths, as Banfield's analysis maintains. A sample of blacks surveyed after periods of rioting in 15 cities overwhelmingly attributed the outbreaks not to characteristics of the rioters themselves but to the discrimination, unemployment, and poor housing within the ghetto. In contrast, but not unexpectedly, whites who were interviewed were far more likely to blame rioters and looters themselves for

the outbreaks of disorder (Campbell and Schuman 1968). In the wake of the 1968 Watts rioting, a research team found that, although only about 15 percent of the black residents took an active part in the rioting, up to one-half were sympathetic and did not see the riot as a spontaneous and meaningless event. Furthermore, rioters included some of the more educated and affluent members of the black community (Sears and McConahay 1969, 1973; Tomlinson 1969).

Overall, then, research appears to favor the social-conflict perspective, which sees urban riots as an outcome of historical conflict within the social order. This view was largely supported by the government commission that reviewed the rioting in the 1960s. The conclusion of the Kerner Commission was that racial discrimination was a central cause of the conflict. American society, the report stated, was tragically divided: "Our nation is moving toward two societies, one black, one white—separate and unequal" (1968, p. 1). This is one reason why in the future the least advantaged minorities (blacks and Hispanics), and not the more advantaged minorities (such as Japanese and Chinese), are likely to be deeply frustrated and involved in rioting.

Society's Response to Rioting

Other than calling out the police and—if things get bad enough, the troops—to quell urban rioting, what has been the longer-term response to such outbreaks? Recent research suggests that two patterns have emerged: (1) the strengthening of the police and (2) increased welfare services to the poor.

First, police forces are beefed up, presumably so that the authorities will be better able to practice surveillance of unrest and curtail future outbreaks of violence in riot-torn areas. Pamela Irving Jackson and Leo Carroll (1981) sampled 90 American cities outside the South with populations over 50,000 and measured the racial composition, level of black activist mobilization, and frequency of riots during the 1960s. They found that police expenditures were related significantly to all three variables; that is, cities that had more riots, with a larger black population, and with more politically organized blacks spent more on their police force in the post-riot period.

A related study corroborates these findings. David Jacobs (1979) studied all urban areas with populations over 250,000 in 1960 and 1970. He found that two variables influenced the size of a city's police force: the income spread in the city (when there was a larger gap between rich and poor, the force was larger) and the size of a city's black population (the more blacks, the more police).

Together, the studies suggest that the urban power structure responds to urban violence through more intensive social control. Concludes Jacobs: It is "likely that the government's monopoly of coercive violence is kept in reserve to ensure that asymmetrical . . . relationships will not be disturbed" (1979, p. 23).

The second societal response—increased social services—appears, on the surface, to offer more hope for the disadvantaged. Frances Fox Piven and Richard Cloward (1971) examined two major periods of urban rioting in the United States: the 1960s confrontations previously described and the riots of the 1930s during the Depression. In the latter case, urban violence grew across the country as the destitution occasioned by the economic collapse spread. The response to these confrontations, as Box 13-9 indicates, was for the government to increase relief payments to the poor. In fact, the 1930s saw the rise of a nationwide welfare system composed of work programs, social security for the aged, and unemployment aid. In the late 1960s the response was the same: the riots, underscoring the plight of the poor, helped induce federal, state, and local governments to increase welfare aid. Millions of people were added to the relief rolls and billions were spent. The riots stopped. It seemed some help had arrived.

It was not to be for long, however. After a relatively brief period of much more liberal relief giving, benefits began to be cut back, as if the government had given the poor welfare to help quiet them down. With the poor thus placated, the violence stopped and militant organizations disbanded. Then, "safe" once more, the govern-

> ## BOX 13-9
> ## Urban Riots in the Depression
>
> Without work a way of life began to collapse. Men could not support their families, people lost their farms and their homes, the young did not marry, and many took to the road. Most people suffered quietly, confused and ashamed by their plight. But not all were so acquiescent. . . . Many began to define their hardships, not as an individual fate, but as a collective disaster, not as a mark of individual failure, but as a fault of "the system. . . ."
>
> Groups of men out of work congregated at local relief agencies, cornered and harassed administrators, and took over offices until their demands were met—which usually meant that money or goods were distributed to them. . . . [For example] Chicago was . . . the scene of frequent "rent riots," especially in the black neighborhoods, where unemployment reached catastrophic proportions and evictions were frequent. Groups of as many as a hundred men, often led by Communist Party members, would assemble to put an evicted family's furniture back into the apartment or house. . . . These tactics frequently culminated in beatings, arrests, and even killings, but they also forced relief officials to give out money for rent payments.
>
> Source: Frances Fox Piven and Richard A. Cloward, *Regulating the Poor* (New York Vintage, 1971), pp. 61–63.

ment proceeded to take away what it had given previously, forcing the poor once more into a desperate scramble for survival at the bottom of the social hierarchy. As Piven and Cloward conclude about the 1930s and 1940s (the same argument would apply to the 1960s and 1970s),

Turbulence had produced a massive federal direct relief program; direct relief had been converted into work relief; then work relief was cut back and the unemployed were thrown upon state and local agencies, which reduced aid to the able-bodied in most places and eventually eliminated it in many. What remained were the categorical-assistance programs for the impotent poor—the old, the blind, and the orphaned. For the able-bodied poor who would not be able to find employment or secure local relief in the days, months, and years to come, the federal government had made no provision. (1971, p. 117)

Recently Larry Issac and William Kelly (1981) have tested Piven and Cloward's thesis by using a comprehensive sample of American cities with populations over 25,000 (670 were examined in 1960 and 1970) and by studying the federal government's welfare expenditures between 1947 and 1976. They found that the cities, by and large, did not respond to the riots by increasing their welfare expenditures but that the federal government did. Interestingly, they also found that the frequency of riots was a better predictor of aid increases than riot severity. Their rather chilling conclusion, following Piven and Cloward, was this:

> [T]he well-being of powerless groups has never been the primary focus of welfare policy in capitalist society; instead, its primary focus has been to regulate the threat which relatively large numbers of powerless people may be capable of generating under certain historical conditions. (Isaac and Kelly 1981, p. 1378)

As if in echo, the Reagan administration proposed cuts in aid to the poor equaling $12 billion for its 1982 budget. Cut about $1 billion each would be food stamps, Medicaid, and Aid to Families with Dependent Children. Cut over $4 billion—almost two-thirds of its 1981 budget—were the very programs that presumably would help the poor the most to get out of their situation: public service jobs, job training, and employment programs. In the years since, the administration has not slackened but, rather, has increased its efforts to cut more and more deeply into social programs that primarily benefit the poor and minorities. All of this would seem to exacerbate the underlying frustrations that appear responsible for urban rioting.

Urban Finances[1]

In April 1975, New York, the nation's largest city, the city with the lion's share of international and national trade, the city with a budget of $11.8

billion (the *combined total* budget for the next 48 largest American cities was only $27.3 billion), stood poised on the brink of bankruptcy, unable to pay its bills. Banks that had been giving the city short-term loans for more than a decade to meet its ever-growing expenses refused to issue more. Without help, total urban collapse was imminent: subways would stop running; police and firefighters would not be paid; the city's hospitals, schools, and welfare agencies would close; the streets would not be cleaned; nor would garbage be collected. The worst imaginable urban nightmare was on the horizon.

The financial crisis that New York faced, and still faces, was only the first and most spectacular of the fiscal collapses that have threatened many of the older industrial cities of the Northeast and Midwest in the last half decade or so. In December 1978 the city of Cleveland actually defaulted, becoming the first American city to do so since the Depression (New York, receiving assistance from the federal government at the last moment, stayed barely solvent.) In 1981 Boston was on the financial brink, unable to pay its teachers or keep its subways running. The same year Detroit was running a $121 million deficit and facing the cheery prospect of the 1982 budget being short another $150 million. St. Louis's story is a bit less severe: it was behind only $10 million in 1981 but expected an increased shortfall of some $70 million in 1982.

A number of factors are responsible. The most obvious culprits are the twin forces that are reshaping cities all over America: the move to the Sunbelt and the decentralization of industry and population (Chapter 3). Both are eroding enormously the Northeastern and Midwestern cities' tax bases.

The Sunbelt and Decentralization

Take the Sunbelt migration. As we have seen, literally millions of Americans and thousands of businesses changed their location in a southerly or westerly direction after about 1960. They took their money and income-generating capacity with them. The northern and midwestern cities, highly dependent on the tax revenues and trade gen-

---

[1] Unless specifically noted otherwise, much of the material in this section is based on Auletta 1979; Morris 1980a; and personal communications with Alan Frishman and Pat McGuire.

TABLE 13-8

Geographical Area of the Eight Most Populous U.S. Cities, 1980

Old Industrial Cities (sq. mi.)		Sunbelt Cities (sq. mi.)	
New York	320	Houston	556.4
Chicago	228	Los Angeles	464
Detroit	139.6	Dallas	350
Philadelphia	129	San Diego	320

Source: *Hammond Almanac, 1980*, 11th ed. (Maplewood, N.J.: Hammond Almanac, Inc., 1980). Reprinted by permission.

erated by these people and firms, found themselves trying to provide services with fewer funds.

Even more of a problem, the fiscal plight of the Snowbelt has been aided, albeit unintentionally, by government policies that favor the Sunbelt. For example, government funds in the form of loans often are used for construction of new homes. Since approximately two out of every three new homes are being built in the Sunbelt, the funds are going there rather than northward (Muchnick 1976). Or consider federal programs that benefit cities directly or indirectly. The Reagan administration has drastically reduced the budget of the Economic Development Administration, which gave out $667 million in loans and grants in 1980. Many of its projects are in the Snowbelt, and many are in stages of partial completion. Consider also that the Reagan administration's decision to support building construction for industry in cities is most likely to redirect immense numbers of dollars to the Sunbelt, where new construction is omnipresent. In contrast, Snowbelt cities sit on locations *already built.* David Muchnick saw the trend as early as 1976. Concerning federal aid, he wrote:

> Philadelphia, Detroit, Baltimore, Washington, D.C., Boston, and Cincinnati will lose over $97 million annually among them. By contrast Houston, Dallas, Memphis, New Orleans, Phoenix, Jacksonville, Fort Worth, Miami, El Paso, and Birmingham will gain over $71 million annually. (1976, p. 22)

Not surprisingly, then, a recent study found that the fiscal strength of most Snowbelt cities has de-

clined while that of Sunbelt cities has improved (Mercer and Goldbert 1984).

What about decentralization, the people and businesses moving out of the center city? Can't the Snowbelt cities find a way to tax those who move to the suburbs? It is doubtful. In the North and Midwest the historical trend has been for suburbs to incorporate independently. They are their own governing bodies, and, not surprisingly, they don't want to finance the center city's budget deficits. They believe, probably rightly, that they generally can provide higher-quality services to their own residents by standing clear of the central city's enormous expenses.

Many southern cities have, thus far, been able to respond effectively to decentralization. In comparison to the virtual absence of annexation in the older industrial cities of the North, Sunbelt cities have annexed vast territories. Between 1950 and 1972, for example, Houston annexed 279.5 square miles and Phoenix pulled in 239.9 square miles. In sharp contrast, the 20 largest older industrial cities put together added only 83 square miles between 1930 and 1972 (Gluck and Meister 1979, pp. 133, 164). Table 13-8 illustrates this by presenting the geographical area of the four most populous old industrial cities of the North in comparison to that of the four most populous cities of the Sunbelt.

Other Factors

A third difference between cities of the two regions is that, in general, Sunbelt cities have not

BOX 13-10
"With a Little Help from Our Friends: Middletown Today"

White, Protestant, mid-American Middletown never was among the great metropolises, of course. But early in this century the Middletowns and the Chicagos of America had something in common: they made decisions for themselves and relied on local resources. According to a team of researchers who have reanalyzed Middletown 50 years after the original study by the Lynds (1929), which we discuss in Chapter 12, the state and federal governments are now involved in providing assistance to a majority of the city's 83,000 citizens. This is particularly evident in the area of social services. Says project director Theodore Caplow: "The Federal Government has in effect taken over all the social welfare functions. . . ." (*Time*, Oct. 16, 1978, p. 109). Moreover, two-thirds of Middletown's households depend on the federal government for some income (*Boston Globe*, March 18, 1979). Team member Penelope Austin reported that "in 1903 . . . all of [Middletown's] general revenue was derived from its own sources. By 1942, 14 percent of the city government general revenue came from intergovernmental sources" (1978, p. 10). By 1975, she concluded, most of the city's general revenue came from nonlocal sources, with the federal government supplying the largest amount (1978, p. 11).

Caplow sums up the situation: "In 1924, the federal government was symbolized [only] by the post office and the American flag. . . ." (*Boston Globe*, March 18, 1979). Although local residents continue to think that few things change in Middletown, the federal government now has a pervasive influence—Austin cites 29 agencies and 976 federal programs that shape in one way or another the lives of Middletowners (1978, p. 6).

also turned over to private enterprise. (Gluck and Meister 1978, p. 216)

On the other hand, northern and midwestern cities, for the last half century, increasingly have paid the cost of elaborate welfare systems, provided the best in police and fire service, maintained city hospitals, excelled in educational services from the elementary to the university level, overseen generally excellent transportation and sanitation services, and given superior pensions to most city employees. Were these all to be abandoned as revenues shrank? Then there are the raw costs of maintaining the city. Since the end of World War II they have gone up enormously. Controlled for inflation, the average city's expenses since 1949 have increased fourfold.[2]

Finally, one other factor deserves mention. For the past few decades the federal government has been helping the Snowbelt cities handle their increased social service programs. As we saw in the last chapter, major federal aid to cities began in the Great Depression of the 1930s, increasing in both amount and proportion in many cities until the 1970s. Cities receiving federal aid became increasingly dependent on the government for crucial monies, as Box 13-10 makes clear.

With the recession of the early 1970s, however, and the fiscal hard times of the last fifteen years, the federal government has begun cutting back the amount of money it gives to cities. These cutbacks have left the cities with two options: abandon programs and face a disgruntled political constituency and declining quality of city life or take up the slack by providing the funds themselves. In either direction lies trouble—political, human, or fiscal.

The New York City Fiscal Crisis: An Example

All these factors are writ large in the New York City financial crisis. Unknowingly at first and then with increasing desperation, the city's government began digging itself into deeper and

provided the level of government services that traditionally are found in the older industrial cities. Houston, for example,

has always had a tradition of privatism. There has never been a great deal of concern about the lower classes, and inner-city Chicano and black neighborhoods have few city services. Middle-class neighborhoods hire their own gardeners to care for nearby city parks while private security guards patrol the streets; garbage collection and other services are

---

[2]Alan Frishman, personal communication.

deeper financial straits, although it by no means can be said that the city was completely to blame for its predicament (suburbanization and the Sunbelt movement were strong factors). Nor can it be said that the city readily abandoned commitments to its citizens as the crisis evolved. Indeed, the opposite is the case. In an effort to be all things to all people, to be America's best city, New York kept taking on *more* fiscal responsibility as the years passed. When the crunch came in 1975, it was as much what Charles Morris (1980) calls "the cost of good intentions" as anything else.

The Onset. In the early 1960s New York had a balanced budget. All seemed well. It wasn't. Trends that had been afoot at least since the 1940s were slowly eroding away its apparently healthy financial situation. For example, in 1944 the G.I. Bill of Rights was passed, allowing returning military personnel cheap VA mortgages. Many began moving to the suburbs. In 1953, New York Governor Dewey approved a bill allowing the city to impose a payroll tax that was never implemented. It is estimated that the tax would have brought in over $400 million per year in the 1970s. In 1958 Mayor Robert F. Wagner allowed city employees to unionize. Demands for fringe benefits and pension funds grew. The city paid most.

In 1961 a new city charter was passed, allowing the mayor to *estimate* city expenses for the coming year; hence, on the basis of higher estimates, the city could borrow or spend more money, even though the *actual revenues* had not been collected and conceivably might never be. In 1964 the state passed a law allowing local governments to borrow against uncollected funds to pay for current expenses. New York began to do this the next year, closing a budget gap for 1965 by issuing a short-term bond to investors. The bond, which the city repaid in 90 days with interest, began an incredible trend. Thereafter, when unable to meet current expenses, the city would issue more bonds. It never had trouble getting the money, for investors would jump at the chance. New York was the most vibrant economic area in the country. Its government and budget had always been sound. But the city's expenses skyrocketed

throughout the 1960s. What was the solution? The city issued more bonds. The bonds *had* to be paid off, however, if the city was to maintain its credit rating. So even more bonds were issued— bonds to pay off bonds. As this cycle repeated itself, the city got further and further behind.

In 1966 the New York State Medicaid law was passed. The City picked up a huge and increasing portion of the tab as the federal government's portion of the payments decreased in the next decade. In 1966 Mayor John V. Lindsay gave in to transit unions' demands for higher salaries and more benefits. In 1967 a city panel settled a police pay dispute by siding with the police for higher salaries. Then, in 1968, President Richard Nixon was elected and began cutting back federal contributions to city programs, which New York City made a commitment to keep going at the same level as before. While all this was going on, individuals, families, and especially businesses were beginning to leave the city in record numbers.

The effect of any one of these factors was minimal in a city with a budget approaching $10 billion, but together the effects were colossal. One example will illustrate: in the mid-1970s Time-Life Books left New York for new headquarters in Alexandria, Virginia. The move may have cost the company about $2 million, but the company expected to save some $4 million in taxes and rental costs in a single year. The city felt additional strain as buildings were left behind by both individuals and industry. Abandonment effectively removes real estate from the tax rolls. In many cases the city took over the management of such property, hoping ultimately to resell to private parties. This occurred, however, in only a small number of cases.

In 1971 Governor Nelson Rockefeller signed an amendment to the local finance law, allowing a municipality to issue one-year bonds to cover shortfalls if it underestimated revenues. The City of New York then began "rolling over" earlier bonds (that is, issued new bonds to pay for bonds due as described earlier). In 1973 the Board of Estimates and the City Council approved a Lindsay budget that could not possibly be paid using known sources. From then on it was only a matter of time.

By 1975 the city had a budget of $12.2 billion. (In 1965 it had been $3.3 billion!) This was the second largest budget in the country—only the federal government's was higher. The city was also in debt some $7 billion in long-term loans and $4.5 billion in short-term loans. The story began to come out, bit by bit. The city was short between $1.2 and $1.5 billion for the year, and no one, once everyone knew what the situation was, would lend the city another dime. New York ran out of money on April 14, 1975. The crisis had arrived.

The Aftermath. The city survived, but it was a cliff-hanger. In the story of its recovery is a lesson for all American cities of the 1980s.

The city was bailed out, first by the federal government and second by the imposition of extremely austere policies for the future. The federal assistance did not come easily; in fact, at first it looked like it wasn't coming at all. Said an October 1975 *New York Daily News* headline likely to go down in history, "[President] Ford to City: Drop Dead." Then the government position softened. A three-year plan was devised to help the city recover; it was renewed at the end of 1978 to run through 1981. The city was allowed to borrow $2.3 billion a year in what were called "seasonal loans," but it *had* to pay back the loans at the end of the year if more were to be forthcoming. This amount was cut to $1.65 billion per year in 1978.

To meet its budget and repay its loans, New York then cut back everywhere. In the years since 1975 there have been mass firings of city employees and job freezes (when somebody leaves or retires the position is not refilled) have been instituted. The city, which had 340,000 employees in 1975, had 180,000 in 1981. Police, to take a single example, had decreased from 30,500 in 1975 to 22,000. For the first time, the city began to charge tuition at the City University of New York. The transit fare was raised to the current level of one dollar. Various hospitals have been closed, and the city's contribution to welfare payments has remained constant in spite of inflation. Park services have been cut and libraries closed. The city has reduced the number of garbage pick-ups. Increased productivity has been expected from all city employees and absenteeism benefits have been cut. Various agencies have been consolidated.

The plan has almost worked. The 1981 budget showed a deficit of $268 million, a veritable pittance compared to the 1975 disaster of well over $1 billion. The city has paid off or refinanced all the staggering $4.5 billion in short-term debts of 1975. In 1979 New York went back on the bond market for the first time since 1975 and paid off all bonds it issued. With the 1982 budget, the city went back in the black for the first time since the crisis began. The city's finances have improved every year since.

Conclusion

Is the urban ship, this boat we are all in together, sinking? Or, on the other hand, might it just begin to float again?

In this chapter we have considered a number of major urban problems—poverty, housing, crime, rioting, and the poor state of many cities' finances. We make no claim that this is an exhaustive list of urban ills. We could have focused on the city's environmental problems (like air pollution or water shortages), the problems of urban transportation, or governmental corruption. There are others.

We chose the ones we did partly because they are serious and of concern to most Americans and partly because they are so obviously interrelated. Together they suggest an important lesson about the city: It is a complex, interlocking whole, a human *creation*. More specifically, any city is a product of the culture in which it exists (a point we made in Chapter 7). American cities, then, have been created by American citizens and, just as surely, the problems of these cities have been created by the same citizenry. No doubt few Americans would have consciously *chosen* to create urban poverty, hasten the deterioration of city housing, foster the conditions for extensive criminal activity (much of it violent), set the stage for urban rioting, or put the city into dire straits monetarily. Yet all these things have happened. They are deep-rooted realities of the American urban scene.

Let us suggest, in conclusion, that these problems are a consequence of the way in which we view the world and do business. Most of the available research tends to support the argument that we have these problems because we profit from their existence, because we wish to protect some vested interests at the expense of others, and/or because we simply don't care enough to do what is necessary to eradicate the problems.

The problem of urban finances reveals perhaps most clearly how the plight of cities is linked to events and changes in the larger society. Cities such as Boston, Detroit, and, most spectacularly, New York face financial crises because, in the search for ever-greener pastures, Americans as individuals, families, and firms have abandoned the older, industrial cities for the Sunbelt or abandoned the inner cities all over the country for the "peace and quiet" of the suburbs. In their wake, they have left the inner city awash with expenses and service commitments it cannot possibly handle without massive aid. But, in a more conservative era, the aid which exists, which is inadequate to begin with, is being cut.

Left behind in the exodus have been the urban poor and minorities and the crumbling houses and factories. With its tax base declining precipitously, the city can't take care of, let alone improve, the lot of all these people and places. So, as time passes, deterioration continues. The poor turn to hustling, to crime, and—when at last the load has become unbearable—to explosive violence. People without such problems wonder what is going on.

If theorists like Herbert Gans are right, poverty and its attendant suffering will never be eradicated until Americans decide that the dysfunctions (the costs) of the problem outweigh the functions (the benefits). The same might be argued about the housing problem, the crime problem, or any other of the problems considered in this chapter. Americans have always been an individualistic lot, seeking personal opportunity first. This has its consequences. On the one hand, as long as there are enough resources like wealth, power, and prestige to go around, there can be some benefits for all. But, as Harvey Molotch (1976) has argued, there almost always are limits to growth. If resources like wealth, power, and prestige are in short supply somebody has to get the short straw. The poor and minorities have received the short straw regarding these resources in the modern American city, and they continue to do so. As a result, social critic Anthony Downs recently contended that "many minority group members live in areas that provide a much lower quality of life in every respect than that enjoyed by most whites. Confronted by a triple handicap of shrinking job opportunities, poor education, and low-quality neighborhoods, these minority citizens are caught in a situation from which there appears to be no escape" (1985, p. 285).

This is not to deny progress on some fronts. Poverty levels decreased markedly until about 1970, and only about 5 percent of all Americans now live in substandard housing—a substantial decrease from the Depression era. Moreover, in the last few years, crime rates have dropped somewhat and urban riots have been much less common. Problems certainly remain, but there is some reason for guarded optimism.

Perhaps the most optimism can be drawn from New York's return from the brink. Whether New York City survived its financial crisis or not was of major consequence to over 7 million people directly, the entire nation and much of the world indirectly. Through wrangling and sacrifice, dedicated individuals and groups, who cared about New York as a collective, human enterprise, worked to turn it around: often a very bitter struggle. New York is not out of the woods by any means yet, but there has been, in the last few years, more and more light showing through the trees. If New York, that labyrinthine, gargantuan, crotchety city of cities can make it back from the brink, why not Boston or Chicago or San Diego or St. Petersburg? All it takes is commitment, work, and judicious planning for the urban future.

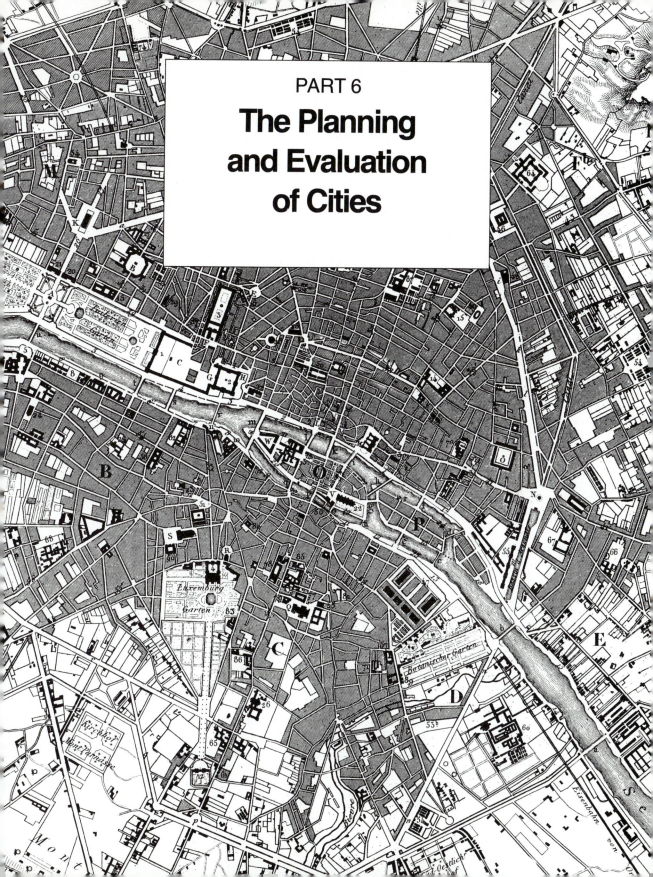

PART 6

The Planning
and Evaluation
of Cities

CHAPTER 14

Planning the Urban Environment

As we have seen, the city doesn't always work well. While occasionally attaining its vaunted status as "pinnacle of human civilization" (for a time in Hellenic Athens perhaps), more typical is the city with significant problems. The last two chapters have demonstrated this with regard to American cities.

In this chapter we shall look to the work of men and women who have reacted to the inadequacies of cities with what are often bold and provocative plans. They believe cities can be made better. Some have tackled the problems of city living at the neighborhood level, while others have conceived of a radical transformation of the city as a whole.

As we might expect, such plans often become the focus of controversy. They frequently collide with established cultural beliefs or with vested economic and political interests. However, a willingness to seriously consider such plans is essential if we are to ensure a continuing dialogue about the quality of urban life and about what we ultimately want our cities to be.

Visions

And when all the world came back
And the light crept up between the shutters
And you heard the sparrows in the gutters,
You had such a vision of the street
As the street hardly understands

T.S. ELIOT, "PRELUDES"

Ebenezer Howard had a vision of the street in the late 1800s. Deeply influenced by Edward Bellamy's novel, *Looking Backward* (a utopian vision of the year 2000 in which all the problems of the city had been eliminated and people lived joyously together), Howard embarked upon an attempt to realize Bellamy's vision in Britain. As he saw it, the industrial city was the core of the problem. People, streaming to these cities in ever-increasing numbers, were suffering overcrowded conditions, misery, and despair.

Howard did not deny that the city had advantages—opportunity, entertainment, diversity—but he believed that the city denied its people the advantages of the country—a healthful environment, a lack of crowding, a sense of freedom. What better way to solve this dilemma than to create a new kind of city that combined the benefits of each setting? As he argued in his *Garden Cities of To-Morrow* in 1898:

> The two magnets must be made one. As man and woman by their varied gifts and faculties supplement each other, so should town and country. The town is the symbol of society—of mutual help and friendly co-operation, of fatherhood, motherhood, brotherhood, sisterhood, of wide relations. . . . The country is the symbol of God's love and care. . . . All that we are and all that we have comes from it. Our bodies are formed of it; to it they return. We are fed by it, clothed by it, and by it we are warmed and sheltered. . . . It is the source of all health, all wealth, all knowledge. . . . Town and country must be married, and out of this joyous union will spring a new hope, a new life, a new civilization. (1898; 1965, p. 48)

To perform the "marriage of town and country," Howard created his Garden Cities plan and set about trying to convince his contemporaries that the plan was not only ethically mandated in terms of human well-being, but practical as well. The outlines of his vision are contained in Cityscape 14-1.

Alas, Howard's vision was, as T. S. Eliot's poem suggests, a vision which the street of his day hardly understood. It struck conservatives as fantastic and liberals as too complex. Said the ultra-liberal *Fabian News*:

> Mr. Howard proposes to pull [our cities] all down and substitute garden cities, each duly built according to pretty colored plans, nicely designed with a ruler and compass. . . . We have got to make the best of our existing cities, and proposals for building new ones are about as useful as would be arrangements for protection against visits from Mr. [H. G.] Wells' Martians [a reference to Wells's novel, *The War of the Worlds*, which depicts a Martian invasion of earth]. (Quoted in Osborn 1965, p. 11)

Undaunted, Howard pushed on. In 1903, in conjunction with a group of businessmen, he established his first garden city, Letchworth, about 35 miles from London. A second city, Welwyn (pronounced "well-en"), was built nearer London in 1919. Although modifications did take place, both were fairly successful at implementing his plans. Until the 1940s, however, they were Britain's only serious attempts at planned new-town development.

The history of urban planning is in many ways writ small in the story of Howard's new towns. As the *Fabian News* indicated, to alter already well-developed cities would be a massive, expensive, and uprooting undertaking. Cities are not only houses and blocks; they are also people and social structures, often with deeply entrenched historical traditions, power relationships, and vested economic interests. Hence, major plans for urban redesign have not always been greeted with rapture. In addition, given the consequences that *bad* city planning has on the lives of so many, it is a task not to be undertaken lightly.

The History of City Planning

Planning in World History

Ebenezer Howard was hardly the first to undertake urban planning on a large scale. Moenjo-Daro, the Indus River Valley civilization of 2500 B.C. that we discussed in Chapter 2, had streets laid out in a distinctive grid pattern, broad avenues obviously planned as thoroughfares, and individual houses designed for comfort and efficiency. Even more impressive were the Mexican cities of Teotihuacán around A.D. 700 and Tenochtitlán (Box 8-1) around A.D. 1500. Both capitals had tremendous size, efficiency, and symbolism. Planned plazas, massive temples, and elaborate gardens were central aspects of these cities. Finally, recall Case Study 7-1, which discussed the tightly controlled plan of Ming Dynasty Peking. Here we saw planned city within planned city, all connected to reveal the important themes of China's culture.

Western cities also show a long history of planning. A great deal of Hellenic Athens was planned, as were the areas used to express the pomp and majesty of Imperial Rome. Even towns

CITYSCAPE 14-1
Sir Ebenezer Howard's Garden Cities of To-Morrow

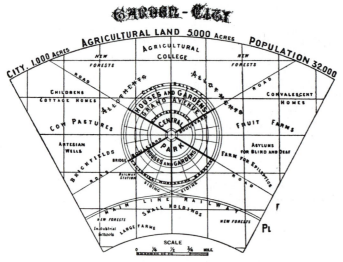

Figure 14-1 *The Garden City and rural belt. Source: Ebenezer Howard,* Garden Cities of To-Morrow *(Cambridge, Mass.: MIT Press, 1965), p. 52. Reprinted by permission.*

Howard's Garden City was to cover about 1,000 acres at the center of a 6,000-acre tract. Figure 14-1 shows the idealized layout of the whole municipal area.

Six magnificent boulevards—each 120 feet wide—traverse the city from centre to circumference, dividing it into six equal parts or wards. In the centre is a circular space containing about five and a half acres, laid out as a beautiful and well-watered garden; and, surrounding this garden, each . . . in its own ample grounds, are the larger public buildings—town hall, principal concert and lecture hall, theatre, library, museum, picture-gallery, and hospital.

The rest of the large space encircled by the "Crystal Palace" is a public park, containing 145 acres, which includes ample recreation grounds within very easy access of all the people.

Running all round the Central Park (except where it is inter-sected by the boulevards) is a wide glass arcade called the "Crystal Palace," opening on to the park. This building is in wet weather one of the favourite resorts of the people, whilst the knowledge that its bright shelter is ever close at hand tempts people into Central Park, even in the most doubtful of weathers. Here manufactured goods are exposed for sale, and here most of that class of shopping which requires the joy of deliberation and selection is done. The space enclosed by the Crystal Palace is, however, a good deal larger than is required for those purposes, and a considerable part of it is used as a Winter Garden—the whole forming a permanent exhibition of a most attractive character, whilst its circular form brings it near to every dweller in the town—the furthest removed inhabitant being within 600 yards.

Passing out of the Crystal Palace on our way to the outer ring of the town, we cross Fifth Avenue—lined, as are all the roads of the town, with trees—fronting which, and looking on to the Crystal Palace, we find a ring of very excellently built houses, each standing in its own ample grounds; and, as we continue our walk, we observe that the houses are for the most part built either in concentric rings, facing the various avenues (as the circular roads are termed), or fronting the boulevards and roads which all converge to the centre of the town. . . . [T]he population of this little city may be . . . about 30,000 in the city itself, and about 2,000 in the agricultural estate. . . .

On the outer ring of the town are factories, warehouses, dairies, markets, coal yards, timber yards, etc., all fronting on the circle railway, which encompasses the whole town, and which has sidings connecting it with a main line of railway which passes through the estate. This arrangement enables goods to be loaded direct into trucks from the warehouses and workshops, and so sent by railway to distant markets, or to be taken direct from the trucks into the warehouses or factories; thus not only effecting a very great saving in regard to packing and cartage, and reducing to a minimum loss from breakage, but also, by reducing the traffic on the roads of the town, lessening to a very marked extent the cost of their maintenance. The smoke fiend is kept well within bounds in Garden City; for all machinery is driven by electric energy, with the result that the cost of electricity for lighting and other purposes is greatly reduced.

Source: Ebenezer Howard, *Garden Cities of To-Morrow* (Cambridge, Mass.: MIT Press, 1965), pp. 50–56.

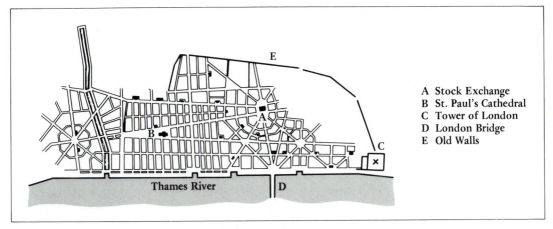

A Stock Exchange
B St. Paul's Cathedral
C Tower of London
D London Bridge
E Old Walls

Figure 14-2 *Sir Christopher Wren's plan for the rebuilding of London, 1666. Source: Arthur B. Gallion and Simon Eisner,* The Urban Pattern, *4th ed. (New York: Van Nostrand, 1980), p. 43. Reprinted by permission of Van Nostrand Reinhold.*

of the Middle Ages had considerable planning. Walls were built for protection, and, within them, various districts were "zoned" for specific activities. There were planned markets, squares, residential quarters, and, always, the medieval church at the city's center. Still later, during the Renaissance, there arose a veritable boom in urban planning.

Why Plan?

The motives of early city planners are important to understand. First, the desire to solve specific urban problems certainly is at the center of much that was done. Underground sewage lines were planned for health reasons, walls for protection, parks for leisure hours, and thoroughfares to facilitate movement.

Second, although we do not know much about Moenjo-Daro, the motives of city planners in Teotihuacán, Tenochtitlán, Peking, and Rome were linked as often to the glorification of those in power as they were to practical concerns. Thus, the Emperor Augustus and his successors, who had been declared gods by the Roman Senate in the first few decades of the Christian era, were "immortalized" by buildings, parks, plazas, and innumerable statues. It also is understandable that city planners would glorify the ruling elite for

yet another reason: the elite, after all, employed them. City planning, therefore, has frequently proceeded "from the top down." Those with wealth and power decide what is to be built and employ planners to realize their desires. Thus the question of *why* people plan cities always is tied up inextricably with the question of *for whom* they are planned. Some plans are meant to favor only some of the city's groups and classes—frequently to the exclusion or detriment of others.

A third focus of urban planning is often the glorification or revivification of important cultural values. Thus, Ming Peking was not only a monument to the all-powerful emperor but a reminder to its citizens of all the beliefs that were central to the Chinese way of life. Of course, not only do values vary across cultures, they also shift across history.

For example, during the Renaissance, the residency of the Pope was reestablished in Rome. Because the church was the most important and wealthiest institution in the Western world, Pope Julius decided to replace the old St. Peter's Basilica with the greatest cathedral and piazza in Christendom. The result was the large, grand Piazza of St. Peter. A long processional way leads the visitor into the massive circular area before the cathedral and then into the cathedral itself. For the faithful, religious reverence is probably the most powerful response to a visit to St. Peter's. For others, awe at the structure is usually paramount. Both reactions were important to the piazza's designers.

Something different is symbolized in Figure 14-2, Sir Christopher Wren's plan for the rebuilding of London after the Great Fire of 1666 (Case Study 2-2). Here, although the magnificent St. Paul's Cathedral (B) is a dominant focus, all roads lead not to the cathedral but to the city's stock exchange (A). The dominant feature of the plan (which ultimately was not adopted) was the financial and trade element of the city's life. London at the time was fast becoming the most powerful economic center in the world. Religion, dominant earlier in British history, was being replaced by economic concerns, and city planning reflected this change.

Three concerns, then, appear again and again in the history of urban design. People plan cities (or parts of them) (1) to solve specific problems, (2) to serve the interests of particular individuals or groups (most frequently the powerful and wealthy), and/or (3) to reflect and intensify (sometimes unconsciously) certain cultural ideals.

Planning in the Industrial Era: 1800–1900

Ebenezer Howard was reacting to the same overcrowded, powerful, and seemingly uncontrollable cities as were the classic sociological theorists of the city—Toennies, Durkheim, Simmel, Park, and Wirth—whom we discussed in Chapter 4. Howard saw little hope for the industrial city, which he believed was a slave to production, greed, and the interests of the few rather than the many. True city planning, he believed, could never exist in such cities because of their size. There were too many forces at work.

In many ways, he was right. Planning on a city-wide scale did not exist in many early industrial cities. While quite a few industrial towns were planned and built during the 1800s—Manchester and Birmingham in England and Pullman, Illinois (Chapter 12), in the United States are good examples—by and large the underlying plan of the industrial era was "efficiency."

For example, when New York—then New Amsterdam—was settled at the tip of Manhattan Island by the Dutch in the early 1600s, street development evolved more or less irregularly, as in many medieval European cities. But, as the city expanded northward, the city founders decided to adopt a rigid gridiron plan that would cover the entire island irrespective of topography. The goals of this plan were efficiency and economics, the trademarks of the industrial era. "Straight-sided and right-angled houses," reported the city commission that adopted the gridiron plan in 1811, "are the most cheap to build and the most convenient to live in" (Gallion and Eisner 1980, p. 49).

In this new trade-dominated city, tradition counted little. Buildings went up ony to be torn down as commercial interests dictated. Indeed, the average life of a Manhattan building today is only about 20 years. Architectural styles, such as Greek facades, are adopted "for show," and not for their deeper symbolism of a revered historic tradition (Goldberger 1979, p. XIV). With the major (and wonderful) exception of Central Park, the whole of New York was fundamentally shaped by the profit motive.

Reaction against this industrial-commercial city began to appear in the United States as problems—such as massive poverty, pollution, and lack of concern for *public* as opposed to *private* interests—became more and more apparent. In urban planning this reaction was tied to the debate over whether the industrial-commercial city would ever be expected to adequately meet the needs of all its citizens.

The "City Beautiful" Movement

The first significant innovation in American city planning was an outgrowth of the 1893 Chicago World's Fair, which showcased architect Daniel Burnham's "White City" (his vision of the opposite of grimy, sooty, industrial cities). Burnham proposed a city built around monumental civic centers, with careful zoning, and focused on citizen participation groups. Inspiring a "City Beautiful" movement, Burnham's ideas had considerable influence among urban planners across the country. Washington, San Francisco, Detroit, Los Angeles, Minneapolis, St. Louis, and Cleveland all initiated City Beautiful projects after the fair.

Yet the movement soon ran into difficulties. Implementation of these beautification and zoning plans was costly; hence, more often than not, corners were cut in an attempt to save. Moreover, for many City Beautiful projects to be successful, private interests, especially businesses, had to be willing to compromise some of their parochial concerns. Many were *not* willing, and, given the reluctance of most American city governments to interfere with private enterprise, the plans—and with them the City Beautiful movement—died.

The real problem, Ebenezer Howard would have said, was that the focus was wrong. Burnham wanted to change the already existing city. This was a mistake. The real solution could only be in the construction of completely new communities.

"Till We Have Built Jerusalem": The New Towns Movement

I will not cease from mental strife,
Nor shall my sword sleep in my hand,
Till we have built Jerusalem
In England's green and pleasant land

WILLIAM BLAKE

With this stanza from the great English poet and artist, William Blake, Sir Ebenezer Howard opened his book *Garden Cities of To-Morrow* in 1898. Howard's belief that his New Towns Movement would solve all of urban society's ills influenced many others both in and beyond his native England.

A Feminist/Socialist New Town in America

One person influenced by Howard was Alice Constance Austin, an upper-class radical from Santa Barbara, California. Convinced of the oppressive nature of the traditional woman's place in society, Austin proposed a series of new towns based upon communal living and kitchenless houses in the early 1900s. Only a "Socialist City," as she called her vision, could relieve women "of the thankless and unending drudgery of an inconceivably stupid and inefficient system, by which her labors are confiscated. . . ." (1935, p. 63).

With help from coinvestors, Austin, like Howard, actually founded her new town, Llano del Rio, in California. But also like Howard she soon found that financing such a venture was fraught with difficulties. After a brief tenure, the Llano group folded in 1917. Although they later resettled in New Llano, Louisiana, Austin's Socialist City movement never attained a great deal more success (Hayden 1978, pp. 286–287).

Later New Towns in Britain

The devastation of London during World War II created a desperate housing shortage and renewed interest in Ebenezer Howard's vision. In 1946 the British New Towns Act was passed, providing for government sponsorship of new urban communities that would relieve overpopulation in London and other cities. These communities—complete with industrial, housing, and commercial areas—were to be built at some distance from larger cities. Indeed, one of the central ideas of the New Towns Act was to limit London's increasing sprawl by surrounding the city with a "green belt"—an idea taken directly from Howard. The new towns then would be constructed beyond the green belt.

Since the passing of the act, thirty-four new towns have been built or started in Great Britain, their success in large measure assured because of government involvement in the form of a public corporation. The first group of new communities, called the Mark I towns, adhered rather closely to Howard's ideas and the successes of Letchworth and Welwyn. They were planned to have about 30,000 residents and to be completely self-contained in terms of industry, housing, education, and transportation facilities. Single-family housing units were predominant, and neighborhoods were to be the focus of social life.

A second wave of new towns—the Mark II group—was begun in the 1950s and 1960s and deviated rather significantly from Howard's original plan. Typified by Cumbernault, outside Glasgow, Scotland, these towns reflected the government's concern that cities of only 30,000 would do little in the long run to alleviate population problems in the larger cities. There also was concern that too many small towns would eat up significant amounts of what Britain had precious little of: land. Thus, the Mark II towns, with population projections of up to 80,000, began to sacrifice greenery for density and to emphasize central (rather than neighborhood) shopping and recreational facilities. The most recent new towns push these concerns even further. One example is the new town of Milton Keynes, west of London, planned for an eventual population of 250,000.

Most of Britain's new towns have survived. People have adjusted quite well to living in this "marriage of the city and country," as Howard called it, and the towns have been eminently successful at providing jobs for their citizens (Michelson 1977). On other levels, however, the new towns have been less successful. Their small number (34) and the limitations they purposely impose on population growth have provided, as some feared, relatively little absorption of the population overspill of the large cities. Moreover, many of the towns are socially homogeneous and rather cliquish, with ethnic and class prejudices quite similar to those encountered in most large cities. Some observers believe this is a product of the planning process itself, with its emphasis on neighborhoods. As sociologists long have noted, in-group solidarity (which neighborhood living facilitates) often creates a corresponding sense of out-group hostility.

Another problem has been the general inflexibility of many of the new-town plans. Rather than recognizing that cities, even small ones, are dynamic entities that must adjust to changing human needs, many new towns have stuck to their original plans past what some observers believe is the point of reason. The result often has been a sense of stagnation, rigidity, and inefficient use of resources (Michelson 1977). As British sociologist Peter Hall suggests, most of the original new-town planners

> . . . were concerned with the production of blueprints, or statements of the future end state of the city. . . . [In] most cases they were far less concerned with planning as a continuous process which had to accommodate subtle and changing forces in the outside world. Their vision seems to have been that of the planner as omniscient ruler, who would create new settlement forms, and perhaps also destroy the old, without interference or question. The complexities of planning in a mixed economy where private interests will initiate much of the development that actually occurs, or in a participatory democracy where individuals and groups have their own, often contradictory notions of what should happen—all these are absent from their writings. . . . (1975, pp. 78–79)

Consequently, what the British new towns have, argues Ray Thomas (1984), is an "image problem." Conceived as architectural wonders that solve major urban problems, the new towns have been overlooked for their more mundane, but *significant*, successes—site development, sewage systems, a continuing centralized planning agency, and, most important of all, economic vitality. As we shall see, these same problems crop up again and again in city planning efforts.

New Towns and Cities in Western Europe, Australia, and Brazil

In one sense the early British new towns were almost anti-city. They were indeed *towns*, their size revealing a distinct dislike of large urban areas and correspondingly large problems. They were also antigrowth. They limited their population strictly, in the belief that more was always less. More population could lead only to disorder and the destruction of the delicate ecological balance between the good life and the surrounding environment.

A concern of more recent new towns, however, is the very opposite. In Holland, Spain, and France, new-town development attempts to stimulate the growth of an entire urban region. Creating jobs around some group of industries, these communities attempt to entice population from the countryside, at the same time keeping down the population of nearby established cities by luring away their residents. In at least some of these cases, the term "new *town*" takes on ironic implications. One such "town," near the Mediterranean port city of Marseilles in France, is expected to have a population of 750,000 people. In a recent conference in the United States, officials from both the Dutch and French new-town programs expressed significant satisfaction with their countries' efforts. In both cases, the new towns have reduced housing pressures in the older cities and curtailed the willy-nilly growth of suburbs (U.S. Dept. of Housing and Urban Development 1985).

A similar "pro-big-city" pattern exists in the Scandinavian countries, particularly Sweden (Michelson 1977), where emphasis is on new towns as more efficient suburbs. Stockholm, like many European and North American cities, began to have a problem with suburban sprawl in the 1950s. In an effort to curb this decentralization, the Swedish government planned a series of satellite cities linked to one another and the central city by efficient transportation. The five cities, known as the Vällingby Complex, are distinct entities but are dependent upon the larger city for goods, many services, and jobs. Each city has approximately 10,000 people living in low-density housing within 300 yards of the subway-station/plaza complex. Despite its general success, recent evidence suggests that, on the whole, life in Vällingby is much the same as life in an American suburb (Popenoe 1977). There are the same difficulties with ethnic sameness and boredom. Perhaps affluent suburban life in any Western country is the same, regardless of the plan.

Australia presents us with a different example—a new *city* designed to be the core of a new urban region centered on the national government. Located in the outback (isolated rural area) Canberra is some 180 miles from the seacoast metropolis of Sydney. Settled as early as 1912, Canberra was to be a new, inland city that would not only house the Australian government but would also begin to develop the Australian hinterland (Robinson 1975). This was no simple task. Canberra was far from Australia's normal trade routes and had no major resources (such as mineral deposits or cheap water power) that would attract investors. Thus, of necessity, the government and the planners have been in complete control (Ebenezer Howard would have liked this).

The result is a physically beautiful city with numerous economic and social difficulties. Economically, the city has suffered because of its location off the beaten track, unavoidable overreliance on a single product (government services), and the implementation of relatively rigid plans into which business fits if it can. For example, since the government controls all land, open bidding for center-city land (a process we discussed in Chapter 6) does not occur. As a result, businesses are scattered throughout the city and the competition that usually keeps prices down has not appeared.

Canberra's plan also has had social consequences. Robinson (1975) reported that the government's insistence on the use of widely dispersed single-family dwellings has hindered the development of a sense of community. Similarly, the city's dependence on one major employer—the government—has tended to create an upper- and middle-class city. This problem has been exacerbated by the inflation-fueled high cost of living. Most low-income families simply cannot afford to live there.

Brasilia, the new inland capital of Brazil, presents a contrasting case. Conceived in the 1950s as a showcase for a modernizing Brazil, the new city is situated some 600 miles from the coastal megalopolis of Rio de Janeiro. Like Canberra, Brasilia was supposed to generate urban development of the interior and siphon off population from the country's older cities. Designed by architect Lucio Costa, its core was meant to serve both as the home of the government and as a residential center. To this end, Costa designed massive office buildings and "superblocks" of apartments. Surrounding the city center, a series of satellite towns—something like those in Vällingby, Sweden—were planned to absorb additional population.

The population of Brasilia in 1957 was 12,000. By 1970 it had grown to over 500,000, an increase much larger and quicker than planned. The city couldn't keep up. Many parts of the original plan were abandoned or modified as people looking for work in the massive construction industry continued to stream into the city. As elsewhere in Brazil and Latin America, those unable to find adequate housing constructed their own out of anything they could find. Thus Brasilia began to evolve huge *favelas* or squatter shantytowns of working-class and poverty-stricken people. Like their counterparts throughout the Third World, these shantytowns lack virtually all the modern amenities; they have no adequate waste removal, transportation, water, or electricity (Epstein 1974). Somewhat ironically, then, this "model" Brazilian city has come to reflect in very short order all the problems that beset the Third World urban situation generally. As if in echo, the same difficulties have beset other state-sponsored new towns in the Third World, such as Chandigarh in India and Ciudad Guyana in Venezuela. All this suggests that new town or not, cities are part of a much larger and more powerful cultural and historical situation than idealistic visions might indicate.

In summary, the distinguishing characteristics of all the contemporary new towns and cities considered thus far is that all have been government sponsored. While some interaction with the private sector has occurred in most cases, it has never been allowed full rein in determining how the city should be planned. The opposite has been the case in the United States. With the exception of one program in the 1930s, modern American new towns are distinguished by their nearly complete dependency on the investments, plans, and ideals of private citizens and corporations.

New Towns in America: Some Examples

First, let us take a moment to consider the exceptions. Only three exist and all had their origin in the Great Depression of the 1930s, when millions of Americans were out of work.

In 1935, President Franklin Delano Roosevelt signed the Emergency Relief Appropriation Act and the National Industrial Recovery Act. One of the provisions of these acts was a federally sponsored project called "Greenbelt Towns." As its name implies, the project was deeply influenced by Ebenezer Howard. Its stated objectives:

1. To give useful work to men on unemployment relief.
2. To demonstrate in practice the soundness of planning and operating towns according to certain garden city principles.

3. To provide low rent housing in healthful surroundings, both physical and social, for families that are in the low-income bracket. (Stein 1957, p. 119)

The three towns constructed as part of the project were Greenbelt, Maryland (13 miles northeast of Washington, D.C.), Greendale, Wisconsin (7 miles from Milwaukee), and Green Hills, Ohio (5 miles north of Cincinnati). There were high hopes that these towns would help to solve big-city problems and contribute significantly to a public-works alternative for ending the Depression.

But the hopes did not come to fruition. First, the towns were planned, as the British new towns had been, to attract their own industry. This never really happened. Built before the era of superhighways and lightweight machinery, they simply did not provide enough economic incentive for major industry to leave the large cities. They thus became, and remain, more like suburbs of the large cities nearby than the independent small cities they were envisioned to be. Second, all such projects require time to develop properly. By the time the towns were getting established, World War II intervened and crucial funding was diverted to military and other objectives. Third, in reaction to the ascendancy to superpower status of the Soviet Union in the postwar era, many argued that these government-sponsored towns smacked of "communism." Intimidated by such rhetoric, in 1949 Congress passed Public Act 65, which allowed the new towns and the greenbelts surrounding them to be sold to private interests. Thus ended the brief tenure of government-sponsored new towns in America.

Nevertheless, the idea of new towns in America is hardly dead. Since the 1920s, private developers with very little government assistance have attempted to build over 100 new urban environments where none existed before (Michelson 1977). A partial list would have to include at least these famous efforts: Baldwin Hills Village near Los Angeles (1941); Park Forest (1947) and Park Forest South (1968) near Chicago; Jonathan, Minnesota (1969); St. Charles, Maryland (1970); and Soul City, North Carolina (1972). But by far the most well-known American new towns are

Radburn, New Jersey (1928); Reston, Virginia (1962); and Columbia, Maryland (1963).

Developed by architect and planner Clarence Stein and later written about at length in his classic and influential *Toward New Towns for America* (1957), Radburn was a direct attempt to develop in the United States a modified version of Ebenezer Howard's garden city. The city is laid out using what Stein called "superblocks," all of which are surrounded by green spaces. Radburn also attempted to provide complete separation of pedestrian and automobile traffic. Stein and cofounder Henry Wright planned access roads only for service purposes and built houses facing the inner green areas, rather than the roads. In 1929 Geddes Smith described Radburn as follows:

> [It is a] town built to *live* in—today and tomorrow. A town "for the motor age." A town turned inside-in—without any backdoors. A town where roads and parks fit together like the fingers of your right and left hands. A town in which children need never dodge motor-trucks on their way to school. (As quoted in Stein 1957, p. 44)

Like so many new towns, however, Radburn ran into financial difficulties as the years passed and was never completed as originally planned.

Reston and Columbia, on the other hand, both near Washington, D.C., are still in the process of realizing their planners' visions. Twenty-five miles from downtown Washington, in suburban Virginia, Reston is the brainchild of developer Robert Simon, who projected an ultimate population of over 70,000 for his "quality urban environment." Planned around two town centers and seven villages of approximately 10,000 residents each, Reston was designed to be as self-sufficient as possible in terms of industry and to provide a broad range of housing, from high-rise luxury apartments to single-family homes on large lots.

Although very beautiful architecturally, the town never attracted the population Simon hoped for. As a result, it began losing money in the late 1960s. Gulf Oil, the town's principal investor, was forced to take over and modify many of Simon's original plans in an attempt to put Reston in the black.

Here we see in high relief the fundamental problem associated with the private development of new towns: Reston *had to turn a profit* to be feasible for its investors. Failing to do so, only two paths remained: the town had to be modified or abandoned.

Columbia, in Maryland, also was designed as a money-maker. Said James Rouse, the town's developer, Columbia's basic goals were "to create a social and physical environment which works for people and nourishes human growth and to allow private venture capital to make a profit in land development and sale" (as quoted in Bailey 1973, p. 16). In order to apply the best thinking available to the execution of his city, Rouse employed a bevy of specialists in the planning phase, including government employees, family counselors, recreationalists, sociologists, economists, educators, health specialists, psychologists, and transportation and communications experts. The result has been the most successful American new town.

Like Reston, Columbia is planned ultimately to have seven villages centered around a downtown. Its population in 1981 was estimated as 110,000, and it is hoped that the city eventually will be a center for a surrounding population of over 250,000. In addition, unlike many American new towns, Columbia was planned to house a low-to-moderate-income group in 300 housing units scattered throughout the city.

Reston and Columbia were products of the 1960s. Encouraged by the partial success these and other new towns had achieved, in 1970 the federal government instituted the New Communities Program, which was to provide federal assistance to private developers in the building of 13 more new towns. The program was a near disaster. It was reduced to a salvage operation by 1974, partially dismantled in 1978, and completely shut down in 1983, when 12 of the 13 communities were unable to meet their financial obligations (Rodwin and Evans 1981; U.S. Dept. of Housing and Urban Development 1985). At present the new-town movement in the United States is all but dead. Why has what seemed to be such a good idea at its inception done so poorly? To find out, we need to review the major goals of the worldwide new-town movement and then examine some criticisms.

Have They Worked? Criticisms of New Towns

All in all, quite a few new towns have been built since Ebenezer Howard sounded the clarion call in 1898. But the tale told by the ledger at this point is muddled, at best. Some, particularly in Europe, have been successful; most have not. Why?

One major goal of most new towns was decentralization. Howard and those who followed thought that the big city was destructive of human life. Overcongestion created major problems in adequate delivery of services and in daily interaction of people, and the city's economic dominance sapped the rest of the region of any vitality. New towns would provide alternative, controlled employment and help distribute population more widely.

Critics argue that new towns really haven't done much along these lines. Regarding population absorption, even in Britain, where new towns have been strongly established for nearly three decades, less than one percent of the population lives in them (Alonso 1970). Moreover, to finance the amount of new housing that would be needed to make a dent in the so-called overpopulation problem is probably impossible. Finally, there is strong evidence—Canberra in Australia and Reston in America are two good examples—that many new towns are not attractive enough to pull in the population they want and need. Hence, Alonso (1970) argues that the improvement of already-existing center-city housing is much more economically efficient.

In terms of the second goal of providing adequate employment and economic advantages, the towns also have had their problems. Few have attracted enough industry or business to employ their residents, frequently despite prodigious efforts. As a result, most American towns have developed a strong suburban flavor—a large proportion of their residents work elsewhere.

Here again, the key factor seems to be cost. It is still more advantageous for most firms to locate in or near the larger cities than to relocate in new towns. Even if firms do relocate outside the central city, as many have in the last two decades, location decisions are based almost exclusively on transportation cost considerations. For instance, firms dependent on trucking are almost certain to relocate on an immediately accessible superhighway rather than a new-town site. So, all things considered, the towns have not been terribly successful at decentralizing population or economic activity. There seems little likelihood that they would do better in the near future.

Another goal was to improve the quality of urban life. The garden city, Howard believed, would be the "new Jerusalem," the "good city" that always had been implicit but hardly ever realized in the city's long and tumultuous history. Provide the right environment, he argued, and people would be happy. Are they?

On the level of life-satisfaction, results are rather mixed. In a study of ten planned communities in the United States (including Columbia, Reston, and Radburn), Lansing, Marans, and Zehner (1975) found 19 percent of these communities' residents saying their lives were "completely satisfying," while 73 percent said life was "pretty satisfying," and 8 percent replied "not very or not at all satisfying." These results seem impressive until they are compared with the results of a national survey of Americans' life satisfaction that indicated 24 percent as "completely satisfied," 66 percent as "pretty satisfied," and 10 percent as "not very or not at all satisfied." When the researchers examined the ten communities individually, they found that the more highly planned communities, like Reston and Columbia, received somewhat higher life-satisfaction scores than the less-planned communities. But this small difference may not be attributable to the community itself. Residents of highly planned communities pay much more for their homes and are more financially secure than their counterparts in less-planned communities; hence, their wealth might be the cause of their greater satisfaction (Michelson 1977).

The issue of income level—or, more generally, social class—is important. A third goal of the new towns was to minimize, if not to eliminate, negative strains and conflicts that often accompany social differences in city living. Has this happened? On one level it is rather difficult to judge, because only Great Britain and a few other countries in the West have made concerted efforts to include members of all social strata in their new towns. In the United States the control of the new town by profit-seeking developers has made most towns so expensive that they are virtually off limits to low-income people. In Canberra in Australia, government policies have produced a similar effect.

But where social-class mixtures do exist, the results have not been encouraging. Brasilia, as we have seen, has evolved major social distinctions between its upper-income and shantytown residents (Epstein 1974), and Michelson (1977) reports on the class-related cliquishness of many British new towns. In the United States, there has been the not-so-encouraging case of Columbia, the one new town that has made an effort to include low-income people. In a recent study of Columbia's poor, Sandberg (1978) found class-bound antagonisms right below the surface. The poor were seen as "different" by the wealthier residents of Columbia and often were shunned or excluded from important aspects of community life. As one working-class mother interviewed by Sandberg put it,

> This is a city, you know, and where you have a city, you have people and you have problems. So all I did for my kids was struggle and work hard and move 'em to a better environment. Things I thought I was gettin' 'em away from, they still exist right here. (1978, p. 225)

Another study, by long-term Columbia resident and social anthropologist Lynne C. Burkhart (1981), has confirmed Sandberg's observations about the importance of class and race in Columbia's daily life.

Next, there is the issue of community control. Ebenezer Howard wanted new towns to be truly "of the people, by the people, and for the people"—that is, environments where the local citizenry—not some abstract state or corporate entity—is in control. Has this happened?

In some cases, only to a limited extent; in others, not at all. A study of Columbia argued that little sense of a community "of the people" has evolved (Brooks 1974). Indeed, Brooks believes that the very nature of the privately developed

new town mitigates against such a sense of community participation. In this most successful of American new towns, Brooks found continuing conflict among developers, the county, and the residents, as well as tensions within all three groups.

Finally, there is the "image" problem mentioned by Thomas (1984). Somehow, to most Westerners, new towns seem somewhat "artificial," the products of someone else's vision. Most Westerners desire the freedom to move and are not enthusiastic about the amount of commitment to community life new towns seem to require. As a result, Thomas argues, the very real successes of new towns at solving important but less "flashy" problems (like sewage and transportation) are ignored or denigrated. Most people, it appears, simply do not want to live in them.

In reviewing new-town development in Britain and Australia, where government involvement has been integral, Robinson (1975) concludes that surprisingly little power is exercised by the people. In both countries government agencies seek almost obsessively to maintain control, as if in fear that the local citizenry would destroy the town vision. The same dominance of local affairs by government agencies and large business concerns is even more prevalent in Brasilia.

Putting it all together, then, the tally could be more impressive. New towns have not significantly decentralized population and economic activity, they cannot claim to have produced a strikingly better urban life or to have eliminated or reduced social tensions, nor can they claim to have created urban environments run by the people.

Most of these problems can be seen at work in the spectacular collapse of the United States' New Communities Program of 1970. In a postmortem, Rodwin and Evans suggest that the following factors led to the program's demise: First, the initial financial burden placed on the private developer, even with federal assistance, was enormous. New towns take time to build and even more time to turn a profit. Most developers could not afford the costs that built up while they were waiting for profit to materialize. Second, the amount of commitment to the program, even from the federal government, was not nearly as strong as necessary to make the new towns successful. New towns are the dream of a few—some city planners, a few public officials, architects, builders, mayors. Many others who could help finance such programs think these efforts could be much more effectively placed elsewhere—in inner-city development, for example, or in the elimination of slum housing. Hence, enthusiasm for the new-towns project was always limited at best. Third, state and local support for the projects was wanting. Because of the federal government's limited backing of the projects, it was imperative that regional authorities help the new towns out in various ways, both political and financial. But such support was hard to come by. There was the lack of enthusiasm just mentioned, as well as financial and political considerations (Rodwin and Evans 1981). The compounded result of these and other factors was a death knell. At present, not only is the New Communities Program dead in America, its resounding failure is unlikely to inspire such programs in the foreseeable future.

In some sense, of course, the new-town *idea* deserves credit. As sociologist Roland Warren writes, speaking of Columbia's developer, James Rouse: "One can but laud . . . the broad social concern and purpose shown by the developer . . . in undertaking a project of this economic magnitude and social audacity and with the degree of human concern that went into it from the onset" (1978, p. 165). The same tribute could be applied even more appropriately to Ebenezer Howard, who aspired to so much in his new towns vision.

Nevertheless, "Jerusalem" has not been built. Robinson (1975, p. 141) sums up the issue bluntly: "the new town is not the panacea for all urban problems." Other visions must be considered.

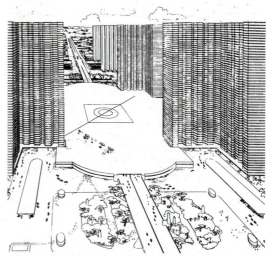

Figure 14-3 *Le Corbusier's Contemporary City. Source: Le Corbusier (with Pierre Jeanneret),* Oeuvre Complete *1910–1929 (Zurich, Switzerland: 1930).*

Ebenezer Howard's ultimate goal for the city was the largest imaginable: a total transformation of urban life. Yet his garden cities, in reality, were rather small. Therein may have lain the fundamental problem, some with more grandiose plans might have argued. To solve the city's problems one does not need little, outlying new towns, but complete new *cities*—more efficient and more humane cities, cities able to handle not just some of the population but all of it. In this section we shall examine three such all-inclusive "visions of the street." All are designed by architects. As we shall see, like new towns, these utopian visions take widely varying forms.

Utopia Unlimited: Architectural Visions

The possible will be attempted only because we have postulated the impossible.

GOETHE

Le Corbusier: The Radiant City

One of the most important figures of modern architecture, the Frenchman Le Corbusier is also one of the most influential of urban planners. In his books, *The City of Tomorrow* (1922) and *The Radiant City* (1933), Le Corbusier outlined his vision of a new urban society. Like Howard before him, Le Corbusier believed the contemporary

Figure 14-4 Frank Lloyd Wright's Broadacre City. Source: Frank Lloyd Wright, The Living City (New York: Horizon, 1978), pp. 198–199. Copyright © The Frank Lloyd Wright Foundation 1958. Reprinted by permission of The Frank Lloyd Wright Memorial Foundation.

metropolis to be a deathtrap. But his solution was the very opposite of Howard's. Widespread decentralization was not the answer; the benefits of concentration of population and social activity in the large city were quite evident. The answer lay in more efficient use of the core. Instead of decreasing density, Le Corbusier proposed *increasing* it, in tall, architecturally magnificent buildings surrounded by huge open spaces. By doing this, Le Corbusier reasoned, up to 95 percent of the available land could be utilized for nonbuilding purposes and a density of up to 1,000 people per acre could be attained. One of Le Corbusier's city plans, called "Contemporary City," is depicted in Figure 14-3.

A second major idea concerned the city's surrounding area. Le Corbusier proposed to do away with the typical Western city's inner-city concentration "by substituting virtually equal densities all over the city. This would reduce the pressure on central business districts, which would in effect disappear. Flows of people would become much more even across the whole city, instead of strong radical flows into and out of the center which characterize cities today" (Hall 1975, p. 75).

Decentralization *with* density, concentrated use of space *and* open space, administrative efficiency *and* spontaneity, organization *and* individuality—all these opposites are intentionally built into Le Corbusier's work. The city was to him the place where such human paradoxes came together. Such opposites need to be exploited and used, not feared.

Although none of Le Corbusier's urban utopias has been built without modification, his influence on city planning was great, and many of his ideas have found partial realization. One classic example is the Alton West estate in Roehampton in southwest London, built after World War II. A second example of a Le Corbusier-influenced project is Manhattan's Stuyvesant Town. Red brick high-rise towers are situated between wide walkways and lawns in this parklike setting constructed in 1947. Although Stuyvesant Town has been controversial, architecture critic Paul Goldberger (1979) believes that its successes outweigh its problems. Still, he recognizes that the satisfaction felt by people living there may be as much a function of their high income as it is of the project itself.

Frank Lloyd Wright: Broadacre City

To the American Frank Lloyd Wright, Le Corbusier's urban vision was anathema. It intensified what he saw as the main problem of the city: overconcentration. Wright was the champion of what he called "organic architecture"—the living union of architectural design with the environment in which it is placed. He reasoned that if the architecture of houses could be so constructed as to be "organic," why couldn't the same be done for entire cities, even whole civilizations?

Basically, like both Howard and Le Corbusier, Wright accepted the integral role of modern technology. Unlike them, however, he planned to increase the space occupied by his utopian city beyond that of any known city, simultaneously lowering its density drastically. He thought his city might easily spread over 100 square miles or more. The idea was that with the help of the automobile, each person could live on her or his own acre of land and still reach neighbors and service facilities with ease.

Figure 14-4 depicts Wright's vision of Broadacre City. A central structure (the tall building in the background) is the local administrative center. At its foot, on the shores of the lake, lies a stadium. In the foreground, the circular building with the spires is the cultural center. Interspersed throughout the area are agricultural fields and dwelling complexes—an idea very much like Howard's. Roads link these areas, and overhead whirl the personal helicopters owned by many Broadacre residents.

Broadacre City was a fusion of what Wright believed to be the ideals of Jeffersonian democracy (fundamentally, that each person should be free to do what he or she likes), the American dream of plenty of land for personal use, and modern technology. He believed as well that people should pay no rent for their land; rather, they would pay a "Single Tax" that would be used for both land payment and public services. After that, they were on their own. No one, not the bank, not the government, could thereafter challenge their right to do with their land as they pleased (Fishman 1977).

Wright's plan even included designs for daily life. He wanted Broadacre City to be the place where, finally, humans could realize their full potential. Everyone would be competent in all important tasks. "In Broadacre City both physical and mental labor would be part of everyone's daily experience. Everyone would have the skills to be a part-time farmer, a part-time mechanic, and a part-time intellectual. Only drudgery would be absent from work" (Fishman 1977, p. 128).

It was never built, of course; not even in part. The plan met with massive criticism during Wright's lifetime (1867–1959). Said critics, Broadacre City was too expensive, too expansive, too radical in all ways. Stung by the negative reaction, Wright lashed out by calling his critics a "mobocracy" and argued anew for his inspired plans. He rewrote his Broadacre treatise, *The Living City*, for the fourth time at age ninety.

Paolo Soleri: The Arcology

While Wright designed and wrote, he also taught—in later years, at his home, Taliesin West, near Phoenix, Arizona. At his side for a time was a young Italian named Paolo Soleri. Like many genius students of other geniuses, Soleri has both taken from and rebelled against his master's teaching. He accepted Wright's central idea that organic architecture could address many of society's ills, but he rejected entirely his teacher's vision of Broadacre City.

Like Le Corbusier, Soleri argues for the dense concentration of people in an urban area. But his vision is that of Le Corbusier with a vengeance, for Soleri has had what must be the strangest dream yet of the city: a completely self-contained unit housing up to *half a million* people in a structure only a few times larger than the Empire State Building and which takes up only the space of a few contemporary city blocks.

Soleri calls his cities "arcologies," or architectural ecologies—environmentally safe, architecturally beautiful, and totally efficient for all human needs. He defines his concept this way: "Arcology is intensively ecological and because of its self-containment is able to be integrally accepted by the natural ecology. It is a belonging of performance, not a belonging of parasitism [like the modern city]" (Soleri 1973, p. 46). The key

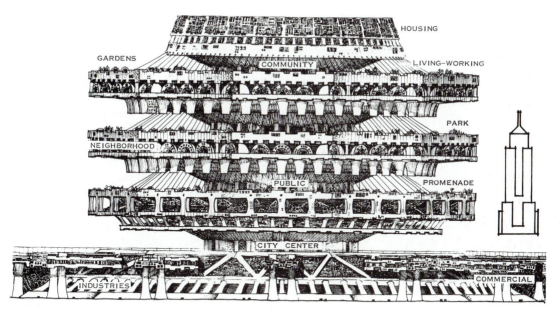

Figure 14-5 *Paolo Soleri's Babel IIB. (The small sketch to the right is the Empire State Building for size comparison.) Source: Paolo Soleri,* Arcology: The City in the Image of Man *(Cambridge, Mass.: MIT Press, 1969), p. 62. Reprinted by permission.*

idea is, at long last, to make the city "in the image of man." The city's job is to concentrate and intensify everything that can help the development of our consciousness. Cities are vital elements of human evolution; hence, dispersed concepts, like Broadacres, do not apply.

In Figure 14-5 we see Soleri's Babel IIB, designed for a population of 520,000. Working from the bottom up, we see the industrial and commercial areas underground; the city center at the point where Babel IIB begins to rise into the air; a public area and a promenade on the first level; a neighborhood and a park (both clearly exposed to the air) on the second level; gardens, a community area (for recreation and the like), and a living/working area on the third level (about 1500 feet high!); and housing at the very top. All service facilities—elevators, heating, and exhaust systems—would be contained in the central core of the city.

Structures like these (Soleri has designed dozens) are so audacious, even in the history of utopian urban planning, that they have met vehement opposition. Critics see the arcologies as

gigantic beehives. Soleri counters by claiming they are "miniatures" compared to today's cities. They occupy a fraction of the land, free up the surrounding countryside for enjoyment, and allow that countryside a chance to return to nature. Imagine this: the population of Los Angeles, which now sprawls over some 500 square miles, contained in 10 to 12 well-dispersed Babels. There would be no freeways, no smog, just beautiful southern California.

Other critics claim that, in such environments, people will be so cramped together that life will be unbearable and their individual identities will be lost. Soleri again says no. Even at populations of 520,000, Babel IIB would only have a density of 268 people an acre. (In comparison, Le Corbusier's "Radiant City" planned for over 1,000 an acre.) Regarding loss of identity, Soleri argues that, on the contrary, personal identity would be enhanced in his arcologies. In the first place, given an arcology's technological efficiency, most people would be freed from the drudgery the inefficient city system of today damns them to. Stores would be nearby, parks a few minutes' walk, the office three floors down. In the second place, the arcology would concentrate—through modern technology's capacity for miniaturization—all the great accomplishments of human history: arts, literature, science. This would place literally everything a human being needs to know at a moment's beck and call. People would find their own identity in an unpressurized way for the first time in human history (Soleri 1973).

But Soleri has not been able to counter effectively the economic criticism. The arcologies, any of them, would be astronomically expensive, both in terms of raw cost and work time. Since there is no precedent that suggests the arcologies will do what Soleri says they will, he has not found the financial help he needs.

Undaunted, he has proceeded on his own. Rising out of the desert at Cortez Junction in Arizona, about an hour's ride north of Phoenix, is Arcosanti, Soleri's prototypical arcology. Arcosanti is planned to be completely self-sufficient and has been under construction for a little more than a decade. Progress is extremely slow. The undertaking is only about 2 percent finished. Yet Soleri holds to his vision. He invests money earned by his books and lectures, solicits private investments, and employs willing workers (mostly students). At the present rate it is doubtful whether Arcosanti will be completed in this century. If more funds aren't forthcoming soon, it may never be completed. However, this is the one utopian urban plan under construction that is still within the complete control of its designer. Soleri hopes to someday demonstrate to the world the feasibility and necessity of implementing his vision on a broader scale.

Utopia's Limitations: A Critique

Planned utopias, like those of Le Corbusier, Wright, and Soleri, certainly have limitations—limitations not unlike those encountered in examining the new-town movement. First, as Arcosanti amply demonstrates, they are often financially impractical. Second, they are often very rigid visions developed by a single person. The utopians seem to assume that everyone will see the basic logic of their vision and share the values that support it (Fishman 1977). How could reasonable people think otherwise? The problem is, reasonable people often *do* think otherwise. Frequently, the utopians have shown a singular unwillingness to bend their concerns to the often legitimate complaints of critics or to the exigencies of the political and economic situation they find themselves in. (To his credit, Paolo Soleri seems more flexible than most planners in this respect. He has changed his designs frequently after dialogue with others.)

Third, most of these plans are sociologically naive. As Peter Hall (1975) notes, the utopians are all architects. As a result they believe that altering the physical world will alter the social world automatically. But the relationship is not so simple. Beautiful designs will not necessarily do away with social differences, racial prejudice, or poverty. As the new towns demonstrated, the larger cultural milieu had a very decided effect on the social life of each newly constructed community. There is little reason to believe it would play any less of a role in utopian cities.

Yet, in the last analysis, we need these utopian thinkers. They are, by their very nature, consciousness raisers. They challenge our thinking about cities, point to obvious problems, and suggest visionary solutions that we "on the street" barely understand. They get us thinking in new ways and critically challenge us to confront our own city experiences. On another level, who can truly say how well a given utopian design may work? When Arcosanti is finished, perhaps we shall find that Paolo Soleri *was* right after all.

Planning the Socialist City

As Le Corbusier, Wright, and Soleri found out, the difficulties of realizing comprehensive urban plans using only private investment are enormous. What then of socialist societies, of countries where urban planning is supported by all the resources of the state? What has been the success of urban planning there?

The Socialist Vision of the City

To begin, socialist theory sees in the city a friend. In fact, after the 1917 Russian Revolution, Lenin claimed that cities represented the possibility for progress toward a socialist society. No doubt Lenin was aware that cities under capitalism had spawned many of the social problems we described in the last chapter. Nevertheless, he believed that, shaped by a socialist culture, cities could become centers of "original ideas, innovations in production, behavior, and thought" (Andrusz 1984, p. 277).

Within socialist societies today, city planning is based on a single broad idea: With the ability to shape the whole society, the government can gradually move toward providing all urban citizens with the highest quality of life, simultaneously eliminating destructive social differences based on race, ethnicity, sex, and class. For this to happen, cities cannot be allowed to grow in the uncontrolled fashion characteristic of capitalist societies (recall, for example, the explosive nineteenth- and twentieth-century growth of London, New York, and Chicago). Furthermore, history abounds with examples of cities controlled by the few and providing little for the many. The socialist city, it is argued, can be different.

More specifically, there are four guidelines by which the vision of a socialist city is to be realized. First, the development of the city must be carefully controlled; for example, population must not be allowed to swell beyond what resources for employment can support. Second, to ensure that the benefits of city life are equally distributed, housing must be constructed in standardized fashion. Furthermore, unlike the pattern common in capitalist societies, various districts of the city should be basically alike: the socialist city must never have "wealthy people living in exclusive residences" while the poor live in "low-rent, burned out industrial areas" (Fisher 1962, p. 252). Third, the city must reflect the dominant interests of the state in socialist society. In the United States, for example, cities have been described as "growth machines" (Chapter 12) serving the interests of a few wealthy landowners; this

is most clearly evident in the urban dominance of the central business district. In the socialist city, on the other hand, business must be scattered throughout the city—essentially equalizing everyone's access to all goods and services. Fourth, and finally, to avoid generating anonymity and social alienation, the city should be constructed as a mosaic of smaller "microdistricts." In this way, even in the midst of a great city, all people can participate meaningfully in social life.

That is the general plan. How has it worked in practice?

Socialist Cities and New Towns

To the American traveller, socialist cities seem radically different from the more familiar cities in the West. To gain a sense of how one might react to a socialist city, look now to Cityscape 14-2, in which one of the present authors (Macionis) describes his first visit to Ljubljana, a major urban center of Yugoslavia.

As this cityscape suggests, the change from a capitalist economy to a socialist system does, indeed, transform a city. But, perhaps even more interesting, are the efforts of socialist societies to build cities from scratch—the construction of new towns. As we have already suggested, planned urban development on this scale generally requires resources available only to governments; in the United States, planning has historically been of smaller scale, and left to private interests.

Some Eastern European New Towns. Begun from scratch, the Polish new town of Nowa Huta stands 10 miles south of Cracow. Principally a steel mill city, Nowa Huta has a population of over 100,000 people, 80 percent of whom are of rural origin. In many ways the city has succeeded within the guidelines of the socialist ideal just outlined. It has adequate urban services and few of the problems (crime and pollution, for example) that plague many older Western cities.

Yet it has not been a complete success. Because of the great expense of comprehensive urban design, building the city has been a hard,

---

CITYSCAPE 14-2
Ljubljana: The "Discovery" of a Socialist City

Ljubljana? For months I had avoided using the word, unsure of the pronunciation (Loob-lee-ah-nah) and only somewhat more certain of its location. Now, aboard an airliner completing the journey from the United States to Yugoslavia, I eagerly awaited first sight of the Alps as a sign that the city was close at hand.

The occasion was spending a semester leading a group of American students to Ljubljana, the capital city of Slovenia, the northernmost province of Yugoslavia. This nation, across the Adriatic Sea to the east of Italy and directly south of Austria, was transformed into a socialist society after World War II.

Of course, the American visitor almost always enters a socialist society with an array of preconceptions about life there. The people are, after all, "communists"— a powerfully negative image in American culture. We easily imagine that "big brother" jealously monitors their every movement. To our pleasant surprise, however, we found people marked by variety, sponaneity, and intense pride.

With a population of some 325,000 (1980), Ljubljana is about the size of Louisville, Kentucky, or Newark, New Jersey. Walking about, one is quickly attracted to the Old City—a district on the banks of the Ljubljanica River dating from the twelfth century. Here, narrow, winding streets delight the pedestrian and provide a sense of history unknown in the United States. Walking north, one finds the newer, industrial center of Ljubljana with wide and straight streets. Yet, typical of socialist cities, there are few neon signs and little of the frantic commercial bustle found in the West. Moreover, Ljubljana has few of the commercial skyscrapers that mark the central area of capitalist cities. Rather, the central region of the city mixes businesses, public buildings, and open spaces. Noteworthy are numerous monuments to heros of the socialist revolution.

Although the average income in Ljubljana is higher than for the country as a whole, residents of the city earn only about half as much as the average American. Further, one finds little of the striking contrast between rich and poor so evident in urban America. The few very large houses—built before World War II—no longer

---

slow process, even with total government involvement. Early residents arrived to find Nowa Huta nearly devoid of the amenities promised. A second problem—also found in the Soviet Union and Yugoslavia—has been the difficulty that previously rural people have had in adapting to an urban, industrial existence:

> They did not know how to use modern technical and sanitary installations. . . . [They] wished to cultivate gardens and maintain livestock. They found in Nowa Huta no place for these activities, and administrators soon found coal in wash basins and pigs on balconies. The former villagers could not find in the new shops the kind of furniture to which they had been accustomed. They brought, therefore, to Nowa Huta their parents' old beds, tables, and shrines, which usually were too big for the small Nowa Huta rooms. . . . The process of adaptation and integration was not as easy as town planners had thought. (Fisher 1962, p. 256)

In another sense Nowa Huta has been too successful. Like Brasilia, it has attracted too many people from the hinterlands too quickly. Its meager facilities are overtaxed and the quality of life has suffered as a result (Fisher 1962).

More successful has been Valenje in northern Yugoslavia. In the center of a coal district, Valenje has a population of about 30,000 and is divided into four standardized microdistricts, each equipped with a school, a shopping center, and public buildings. The administrative city center coordinates the entire complex. Fisher suggests that, when completed, Valenje is likely to be "an ideal urbanistic and architectural expression of socialist [values]" (1962, p. 257).

New Towns in the Soviet Union. As the most powerful socialist society in the world, the Soviet Union has led the way in constructing new towns. In a 50-year period after 1926, over 1,100 such towns were built, providing housing for more than 40 million people. Because urbanization has been more rapid in the Soviet Union than in the United States, and also as a result of massive devastation of its cities during World War II, the So-

contain rich families but are home to organizations. The people of Ljubljana do see some neighborhoods as better than others, but such differences are slight from the American's point of view. Just as important, one finds no abandoned houses or deteriorated slum areas that are commonplace in large American cities.

Housing in Yugoslavia is defined as a social resource. Thus while most people own their own apartments, no one may own more than two residences. Since the war, the city has rapidly constructed more than 100,000 apartment units, but can barely keep up with demand. Most apartment buildings are about eight stories high and form microdistricts according to large-scale socialist urban planning. Individual apart-

ments are small by American standards, and they are generally uniform in appearance, further reducing the differences from one neighborhood to the next.

The visitor to Ljubljana immediately senses the relative safety of the busy streets. As noted in Chapter 13, fear of crime greatly limits activity in American cities. But in Ljubljana, there are almost no areas to be avoided for this reason.

While the safety of Ljubljana greatly increases the visitor's enjoyment, the city lacks the excitement of capitalist cities. The old saying that "the city never sleeps" does not apply to Ljubljana; with only a handful of night-spots, this is a quiet city after about 11 o'clock in the evening. Further, the range of life-styles is quite

narrow, due to the relative economic quality as well as the socialist emphasis on social responsibility rather than individual differences. Thus, there are no evident vice districts, gay communities, or countercultural centers common in American cities. The visitor also notes the virtual absence of a familiar mode of urban expression: graffiti. To the Yugoslavs, such acts are deemed antisocial examples of western decadence. Perhaps this explains why occasional graffiti are inevitably linked to the western "punk" life-style and are invariably written in English.

Ljubljana is distinctive—it is a *socialist* city that shows how economic systems can shape urban life.

Source: John J. Macionis.

---

viet Union has faced a desperate need for urban housing. New towns have been a major part of the strategy to meet this challenge.

Soviet new towns reflect many of the principles of socialist planning we have already noted. Housing is typically uniform in design, providing only about 100 square feet of living space for each person. Furthermore, the government heavily subsidizes costs so that, on the average, only about 5 percent of an individual's earnings are spent for housing.

In many respects, Soviet new towns have been successful. First, and most important, they have gone a long way toward meeting the demand for housing. Second, in virtually all the new towns, social differences based on income and ethnic background have been minimized. There is little evidence, for example, of the striking contrasts among neighborhoods typical of Western, capitalist cities. Third, new towns have greatly contributed to the economic development of regions within the vast hinterland of the Soviet Union.

On the other side of the coin, however, a number of criticisms have been made. First, governmental regulation of housing provides a means by which citizens are subject to political control; those who voice criticism of the system, for example, may find themselves placed lower on already-long waiting lists. Second, although relatively small differences in income characterize Soviet society, there are considerable personal differences in power. Those with connections to the Communist party, for example, are often able to gain the most desirable housing at the expense of others. Third, and finally, the elimination of social differences in new towns has often been accomplished through systematic repression of ethnic and religious traditions—the plight of many Soviet Jews is the most well-known case in point (Inkeles 1962; Underhill 1976).

Moscow. This leading socialist city has a more complex story. In the early part of this century, when Russia was still a Tsarist nation, Moscow was a huge city of impoverished peasants with a

Modern apartment buildings in the newly developed suburb of Kount-sevo near Moscow. Whether in the socialist bloc or in the West, grand plans such as these often result in sterile buildings. (© Paolo Koch/Rapho/Photo Researchers)

relatively small middle class and a smaller, very powerful, elite. Today it is one of the great modern cities of the world, the epicenter of one of the world's two superpowers. It is a city, as Mike Davidow (1976) reports, of quick and efficient mass transportation, extremely low unemployment, very little street crime, no racial or ethnic ghettos, and little danger of the bankruptcy that threatens many modern American cities and their residents. This is an impressive achievement, to say the least.

Yet Moscow's success has not been achieved without costs. Berry and Kasarda (1977) suggest that the policy of standardization, coupled with the Soviet Union's desire to industrialize rapidly, has led to housing being given short shrift. There is simply not enough quality housing, and what

does exist often is accused of having an almost mind-deadening sameness.

A related problem is overpopulation. Satellite cities (not suburbs) have been established on Moscow's perimeter, beyond a 6-mile-wide greenbelt, but in-migration continues. The city's population was over 6 million in 1960, more than 7 million in 1970, and reached 8.1 million in 1980. It is assumed the Moscow region will have over 50 million inhabitants by the year 2000 (Frolic 1976, p. 277)—a megalopolis by any standard.

A third problem grows out of the second. Moscow is experiencing a declining ability to provide such services as adequate transportation and waste removal, it is becoming more and more polluted, and it experiences continual shortages of consumer goods (Cattell 1976). One Soviet observer suggests that despite its tremendous strides Moscow's planners have had to slip away from the original, small-scale, humanistic orientation of Marxist ideology and turn instead to a "plan designed mainly to cope with the problems of managing bigness" (Frolic 1976, p. 284). In these respects at least, Moscow resembles its Western counterparts.

Evaluation

No knowledgeable urbanist can deny the successes of socialist urban planning. By and large, socialist cities are safe, clean, and without the extreme poverty that we have seen in much of the rest of the world's cities. A great deal of progress has been made toward the ideal that all the city's citizens "should have equal access with minimal outlays of journey time and effort, whether on foot or by public transport, to all the material, cultural, and welfare goods and services that they require" (French and Hamilton 1979, p. 9).

Yet, the success, as elsewhere, has been mixed. First, labor, technology, and finances have not always been adequate to meet all needs, and productive capacity lags behind most Western cities. Second, despite concerted attempts to limit population growth, many socialist cities are becoming overpopulated, and are finding that pollution is on the rise, that expenses steadily increase, and that their quality of life has suffered as a result.

A third problem is more unsettling in view of socialist philosophy. Recently, as job opportunities have increased, a socialist version of class differences has emerged in many cities, although in this instance the elites turn out not to be the Tsarist royalty or the rich merchant class but Communist party officials, industrial leaders, and technological or scientific experts (French and Hamilton 1979). Szelenyi puts it baldly in his study of urban inequalities in European socialist countries: "Housing inequalities are being created now, as those with higher incomes get the better housing; and these inequalities are being created by administrative allocation, [that is] by the distinctively socialist mechanism which was supposed to replace the capitalist market method of allocation" (1983, p. 6). Bater's (1984) study

of Soviet cities also finds extensive evidence of such favoritism.

A last issue concerns the cultural values that are being implemented in the socialist city. These cities have been thoroughly planned with the values of standardization and state control at their core. The result has been the elimination of much of the diversity and spontaneity that characterize Western cities. Socialist cities don't have the exciting bright lights of London's West End, or the clash of architectural styles of New York, or the ethnic enclaves of San Francisco, Paris, or Montreal. As a result, most Westerners react to socialist cities with reserve, even condemnation. Yet Western cities, as we have so often seen, are usually much less safe and clean, and reveal far more poverty and obvious human suffering than their socialist counterparts.

This leads us to a crucial issue in city planning. The essence of planning is to make choices among alternatives while guided by beliefs about what it is good for human beings to do or be. As value choices are implemented, the city becomes one thing and not another. Perhaps city planners can't eat their cake and have it too. A decision in favor of standardization and total control, for example, may eliminate much urban diversity and spontaneity. Conversely, a decision that reflects more individualistic values may make equalization of resources and opportunity extremely difficult to attain.

Another possibility exists, however. Perhaps the problem is not only valuational. Perhaps the city itself is so complex that it will resist to some degree *any* plan—capitalist or socialist—that is applied to it.

Meanwhile . . . Downtown: More Focused Urban Planning

Socialist *and* capitalist city builders have had great difficulty in altering their cities. The problem, some planners suggest, is that the plans we have considered thus far are too grandiose, too big. The claim is that *any* comprehensive urban plan will come to a bad end. The city is simply *too complex a phenomenon* to be controlled as though it were a programmable computer. These planners would argue that the only type of urban planning likely to succeed is circumscribed planning, planning that is focused on a more limited aspect of city life—say, the use of neighborhoods or parks. These smaller chunks of the urban scene are understandable and manageable. The city as a whole never is.

Sidewalks, Neighborhoods, and Local Initiative

There has been a reaction in recent years, particularly in Western societies, against the comprehensive visions of people like Ebenezer Howard, Paolo Soleri, and the socialist city planners. Robert Fishman summarizes the reaction this way:

> *Its most profound source, I believe, is the loss of confidence in the reality of a common good or purpose which can become the basis of city life.* The planner's claim to be serving the interests of all . . . is now seen as either a foolish delusion or, worse, a hypocritical attempt to impose his own limited values on everyone else. . . . [Comprehensive] planners saw the chaos and diversity of the great city as a kind of disease and the worst enemy of social harmony. Their critics have no desire to conform to an all-embracing harmony that leaves people unable to plan for themselves. They put their trust in diversity and see in urban disorder the last, best hope for individual freedom and self-realization. (1977, p. 267; emphasis added)

Leading this reaction has been Jane Jacobs, author of *The Death and Life of Great American Cities* (1961). Jacobs believes that the greatest values of the city are *intensity* and *diversity*; hence, anything that diminishes these qualities (comprehensive planning, by definition) leads to the "death" of great cities. The city's "life" is its myriad interactions and multiple uses of its streets, parks, sidewalks, and neighborhoods. These interactions and uses, Jacobs suggests, are never *planned* in any rigid sense. The people of the city *invent* them, as they go along, to meet their own needs and to solve their own problems.

Consider sidewalks. In any vital city area, a sidewalk has uses far beyond easing the passage of pedestrians. In neighborhoods, sidewalk stoops

Neighborhoods where residents make ongoing use of public spaces are vital and exciting. Jane Jacobs believes that curtailing the spontaneous use of the urban environment would signal the death of the city. (Jan Lukacs/EPA)

are places to sit and visit and corners are places to "hang out." Even in more anonymous districts, similar things happen. Around Sunset Strip in Los Angeles, a well-known "crowd" hangs out; a different type of crowd occupies the Harvard Square area of Boston. Second, sidewalk street life can serve as a means of public surveillance, through which people come to know each other and identify strangers. Jacobs argues, for example, that in areas where street life abounds, crime rates are lower. As if in acknowledgment of Jacob's thesis, people in major cities across the United States, one evening in August 1985, sat on their doorsteps and walked out on the streets where they lived, in an organized effort to dissuade criminals and "reclaim the night." Third, sidewalks are learning environments for children, through which they learn about the city, themselves, their neighborhood, and the rules of urban social life.

BOX 14-1
Jane Jacobs's Goals of City Planning

Consider, for a moment, the kind of goals at which city planning must begin to aim, if the object is to plan for city vitality.

Planning for vitality must stimulate and catalyze the greatest possible range and quantity of diversity among uses and among people throughout each district of a big city; this is the underlying foundation of city economic strength, social vitality and magnetism. To do this, planners must diagnose, in specific places, specifically what is lacking to generate diversity, and then aim at helping to supply the lacks as best they can be supplied.

Planning for vitality must promote continuous networks of local street neighborhoods, whose users and informal proprietors can count to the utmost in keeping the public spaces of the city safe, in handling strangers so they are an asset rather than a menace, in keeping casual public tabs on children in places that are public.

Planning for vitality must combat the destructive presence of border vacuums, and it must help promote people's identification with city districts that are large enough, and are varied and rich enough in inner and outer contacts to deal with the tough, inescapable, practical problems of big-city life.

Planning for vitality must aim at unslumming the slums, by creating conditions aimed at persuading a high proportion of the indigenous residents, whoever they may be, to stay put by choice over time, so there will be a steadily growing diversity among people and a continuity of community both for old residents and for newcomers who assimilate into it.

Planning for vitality must convert the self-destruction of diversity and other cataclysmic uses of money into constructive forces, by hampering the opportunities for destructiveness on the one hand, and on the other hand by stimulating more city territory into possessing a good economic environment for other people's plans.

Planning for vitality must aim at clarifying the visual order of cities, and it must do so by both promoting and illuminating functional order, rather than by obstructing or denying it.

Source: Jane Jacobs, *The Death and Life of Great American Cities* (New York: Random House, 1961), pp. 408–409.

Finally, street life can be the crucial support of a sense of community in a city area. Such areas as Philadelphia's South Philly, New York's Lower East Side or the Village, New Orleans's French Quarter or Garden District, or San Francisco's Nob Hill or Haight-Ashbury all maintain a positive identity based on their street life.

Nobody really can plan such uses and neighborhoods, Jacobs says. Take the issue of size. How large is a neighborhood? How should we plan it ideally? The socialist city planners might answer that a neighborhood comprises between 6,000 and 12,000 people. Jacobs would counter by claiming that this is a rigid, arbitrary, even dangerous estimate. Some "real" neighborhoods—those that have been created spontaneously by their residents—are very small, others are large, others in between. Indeed, perhaps we should not attempt to define the "neighborhood" at all:

If we look at successful street-neighborhood networks in real life, we find . . . whenever they work best, street neighborhoods have no beginnings and ends setting them apart as distinct units. The size even differs for different people from the same spot, because some people range further, or hang around more, or extend their street acquaintance farther than others. Indeed, a great part of the success of these neighborhoods depends on their overlapping and interweaving, turning the corners. (Jacobs 1961, p. 120)

In general, then, Jacobs lauds local planning initiatives and loathes grandiose designs. What city planners should do, she says, is facilitate diversity and vitality and *let local people do the rest.* This is city planning with a virtually "hands-off" attitude. Box 14-2 outlines Jacob's suggestions to a city planning board.

The next-to-last proposal Jacobs makes in the

box reflects her advocacy of channeling local funds for local residents' use. This often has not been an easy task in cities, because historically most local funds have been conrolled by banks. Since banks are corporate entities out to make a profit, they have been rather reserved about investing in projects or areas that wouldn't turn that profit.

Reflecting this attitude is the policy of "red-lining," in which a bank or insurance company quite literally draws a red line on the map around any area in a city it considers a poor investment. Typically, red-lined areas are ethnic or racial ghettos or deteriorating areas.

One such red-lined area was Brooklyn's Park Slope district. Once prosperous, it had declined in recent years to a neighborhood of seedy bars, teenage hangouts, and ever-worsening housing. The area currently is settled by a very heterogeneous population, most of whom are low- and moderate-income blacks, Puerto Ricans, and whites. When some of these local residents asked a few years ago for rehabilitation loans, they were turned down flat by one of the area's major banks, Greater New York. What happened next is described in Cityscape 14-3. One can imagine Jane Jacobs's applause. This is the urban "planning" she supports most vigorously: people working for themselves to make the city fit their needs as *they* define those needs.

Open Spaces: Squares, Parks, and Architecture

Not everyone who shares the belief in more focused city planning, of course, goes as far as Jacobs. Some argue that while holistic city planning is not desirable, good planning can be more comprehensive than Jacobs advocates.

One such advocate is August Heckscher (1977), who recently spent two years visiting such cities as Omaha, Dallas, Cincinnati, Buffalo, Rochester, and Milwaukee. Heckscher contends that the city is fundamentally an organization of *space*. How a city organizes that space determines the "living" success or failure of that city; thus,

Each city is a place of its own, its uniqueness determined in large measure by patterns created by the alternation of structure and void, of buildings and spaces between. The large green spaces, parks and parkways, river banks and waterfronts, give to a city a coherence that allows the urban dweller to have a feeling of the whole. . . . What is expressed in open spaces is the essential quality of urban life—its casualness and variety, its ability to crystallize community feeling. (Heckscher 1977, p. 4)

For example, Heckscher contends that the spatial organization of cities reflects our deepest cultural values. Grounded in the values of individualism, freedom, expansion, and business success, American cities typically adopted a grid pattern. With a grid, vistas are opened up; people could look down whole streets, even out to the countryside; regularity is introduced; control is suggested. Curved streets and irregular building patterns, on the other hand, like those of medieval towns and many rural areas, were thought to be enclosing, limiting, unpredictable, not future-oriented.

Heckscher takes Philadelphia as a case in point (refer to Figure 6-3). Planned in 1682 by William Penn, Philadelphia's grid is nothing if not an embodiment of the new country's values. Penn established his city at the narrowest point of land where the Schuylkill and Delaware Rivers met, and he bounded the city on the north by a greenbelt to be known as Liberty Lands. He placed a park in each of the quadrants of the city and set a major square at Center City, which was reached by four broad, open avenues. The inner-city area, divided up by the grid, was then sold in standardized parcels that Penn vigorously promoted (refer to Box 3-2). The values of open vistas, efficiency, and economic success are all preeminently evident in this single design.

Heckscher believes deeply in the necessity of squares, parks, architecture, and artwork in the city. They are especially important in cities, like those in America, that are dominated by economic concerns. They serve to remind people that there are "other things" to life. Squares provide small, natural meeting and conversing places, as well as the setting for more formal oc-

CITYSCAPE 14-3
Breaking the Bank:
Community Initiative in Park Slope

Greater New York's refusal to offer mortgages or rehabilitation loans [to local residents] irked Herb Steiner, owner of a small Park Slope factory that manufactures postage-stamp dispensers. A resident of the neighborhood since 1971, Steiner organized like-minded neighbors into a community group, South Brooklyn Against Investment Discrimination (AID), to bring pressure on the bank's lending policies. "At our first meeting with bank officials," says Steiner, "they threw crime, rent control, and the South Bronx at us. The impression they gave us was, 'What institution in its right mind would invest in this hellhole?'"

When subsequent meetings produced similar acrimony, AID escalated its anti-redlining tactics. It hung red banners from the bank's facade, proclaiming it "Big Red." It released red balloons into the air and painted a thick red line around the bank building. When the bank still refused to budge, the group decided to play its trump card. For months, members manned tables at nearby street corners, preparing for a "withdrawal week." Some 1,200 of the bank's depositors signed pledge cards committing themselves to withdrawing their funds. Finally, in July 1977, AID called in its mark-

ers, and by week's end $863,000 had been withdrawn from the bank and deposited in financial institutions with better local lending records.

Still the bank held fast, and AID began the tedious process of preparing a second withdrawal week. Then, the week before this new offensive was to be carried out, the bank relented, agreeing to an "affirmative action" program by which it pledged to originate $25 million in New York City mortgages in 1978, including $2.5 million for Park Slope. . . . AID was not appeased. Steiner felt that the sums involved were trivial. . . .

It was in the midst of this standoff, in April 1978, that Greater New York applied to the FDIC [Federal Deposit Insurance Corporation] for approval of a new branch on Manhattan's Upper East Side, the city's silk-stocking district. To Park Slope residents, the move seemed but a further indication of the bank's efforts to distance itself from Brooklyn, and they were intent on calling that fact to the attention of federal regulators.

In the past, AID would have had few hopes of actually stopping the application from going through, given the prevailing interpretation of public "convenience and needs." But things were to be dif-

ferent this go-round. A few months earlier, the CRA [Community Reinvestment Act—which requires the FDIC to ask that banks meet the credit needs of local residents] had become law, and AID moved quickly to test its procedures. . . . The group submitted to the FDIC an 85-page petition documenting its redlining charges [and claiming that] the mortgage record of Greater New York was a "shame and a scandal."

Then, in April, in the first such action under the CRA, the FDIC rejected the bank's branch application. Though Greater New York's mortgage record has improved in recent months, declared the FDIC, the bank's lending activity "cannot yet be said to be at an acceptable level."

Greater New York's operations are managed from its stately colonial-style building on Madison Avenue in midtown Manhattan. Bank president Jerome Maron says the CRA has "forced me to choose between Scylla and Charybdis." The bank will comply with the law by more actively seeking loans in Park Slope and other Brooklyn neighborhoods. . . .

Source: Michael Massing, "Breaking the Bank: The Community Reinvestment Act," *Saturday Review*, September 15, 1979, pp. 22, 24.

---

casions such as political rallies and concerts. They provide a crucial physical and psychological break in the city's pattern. New Orleans's Jackson Square, located in the French Quarter, is one such functional square. Others include Union Square in San Francisco, City Hall Square in Toronto, and Washington Square in New York.

Parks are equally important. *New York Times*

architecture critic Paul Goldberger (1979) speaks for many others in saying that one of New York's finest accomplishments is Central Park, 843 acres on the upper half of Manhattan Island, which preserves a bit of country in the city. Some of the joys of Central Park are described in Cityscape 14-4.

Although Central Park is the most well known, virtually every major American city has a

CITYSCAPE 14-4
Saturday in the Park

New York has a special charm for [residents] on a summer weekend, when the town empties out, when the trucks and commuters and commuter cars are gone. The air is cleaner, the city is quieter, and the peaceful, empty avenues seem especially wide and beautiful. When we've had enough of the peace and quiet, we head for Central Park, where the action is. . . .

There was the usual holiday jam at the Seventy-second Street entrance: crowds around the ice-cream and pretzel stands and a tangle of bikes and baby strollers, as cyclists and parents tried to work their way through the crowd and into the park. Just inside the entrance on my left, [a] playground was crowded with holiday fathers. . . .

On my right, across the road from [the] playground, a broad lawn slopes down to the Model Sailboat Pond with the Model Boathouse (a gift of the Kerbs family) alongside it. Press your nose against the boathouse door, and when your eyes have got used to the dark interior, you can see all the elaborate boats in dry dock: Columbus's fleet, pirate ships, whaling vessels, all fully rigged, and Spanish warships complete down to the galley slaves at the oars. The hobbyists who built them hold a regatta on a Sunday in June, and if you're here on the right Sunday it's something to see.

At the far end of the pond is the Alice in Wonderland Statuary, a gift of the Delacorte family, depicting the Mad Tea Party in bronze. A gigantic Alice presides over the tea table where the Dormouse, Cheshire Cat and March Hare are dominated by the Mad Hatter, or at least by the height of his mad hat. Older children climb to the top of Alice's head and sit on it, younger ones climb to the top of the Mad Hatter's hat, and toddlers crawl or stagger in and out among the giant mushrooms under the tea table. . . .

The foot of Dog Hill is at Seventy-sixth Street and the hill slopes gradually upward to Seventy-ninth, rolling backward in a broad sweep as it rises. We claim it's the largest canine social hall in the world. On a sunny weekend afternoon, there'll be forty or fifty dogs charging around, two or three of whom always appoint themselves as welcoming committee and streak all the way down to the foot of the hill to greet every new arrival. It's the dream of my life to make enough money (which I won't) or leave enough money when I die (which I might) to donate a dog drinking fountain to the Hill. . . .

Beyond the bandshell, the Mall itself runs through the park for several blocks. Today's warm weather had brought out the food vendors . . . shish-kebab stands presided over by enterprising

families, two young black men . . . broiling chicken and corn-on-the-cob over a charcoal fire, a middle-aged couple . . . cooking tacos and four young people sat behind a long table with two signs, one advertising "SMILE! BE HAPPY!" and a smaller one advertising "Magic Foods to Turn You On!" The magic foods were apples, bananas, peaches, watermelon slices and coconuts. At one table, two girls were selling their homemade date-nut and pumpkin breads. . . .

The size of the park—it's more than twice the size of Monaco—is a great boon on summer evenings. Down at the Wollman Skating Rink (gift of the Wollman family) the Schaefer Music Festival features rock-and-roll concerts (sponsored by the Schaefer Brewing Company). And loud as they are, the rock concerts are so far away that they never interfere with Mahler or Puccini holding forth on the Sheep Meadow—which in turn can't be heard by the actors or audience at the Shakespeare theatre—which doesn't interfere with the sounds of the free Jazz Festival or Harlem Dance Theatre performance going on up on the Harlem Mall.

Source: Helene Hanff, *Apple of My Eye* (Garden City, N.Y.: Doubleday, 1978), pp. 175–185.

large park designed for the recreation and informal social use of its citizens. Atlanta has Piedmont Park (185 acres), Chicago has Grant Park (305 acres), and San Diego has Balboa Park (1,158 acres). There is Schenley Park in Pittsburgh (456 acres) and Griffith Park in Los Angeles (4,063 acres), and Philadelphia has the largest city park in the world, Fairmount Park (4,079 acres).

The architecture of individual buildings is also crucial in giving a city its flavor and excitement. Indeed, Heckscher believes that urban architecture is probably the single most important element in shaping the quality of the urban experience. Buildings generate human *feelings*. New York's skyline is the most famous example of a complex architectural effect (see Box 6-2), but individual buildings have similar effects. Frank Lloyd Wright's Guggenheim Museum in New York always creates a response, as do San Francisco's brightly painted Victorian houses. Even the inside of a building elicits our response. Walking through the world's great cathedrals—St. Paul's in London or Notre Dame in Paris, for example—creates a very different experience from the inside of a modern apartment building or a dilapidated tenement.

Of course, architecture affects each of us in different ways. Conway (1977) and others have found that some people respond to skyscrapers positively, others negatively. For example, to provide views of the entire city and as symbols of economic success, tall buildings are great; for views of the rest of the city's architecture, they are often an obstruction. On another level, for efficient use of limited downtown space, high-rise apartment complexes are superb; for watching your kids playing, they are a problem.

Architecture also gives a city a sense of its own history. Many have advocated saving the city's architecture as an act of vital historical preservation. Without its history, the city loses its roots. Urban art serves a similar function. It not only beautifies the city and stimulates the viewer's aesthetic sense, it also serves a cultural and historical purpose.

Heckscher, however, does not advocate a staid approach to the creative use of urban space. Experimentation and change must play a crucial role:

Classic city design called for monuments, circles, arches, and other devices to mark and celebrate [the city]. It is not suggested that these be imitated (although many of them merit preservation); rather that by contemporary urban planning the same effect be secured. The means available to today's planner include such devices as "portal" parks, malls, walkways and plazas, lighting and landscaping, and, not least, an adroit use of modern sculpture and wall paintings. (1977, p. 49)

In the last analysis, Heckscher believes, with Jacobs, that the city's space should have manifold uses. We must learn to see these uses, preserve them, and, where possible, plan for them. A plaza is more than an open space. It is a place where people can congregate and enjoy one another, a wholly different experience from that of the workaday street.

Recently, William H. Whyte did a study of the social life of small urban spaces. He found that many people doted on them, that they added enormously to a city's vital élan. As he wrote of the Seagram Plaza in midtown Manhattan, "On a good day, there would be a hundred and fifty people sitting, sunbathing, picnicking and schmoozing—idly gossiping, talking 'nothing talk'" (1980, p. 14). Further, Whyte found that people actively choose to go to such places in contrast to more isolated parts of the city.

[People] go to the lively places where there are many people. And they go there . . . not to escape the city but to partake of it. . . . The multiplier effect is tremendous. It is not just the number of people using [these small urban places], but the larger number who pass by and enjoy them vicariously, or the even larger number who feel better about the city center for knowledge of them. For a city such places are priceless, whatever the cost. (1980, pp. 100–101)

To do away with such small, open spaces would be to do away at one fell swoop with all the vibrant interactions that go on in them. We must be very careful, say Whyte, Heckscher, and Jacobs, not to see the city just in terms of economic efficiency or political ideals or some grandiose philosophy. The city is full of *people*, whose needs and interests are much more complex and varied than any abstract ideals admit.

The Syntax of Cities

Throughout this chapter we have encountered urban planners deeply at odds with one another. Some—like Howard—are in favor of almost totally planned urban environments. Others—Jacobs, Heckscher, and Whyte—argue for more limited city planning, planning "as if people mattered," planning in favor of a certain amount of urban disorder. Recently a theory has emerged suggesting that acrimonious debate between large- and small-scale planners may be unnecessary. Both may be partially right in their assertions.

This is the voice of British architect Peter Smith (1977), who suggests that the human mind is governed by a "syntax"—a set of "rules of communication" that result from how the mind perceives its environment. Drawing on recent physiological and psychological research, he argues that in the human brain, the left hemisphere, which controls the right side of the body, is in charge of the brain's linear, rational, and orderly abilities; while the right hemisphere, controlling the left side of the body, is overseer of the brain's impressionistic, spontaneous, emotional, and aesthetic capacities. As we have just seen, much of the literature on urban planning reflects a debate between those who favor, in Smith's terms, one type of brain functioning over the other. But Smith argues that both aspects of mental functioning are ineradicable. People want order and stability (a left-hemisphere need) *and* spontaneity and novelty (a right-hemisphere need).

Smith's point for city planners, of course, is that both levels are fundamental and must be taken into account if we are to have successful urban planning. The trick is to find the balance, not to eliminate one or the other. We must have order in the city, but not too much (left hemisphere). We also must have spontaneity and aesthetic beauty, but, once again, not too much (right hemisphere). Too much regularity and order stultifies an urban setting, which can make people dull and unresponsive. Too much disorder, on the other hand, makes the city unpredictable and creates in people a feeling of unease, even fear. Smith would say that the great risk Howard and the socialists run is the creation of boring and deadening cities, whatever the political and economic successes. Conversely, the great risk run by planners in the Jane Jacobs mold is the creation of cities with so many individual interests that chaos results. In such cities a collective vision of the city's long-term goals would be difficult, if not impossible, to achieve.

Rouse Revisited: Big-Little Plans

James Rouse is probably the premier urban planner in America today. Columbia, Maryland, the totally planned community we reviewed earlier in this chapter, was his brainchild. As we suggested,

Columbia has not been the raging success it was initially envisioned to be. Undaunted, Rouse has shifted his attention to other projects of urban regeneration in recent years. Most of these have been *spectacularly* successful. Interestingly, they are neither comprehensive, all-encompassing visions like Columbia, nor small-scale, local efforts like those championed by Jane Jacobs. They are in-between—sort of big-little plans. "Big" in the sense that they take the needs of the whole city into account as well as its history, and "little" in the sense that they are localized—taking up only a small portion of the city's space. Thus, these plans express Smith's notion of the syntax of the city. The most well-known of Rouse's recent efforts are the Faneuil Hall complex in Boston, New York's South Street Seaport, Baltimore's Inner Harbor, and the Grand Avenue Mall in Milwaukee.

All of these projects have reclaimed portions of a dying center city. Rouse saw no reason that the deterioration of downtown in most Eastern American cities in the 1960s had to continue. Said he: "We have lived so long with grim, congested, worn out inner cities and sprawling, cluttered outer cities, that we have subconsciously come to accept them as inevitable and unavoidable. Deep down in our national heart is a lack of conviction that cities can be beautiful, humane, and truly responsive to the needs and yearnings of our people" (cited in Demarest 1981, pp. 37–9).

So he set to work. Before Rouse began, the Faneuil Hall area of Boston had become as tawdry as one could imagine. The site of the city center in Revolutionary War days, the area abounded with old, dilapidated warehouses that abutted on the harbor. No one lived there, only a few business firms remained: the locale could have been called "down and out" in a generous moment.

Today, it is transformed. The old warehouses have been outwardly maintained, but the inner cores modernized. Faneuil Hall has been revamped in the same manner. Inside are food shops that run its football-field length. On either side of the Hall are pedestrian areas with benches, outdoor eating areas, and places where street musicians play. The refurbished old warehouses on either side are now the place of business of high-quality shops. On any summer day, the place is teeming with people—locals, tourists, visitors from the suburbs. Looking at the project from the vantage point of one of the high rises in the area or from the harbor, one sees how Rouse's vision works: the new buildings mimic or harmoniously blend with the old buildings of the area. Perhaps most important, the businesses in the project are profitable—crucial in a capitalist system—and the success of the Faneuil Hall project has stimulated development in the whole downtown area of Boston. Nearby, other warehouses are being converted to co-ops, the Italian North End is undergoing renewal, and the regeneration is spreading into other parts of nearby Boston. Much the same has happened in Baltimore's Inner Harbor and, on a smaller scale, in New York's South Street Seaport.

Critics maintain that Rouse's inner city successes pander to the wealthier elements of the urban area and do little for the poor. There is truth in this accusation. Still, if one conceives of the city as *many* problems, certainly Rouse's changes have helped alleviate one: deteriorating inner-city locales have been replaced with thriving, vibrant places. They have helped bring the center areas of some cities back from the brink and, at the same time, have maintained a sense of linkage with the city's history. If, as Rouse says, "The only legitimate purpose of a city is to provide for the life and growth of its people" (cited in Demarest 1981, pp. 36–7), then perhaps *one* way of doing this is to use big-little plans like Rouse's.

The Realities of Urban Planning

There is still more to be considered. Whatever the philosophical stance one ultimately takes about urban planning, that planning always must be implemented in the city itself—an extremely complex physical, social, and cultural milieu. There are always traditions, vested interests, and environmental conditions that must be contended with. These are the realities urban plan-

ners must deal with. Let's take a few moments in conclusion to consider a few of them.

Economics and Politics

Major alterations in the urban landscape are extremely expensive to bring about, whether in capitalist or socialist nations. The history of city planning is a graveyard of ideas that never received the necessary economic support. Without government backing, Ebenezer Howard could establish only two garden cities. Even with government support, the British new-town effort has been limited or modified because of economic considerations. In the United States, Stein's Radburn, New Jersey, was never completed because of financial difficulties, and Reston, Virginia, has been in dire straits for the same reason. Partially because of its expense (and partially because of its audacity), Frank Lloyd Wright's Broadacre City was never built; and, for lack of funds, Paolo Soleri's Arcosanti grows excruciatingly slowly. Socialist cities, as well, have been delayed because government funds have been lacking or diverted to other areas—to military or agricultural expenses, for example. Even the most limited of city plans—plazas, monuments, sculpture—often go begging for economic reasons.

Politically, especially in Western cities, significant city plans are almost always surrounded by controversy, as interest group vies with interest group to satisfy its own particular vision of the city or meet its own more narrowly defined needs. Consider Cityscape 14-5, in which Norman Krumholz, past executive director of Cleveland's City Planning Commission, discusses his successes and failures as a city planner. Note that all of Krumholz's projects are relatively small in scale. Moreover, there is every reason to believe that the difficulties he ran into are typical; city planning may be "fun 'n' games" but implementation of that planning almost never is. Here are some examples.

Philadelphia. In what was once William Penn's proud city a major controversy is brewing. A developer has recently proposed a new complex that

---

CITYSCAPE 14-5

The Realities of City Planning in Cleveland

[One] of our successes had to do with a highway proposal, the Clark Freeway. It was authorized by the regional planning agency over our vociferous objection. We produced an analysis that showed the proposal offered practically nothing to the City of Cleveland at considerable costs to the city and the people of the city. Our recommendation to then Mayor Carl Stokes was that we challenge the regional agency and try to get them to rescind that highway decision. This led to a suit in Federal Court and [an attempt to decertify] the Northeast Ohio Areawide Coordinating Agency. [Finally] . . . we put eight more representatives on the agency board and . . . rescinded the controversial Clark Freeway proposals. So I think we

have to consider that kind of a major win.

In addition, in the spring of 1975, the City Planning Commission Staff and I created the framework for the negotiations for the transfer of the Cleveland Transit System to the Regional Transit Authority. . . . [We] were successfully able to bargain for reduced fares. We have a 25-cent fare now and reduced fares for the aged and the handicapped who are heavily transit dependent. . . . We got increased service. . . . We got [better] route spacing, so there is less distance to walk for a transit vehicle. We got a supplementary service called Community Responsive Transit, which resembles dial-a-bus right now, in the transit dependent neighborhoods

of the city. We think we worked out a good deal on the transit negotiations. . . . But it was a long battle. . . .

Those have been a number of important successes, but we do not always fight and win; we got bombed a lot more than we won, and we lost maybe 80% of the deals we got involved with. Let me recount some of the ones we have lost. The first issue was a rezoning issue. When I first got to Cleveland, a developer wanted to impose very high densities for residential development on an abandoned amusement park that faced Lake Erie. We insisted, as a condition for the rezoning, that he dedicate 300 feet of the depth of the frontage on the lake to the public for a park. Our insistence,

---

would include a building over 750 feet high—a skyscraper to be sure, but nothing like those twice that height in other cities. The complex would create many jobs in the construction process and many others in business, hotel, retail, and food services after completion. Moreover, like those of Baltimore and Boston, Philadelphia's downtown is in great need of rejuvenation. Although this may sound like a good idea, there are some difficulties. The 548-foot height of the Philadelphia City Hall, the city's landmark since 1894, has long been an informal restriction on upward development. The new complex would overshadow City Hall by 200 feet, thus breaking a strong link with tradition. The absence of higher skyscrapers has kept Philadelphia, in the eyes of many of its citizens, a more human-scale city, a city where people are not dwarfed by uncontrolled business interests. Once the height barrier is smashed, say proponents, ever-taller skyscrapers will follow and Philadelphia's manageability will be lost forever (Robbins 1984, p. 22). Which priorities are most

important here—tradition and manageability or economic revitalization?

Detroit. There is no doubt that until the revival of the automobile industry in the last few years, Detroit was a city in trouble. As the white population moved in droves to the suburbs, removing tax dollars from the city, the downtown declined rapidly, a large percentage of its housing stock becoming slumlike. Indeed, the situation was so bleak that in the November elections of 1984 the suburb of East Detroit considered changing its name officially to Erin Heights so that it could dissociate itself from its parent city.

Then, in 1980, General Motors proposed to build a new plant within the city limits if the city would provide the needed land (Jones and Bachelor 1984). On paper the idea seemed good. The plant would bring in jobs, tax revenues, and support industries. City officials were excited. However, problems arose. For one thing, in order to get GM to commit to building the plant in Detroit

of course, was illegal, but nobody cared about that. Anyhow, we successfully got the City Planning Commission to disapprove the zoning proposal, but we were overridden in the City Council by a 32 to 1 vote. The one member who supported us did so for the wrong reason; he had thought a different bill was coming up, and he voted the other way. Then we got involved in disapproving a proposed $350 million downtown tower investment because we felt it was a phony deal; the city was going to be asked to make massive capital improvements that were hidden in the legislation with no quid pro quos. That is to say, there did not seem to be any new jobs for city residents, particularly the unemployed. . . . We opposed it, and the City Planning Commission disapproved it. The President of the City Council called the City Planning Commission a "bunch of baboons," called for my resignation, and so on. Then the City Council overrode us—I think by 31 to 2. We have 33 city councilmen, so we did a little better on that one. . . .

What have we learned from all this? . . . The planner and public administrator in general want to address a problem only in terms of their own professional skills, and then they want to stop. . . . That is clearly not enough.

It is not enough if we are really serious about affecting outcomes, and that must be part of the definition of a city planner. . . . In matters of public policy, the people who decide are politicians. . . . It seems to me we have to be prepared to spend some time and take some risks in the political arena to work toward the goal of improved city conditions. If we are serious about our work, we have to understand much more clearly that decision-making is a long-term, continuing process, and so is implementation. It is not a single, clear act that just happens in time, after which we may go back to sleep.

Source: Norman Krumholz, "Cleveland: Problems of Declining Cities," in Anthony James Catanese and W. Paul Farmer, eds., *Personality, Politics, and Planning* (Beverly Hills, Calif.: Sage, 1978), pp. 65–70.

and not in some other city, the city had to give the company substantial tax breaks, thereby deferring the revenues so desperately needed. For another thing, a site had to be found. After considering various possibilities, the city and GM settled on an area known as Poletown, originally settled by Polish immigrants. But the people who still lived in Poletown were understandably unenthusiastic about being moved out. They formed a citizen's group and protested vigorously to the city—and even to the Michigan Supreme Court—but to no avail. The city was given the right of eminent domain to take their land, reimburse them at a "fair price," and destroy their homes. By the end of 1983, over 3,500 people and 150 small businesses had been relocated and 1,500 buildings demolished. To prepare the site adequately for GM, the city had to spend $200 million!

Jones and Bachelor (1984) suggest that this case illustrates numerous city-planning issues. Should a corporation be able to dictate (by threatening to relocate elsewhere) to a city government? Should city officials, who after all don't *live* on the site to be demolished, have the power to destroy a community of long standing? How can citizens *really* fight city hall on such issues? And, just as important, did Detroit give up so much in terms of tax incentives and spending to get the site ready that the GM plant would actually provide few financial benefits to the city?

These are not easy questions. They point to the fact that any implementation of urban planning inevitably involves trade-offs. Some will benefit at the cost of others. To illustrate further, let us consider one final case.

Austin. Like many cities, Austin, the capital of Texas, a thriving Sunbelt city, has an emergency medical service (EMS), a corps of ambulances and medical staff that respond to distress calls from various locations in the city. During the 1970s, Austin grew rapidly, increasing its population nearly 200,000—from 360,000 to 537,000. Concerned with the quality of care and the cost of delivering such life-and-death service, the Austin city government hired David Eaton and his associates (1985) to analyze the situation and suggest alternatives.

What Eaton found was a situation where interest groups were in intense competition with one another—doctors' demands for the highest quality of care came up against government officials' concern for the cost of the service, and different neighborhoods' demands that *their* locale get rapid and competent response. To make matters more complicated, the city's neighborhoods reflected the interests of three different racial groups—blacks, Hispanics, and Anglos (whites). Finally, the city wanted to build a service that would take into account projected needs as the population grew in the coming decades.

However implemented, the EMS had to serve some of these interests more than others. That was the bottom line, the reality of the situation. (To take just one case: the city's blacks and Anglos live in essentially segregated districts. Providing the most rapid service to one district would mean not being able to provide that service to a district located in another direction.) The problem thus was twofold: to discover just what the city's options were and then to make a choice among them.

To solve the first problem, Eaton's group used a sophisticated computer analysis which divided the city into districts and then determined how much it would cost the city to get the most rapid and high-quality service to any given interest group. Then they determined what type of service the rest of the city would get if interest group A got the highest quality service. The end result was a series of plans from which the city could choose to solve the second problem: how to implement an EMS for the city of Austin.

Eaton's plans put the city government in a pretty touchy position. As already noted, the adoption of any *one* plan meant that some interest groups would be served more than others. Somebody was sure to yell "Foul!" no matter *what* was done.

The method finally adopted to solve the dilemma is interesting and instructive. The city government held a series of public meetings where members of each interest group could ex-amine all the plans and speak their mind regarding them. In this way, each group had a chance to influence the government's final decision.

After all the hearings, the government adopted an EMS plan that would service 87 percent of all calls from all areas of the city within five minutes—a remarkably efficient solution. Nevertheless, not all interest groups were served equally. The plan called for the EMS to respond most quickly to calls from the city's black neighborhoods, second most quickly to calls from the Hispanic neighborhoods, and least quickly to calls from the Anglo areas. The city government chose this solution (despite the fact that the majority of government members were Anglo) because it recognized, as a result of the arguments presented at the hearings, that violence levels were greater in the black and Hispanic areas and that these groups typically did not have their own doctors. Hence, without an efficient EMS there was a much greater threat to life for individuals in these groups than for individuals from Anglo populations.

This is a most laudable and perhaps surprising outcome to a complex problem. It should remind us of a very serious issue: *For whom* do we plan cities? As our discussion of urban renewal in the last chapter revealed, city-planning projects have often served elites. In the history of city planning the story is the same: the poor and minorities have fared less well almost by definition. As Bachrach and Baratz (1970) have shown in their study of city politics and planning in Baltimore, all political systems seem to rest upon a set of beliefs, values, and behavioral patterns that benefit those in power. A recent study by Walton (1982) concluded much the same. Walton found that in the Reagan administration's proposed "urban enterprise zones" plan, by which businesses would be encouraged to locate new facilities in inner-city slum areas, benefits would accrue mainly to the firms in the form of massive tax breaks. The poor living in the enterprise zones would benefit little, if at all.

Marxist critic Michael Smith has written recently, "In capitalist societies, urban planners have tended to serve the values and interests of corporate capitalist city builders and suburban developers . . . [P]lanners work within limits set by those who can pay their bills" (1979, p. 253). More recent studies by Boyer (1983) and Steinberger (1985) reach the same conclusions. But the socialist countries have not been all that much better regarding the question of whose plans are implemented. The state is in control and makes decisions for everyone, often with little public consultation.

All these reminders make the Austin decision all that more remarkable. Through a careful process of analysis of all available options and a hearing of all arguments by all parties interested in the problem, the city government made a decision that advantaged the poorer and minority populations of the city more than the rich majority. It *is* atypical, but it does show that such solutions *can* be reached if a city's people are knowledgeable of the decisions affecting their lives and, in addition, are allowed to influence those decisions in a reasonable way.

The Difference That Values Make

This brings us to what is probably the most important reality. In the final analysis, urban planning is always a question of values: *which* and *whose* are the key issues. From the beginning of this chapter we have seen that city planning was always imbued with cultural or historical values. In Catholic Rome we found planning that glorified the church; in monarchic France we saw planning that glorified the king; in nineteenth- and twentieth-century New York, we found planning that augmented the pursuit of the almighty dollar.

Values also permeate, explicitly or implicitly, the work of urban planners. In his review of Jane Jacobs's *Death and Life of Great American Cities*, Herbert Gans (1962, pp. 170–175) suggests that Jacobs is a typical product of Western society. She complains that city planning has not been successful because it has not been left up to the people. What could be more Western, more North American, Gans asks, than this complaint that we need greater emphasis on the importance of the individual, the small group, and local initiative? Gans suggests that Jacobs misses the crucial role played in the success or failure of urban planning

by larger social patterns, such as racial discrimination and financial destitution.

Significantly, the same values implicitly lauded by Jacobs appear in virtually all American city planning. Even planners like Columbia's James Rouse, who specifically *rejects* the American idea that money is everything, have a bottom-line commitment to the profit motive. Said Rouse in an interview:

> The business mentality today is that the pursuit of profit is the purpose of life, and that people come second or third. I think that's deplorable. It's why development has such a bad name and why cities suffer from so much ugliness. What should be important is to produce something of benefit to mankind. If that happens, then the profit will be there. (Pawlyna 1981, p. 64)

Similarly, given all his vehement opposition to building cities in the traditional American manner, Frank Lloyd Wright's Broadacre City plan was steeped in Americana: he envisioned a city where the individual was beholden to no one and where the privately owned parcel of land, car, or helicopter would predominate.

It is likely that Gans would be as critical of these designs as he is of Jane Jacobs's proposals. While they must be applauded for their refreshingly different approach to city building, if their underlying values are the same as the values of more traditional city planners, what is to keep many of the old problems from reemerging? Indeed, in our discussion of Rouse's Columbia, we saw that the old problems *did* reemerge: racial and class tensions, an unwillingness to put community welfare above individual desires, and a desire to maximize profit have all played their part in keeping Columbia from fully realizing its ideals.

Similarly, because most Americans are deeply committed to the values of individuality and personal profit, all-inclusive plans like Le Corbusier's, Soleri's, or those of socialist cities are dreaded like the plague. Such plans appear to demand subscription to, even submersion in, the group. Since such a commitment would severely limit their vision of "individual initiative," most Americans involved in city planning have fought long and hard to keep the government's role in matters urban to an absolute minimum.

Indeed, perhaps *the* characteristic element of American urban planning has been the *lack* of such planning on the state and federal levels throughout our history. From the 1600s on, American cities have grown and changed with extremely limited intervention by any governmental form larger than the city itself. Occasionally, a national plan is developed, like the Model Cities program of the 1960s and the New Towns Act of the last decade. But these are small, piecemeal efforts, designed to be implemented in only a few areas. Furthermore, the general impetus behind the Reagan administration's New Federalism philosophy is not to get the federal government *more* involved in national programs, but less. Hence, sweeping programs for correcting the problems of our cities are not likely to be forthcoming.

This is nothing new. Quite simply, Americans have no overall plans or policies for their cities *because they do not want them.* Our national urban policy, really, is to have *no* national urban policy. If private sector investors, like Jim Rouse, can't make our cities better, if limited programs, like the New Towns Act, can't help, then we'll have to live with the consequences (which as we have seen, particularly in chapters 11 through 13, are considerable). French and Hamilton sum up well:

> State intervention and control [in cities] in Western countries is aimed at, and can only hope to achieve, the amelioration of the inadequacies of the existing system because planning has to operate within the limits imposed by private ownership of land and buildings, private control of investment, and the greater freedom of choice and action possessed by the individual, *even when such action may not be in the public interest.* (1979, p. 19; emphasis added)

Of course, the obverse applies in socialist countries like the Soviet Union: individual choice and local differences are seen as a distinct threat to the wider collective vision.

So the last reality of urban planning is its linkage to (often unperceived) cultural values. Different societies support different forms of city planning, not because they are able to demonstrate conclusively that their form of planning is inher-

ently superior to any other, but because they believe *a priori* that it *is* superior. Hence, to be consistent with their own cultural values, they must prefer one type of plan automatically, while, equally automatically, rejecting another. Whatever the evidence, it is doubtful that Jane Jacobs's type of argument will make much headway in the socialist countries in the near future. By the same token, it is difficult to imagine future American city planners advocating organizing the city collectively, as modern Moscow has done. If they did, the catcalls would be heard all over town.

Conclusion

Can we honestly say that one type of city planning has been spectacularly more effective than any other? Our review suggests a number of conclusions.

First, all the evidence suggests that changing the city's physical plant is not enough. In new towns the world over, from Ebenezer Howard's Letchworth to James Rouse's Columbia to Lucio Costa's Brasilia, despite the best intentions, the old, *culturally based* problems reemerge. People still exhibit harmful prejudices, class separations, and income differences; and larger cultural forces—such as the rush to cities in Latin America—continue to play their part. While changing the city physically is *necessary*, it is not *sufficient* to create the idealistic living environment envisioned by almost all city planners. We must be sophisticated, sociologically as well as architecturally.

Second, it is safe to say that none of the planning experiments of the last century has been an unqualified success. New towns have not solved the problems of the larger cities, nor have they been able to solve many of their own difficulties. Utopian designs (to the degree that they have been actualized) show similar limitations. Likewise, socialist cities, despite significant strides at eliminating some of the more egregious faults (such as crime and poverty) of capitalist cities, still face major problems of production, overpopulation, individual initiative, and, not least, vitality. Finally, small-scale efforts, such as those proposed by Jane Jacobs, August Heckscher, William Whyte, and James Rouse in his revamping of inner-city areas, are piecemeal, often pit interest groups irreconcilably against one another, and usually leave untouched the larger problems of the city—such as racial prejudice and income differentiation. While more widespread implementation of any of these planning styles doubtless would produce benefits, it is unlikely that any would do much more than it has already at solving the city's multiple ills. There seem to be inherent strengths *and* weaknesses in each.

Third, we always must bear in mind that urban planning occurs within a framework of certain ineradicable realities. Economic and political considerations influence the ability of any plan to be implemented successfully. If it costs too much, it won't be done. If sponsored by the rich, it probably won't help the poor very much. If any group is offended, the plan will be resisted. If it's sponsored by the government or a corporate entity, the planner will probably have to serve *their* interests, not her or his own. Ignorance or obliviousness to such realities on the part of urban planners is foolhardy at best, disastrous at worst.

In the end, of course, the most important reality facing urban planning has to do with values. For centuries, peoples' cultural biases and personal interests have subtly or overtly influenced and controlled what urban plans they were willing to countenance. Today, the valuational differences that separate socialist and capitalist societies perform the same controlling function. Individualist plans are anathema in the socialist bloc; collectivist visions are not brooked in the capitalist countries.

The irony of this standoff, if Peter Smith's recent theory about the syntax of cities is correct, is that the urban plans that may work best at alleviating the city's difficulties probably combine elements of *both* approaches. Smith's work suggests we need both overarching order and control (long stressed in socialist planning) and freedom to choose (the focus of most capitalist planning) if we are to attain the best possible urban environment. To preclude either is to court defeat from the outset. Yet, given their uncritical commitment to a cultural ideology, this often seems to be what urban planners are bent on doing. To gain some distance from this parochial "value bind," it would seem essential that future urban planners immerse themselves deeply in the visions of planners elsewhere and try to understand both the reasons for such ideas and the resistances they might feel toward them.

Last, it seems to us there should be an overarching set of questions to guide urban planning. *Why* is a plan being undertaken in the first place? *Who* does the plan really benefit? *What* is the relationship between this plan and the long- and short-term goals and welfare of the city overall? Guiding all of these questions, we also suggest, should be a clearly stated fundamental value concern: a commitment to the health and welfare of *all* people who live in the city, considered both individually and collectively. Without such a focus, city planners cannot help but repeat the failures of the past. With such an orientation, it is possible that in time a vision of the street might emerge that perhaps—just perhaps—all citizens could understand.

CHAPTER 15

The Good City and the Future of Cities

'This music crept by me upon the waters'
And along the Strand, up Queen Victoria
*   Street.*
O City city, I can sometimes hear
Beside a public bar in Lower Thames Street,
The pleasant whining of a mandolin
And a clatter and a chatter from within
Where fishmen lounge at noon; where the
*   walls*
Of Magnus Martyr hold
Inexplicable splendour of Ionian White
*   and gold.*

T. S. ELIOT, "THE WASTE LAND"

Having made our visit to cities around the world, past and present, we come full circle. What, finally, can we say about the good city and the likely future of cities? For the last 14 chapters we have considered the complex elements that comprise the urban phenomenon. We have seen that the city began some 10,000 years ago and has gone through a long process of development, destruction, and rebirth (chapters 2 and 3). We have seen, as well, that cities generally do not fit the negative stereotypes some people hold about them (Chapter 4), that they create a unique social psychological experience (Chapter 5), that they are

inextricably linked to the physical environment in which they exist (Chapter 6), and that they are indelibly shaped by the culture in which they exist and the unique histories they possess (chapters 7 through 10).

But the city's promise has always been more than simply providing a distinctive way of life. The city has always held out the promise of a *better* way of life, a more affluent, more sophisticated, more humane life. In chapters 11 through 13 we considered how well this promise has been fulfilled in a detailed examination of the American city. While certainly the promise has been fulfilled for many urbanites, not much digging was necessary to discover that it has not been fully realized for everyone. Many continue to suffer the indignities of poverty and racial discrimination. Moreover, we found that our American cities as a whole are languishing under heavy burdens: poverty, crime, pollution, financial crises. The situation is much worse in many other cities of the world.

The key word that leaps out from the T. S. Eliot poem that begins this chapter is "sometimes": *sometimes* the city lives up to its promise of providing the best that life can offer. Significantly, this uplifting passage appears in a poem otherwise dedicated to a scathing critique of modern society and its urban life. "The Waste Land," according to Eliot, is more prevalent than the city's "inexplicable splendor." Can we hope for a more humane urban future?

This is a question fueled by more than academic interest. The world is becoming ever more urban (Table 1-1). If we cannot create better cities, we may doom future urban citizens to even greater difficulties than those experienced by their forebears.

We began our examination of the possibilities of a more humane city in Chapter 14 by considering the actual plans that thinkers, architects, and city planners have proposed for making better cities. We found strengths, weaknesses, and biases in all these plans.

However, there might be another way to consider the issue: we could develop some prototypical idea of what the best city might be—a model of the good city. One purpose of this final chapter is to examine what the characteristics of such a city might be, to see whether such cities exist today, and to evaluate the possibility of creating such cities in the future. The best way to begin this process is to find out what others have considered good or great cities.

The Debate Over the Good City: More Visions

Whitman

The great city is that which has the greatest man or woman;

If it be a few ragged huts, it is still the greatest city in the whole world . . .

The place where the great city stands is not the place of stretch'd wharves, docks, manufactures, deposits of produce . . .

Nor the place of the tallest and costliest buildings, or shops selling goods from the rest of the earth,

Nor the place of the best libraries and schools—nor the place where money is plentiest,

Nor the place of the most numerous population. . . .

Where thrift is in its place, and prudence is in its place;

Where the men and women think lightly of the laws;

Where the slave ceases, and the master of slaves ceases;

Where the populace rise at once against the never-ending audacity of elected persons . . .

Where the citizen is always the head and ideal—and President, Mayor, Governor, and what not, are agents for pay;

Where children are taught to be laws to themselves, and to depend on themselves;

Where equanimity is illustrated in affairs;

Where speculations on the Soul are encouraged;

Where women walk in public processions in the streets, the same as the men;

Where they enter the public assembly and take places the same as the men;

Where the city of the faithfullest friends stands . . .

There the great city stands.

WALT WHITMAN, "SONG OF THE BROAD-AXE"

The nineteenth-century American poet, Walt Whitman, thought he knew what the good city was. It was people with a particular type of *attitude*: tolerant of one another, wary of external domination, and oriented to the fulfillment of their personal needs. Noble sentiments; sentiments virtually all of us could share.

But is Whitman's vision an *adequate* model for the good city? With a few strokes of his pen he has dispensed with the importance of the city's buildings, economic arrangements, educational facilities, and size of population. Surely this would have made many of the people we encountered in Chapter 14 nervous. To pick just two examples: to Ebenezer Howard, planning a vital economy and limiting population were essential ingredients in constructing the good city; to August Heckscher the careful arrangement of a city's space—its buildings, parks, art—was integral in fostering good city life.

Howard and Heckscher likely would argue that Whitman is being too "social-psychological" in

---

BOX 15-1
The Heavenly City of God

Then I saw a new heaven and a new earth. . . . And I saw the holy city, new Jerusalem, coming down out of heaven from God, prepared as a bride adorned for her husband; and I heard a great voice from the throne saying, "Behold, the dwelling of God is with men. He will dwell with them, and they shall be his people, and God himself will be with them; he will wipe away every tear from their eyes, and death shall be no more, neither shall there be mourning nor crying nor pain any more, for the former things have passed away."

. . . [The city] had a great, high wall, with twelve gates, and at the gates twelve angels, and on the gates the names of the twelve tribes of the sons of Israel were inscribed. . . . The city lies four-square, its length the same as its breadth. . . . The wall was built of jasper, while the city was pure gold, clear as glass. And the twelve gates were twelve pearls, each of the gates made of a single pearl. . . .

And I saw no temple in the city, for its temple is the Lord God the Almighty and the Lamb . . . and the kings of the earth shall bring their glory into it, and its gates shall never be shut by day—and there shall be no night there; they shall bring into it the glory and the honor of the nations. But nothing unclean shall enter it, nor any one who practices abomination or falsehood, but only those who are written in the Lamb's book of life.

Then he showed me the river of the water of life, bright as crystal, flowing from the throne of God and of the Lamb through the middle of the street of the city; also, on either side of the river, the tree of life with its twelve kinds of fruit, yielding its fruit each month; and the leaves of the tree were for the healing of the nations. There shall no more be anything accursed . . . and his servants shall worship him; they shall see his face, and his name shall be on their foreheads. And night shall be no more; they need no light of lamp or sun, for the Lord God will be their light, and they shall reign for ever and ever.

Source: Book of Revelations, *New Testament* (R.S.V.), Chaps. 21–22.

---

his vision of the great city. He hasn't looked deeply enough to see that the urban dweller's attitudes are part and parcel of a much more complex set of forces. Both would argue further that Whitman's "right attitudes" can be fostered in people only when the city's other major elements—its relationship to its physical setting and to the broader culture—are organized in such a way as to support and encourage the growth of these ideals.

This is a solid critique. Whitman's vision *is* too simple. The question is not whether tolerance and a concern for personal fulfillment are important attitudes for urban citizens to possess (most would agree they are); the question is what arrangement of the city's elements is likely to bring them about. With this in mind, let's turn to other conceptions.

Plato's Laws

As we saw in Case Study 7-2, the Greeks of the Hellenic period put significant effort into making Athens the good city. Where it fell short, Plato offered them an even greater ideal. The best city,

he wrote in *The Laws*, should be located near the middle of the country with an acropolis at its center. It should be divided into 12 major districts and subdivided into 5,040 plots (a number chosen because it is divisible by any number from one to ten). Each plot then should be assigned so as to provide each household with land of equal quality. Overall, the city should have no more than 5,000 households, and property should be inheritable only by sons or the husbands of daughters. If families had too many children, "excess" children were to be adopted or transferred to other areas so that a stable population could be ensured. The citizenry (remember only *males* were citizens) would be divided into priests, artisans, farmers, warriors, and philosophers. The latter always would be the city's leaders ("kings," Plato says) because of their specialized knowledge in human affairs (Rosenau 1972, pp. 19–20).

St. John's Revelation

Plato's version of the good city is very much a city of the material world. The Christian tradition is quite different. In that vision, the last thing we

Figure 15-1 *Scamozzi's Ideal City*
Source: Helen Rosenau, The Ideal City *(New York: Harper & Row, 1972), p. 60. Reprinted by permission of Curtis Brown Academic Ltd. on behalf of Helen Rosenau.*

want is a city governed by *human* ideals. As history has demonstrated time and again, that always leads to disaster. Rather, what is needed is a city ruled by God, a city where people are so spiritually oriented that all the petty problems of this world fade away. Box 15-1 contains the essence of St. John's vision of the Heavenly City of God.

The interesting thing about Plato's this-worldly and John's other-worldly versions of the good city is that both, like Whitman's, are partial visions. Plato focuses on the arrangement of physical space and assigns immutable social rules. He assumes that, if his "laws" are lived up to, all the city's inhabitants will be happy. John's vision is more like Whitman's. He suggests that if people were only spiritual enough, the heavenly city would appear and all earthly desires would be fulfilled automatically. Neither vision suggests the necessity of considering *all* the elements of the city we have studied: its physical environment, the experience it creates, and the all-important cultural setting that guides the city's daily life.

Something else may be noted about Plato's and John's visions. Like the city planners' visions

of Chapter 14, they are both firmly rooted in the values and cultural concerns of their time, place, and group. Plato's good city is an integration of the cities of his day with Greek cosmology, and John's heavenly city is a combination of Christian religious values and the actual Middle Eastern cities of the pre-Christian era (Rosenau 1972, Chap. 1).

Scamozzi's Ideal City

Examine next Vincenzo Scamozzi's Ideal City of the sixteenty-century Italian Renaissance (Figure 15-1). His city is walled, has 12 gates, a grid plan, a large central square for church and city government, and four other symmetrically placed squares for marketing activities. On reflection, we can see easily that Scamozzi's city is linked to the social concerns and values of *his* time. The wall is a remnant of an era when the need for city protection was pronounced; the 12 gates are a link to the Christian biblical tradition of St. John's Heavenly City; the church at the center reflects the same religious heritage and its importance in

Italian life; the city hall symbolizes the growing role of municipal government; and the grid plan is representative of the emerging importance in urban affairs of trade and efficient use of space.

Doxiadis: Ecumenopolis

Finally, let us move to the present and consider the all-encompassing vision of Greek planner C. A. Doxiadis (1974). Unlike any of the good city proponents we have considered thus far, Doxiadis sees the trend to ever larger cities—even to megacities of 10 million or more—as natural and even desirable. As cities grow in size, they will form linked urban areas with no real rural space between them, as has already happened in parts of the United States and Europe. Such urban areas will be the "city of the future," which Doxiadis dubs "Ecumenopolis," after his notion that such a city will be of all races, colors, and creeds.

Since we are already well on our way to Ecumenopolis, Doxiadis thinks, the city planner's task is to identify true human needs and how the city can facilitate their satisfaction. We need to usher in the transitional phase of "Anthropopolis," the city of human development. We can now consider some of Doxiadis's ideas about fundamental human needs and what we need to do to satisfy them in the urban environment.

He suggests that people have always lived by five basic principles: (1) seeking to maximize potential contacts with other people and things (water, food, etc.); (2) minimizing their effort in doing so; (3) optimizing their use of space; (4) optimizing their relationship with other elements in the system of life—nature, society, networks of communication; and (5) optimizing the relationship of all these principles with each other. Since the growth of megacities is inevitable, the job of creating the good city is basically *technical*—understanding how to maximize all of these principles and then applying this knowledge to existing cities. If a city is too densely populated—that is, people are not maximizing their use of space (principle 3 above)—then we need to find a way to spread them out. This applies to all the principles in all cities.

Beyond the specifics of Doxiadis's plan, consider how thoroughly "modern" his ideas are. For him, growth is inevitable and desirable, and the solution to our urban woes is basically a "fix-it" job. This sounds like planning a superhighway or simply taking your TV to the repair shop. It also is instructive to contrast Doxiadis's views with those of St. John. Writing in a period when religion was dominant, St. John saw the good city only coming about when people believe in God more fully. Writing in technical and scientific times, Doxiadis doesn't mention religion at all. Rather, he focuses on the effects of *modern, rational technology* on urban living.

Rasmussen and Bauer: The Debate over the Ideal City

Next, consider the contrasting positions taken by Steer Eiler Rasmussen and Catherine Bauer, both contemporary urban critics. First, Rasmussen asserts that to

> search for the ideal city today is useless. For all cities are different. Each has its own spirit, its own problems, and its own pattern of life. As long as the city lives, these aspects continue to change. . . . In fact, the concept is obsolete; there is no such thing.
>
> When we turn to the cities of the Renaissance, it is easy to see why the notion of the ideal city made some sense in those times. . . . In a [Renaissance] town, houses were all of the same kind. . . . The contour of the town was rigidly shaped by its geometrically-designed fortifications. . . .
>
> Today . . . the town planner must meet his problems without any sort of prejudice about how a city should look. . . . He . . . is like a doctor or educator who studies [individual] human beings and finds out how to guide their development. . . .
>
> The modern city is determined by the flexible laws of its interior life. Unlike geometrical rules, these laws are not universal. . . . What is right in one place may be wrong in another. (1955, pp. 367–368)

Now, contrast Bauer's view:

[T]he modern city poses the universal dilemma of our times—society versus freedom. The good city must protect minimum living standards but at the same time provide an environment favorable to creative experiment, freedom of initiative, and maximum consumer choice. . . .

Faced with these complex requirements, is there any point in continuing the old search for a definite concept of the ideal city? Is there any use in seeking for a generalized physical form that would, in theory at least, best satisfy our necessities? . . .

The answer is yes. It is absolutely necessary to develop *images* of the present-day ideal city. . . . Experience during the last twenty years underlines the need for ideal images . . . [W]ithout the guidance of ideals . . . [we have produced] great barrack blocks of public housing which are all too often managed like an old-fashioned asylum or mental institution. There are vast suburban Federal Housing Administration projects with thousands of identical boxes for families who are equally identical in age, income, and race. . . . There are also expensive slum clearance and redevelopment projects, apparently adding to the congestion and sharpening the race relations problem. . . . (1955, pp. 369–370)

Rasmussen's argument for the uniqueness and individuality of cities and Bauer's focus on the common elements of cities are reflective of what is probably the most crucial value debate of *our* time, the debate between individual interests and collective responsibilities, a debate that we have seen take a most virulent tone in the confrontations of proponents of capitalist and socialist cities in the last chapter.

Evaluation

Two considerations have emerged thus far in considering a model of the good city. First, it would seem imperative that an adequate model of the good city would have to be *integrative*. It would have to take into account all the major elements of urban existence—the city's environmental setting, its links to the larger culture, its historical uniqueness, and the experience it creates.

Second, if thinkers like Plato, Scamozzi, Rasmussen, and Bauer are any example, it would seem unavoidable that a model of the good city

also will be *value laden*. Of necessity, it would have to say that *this* way of organizing urban life is better than *that*. Taking such value positions, of course, is always tricky business. People, as we have seen, often radically disagree with one another as to what is valuable. How can we say objectively which values are most important?

Probably we cannot. As our discussion illustrates, any model of the good city will reflect, whether we wish it to or not, the creator's personal values and, in some form, the values of his or her social class, culture, and historical period. To us, products of twentieth-century Western culture, Plato's vision of the good city probably seems a bit sterile and "force fed," without much room for change or choice. To many in Plato's circle it probably seemed well-nigh perfect. These same considerations apply to the model of the good city we will present in the pages to follow. It is a product of a certain set of personal, class, cultural, and historical values. It cannot be otherwise.

This lack of ultimate objectivity should not dissuade us, however, from *trying* to create a model of the good city. In the end, we side with Bauer and not Rasmussen. Although for historical, cultural, or locational reasons each city truly is unique and therefore requires some type of special consideration not likely to be relevant in other cities, there *are* commonalities. Not to consider these commonalities is to make an implicit value judgment that allows the forces already at work in the city go on working without our intervention. On the other hand, to consider such commonalities and consciously decide whether some of them are conducive to the city's life (and hence should be encouraged) while others are destructive of that life (and hence should be discouraged), is to stimulate the debate on urban life and push our understanding of cities further. In other words, simply *proposing* a model of the good city is an exercise in value exposure (of the values already present in the urban setting) and value clarification (of the values being proposed).

There is another, less subtle, reason for constructing a model of the good city. Like those who have preceded us in such an endeavor—Whitman, Scamozzi, Doxiadis, and the like—we, too, believe that the city is not all it could be and that, as a result, the lives of the city's inhabitants are less fulfilling than they might be. Consequently, we, the authors of this book, also want to influence how people interested in cities think about them, act in them, even act to change them.

What are these values and how do they form the basis for our model of the good city? What do we mean by a phrase such as "the city's people are leading less fulfilling lives than they might be"?

To get at these questions we will begin with a comment from urban planner Kevin Lynch's recent book, *A Theory of Good City Form* (1981). Lynch thought that the best way to begin thinking about ideal city form was to begin with the observation "that the human species has certain basic requirements for survival and well-being, and that in any given culture there are important common values" that are related to and support such survival and well-being (1981, p. 103). In other words, Lynch begins with the notion that people *need* certain things in order to survive and that it is the job of the city to provide those things.

Such an approach to the good city might be called a "need theory model." Let us be even more specific. We would argue that *the good city is an urban setting able to meet all the basic needs of its citizens adequately.* Further, we would argue, following anthropologist Ashley Montagu (1958), that *the basic needs of people are essentially of three types: physical* (such as food, shelter), *mental* (such as love, security, stimulation), *and social* (a sense of community and meaningful participation). In other words, if a given city were able to provide all its citizens with adequate amounts of food and shelter and another city were not, then, on the criterion of physical needs satisfaction, we would judge the first city to be a better city.

But of course it is more complex than this example suggests. We are interested here in *three* basic types of human needs, and it is entirely possible that a city may do well in satisfying one need and not another. For example, as noted in chapters 5 and 10, contemporary Chinese cities appear to have eradicated hunger and the ravages of poverty for their entire citizenry. In comparison, as we saw most distressingly in chapters 12 and 13, significant portions of the population of American cities are still visited by these twin scourges. Considering another basic need, however, that for mental stimulation, the balance appears to shift in favor of the American city. Despite the existence of considerable poverty within them most major American cities are vibrant and intellectually alive. Chinese cities, on the other hand, are not as vital because people do not have as much freedom, and seem to be chafing at the bit somewhat as a result. The trick, it would seem, is for a city to be able to satisfy all three levels of need simultaneously.

But—has any city ever done this? Is it even possible? To find out we need to take a look at what others have thought were particularly good cities and see whether these three types of needs are being satisfied. Moreover, even if these cities are not completely successful in this complex task, we can learn from them. We can learn what conditions of social structure appear to facilitate the satisfaction of different human needs. And that, after all, is the truly important policy question regarding the good city. If we could construct a model of the social structural characteristics that promote the satisfaction of these three types of human need—then we would have a tool not only to *evaluate* existing cities, but also a tool that would suggest how cities might be *reorganized* cities to meet more of the needs of more of their people in the future.

Thus, the next step is to look at what supposedly are good cities. However, once again, we would expect opinions to differ as to which cities provide the higher quality of life. Europeans laud London or Paris; Canadians tout Vancouver, Montreal, and Toronto. In the United States the same case is made for Boston, Chicago, New York, Washington, New Orleans, and (despite the smog) Los Angeles. Nevertheless, poll after poll shows that most Americans rate none of these cities as America's best. That honor goes, time and again, to San Francisco (Davis 1971); hence, we will begin our search for a truly useful model of the good city there.

San Francisco's unique setting gives it much of its charm. The city has built itself around and over its many hills. See the front cover for a view of downtown with Coit Tower in the foreground. (John J. Macionis)

CASE STUDY 15-1
San Francisco: America's Good City?

The Physical Setting

To begin with, the site that the city occupies is spectacular. Situated on the northernmost part of an extremely hilly peninsula within the limited space of a few square miles, San Francisco ranges from sea level to a height of 934 feet. The hills create vista upon vista of the city, the San Francisco Bay, and the striking Bay Area (including the cities of Berkeley and Oakland and the counties of Contra Costa, Marin, and San Mateo). For most of the year the surrounding land masses are a stunning gold and, in spring, a lush green. It hardly ever snows and the daily average temperature, year round, is 55 degrees.

The city's famous fog is also a product of its setting. As the land cools, fog advances over the city from the Pacific. Impeded by the hills, the fog is often trapped in valleys or in the narrow entrance to San Francisco Bay known as the Golden Gate.

In sum, San Francisco has a remarkable environment. No one has ever captured the excitement of this setting better than Herb Caen, whose odes of joy to his city have appeared in the *San Francisco Chronicle* for more than 30 years. A sample is presented in Cityscape 15-1.

San Francisco's Culture of Civility

Sociologists Howard S. Becker and Irving Louis Horowitz (1971) claim that San Francisco is the one city in the United States capable of tolerating nearly every type of life-style and human activity. This they call the city's "culture of civility" (see Box 15-2), a mind-set very akin to the tolerance championed by Walt Whitman a century ago.

As a result of its culture of civility, San Francisco has become a haven for groups out of the

American mainstream—homosexuals, political radicals, radical feminists, and religious and "human potential" cults of all kinds, most of whom live their life-styles openly. But rather than fearing such groups, San Franciscans have generally learned to enjoy their presence. In many other cities, Becker and Horowitz argue,

> people assume, when they see someone engaging in proscribed activity, that there is worse to come. "Anyone who would do that (take dope, dress in women's clothes, sell his body or whatever) would do anything. . . ." Common sense ignores the contrary cases around us everywhere: professional criminals often flourish a legionnaire's patriotism . . . homosexuals may be good family providers. . . . Deviance, like conforming behavior, is highly selective. . . . San Francisco's culture of civility, accepting that premise, assumes that if I know that you steal or take dope or peddle your ass, that is all I *know*. (1971, pp. 6–7)

Also because of their culture of civility, San Franciscans engage in frequent interaction with members of these unconventional groups and have learned that the stereotypes of these groups are fundamentally incorrect. Hippies, for example, are not drug-crazed maniacs but simply human beings spending their days differently from others (Becker and Horowitz 1971, p. 7).

Not surprisingly, most San Franciscans rate their city highly. Robert Wuthnow (1976) reports that an overwhelming 85 percent of Bay Area residents said they were satisfied with their community.

In short, there is good evidence that suggests that San Francisco is, in many respects, a pretty good city. It apparently has a very positive relationship with its physical environment, a vital, heterogeneous population, and it creates, for many, an entrancing, almost mesmerizing urban experience. Cityscape 15-2 presents a typical case of infatuation with San Francisco.

What accounts for this success? We turn to the city's history for an answer.

History

Backwater: 1776–1847. In Cityscape 1-1 we presented Richard Henry Dana's impression of early San Francisco. When Dana first visited the Bay

---

BOX 15-2
Openness and Tolerance in San Francisco

Walking in the Tenderloin [vice district] on a summer evening, a block from the Hilton, you hear a black whore cursing at a policeman: "I wasn't either blocking the sidewalk! Why don't you motherfucking fuzz mind your own goddamn business!" The visiting New Yorker expects to see her arrested, if not shot, but the cop smiles good-naturedly and moves on, having got her back into the doorway where she is supposed to be.

You enter one of the famous rock ballrooms and, as you stand getting used to the noise and lights, someone puts a lit joint of marijuana in your hand. The tourist looks for someplace to hide, not wishing to be caught in the mass arrest he expects to follow. No need to worry. The police will not come in, knowing if they do they will have to arrest people and create disorder.

Candidates for the city's Board of Supervisors make their pitch for the homosexual vote, estimated by some at 125,000. They will not be run out of town; the candidates' remarks are dutifully reported in the daily paper, as are the evaluations of them by representatives of SIR, the Society for Individual Rights.

The media report (tongue in cheek) the annual Halloween Drag Ball, for which hundreds of homosexuals turn out at one of the city's major hotels in full regalia, unharassed by police.

One sees long-haired, bearded hippies all over the city, not just in a few preserves set aside for them. Straight citizens do not remark their presence, either by gawking, hostility or flight.

Nudie movies, frank enough to satisfy anyone's curiosity, are exhibited in what must be the largest number of specialty movie houses per capita in the country. Periodic police attempts to close them down (one of the few occasions when repression has been attempted) fail.

Source: Howard S. Becker and Irving Louis Horowitz, "The Culture of Civility," in Howard S. Becker, ed., *Culture and Civility in San Francisco* (New Brunswick, N.J.: *Trans-Action*, 1971), pp. 4–5.

Area in 1835–1836, the town was called "Yerba Buena" ("Good Herbs") and was the northernmost outpost in the Spanish colonial system (Chapter 8). Settled first in 1776, the small garrison and community fell into disuse and disrepair

---

CITYSCAPE 15-1
Herb Caen's San Francisco: Baghdad-by-the-Bay

San Francisco, to me, is like a house of cards: post cards in glowing colors stacked against the hills that march from the Bay on one side to the Pacific Ocean on the other.

The real magic of the city lies in the way these snapshots remain in the mind, no one impressed more sharply on the consciousness than the next. And when I am far away, the city's myriad details come floating back to me as though they were unwinding endlessly on the movie screen of my memory.

Each picture is sharp and complete, glamorized a little by a wisp of fog in one corner and a pennant streaming in the wind atop a skyscraper. It's a sentimental, perhaps corny, way to look at a city, but the San Franciscan is hopelessly sentimental, and I am hopelessly San Franciscan.

To me, my city is Baghdad-by-the-Bay, and my mind is lined—yes, even cluttered—with its pictures, ranged side by side. Like this:

By the dawn's early light Coit Tower standing starkly silhouetted against the first faint flush in the east. . . . A sun-and-windswept corner on Montgomery Street, where you can look west and see a wall of thick, dirty fog rising genie-like from the Pacific, while a finger of whiter, puffier stuff feels its way into the Bay, twisting this way and that till it conforms to every contour, snugly and coldly. . . .

The smug majesty of the City

Hall's famed dome, higher (and dirtier) than Washington's, and so far above the conniving that goes on beneath it. . . . The few surviving little wooden houses of Telegraph Hill, clinging together for mutual protection against concrete newcomers slowly pushing them out on a limb. . . . And Fisherman's Wharf at 7 A.M., with its tiny fleet of tiny ships lined up in neat display, and proud sea gulls strutting past to review them. . . .

. . . That occasional white ferryboat drifting over from Oakland and dipping respectfully beneath the aloof bridge that doomed so many of its sidewheeling sisters. . . . And block after block of flatiron buildings along Columbus Avenue—sharp edges of a city that grew in too many directions at once.

The incongruity of a lonely foghorn calling somewhere in the Bay as you stroll hatless down a sun-swept street—and the grotesque sight of this jumbled city from Twin Peaks, a sardonic, hysterical travesty on the dreams of those who stood there after the Great Fire and planned the Perfect City. . . . Long-forgotten cable-car slots wandered disconsolately and alone up steep hills that are now flattened, with a contemptuous snort, by high-powered, twin-engined busses. . . . University of California's Medical Center (where they discovered vitamin E) rearing up like a spectacular movie set against the darkness of Mount Sutro and Parnassus Heights, while in the pre-

dawn hush of Golden Gate Park, far below, squirrels sit unafraid in the middle of the silent roads, and ducks waddle importantly along the bridle paths. . . . The full magnificence of the Pacific bursting into your consciousness as you swing past the Cliff House. . . . And the monumental mechanical madness of the Kearny, Geary, Third, and Market intersection, where traffic, honking the horns of its dilemma, squeezes painfully through a bottleneck with a "Stop" sign for a cork. . . .

. . . And the eye-bulging sight, from atop the Fifteenth Avenue hill, of the little white new houses marching through the Sunset District toward the Pacific like stucco lemmings that decided, just in time, not to hurl themselves into the sea. . . .

The crowded garages and the empty old buildings above them, the half-filled night clubs and the overfilled apartment houses, the saloons in the skies and the families huddled in basements, the Third Street panhandlers begging for handouts in front of pawnshops filled with treasured trinkets, the great bridges and the rattletrap streetcars, the traffic that keeps moving although it has no place to go, the thousands of newcomers glorying in the sights and sounds of a city they've suddenly decided to love, instead of leave. . . .

This is Baghdad-by-the-Bay!

Source: Herb Caen, *Baghdad-by-the-Bay* (Garden City, N.Y.: Doubleday, 1949), pp. 1–5.

---

over the ensuing 70 years because of Spanish unwillingness to invest heavily in so distant a region.

But the Bay Area was too spectacular not to attract the eyes of westward-moving Americans. Fired by stories (like Dana's) of a magnificent inland sea (the bay), easterners began to arrive in northern California in the 1830s and 1840s.

Mary Ann Singleton's San Francisco: Taking the Plunge

Mary Ann Singleton was twenty-five years old when she saw San Francisco for the first time.

She came to the city alone for an eight-day vacation. On the fifth night, she drank three Irish coffees at the Buena Vista, realized her Mood Ring was blue, and decided to phone her mother in Cleveland.

"Hi, Mom. It's me."

"Oh, darling. Your daddy and I were just talking about you. There was this crazy man on "McMillan and Wife" who was strangling all these secretaries, and I just couldn't help thinking . . ."

"Mom . . ."

"I know. Just crazy ol' Mom, worrying herself sick over nothing. But you never can tell about those things. Look at that poor Patty Hearst, locked up in that closet with all those awful . . ."

"Mom . . . long distance."

"Oh . . . yes. You must be having a grand time."

"God . . . you wouldn't believe it! The people here are so friendly I feel like I've . . ."

"Have you been to the Top of the Mark like I told you?"

"Not yet."

"Well, don't you dare miss that! You know, your daddy took me there when he got back from the South Pacific. I remember he slipped the bandleader five dollars, so we could dance to 'Moonlight Serenade,' and I spilled Tom Collins all over his beautiful white Navy . . ."

"Mom, I want you to do me a favor."

"Of course, darling. Just listen to me. Oh . . . before I forget it, I ran into Mr. Lassiter yesterday at the Ridgemont Mall, and he said the office is just falling apart with you gone. They don't get many good secretaries at Lassiter Fertilizers."

"Mom, that's sort of why I called."

"Yes, darling?"

"I want you to call Mr. Lassiter and tell him I won't be in on Monday morning."

"Oh . . . Mary Ann, I'm not sure you should ask for an extension on your vacation."

"It's not an extension, Mom."

"Well, then why . . ."

"I'm not coming home, Mom."

Silence. Then, dimly in the distance, a television voice began to tell Mary Ann's father about the temporary relief of hemorrhoids. Finally, her mother spoke: "Don't be silly, darling."

"Mom . . . I'm not being silly. I like it here. It feels like home already."

"Mary Ann, if there's a boy . . ."

"There's no boy. . . . I've thought about this for a long time."

"Don't be ridiculous! You've been there five days!"

"Mom, I know how you feel, but . . . well, it's got nothing to do with you and Daddy. I just want to

---

When war broke out between Spain and the United States in 1846, California became part of the United States.

On July 9, 1846, the USS *Portsmouth* sailed into the bay, anchored at Yerba Buena, disembarked sailors and marines, and claimed all of California for the United States. Most of the Spanish fled. Not a shot was fired. A year later, the commanding officer of the *Portsmouth*, now chief magistrate, changed the town's name to San Francisco. The population was well under 1,000. Less than two years later, the population was over 30,000 and the sleepy backwater was a boom town of unprecedented proportions.

Incredible San Francisco: 1848–1874. The cause was gold. In January 1848, Captain John Sutter made a strike in the foothills of the Sierra Nevada mountains, 100 miles east. At first, town residents were unimpressed: no one was sure what the real value of gold was. But they began to get a glimmering later in the year when a miner sold his poke for $8 an ounce and *California Star* publisher Sam Brennan strode down Montgomery Street holding aloft a bottle of nuggets crying "Gold! Gold! Gold! on the American River!" (Lewis 1966, p. 49).

Gold fever struck. Many San Franciscans abandoned their homes and raced to the gold fields. By the end of 1848 the settlement was like a ghost town, but not for long. Word of the strike spread around the world, and San Francisco was deluged with frenzied gold seekers from everywhere. "Farmers abandoned their farms; workmen their jobs; clerks quit their counting houses; preachers their pulpits. One quarter of Nan-

start making my own life . . . have my own apartment and all."

"Oh, that. Well, darling . . . of course you can. As a matter of fact, your daddy and I thought those new apartments out at Ridgemont might be just perfect for you. They take lots of young people, and they've got a swimming pool and a sauna, and I could make some of those darling curtains like I made for Sonny and Vicki when they got married. You could have all the privacy you . . ."

"You aren't listening, Mom. I'm trying to tell you I'm a grown woman."

"Well, act like it, then! You can't just . . . run away from your family and friends to go live with a bunch of hippies and mass murderers!"

"You've been watching too much TV."

"O.K. . . . then what about The Horoscope?"

"What?"

"The Horoscope. That crazy

man. The killer."

"Mom . . . The Zodiac."

"Same difference. And what about . . . earthquakes? I saw that movie, Mary Ann, and I nearly died when Ava Gardner . . ."

"Will you just call Mr. Lassiter for me?"

Her mother began to cry. "You won't come back. I just know it."

"Mom . . . please . . . I will. I promise."

"But you won't be . . . the same!"

"No. I hope not."

When it was over, Mary Ann left the bar and walked through Aquatic Park to the bay. She stood there for several minutes in a chill wind, staring at the beacon on Alcatraz. She made a vow not to think about her mother for a while.

Back at the Fisherman's Wharf Holiday Inn, she looked up Connie Bradshaw's phone number. Connie was a stewardess for

United. Mary Ann hadn't seen her since high school: 1968.

"Fantabulous!" squealed Connie. "How long you here for?"

"For good."

"Super! Found an apartment yet?"

"No . . . I . . . well, I was wondering if I might be able to crash at your place, until I can . . ."

"Sure. No sweat."

"Connie . . . you're single?"

The stewardess laughed. "A bear shit in the woods?"

Source: Armistead Maupin, *Tales of the City* (New York: Harper & Row, 1978), pp. 1–3.

---

tucket Island's voting population went west in nine months" (Moorhouse, 1979, p. 49). These migrants were the "forty-niners."

Writing in 1852, Thomas de Quincy argued that most of the gold rush was a swindle, that the "gold-just-lying-around-to-be-picked-up" stories were fabrications concocted by a few unscrupulous souls to bamboozle people into selling their worldly goods cheaply or into buying nonexistent gold mines in the desert. De Quincy was right. Few really did "get rich quick." But swindle or not, the gold rush created the foundation for modern San Francisco. It was the only port able to serve the gold fields, and there certainly *was* money to be made in outfitting miners, building offices and homes in the booming city, and providing "entertainment" for the men of "the wild west."

Gold-rush San Francisco was as lawless and wide-open a city as could be imagined. There were 1,000 murders between 1849 and 1856. Knife fights, kangaroo courts, and lynchings took place in the streets. There were local gangs—one called "The Hounds" because of how they pursued their victims—who thrived on racial hatred, attacking Mexicans, Peruvians, and anyone else who was not white. To curtail this, there emerged equally vicious vigilante groups. There were saloons galore, prostitutes on every street, over 1,000 gambling casinos, and liquor literally everywhere. One observer of the times recalled those days in a letter written in 1856:

> It was a Sunday morning in December, 1849, when landing from the Panama steamer I wended my way with the throng to Portsmouth Square, this being at the time the great resort of the deni-

zens of this rising metropolis. . . . [At one building a preacher was] discoursing from the text, "The way of the transgressor is hard." It was a scene I shall never forget. On all sides of you were gambling houses, each with its brand of music in full blast. Crowds were going in and coming out; fortunes were being lost and won; terrible imprecations and blasphemies rose amid the horrid wail, and it seemed to me pandemonium was let loose." (Cited in Asbury 1933, p. 21)

And a *New York Evening Post* reporter, after witnessing this scene, wrote back East that "the people of San Francisco are mad, stark mad."

By the late 1850s the gold began to peter out and the city became a bit calmer. Many miners left, many ramshackle tents disappeared, city (rather than vigilante) law was created, and duly elected citizens took over the city's government.

Then it happened again. In 1859 a huge silver deposit—the famous Comstock Lode—was found on the far side of the Sierra Nevada. In the next 15 years over $300 million in silver was taken from the lode and passed through San Francisco. The prospectors and all those who served them descended on the city once more. Although some of the lawlessness returned, it was better controlled. With an organized city government, the rowdier elements of the silver and shipping trade were relegated to an area of the city known as "the Barbary Coast," which became one of the most infamous sites of urban decadence since Babylon itself (see Box 15-3).

Once again the city grew incredibly quickly. Adding to the growth was the opening of the first transcontinential railroad in 1869, which allowed easy shipment of all West Coast and Pacific goods to the lucrative city markets of the East. By 1870 the city's population had reached 150,000. Millionaires' mansions began to appear on Nob Hill, based on fortunes made in silver, shipping, the railroads, and banking. The city became the "high culture" showcase of the West, with great theaters and hotels offering the best that money anywhere could buy. Literary notables, such as Bret Harte and Mark Twain, came to the city, establishing a tradition of bohemian culture that was to find later expression in the Beat movement of the 1950s and the hippies of the 1960s.

Racial and Political Tensions: 1875–1906.
When the Comstock Lode began to play out in the late 1870s, a severe recession set in, bringing to the surface a problem long dormant: the city's ambivalence toward its large Chinese population. The Chinese had arrived in San Francisco first during the gold rush. At the time, they were welcomed because of their industriousness and their willingness to work for very low wages at jobs others did not want. Most became servants, cooks, gardeners, messengers, and launderers. Their numbers grew, from 4,000 in 1853 to over 15,000 in the 1870s, and many became more successful, cornering such industries as clothing manufacture and cigar making. When the post-Comstock recession deepened, the continuing willingness of the Chinese to work for low wages created a competitive conflict with whites. An anti-Chinese slate was elected in 1875, and the new mayor, Andrew Bryant, oversaw the passing of a series of laws patently aimed at restricting Chinese freedom and competitive advantage.

With the city still in recession, in July 1877 some jobless laborers destroyed much of Chinatown. "The mob roved unchecked through the narrow streets and alleys of the quarter, smashing windows, kicking down doors of laundries and other places of business, and setting fire to their interiors, then cutting the hoses of firemen when they arrived to put out the blazes" (Lewis 1966, p. 140). Bryant called out the police to stop the riots, but they were unequal to the task. On July 25, about 5,000 anti-Chinese rioters again converged on Chinatown and other areas of the city. Faced with chaos, San Franciscans formed a vigilante group (as they had in the 1850s), called themselves "The Committee for Safety," and battled with the rioters throughout the city. The rioters finally were quelled by a combination of vigilantes, sailors and marines, and local citizenry backing up the city's police. Although the worst was over, the racial tension between Chinese and whites continued in the coming decades, and between 1882 and 1900 a series of

---

BOX 15-3
Life and Death on the Barbary Coast

Many San Franciscans were scandalized by what went on in the Barbary Coast and took steps to have it closed down (they failed until 1917). To alert the public, some wrote moralistic pamphlets like the following. Despite the moralizing, the description is basically accurate.

"Barbary Coast" proper is in the northerly part of the city, comprising both sides of Broadway and Pacific streets, and the cross streets between them, from Stockton street to the water front. . . . Like the malaria arising from a stagnant swamp and poisoning the air for miles around, does this stagnant pool of human immorality and crime spread its contaminating vapors over the surrounding blocks on either side. . . .

In the early days of San Francisco, Barbary Coast was the place of refuge and security for the hundreds of criminals that infested the city. When they had passed within its boundary, they were strongly fortified against any

assault that the officers of the law might lead against them. It was, in those days, an easy matter for a stranger to enter this fortress of vice, but when once behind the walls he was exceedingly fortunate who had the opportunity to depart, taking with him his life. Then villains of every nationality held high carnival there. . . .

Even in the presence of a strong police force, and in the face of frowning cells and dungeons, it is unsafe to ramble through many of the streets and lanes in this quarter. Almost nightly there are drunken carousals and broils, frequently terminating in dangerous violence; men are often garroted and robbed, and it is not by any means a rare occurrence for foul murder to be committed. "Murderer's Corner" and "Deadman's Alley" have been rebaptized with blood over and over again, and yet call for other sacrifices.

Barbary Coast is the haunt of the low and vile of every kind. The petty thief, the house burglar, the tramp, the whoremonger, lewd

women, cutthroats and murderers, all are found there. Dance houses and concert saloons, where blear-eyed men and faded women drink vile liquor, smoke offensive tobacco, engage in vulgar conduct, sing obscene songs, and say and do everything to heap upon themselves more degradation, unrest and misery, are numerous. Low gambling houses thronged with riot-loving rowdies in all stages of intoxication are there. Opium dens, where heathens and God forsaken women and men are sprawled in miscellaneous confusion, disgustingly drowsy, or completely overcome by inhaling the vapors of the nauseous narcotic, are there. Licentiousness, debauchery, pollution, loathsome disease, insanity from dissipation, misery, poverty, wealth, profanity, blasphemy and death, are there. And Hell, yawning to receive the putrid mass, is there also.

Source: B. S. Lloyd, *Lights and Shade in San Francisco* (San Francisco, 1876).

---

federal laws known as the "Exclusion Acts" were passed, strictly limiting the influx of Chinese to the country.

There were important political conflicts during this period as well. Violence frequently broke out between newly formed unionists and owners. The greatest prize in this contest was control of the city government. Whichever group controlled city hall also controlled the docks and the railroads and was able to practice favoritism by awarding city building commissions.

In the period from 1880 to the early 1900s, various political machines gained control of the city's government. The most notorious of these was the administration of Mayor Eugene

Schmitz. Elected in 1901, 1903, and 1905, on the Union Labor ticket, Schmitz allowed Abe Reuf, his campaign manager and a lawyer, nearly complete control of city hall. Extortion and privilege soon were rampant, with Reuf being paid a small fortune in "legal fees" by various local companies. Finally exposed, the Schmitz-Reuf graft operation was about to be brought to trial when, on April 18, 1906, a huge earthquake destroyed much of what many called "the Sodom-by-the-Sea."

The Earthquake and Regeneration: 1906–1917.
We have described already in Cityscape 6-1 the massive destruction brought by the San Fran-

The aftermath of the tragic earthquake that destroyed much of San Francisco in 1906. (Bettmann)

cisco earthquake. The city lost over 28,000 buildings and had estimated financial losses of $500 million. Insurance companies paid out a staggering sum in claims, resulting in a building boom not seen since the gold and silver rush days. Like the mythical phoenix and so many other cities in history, San Francisco rose from its own ashes.

The task of rebuilding the city awakened a sense of civic pride. Determined to make the city "The Paris of America" (a campaign slogan of 1910), a collective effort was made to clean up the city's long-tolerated public corruption, crime, and vice.

The graft trials that had been about to get underway when the earthquake struck went into full swing between 1906 and 1910. Schmitz, Reuf, and numerous others went to jail, and "bossism,"

though not completely dead, was wounded severely. The Barbary Coast was closed down. A series of laws was passed between 1910 and 1913 which made it illegal for women to serve liquor in the district, for new saloons to open up, and for dancing to be done where liquor was served. The final blow against the Coast came in 1917, as detailed in Box 15-4.

The Golden Gate: 1918–Present. The closing of the Barbary Coast symbolized the end of San Francisco's wildest days. With a well-established economy based primarily on banking, shipping, and white-collar industries, it has continued to grow. Its population reached 700,000 in 1950 and has remained near that figure since. To accommodate this growth, the city built its airport in 1927, completed a massive water pipeline

---

BOX 15-4
The End of the Barbary Coast

Early in February 1917 the police raided and closed every brothel in the uptown area, and on February 14 a blockade was instituted against the Barbary Coast. The entire quarter was surrounded by policemen, no man was permitted to enter unless he could prove that he was engaged in legitimate business, and the prostitutes were ordered to vacate the cribs, cow-yards, and parlor houses. They were allowed a few hours in which to pack and remove their belongings, but by midnight the red-light district was deserted; eighty-three brothels had been closed and 1,073 women had been driven from their quarters. A hundred Chinese girls were evicted from the few bagnios which remained in operation on Grant Avenue. Two days later forty Barbary Coast saloons and dives closed their doors through lack of business, and within a week the remainder of the resorts had likewise abandoned the field.

The Barbary Coast was as dead as the proverbial doornail. . . . Of its ancient glories nothing remains excepting a few battered facades, the tattered remains of signs, and the plaster nymphs and satyrs in the entrance lobby of the old Hippodrome, now befouled by dirt and penciled obscenities.

Source: Herbert Asbury, *The Barbary Coast* (Garden City, N.Y.: Doubleday, 1933), pp. 312–314.

---

the hippies, the other wing of the 1960s counterculture, appeared in the city's Haight-Ashbury district, replete with psychedelia and acid rock. Notoriety continued in the 1970s. Patty Hearst, daughter of the owner of the Hearst newspaper syndicate, was captured by the Symbionese Liberation Army, a radical group based in Berkeley, and finally recaptured by authorities in San Francisco after months of hiding out and a massive shoot-out in southern California. The Reverend Jim Jones's People's Temple flourished and then took itself to Guyana, where over 900 people were massacred at Jones's order in November of 1978. In the same month, Mayor George Moscone and City Board Supervisor Harvey Milk were brutally murdered by a disgruntled former board member while at their desks at City Hall.

Taking over for Moscone as mayor was Diane Feinstein. Elected in her own right in 1979, Feinstein has weathered numerous problems, such as a direct confrontation with the police department (she fired the chief), a citywide teacher's strike, and a transportation crisis. She also has kept the city solvent. For her 1982 budget, Feinstein announced a 10.4 percent expenditure increase (most northwestern and midwestern cities are cutting back desperately) and her intention to hire much-needed police, bus, and streetcar workers. Nonetheless, she realizes frugal times are here; as she said in an interview, "We have significantly less purchasing power than in past years, but so far the impact has only been on the surface" (*Time*, 1981, p. 32). The budgetary cushion has continued. In 1984 the city had a surplus of some $130 million, a rather remarkable feat given the financial straits that many American cities find themselves in.

In recent years the city has become no less interesting. In the past decade it has become a kind of gay person's mecca. It is estimated that fully 20 percent of the city's residents are of homosexual preference. However, while there was once considerable tension between the gay and heterosexual communities, this seems to have lessened over the years, paralleling the historical tendency of groups in the city to "live and let live." Says City Supervisor Harry Britt: "We have

from the Sierra Nevada, and constructed the San Francisco-Oakland Bay Bridge and the Golden Gate Bridge in the 1930s—the latter considered by many to be the most beautiful suspension bridge in the world. Moreover, the city has remained one of the country's great urban tourist attractions.

Nevertheless, being less wild has hardly meant being sedate. In the 1950s the Beat movement began in San Francisco, under the tutelage of such figures as Lawrence Ferlinghetti (whose famous "City Lights" bookstore in the North Beach district is still open), poet Allen Ginsberg, and novelist Jack Kerouac. In the 1960s, the radical student movement began in the Bay Area with numerous demonstrations and confrontations at the University of California in Berkeley and at San Francisco State. At the same time,

fights going on in this town, but we don't have fights between gays and straights" (*Time*, July 16, 1984, pp. 22–23). In 1984 the city became one of few in the country to introduce an ordinance against high-rise buildings, when its voters accepted a proposal to ban all skyward building that would impair the access of sunlight to the city's public parks. Supervisor Bill Maher interpreted the vote this way: "San Franciscans are very concerned with the quality of life in their city and they're prepared to make some trade-offs. It's the first time that voters said 'Wait a minute, there's a limit to growth'" (Turner, 1984, p. A 14). And, in 1986, San Francisco joined only a handful of other American cities when it voted to eliminate all of the city's investments in racially torn South Africa (*New York Times*, January 29, 1986). In short, San Francisco continues to be an eccentric, exciting, and extremely socially conscious version of the American city.

The Social Construction of Urban Excellence

Cities are human creations, the product of billions of decisions made in response to historical, environmental, and cultural exigencies. The source of San Francisco's contemporary excellence lies in the decisions its inhabitants have made since its founding.

For instance, take the gridiron street plan that characterizes not only the city's flat sections but the hilly areas as well. Lewis Mumford thinks the plan a disaster:

> On steep hilly sites, like that of San Francisco, the rectangular plan, by failing to respect the contours, placed a constant tax upon the time and energy of the inhabitants, and inflicted on them daily economic losses, measurable in tons of coal and gallons of gasoline wasted, to say nothing of undoing the major esthetic possibilities of a hillside that is intelligently platted. (1961, p. 423)

This is all true, of course, except for the last point. As John Dos Passos pointed out in the observations about the city's hills that opened Chapter 6, the grid has been a happy accident that has very much *enhanced* the city esthetically.

This is an important point. Often the effects of urban decisions are unforeseen. This is partly the case with the city's much-touted culture of civility. While today's San Francisco is relatively sanguine about its "different" groups and often works to protect their rights, in history the city was less tolerant. Recall that many early San Franciscans were hardly pleased about the forty-niners, the Chinese, the bohemians, the unionists, and the denizens of the Barbary Coast. Even so, the economic, political, and social welfare of the city in large part rested on these groups at various points in history; hence, over the years, San Franciscans learned to live with such groups. After awhile, the groups became so merged with the city that it seemed as though they had always been there. This process has resulted, more by accident than conscious design, in a growing respect for social differences—a culture of civility—and a weakening of the social forms that often limit urban tolerance, such as organized religion and political conservatism (Wuthnow 1976).

On the other hand, the creation and preservation of the city's excellence frequently has been most intentional. Before the earthquake of 1906, plans were underway to completely redesign the city to take advantage of its reputation as the "Paris of the West." City planner Daniel Burnham—the person responsible for the City Beautiful Movement discussed in the last chapter—was hired, and produced an elaborate plan for reconstructing the city in an Athenian and Parisian style. In one area of downtown the grid would have been significantly altered, to be replaced by a civic center approached by various radially arranged roads. Telegraph Hill was to be redesigned completely, with an acropolis-like building on top approached by winding roads in the European style. Copies of Burnham's plan were being distributed in City Hall in mid-April of 1906, when the earthquake dashed all hopes for its implementation (Scott 1959).

More successful have been the city's postearthquake efforts to preserve its unique heritage. Three routes of the cable car system have been maintained at significant cost to the city, and San Franciscans positively dote on the wooden Victorian houses that survived the 1906 destruction. Many are bought, repaired, painted in incredible colors and designs, and kept in immaculate condition—not for tourists but for the pleasure of San Franciscans themselves.

The Social Construction of Urban Problems

But we must not be too idealistic about San Francisco. Along with its excellent qualities, it also has created its share of problems. H. H. Bancroft described the gold rush era as a period of "moral, political, and financial night." Similar critiques could be made of the city's treatment of minorities and tolerance for widespread graft and vice through the early twentieth century. All these conditions existed because San Franciscans willed or allowed them to.

Furthermore, describing the modern city, Fred Davis (1971) has suggested that much of San Francisco's success rests on a "mystique" about its "goodness" that, at deeper levels, is disappearing or patently untrue. For example, Davis reports that there has been serious degradation of the city's environment, with drastic increases in smog, great loss of open space, and massive traffic congestion in recent years. Similarly, Hippler (1974), in a study of Hunter's Point, one of the city's black ghettos, made clear that the problems of being black in urban America are as real in San Francisco as anywhere, and Wiseman's (1970) analysis of the city's skid row district underscores the point in the desperate situation of the city's homeless. Wirt's (1974) analysis of the city's political structure depicts serious problems, revealing the government to be characterized by terrific ethnic conflicts and insensitivity to underprivileged groups, an interpretation supported by a more recent study by Whitt (1982). Examining the construction of BART (the Bay Area Rapid Transit), Whitt concludes that BART came into being primarily to serve the region's business interests. This meant political maneuvering to put stations at particular points favorable to business at the expense of stations for the city's low-income residents. In addition, Wuthnow (1976) reports that the Bay Area ranks among the highest in the nation in rates of suicide, alcoholism, divorce, and crime. Finally, Morain (1985) has shown that San Francisco, like American cities everywhere, is paying a steep human price for the gentrification of many neighborhoods. As the more affluent move in, the poor are forced to double up or move out of the city entirely.

As in the case of the city's successes, then, human decisions or lack thereof are the perpetrators of these problems. By not being consciously attentive to encroachments on its valued environment, the city has lost ground in this crucial area. Similarly, San Franciscans, apparently as a result of prejudice or disinterest, have allowed racial discrimination, political inefficiency, and economic stagnation to mar their city.

Evaluation

This case study of San Francisco suggests two important things about a model of the good city. First, both San Francisco's success and its problems are *socially constructed* phenomena, the product of decisions made or *not* made (the latter being simply a decision of disinterest). Sometimes decisions have had a beneficial effect, sometimes not. Sometimes the effects of decisions have been intended consciously, sometimes not. In all cases, however, the effects of decisions are real and have had real consequences. This should suggest that cities, as human creations, can be controlled and directed intentionally. This should in turn suggest that, given adequate resources (time, energy, money, materials, *desire*), the creation of a truly good city is a real possibility.

Second, in terms of the definition of the good city given earlier, San Francisco presents a bit of a mixed bag. Its greatest strengths appear to be its ability to stimulate people (the mental need criterion) and to give them a sense of community (the social needs criterion). However, on other needs, it doesn't fare as well. There are thousands of poverty-stricken people in the city, housing is inadequate for many, and there is considerable unemployment. Clearly, the city does not do very well in meeting the physical needs criterion, at least for a significant proportion of its people. Nor does it seem to perform well in providing security for all its citizens (another mental need). Crime rates and suicide rates are high, and urban violence is prevalent, particularly in the minority areas.

Even if it isn't the ultimate good city, however, on another level San Francisco still has something important to teach us about urban excitement and a sense of community. The city stands out because of the sense of tolerance and openness fostered by its culture of civility. True, much of the culture of civility came about as a sort of historical accident. Nevertheless, once in place, the people of the city cherished and worked hard to protect this vital quality. In other words, if people in cities elsewhere wish to create a greater sense of tolerance, openness, and civic pride in their urban environment, they might look to San Francisco and its history for clues about how a culture of civility could be actively generated.

Of course, one can imagine arguments about whether a culture of civility and a strong sense of community are traits that are really good for all cities. Yet even San Francisco's weaknesses concerning these traits are instructive. For example, when tolerance became license—as happened in the gold rush days and on the Barbary Coast—elements destructive to the city's entire fabric were set loose. Similarly, when tolerance was lost completely—as in the anti-Chinese riots of the 1870s—the Chinese, the rioters, the city's physical plant, and its reputation all suffered, not to mention the millions of dollars the rioting cost the city, private individuals, and businesses.

In the same vein, consider the outcome of the loss of a sense of civic responsibility in the city's leaders. When government turned into "bossism" of the type promulgated by Eugene Schmitz at the turn of the century, once again the whole city suffered. In contrast, when involvement in Jim Jones's People's Temple became all-absorbing for a few San Franciscans, the ability of these individuals to be critical of their social environment was lost completely. They became puppets. These extremes suggest that there may be a minimum standard of community responsibility that citizens must maintain if a city is to prosper; at the same time, there also

may be a point at which involvement becomes excessive and detrimental to both individual and collective well being.

The key to considering any possible trait that the good city should have is to ask what would happen if that trait were not present or, as we did above, what would happen if it were pushed to extremes. What would the consequences be? This question should be answered by looking at that trait in different urban settings.

This is exactly where our case study of San Francisco has its limitations. Surely there are other positive traits that must be considered in constructing a model of the good city. With this in mind, we next turn to studies which have tried to examine the overall quality of life in American cities.

Studies of the Quality of Urban Life

Boyer and Savageau

Richard Boyer and David Savageau (1984) claim that the widespread view of San Francisco as America's best city is not completely accurate. After a detailed study of all American cities, they concluded that America's best city is . . . Pittsburgh. *Pittsburgh?* That smoky, industrial city of steel mills? Correct—and Boyer and Savageau claim they have the evidence to prove it.

Impatient with unsophisticated opinion polls about good cities, Boyer and Savageau ranked the 329 MSAs of the 1980 census according to their overall quality of life. To do this, they chose nine general dimensions (we might call them "values") that they believe are the major components of the quality of urban life: climate, housing, health care, crime, transportation, education, the arts, recreation, and economics. Using statistics compiled by the census bureau, they calculated a rating in each dimension for each city and then a combined overall rating for each city. New York, for example, ranked first in the dimensions of transportation, the arts, and health care, but last (worst) in the dimension of crime.

Pittsburgh's overall ranking at the top is not so surprising, say Boyer and Savageau. They point out that Pittsburgh has undergone considerable downtown renovation in the last two decades, the virtual shutdown of the steel mills has alleviated the smog problem, and the city now has a modern corporate-service economy. Residents have enjoyed these improvements for years; Boyer and Savageau's objective measures show the city to be much better than national public opinion (decades behind the times) held it to be. Following Pittsburgh in descending order were Boston, Raleigh-Durham, North Carolina; San Francisco (the opinion polls were not far off, after all); Philadelphia; Nassau-Suffolk, New York; St. Louis; Louisville, Kentucky; Norwalk, Connecticut; and Seattle.

Pierce

Geographer Robert Pierce (1984) argues that Boyer and Savageau's analysis is too simplistic: it assumes that the nine dimensions are equally valued in the minds of city residents. Surely, says Pierce, a low crime rate, to take just one example, is of greater importance to most people than a lively arts program. To examine the relative subjective importance of Boyer and Savageau's nine dimensions, Pierce asked more than 1,000 residents of New York State to rank them. He found that some dimensions were consistently more important than others: climate, crime, economics, and housing ranked highest.

Armed with this information, Pierce returned to the census data and gave these dimensions a higher value in overall scoring. Thus, his list of America's best cities is radically different from Boyer and Savageau's. Tied for first place are Greensboro, North Carolina, and Knoxville, Tennessee. Following in descending order are Asheville, North Carolina; Nashville, Tennessee; Raleigh-Durham, North Carolina; Charleston, West Virginia; Wheeling, West Virginia; Evansville, Indiana; and Anaheim, California. Of Pierce's top ten, only Raleigh-Durham appears on the Boyer and Savageau list. Most of Pierce's cities are located in North Carolina, Tennessee, and West Virginia—hardly places associated in the national mind with images of best cities. Finally, note that all of these cities are fairly small in population—no multimillion-people cities like San Francisco, Philadelphia, Seattle, St. Louis, or Pittsburgh as on Boyer and Savageau's list. This suggests that small cities may be able to meet peoples' priorities more easily.

Note, too, that the dimensions chosen by people in Pierce's poll are closely reflective of the basic needs we suggested must be satisfied by "the good city": the desire for a pleasant climate, decent housing, and a vibrant economy are directly related to the physical needs criterion. The concern that crime rates be low is connected to the needs for physical safety and mental security. In other words, people know intuitively what their own basic needs are. Once these are satisfied they can turn to other, less vital needs—transportation, a solid educational system, recreational facilities, adequate health care, and a vibrant program in the arts. To put it another way, Pierce's results suggest that if we are to build better cities, we had best attend to "first things first"—we should make sure that people are warm and fed and physically and mentally secure before we spend enormous amounts of money, time, and effort on needs of lesser importance.

Liu

In comparison to the above studies, the one conducted by Ben-Chieh Liu is the most sophisticated of all. In 1976 Liu published a study that examined the qualify of life in the 243 MSAs in the United States that were included in the 1970 census. He focused on five key dimensions of city life:

1. Economics
2. Politics
3. The environment
4. Health and education
5. Social relationships

He decided on these dimensions (and not others) for the following reasons: First, they were *universal* dimensions; cities anywhere at any time could be said to operate in terms of them. Second, they were dimensions that could be *commonly understood* by all the city's inhabitants. Third, they were dimensions that could have *policy implications* for improving city life. Fourth, they were *flexible* enough to account for any urban life-style currently existing or foreseeable in the future. Finally, they were easily amenable to *scientific study* (Liu 1976, pp. 53–54).

Liu made his own value concerns absolutely clear. He was interested primarily in developing a broad conception of urban well-being and believed that his five dimensions were principal elements of that well-being. He went further. Reasoning that cities have both collective (citywide) and individual aspects, he decided to measure the quality of city life on both levels, something that the Boyer and Savageau and Pierce studies did not do. A good city, he implied, would satisfy its individual citizens as it sustained its own community life and general vitality.

To rate each city's performance on the five dimensions, Liu studied over 120 aspects of city life, which he called "factors." A few of these are listed in Table 15-1. For example, to measure a city's level of economic well-being, Liu examined the level of income per capita and savings per capita (both individual well-being factors) and percent of families above the poverty level and the unemployment rate (both collective well-being factors), among others. In considering the quality of a city's social life, Liu considered the ratio of black to white income, the ratio of male to female professional employment, and income inequality between the central city and the suburbs—all factors he believed measured an individual's urban advantages. On the community level of this social dimension, Liu considered such traits as the percent of homes with plumbing; the number of volumes in public libraries per 1,000 people in the population; and the number of dance, music, and drama events in the area.

As in Pierce's study, Liu's factors in each dimension were weighted on the basis of how important they were in comparison to all other factors in the dimension (for example, in the economic dimension, Liu gave the factor "personal income per capita" five times the weight of

"savings per capita"). Then, Liu computed an overall "quality" score for each dimension by adding the scores for all factors in that dimension and dividing the total by the number of factors.

Considering Liu's five main dimensions, his 120 measures of these dimensions, and his weighting procedure, we see that he too is interested in the question of how well cities meet the needs of their citizens. His dimensions reflect the same concerns we mentioned previously—namely that, first and foremost, it is the obligation of cities (if they are to be considered good cities) to provide ways for all their citizens to satisfy their physical, mental, and social needs.

To compare cities of fairly equal size, something that Boyer and Savageau did *not* do and were criticized for, Liu divided the 243 American MSAs into three groups: large cities (populations over 500,000), medium cities (populations between 200,000 and 500,000), and small cities (populations between 50,000 and 200,000). Using a complicated method of scoring, he determined a score for each city on each of his five dimensions. He then averaged those scores to produce an overall quality-of-life score for each city. Finally, Liu rated each city, on the basis of its overall score, as follows: an "A" rating indicated a city of "outstanding" quality of life; a "B" rating characterized "excellent" urban quality; and "C," "D," and "E" ratings were for "good," "adequate," and "substandard" qualities of life, respectively.[1] By assigning these "letter grades," Liu intended to show that small differences in overall scores were not necessarily indicative of major quality-of-life differences between cities (Liu 1976, pp. 78–92, 208–211).

Taken together, Liu's methods are much more complex and sophisticated than those of either Boyer/Savageau or Pierce. For this reason, his results deserve our careful consideration.

---

[1]Assignments to category were made by consulting standard deviation scores. Cities scoring one full standard deviation above the mean were placed in the "A" category; cities one full standard deviation below were given an "E" rating. All others were assigned categories in between depending on their distance from the mean (Liu 1976, p. 88).

TABLE 15-1

Some of Liu's Factors for Measuring Quality-of-Life Dimensions

Economic Dimension

Individual Economic Well-Being
1. Personal income per capita
2. Savings per capita
3. Percent of owner-occupied homes

Collective Economic Well-Being
1. Percent of families above poverty level
2. Degree of economic concentration in city
3. Production value per worker: construction

Political Dimension

Individual Activities
1. Availability of information: local Sunday paper distribution per 1,000 population
2. Percent of homes with TV available
3. Local radio stations per 1,000 population

Local Government Factors
1. Professionalism: average monthly earnings: teachers
2. Professionalism: average monthly earnings: other full-time employees
3. Professionalism: entrance salary: patrolmen

Environmental Dimension

Individual and Institutional Environment
1. Air pollution: average level: total suspended particulates
2. Air pollution: average level: sulphur dioxide
3. Visual pollution: average annual inversion frequency

Natural Environment
1. Mean annual inversion frequency
2. Possible annual days of sunshine
3. Number of days with thunderstorms

Health and Education Dimension

Health: Individual Aspects
1. Infant mortality per 1,000 live births
2. Death rate per 1,000 population

Education: Individual Aspects
1. Median school years: persons over 25
2. Percent, 4 years high school or more: persons over 25

Health: Collective Aspects
1. Dentists per 1,000 population
2. Physicians per 1,000 population

Education: Collective Aspects
1. Per capita local government expenditures
2. Percent of persons with 4 years of college or more: persons over 25

Social Dimension

Possibilities for Individual Development
1. Labor force participation rate
2. Mean income per family member
3. Percent of married couples with own home

Individual Equity
1. Race: ratio of black-white income level
2. Race: ratio of black-white employment level
3. Race: ratio of black-white professional employment level

Community Living Conditions

General Conditions
1. Percent, homes with plumbing
2. Percent, homes with more than 1 person per room
3. Percent, homes with telephone available

Facilities
1. Number of banks per 1,000 population
2. Number of retail trade establishments per 1,000 population
3. Number of books in public library per 1,000 population

Source: Adapted from Ben-Chieh Liu, *Quality of Life Indicators in U.S. Metropolitan Areas* (New York: Praeger, 1976), pp. 54–79. Copyright © 1976 Praeger Publishers, Inc. Reprinted by permission of Praeger Publishers.

TABLE 15-2
Quality-of-Life Scores and Ratings for 35 Large American Cities

Rank	City	Overall Score*	Rating
1	Portland, Ore.	1.75	A
2	Sacramento, Calif.	1.63	A
3	Seattle-Everett, Wash.	1.63	A
4	San Jose, Calif.	1.52	A
5	Minneapolis/St. Paul, Minn.	1.52	A
6	Rochester, N.Y.	1.50	A
7	Hartford, Conn.	1.48	A
8	Denver, Colo.	1.48	A
9	San Francisco-Oakland, Calif.	1.45	A
10	San Diego, Calif.	1.43	A
11	Milwaukee, Wis.	1.39	A
12	Grand Rapids, Mich.	1.39	A
13	Salt Lake City, Utah	1.37	A
14	Anaheim, Calif.	1.33	B
15	Buffalo, N.Y.	1.33	B
16	Oklahoma City, Okla.	1.27	B
17	Omaha, Neb.	1.26	B
18	Albany-Schenectedy-Troy, N.Y.	1.25	B
19	Syracuse, N.Y.	1.23	B
20	Washington, D.C.	1.23	B
21	Los Angeles-Long Beach, Calif.	1.22	B
22	Columbus, Ohio	1.19	B
23	Boston, Mass.	1.19	B
24	Cleveland, Ohio	1.11	B
25	Toledo, Ohio	1.10	B
26	San Bernardino-Riverside-Ontario, Calif.	1.08	C
27	Houston, Tex.	1.05	C
28	Phoenix, Ariz.	0.98	C
29	Akron, Ohio	0.97	C
30	Cincinnati, Ohio	0.97	C
31	Honolulu, Hawaii	0.96	C
32	Dayton, Ohio	0.95	C
33	New York, N.Y.	0.91	C
34	Dallas, Tex.	0.90	C
35	Indianapolis, Ind.	0.90	C

*Derived from combining and averaging the individual scores for each city on the dimensions of economic, political, environmental, health and educational, and social relationships (see text and Table 15-3). Mean score = 0.99; standard deviation = 0.37.

Source: Adapted from Ben-Chieh Liu, *Quality of Life Indicators in U.S. Metropolitan Areas* (New York: Praeger, 1976), Table 16. Copyright © 1976 Praeger Publishers, Inc. Reprinted by permission of Praeger Publishers.

Large Cities. Liu classified 65 MSAs as large. The overall quality-of-life scores and ratings for the top 35 MSAs are listed in Table 15-2.

The first thing of note in the table is that, of the usual claimants to America's "good city" title in public opinion polls, only San Francisco appears in the "A" ("outstanding") category. Washington, Los Angeles, and Boston all receive "B" ("excellent") ratings, while New York only rates a "C" ("good"). Other prominent large cities (not shown on the table) fare no better. Chicago got a "C" as did the Sunbelt cities of Dallas, Houston,

TABLE 15-3
Rankings and Ratings of Selected Large MSAs on Five Quality-of-Life Dimensions

City	Economic Ranking	Economic Rating	Political Ranking	Political Rating	Environmental Ranking	Environmental Rating	Health/Education Ranking	Health/Education Rating	Social Ranking	Social Rating
Top 5 Western*										
Portland, Ore.	3	A	8	A	11	A	9	A	1	A
Sacramento, Calif.	40	C	7	A	1	A	8	A	5	A
Seattle-Everett, Wash.	20	B	19	B	2	A	6	A	2	A
San Jose, Calif.	36	C	25	B	7	A	1	A	15	B
Denver, Colo.	33	C	16	B	24	C	3	A	4	A
Top 5 Midwestern										
Minneapolis-St. Paul, Minn.	25	B	9	A	20	B	7	A	9	A
Milwaukee, Wis.	16	B	12	A	32	C	19	B	8	A
Grand Rapids, Mich.	14	B	5	A	31	C	21	B	30	C
Columbus, Ohio	35	C	21	B	38	C	23	B	14	B
Cleveland, Ohio	4	A	28	C	60	E	32	C	24	B
Top 5 Northeastern										
Rochester, N.Y.	11	A	3	A	13	B	13	A	50	D
Hartford, Conn.	22	B	6	A	40	C	5	A	23	B
Buffalo, N.Y.	32	C	1	A	45	D	25	B	18	B
Albany-Schenectedy-Troy, N.Y.	47	D	2	A	53	D	14	B	25	B
Syracuse, N.Y.	51	D	4	A	42	D	15	B	20	B
Top 5 Southern										
Houston, Tex.	2	A	53	E	26	C	33	C	29	C
Dallas, Tex.	1	A	64	E	21	B	39	D	35	C
Richmond, Va.†	10	A	39	C	41	D	50	D	60	E
Atlanta, Ga.†	7	A	56	E	52	D	37	D	44	D
Fort Lauderdale-Hollywood, Fla.†	12	A	47	D	36	C	58	E	26	B

*As ranked by Liu's "Overall" Quality of Life Index (see Table 15-2).
†Not in Table 15-2; ranked lower than 35 nationwide.

Source: Adapted from Ben-Chieh Liu, *Quality of Life Indications in U.S. Metropolitan Areas* (New York: Praeger, 1976), Tables 1–5. Copyright © 1976 Praeger Publishers, Inc. Reprinted by permission of Praeger Publishers.

and Phoenix. "D" ("adequate") ratings were assigned to Detroit, St. Louis, Pittsburgh, and Atlanta; while Philadelphia, New Orleans, and Miami were all given an "E" ("substandard").

Second, consider that the "A" rating is dominated by western cities. Table 15-3, which presents the ranking and ratings on all five of Liu's dimensions for the top five cities in each major geographical region of the country, provides information about why this pattern may have emerged.

A general reading of Table 15-3 suggests the following: on the economic dimension, the five southern cities are doing very well indeed. They are followed fairly closely by midwestern and western cities, with northeastern cities, part of the old industrial region of the country, bringing up the rear. On the political dimension, northeastern cities are dominant, gaining "A" ratings for governmental efficiency and responsiveness. (Recall our discussion of New York's attempt to be "all things to all people" in Chapter 13.) Western and midwestern cities, about equal overall, follow closely behind, with southern urban areas doing quite poorly on this dimension. However, we can see why the western cities gained higher overall quality-of-life scores (Table 15-2) when we look at the remaining three dimensions. The western cities clearly outrank and outrate the other geographical areas in terms of quality of environment, health and educational services, and social life.

Why did the western cities do so well in these three dimensions? First, since most western cities are not engaged in heavy industry, their attack on the environment in terms of pollution and depletion of resources is not as intense as in their industrial counterparts east of the Rocky Mountains (Liu 1976, p. 137). Second, the outstanding environmental quality of western cities is clearly a contributing factor to a high rating for the health dimension as well. Third, the relative affluence gained by many middle- and upper-middle-class migrants to these cities since World War II has contributed heavily to the excellence of the region's educational facilities. New schools, good materials, and highly paid teachers are commonplace. Finally, western cities are America's newest "social frontier." Virtually unsettled before the twentieth century, many of these cities, of necessity, have developed their own variation of San Francisco's "culture of civility," while other regions of the country—the Midwest (although this area least), the Northeast, and the South—all with well-entrenched social traditions, seem to have less open and tolerant social relationships according to the table. The result is that people are somewhat freer to live their lives as they choose in the West, so the cities they reside in score better on this dimension.

Medium and Small Cities. Table 15-4 presents Liu's overall scores for the top ten medium and small cities in the country. All have "A" ratings. The table indicates both similarities to and differences from Table 15-2. The Midwest dominates both medium and small cities, although western cities are quite strong in the medium category. As in the "A" category of Table 15-2, few northeastern and no southern cities appear.

A second pattern is of even greater interest. The small MSAs have generally higher quality-of-life scores than the medium MSAs. Comparing the small MSA scores with those of the top ten cities in Table 15-2 makes the point even more strongly. The top nine small MSAs have a higher score than all the large MSAs save one—Portland, Oregon. Nor is this a random finding. The average quality-of-life score for Liu's 65 large MSAs was .97; for the 83 medium MSAs it was .98; for the 95 small MSAs it was 1.22. Cities under 500,000 thus appear to have a higher quality of life. Perhaps garden-city designer Ebenezer Howard (Chapter 14) was right about the benefits of smaller cities after all.

This finding is buttressed by yet another pattern Liu uncovered. Large MSAs with vital economies (the southern cities in Table 15-3 provide an example) apparently experience something of a trade-off; that is, the higher their economic rating, the more likely they were to score on the low side in one or more of the other quality-of-life dimensions. Liu found this relationship to be particularly pronounced between the economic and environmental dimensions: the thriving economies of large cities were very frequently associated with poor environmental quality. Medium and small cities were not nearly so likely to experience this trade-off; in those that had vital economies, environmental quality ratings also were high.

The Case for Smaller Cities

The reasons for this quality-of-life advantage in smaller cities may not be too difficult to discern (recall that Pierce too found that when people's needs were ranked, smaller cities seemed to meet the overall spectrum of needs more easily). For

---

TABLE 15-4
Quality-of-Life Scores for Ten Medium and Ten Small American Cities

Rank	City	Overall Score*
Medium Cities		
1	Eugene, Ore.	1.73
2	Madison, Wis.	1.70
3	Appleton-Oshkosh, Wis.	1.62
4	Santa Barbara, Calif.	1.58
5	Stamford, Conn.	1.57
6	Des Moines, Iowa	1.54
7	Lansing, Mich.	1.53
8	Kalamazoo, Mich.	1.53
9	Fresno, Calif.	1.51
10	Ann Arbor, Mich.	1.45
Small Cities		
1	LaCrosse, Wis.	1.91
2	Lincoln, Neb.	1.85
3	Topeka, Kans.	1.81
4	Green Bay, Wis.	1.75
5	Ogden, Utah	1.72
6	Sioux Falls, S.D.	1.69
7	Fargo, N.D.–Moorhead, Minn.	1.69
8	Bristol, Conn.	1.66
9	Danbury, Conn.	1.65
10	Lafayette-West Lafayette, Ind.	1.62

*Derived from combining and averaging the individual scores for each city on the dimensions of economic, political, environmental, health and educational, and social relationships (see text).
Medium cities: mean score = 0.98; standard deviation = 0.36.
Small cities: mean score = 1.22; standard deviation = 0.38.

Source: Adapted from Ben-Chieh Liu, *Quality of Life Indicators in U.S. Metropolitan Areas* (New York: Praeger, 1976), Tables 17, 18. Copyright © 1976 by Praeger Publishers, Inc. Reprinted by permission of Praeger Publishers.

---

example, consider both economics and politics: smaller cities have economic and political systems that are much more manageable. Trade relationships and political affiliations are known widely, and the number of people involved is much smaller than in a large city. Not only may this contribute to a greater sense of community in the city, it also can make the actors on the urban scene more accessible to one another. Control of and intervention in problematic situations, therefore, may be much easier.

The case for smaller cities is grounded in still other evidence. We have seen already that violent crime rates are highest in the largest cities (Table 13-5). This relationship has been demonstrated again and again by sociologists (Archer et al. 1978). In a related study Verbrugge and Taylor (1980) found that large city size was a much better predictor of negative attitudes toward a city than density (how many people there are in a given area). As they concluded: "Simply put, living in Baltimore (a *large* place) versus Hagerstown, Maryland (a *small* place) may make more difference than living in a neighborhood of row houses (a *dense* place) versus separate houses (a less dense area)."

Furthermore, Molotch (1976) has found that continuing city growth benefits the city's elites at the expense of other citizenry. One way this happens is that larger cities generate greater income differences between social classes (Haworth et al. 1978) and, perhaps not surprisingly, greater income differentials between races (Nord 1984). Finally, in a set of studies similar to Liu's, Elgin et al. (1974) found that for *all* major dimensions of life other than the economic—that is, for social relationships and the environmental, political, and health/educational dimensions—quality was correlated *inversely* with the size of the city. That is, as city size went up, the measured quality of these dimensions went down.

The fly in the ointment is the economic dimension. Apparently, until a city becomes a megalopolis, somewhere between the 3- and 9-million population mark, there seems to be a continuing and positive correlation between city size and income level: larger cities generate more income. It is not even clear that being in the 3-to-9-million population range decreases a city's economic productivity (Alonso 1975, p. 443).

We thus arrive at a predicament. If the preceding evidence is to be believed, when we consider all five of Liu's aspects of life—social relationships, environmental quality, political responsiveness, health and education provisions, *and* economic well-being—it seems that smaller cities are likely to provide, overall, a more humane and more satisfying urban life. On the other hand, a larger percentage of people are likely to get richer in a big city.

Reflecting on the nature of the city in the fifth century B.C., Aristotle said that people first came to the city for security; then, seeing the city's great attributes, they stayed there "to live the good life." By the fifteenth century A.D. the cities of Europe were being transformed into money-making machines. Ever since, seeing a chance to end the poverty they have lived with for millennia, people have streamed to the modern city seeking their fortune. Of course, like the people of Aristotle's day, they also sought the other benefits of the city. They, too, saw the city as the fountainhead of the good life, the provider of excitement and new ideas. But, as we saw in earlier chapters, the economic dimension became paramount. People kept coming . . . and coming . . . and coming. As their numbers mounted, the city's ability to provide the aspects of the good life beyond the economic began to decline. Many people *did* become richer but in other respects began to find themselves in a less than ideal environment—crime rose, for example. Not surprisingly, in Europe and North America, many who could afford to left for the suburbs. They're still leaving.

There is a double irony in the exodus, however. On the one hand, the departing millions have left the center city high and dry, unable to fend for itself in many respects (Chapter 13); thus, they have hastened the erosion or destruction of the very vitality that made the city great in the first place. On the other hand, as we saw in Chapter 11, the suburbs themselves often have certain detriments. Increased commuting costs and a lack of the intense vitality of the city that stimulates personal and community growth are just two.

The crux of the matter seems to be this: Among all forms of human settlement, only the city produces the environment where virtually *all* human possibilities exist. Only the city provides the mix of variables that prods human life into continual change and growth. This ability of the city to "center" everything human has never been expressed more eloquently than in Victor Hugo's words about Paris, in Box 15-5.

But the evidence we have just considered suggests that *smaller* cities do this best. Bigger is not always better. In this context, we might recall for a moment the cities that often are considered the greatest in history—Hellenic Athens (Chapter 7), the Italian Renaissance city-states, and Elizabethan London (Chapter 2). All were small cities. All were small enough so that most of the actors could be known to one another, small enough so that planning could be controlled. London was the largest, approaching the half-million mark. Moreover, none focused exclusively on any one aspect of life to the exclusion of others. The merchant thrived alongside Shakespeare. All possibilities existed together. Aristotle would have said that the success of these cities was no accident.

BOX 15-5
Paris Is the Ceiling of the Human Race

Paris is the expression of the world. . . . Paris is a sum total. Paris is the ceiling of the human race. All this prodigious city is an epitome of dead and living manners and customs. He who sees Paris seems to see all history. . . . All that can be found anywhere can be found in Paris. The fishwoman of Damarsais can hold her own with the herb-woman of Euripides, the discobolus Vejanus lives again in Forioso the rope-dancer. . . . Damasippus the curiosity-broker would be happy among the old curiosity shops. . . .

Ransack your memory for something which Paris has not. . . . [The] cemetery of St. Médard turns out quite as good miracles as the Oumoumil mosque at Damascus. . . . Paris combines in one wonderful [place] the Greek nudity, the Hebrew ulcer, the Gascon jest. . . . Paris does more than lay down the law; it lays down the fashion; it lays down the routine . . . what a marvel is such a city! How strange a thing that all this mass of what is grand and what is ludicrous should be so harmonious, that all this majesty is not disturbed by all this parody, and that the same mouth can today blow the trumpet of the last judgment and tomorrow a penny whistle.

Such is Paris. The smoke of its roofs is the idea of the universe. A head of mud and stone, if you will, but, above all, a moral being. It is more than great, it is immense. Why? Because it dares.

To dare; progress is at this price.

Source: Victor Hugo, *Les Miserables* (New York: Modern Library, 1938), pp. 499–502.

crease as desirable, especially within our own interest group. Not that this is peculiar, for such an attitude is commonplace around the world and across centuries. *It is, however, obsolete.* (1983, p. 1; our italics)

Of course, it is difficult to say exactly what size is too great and what size too small. The key is to strike a balance between size and the quality of environmental, social, political, and economic life. If there are too few people, the kind of stimulation portrayed by Victor Hugo in Box 15-5 will not emerge. The small, village-style community suggested by Ferdinand Toennies's concept of *gemeinschaft* (Chapter 4), whatever its attributes (which some people quite legitimately prefer), is not a city. Not having the city's critical mass, it cannot provide the stimulation and intensification of life that is the city's hallmark. Just as surely, if a city has too many people, stimulation quickly becomes overstimulation and the quality of life (all dimensions but the economic) declines. Urban planner Robert Goodman, in considering the balance between economics and politics, says that each population should work out its own formula concerning size:

> The size of the governing unit, be it called a commune, a neighborhood or a city, would be determined by arrival at a balance between the size necessary to produce certain products economically and the size at which people have an ability to actively participate in governing themselves. (1971, pp. 177–178)

Regarding a city, however, we might hazard this guess: it would seem reasonable, on the basis of the data we have encountered, that the population of the good city might hover somewhere between the 50,000 and 500,000 marks. Anything under 50,000, more than likely, would be too small; and anything above half a million, most assuredly, would be too big.

A Model of the Good City

With these comments we conclude our search for the attributes of the good city. Perhaps the most interesting thing about the studies by Boyer and

The best city, he said, should be small enough to be taken in "at a single view" (Mumford 1961, p. 186).

In other words, urban Americans have to come to grips with their notion that growth of almost any kind is almost always good. As Ralph Thomlinson concluded after an analysis of the projected population overgrowth of Los Angeles in the coming decades,

> Growth is not necessarily good, and slow growth is usually better than rapid growth; often no growth is best of all. Americans are accustomed to rapid growth, and many of us see population in-

Savageau, Pierce, and Liu is not their *disagreement* on which city is America's best, but their *agreement* on the general characteristics we need to consider if we wish to evaluate the quality of our cities. All, whether they acknowledge it or not, use what we have called here a "needs model" of the good city. They suggest, as do we, that better cities meet the physical, mental, and social needs of their citizens more adequately than other cities.

Further, a study of the qualities of America's good cities has given us a fairly good idea of what social structural characteristics most likely to be conducive to satisfying people's basic needs spectrum. We offer a list of such characteristics here and suggest that it can be used as a model by which to judge the adequacy of any city regarding its quality of life. Specifically, a good city will have:

1. A nonexploitive relationship with its environment.

2. A responsive government run by leaders dedicated to the common good.

3. A thriving economy, able to meet men's and women's physical and recreational needs without undue strain.

4. Adequate health, transportation, housing, artistic, and educational facilities.

5. An open, tolerant, stimulating, social structure without great inequality.

6. A citizenry that identifies with and is committed to the positive life of the city.

7. A relatively small size (probably between 50,000 and 500,000) in order to maintain all the above positive traits in balance with one another.

To this list we would add an eighth characteristic suggested by Kevin Lynch (1981). For Lynch (whose work we encountered first in Chapter 5, a good city should be "legible."[2] That is, a city should have a visual and physical form that makes

us "feel at home," that provides security and enhances our intellectual and emotional experience. As he puts it, a good city must be "clearly perceived and mentally differentiated"; it must be easily "structured in time and space by its residents"; in short, it must provide a "match between environment, our sensory and mental capabilities," and our personal and cultural values (1981, p. 118).

We hasten to add that this is a beginning, tentative list of good city traits; it is probably not exhaustive and we make no claim that it is completely correct. Much work need to take place before we achieve a fully adequate model. Nor do we deny that this model is shaped by the *values* of our time, our culture, and our own experiences. For example, the list emphasizes the need for responsive government and an open and tolerant social structure. These are values that would head almost any list of the fundamental beliefs of Western, democratic societies (Williams 1970). Because all the traits on our list are value-loaded, they are open to debate. Plato probably would not have been very happy with a model so "open," a model with no hard and fast "laws" for social behavior. Certainly St. John would have been dubious about any model that ignores an overarching religious commitment as the cornerstone of the good city. We leave it to the reader to carry on the debate.

In the end, however, we would argue that our model is not *hopelessly* biased. We think available evidence suggests that a city with these traits *is* more humane. There is evidence that when people's basic needs are met, they are both healthier and happier. For instance, people who are fed properly *develop* properly in a physical sense; people who do not receive adequate nutrition are frequently malformed irreversibly both physically and mentally (Montagu 1974). This is so obvious as to be almost a cliché. Yet, individually and collectively, we seem to forget; as a result, we allow significant numbers of people in our cities to be malnourished. Similarly, the study by Blau and Blau (1982) which we reviewed in Chapter 13 showed conclusively that urban violence is associated with mental frustration induced by income inequalities. If we wish to reduce or eliminate

---

[2]Lynch uses the word "sense" (1981, p. 118). "Legible," however, is consistent with his earlier work (1960) and fits with the discussion in Chapter 5.

such violence, then, we need to find ways to reduce such inequalities.

In sum, we suggest that cities should actively try to develop or strengthen the traits on our list. Unfortunately, many cities, particularly in the non-Western areas of the world, appear to be moving *away* from the acquisition of these traits. Still, if cities are socially constructed realities, as we have claimed, it is yet possible that they can be changed in more fortuitous directions. As we saw in chapters 12 through 14, however, bringing about significant urban change is hardly simple. Cities operate within their historically and culturally created traditions, shaped by many vested interests not likely to be very enthusiastic about major change. For these reasons, it would be a good idea to take a brief look at what the future of cities is likely to be, before suggesting remedies.

The Future of Cities: Trends and Concerns

The World: Population Growth and Scarce Resources

The most probable worldwide urban population trend was suggested in Table 1-1. Even if the argument in the preceding section is correct—that smaller cities produce a higher quality of urban life than larger cities—it is unlikely that the incredible surge toward population growth in most of the world's cities will abate in coming years. By the year 2000, most experts expect that nearly half of the world's expected population of 7 billion people will live in cities. Furthermore, the world's largest cities—all expected to be in the Third World (Mexico City, Chongqing, Calcutta, and Cairo are examples)—are likely to have populations approaching 30 million! Some urbanists, such as Greek city planner Constantine Doxiadis (1969), believe that world population is not likely to level off until it reaches nearly 12 billion sometime in the twenty-first century, when nearly 10 billion people will be residing in cities.

Such growth inevitably will make more problematical another already visible trend: the strain on production and resources. As more people move into them, the cities will have to increase their supplies of water, food, energy, housing, and consumer goods and use their space more efficiently. Mounting evidence suggests that this is becoming ever more difficult. Our profiles of non-Western cities in chapters 8 through 10 showed just about all of them falling increasingly behind. Recall Jan Morris's phrase (Chapter 10): "India struggles, India sinks!" The urban future for these areas appears dim indeed. Yet opinions differ: two major scenarios have been hypothesized.

Hypothesis I: Apocalypse Now (or at Least Soon). The most well-known hypothesis related to uncontrolled population growth and resource depletion is that of Donella Meadows, Dennis Meadows, and their associates. In *The Limits of Growth*, they argued:

> If the present growth trends in world population, industrialization, pollution, food production, and resource depletion continue unchanged, the limits to growth on this planet will be reached sometime within the next one hundred years. The most probable result will be a rather sudden and uncontrollable decline in both population and industrial capacity. (1972, p. 23)

Constructing their argument on a series of computer analyses based on hypothetical trends, Meadows and Meadows predicted that even a doubling of resource capacity and technological ability in some areas could only forestall the coming disaster. Hence, there is only one solution: stop growth; redistribute the wealth of those nations and cities who "have" to those who "have not" to achieve greater equality; and have everyone, worldwide, own up to the fact that a very limited standard of living must be maintained if the human race is to survive.

A related argument is put forth by Michael Lipton (1976). He argues that the world currently is bedeviled by what he calls an "urban bias." Cities prosper in all societies—capitalist, socialist, Third World—at the expense of rural areas. The cities take the raw materials from the countryside and process them, primarily for their own use. The cities "corner the market" on the most talented people and the best services. They also

As the world population grows and becomes increasingly urban, se-curing adequate resources to meet the needs of all will be a critical problem. This woman begging outside the church in Taxco, Mexico, symbolizes the plight of billions. (F.B. Grunzweig/Photo Researchers)

control the wealth and the political machinery. In return they give little back to rural areas. Because of all this, the bulk of the world's population (70 percent of whom continue to live in rural areas) is being exploited unconscionably.

There are data to support this view. In Chapter 8 we presented evidence (Table 8-1) that city dwellers are wealthier, on the average, than rural dwellers in Mexico. But the same pattern holds worldwide: in all areas of the world, the poverty level is significantly greater in rural areas when compared with cities (Linn 1983).

Moreover, the situation is getting worse. Because the rural poor are so poor, they cannot muster the economic or political resources to better their situation. They thus fall even further be-hind. Most city dwellers, committed to maintain-ing and increasing their own benefits, could not care less about the fate of these billions. The only solution, Lipton suggests (similar to the assess-ment by the Meadows of the resources predica-ment), is for the "haves" to help the "have nots" immediately and massively.

> [What] is needed is simple: a much larger share of all sorts of developmental resources—savings, aid, brains, dollars, administrators—for rural areas and agriculturalists; and, within these, concentra-tion of resources on the poor [and the] weak. . . . (1976, p. 328)

E. F. Schumacher, the noted British econo-mist, agreed (1973). If the problem is that wealth draws people from the impoverished countryside to cities, then the solution is to increase the wealth of the countryside. To this end, Schumacher recommended that Third World countries encourage the self-sufficiency of their rural people. However, he did *not* suggest that this be done by bringing modern technology to the rural areas. On the contrary, like the Meadows, he believed that the only way to solve the current world resource problem is to *reduce* our overall economic standard of living. He argued that we all have unnecessary material comforts anyway, and that the desire to have ever more must be curtailed. In the name of progress, we greedily deplete the world's resources, in the process creating poverty for billions of people.

The solution, then, is for all of us—not just the peoples of the Third World—to subscribe to what Schumacher called a "Buddhist economics." Buddhists live a simple life, keeping only the material essentials, and concentrating their "wealth" in areas such as the quality of their relationships. That, thought Schumacher, is a life worthy of emulation. A world based on a Buddhist economics would, in the long run, solve the crisis of resource depletion. Such an attitude could also encourage rural areas, villages, and towns to more efficiently develop existing technology. Improving the rural standard of living in this way would reduce the rush to the cities throughout the Third World.

Hypothesis II: Things Are Getting Better (Be Patient). The opposing viewpoint suggests that the so-called urban and world crisis is not as bad as Meadows and Meadows, Lipton, and Schumacher suggest. Walt Rostow (1978) argues that the history of the last 200 years indicates that there have been numerous periods of relative abundance and scarcity. What controls the ascendancy of either period is technology. In one era, a particular technology is sufficient. In the preindustrial period, for example, hand labor and beasts of burden met the needs of most of the population. When people began streaming into cities in ever-increasing numbers in the late Middle Ages, however, the old technology no longer was adequate. Many began to suffer. A period of scarcity set in.

The response was a more efficient technology—the industrial, mechanized variety. This technology could process materials (Eli Whitney's cotton gin) and food (Cyrus McCormick's reaper) more efficiently. A period of increasing affluence began.

Further, Rostow suggests that each new phase of abundance has moved city and world standards of living upward. He would say that it is no accident that a recent study found that the average Bostonian of 1875 spent 94 percent of total income on food, housing, and other necessities, while the Bostonians of 1975 had to spend only 56 percent of their available income on the same items.

Rostow agrees that we currently are facing a "scarcity" phase: technology and the economy have lagged behind population growth. Yet, this crisis, he argues, is no different from past periods of scarcity and in time will generate its own solution if we let it and if we practice greater international cooperation and distribute goods and services to areas of the world with the greatest difficulties. He would see microelectronic technology, the progressive "white-collarization" of Western cities, and the increasing industrialization of Third World cities as part of this process of finding a solution to present problems.

This position has been basically supported in a study of dependency in 72 Third World countries. Delacroix and Ragin (1981) argue that, while exploitation of Third World countries by advanced societies has had a negative effect, the most useful and historically proven road to improving the situation is the development of local resources.

In addition, some demographers do not believe we are on the verge of an overpopulation catastrophe. In a recent study of world fertility trends, Amy O. Tsui and Donald J. Bogue (1978) argue that the worst is past, that world population growth rates are slowing, and that (as Rostow predicts) by the end of the first quarter of the twenty-first century, local economies all over the world will have "caught up" with the overpopulation problem.

Then there is the issue of the city itself. As we mentioned in Chapter 10, Jane Jacobs (1984) has recently argued that the city is *not* the cause of society's ills. From their origin around 8000 B.C., cities have always been the *main* generators of the wealth of nations. Across history, cities have attracted an increasing proportion of humanity because they are uniquely able to improve the quality of life. To arbitrarily reduce their size, to redistribute their income to the rural areas, and to keep people from coming to them would be the height of folly to Jacobs. This would dismantle the most likely solution to our current predicament.

Thus, the solution for Jacobs is radically different than that proposed by Meadows and Meadows, Lipton, and Schumacher. She would have us, for the most part, leave the urban process alone. She *would*, however, want to convince Third World countries that they would benefit more if their cities traded almost exclusively with each other. As we explained in Chapter 10, much current trade in the Third World is centered on First and Second World cities, to the detriment of poorer societies. But urban trade among cities *at the same level of development* pulls these cities up by their own bootstraps.

Evaluation. At present, it is impossible to say that one or the other of these hypotheses is entirely correct. Both use essentially the same data to come up with contradictory predictions. Each accuses the other of political motives. Many of the "apocalypse-now" theorists claim that the "getting-better" theorists are essentially apologists for the status quo and the powers that currently oppress the rest of the world. Many of the "getting-better" theorists accuse the "apocalypse-now" theorists of being misguided ideologues bent on the destruction of the very system that has pulled the greatest proportion of the world population ever from rags to, if not riches, at least more-than-adequate economic well-being.

Nevertheless, all the evidence suggests that overwhelming population growth and parallel resource scarcity are going to be major patterns in most world cities for the next few decades. This assures that not only will these cities move further and further away from the model of the good city we have proposed, but that the suffering that

exists in most of these cities now surely will get worse before it gets better. To alleviate that suffering, some form of increasing contribution by the countries that "have" would seem absolutely essential.

In the last analysis, however, any plan that would aid the development of the world's languishing cities has to be developed by the local population, not outsiders. As Gunnar Myrdal has argued,

> [Any plan] must be guided by a broad conception of the current attitudes of the country, its natural resources and people, its trading position in the world, and so on. It must conform to the major ambitions and valuations of the government. . . . Further, it must permit a working compromise between the various social and political forces— pressures, vested interests, ideals, and the heavy obstacles presented by prevailing attitudes and institutions. (1971, p. 440)

Myrdal goes on to state that, once approved, the plan must be given massive support, a "big push" to get things going. But he is also wise enough to see that such a push cannot be limited to economic factors. It must be a plan for total development of the social system. If the plan is restricted to economic development, a truly viable society will never emerge, and the mistake made by so many other areas of the world—making the assumption that economic development is the end-all and be-all of human existence—will be made all over again.

The United States

The outlook is less bleak in this part of the world. Despite declining productivity in recent years, this country still maintains one of the highest standards of living in the world, and its cities, while in trouble, are not at the point of near-collapse that some non-Western cities find themselves in. (Some scholars, like Meadows and Meadows [1972] and Barry Commoner [1975], would argue that the reason for the continued relative urban well-being in this country is our exploitative posture to the rest of the world.)

Certainly, all the evidence suggests that Sunbelt growth and urban decentralization will continue in great strength. There seems to be no way to keep people up in Boston (or Chicago or . . .) after they've seen Atlanta (or Houston or . . .). Similarly, there appears to be no way to keep those who can leave in the central cities after they've seen the suburbs. Finally, there is the growing trend of American cities to become white collar and service-oriented in their occupational structure, thereby becoming, except for isolated racial and ethnic ghettos, havens of the rich and the so-called "yuppie generation." Let us take a moment to look at each of these trends.

The Sunbelt. There are both positive and negative aspects to the Sunbelt's growth. On the positive side is a thriving economy, a revitalized position of national prominence and influence, and growth along major "high culture" dimensions (Houston is now the country's second most important art center after New York, and Los Angeles holds the same position for theater).

But the growth of the Sunbelt is extremely rapid and bodes to be seriously unsettling before long. As the population crunch continues, we have evidence of increasing problems with resources (water, air quality, and housing are three areas already causing much consternation) and increasing difficulties on the social front, as ethnic and racial groups confront one another and as competition for land and jobs grows more intense (the confrontation between Mexican immigrants and other groups in southern California cities is already acute). Unless Sunbelt cities do something to control their growth, many may find themselves overwhelmed before the 1980s are out.

Instituting such controls may be extremely difficult. On one hand, given their commitment to total freedom of choice regarding geographical mobility, Americans are not likely to approve of any form of restriction. For this reason, no city is likely to be successful in limiting in-migration. On the other hand, even with the annexation of suburbs that has been occurring in Sunbelt states (Chapter 13), more and more of the population is moving beyond the central city's political control.

Decentralization and the Inner City. As Table 1-2 shows, many major American cities are still growing. But the suburbs, and not the central cities, are everywhere growing fastest of all (see Table 3-5). Thus, it is becoming increasingly correct to speak of the American city not as the traditional downtown but as an entire MSA of which the core forms only a part. An example from Florida, one of the Sunbelt states experiencing the fastest growth, will illustrate. During the 1970s, according to John Herbers (1981a, p. 12), the cities of Tampa, St. Petersburg, and Orlando "spilled over their boundaries" causing nearby small counties to grow enormously.

The trend is the same everywhere: North, Midwest, and West. The inner cities are being abandoned, and gone with the escaping population is wealth and, increasingly, political clout. Central cities are facing a surrounding population that is increasingly powerful as well as politically conservative. All across the country, political lines are being redrawn in favor of the suburbs and outlying districts.

Once again, this process has a disturbing racial tinge. In a study of residential segregation in Detroit, Farley and his associates (1978) found that suburbs are predominantly white by design. Many blacks are able to afford the higher housing prices of the suburbs and do, indeed, want to move into these areas. Many whites appear to be determined to keep blacks out of their suburbs, however, and devise various ways to do so.

The decentralization trend also does not augur well for the problems that central city governments face. Economic aid to cities has already been drastically cut by the Reagan administration. Cities, by and large, are so financially strapped by the exodus of affluent taxpayers to the suburbs that they could not make up the difference even if they wanted to.

There are some bright signs, however. Decentralization has meant that small cities around the country have grown, just the sort of change that our model of the good city would applaud. If those who move to such areas find ways of keeping a hold on their own cities' growth, many of the positive attributes of the good city can be maintained. Said Marta Belish, executive director of the Roseville (a growing town north of Sacramento, California) Chamber of Commerce in a *New York Times* article in 1981: "People think we're going to become 'another San Jose,' but I think they're wrong. We've seen what progress has done to San Jose, and the people here won't let it happen."

Ironically, if northern and midwestern cities survive the crises that decentralization and the Sunbelt exodus have precipitated, there may be a silver lining yet. They are becoming smaller through no choice of their own. As they do, they may find their quality of life increasing. Certainly the air should get cleaner, the burden on city services will be reduced, the congestion will lessen, and so on. Such cities also will be forced to find alternative sources of revenue as their qualifications for federal assistance dwindle. They will have to rely more on local initiative, programs, and people—all traits that approximate more closely our model of the good city.

There are a few signs that this is happening. One example is Stamford, Connecticut. Until the mid-1960s, this small city was losing population and industry. Then began a resurgence caused by the decentralization of New York City, some 50 miles away. Companies began leaving New York for all the reasons we cited in Chapter 3—poor transportation, high taxes, outmoded plants, and escalating operating costs—and some relocated in Stamford. This process drew other corporations to Stamford, and by the mid-1980s the Stamford area had more "Fortune 500" companies than all American cities except New York and Chicago (Lueck 1985).

The city has been transformed. Goldberger (1985) describes it:

> Corporate headquarters rise where old, decaying commercial buildings stood a few years ago. An eight-year-old high-rise hotel is so successful it is doubling in size. And a downtown shopping mall is filled with fashionable boutiques, one of which, Bottega Veneta, advertises its locations as "Rome—New York—Beverly Hills—Stamford." . . . From the Connecticut Turnpike, Stamford now provides a vista that more closely resembles a new city in the Sunbelt than an old city in the Northeast.

But, as so frequently seems to be the case in American cities, what appears to be a golden opportunity to transform a dying urban area into something approximating a good city may be lost. The only reality in Stamford's rebirth, it seems, is the reality (and values) of the marketplace. The idea that other urban values are important—community and interaction, for example—does not appear to have occurred to anyone. Goldberger reports that the city's old, functional street pattern has been destroyed and replaced by nothing useful; the new downtown has been built for the automobile and not for people; downtown activity in the evening is almost nonexistent; and the architecture of the city is dull and "mallish." In other words, locked into the philosophy of the marketplace, the city is denied the promise of being a *complete* human environment. Gentrification and lots of money do not spell "the good city."

Finally, increasing decentralization causes still other worries. We argued earlier that it was the particular configuration of the central city itself that was responsible for the most positive aspects of urban life. The city throws people with different backgrounds and ideas together and demands that they deal with the encounter. It is that encounter which has, historically, produced some of humankind's brightest moments—Hellenic Athens, for instance. It is that encounter which has created the immensely stimulating and humanizing experience that is Herb Caen's San Francisco (Cityscape 15-1) and Victor Hugo's Paris (Box 15-5). Decentralization, unless it effectively transfers that experience to smaller cities (which it may), threatens this most valuable aspect of the good city: the insistence that we become more than we were, that we deal with complacency, that we change.

As a society, Americans have historically had a mixed view of the city. The current decentralization move reflects this ambivalence. Our historical pattern has been to move to cities, get what we want (most frequently wealth), and get out. The city was (is) to most a "nice place to visit," a place to make a living, not a place to live. But what we lose by living in the suburbs could be one of the most important means we have for enhancing and developing our humanity to the fullest: the dynamism of the city itself.

The Postindustrial City of the 1980s. But isn't the core of the American city being transformed in many places by the move to a postindustrial economy based on white-collar, service-oriented occupations? Aren't the mostly affluent people who are involved in this shift generating, once more, the art, good food, and vibrant street life that are the distinguishing features of the good city in history?

The answer to this question is a qualified yes. The gentrification movement is now clearly a trend in the American urban landscape. Portions of many cities, from business headquarters to residential areas, are being transformed as the postindustrial economy takes hold. But we must be careful to note just how limited a phenomenon gentrification still is and how unequally its benefits are shared among different categories of urbanites.

The process currently involves only about 10 percent of the city's inhabitants. Yet this small portion carries considerable economic clout that often hurts the interests of the less-privileged majority. For example, renting an apartment in Manhattan usually costs almost $1,000 a month (Carmody 1984). Not surprisingly, such high rents are driving out poorer residents. Middle-class residents are in danger of losing their stable rents as white-collar demand for apartments forces prices up (Hopkins 1985). Moreover, gentrification and the expansion of the service-oriented economy have done nothing to change the poorest areas of major cities: New York still has its Harlem and South Bronx; Chicago, its South Side; Los Angeles, its Watts.

The Future of Cities: Possibilities for Change

Tuning the lyre and handling the harp are no accomplishments of mine, but rather taking in hand a city that was small and inglorious and making it glorious and real.

THEMOSTICLES, GREEK STATESMAN, FIFTH CENTURY, B.C.

In the rest of the world, the hope for an urban place of dignity and serenity is probably "on hold" for the next few decades. There are some signs in the United States that the city is regenerating in a positive direction. But these signs are balanced by less favorable ones: our cities are still riven with dissension, with great inequalities of wealth, power, and prestige, with racial discrimination, and with environmental and population problems that even the best cities cannot seem to solve.

One of the main reasons for this set of difficulties, we believe, is that, historically, the city has been so infrequently the object of careful attention. Living in cities for 10,000 years, humanity has only rarely asked what cities are, why they work well or badly, and what cities *should* be. For most of our forebearers, and probably for us as well, cities have been—and are—seen as places to use, places to "make a living," not as places to construct a meaningful life with other people in a common community. In light of this indifference, there should be little surprise at the fact that urban problems have been—and are—common and that these cause considerable human suffering.

In a very important sense, the history of the city has been a history of opportunity-seeking followed by overload. As we saw in Chapter 2, cities first began as places of tremendous opportunity—economic, political, intellectual. Over the centuries people came to them and found them most capable of meeting important needs. Others got the idea and came too. In most societies (the ancient Greeks are a notable exception), there was no attempt to control city growth. Cities grew bigger, and bigger, and bigger still. With such growth came overload. The city became so big the actors didn't know one another. People were so interested in meeting their own personal needs that they forgot about the city as an entity which needed care. Problems developed. Some attempts at solving the problems were tried but most solutions didn't work very well. So, especially in the United States, many people moved on to the proverbial "greener pastures," another city, the suburbs, someplace where the opportunity was supposed to be greater, or where the living was supposed to be easier. For a time it probably was, but, once again, it was not long before word got out that there was a better place and the overload part of the cycle developed once again.

But this is not inevitable. Although complex, we have tried to show throughout this book that the city is a human creation. It can be a human *recreation* as well. We have learned *something* about the way cities work. We also are beginning to have the knowledge of how to make them into more healthful, exciting, and secure environments in which to live, if only we decide to undertake the formidable task of making them so.

Our model of the good city suggests that better cities can be socially constructed if we try to improve the quality of city life by cultivating the eight characteristics suggested earlier. But such cities will not appear as if by magic. Cultural values and traditions, vested interests, and the main urban trends we have just discussed will continue to shape significantly the cities of the future.

Hence, there must be a *commitment* on the part of groups and individuals to bring about better cities. Similarly, *noncommitment* to urban action must also be recognized as a decision with powerful consequences. Inactivity allows forces at work in the city to persist, with familiar consequences. Better, then, to make a conscious effort toward promoting the traits we believe to enhance the positive good of the city.

So the final question is: What can be done to effect positive urban change? A few cases are suggestive.

Collective Action

We have stressed throughout this book the strength of the city's link to the values of the wider culture. This link implies that significant social change (short of an out-and-out revolution) must be consistent with the prevailing cultural-urban ideology. Thus, in New York, sweat equity has worked in the South Bronx (Cityscape 13-2) and

"breaking the bank" has been effective in Brooklyn (Cityscape 14-3) because people have banded together and produced effective change by forcing "the system" to accommodate their interests. Similarly, the most successful American new towns (Chapter 14) are those (like Columbia) that have allowed developers to make a profit and at the same time have fostered some element of community participation.

Individual Action

On the surface, collective action to improve the urban future seems, however difficult, somehow much easier than individual action. It is often said that the modern city is too big for one person to have an effect.

In answer to a question about what the individual could do to help bring the good city into being, the late Kingsley Birge gave the following advice: Everyone in the city has to live somewhere. Begin there. With the means available, each person could decide what would be the best home he or she could have. Having developed some personal model of "the good home," that person could set about creating, room by room, an ideal environment—putting in the kind of furnishings, art, music, that brought the greatest pleasure. As necessary, compromises with neighbors or other family members could be made so that everyone's interests were served as much as possible. This is very close to what has been happening with the sweat-equity movement just mentioned. Individuals are building "good homes," negotiating with banks, landlords, local businesses, and city officials in the process, and, in many cases, are contributing to a healthier city.

Or consider the effect of Paul Lattimore on the small Upstate New York city of Auburn. Two decades ago, Auburn, like so many small American cities, was in dire straits. Its industry was dead or dying, its young people were moving out, its tax base was declining. Then, in 1968, Lattimore was elected mayor. A city council member for more than a decade, he had learned not only what ailed his city but how the city worked. Using his own experience-based model of a good city, Lattimore decided that what the city needed most was an economic shot in the arm: new industrial investment. But how could he attain this in economically depressed Upstate New York?

Lattimore commissioned an independent firm at a cost of $30,000—which many in the city thought was an utter waste of money—to determine if the city was a viable area for industrial investment. The study concluded in the affirmative. Lattimore then sent the results of his study to all embassies of countries he knew were interested in establishing industrial plants in the United States. The Japanese responded to his report with interest. Visiting Japan, Lattimore convinced a Japanese steel firm that Auburn was the place to locate a new steel miniplant. The Japanese poured $15 million into their plant and created 240 well-paying jobs for local residents. The money in investments and wages helped revitalize Auburn's faltering economy and stem the tide of departing young people.

Success fed upon itself. On the evidence of the steel firm's success, other industries recently have located in Auburn, thereby stimulating the city even more. Lattimore was instrumental in having McDonald's fast-food chain locate its roll-making plant for Upstate New York in Auburn ("We're rolling in dough," he said). In 1980 another study prompted by Lattimore discovered that underneath Cayuga County (Auburn's county) lay one of the richest natural-gas deposits in the United States. Because of this discovery, the Miller Brewing Company decided to locate its new brewery near Auburn, and still more money and more jobs poured into the area. With the money generated, the city has built a large downtown shopping mall and undertaken renovation of many of its key buildings. Today, largely as the result of the efforts of one individual and his associates, the city of Auburn is thriving. In the process, Lattimore was reelected for an unprecedented four terms and served a term as National Chairperson of the President's Commission on Small Cities.

Of course, one critical response to Lattimore's success is to note that Auburn was turned around because it is a *small* city. That is partly true. There is no doubt that the small size of Auburn allowed Lattimore to have a pronounced effect on the whole city. Still, working in larger cities is also

possible. The policies of the mayors of New York, Dallas, or Albuquerque can be as powerful as those of Lattimore. Furthermore, one does not have to hold political office to have a positive effect on urban affairs. Curtis Sliwa's Guardian Angels—the group that fights crime by patrolling neighborhoods and public transportation—was so successful in New York that other cities also started Guardian Angel chapters. Now, Sliwa is the head of a national organization of Guardian Angels with branches in dozens of American cities—from Syracuse to New Orleans, from Boston to Los Angeles.

Individuals *can* make a difference, even in the face of stiff resistance. The commitments to producing meaningful urban change is the first step.

Politics, Economics, and the Idea of the Good City

As we said at the end of Chapter 14, political and economic realities always limit the best-intentioned of visions. Lattimore in his years as mayor was often embroiled in controversy and debate. Said he, "I never intended to win a popularity contest."

Such conflict seems unavoidable. Plans to alter a city in one way inevitably affect the lives of citizens in another way. For example, a new superhighway that alleviates the city's congestion problem may destroy a vital neighborhood; or a shopping mall in one area of the city may sap the economic lifeblood of another area. Even more complicated, emphasizing some values in city planning inevitably means that other values must be downplayed. Roland Warren (1970a) notes that, if a city opts for strengthening neighborhood autonomy, then identification with the city as a whole is likely to be weakened. For people with commitments to projects that benefit particular neighborhoods, projects designed for the benefit of the entire city—a new subway system, for example—are less likely to be seen as vital (and vice versa).

Yet, as Michael Smith (1979) has pointed out, such intergroup debate, if allowed and encouraged and if the groups involved have roughly equal access to the city's power sources, can be stimulating, democratic in the best sense, and corrective. Such debate can facilitate better understanding among all parties and result in compromises that benefit more than just a single group.

In addition, due to limited economic resources, only some projects for urban revitalization are possible. Investment in improved public housing may mean the city's street repair and park renovation projects will have to go wanting.

If such political conflicts and economic trade-offs are inevitable, how can they be resolved? As in the past, will groups of people relentlessly compete?

Roland Warren (1970a, 1970b) has argued that the arbiter in urban decision making should be a value-based, evidence-supported model of the good city. Such a model states that, as far as we know, *this* alternative will lead to a better quality of urban life for all than *that* alternative. Such a model can be used to evaluate alternative courses of action. At the very least, such a model could provide a list of priorities.

Of course, using such a model presupposes making the jump from considering only our own parochial interests to considering the best interests of the entire city. This is particularly difficult, "self-interest" having the high value it does in our society. The trick is to see that in terms of the whole round of life, the *collective* interest is our own *self*-interest as well. We may become personally powerful, but at the cost of good relations with our colleagues if we have stepped on them on our way to the top. We may work extremely hard to become rich, but pay the price of undermining our personal lives.

We are more than what we make, more than what we have. We, the majority who live in the city, *are* the city. The care of the one is the care of the other. Few have said this better than Lawrence Haworth in his book, *The Good City*:

> The person is part of the community he [or she] serves and if it is rightly ordered, both [community and individual] grow by serving it and share in the goods that the community sustains. In a genuine

community the antithesis between living for oneself and living for others, selfishness and altruism, is transcended. The self and the others are incorporated in a venture that serves at once as the ground of their self-fulfillment and the focus of their duties. None lives for himself [or herself] alone, nor yet merely for the others: all live for a community which is *theirs*. (1966, p. 62)

If we cannot see the truth in Haworth's suggestions, we doom the good city from the start.

The evidence suggests that cities seem to do better when they have vital economies; responsive governments; nonexploitative relationships with their physical environments; superlative health, transportation, housing, artistic, and educational facilities; open, tolerant, and relatively egalitarian social structures; and the quality of being "legible" and relatively small in population. Whatever brings us closer to those ends is what we should do.

Lewis Mumford said that the supreme role of the city in history was its ability to magnify all the dimensions of human life—positive and negative. The historical magnification of the negative cannot be denied; the city has frequently magnified excessive self-interest and unconcern and has been the site of enormous suffering. Occasionally, almost by accident, it has magnified something else; the city has been the locus of the "inexplicable splendor" that T. S. Eliot spoke of at the beginning of this chapter. Accidental or intended, those moments of urban triumph have been real. With our growing knowledge of *what the city should be*, such moments could become more common. We could create better cities, even good cities, should we desire to. However, to do so we must put our undivided attention on magnifying the positive.

> We must restore to the city the maternal, life-nurturing functions, the autonomous activities, the symbiotic associations that have been neglected or suppressed. For the city should be an organ of love; and the best economy of cities is the care and culture of [human beings]. (Mumford 1961, p. 575)

Exactly.

References

Aaron, H. J. 1972. *Shelter and Subsidies*. Washington, DC: Brookings Institution.

Abrahamson, Mark, and Valerie J. Carter. 1986. "Tolerance, Urbanism and Region." *American Sociological Review* 51: 287–294.

Abrams, C. 1967. "The Future of Housing." In *Urban Renewal: People, Politics, and Planning*, edited by J. Bellush and M. Hausknecht. Garden City, NY: Doubleday.

Abu-Lughod, Janet. 1969. "Testing the Theory of Social Area Analysis: The Ecology of Cairo, Egypt." *American Sociological Review* 34: 198–212.

———. 1980. *Rabat: Urban Apartheid in Morocco*. Princeton, NJ: Princeton University Press.

———. 1984. "Culture, 'Modes of Production,' and the Changing Nature of Cities in the Arab World." Pp. 94–119 in *The City in Cultural Context*, edited by John A. Agrow, John Mercer, and David E. Sopher. Boston: Allen and Unwin.

Achor, Shirley. 1978. *Mexican-Americans in a Dallas Barrio*. Tucson: University of Arizona Press.

Albon, Joan. 1971. "Retention of Cultural Values and Differential Urban Adaptation in a West Coast City." *Social Forces* 49: 385–393.

Aldrich, H. E. 1973. "Employment Opportunities for Blacks in the Black Ghetto: The Role of White-Owned Business." *American Journal of Sociology* 78: 1403–1425.

Alihan, Milla. 1938. *Social Ecology*. New York: Cooper Seiare.

Alonso, William. 1970. "What Are New Towns For?" *Urban Studies* 7: 35–45.

———. 1971. "A Theory of the Urban Land Market." Pp. 154–159 in *Internal Structure of the City*, edited by Larry S. Bourne. New York: Oxford University Press.

———. 1975. "The Economics of Urban Size." Pp. 434–451 in *Regional Policy*, edited by John Friedmann and William Alonso. Cambridge, MA: MIT Press.

Andelman, D. A. 1974. "The City Crime Wave Spreads to the Suburbs." Pp. 196–200 in *Suburbia in Transition*, edited by L. Masotti and J. Hadden. New York: New Viewpoints.

Andersen, Kurt. 1983. "The New Ellis Island." *Time* 121 (June 13): 18–22, 24–25.

Anderson, Martin. 1964. *The Federal Bulldozer*. New York: McGraw-Hill.

Anderson, Nels. 1923. *The Hobo: The Sociology of the Homeless Man*. Chicago: University of Chicago Press.

Andruss, Gregory D. 1984. *Housing and Urban Development in the USSR*. Albany, NY: SUNY.

Archer, Dane, Rosemary Gartner, Robin Akert, and Tim Lockwood. 1978. "Cities and Homicide." *Comparative Studies in Sociology* 1: 73–95.

Architectural Forum. 1951. "Slum Surgery in St. Louis." April, pp. 128–136.

Arguedes, Alicides. 1920. *Vida Criolla: La Novela de la Ciudad*. Paris: Liberia P. Ollendorff.

Armstrong, Regina Belz. 1972. *The Office Industry*. Cambridge, MA: MIT Press.

Asbury, Herbert. 1933. *The Barbary Coast*. Garden City, NY: Doubleday.

———. 1940. *The Chicago Underworld*. New York: Ace.

Auletta, Ken. 1979. *The Streets Were Paved with Gold*. New York: Random House.

Austin, Alice Constance. 1935. *The Next Step*. Los Angeles: Institute.

Austin, Penelope Canan. 1978. "The Federal Presence in Middletown, 1937–1977." Paper presented to the American Sociological Association.

Bachrach, Peter, and Morton S. Baratz. 1970. *Power and Poverty*. New York: Oxford University Press.

Bahr, H. 1973. *Skid Row: An Introduction to Disaffiliation*. New York: Oxford University Press.

Bailey, James, ed. 1973. *New Towns in America*. New York: Wiley.

Baldassare, Mark. 1979. *Residential Crowding in Urban America*. Berkeley: University of California Press.

Baltzell, E. Digby. 1958. *Philadelphia Gentlemen*. Glencoe, IL: Free Press.

———. 1964. *The Protestant Establishment*. New York: Vintage.

———. 1979. *Philadelphia Gentleman: The Making of a National Upper Class*. Philadelphia: University of Pennsylvania Press.

———. 1980. *Puritan Boston and Quaker Philadelphia*. New York: Free Press.

Banerjee, Nirmala. 1982. "Survival of the Poor." Pp. 175–187 in *Towards a Political Economy of Urbanization in Third World Countries*, edited by Helen I. Safa. New York: Oxford University Press.

Banfield, Edward C. 1970. *The Unheavenly City*. Boston: Little, Brown.

Banfield, Edward C. 1974. *The Unheavenly City Revisited*. Boston: Little, Brown.

Banfield, Edward C., and James Q. Wilson. 1963. *City Politics*. Cambridge, MA: Harvard University and MIT Presses.

Barbanel, Josh. 1985. "On the Streets, Tough Test for New Homeless Policy." *New York Times*, Nov. 15, pp. B1, B5.

Barron, James. 1985. "Battling an Unwelcome Image as Least Wonderful U. S. Town." *New York Times*, Jan. 10, p. A17.

Barthelme, Donald, 1970. *City Life*. New York: Dutton.

Bascom, William, 1955. "Urbanization Among the Yoruba." *American Journal of Sociology* 60: 446–454.

———. 1963. "The Urban African and His World." *Cahiers d'Etudes Africaines*: 163–183.

Bater, James H. 1984. "The Soviet City." Pp. 369–375 in *Urban Innovation Abroad*, edited by Thomas Blair. New York: Plenum.

Bauer, Catherine. 1955. "Commentary." Pp. 369–372 in *The Metroplis and Mental Life*, edited by Robert M. Fisher. New York: Russell and Russell.

Becker, Howard S., and Irving Louis Horowitz. 1971. "The Culture of Civility." Pp. 4–19 in *Culture and Civility in San Francisco*, edited by Howard S. Becker. New Brunswick, NJ: Trans-Action.

Belkin, Lisa. 1983. "Jersey Town: A Feeling of Community." *New York Times*, Sept. 14, p. B1.

Bell, Wendell, and Marion Boat. 1957. "Urban Neighborhoods and Informal Social Relations." *American Journal of Sociology* 62: 391–398.

Bellush, J., and M. Hausknecht, eds. 1967. *Urban Renewal: People, Politics, and Planning*. Garden City, NY: Doubleday.

Berger, B. 1960. *Working Class Suburb*. Berkeley: University of California Press.

Berger, Glenn H., ed. 1967. *The Urban Explosion in Latin America: A Continent in Process of Modernization*. Ithaca, NY: Cornell University Press.

Berry, Brian J. L. 1961. "City Size Distribution and Economic Development." *Economic Development and Cultural Change* 9: 573–581.

———. 1985. "Islands of Renewal in Seas of Decay." Pp. 69–98 in *The New Urban Reality*, edited by Paul E. Peterson. Washington, DC: Brookings Institution.

Berry, Brian J. L., and Frank Horton. 1970. *Geographical Perspectives on Urban Systems*. Englewood Cliffs, NJ: Prentice-Hall.

Berry, Brian J. L., and John D. Kasarda. 1977. *Contemporary Urban Ecology*. New York: Macmillan.

Berry, Brian J. L., and Philip H. Rees. 1969. "The Factorial Ecology of Calcutta." *American Journal of Sociology* 74:445–491.

Best, Alan C. G., and Harm J. de Blig. 1977. *African Survey*. New York: Wiley.

Blau, Judith R., and Peter M. Blau. 1982. "Metropolitan Structure and Violent Crime." *American Sociological Review* 47:114–128.

Blauner, Robert. 1969. "Internal Colonialism and Ghetto Revolt." *Social Problems*: 393–408.

Blumenfeld, Hans. 1964. *The Modern Metropolis*. Cambridge, MA: MIT Press.

———. 1969. "The Modern Metropolis." Pp. 166–177 in *American Urban History*, edited by A. B. Callow, Jr. New York: Oxford University Press.

Bogue, D. "Urbanism and Metropolitanism." Pp. 21–22 in *The Suburban Community*, edited by W. Dobriner. New York: Putnam.

Bonavia, David. 1978. *Peking*. Amsterdam: Newsweek.

Bookchin, Murray. 1975. *The Limits of the City*. New York: Harper Torchbooks.

Booth, Alan, David R. Johnson, and John N. Edwards. 1980. "In Pursuit of Pathology: The Effects of Human Crowding." *American Sociological Review* 45: 873–878.

Borukhov, Eli, Yona Ginsberg, and Elia Werczberger. 1979. "The Social Ecology of Tel Aviv." *Urban Affairs Quarterly* 15: 183–205.

Bose, Ashish. 1976. "Urbanization in India: A Demographic Perspective." Pp. 289–340 in *Patterns of Urbanization: Comparative Country Studies*,

Vol. 1, edited by Sidney Goldstein and David F. Sly. Dolhain, Belgium: Ordina.

Bose, Nirmal Kumar. 1973. "Calcutta: A Premature Metropolis." Pp. 251–262 in *Cities: Their Origin, Growth and Human Impact*. San Francisco: Freeman.

Boskoff, Alvin. 1970. *The Society of Urban Regions*. 2nd ed. New York: Appleton-Century-Crofts.

Boston Globe. 1979. "Taking the Pulse of Middletown." March 18, pp. 1–2.

Bott, Elizabeth. 1957. *Family and Social Network*. London: Tavistock.

Bottomore, T. B. 1966. *Classes in Modern Society*. New York: Pantheon.

Bouvier, Leon F. 1981. *Immigration and Its Impact in U.S. Society*. Washington, DC: Population Reference Bureau.

Boyer, M. Christine. 1983. *Dreaming the Rational City*. Boston: MIT.

Boyer, R. E., and K. A. Davies. 1973. "Urbanization in Nineteenth Century Latin America: Statistics and Sources." *Statistical Abstract of Latin America*. July supplement.

Boyer, Richard, and David Savageau. 1984. *Places Rated Almanac*. Chicago: Rand McNally.

Bradburn, Norman. 1969. *The Psychology of Well-Being*. Chicago: Aldine.

Bradbury, Katherine, Anthony Downs, and Kenneth Small. 1982. *Urban Decline and the Future of American Cities*. Washington, DC: Brookings Institution.

Bradshaw, York W. 1985. "Dependent Development in Black Africa." *American Sociological Review* 50: 195–207.

Brelsford, W. V., ed. 1960. *Handbook to the Federation of Rhodesia and Nyasaland*. Salisbury, Rhodesia: Government Printer.

Bridenbaugh, Carl. 1938. *Cities in the Wilderness*. New York: Ronald Press.

Brooks, Richard Oliver. 1974. *New Towns and Communal Values: A Case Study of Columbia, Maryland*. New York: Praeger.

Brooks, Van Wyck. 1936. *The Flowering of New England*. New York: Modern Library.

Bruce, J. M. 1970. "Intergenerational Occupational Mobility and Visiting with Kin and Friend." *Social Forces* 49: 117–127.

Brush, John E. 1961. "The Morphology of Indian Cities." Pp. 57–70 in *India's Urban Future: Seminar on Urbanization in India*. Berkeley: University of California Press.

Bryon, Robert. 1950. *The Road to Oxiana*. London: Methuen.

Buckland, Robert. 1968. *Share My Taxi!* London: Michael Joseph.

Bunker, Stephen G. 1984. "Modes of Extraction, Unequal Exchange, and the Progressive Underdevelopment of an Extreme Periphery: The Brazilian Amazon, 1600–1800." *American Journal of Sociology* 89: 1017–1064.

Burgess, Ernest W. 1925. "The Growth of the City." Pp. 47–62 in *The City*, edited by Robert E. Park and Ernest W. Burgess. Chicago: University of Chicago Press.

Burkhart, Lynne C. 1981. *Old Values in a New Town*. New York: Praeger.

Burn, A. R. 1970. *Greece and Rome*. Glenview, IL: Scott, Foresman.

Burns, John F. 1985. "Canton Booming on Marxist Free Enterprise." *New York Times*, Nov. 15, pp. A1, A14.

Butterworth, Douglas, and John K. Chance. 1981. *Latin American Urbanization*. New York: Cambridge University Press.

Cahnman, Werner, and Rudolf Heberle. 1971. *Ferdinand Toennies, On Sociology: Pure, Applied and Empirical*. Chicago: University of Chicago Press.

Calhoun, J. B. 1962. "Population Density and Social Pathology." *Scientific American* 206: 139–148.

Callow, A. B., Jr., ed. 1969. *American Urban History*. New York: Oxford University Press.

Campbell, Angus, and Howard Schuman. 1968. *Racial Attitudes in Fifteen American Cities*. Ann Arbor, MI: Institute for Social Research.

Carlton, Eric. 1977. *Ideology and Social Order*. London: Routledge and Kegan Paul.

Carmody, Deirdre. 1981. "New York is Facing 'Crisis' on Vagrants," *New York Times*, June 28, pp. 1, 34.

———. 1984. "Hard to Find, Harder to Afford." *New York Times*, July 19, pp. 131, 136.

Castells, Manuel. 1977. *The Urban Question*. Cambridge, MA: MIT Press.

———. 1978. *City, Class, and Power*. New York: St. Martins.

Cattell, David T. 1976. "Soviet Cities and Consumer Welfare Planning." Pp. 257–275 in *The City in Russian History*, edited by Michael F. Hamm. Lexington, KY: University of Kentucky Press.

Chandler, Tertius, and Gerald Fox. 1974. *3000 Years of Urban History*. New York: Academic Press.

Chang, Kwang-Chih. 1977. *Archaeology of Ancient China*. New Haven, CT: Yale.

Childe, V. Gordon. 1950. "The Urban Revolution." *Town Planning Review* 21: 3–17.

Choldin, Harvey M. 1978. "Urban Density and Pathology." *Annual Review of Sociology* 4: 91–113.

Choldin, Harvey M. 1985. "Review of *Overcrowding in the Household*." *Contemporary Sociology* 14: 409–410.

Choldin, Harvey M., C. Hanson, and R. Bohrer. 1980. "Suburban Status Instability." *American Sociological Review* 45: 972–983.

Christaller, Walter. 1966. *Central Places in Southern Germany*. Englewood Cliffs, NJ: Prentice-Hall.

Ciardi, John. 1959. *How Does a Poem Mean?* Boston: Houghton Mifflin.

Clark, Kenneth. 1980. "The Role of Race." *New York Times Magazine*, Oct. 5, pp. 25–33, 90–91.

Cleveland *Plain Dealer*. A. P. Report, June 30, 1979.

Clinard, Marshall B. 1978. *Cities with Little Crime*. London: Cambridge University Press.

Cloward, Richard H., and Lloyd E. Ohlin. 1960. *Delinquency and Opportunity*. Glencoe, IL: Free Press.

Coe, Michael D., and Robert A. Diehl. 1980. *In the Land of the Olmec*. Austin, TX: University of Texas Press.

Cohen, Mark Nathan. 1977. *The Food Crisis in Prehistory*. New Haven, CT: Yale University.

Coleman, John R. 1983. "Diary of a Homeless Man." *New York*, Feb. 21, pp. 26–35.

Coleman, Richard P., and Bernice L. Neugarten. 1971. *Social Status in the City*. San Francisco: Jossey-Bass.

Coleman, Richard P., and Lee Rainwater. 1978. *Social Standing in America*. New York: Basic Books.

Commoner, Barry. 1975. "Poverty Breeds 'Overpopulation.'" *Ramparts*, Aug./Sept., pp. 21–25, 58–59.

Conway, Donald J., ed. 1977. *Human Response to Tall Buildings*. Stroudsburg, PA: Dowden, Hutchinson, and Ross.

Conway, W. G. 1977. "People Fire in the Ghetto Ashes." *Saturday Review*, July 23, pp. 15–16.

Cornelius, Wayne. 1975. *Politics and the Migrant Poor in Mexico City*. Stanford, CA: Stanford University Press.

Costello, V. F. 1977. *Urbanization in the Middle East*. New York: Cambridge University Press.

Cottrell, John, and the Editors of Time-Life. 1979. *The Great Cities: Mexico City*. Amsterdam: Time-Life.

Counts, G. S. 1925. "The Social Status of Occupations: A Problem in Vocational Guidance." *School Review* 33: 16–27.

Cox, Harvey. 1965. *The Secular City*. New York: Macmillan.

Cressey, Paul G. 1932. *The Taxi Dance Hall*. Chicago: University of Chicago Press.

Crossette, Barbara. 1985. "The Politics of Ruling and Romance in Singapore." *New York Times*, April 11, p. A2.

———. 1986. "In Jakarta." *New York Times*, April 22, p. A2.

Dahl, Robert A. 1961. *Who Governs?* New Haven, CT: Yale University Press.

Dana, Richard Henry. 1947. *Two Years Before the Mast*. New York: Heritage; originally published 1862.

Davidow, Mike. 1976. *Cities Without Crisis*. New York: International Publications.

Davidson, Basil. 1959. *The Lost Cities of Africa*. Boston: Atlantic-Little, Brown.

Davidson, C., and C. M. Gaitz. 1974. "'Are the Poor Different?' A Comparison of Work Behavior and Attitudes among the Urban Poor and Non-Poor." *Social Problems* 22: 229–245.

Davidson, Spencer. 1985. "The World's Largest City." *Time*, Aug. 9, p. 29.

Davie, Maurice R. 1937. "The Pattern of Urban Growth." In *Studies in the Science of Society*, edited by George Murdock. New Haven, CT: Yale University Press.

Davis, Fred. 1959. "The Cabdriver and His Fare." *American Journal of Sociology* 65: 158–165.

———. 1971. "The San Francisco Mystique." Pp. 152–162 in *Culture and Civility in San Francisco*, edited by Howard S. Becker. New Brunswick, NJ: Trans-Action.

Davis, Kingsley. 1969, 1972. *World Urbanization, 1950–1970*. Vols. 1, 2. Berkeley, CA: Institute of International Studies.

———. 1973. "Burgeoning Cities in Rural Countries." Pp. 219–223 in *Cities: Their Origin, Growth and Human Impact*. San Francisco: Freeman.

———. 1974. "The Urbanization of the Human Population." Pp. 160–177 in *An Urban World*, edited by Charles Tilly. Boston: Little, Brown.

Davis, Kingsley, and Hilda Hertz Golden. 1954. "Urbanization and Development in Pre-Industrial America." *Economic Development and Cultural Change* 3: 6–26.

Dear, Michael, and Alan Scott. 1981. *Urbanization and Urban Planning in Capitalist Society*. London: Methuen.

Delacroix, Jacques, and Charles C. Ragin. 1981. "Structural Blockage: A Cross-National Study of Economic Dependency, State Efficacy, and Underdevelopment." *American Journal of Sociology* 86: 1311–1347.

Demarest, Michael. 1981. "He Digs Downtown." *Time*. Aug. 24, pp. 36–43.

Deshpande, C. D., and L. S. Bhat. 1975. "India." Pp. 358–376 in *Essays in World Urbanization*, edited by Ronald Jones. London: George Philip.

Diaz, Bernal. 1956. *The Discovery and Conquest of Mexico*. New York: Farrar, Straus, and Cudahy.

Dickens, Charles. 1853. *Bleak House*. London: Chapman and Hall.

DiGiovanni, Frank F. 1984. "An Examination of Selected Consequences of Revitalization in Six U.S. Cities." *Urban Studies* 21: 245–259.

Dike, Azuka A. 1979. "Misconceptions of African Urbanism: Some Euro-American Notions." Pp. 19–29 in *Development of Urban Systems in Africa*, edited by R. A. Obudho and Salah El-Shakhs. New York: Praeger.

Dobriner, W. 1963. *Class in Suburbia*. Englewood Cliffs, NJ: Prentice-Hall.

Dobson, R. B. 1977. "Mobility and Stratification in the Soviet Union." *Annual Review of Sociology* 3: 297–329.

Domhoff, G. William. 1978. *Who Really Rules? New Haven and Community Power Reexamined*. New Brunswick, NJ: Trans-Action Books.

————. 1983. *Who Rules America Now? A View for the '80's*. Englewood Cliffs, NJ: Prentice-Hall.

————. 1984. "The Growth Machine and the Power Elite: A Theoretical Challenge to Pluralists and Marxists Alike." Presentation at Annual Meeting of the American Political Science Association, Washington, DC.

Donaldson, S. 1969. *The Suburban Myth*. New York: Columbia University Press.

Dos Passos, John. 1969. "San Francisco Looks West." Pp. 484–489 in *City Life*, edited by Oscar Shoenfeld and Helen MacLean. New York: Grossman; essay originally published 1944.

Doumas, Christos. 1974. *Santorini*. Athens: Hannibal.

Downs, Anthony. 1968. *Who Are the Urban Poor?* New York: Committee for Economic Development.

————. 1970. *Urban Problems and Prospects*. Chicago: Markham.

————. 1973. *Opening Up the Suburbs*. New Haven, CT: Yale University Press.

————. 1985. "The Future of Industrial Cities." Pp. 281–294 in *The New Urban Reality*, edited by Paul E. Peterson. Washington, DC: Brookings Institution.

Doxiadis Associates International. 1973. *Nigeria: Development Problems and Future Needs of Major Urban Centers—Existing Conditions and Present Needs in Kano*. Report No. 4, DOX-N16-A10.

Doxiadis, Constantine A. 1969. "Ecumenopolis: World City of Tomorrow." *Impact of Science on Society* 19.

————. 1974. *Antropopolis*. New York: Norton.

Dubos, René. 1972. "Reports of the Death of New York Are Greatly Exaggerated," *American Scholar* 3 (summer).

Duncan, Beverly. 1956. "Factors in Work-Residence Separation: Wages and Salary Workers." *American Journal of Sociology* 21: 48–56.

Duncan, Greg J., Mary Corcoran, Patricia Gurin, and Gerald Gurin. 1984. *Years of Poverty, Years of Plenty*. Lansing, MI: University of Michigan Press.

Duncan, Otis Dudley. 1955. "Social Area Analysis." *American Journal of Sociology* 61: 84–85.

Duncan, Susana. 1977. "Mental Maps of New York." *New York*, Dec. 19, pp. 51–62.

Durkheim, Emile. 1964. *The Division of Labor in Society*. New York: Free Press; originally published 1893.

Eaton, David, et al. 1985. "Determining Emergency Medical Service Vehicle Deployment in Austin, Texas." *Interfaces* 15: 96–108.

Edmonston, Barry, and Thomas M. Guterbock. 1984. "Is Suburbanization Slowing Down?" *Social Forces* 62: 905–925.

Elgin, Dane, Tom Thomas, Tom Logothetti, and Sue Cox. 1974. *City Size and Quality of Life*. Washington, DC: National Science Foundation.

Engels, Friederich. 1958. *The Condition of the Working Class in England*. Trans. by W. O. Henderson and W. H. Chaloner. New York: Macmillan.

Epstein, David G. 1974. *Brasilia, Plan and Reality*. Berkeley: University of California Press.

Ervin, Delbert J. 1984. "Correlates of Urban Residential Structure." *Sociological Focus* 17: 59–75.

Evans, Peter B., and Michael Timberlake. 1980. "Dependence, Inequality, and the Growth of the Tertiary." *American Sociological Review* 45: 531–552.

Fallows, James. 1983. "Immigration: How It's Affecting Us." *The Atlantic*, November, pp. 45–52, 55–62, 66–68, 85–90, 94, 96, 99–106.

Faris, Robert E. L. 1967. *Chicago Sociology: 1920–1932*. Chicago: University of Chicago Press.

Farley, R. 1976. "Components of Suburban Population Growth." Pp. 3–33 in *The Changing Face of the Suburbs*, edited by B. Schwartz. Chicago: University of Chicago Press.

Farley, Reynolds, et al. 1983. "Chocolate City, Vanilla Suburbs." Pp. 293–315 in *Cities and Urban Living*, edited by Mark Baldassau. New York: Columbia University.

Fava, S. F. 1956. "Suburbanism as a Way of Life." *American Sociological Review* 21: 34–37.

Feldman, S.D., and S. W. Thielbar. 1975. *Life Styles*, 2nd ed. Boston: Little, Brown.

Finger Lakes Times. 1981. "British Street Violence Spreads to North London," July 8, p. 1.

Firebaugh, Glenn. 1979. "Structural Determinants of Urbanization in Asia and Latin America, 1950–1970." *American Sociological Review* 44: 199–215.

Firey, Walter. 1947. *Land Use in Central Boston*. Cambridge, MA: Harvard University Press.

Fischer, Claude. 1971. "A Research Note on Urbanism and Tolerance." *American Journal of Sociology* 76: 847–856.

———. 1973. "Urban Malaise." *Social Problems* 52: 221–235.

———. 1975. "Toward a Subcultural Theory of Urbanism." *American Journal of Sociology* 80: 1319–1341.

———. 1981. "The Public and Private Worlds of City Life." *American Sociological Review* 46: 306–316.

———. 1984. *The Urban Experience*. 2nd Edition. New York: Harcourt Brace Jovanovich.

Fischer, Claude, R. M. Jackson, C. A. Stueve, K. Gerson, and L. M. Jones. 1977. *Networks and Places*. New York: Free Press.

Fisher, Jack. 1962. "Planning the City of Socialist Man." *American Institute of Planners* 28: 251–265.

Fishman, Robert. 1977. *Urban Utopias in the Twentieth Century*. New York: Basic Books.

Formos, Walter. 1986. "Growth of Cities Is Major Crisis." *Popline* 8: 4.

Fox, Richard. 1977. *Urban Anthropology*. Englewood Cliffs, NJ: Prentice-Hall.

Freedman, Jonathan. 1978. *Happy People*. New York: Ballantine.

Freedman, Jonathan, S. Klevansky, and P. Ehrlich. 1971. "The Effects of Crowding on Human Task Performance." *Journal of Applied Social Psychology* 1: 7–25.

Freedman, Leonard. 1969. *Public Housing: The Politics of Poverty*. New York: Holt, Rinehart and Winston.

Freeman, Jo. 1980. "Women and Urban Policy." *Signs: Journal of Women in Culture and Society* 5, 3 (spring) supplement: 4–21.

French, R. A., and F. E. Ian Hamilton. 1979. "Is There A Socialist City?" Pp. 1–22 in *The Socialist City*, edited by R. A. French and F. E. Ian Hamilton. New York: Wiley.

Frey, William H. 1980. "Central City White Flight." *American Sociological Review* 44: 425–448.

Friedrich, Otto. 1984. "And if Mexico City Seems Bad . . ." *Time*, Aug. 6, pp. 36–39.

Fried, Morton H. 1967. *The Evolution of Political Society*. New York: Random House.

Frisbie, W. 1976. *The Scale and Growth of World Urbanization*. University of Texas Population Research Center.

Frolic, B. M. "The New Moscow City Plan." Pp. 276–288 in *The City in Russian History*, edited by Michael F. Hamm. Lexington: University of Kentucky Press.

Fuguitt, Glenn V. 1984. "The Nonmetropolitan Population Turnaround." *Annual Review of Sociology* 21: 259–280.

Gallion, Arthur B., and Simon Eisner. 1980. *The Urban Pattern*, 4th ed. New York: Van Nostrand.

Gans, Herbert. 1962a. "City Planning and Urban Realities." *Commentary* 33: 170–175.

———. 1962b. *The Urban Villagers*. New York: Free Press.

———. 1968. "Urbanism and Suburbanism as Ways of Life: A Re-evaluation of Definitions." Pp. 34–52 in *People and Plans*. New York: Basic Books.

———. 1972. "The Positive Functions of Poverty." *American Journal of Sociology* 78: 275–289.

———. 1982. *The Urban Villagers: Group and Class in the Life of Italian Americans*. New York: Free Press.

Georgano, G. N. 1973. *A History of the London Taxicab*. New York: Drake.

Gibbon, Edward. 1879. *The Decline and Fall of the Roman Empire*. London.

Gilbert, Alan, and Josef Gugler. 1983. *Cities, Poverty, and Development*. New York: Oxford University.

Ginsburg, Norton. 1972. "Planning the Future of the Asian City." Pp. 269–284 in *The City as a Center of Change in Asia*, edited by D. J. Dwyer. Hong Kong: Hong Kong University Press.

Giovannini, Joseph. 1983. "I Love New York and L.A., Too." *New York Times Magazine*, Sept. 11, pp. 145, 147–149.

Glaab, Charles N. 1963. *The American City: A Documentary History*. Homewood, IL: Dorsey Press.

Glaab, Charles N., and A. Theodore Brown. 1967. *A History of Urban America*. New York: Macmillan.

Glasgow, Douglas G. 1980. *The Black Underclass*. San Francisco: Jossey-Bass.

Glazer, Nathan, and Daniel P. Moynihan. 1969. "Beyond the Melting Pot." Pp. 225–243 in *American Urban History*, edited by A. B. Callow, Jr. New York: Oxford University Press.

———. 1970. *Beyond the Melting Pot*, 2nd ed. Cambridge, MA: MIT Press.

Gluck, Peter R., and Richard J. Meister. 1979. *Cities in Transition*. New York: New Viewpoints.

Goffman, Erving. 1971. *Relations in Public*. New York: Basic Books.

Goldberger, Paul. 1979. *The City Observed: New York*. New York: Vintage.

———. 1985. "Stanford's New Look." *New York Times*, March 11, pp. 41, 84.

Goodman, Robert. 1971. *After the Planners*. New York: Simon and Schuster.

Goodwin, L. 1971. Research reported in "Viewing the Poor." *Transaction* 5: 16.

Gordon, David. 1977. "Capitalism and the Roots of Urban Crisis." In *The Fiscal Crisis of American Cities*, edited by R. E. Alcaly and D. Mermelstein. New York: Random House.

Gordon, Margaret T., Stephanie Riger, Robert Le Bailly, and Linda Heath. 1980. "Crime, Women, and the Quality of Urban Life." *Signs: Journal of Women in Culture and Society* 5, 3 (spring), supplement: 144–159.

Gordon, R., K. Gordon, and M. Gunther. 1960. *The Split Level Trap*. New York: Bernard Geis.

Gottlieb, Martin. 1985. "Battery Project Reflects Changing City Priorities." *New York Times*, Oct. 18, pp. B1–B2.

Gottmann, Jean. 1961. *Megalopolis*. New York: Twentieth Century Fund.

Gouldner, Alvin. 1965. *Enter Plato*. New York: Free Press.

Gove, Walter R., and Michael Hughes. 1980. "In Pursuit of Preconceptions: A Reply to the Claim of Booth and His Colleagues That Household Crowding Is Not an Important Variable." *American Sociological Review* 45: 878–886.

Gove, Walter R., Michael Hughes, and O. Galle. 1979. "Overcrowding in the Home: An Empirical Investigation of Its Pathological Consequences." *American Sociological Review* 44: 59–80.

Gray, Robert. A *History of London*. 1978. London: Hutchinson.

Green, Constance. *American Cities*. 1957. Welwyn Garden City, Eng.: Broadwater Press.

Green, Mark. 1985. "Why the Budget Law Is Bad for New York." *New York Times*, December 19, pp. A31.

Green, Robert L. 1977. *The Urban Challenge: Poverty and Race*. Chicago: Follett.

Greene, William Chase. 1923. *The Achievement of Greece*. Cambridge, MA: Harvard University Press.

Greer, Scott. 1962. *The Emerging City*. New York: Free Press.

———. 1965. *Urban Renewal and American Cities*. Indianapolis: Bobbs-Merrill.

Griffitt, W., and R. Veitch. 1971. "Hot and Crowded: Influence of Population Density and Temperature and Interpersonal Affective Behavior." *Journal of Personality and Social Psychology* 17: 528–548.

Grove, Walter R., and Michael Hughes. 1983. *Overcrowding in the Household*. New York: Academic Press.

Gugler, Josef, and William G. Flanagan. 1977. *Urbanization and Social Change in West Africa*. New York: Cambridge University Press.

Haberman, Clyde. 1984. "Down in the Subway, It's (Oof!) a Different Japan." *New York Times*, Jan. 23, pp. A2.

———. 1985. "Japanese Ponder the Puzzle of the Bad Samaritans." *New York Times*, Jan. 31, pp. A2.

Hackler, Tim. 1979. "The Big City Has No Corners on Mental Illness." *New York Times Magazine*, Dec. 19.

Hall, Edward. 1966. *The Hidden Dimension*. Garden City, NY: Doubleday, chap. 13.

Hall, Peter. 1975. *Urban and Regional Planning*. London: Pelican.

———. 1979. *World Cities*, 2nd ed. New York: McGraw-Hill.

———. 1984. "Geography," pp. 21–36 in *Cities of the Mind*, edited by Lloyd Rodwin and Robert M. Hollister. New York: Plenum.

Hamblin, Dora Jane. 1973. *The First Cities*. New York: Time-Life.

Hamilton, Edith. 1942. *The Greek Way*. New York: Norton.

Hance, William A. 1970. *Population, Migration, and Urbanization in Africa*. New York: Columbia University Press.

Hanson, Frank. 1980. "Arson: Its Effects and Control." *Fire Surveyor* 9: 32–36.

Hardoy, Jorge E. 1975. "Two Thousand Years of Latin American Urbanization." Pp. 3–56 in *Urbanization in Latin America*, edited by Jorge E. Hardoy. Garden City, NY: Anchor.

Harris, Chauncey D., and Edward L. Ullman. 1945. "The Nature of Cities." *Annals* 242: 7–17.

Harris, Marvin. 1958. "Portugal's African 'Wards.'" *Africa Today*.

———. 1977. *Cannibals and Kings*. New York: Vintage.

Harvey, David. 1973. *Social Justice and the City*. Baltimore: Johns Hopkins.

Hawkes, J. 1973. *The First Great Civilizations*. New York: Knopf.

Hawley, Amos. *Urban Society*. 1971. New York: Ronald Press.

———. 1984. "Human Ecological and Marxian Theories." *American Journal of Sociology* 89: 904–917.

Hawley, Amos, and Otis Dudley Duncan. 1957. "Social Area Analysis: A Critical Appraisal." *Land Economics* 33: 337–344.

Haworth, C. T., J. E. Long, and D. W. Rasmussan. 1978. "Income Distribution, City Size and Urban Growth." *Urban Studies* 15: 1–7.

Haworth, Lawrence. 1966. *The Good City*. Bloomington, IN: University of Indiana Press.

Hayden, Delores. 1978. "Two Utopian Feminists and Their Campaigns for Kitchenless Houses." *Signs: Journal of Women in Culture and Society* 4: 274–290.

Hayner, Norman. 1936. *Hotel Life*. Chicago: University of Chicago Press.

Heckscher, August, with Phyllis Robinson. 1977. *Open Spaces: The Life of American Cities*. New York: Harper & Row.

Heilbroner, R. 1975. *The Making of Economic Society*. Englewood Cliffs, NJ: Prentice-Hall.

Heilbrun, James. 1974. *Urban Economics and Public Policy*. New York: St. Martin's.

Heng, Liang, and Judith Shapiro. 1984. *Son of the Revolution*. New York: Vintage.

Herbers, John. 1981a. "Redrawing Will Form Districts with New Priorities." *New York Times*, June 19, p. 12.

———. 1981b. "Blacks Returning to Southern Cities," *New York Times*, July 5, pp. A1, A9.

———. 1985. "Cities Attract More Offices, Less Housing." *New York Times*, Oct. 21, pp. A1, A18.

Herskovits, Melville J. 1962. *The Human Factor in Changing Africa*. New York: Knopf.

Hinds, Michael. 1986. "Baltimore's Story of City Homesteading." *New York Times*, January 16, pp. C1, C6.

Hippler, Arthur E. 1974. *Hunter's Point*. New York: Basic Books.

Hirschman, Charles. 1983. "America's Melting Pot Reconsidered." *Annual Review of Sociology*. Vol. 9. Palo Alto, CA: Annual Reviews, Inc., pp. 397–423.

Hirschman, Charles, and Morison G. Wong. 1984. "Socioeconomic Gains of Asian Americans, Blacks, and Hispanics: 1960–1976." *American Journal of Sociology* 90: 584–607.

Hodge, Robert W., et al. 1964. "Occupational Prestige in the United States." *American Journal of Sociology* 70: 286–302.

Hoge, Warren. 1983. "For Every One We Reach There Are 1000 We Don't Touch." *New York Times*, Sept. 11, pp. 8E.

Hohenberg, Paul M., and Lynn Hollen Lees. 1985. *The Making of Urban Europe, 1000–1950.* Cambridge, MA: Harvard University Press.

Holt, W. Stull. 1969. "Some Consequences of the Urban Movement in America." Pp. 41–52 in *American Urban History*, edited by A. B. Callow, Jr. New York: Oxford University Press.

Holusha, John. 1985. "Midwest Cities Find New Economic Life on Old Waterfronts." *New York Times*, Sept. 30, pp. A1, B12.

Hoover, Edgar M., and Raymond Vernon. 1959. *Anatomy of a Metropolis.* Cambridge, MA: Harvard University Press.

Hopkins, Ellen. 1985. "The Dispossessed." *New York Magazine*, May 13, pp. 48–61.

Howard, Ebenezer. 1965. *Garden Cities of To-Morrow*, Cambridge, MA: MIT Press.

Howell, Joseph T. 1973. *Hard Living on Clay Street.* Garden City, NY: Anchor.

Hoyt, Homer. 1939. *The Structure and Growth of Residential Neighborhoods in American Cities.* Washington, DC: Federal Housing Administration.

Hunter, Albert. 1978. "The Persistence of Local Sentiments in Mass Society." Pp. 133–162 in *Handbook of Contemporary Urban Life*, edited by David Street and associates. San Francisco: Jossey-Bass.

Hunter, Floyd. 1963. *Community Power Structure.* Garden City, NY: Doubleday.

Hwang, Sean-Shong, et al. 1985. "The Effects of Race and Socioeconomic Status on Racial Segregation in Texas, 1970–1980." *Social Forces* 63: 732–747.

Infield, Tom. 1985. "Two Decades of Transition and Tension." *Philadelphia Inquirer*, Nov. 24, pp. 14, 204.

Inkeles, Alex. 1962. "Soviet Nationality Policy in Perspective." P. 300 in *Russia Under Khrushchev: An Anthology from Problems of Communism*, edited by Abraham Blumberg. New York: Praeger.

Inkeles, Alex, and David Smith. 1974. *Becoming Modern.* Cambridge, MA: Harvard University Press.

Irwin, John. 1977. *Scenes*. Beverly Hills, CA: Sage.

Isaac, Larry, and William R. Kelly. 1981. "Racial Insurgency, the State, and Welfare Expansion." *American Journal of Sociology* 86: 1348–1386.

Iyer, Pico. 1984. "Capitalism in the Making." *Time*, April 30, pp. 26–31, 35.

Jackson, K. 1973. "The Crabgrass Frontier: 150 Years of Suburban Growth in America." Pp. 196–221 in *The Urban Experience: Themes in American History*, edited by R. Mohl and J. Richardson. Belmont, CA: Wadsworth.

Jackson, Pamela Irving, and Leo Caroll. 1981. "Race and the War on Crime." *American Sociological Review* 46: 290–305.

Jacobs, David. 1979. "Inequality and Police Strength." *American Sociological Review* 44: 913–925.

Jacobs, Jane. 1961. *The Death and Life of Great American Cities.* New York: Random House.

———. 1970. *The Economy of Cities.* New York: Vintage.

———. 1984. *Cities and the Wealth of Nations.* New York: Random House.

Jacobs, Jerry. 1984. *The Mall.* Prospect Heights, IL: Waveland Press.

Jaffee, David. 1985. "Export Dependence and Economic Growth." *Social Forces* 64: 102–118.

James, George, 1986. "City Homesteaders Bid on Dreams." *New York Times*, May 14, pp. B1, B6.

Johnson, Dirk. 1986. "Suburban Frontier: New Settlers Adjust." *New York Times*, April 30, pp. B1, B5.

Johnston, R. J. 1976. "Residential Area Characteristics." Pp. 193–235 in *Social Areas in Cities*. Vol. 1, *Spatial Processes and Form*, edited by D. T. Herbert and R. J. Johnston. New York: Wiley.

Jones, Bryan D., and Lynn W. Bachelor. 1984. "Local Policy Discretion and the Corporate Surplus." Pp. 245–268 in *Urban Economic Development*, edited by Richard D. Bingham and John P. Blair. Beverly Hills, CA: Sage.

Kadushin, Charles. 1983. "Mental Health and the Interpersonal Environment." *American Sociological Review* 48: 188–198.

Karp, D., G. Stone, and W. Yoels. 1977. *Being Urban*. Lexington, MA: D. C. Heath.

Kasarda, J. "The Changing Occupational Structures of the American Metropolis: Apropos the Urban Problem." Pp. 113–136 in *The Changing Face of the Suburbs*, edited by B. Schwartz. Chicago: University of Chicago Press.

Kasarda, John D. 1983. "Entry-Level Jobs, Mobility, and Urban Minority Employment." *Urban Affairs Quarterly* 19: 21–40.

Katz, Z. 1973. "Insights from Emigrés and Sociological Studies of the Soviet Economy." In *Soviet Economic Prospects for the Seventies*. Washington, DC: U.S. Government Printing Office.

Keats, J. 1956. *The Crack in the Picture Window*. New York: Ballantine Books.

Keller, Suzanne. 1968. *The Urban Neighborhood*. New York: Random House.

Kemp, Barry J. 1977–1978. "The Early Development of Towns in Egypt." *Antiquity* 51–52: 185–200.

Kemper, Robert V. 1977. *Migration and Adaptation*. Beverly Hills, CA: Sage.

Kenyon, Kathleen. 1957. *Digging Up Jericho*. London: Ernest Benn.

Kenyon, Kathleen. 1970. *Archeology in the Holy Land*. New York: Praeger.

Kerner Commission. 1968. *Report of the National Advisory Commission on Civil Disorders*. Washington, DC: U.S. Government Printing Office. Republished by Bantam Books, New York, 1968.

Kiefer, Michael. 1984. "New Faces Old Dreams." *Chicago* 33: 126–135.

Kim, Illsoo. 1984. "The Korean Fruit and Vegetable Business." Pp. 107–117 in *The Apple Sliced: Sociological Studies of New York*, edited by Vernon Boggs et al. New York: Bergin and Garvey.

King, S. 1974. "Suburban Downtowns: The Shopping Centers." Pp. 101–104 in *Suburbia in Transition*, edited by L. Masotti and J. Hadden. New York: New York Times Books.

Knauss, Peter R. 1972. *Chicago: A One Party State*. Champaign, IL: Stipes.

Komroff, Manuel, ed. 1964. *The Travels of Marco Polo*. Norwalk, CT: Heritage.

Kornberg, W. 1975. "A Pre-Columbian Metropolis." *Mosaic*. Sept.-Oct., pp. 26–33.

Kozlay, Charles Meeker, ed. 1914. *The Writings of Bret Harte*.

Kuroda, Toshio. 1976. "Urbanization and Population Redistribution in Japan." Pp. 433–464 in *Patterns of Urbanization: Comparative Country Studies*. Vol. 2, edited by Sidney Goldstein and David F. Sly. Dolhain, Belgium: Ordina.

Kusner, Kenneth L. 1983. "Black Urban History in the U.S." Pp. 71–92 in *Black History*, edited by Patricia J. F. Rosef et al. New York: Haworth Press.

Kurian, George T. 1984. *The New Book of World Rankings*. New York: Facts on File Publications.

La Gory, Mark, Russell Ward, and Thomas Juravich. 1980. "The Age Segregation Process." *Urban Affairs Quarterly* 16: 59–80.

Lamberg-Karlovsky, C.C., and Martha Lamberg-Karlovsky. 1973. "An Early City in Iran." Pp. 28–37 in *Cities: Their Origin, Growth and Human Impact*. San Francisco: W. H. Freeman.

Landesco, John. 1929. *Organized Crime in Chicago*. Chicago: University of Chicago Press.

Langan, Patrick A., and Christopher A. Innes. 1985. *The Risk of Violent Crime*. Washington, DC: U.S. Government Printing Office, Bureau of Justice Statistics.

Langer, William L. 1973. "The Black Death." Pp. 106–111 in *Cities: Their Origin, Growth and Human Impact*. San Francisco: W. H. Freeman.

Lansing, John B., Robert W. Marans, and Robert B. Zekner. 1975. *Planned Residential Environments*. Ann Arbor, MI: Institute for Social Research, University of Michigan.

Lao, She. 1979. *Rickshaw*. Honolulu: University of Hawaii.

Laska, Shirley Broadway, and Daphne Spain, eds. 1980. *Back to the City: Issues in Neighborhood Renovation*. New York: Pergamon Press.

Laslett, P. 1971. *The World We Have Lost*. New York: Scribner's.

Leakey, Richard, and Roger Lewis. 1977. *Origins*. New York: Dutton.

Le Corbusier (with Pierre Jeanneret). 1930. *Ouevre Complete 1910–1929*. Zurich, Switzerland.

Lee, Barrett A., et al. 1985. "Testing and Decline-of-Community Thesis: Neighborhood Organizations in Seattle, 1929 and 1979." *American Journal of Sociology* 89: 1161–1188.

Leeming, Frank. 1963. *Street Studies in Hong Kong*. New York: Oxford University Press.

Lenski, Gerhard, and Jean Lenski. 1987. *Human Societies: An Introduction to Macrosociology*. 5th Edition. New York: McGraw-Hill.

Leonard, Olin. 1963. "La Paz, Bolivia." Pp. 173–178 in *Readings in Latin American Social Organization and Institutions*, edited by Olin Leonard and Charles Loomis. East Lansing, MI: Michigan State University Press.

Leons, Barbara. 1978. "Race, Ethnicity, and Political Mobilization in the Andes." *American Ethnologist* 5: 484–494.

Levy, Maury Z., ed. 1979. "The Powers That Be." *Philadelphia*. Sept., pp. 159–172, 255.

Lewis, Oscar. 1960. *Tepotzlan: Village in Mexico*. New York: Holt, Rinehart and Winston.

———. 1961. *The Children of Sanchez*. New York: Random House.

———. 1966a. *La Vida*. New York: Random House.

———. 1966b. *San Francisco*. Berkeley, CA: Howell-North.

Lewis-Beck, Michael S. 1979. "Some Economic Effects of Revolution Models, Measurement and the Cuban Evidence." *American Journal of Sociology* 84: 1127–1149.

Liebow, Eliot. 1967. *Tally's Corner*. Boston: Little, Brown.

Lindsey, Robert. 1986. "Rush Is to Interior as California Growth Shifts." *New York Times*, January 16, pp. A1, A14.

Lineberry, R. L., and I. Sharkansky. 1978. *Urban Politics and Public Policy*. 3rd ed. New York: Harper & Row.

Linn, Johannes F. 1983. *Cities in the Developing World*. New York: Oxford University.

Linsky, Arnold S. 1965. "Some Generalizations Concerning Primate Cities." *Annals of the Association of American Geographers* 55: 506–515.

Lipset, S. M., and R. Bendix. 1967. *Social Mobility in Industrial Society*. Berkeley: University of California Press.

Lipton, Michael. 1976. *Why Poor People Stay Poor*. Cambridge, MA: Harvard University Press.

Lipton, S. Gregory. 1977. "Evidence of Central City Revival." *Journal of the American Institute of Planners* 43: 136–147.

Liu, Ben-Chieh. 1976. *Quality of Life Indicators in U.S. Metropolitan Areas*. New York: Praeger.

Lloyd, Peter C. 1967. *Africa in Social Change*. Baltimore: Penguin.

———. 1973. "The Yoruba: An Urban People?" Pp. 107–123 in *Urban Anthropology*, edited by A. Southall. New York: Oxford University Press.

Loewe, Michael. 1964. *Imperial China*. New York: Praeger.

Lofland, Lyn. 1973. *A World of Strangers*. New York: Basic Books.

———. 1983. "Understanding Urban Life." *Urban Life*, 491–511.

Logan, John R., and Mark Schneider. 1984. "Racial Segregation and Racial Change in American Suburbs, 1970–1980." *American Journal of Sociology* 89: 874–888.

Lohr, Steve. 1983. "The Cloud Over Hong Kong." *New York Times Magazine*, August 14, pp. 26–31.

London, Bruce, and William G. Flanagan. 1976. "Comparative Urban Ecology: A Summary of the Field." Pp. 41–66 in *The City in Comparative Perspective*, edited by John Walton and Louis H. Masotti. Beverly Hills, CA: Sage.

Long, L., and P. Glick. 1976. "Family Patterns in Suburban Areas. Recent Trends." Pp. 39–67 in *The Changing Face of the Suburbs*, edited by B. Schwarz. Chicago: University of Chicago Press.

Lowe, Jeanne R. 1967. *Cities in a Race with Time*. New York: Random House.

Luech, Thomas J. 1985. "An Office Boom Transforms Once-Ailing Connecticut City." *New York Times*, March 10, pp. 1, 46.

Lu, Zifen. 1984. "Garden City Grows." *China Daily*, Oct. 17, p. 1.

Lynch, Kevin. 1960. *The Image of the City*. Cambridge, MA: MIT Press.

———. 1981. *A Theory of Good City Form*. Cambridge, MA: MIT Press.

———. 1984. "Reconsidering *The Image of the City*." Pp. 151–161 in *Cities of the Mind*, edited by Lloyd Rodwin and Robert M. Hollister. New York: Plenum.

Lynd, R., and H. Lynd. 1929. *Middletown*. New York: Harcourt, Brace and World.

———. 1937. *Middletown in Transition*. New York: Harcourt, Brace and World.

McCabe, James D., Jr. 1970. *Lights and Shadows of New York Life*. New York: Farrar, Straus and Giroux; originally published 1872.

McClellan, G. S. 1974. *Crisis in Urban Housing*. New York: W. H. Wilson.

McDowell, Bart. 1984. "Mexico City: An Alarming Giant." *National Geographic* 166: 139–174.

MacFarquhar, Roderick. 1972. *The Forbidden City*. New York: Newsweek.

Macionis, John J. 1978. "The Search for Community in Modern Society: An Interpretation." *Qualitative Sociology* 1: 130–143.

McKelvey, Blake. 1969. *The City in American History*. London: Allen and Unwin.

Madge, J. 1962. *The Origins of Scientific Sociology*. New York: Free Press.

Malloy, James. 1970. *Bolivia: The Uncompleted Revolution*. Pittsburgh: University of Pittsburgh Press.

Mangin, William. 1973. "Squatter Settlements." Pp. 233–240 in *Cities: Their Origin, Growth and Human Impact*. San Francisco: W. H. Freeman.

Mann, A. 1963. "Introduction" to W. O. Riordon, *Plunkitt of Tammany Hall*. New York: Dutton.

Mann, Leon. 1973. "Learning to Live with Lines." In *Urbanman*, edited by John Helmer and Neil A. Eddington. New York: Free Press.

Maraini, Fosco. 1976. *Tokyo*. Amsterdam: Time-Life.

Markson, E. W., and B. B. Hess. 1980. "Older Women in the City." *Signs: Journal of Women in Culture and Society* 5, 3 (spring), supplement: 127–141.

Marlin, John Tepper, Immanuel Ness, and Stephen T. Collins. 1986. *Book of World City Rankings*. New York: Free Press.

Marquand, J. P. 1943. *So Little Time*. Boston: Little, Brown.

Marsh, R. 1963. "Values, Demand and Social Mobility." *American Sociological Review* 28: 565–575.

Marshall, Harvey, and John Stahura. 1979. "Black and White Population Growth in American Suburbs: Transition or Parallel Development?" *Social Forces* 58: 305–328.

Marshall, Leon S. 1969. "The English and American Industrial City of the Nineteenth Century." Pp. 148–155 in *American Urban History*, edited by A. B. Callow, Jr. New York: Oxford University Press.

Martines, L. 1979. *Power and Imagination: City-States in Renaissance Italy*. New York: Knopf.

Marullo, Sam. 1985. "Targets for Racial Invasion and Reinvasion." *Social Forces* 63: 748–774.

Masotti, L., and J. Hadden, eds. 1974. *Suburbia in Transition*. New York: New York Times Books.

Massey, Douglas S., and Brooks Bitterman. 1985. "Explaining the Paradox of Puerto Rican Segregation." *Social Forces* 64: 306–331.

Massey, Douglas S., and Brendan P. Mullan. 1984. "Processes of Hispanic and Black Spatial Segregation." *American Journal of Sociology* 89: 836–873.

Mayer, Harold M., and Richard C. Wade. 1969. *Chicago: Growth of a Metropolis*. Chicago: University of Chicago Press.

Mayhew, Bruce H., and Roger L. Levinger. 1976. "Size and Density of Interaction in Human Aggregates." *American Journal of Sociology* 82: 86–110.

Meadows, Donella H., Dennis L. Meadows, Jorgen Randers, and William W. Behrens, III. 1972. *The Limits to Growth*. New York: Universal.

Meier, Richard. 1972. "Notes on the Creation of an Efficient Megalopolis: Tokyo." Pp. 557–580 in *Human Identity in the Urban Environment*, edited by Gwen Bell and Jacqueline Tyrwhitt. Baltimore: Penguin.

Mercer, John, and Michael A. Goldberg. 1984. "The Fiscal Condition of American and Canadian Cities." *Urban Studies* 21: 233–243.

Merry, Sally E. 1981. "Defensible Space Undefended: Social Factors in Crime Control Through Environmental Design." *Urban Affairs Quarterly* 16: 397–422.

Merton, R. K. 1968. *Social Theory and Social Structure*. New York: Free Press.

Meyer, Karl. 1979. "Love Thy City: Meeting the American Metropolis." *Saturday Review*, April 28, pp. 16–20.

Michelson, William. 1977. "Planning and Amelioration of Urban Problems." Pp. 562–640 in *Contemporary Topics in Urban Sociology*, edited by Kent P. Schwirian et al. Morristown, NJ: General Learning Press.

Milgram, Stanley, et al. 1972. "A Psychological Map of New York City." *American Scientist* 60: 194–200.

Miller, William. 1962. "American Historians and the Business Elite." Pp. 309–328 in *Men in Business*, edited by William Miller. New York: Harper & Row.

Miller, Zane L. 1973. "The Black Experience in the Modern American City." In *The Urban Experience*, edited by F. A. Mohl and J. F. Richardson. Belmont, CA: Wadsworth.

Millon, René. 1970. "Teotihuacán: Completion of Map of Giant Ancient in the Valley of Mexico." *Science* 170: 1077–1082.

———. 1973. "Teotihuacán." Pp. 82–92 in *Cities: Their Origin, Growth and Human Impact*. San Francisco: W. H. Freeman.

Mills, C. Wright. 1956. *The Power Elite*. New York: Oxford University Press.

Miner, Horace. 1953. *The Primitive City of Timbuctuo*. Princeton, NJ: Memoirs of the American Philosophical Society 32.

Molotch, Harvey. 1976. "The City as a Growth Machine." *American Journal of Sociology* 82: 309–333.

Montagu, Ashley. 1958. *The Direction of Human Development*. New York: Harper & Row.

———. 1972. "Sociogenic Brain Damage." *American Anthropologist* 74, 1045–1061.

———. 1974. "Sociogenetic Brain Damage." Pp. 45–73 in *Culture and Human Development*. Englewood Cliffs, NJ: Prentice-Hall.

Moody, J. 1967. "Paul Staidinger: An Early European Traveller to Kano." *Kano Studies*, June.

Moore, Joan, and Harry Pachon. 1985. *Hispanics in the United States*. Englewood Cliffs, NJ: Prentice-Hall.

Moorhouse, Geoffrey. 1979. *San Francisco*. Amsterdam: Time-Life.

Morain, Dan. 1985. "S.F. Moves: Yuppies in, the Poor Out." *Los Angeles Times*, April 5, pp. 1, 22–23.

Morganthau, Tom. 1982. "Reagan's Polarized America." *Newsweek*, April 5, pp. 17–19.

Morris, Charles. 1980. *The Cost of Good Intentions*. New York: W. W. Norton.

Morris, Jan. 1976. "Entering L.A.: Historical Monument." *Rolling Stone*, July 1, pp. 28–32, 77–84.

———. 1978. "London Intermezzo." *Rolling Stone*, April 20, pp. 55–60.

———. 1980a. *Destinations*. New York: Oxford University Press/Rolling Stone.

———. 1980b. "India Struggles, India Sinks." *Rolling Stone*, Oct. 2, pp. 42–45.

Mosley, Michael E. 1975. "Chan Chan." *Science* 187: 219–225.

Mowner, Ernest. 1927. *Family Disorganization*. Chicago: University of Chicago Press.

Muchnick, David M. 1976. "Death Warrant for the Cities?" *Dissent* (winter): 21–32.

Muller, Peter O. 1981. *Contemporary Suburban America*. Englewood Cliffs, NJ: Prentice-Hall.

Mumford, Lewis. 1961. *The City in History*. New York: Harcourt, Brace and World.

Murphy, Rhodes. 1980. *the Fading of the Maoist Vision: City and Country in China's Development*. New York: Methuen.

———. 1984. "City as a Mirror of Society." Pp. 186–204 in *The City in Cultural Context*, edited by John A. Agnew, John Mercer, and David E. Sophen. Boston: Allen and Unwin.

Myrdal, Gunnar. 1971. *Asian Drama*. New York: Vintage.

Nam, Charles B., and Susan Gustavul Philliber. 1984. *Population: A Basic Orientation*. 2nd. Edition. Englewood Cliffs, NJ: Prentice-Hall.

Nathan, R. P. 1979. "New Crisis Downtown?" *Transaction* 5(Sept.-Oct.).

National Opinion Research Center (N.O.R.C.). 1947. "Jobs and Occupations: A Popular Evaluation." *Opinion News* 9: 3–13.

———. 1983. *General Social Surveys, 1972–1983: Cumulative Codebook*. Chicago.

Newman, Oscar. 1972. *Defensible Space*. New York: Macmillan.

Newsweek. 1981. "The Plague of Violent Crime." March 23, pp. 46–54.

Ng'Weno, Hilary. 1984. "Africa Seems Destined for Misery." *Newsweek*, November 19, p. 27.

Nicholas, Ilene. 1982. "Extinct Cities." In *Cities*, edited by Lisa Taylor. New York: Cooper-Hewitt Museum.

Nolan, Patrick D. 1983a. "Status in the World Economy and National Structure and Development." *International Journal of Comparative Sociology* 24: 109–120.

———. 1983b. "Status in the World System, Income Inequality, and Economic Growth." *American Journal of Sociology* 89: 410–419.

Nord, Stephen. 1984. "Urban Income Distribution, City Size and Urban Growth: Some Further Evidence." *Urban Studies* 21: 325–329.

Nossiter, B. 1978. *Britain: A Future That Works*. London: Andre Deutsch.

Oldenburg, Don. 1985. "Cities Fighting War of Images to Attract Jobs." *Rochester Democrat and Chronicle*, December 22, pp. 17a, 17b.

Osborn, Frederick J. 1965. Pp. 9–28, "Preface" to Ebenezer Howard, *Garden Cities of To-Morrow*. Cambridge, MA: MIT Press.

Padilla, Elena. 1958. *Up from Puerto Rico*. New York: Columbia University Press.

Palen, J., and L. Schnore. 1965. "Color Composition and City-Suburban Differences." *Land Economics* 41 (February).

Park, Robert E. 1950. *Race and Culture*. Glencoe, IL: Free Press.

———. 1967. "The City: Suggestions for the Investigation of Human Behavior in the Urban Environment." Pp. 1–46 in Robert E. Park and Ernest W. Burgess, *The City*. Chicago: University of Chicago Press; originally published 1916.

Pawlyna, Andrea. 1981. "James Rouse, A Pioneer of the Suburban Shopping Center, Now Sets His Sights on Saving Cities." *People*, July 6, pp. 63–71.

Pear, Robert. 1985. "Gain Made by Blacks as Mayors." *New York Times*, March 22, p. A10.

Peattie, Lisa R. 1974. "The Concept of 'Marginality' as Applied to Squatter Settlements." Pp. 101–109 in *Latin American Urban Research*. Vol. 4, edited by Wayne A. Cornelius and Felicity M. Trueblood. Beverly Hills, CA: Sage.

Pedersen, Paul O. 1967. *Modeller for Befolkningsstrucktur og Befolkningssudvikling i Storbymorader Specielt med Henblik pa Storkobenhavn*. Copenhagen, Denmark: Stat Urban Planning Insitute.

Perlman, J. E. 1976. *The Myth of Marginality: Urban Poverty and Politics in Rio de Janeiro*. Berkeley: University of California Press.

Peterson, Joyce. 1965. *The New York I Love*. New York: Tudor.

Peterson, William. 1969. *Population*, 2nd ed. New York: Macmillan.

Petras, James, and Maurice Zeitlin, eds. 1968. *Latin America: Reform or Revolution?* Greenwich, CT: Fawcett.

Pierce, Robert M. 1984. "Rating America's Cities." Paper presented to the Annual Meeting of American Geographers. Washington, DC, April.

Pirenne, Henri. 1952. *Medieval Cities*. Princeton, NJ: Princeton University Press; originally published 1925.

Piven, Frances Fox, and Richard A. Cloward. 1971. *Regulating the Poor*. New York: Vintage.

Polsby, N. W. 1959. "Three Problems in the Analysis of Community Power." *American Sociological Review* 24: 796–803.

Popenoe, David. 1977. *The Suburban Environment*. Chicago: University of Chicago Press.

Portes, Alejandro. 1977. "Urban Latin America: The Political Condition from Above and Below." Pp. 59–70 in *Third World Urbanization*, edited by Janet Abu-Lughod and Richard Hay, Jr. Chicago: Maaroufa.

Portes, Alejandro, and John Walton. 1976. *Urban Latin America*. Austin: University of Texas Press.

Prokesch, Steven E. 1985. "U.S. Companies Weed Out Many Operations." *New York Times*, Sept. 30, pp. A1, D5.

Public Broadcasting System. 1985. "Adam Smith in the New China—From Marx to Mastercard." Television broadcast, June 12.

Pynoos, Jon, Robert Schafer, and Chester W. Hartman, eds. 1973. *Housing Urban America*. Chicago: Aldine.

Rainwater, Lee. 1970. *Behind Ghetto Walls*. Chicago: Aldine.

Rasmussen, Steen Eiler. 1955. "Commentary." Pp. 367–369 in *The Metropolis and Mental Life*, edited by Robert M. Fisher. New York: Russell and Russell.

Reid, T. R. 1985. "Mall-Adjusted Americans Fuel Amazing Money Machines." *Washington Post*, Aug. 30, pp. A1, A12.

Reiss, A. J., Jr. 1964. Pp. 60–83 in *Louis Wirth: On Cities and Social Life*, edited by A. J. Reiss, Jr. Chicago: University of Chicago Press; originally published in *American Journal of Sociology* 44: 1–24.

Reissman, L. 1964. "Readiness to Succeed: Mobility Aspirations and Modernism among the Poor." *Urban Affairs Quarterly* 4: 379–395.

Reitzes, Donald C. 1983. "Urban Images: A Social Psychological Approach." *Sociological Inquiry* 53: 314–332.

Republica de Bolivia, Ministerio de Planeamcento y Coordinacim, Instituto Nacional de Estradishica Resultos Provisionales. Dept. de La Paz Censo. Nacional de Populacion y unuemda. Vol. 4.

Richards, J. M. 1972. "Lessons from the Japanese Jungle." Pp. 590–594 in *Human Identity in the Urban Environment*, edited by Gwen Bell and Jacqueline Tyrwhitt. Baltimore: Penguin.

Riesman, D. 1958. "The Suburban Sadness." Pp. 375–408 in *The Suburban Community*, edited by W. Dobriner. New York: G. P. Putnam's Sons.

Rimer, Sara. 1984. "The Other City." *New York Times*, Jan. 30, pp. B1, B4.

Robbins, William. 1984. "Philadelphians Split on Curbing Building Height." *New York Times*, April 15, p. 22.

Roberts, M. Hugh P. 1979. *An Urban Profile of the Middle East*. New York: St. Martin's.

Robinson, Albert J. 1975. *Economics and New Towns*. New York: Praeger.

Robinson, C. H. 1897. *Hausaland, Or Fifteen Hundred Miles Through the Central Sudan*. London: Simpson, Low, and Marston.

Rodwin, Lloyd. 1981. *Cities and City Planning*. New York: Plenum.

Rodwin, Lloyd, and Hugh Evans. 1981. "The New Communities Program and Why it Failed." Pp. 115–136 in *Cities and City Planning*, edited by Lloyd Rodwin. New York: Plenum.

Roebucks, Janet. 1974. *The Shaping of Urban Society*. New York: Scribner's.

Rokove, Milton L. 1975. *Don't Make No Waves, Don't Back No Losers*. Bloomington: Indiana University Press.

Romm, J. 1972. *Urbanization in Thailand*. New York: Ford Foundation.

Rosenau, Helen. 1972. *The Ideal City*. New York: Harper & Row.

Rosenblatt, Roger. 1981. "A Mayor for All Seasons." *Time*, June 15, pp. 22–28.

Rosenthal, J. 1974. "The Rapid Growth of Suburban Employment." Pp. 95–100 in *Suburbia in Transition*, edited by L. Masotti and J. Hadden. New York: New York Times Books.

Rostow, Walt W. 1978. *The World Economy: History and Prospect*. Austin: University of Texas Press.

Russell, George. 1984. "People, People, People." *Time*, Aug. 6, pp. 24–25.

Ryan, William. 1971. *Blaming the Victim*. New York: Vintage.

Sale, Kirkpatrick. 1976. *Power Shift: The Rise of the Southern Rim and Its Challenge to the Eastern Establishment*. New York: Vintage.

Sancton, Thomas A. 1984. "The Hong Kong Agreement." *Time*, Oct. 4, pp. 8–14.

Sandberg, Neil. 1978. *Stairwell 7: Family Life in the Welfare State*. Beverly Hills, CA: Sage.

Schaefer, R. T. 1975. *Racial and Ethnic Groups*. Boston: Little, Brown.

Scheider, Kenneth R. 1979. *On the Nature of Cities*. San Francisco: Jossey-Bass.

Schlesinger, Arthur. 1969. "The City in American Civilization." Pp. 25–41 in *American Urban History*, edited by A. B. Callow, Jr. New York: Oxford University Press.

Schnore, Leo. F. 1963. "The Socio-Economic Status of Cities and Suburbs." *American Sociological Review* 28: 76–85.

———. 1965. "On the Spatial Structure of Cities in the Two Americas." In *The Study of Urbanization*, edited by Philip M. Hauser and Leo F. Schnore. New York: Wiley.

———. 1972. *Class and Race in Cities and Suburbs*. Chicago: Markham.

Schnore, Leo F., C. Andre, and H. Sharp. 1976. Pp. 89–94 in *the Changing Face of the Suburbs*, edited by B. Schwartz. Chicago: University of Chicago Press.

Schreiner, Tim. 1984. "Fewer Join Country Living Renaissance." *USA Today*, April 30, pp. 1A, 2A.

Schumacher, E. F. 1973. *Small is Beautiful*. New York: Harper & Row.

Scott, Mel. 1959. *The San Francisco Bay Area*. Berkeley: University of California Press.

Sears, David O. 1973. *The Politics of Violence: The New Urban Blacks and the Watts Riot*. Boston: Houghton Mifflin.

Sears, David O., and J. B. McConahay. 1969. "Participation in the Los Angeles Riot." *Social Problems* 17: 3–20.

Seeley, J., R. Sim, and E. Loosley. 1956. *Crestwood Heights*. Toronto: University of Toronto Press.

Sennett, Richard. 1969. *Classic Essays on the Culture of Cities*. Englewood Cliffs, NJ: Prentice-Hall.

Shaw, Clifford R., et al. 1929. *Delinquency Areas*. Chicago: University of Chicago Press.

Shaw, Clifford R., and Henry McKay. 1931. *Social Factors in Juvenile Delinquency*. Chicago: University of Chicago Press.

———. 1969. *Juvenile Delinquency and Urban Areas*. Rev. ed. Chicago: University of Chicago Press; originally published 1942.

Shenon, Philip. 1984. "Twenty-Two Indicted in a 'Terror' Plot to Force Tenants Out." *New York Times*, May 2, pp. A1, B4.

Shevky, Eshref, and Wendell Bell. 1955. *Social Area Analysis*. Stanford, CA: Stanford University Press.

Shevky, Eshref, and Marilyn Williams. 1949. *The Social Areas of Los Angeles*. Berkeley: University of California Press.

Sidel, Ruth. 1974. *Families of Fengsheng*. Baltimore: Penguin.

———. 1978. *Urban Survival: The World of Working Class Women*. Boston: Beacon.

Simmel, Georg. "The Metropolis and Mental Life." Pp. 409–424 in *The Sociology of Georg Simmel*, edited by K. Wolff. New York: Free Press; originally published 1905.

Sipes, Richard. 1973. "War, Sports, and Aggression." *American Anthropologist* 75: 64–86.

Sjoberg, Gideon. 1965. *The Preindustrial City*. New York: Free Press.

———. 1973. "The Origin and Evolution of Cities." Pp. 19–27 in *Cities: Their Origin, Growth and Human Impact*. San Francisco: W. H. Freeman. pp. 19–27.

Slovah, Jeffrey S. 1985. "City Spending, Suburban Demands, and Fiscal Exploitation." *Social Forces* 64: 168–190.

Sly, David F., and Jeffrey Tayman, 1980. "Metropolitan Morphology and Population Mobility." *American Journal of Sociology* 86: 119–138.

Smith, Michael P. 1979. *The City and Social Theory*. New York: St. Martin's.

Smith, Peter F. 1977. *The Syntax of Cities*. London: Hutchinson.

Smolowe, Jill. 1984. "Japan's Aimless Generation." *Newsweek*, Oct. 8, pp. 10–14.

Soleri, Paolo. 1973. *The Bridge Between Matter and Spirit Is Matter Becoming Spirit*. Garden City, NY: Anchor.

Sorkin, Alan L. 1978. *The Urban American Indian*. Lexington, MA: Lexington.

Spectorsky, A. C. 1957. *The Exurbanites*. New York: Berkley.

Spengler, Oswald. 1928. *The Decline of the West*. New York: Knopf. Excerpted in Richard Sennett, ed., *Classic Essays on the Culture of Cities*. Englewood Cliffs, NJ: Prentice-Hall, 1969.

Srole, Leo. 1972. "Urbanization and Mental Health: Some Reformulations." *American Scientist* 60: 576–583.

Stack, Carol. 1974. *All Our Kin*. New York: Harper & Row.

Stahura, John, C. Ronald Huff, and Brent L. Smith. 1979. "Crime in the Suburbs." *Urban Affairs Quarterly* 15: 291–316.

Starr, Roger. 1985. "Crime." *New York Times Magazine*, Jan. 27, pp. 19–25, 58–60.

Stavrianos, L. S. 1983. *Global History: The Human Heritage*. 3rd Edition. Englewood Cliffs, NJ: Prentice-Hall.

Steffens, Lincoln. 1948. *The Shame of the Cities*. New York: Peter Smith; originally published 1904.

Stein, Clarence. 1957. *Toward New Towns for America*. Cambridge, MA: MIT Press.

Steinberger, Peter J. 1985. *Ideology and the Urban Crisis*. Albany, NY: State University of New York.

Steinnes, Donald N. 1982. "Suburbanization and the 'Malling of America'." *Urban Affairs Quarterly* 17: 401–418.

Stengel, Richard. 1985. "When Brother Kills Brother." *Time*, September 16, pp. 32–33, 35–36.

Sterne, Michael. 1978. "It'll Take More Than Money to Save the South Bronx." *New York Times*, February 26, E5.

Stevens, William K. 1979. "Old Cities, New Cities: Energy in the 80s." *New York Times*, Dec. 9, pp. F1, F5.

———. 1984. "On Sidewalks of Bombay, Life Has a Silver Lining." *New York Times*, May 8, p. A2.

Still, Bayrd. 1974. *Urban America*. Boston: Little, Brown.

Stokols, D., M. Rall, B. Pinner, and J. Schopler. 1973. "Physical, Social and Personal Determinants of the Perception of Crowding." *Environmental Behavior* 5: 87–115, 421–440.

Strong, Josiah. 1885. *Our Country: Its Possible Future and Its Present Crisis*. New York: Baker and Taylor.

Sunday Times. 1978. "The Siege of London." Aug. 20, pp. 33-34.

Sutherland, Edwin H. 1937. *The Professional Thief*. Chicago: University of Chicago Press.

Suttles, Gerald D. 1968. *The Social Order of the Slum*, Chicago: University of Chicago Press.

———. 1984. "The Cumulative Texture of Local Urban Culture." *American Journal of Sociology* 90: 283–304.

Sweetser, Frank. 1965. "Factor Structure as Ecological Structure in Helsinki and Boston." *Acta Sociologica* 26: 205–225.

Szelenyi, Ivan. 1983. *Urban Inequalities Under State Socialism*. New York: Oxford University Press.

Taeuber, Karl, and Alma Taeuber. 1965. *Negroes in Cities*. Chicago: Aldine.

Terrill, Ross. 1975. *Five Cities of China*. Boston: Atlantic-Little, Brown.

Thernstrom, Stephen. 1965. "Yankee City Revisited." *American Sociological Review* 30: 236–242.

———. 1969. "Immigrants and WASPs: Ethnic Differences in Occupational Mobility in Boston, 1890–1940." In *Nineteenth Century Cities*, edited by Stephen Thernstrom and Richard Sennett. New Haven, CT: Yale University Press.

———. 1973. *The Other Bostonians*. Cambridge, MA: Harvard University Press.

Thomas, D. 1980. "The Urban Fringe: Approaches and Attitudes." Pp. 17–30 in *Suburban Growth*, edited by J. H. Johnson. Aberdeen: Aberdeen University Press.

Thomas, Jim. 1983. "Toward a Critical Ethnography." *Urban Life* 11: 477–490.

Thomas, Ray. 1984. "Britain's New Towns." Pp. 369–375 in *Urban Innovation Abroad*, edited by Thomas Blair. New York: Plenum.

Thomlinson, Ralph. 1972. "Bangkok: 'Beau Ideal' of a Primate City." *Population Review* 16: 32–37.

———. 1983. "The Demographic Outlook for Los Angeles, 1980–2000." *California Sociologist* 1–21.

Thrasher, Frederick. 1929. *The Gang*. Chicago: University of Chicago Press.

Time. 1978. "Middletown Revisited." Oct. 16, pp. 106, 109.

———. 1980. "I Feel So Helpless, So Hopeless." June 16, pp. 20, 23, 24, 26.

———. 1981. April 13, p. 59.

Tobin, G. 1976. "Suburbanization and the Development of Motor Transportation: Transportation Technology and the Suburbanization Process." Pp. 95–111 in *The Changing Face of the Suburbs*, edited by B. Schwartz. Chicago: University of Chicago Press.

Tocqueville, Alexis de. 1955. *The Old Regime and the French Revolution.* New York: Anchor Books; originally published 1856.

Todaro, M. P. 1977. *Economic Development in the Third World.* New York: Longman.

Toennies, Ferdinand. 1963. *Community and Society.* New York: Harper & Row; *Gemeinschaft und Gesellschaft*, originally published 1887.

Tomlinson, T. M. 1969. "The Development of a Riot Ideology among Urban Negroes." Pp. 226–235 in *Racial Violence in the United States*, edited by Allen D. Grimshaw. Chicago: Aldine.

Tsui, Amy Ong, and Donald J. Bogue. 1978. "Declining World Fertility: Trends, Causes, Implications." *Population Bulletin* 33: 3–56.

Turner, Frederich C. 1976. "The Rush to Cities in Latin America." *Science* 192: 955–962.

Turner, Wallace. 1984. "High Rises Curbed in San Francisco." *New York Times*, June 10, p. A1.

———. 1985. "Portland, Oregon, Has a New Mayor and a New Style." *New York Times*, Feb. 8, p. A16.

Ullman, Edward L. 1941. "A Theory of Location for Cities." *American Journal of Sociology* 46: 853–864.

———. 1962. "Presidential Address: The Nature of Cities Reconsidered." *Regional Science Association: Papers and Proceedings* 9: 7–23.

Underhill, Jack A. 1976. *Soviet New Towns: Housing and National Urban Growth Policy.* Washington, DC: U.S. Dept. of Housing and Urban Development.

U.S. Bureau of the Census. 1973. *We the Americans: Our Cities and Suburbs.* Washington, DC: U.S. Government Printing Office.

———. 1980. *Statistical Abstract of the United States, 1980.* Washington, DC: U.S. Government Printing Office, Table 1418.

U.S. Dept. of Housing and Urban Development (HUD). 1975. *Women and Housing: A Report on Sex Discrimination in Five American Cities.* Washington, DC: U.S. Government Printing Office.

Valentine, Betty Lou. 1978. *Hustling and Other Hard Work.* New York: Free Press.

Van Arsdol, Maurice D., Santo F. Camilleri, and Calvin F. Schmid. 1958a. "The Generality of Urban Social Area Indexes." *American Sociological Review* 33: 277–284.

———. 1958b. "An Application of the Shevky Social Area Indexes to a Model of Urban Society." *Social Forces* 37: 26–32.

———. 1961. "An Investigation of the Utility of Urban Typology." *Pacific Sociological Review* 4: 26–32.

Van Valey, T. L., W. C. Roof, and J. E. Wilcox. 1977. "Trends in Residential Segregation." *American Journal of Sociology* 82: 826–844.

Verbrugge, Lois M., and Ralph B. Taylor. 1980. "Consequences of Population Density and Size." *Urban Affairs Quarterly* 16: 135–160.

Vidich, Arthur, and Joseph Bensman. 1968. *Small Town in Mass Society.* Princeton, NJ: Princeton University Press.

Vidich, Charles. 1976. *The New York Cab Driver and His Fare.* Cambridge, MA: Schenkman.

Vining, Daniel J. 1985. "Growth of Core Regions in the Third World." *Scientific American* 282: 42–49.

Vogel, Ezra. 1979. "The Miracle of Japan." *Saturday Review*, May 26, pp. 18–23.

Von Hagen, Victor. 1961. *The Ancient Sun Kingdom of the Americas.* Cleveland, OH: World.

Wade, Richard C. 1982. "The Suburban Roots of the New Federalism." *New York Times Magazine*, Aug. 1, pp. 20–21, 39, 46.

Walton, John. 1979. "Urban Political Movements and Revolutionary Change in the Third World." *Urban Affairs Quarterly* 15: 3–22.

———. 1981. "The New Urban Sociology." *International Social Science Journal* 33.

———. 1982. "Cities and Jobs and Politics." *Urban Affairs Quarterly* 18: 5–17.

Ward, Barbara. 1962. *The Rich Nations and the Poor Nations.* New York: Norton.

Warner, Sam Bass, Jr. 1962. *Streetcar Suburbs.* Cambridge, MA: Harvard University and MIT Presses.

Warner, W. Lloyd, and P. S. Lunt. 1942. *The Social Life of a Modern Community.* New Haven, CT: Yale University Press.

Warren, Roland L. 1970a. "The Good Community—What Would It Be? *Journal of the Community Development Society* 1: 1, 14–23.

———. 1970b. "Toward a Non-Utopian Normative Model of the Community." *American Sociological Review* 35: 219–228.

———. 1978. "Some Observations on the Columbia Experience." Pp. 158–168 in *Psychology of the Planned Community*, edited by Donald C. Klein. New York: Human Sciences.

Washington Post. 1981. "News Reports of British Urban Riots," July 6.

Wattel, H. 1958. "Levittown: A Suburban Community." Pp. 287–313 in *The Suburban Community*, edited by W. Dobriner. New York: G. P. Putnam's Sons.

Weaver, Muriel Porter. 1972. *The Aztecs, Maya and Their Predecessors*. New York: Seminar Press.

Weber, Adna Ferrin. 1899. *The Growth of Cities*. New York: Columbia University Press.

Weber, Max. 1946. *From Max Weber: Essays in Sociology*, translated and edited by H. Gerth and C. W. Mills. New York: Oxford University Press.

———. 1966. *The City*. New York: Free Press.

Wee, Ann. 1972. "Some Social Implications of Rehousing Programmes in Singapore." Pp. 216–231 in *The City as a Center of Change in Asia*, edited by D. J. Dwyer. Hong Kong: Hong Kong University Press.

Weil, Thomas, et al. 1974. *Asia Handbook for Bolivia*. Washington, DC: American University Press.

Weisner, Thomas S. 1981. "Cities, Stress, and Children." Pp. 783–808 in *Handbook of Cross-Cultural Human Development*, edited by Ruth H. Moore, Robert L. Monroe, and Beatrice B. Whiting, eds., New York: Garland.

Weillisz, Christopher. 1983. "Bronx Neighborhood: 'One Big Family'." *New York Times*, Sept. 14, p. B1.

Wellman, Barry. 1979. "The Community Question: The Intimate Networks of East Yorkers." *American Journal of Sociology* 84: 1201–1231.

Wenke, Robert J. 1980. *Patterns in Prehistory*. New York: Oxford University Press.

Wertheim, W. F. 1964. *East-West Parallels: Sociological Approaches to Modern Asia*. Chicago: Quadrangle.

Whiteford, Andrew. 1977. *An Andean City at Mid-Century*. East Lansing: Michigan State University Press.

Whitt, J. Allen. 1982. *Urban Elites and Mass Transportation*. Princeton, NJ: Princeton University Press.

Whyte, William F. 1943. *Street Corner Society*. Chicago: University of Chicago Press.

Whyte, William H., Jr. 1956. *The Organization Man*. Garden City, NY: Anchor Books.

———. 1974. "The Best Street Life in the World . . ." *New York Magazine*, July, pp. 26–33.

———. 1980. *The Social Life of Small Urban Spaces*. Washington, DC: Conservation Foundation.

Wilford, John Noble. 1985. "A Legendary 'Lost City' in Andes Gives Hint of Mysterious Culture." *New York Times*, February 1, pp. A1, A11.

Willett, F. 1971. "A Survey of Recent Results in the Radio-Carbon Chronology of Western and Northern Africa." *Journal of African History* 12.

Wilkie, R. W. 1968. "On the Theory of Process in Human Geography." Master's thesis, Department of Geography, University of Washington.

Williams, Robin. 1970. *American Society*. 3rd Edition. New York: Knopf.

Williams, Roger. 1978. "The Assault on Fortress Suburbia." *Saturday Review*, Feb. 18, pp. 17–24.

Willits, Fern K., Robert C. Bealer, and Donald M. Crider. 1973. "Leveling of Attitudes in Mass Society." *Rural Sociology* 38: 36–45.

Wilson, Kenneth L., and Alejandro Portes. 1980. "Immigrant Enclaves: An Analysis of the Labor Market Experiences of Cubans in Miami." *American Journal of Sociology* 86: 295–319.

Wilson, Thomas C. 1985a. "Urbanism and Tolerance: A Test of Some Hypotheses Drawn from Wirth and Stouffer." *American Sociological Review* 80: 117–123.

———. 1985b. "Settlement Type and Interpersonal Estrangement." *Social Forces* 64: 139–150.

Wilson, Thomas C. 1986. "Community Population Size and Heterogeneity." *American Journal of Sociology* 91: 1154–1169.

Wilson, William J. 1980. *The Declining Significance of Race*. Chicago: University of Chicago Press.

Wirt, Frederick. 1974. *Power in the City*. Berkeley: University of California Press.

Wirt, Frederick, et al. 1976. *On the City's Rim: Politics and Policy in Suburbia*. Lexington, MA: D. C. Heath.

Wirth, Louis. 1938. "Urbanism as a Way of Life." *American Journal of Sociology* 44: 1–24.

———. 1964. *On Cities and Social Life*. Chicago: University of Chicago Press.

Wiseman, Jacqueline. 1985. "Stations of the Lost." *Los Angeles Times*, April 5, pp. 22–23.

Wolfe, Linda. 1983. "Friendship in the City." *New York*, July 18, pp. 20–28.

World Development Report 1984. Fairfield, NJ: Oxford University Press.

Wren, Christopher S. 1984a. "China's Cities to Get More Capitalism." *New York Times*, Oct. 14, p. A2.

———. 1984b. "Deng's Goals for China." *New York Times*, Oct. 28, p. H6.

Wright, Arthur F. 1977. "The Cosmology of the Chinese City." Pp. 33–74 in *The City in Later Imperial China*, edited by G. William Skinner. Stanford, CA: Stanford University Press.

Wright, Frank Lloyd. 1958. *The Living City*. New York: Plume.

Wurdock, Clarence J. 1981. "Neighborhood Radical Transition: A Study of the Role of White Flight." *Urban Affairs Quarterly* 17: 75–89.

Wuthnow, Robert. 1976. *The Consciousness Reformation*. Berkeley: University of California Press.

Yazaki, Takeo. 1973. "The History of Urbanization in Japan." Pp. 139–162 in *Urban Anthropology*, edited by Aidan Southall. New York: Oxford University Press.

Yeung, Yue-man. 1976. "Southeast Asian Cities." Pp. 285–310 in *Urbanization and Counter-Urbanization*, edited by Brian J. L. Berry. Beverly Hills, CA: Sage.

Zorbaugh, Harvey. 1928. *The Gold Coast and the Slum*. Chicago: University of Chicago Press.

Acknowledgments

Quotations from the following works are used with permission of the sources credited here. Pages on which the quotations appear are given in **boldface** in parentheses. Tables, figures, and photos are used with permission of sources given in text captions that accompany the material.

Chapter 1

T. S. Eliot, "The Waste Land" and "The Love Song of J. Alfred Prufrock," *Collected Poems 1909–1962.* Copyright 1936 by Harcourt Brace Jovanovich, Inc.; copyright © 1963, 1964 by T. S. Eliot. Reprinted by permission of Harcourt Brace Jovanovich, Inc. and Faber and Faber, Inc. **(2; also see 402, 438)**

Paul Theroux, *The Family Arsenal.* Copyright © 1976 by Paul Theroux. Reprinted by permission of Houghton Mifflin Company. **(14)**

Joseph B. Treaster, "Puerto Rico Cites Peril of Shantytowns," *The New York Times*, October 11, 1985. Copyright © 1985 by The New York Times Company. Reprinted by permission of The New York Times Company. **(19)**

Upton Sinclair, *The Jungle.* Published by Viking Press in 1947. Reprinted by permission of Viking Penguin, Inc. **(22–23)**

Chapter 2

Lewis Mumford, *The City in History*, pages 229–232. © 1961 by Lewis Mumford. Reprinted by permission of Harcourt Brace Jovanovich, Inc. **(47; also see 193)**

Robert Gray, *A History of London.* Published by Hutchinson in 1978. Reprinted by permission of Century Hutchinson Limited, London. **(57, 58)**

Chapter 3

Richard C. Wade, "Urban Life in Western America, 1790–1830," *American Historical Review*, October 1958. Reprinted by permission of Richard C. Wade. **(70)**

Chapter 4

Tim Rice, "Eva, Beware of the City," from the opera *Evita.* Music by Andrew Lloyd Webber. Lyrics by Tim Rice. Copyright © 1977 by Evita Music Ltd., London, England. All rights reserved. Sole selling agent for the entire Western Hemisphere, Leeds Music Corporation, New York, NY. Reprinted by permission of MCA Music. **(102)**

Tim Hackler, "The Big City Has No Corner on Mental Illness," *The New York Times Magazine*, December 19, 1979. Copyright © 1979 by The New York Times Company. Reprinted by permission of The New York Times Company. **(124)**

Chapter 5

Alfred Kazin, *A Walker in the City.* Copyright 1951, 1979 by Alfred Kazin. Reprinted by permission of Harcourt Brace Jovanovich, Inc. **(135)**

Malvina Reynolds, "Little Boxes." Words and music by Malvina Reynolds. © 1962 Schroder Music Company (ASCAP). Reprinted by permission of Schroder Music Company, 1450 6th Street, Berkeley, CA 94710. (305)

William M. Dobriner, *Class in Suburbia*. © 1963 by Prentice-Hall, Inc. Reprinted by permission of the publisher, Prentice-Hall, Inc., Englewood Cliffs, NJ 07632. (310–311)

Chapter 12

Helene Hanff, *Apple of My Eye*, pages 88–89. Copyright 1978 by Helene Hanff. Reprinted by permission of Helene Hanff and Collins & Sons, Ltd. (318; also see 166, 428)

Piri Thomas, *Down These Mean Streets*. Copyright © 1967 by Piri Thomas. Reprinted by permission of Alfred A. Knopf, Inc. (332–333)

Carl Sandburg, "Chicago," *Chicago Poems*. Copyright 1916 by Holt, Rinehart and Winston, Inc.; renewed 1944 by Carl Sandburg. Reprinted by permission of Harcourt Brace Jovanovich, Inc. (348)

Chapter 13

Edward C. Banfield, *The Unheavenly City Revisited*. © 1968, 1970, 1974 by Edward C. Banfield. Reprinted by permission of Little, Brown and Company. (362–363)

William Ryan, *Blaming the Victim*. Published by Pantheon Books in 1970 and Vintage Books in 1972. Reprinted by permission of Pantheon Books, a Division of Random House, Inc. (365)

Ann Petry, *The Street*, pages 152–153. Copyright 1946, copyright © renewed 1974 by Ann Petry. Reprinted by permission of Houghton Mifflin Company. (369; also see 136, 140–141, 292)

Roger Williams, "The New Urban Pioneers," *Saturday Review*, July 23, 1977. Copyright © 1977 by *Saturday Review*. All rights reserved. Reprinted by permission of *Saturday Review*. (380–381)

Guardian Angels, interview material originally broadcast on "Horizons," June 18, 1980. © 1980 National Public Radio. Reprinted courtesy of National Public Radio, Washington, D.C. (386–387)

Chapter 14

T. S. Eliot, "Preludes," *Collected Poems 1909–1962*. Copyright 1936 by Harcourt Brace Jovanovich, Inc.; copyright © 1963, 1964 by T. S. Eliot. Reprinted by permission of Harcourt Brace Jovanovich, Inc. and Faber and Faber, Inc. (402; also see 2, 438)

Ebenezer Howard, *Garden Cities of To-Morrow*. Published by MIT Press in 1965. Reprinted by permission of The MIT Press, Cambridge, MA. (404)

Jane Jacobs, *The Death and Life of Great American Cities*. Copyright © 1961 by Jane Jacobs. Reprinted by permission of Random House, Inc. (425)

Michael Massing, "Breaking the Bank," *Saturday Review*, September 15, 1979. © 1979. Reprinted by permission of *Saturday Review*. (427)

Helene Hanff, *Apple of My Eye*, pages 175–185. Copyright 1978 by Helene Hanff. Reprinted by permission of Helene Hanff and Collins & Sons, Ltd. (428; also see 166, 318)

Norman Krumholz, "Cleveland," *Personality, Politics, and Planning*, edited by James Catanese and W. Paul Farmer. Published by Sage in 1978. Reprinted by permission of Norman Krumholz, Cleveland City Planning Director, 1969–1979. (432–433)

Chapter 15

T. S. Eliot, "The Waste Land," *Collected Poems 1909–1962*. Copyright 1936 by Harcourt Brace Jovanovich, Inc.; copyright © 1963, 1964 by T. S. Eliot. Reprinted by permission of Harcourt Brace Jovanovich, Inc. and Faber and Faber, Inc. (438; also see 2, 402)

Herb Caen, *Baghdad-by-the-Bay*, originally published in 1949. Copyright © 1979 by Herb Caen. Reprinted by permission of Doubleday & Company, Inc. (447)

Armistead Maupin, *Tales of the City* (New York: Harper & Row, 1978), pages 1–3. Copyright © 1978 by The Chronicle Publishing Company. Reprinted by permission of Harper & Row, Publishers, Inc. (448–449)

Index